Robert Bolt

'Errors, like straws, upon the surface flow;
He who would search for pearls must dive below'

John Dryden

ADRIAN TURNER

ROBERT BOLT

Scenes From Two Lives

HUTCHINSON
LONDON

1 3 5 7 9 10 8 6 4 2

This edition first published in 1998 by Hutchinson

Random House (UK) Limited
20 Vauxhall Bridge Road
London SW1V 2SA

Random House Australia (Pty) Ltd
20 Alfred Street
Milsons Point, Sydney
New South Wales 2016 Australia

Random House New Zealand Limited
18 Poland Road, Glenfield
Auckland 10 New Zealand

Random House South Africa (Pty) Limited
Endulini, 5A Jubilee Road
Parktown 2193, South Africa

A CIP record for this book is available from the British Library

Papers used by Random House UK Limited are natural,
recyclable products made from wood grown in sustainable forests.
The manufacturing processes conform to the environmental
regulations of the country of origin

ISBN 0 09 180176 1

Typeset in Plantin by SX Composing DTP, Rayleigh, Essex
Printed and bound in Great Britain by
Mackays of Chatham PLC

Random House UK Limited Reg. No. 954009

CONTENTS

PART THREE: FUCKING HELL

INTRODUCTION AND ACKNOWLEDGEMENTS

Script Extract: Augustus (1977)

The scene is a dinner party at a country house, attended by the artist Augustus John and several socialites:

He drinks a glass of port. He is seated by a lovely young DEBUTANTE at the big round dining-table. On SOUND the murmur of polite and clever conversation.

DORELIA in a silver lame dress glances at

OTTOLINE leaning forward, listening to the Debutante whose eyes wander speculatively over AUGUSTUS, romantic in his glittering white shirt and moleskin gypsy jacket.

Her other neighbour is a pale-faced man with sharp blue eyes and a reddish beard (GB SHAW, but let's not say so). He is not pleased that her attention is away from him.

> DEBUTANTE
> But you'd live in a caravan all the time?

> AUGUSTUS
> Yes.

> DEBUTANTE
> Honestly?

> AUGUSTUS
> Yes.

> DEBUTANTE
> You're romantic.

SHAW grunts.

Aren't you romantic, Mr Shaw?

SHAW
No my dear, I'm an Artist.

It makes a silence. AUGUSTUS glances at him dangerously. SHAW smiles challengingly:

SHAW
Art and Life are not the same. Are they Mr John?

AUGUSTUS
Yes.

DEBUTANTE
Oh Good!

SHAW
You've fallen for his gypsy jacket. Art's a job of work my dear.

AUGUSTUS
If Art's a job of work, so's Life.

A clever-looking BISHOP smiles and:

BISHOP
It is, Mr John, it is.

AUGUSTUS looks at him balefully and:

AUGUSTUS
It fucking well isn't.

Appalled silence.

I cannot claim to have known Robert Bolt well, having met him on no more than four occasions, and then only casually. Doubtless his family and friends, after reading this book, will claim that I did not know him at all and that, surely, is the penalty which all biographers must pay and live with.

Robert suffered a stroke in 1979, leaving him partially paralysed and with his speech seriously impaired. Many people I met during the course of writing this book said how sad it was that I never knew the original Robert, the combative Robert, the man who could light up a room by the electric currency of words.

Our first encounter was in 1984 when I was writing a feature for *The Times* about the making of the film, *The Bounty*. I called Robert's agent, the legendary Margaret Ramsay, to request an interview and within an hour she called back to say that Robert could see me that very afternoon. She gave me the name and address of a hospital in London. The fact that Robert was willing to be interviewed from his hospital bed impressed me – few people would have agreed to meet the press in such circumstances – and I was immediately struck by his refusal to let illness defeat him, by his obvious though not intimidating intelligence and by his piercing blue eyes, so sharp they might have seen in the dark.

Speech was difficult for him and whenever he had trouble with a word or a sentence he would purge his dysphasic system by roaring out 'FUCK–ING–HELL!' This became a sort of trademark; everyone who knew Robert had experienced it and whole restaurants were frequently stunned into appalled silence by it. 'Of course,' as he would say, chuckling at the black comedy of it all.

I next met him at the National Film Theatre, where I then worked, then at a party at David Lean's house in Docklands and, finally, at Lean's memorial service at St Paul's Cathedral in 1991. It will be understood immediately, therefore, that I approached this book from the film side of things, not the theatre, and I dare say that a theatre critic would have written a completely different book.

In 1994 I published a modest account of the making of *Lawrence of Arabia* which dealt largely with the prolonged and bitter dispute over the authorship of the screenplay. When I interviewed Robert by fax in 1992 he answered my questions patiently and seemed unconcerned about my evident sympathy for his predecessor on the film, a blacklisted writer named Michael Wilson. The following year, after I had edited Kevin Brownlow's monumental and surely definitive biography of David Lean, I realised that a biography of Robert was the next logical step. His work with David Lean was, after all, just one aspect of a remarkable life and career.

Apart from his childhood, education and wartime experiences, there were the radio plays, his startling success as a playwright, the films he made without David Lean and the films he wrote which were never made. There were the four marriages, his life as a schoolteacher, his brushes with scandal, his brief imprisonment, the tragedy of his daughter's death, his son's drug addiction and his own crippling illness. Robert Bolt was far more than merely 'the writer of *Lawrence of Arabia*, *Doctor Zhivago* and *A Man For All Seasons*' and if he never wrote the truly great play, his whole life – as one of my interviewees, John Sergeant, said – was a morality play in itself.

I first made contact with Robert's son, Ben, who managed to camouflage any concerns he may have had and immediately offered his full support, setting aside plans to write a book himself. Despite the demands made on him as a film director, Ben sent many letters and faxes on my behalf and gave me access to a great deal of Robert's private correspondence, screenplays and playscripts, as well as scrapbooks of newspaper clippings. Ben's wife, Jo – one of three Jos in Robert's life – was also a mine of information and insight, unstinting in her time and encouragement. I owe them both the deepest gratitude for without them the book simply could never have been written.

Sarah Miles, Robert's widow, was writing her third volume of memoirs, *Bolt From the Blue*, but as soon as that was completed she invited me to her home on many occasions when she cooked, entertained and talked for hours into my tape recorder. She also gave me unlimited ·and unsupervised access to Robert's filing cabinets from which I would gather armfuls of material and disappear until I was ready for another act of plunder. I am grateful for her patience and, most of all, for her trust and friendship.

Robert's and Sarah's son, Tom, changed his mind about seeing me as the book was nearing completion. His timing was propitious for his unexpected and very welcome appearance gives this story, in musical terms, its recapitulation.

I must also acknowledge here Robert's third wife, Ann Queensberry, who endured several hours of relentless and what must at times have seemed like heartless questioning. Her stamina during what could only have been a terribly painful and exhausting experience fills me with respect.

Robert's first wife, now the novelist Jo Riddett, politely but firmly declined to be interviewed. Sections of the book are undoubtedly the weaker without her contribution and I can only ask for her understanding and forgiveness if she feels she has been unfairly portrayed.

There are many others to acknowledge: Roger L Mayer, President and Chief Operating Officer of Turner Entertainment Co., enabled me to inspect some of the legal files of Metro-Goldwyn-Mayer, now held under the corporate roof of Ted Turner. Andrew Velcoff and, especially, Kristen Ramsey of Turner Broadcasting's legal department, facilitated my visit to steamy Atlanta a week before the start of the Centennial Olympic Games. Few writers in recent years have been given access to the voluminous MGM files and I hope that my incursion may have helped to ease the path for future film historians.

At the BBC's Written Archives Centre in Caversham, near Reading, I discovered – to my delight and great relief – a wealth of material relating to Robert's years as a radio dramatist. So comprehensive, well preserved and catalogued are the BBC's archives that an entire book could have been written about this period in Robert's life. My thanks to Jacqui Kavanagh and Susan Knowles for making my visits there so richly rewarding.

Also in Reading, at the University, archivist Michael Bott is the custodian of a remarkable collection of letters which record the making of *Lawrence of Arabia* and *Doctor Zhivago* and much else besides. These letters, which were donated by David Lean's professional and personal partner for seven years, Barbara Beale, give a unique insight into the working methods of Robert Bolt and David Lean. Michael Bott also drew to my attention the archives of the publishing house Heinemann, which revealed some fascinating material about the thwarted publication of the screenplay for *Lawrence of Arabia*.

In 1992, Paul Jarrico gave me access to the papers of his brother-in-law, Michael Wilson, which I used extensively in my book on *Lawrence of Arabia*. Some of this research, which was conducted at the University of California Los Angeles, is to be found in the present volume. I am delighted that my own work, as well as that of other writers, scholars and filmmakers, has finally led to a public acknowledgement of Wilson's work on *Lawrence*, while not in the least detracting from Robert's own remarkable contribution.

Fred Zinnemann – who sadly died during the writing of the book – not only agreed to be interviewed, he allowed me to inspect his personal papers at the Margaret Herrick Library at the Academy of Motion Picture Arts and Sciences in Los Angeles. My visit to this library, a model of its kind, was made effortless by Sam Gill who also dug out some of the John Huston papers which contained a piquant footnote to Robert's career which I would never have discovered myself. Also at the Academy, Scott Curtis was extremely helpful in solving a mystery about Captain Cook, and Lorraine LoBianco showed me, at a moment's notice, videotapes of the three Oscar ceremonies at which Robert was nominated.

Frith Banbury, who directed *Flowering Cherry* and *The Tiger and the Horse* also agreed to be interviewed and enabled me to inspect his papers which are deposited at the Harry Ransom Humanities

Research Center at the University of Texas, Austin. Melissa Miller, Rachel Howarth and Bill Fagelson dealt with my enquiries with speed and enthusiasm despite the fact that my visit coincided with a major refurbishment of their facility.

Paul Richardson and Caroline Dawnay enabled me to inspect the original Diaries of Kenneth Williams and generously gave permission to publish several entries which were, for various reasons, not included in the published edition. My thanks to them as well for providing copies of many letters which Robert wrote to Williams over a twenty year period.

At Millfield School, near Street in Somerset, archivist Barry Hobson gave me some valuable correspondence as well as introductions to Robert's teaching colleagues and former pupils. In Bishopsteignton, Devon, Sheila Robbins not only provided me with a vivid picture of life in her village, circa 1951, she also enabled me to speak to two of her nephews who had starred in Robert's very first plays. At Her Majesty's Prison at Drake Hall, Staffordshire, the governor Geoff Hughes kindly took me on a tour of the installation, including the cell blocks where Robert spent a fortnight in 1961. Colin Chambers of the Royal Shakespeare Company, who was writing a biography of Margaret Ramsay, was generous with his encyclopaedic knowledge and also gave me copies of several vital letters.

It became a sort of ritual: I would drive out of London, invariably to Dorset, Devon or Somerset, to visit a colleague or former girl-friend of Robert's. They would offer refreshment and as I waited in the living room there on the coffee table would be a neat stack of letters and, sometimes, photographs.

I have been exceedingly fortunate in my subject: Robert not only wrote many hundreds of letters, the recipients invariably kept them. If this book has any strength at all it lies in this marvellously evocative and informative correspondence which I have quoted from at length. And since my subject was a dramatist – and a notoriously articulate talker – I made the decision to present the book as far as possible in dialogue; that is to say, using letters and interviews where other biographers might have chosen to paraphrase or to put thoughts into people's mouths. Robert's life seems to have been a clamour of often dissenting voices and so, in a way, is this book.

I have also decided to quote from Robert's letters *exactly* as they were written, without any attempt to correct spelling mistakes (this becomes acute after his stroke). The reader can therefore be assured that there are no typographical errors; that, for instance, Mr

Knightley in Jane Austen's *Emma* was written as 'Mr Nitely,' 'Falstaff' as 'Falstaf' and 'Gandhi' as 'Ghandi.' Nor, as a consequence, at least as far as Robert's letters are concerned, are there any of those irritating, italicised [*sic*]s to disrupt the flow.

Apart from Robert's first wife, only one other person formally declined to be interviewed. This was Felicity Kendal with whom Robert had a brief affair and a rather longer friendship in the late Seventies. Doubtless Ms Kendal had good reasons for not speaking to me, but her recourse to her solicitor was frankly astonishing. Rather than obtain from others secondhand accounts of her relationship with Robert, I have chosen to write her out of his life altogether.

The list that follows is inevitably long: everyone named on it either agreed to be interviewed or helped in myriad ways. Many of those named also gave permission for their letters to be quoted. My deepest thanks to them all: Lord Attenborough; Den Back; Mr and Mrs Wyndham Bailey; Roy Battersby; Barbara Bloom; Sydney and Jaya Bolt; Carolyn (Pfeiffer) Bradshaw; Malcolm Brown; Kevin Brownlow; Derek Bryan; Michael Bryant; Simon Callow; Leslie Caron; Julia Cave; Judi Cheng; Ronnie Colsen; Pippa Cross; Lord Dacre; the Editor and staff of the Dawlish Gazette; Tor Douglas; John Dunn; Margaret (Chapman) Durden; Liz Dyckhoff; Valerie Eaton Griffith; Madeleine L'Engle; George Englund; Quentin Falk; Mia Farrow; Gary Fishgall; Jon Finch; John Florescu; John Fowles; Roger and Liza Gard; Fernando Ghia; Shelley Groves; Sir Peter Hall; Laurence Harbottle; Gillian Harrison; Ronald Harwood; Jack Hazan; Charlton Heston; George Roy Hill; Eric John; Kenneth Jupp; Michael and Liz Kellaway; Dr Paul Knapman; Joyce Knowland; Mrs Burt Lancaster; Norman Lear; Roy Lockett; Barbara (McClelland) Lover; Bernard McCabe; Herbert McCabe; Naomi (Keanie) May; John Miller; Christopher Morahan; Oswald Morris; Elijah Moshinsky; Julie (Laird) Nightingale; Barry Norman; Trevor Nunn; Sir Anthony Nutting; Ron Paquet; Jay Parini; Sian Phillips; Mr and Mrs Steve Puddephatt; Lord Puttnam; Lord Quinton; Corin Redgrave; Lady Redgrave; Stella Richman; Laura Rivkin; Mr and Mrs Anthony Rossiter; Lady Charlotte (Taylor) St Johnston; David and Sarah Salmon; Ralph Sanders and Mavis Stuckey of the Dawlish Museum; Alan Sapper; Richard Sarafian; Paul Scofield; John Sergeant; Mary Selway; Mark Shivas; the late Len Smith; Barry Spikings; John Standing; Elaine Steinbeck; Oliver Stone; Vaea Sylvain; David Thompson; Terry Thompson; Colin Vaines; Sqn. Ldr Peter Wallis; Stephen Walters;

Michael Wearing; Paula Weinstein; Mary Wesley; Dora Wigg; Bernie Williams.

Final thanks are due to Derek Elley who read the first drafts of the beginning, middle and end of the manuscript (though not necessarily in that order) and kept me on track when the branch lines looked so tempting. His criticisms and encouragement were a godsend. My thanks, too, to my agent, Laura Morris, who secured this project with Hutchinson with astonishing speed. And at Hutchinson, Paul Sidey has been exceptionally kind, enthusiastic and patient, as has his assistant, Sophie Wills. Ilsa Yardley proved the most eagle-eyed copy editor.

My wife, Andrea, somehow endured my absences, even when I was at home. This book is dedicated to her, with much love.

Adrian Turner
London and Los Angeles, October 1997.

PART ONE

NOT FIT FOR PARADISE

'I am in hell!'

Fletcher Christian to William Bligh

'The bugger of writing for a brilliant film director
is that while you are certainly writing for a superior skill
you may be writing for an inferior mind.'

Robert Bolt on working with David Lean

ONE

TO THE SOUTH SEAS

'The road of excess leads to the palace of wisdom.'

William Blake

In the summer of 1977, Robert Bolt's life was in free-fall. He was fifty-two and the fame and fortune which attended him in the previous decade had to some extent evaporated and so had the relative stability of his personal life. The last film to bear his name, *Lady Caroline Lamb*, which also marked his début as a director, had been a mixed blessing, and his latest play, *State of Revolution*, which was running at the Lyttelton, had not been well received and would soon be removed from the National Theatre's repertory.

Prior to 1973, everything that Robert had written had come to fruition very much as he intended – plays such as *A Man For All Seasons*, *The Tiger and the Horse* and, his personal favourite, *Gentle Jack*, as well as five feature films – *Lawrence of Arabia*, *Doctor Zhivago*, *A Man For All Seasons*, *Ryan's Daughter* and *Lady Caroline Lamb*. He had become the highest paid screenwriter in the world, yet people close to him, most notably his agent and confidante Margaret Ramsay, had accused him of selling out. More than that, Ramsay was telling all her new clients that Robert was an example of what not to become.

Robert recognised within himself an imbalance between artistic integrity and creature comforts and in some ways this might be said to have been his major dramatic theme, the conflict between men of reason and men of the flesh, a conflict between the Classical and the Romantic. His family, friends and colleagues mirrored this tension: his first wife, Jo, was described by Peter Hall as having a 'fearsome integrity', while his brother, Sydney, preferred to teach at a Cambridge polytechnic rather than at the University. Colleagues such as David Lean or Sam Spiegel, on the other hand, offered Robert a world of limitless wealth, Rolls-Royces, private yachts, grand hotels and the exercise of power.

A close friend of Robert's, Mike Kellaway, was a sculptor whose lack of fame seemed inextricably bound up with his notion of what an artist's life should be: a struggle. Although some of Kellaway's work left Robert at a rare loss for words, other pieces found their way into his houses and gardens, bizarre monuments to Kellaway's lack of compromise and Robert's beneficence. Just as Robert occasionally goaded Sydney about teaching pupils who were unworthy of his academic gifts, Kellaway was treated to homilies on the importance of money and ambition.

'It maddens me that you should still be teaching at the Slade,' Robert once said to Kellaway. 'What maddens me most of all is that you should toy with the idea that this is merited. I admire your tenacious determination not to throw up the intellectual sponge but are you sure that it is a sponge you have there? It may be a bag of old bricks. The only instrument heavy and sharp enough to break through my own philosophic conceits is my greed for success and for money, which is why I wish you would be greedier.'[1]

Robert's greed almost led him to price himself out of the market, for by the summer of 1977 he was encountering problems. Whereas film producers once found it hard to say 'no' to any screenplay signed by Robert Bolt, they now considered it easy. A screenplay about South American Indians, entitled *Guarani*, was admired by every studio in Hollywood, though none of them wanted to make it. Robert's screenplay of *Gandhi* had been rejected twice, by David Lean and by Richard Attenborough. And *State of Revolution* had only reached the stage of the Lyttelton after several rewrites demanded by Robert's close friend, Peter Hall.

Robert still bore the scars left by his highly publicised divorce from his second wife, the actress Sarah Miles. This followed a bizarre scandal in which Sarah's business manager and lover, David Whiting, had been found dead in her motel room in Gila Bend, Arizona, where she was filming a Western with Burt Reynolds. Pursued by the press, who accused her of murder, Sarah decided to seek privacy and seclusion in Los Angeles and, in so doing, lost custody of her son Tom, a difficult child (named after Sir Thomas More) whose academic and emotional problems gave Robert the greatest cause for concern. Robert saw the three grown-up children from his first marriage – Sally, Ben and Joanna – irregularly though relations with them were affectionate.

The divorce from Sarah obliged Robert to sell the idyllic waterside house in Byfleet, Surrey, which they owned jointly. He gave a lavish 'house-cooling party', replete with fireworks, a fat pig on a barbecue and a glittery guest list which included Albert Finney, Antonia Fraser, Rex Harrison and Kenneth Williams. After the party, he threw his unwanted books on the bonfire – his secretary, Gillian Harrison, wondered why he did not give them to charity – and moved out of the house which now held so many sour memories, most of them associated with Whiting.

He rented an apartment in one of the concrete towers at the Barbican in London and bought a beautiful, secluded fifteenth century manor house in Littlehempston, Devon. It was in Devon that Robert had begun his adult life as a teacher and father; he felt at home there and was looking forward to getting down to some serious writing in his study with its views of rolling hillsides and a rushing stream.

Being a generous man by nature and, consequently, something of a spendthrift, he had relatively little money. The renovation of the Old Manor, which was undertaken by a friend of his, Charlotte Taylor, had consumed most of his capital and what money he had left was being taken from him by Britain's Labour government, whose avowed intention was to 'tax the rich until the pips squeak'. A thoroughly committed socialist like Robert had only one course of action: he needed an excuse to leave the country for a year and, by doing so, to deny the government his personal contribution to their programme of welfare reforms.

Robert had nothing on the immediate horizon to engage his attention, having just turned down a lucrative offer to write an adaptation for television of James Clavell's bulky novel of Japanese history, *Shogun*. Then came a rather less lucrative offer to write a screenplay for Stella Richman, a television executive who, in partnership with David Frost, wanted to break into feature films.

Richman had bought the screen rights to Michael Holroyd's biography of the artist, Augustus John, an esoteric subject for a film which had enough sexual angles to make it commercially viable, she thought. Robert was to be paid $100,000 on delivery of the first draft and a further $67,000 for a second draft if the project went ahead. 'Fred Zinnemann came to see me,' recalled Richman, 'because he was interested in making the film and knew I had just bought the book. He was fascinated by Augustus as an old man, the deterioration. I said to Zinnemann that I could only think of Robert Bolt to write the script but because he was so famous I didn't dare ask him. But Zinnemann said why not, just call him up. So I approached Robert through his agent, Peggy Ramsay, and we made a deal. Robert was interested in the three women who were instrumental in Augustus's life – his sister, his wife and his major mistress. I was happy to go along with that as long as Michael Holroyd was happy.'[2]

Augustus John, who had fallen rapidly from critical favour since his death in 1961, was once a near neighbour of Robert's in Hampshire. The fact that John had painted some of the most famous portraits of T. E. Lawrence and had been a member of Bertrand Russell's Committee of 100, taking part in the famous anti-nuclear demonstration of 17 November 1961, while Robert languished in jail for his own CND activities, would certainly have drawn Robert to the subject. It is also possible that he saw in his new subject the sort of professional Bohemian he often aspired to be. And there was also the idea that John was attractive to women purely because he was an artist. It was this theme which had preoccupied Robert and David Lean when they made *Doctor Zhivago*.

Most of all, though, Robert wanted the money and following a series of amiable meetings with Richman and Holroyd, he swiftly wrote a first-draft screenplay. Holroyd was delighted by Robert's work and Richman seemed confident that she could raise the finance for it.

As Robert was finishing his first draft of *Augustus*, he was startled to receive an invitation to join David Lean on the island of Bora Bora in the South Pacific. Robert had seen little of Lean since they had made *Ryan's Daughter* in 1970. He had become accustomed to Lean's disappearances and long silences: the director was a compulsive traveller who made few friends even among his most regular collaborators. It says much for professional loyalty and the respect in which Lean was held that, when he wanted them, his colleagues could be relied upon to drop everything – family, work, past resentments – and travel across the world at his behest. There was also, of course, the prospect of a handsome pay cheque since a Lean production was in no way lean.

It was Phil Kellogg, Lean's former agent and now his producer, who told Robert that Lean proposed making a new version of *Mutiny on the Bounty*. Having settled more or less permanently in the islands of Polynesia, Lean was determined to make a film there in order to convey to the world his rapture at the lagoons and jagged volcanic peaks. He worked briefly on a biography of Captain Cook, then a film of Alan Moorehead's study of colonialism in the South Seas, *The Fatal Impact*. But when Lean read Richard Hough's *Captain Bligh and Mr Christian*, which was a fresh account of the naval mutiny of 1789, he was astonished by the complexity and richness of the story, as well as its striking divergence from the familiar MGM films of 1935 and 1962. The truth of the *Bounty* mutiny and its even more dramatic aftermath was far stranger than any fiction.

Robert was at once thrilled by the idea. 'Now don't get silly and impatient,' he wrote to Lean. 'You only found this project a week ago yourself. I haven't even read it. And here I am committing myself to it and you, which as you know is a thing I don't do lightly. If you go and get another writer you'll just waste time and money and then call me in anyway. No, I don't think I'm the best writer in the world, I do think I'm a good writer for this particular film. The background, the themes, the characters are right up my alley. Perhaps even too obviously so. We mustn't do merely what we've done before. There really is in this one the opportunity for what we've always wanted – a strong narrative *plus* a bit of freewheeling magic.'[3]

Robert would naturally have wanted to convey to Lean his fullest enthusiasm about the project and he was right in his assessment of the story: the conflict between Christian and Bligh was a precise mirror image of the conflict which motivated Robert as a man and as a writer. Within a month he had familiarised himself with the historical background – the voyage to Tahiti, the mutiny, the doomed search for the mutineers by Edwards in the *Pandora*, the fate of the mutineers on their island refuge of Pitcairn – and sent Kellogg a brilliant summary of the film's principal themes:

> I'm convinced we're on to something very good and I can't wait to start on the actual script. For me, the most amazing and significant stuff is that incredible mutual slaughter which broke out on Pitcairn, and the reasons for it, part racial, part merely human. We're evidently not fit for Paradise. We need civilisation and we need our *own* civilisation. I'm sure that Fletcher Christian was a Romantic – I mean part of the Romantic Movement which found its apotheosis in Byron and Shelley. They believed in Man's innate goodness and the Noble Savage; they thought that rationality was the root of evil and Freedom the root of good. It's all bound up with the French Revolution and other revolutionary movements of the time.
>
> Bligh is the opposite, a scientist, rationalist, disciplinarian. He knows far more about human nature than Christian. But he

knows himself to be forbidding, respected but not liked. He would be charmed by and he would envy Christian's magnetism, popularity, easygoing ways with the men and his way with the girls. So long as he has Christian as his own protégé, his admiring younger brother as it were, he could tolerate all that. But when Christian, in the South Seas, goes his own natural way, all the slackness inherent in his easygoing ways would become doubly apparent to Bligh *because he is partly to blame*. He would react violently back to discipline, the whip and the nagging. And this to Christian would seem unfair, malignant, a crazy persecution.

Anyway, that's very roughly how I see the story in terms of *theme*. And, alas, I can't write a story without a theme. Please show this to David.[4]

While spending a year at a luxury resort hotel in the South Seas may have suited Lean perfectly, people who knew Robert foresaw disaster. He liked theatres, cinemas, restaurants, socialising, and Bora Bora offered none of this. He liked, in fact, *his own civilisation* and wondered how he could possibly cope without it.

Stella Richman remembered Robert fighting a battle within himself as to whether he should go or not: 'It was a terrible mistake for him to go,' she said, 'everyone saw that, but there was nothing anyone could say to stop him. Robert said, "I must go. I can't refuse David. This is going to be his last film and I must write it for him." We all said, "Of course you must." '[5]

On 28 August 1977 Robert began the long journey to Bora Bora. He deposited Tom with Sarah, who was living in a house in Kensington, and headed for the airport. Tom would remain in London until Sarah flew with him to Los Angeles. Then Julie Laird, who was Tom's nanny as well as Robert's research assistant, would fly out to LA, collect Tom from Sarah, and fly on to Bora Bora.

'Robert didn't want to go,' said Sarah, 'but he couldn't let David Lean down. It was obviously going to be difficult for him and he had to take our son Tom with him. We had discussed this a lot and we thought that Tom would be better off having an adventure than in some third-rate school in Los Angeles.'[6]

Robert's secretary, Gillian Harrison, also had misgivings: 'After the divorce, the selling of the house and various other problems, Robert was crazy to go,' she said. 'I thought he was heading for a nervous breakdown.'[7]

Robert's own misgivings are expressed in a letter to Debbie

Condon, a woman he loved deeply who had chosen to marry someone else. On the slightly drunken eve of his departure he wrote: 'Off-pissed I am that you seeing shan't be Bora Bora I go to. I partly look forward to, partly dread the prospect of the Southern Seas. I'm afraid my *main* reason is the money (I tell myself). David is a dreadfully demanding man but he does make very good films. I wish I had someone other than Tom to take with me.'[8]

Robert left his beloved Old Manor in the capable hands of Harrison and his children, and begged them to make as much use of it as they liked. He knew he had no alternative but to take his nine-year-old son Tom with him, even though the boy's education – he could barely read or write – would suffer still further, a fact that Robert, a former schoolteacher, found hard to accept. He consoled himself with the thought that Tom might benefit in other ways and they would at least be together.

Just before Robert left for Bora Bora, word came that Lean now proposed making two films about the *Bounty*, a decision which would prolong Robert's stay and effectively double his fee. The assignment would now earn him $1 million, plus expenses and a hefty percentage of the profits. Robert would write the two pictures for Lean, pay no income tax and return home refreshed, tanned and rich.

Paradise, though, was to exact a heavy penalty.

THE LITTERED LAGOON

'Though we travel the world over to find the beautiful, we must carry it with us or we find it not.'

Ralph Waldo Emerson -

Bora Bora, which lay 160 miles north-west of Tahiti, was once the home of a warmongering tribe of Polynesians who launched regular raids against the nearby island of Huahine and against Tahiti itself. By the time Robert arrived in early September 1977 the descendants of these ferocious warriors performed their war dances for the tourists, who lived in thatched cottages, frolicked in the lagoon and drank cocktails with pink umbrellas.

When the eighteenth-century sailors arrived, after a long slog across the Atlantic and round Cape Horn, they literally couldn't believe their eyes. The surpassing beauty of the landscape was matched by the people who lived there. Apart from the odd skirmish and human sacrifice, it was a world of plenty, with no dangerous animals or reptiles, not even malarial mosquitoes. The explorers and sailors took home such stories of food without end and sex without guilt that a myth of Paradise, a Garden of Eden, rapidly gained currency in British and French society. Bougainville named Tahiti New Cytherea, after the birthplace of Aphrodite, and expedition artists portrayed Tahitian women as water nymphs, half naked and wholly inviting. Rousseau's Noble Savage, it seemed, was not merely a philosophical proposal; it actually had an address in the middle of the Great South Sea.

Within fifty, even twenty, years it was all over. In fact, it was the voyage of the *Bounty* which sealed Tahiti's fate since it was the first specifically mercantile voyage to the South Pacific. When the Admiralty commissioned Bligh to collect breadfruit from Tahiti and transport them to the West Indies, where they would be cultivated and fed to the slaves, the Age of Enlightenment was irrevocably harnessed to the age of enslavement.

After a period of British rule in Tahiti the French took over, at first harshly, and the Tahitians fell victim to diseases like influenza and syphilis, as well as the most deadly disease of all, religion, which was carried by the missionaries. Even so, the South Seas dream persisted: Herman Melville, Pierre Loti, Paul Gauguin, Robert Louis Stevenson, Jack London and Somerset Maugham all went there in search of the primitive. And if they didn't find it on Tahiti or Bora Bora they moved on to the remote Marquesas and if they didn't discover it there, well, they simply imagined it.

Bora Bora's serene slumber was interrupted in 1929, when the film-maker F. W. Murnau filmed *Tabu* there, then by the Second World War when it was invaded by several thousand American marines, one of whom was James Michener, whose stories of the island's beauty merely perpetuated the old South Seas myth. On departure, they left behind an airstrip and several hundred incongruously blond children.

Part of the 1962 version of *Mutiny on the Bounty* was shot there, taking advantage of the island's first resort, the Hotel Bora Bora, where the most prized rooms were a group of six thatched bungalows built on stilts directly over the water. The seventy-year-old David Lean and his thirty-year-old girl-friend, Sandy, had the bungalow furthest from the hotel, the only one of the six to enjoy the staggering view down the lagoon towards the sacred, tombstone shaped volcanic plug called Otemanhu. Today, this room costs $700 a night plus tax; in 1977 it was $150.

Robert was installed in a large beach bungalow with two bedrooms and a sitting room. To begin with, he marvelled at his surroundings: 'It is insanely beautiful,' he wrote in the first of his letters to his children. 'The sea is the colour of stained glass windows, mostly blues and greens, but blazing with light. One thing I hadn't realised is that the lagoons are very shallow. As deep as thirty or forty feet here and there but mostly four or five and often less than three. David and Sandy have a Boston Whaler, a modern outboard boat, so we are independent of the drunkenly expensive facilities provided by the hotel. We have seen shark, stonefish and dozens of manta which are like something from a poet's nightmare, so alien and lovely; they "fly" like giant bats in slow motion. In short it's a wonderful place but I should say somewhat lacking in variety. Six weeks, yes. Six months, no.'[1]

After a week, Robert reported that he felt fitter than he had in years. He was swimming a mile a day, getting in lots of fishing and going to bed before ten each evening. Lean, though, was never seen in the water. He liked nothing better than to perch on his terrace and gaze at the ocean for hour after hour, day after day. Sometimes he would ask Sandy to fetch his trusty old Leica and he would snap through an entire roll, catching the shift in the clouds, the reflection on the water, the spray on the distant reef or, if he was quick enough, the flashing red tail on a cruising tropic bird. There is surprisingly little land in his pictures and rarely any people; Lean seemed to be as obsessed by the empty expanse of the sea as he was by the desert when he made *Lawrence of Arabia*.

He quickly began to irritate Robert. It was as if Lean had matched the perfection of the landscape with his own appearance. He and Sandy were always immaculate and they had even embellished their overwater bungalow with furnishings and china imported from Sweden. 'My life-style gets on his nerves,' Robert told Gillian Harrison. 'His gets on mine; wherever he goes he sets up this elaborate daily ritual and entourage, like Louis XV at Versailles but suburban. There is some corner of a foreign field which is forever Croydon.'[2]

When Robert arrived, Lean had gathered his loyal disciples. There was Phil Kellogg, the producer and former agent who had the reputation of being a gentleman which, in Hollywood, means lacking toughness; it was said that Kellogg only liked to be the bearer of good tidings. There was John Box, the production designer, the man who had built Akaba and Moscow in Spain for *Lawrence* and *Zhivago*. And there were Eddie Fowlie and his wife, Kathleen. Fowlie was not only Lean's prop man, he was his best friend, a rough diamond with a shock of silver hair who knew how to drum up two dozen elephants at the drop of a hat. It was Fowlie who had given Lean a copy of Richard Hough's book, setting in motion the epic that was to follow.

Robert had only been in Bora Bora for a fortnight when the *Bounty* project underwent the first of its convulsions. An executive at Warner Bros, John Calley, had agreed to finance the picture, having been persuaded that Lean was only interested in filming Bligh's heroic 3400 mile open boat voyage following the mutiny. But when Lean told Calley that he wanted to make the entire story and would require an exact replica of the *Bounty*, which would have to be built from scratch, Calley began to worry about the budget. Lean then announced that he wanted to make two films and Calley knew he could never persuade his board to agree to it. Finally, when John Box abruptly quit the production and arrived in Los Angeles with horror stories about Lean's soaring ambition and the budget needed to support it, Calley withdrew his support and put the project into turnaround.

It so happened that the Italian producer, Dino De Laurentiis, was on Bora Bora setting up a remake of John Ford's *Hurricane*. The Hotel Bora Bora turned down De Laurentiis's booking for his cast and crew, so he decided to build his own hotel, the Marara, at the other end of the beach. When Kellogg needed to fly to Los Angeles to meet Calley, De Laurentiis gave him a lift in his private plane and somewhere over the Pacific he agreed to finance both films, as well as the replica *Bounty*. The first film was to be called *The Lawbreakers* and the second, *The Long Arm*.

On 6 October 1977 Julie Laird arrived in Bora Bora with Robert's son, Tom. Robert had met Julie at a dinner party in London only a month or two before. She was in her early thirties and had been an actress, until she married an Irish builder and went to live on the top of a hill in County Cork. When the marriage failed, Julie returned to London, getting a job as a researcher at the Victoria and Albert Museum.

'At the dinner party', said Julie, 'I told a story about when I lived in Ireland. At the bottom of our hill was an old stone building, a pigsty really, which belonged to an old man named Mack. My husband, Bill, wanted to buy the building and make something wonderful out of it. So every evening Bill went down for a chat with Mack. One day, Bill looked up and saw a light bulb on a tree with a flex hanging down, connected to nothing. Bill said, "Mack, what's that bulb for?" And Mack said, "Sure it gives off such a powerful light when the sun's shining through it." Robert never forgot that story.'

Totally charmed by Julie, Robert conspired to meet her on several more occasions. One evening he said he was going to Tahiti and that he wanted her to go with him. 'I can't face David Lean on my own,' he told her.

'It was quite out of the blue,' said Julie, 'so I told him I would think about it. Then he rang and said, "How much are they paying you at the V&A?" I said sixty pounds a week. He said, "I'll pay you sixty pounds a week, you'll live absolutely free and you can let your flat to bring in more cash. It'll set you up." There was a pause, then he said, "And you can bring Tom with you." He'd got it all worked out.

*

I had told Robert that I was the last person to look after Tom. I had no children and I'd no experience of them. But he said, 'Then you're exactly what he needs.' When I arrived in Los Angeles to collect Tom from Sarah they were both in a state. They're very close in a way but, wow, it's not to be tampered with if you're an outsider. I had to more or less drag Tom out of the house screaming.

Robert met us at the airport in the middle of the night and took us to the hotel where David Lean had stayed up to see what I was like. He hadn't welcomed the idea of a 'museum' person joining his unit. He said, 'You look awfully pale.'[3]

Robert and Julie enjoyed each other's company. They giggled a lot, listened to Mozart records and every morning at six o'clock they snorkelled beneath Lean's overwater bungalow and made V-signs like a pair of school children. Apart from the work, the reason for it all, they found their situation entirely ridiculous, which it often was, as in the ludicrous saga of the pawpaw and the hotel gardener:

> The Tahitian gardener is one of the very great bores of all time [Robert told his children]. He greets me every morning with entirely spurious bonhomie and gifts of pawpaw – a greenish fruit tasting like potato soaked in melon juice – for which he receives obligatory gifts of cigarettes, beer and matches. His appetite for these is insatiable; our appetite for pawpaw is strictly limited.
>
> His supply of pawpaw is flexible and large because he steals them from other people's gardens. My method of disposal was to wait until night and fling them far out to sea. But pawpaws float and the evidence accumulated. So Julie takes them into the Chinese store where she furtively slips them into the racks along with other pawpaw, a sort of reverse shoplifting which would seem bizarre in Fulham High St but here seems quite sensible. Of such things are my days composed. Keep writing for God's sake.[4]

To an outsider – and perhaps to Lean and Sandy – Robert and Julie were behaving as if they were lovers, even honeymooners, like so many of the hotel's American and Japanese guests. But the truth was rather more complicated.

> It was something we both avoided [said Julie]. I thought that a job was a job and I was being paid. He asked me very sweetly once, 'Do you want me to go to bed with you? I'm not very good at it.' I was deeply embarrassed and said, 'Look, as far as I'm

concerned it's never been a question of the Olympics. I just don't think it's a good idea.' Then there was one beautiful evening, following a tense dinner with David and Sandy, when we went out in our pirogue to see a cruise liner moored in the bay. Robert said to me, 'Look, when this is all over and when I get back to England . . .' And I said, 'Don't say another word. Just leave it. This isn't real, nothing down here is sensible' and I think he appreciated that.

Years later I told him how glad I was that nothing had happened between us. It meant we had never let each other down and that we never got into an area we couldn't handle. I think he was comforted by that because he had so many emotional problems, especially with women. He said to me, 'I work or I screw. A lot of us men are absolutely useless in this area.' I think he meant it. He also had problems with his children because he wasn't always sure if he really loved them or not. It was a question of, well, how are you supposed to feel? Looking back, I think I was safer with Robert by not becoming too close.[5]

As soon as he started work on the script, Robert knew he was in for a hard time. Lean had changed in small but infuriating ways since they had last worked together on *Ryan's Daughter*. Because Lean thought the *Bounty* project might be his swan-song, the films had to be truly great, ultimate epics. He cared little about what they might cost because he believed – wrongly as it turned out – that De Laurentiis had given him an open cheque. And in order to realise this great work, Lean wanted Robert to write a grand procession of major sequences in which Lean's artistry would dazzle the world.

Robert knuckled under and dreamed of England. 'Lotus eating I am not,' he wrote to Gillian Harrison. 'The food at this violently expensive hotel would disgrace a British restaurant in the middle of an air raid. I would give anything for a Salcombe Smokey and a Devonshire cream tea.'[6]

When Gillian read Robert's catalogue of complaints, many of them directed at Lean, she understood at once what the problem was: 'It is sad to know that your great affection for David is being nibbled by irritation,' she wrote. 'I suppose to live at such proximity with him must be getting on your nerves. He must be moving out of that way of life which you originally shared with him – middle age – he must be seventy. In other words, he is getting old and you aren't.'[7]

After a month, Tom had become a major concern for Robert and for Julie, who had to cope with him when Robert was closeted with Lean, which was most of the time. Through no fault of his own, Tom was entirely unsuited to life at Bora Bora. He could be sullen one day, hysterical the next and was generally disruptive around the hotel, which endeavoured to maintain a quiet, country club atmosphere. Tom had also been sent to a school in the island's only village, Vaitape, and because the lessons were all in French he couldn't understand a thing. Robert noted ruefully that instead of learning French, Tom was forcing the other children to speak English. 'This place and this life are no good for him,' he told Gillian Harrison. 'Julie is being perfect; affectionate, attentive, crisp and conscientious. I am doing my best which, after a day with David, isn't very good I fear. The climate is bad for kids. Tom's always precarious metabolism and sensitive skin have produced a constellation of running sores and a general mood of tearful depression. He's not allowed into the sea which in this, the rainy season, is a soup of bacteria and coral polyp. And he's learning nothing at school; if anything he's regressing. The hotel this morning looks like a carelessly administered Japanese death camp. Perhaps it is.'[8]

If Robert was trying to cope with Tom's specific set of problems, Lean was another sort of problem. Both were equally draining. 'David is even less flexible and more self-certainly shut-minded than I remember him,' Robert told his other children. 'He remains I think a near genius or at least a master craftsman, but personally is less rewarding and more demanding than Thomas. Between him and Thomas there is the natural antipathy of perfect similarity. On David's side there is authority, but Thomas has youth. . . . The boredom and the melancholy are beyond expression and would be beyond endurance were it not for the work and my frantic need of the ambrosial payment.'[9]

'Tom was a curious child,' said Julie. 'I don't think I was good with him and when he got septicaemia I knew he'd be much better off in England at a proper school. But he was terribly brave and seemed to accept all the things that were happening to him. Then he could go completely berserk for no apparent reason. So I persuaded Robert to let me take him home and it was also agreed with David that I should do research work on the film in London.'[10]

The oppressive weather had made everybody fractious and even getting Julie and Tom to Papeete, the capital of Tahiti, where they would meet the plane for Los Angeles, turned into a maze of crossed wires:

All *sorts* of stimulus here just now [reported Robert]. Sarah is going to have Tom for Christmas, unless of course she isn't. That we shall find out tomorrow when Julie deposits him (or doesn't) in LA with Sarah. Julie was booked out of here for Papeete tonight to spend the night there before proceeding to LA. But then Dino De Laurentiis said no, use our plane tomorrow and reduce it all to a day-trip. Yes, we said, how lovely. Aha, they said, our private plane is poorly. Oh we said, never mind, it's the thought that counts. No no, said David Lean, we'll charter a private plane. So now here we are with three distinct possibilities none probable and the LA plane will leave Papeete tomorrow with or without Tom and Julie. Small wonder that ordinary people envy us film folk the dash and high colouring of our privileged lives.[11]

Julie and Tom left Bora Bora by scheduled inter-island flight on 17 December 1977. 'On the plane to Los Angeles, Tom said to me, "Will we see each other again?" and I said I didn't know. Then he said, "You are the only person who is completely honest. You don't pretend to like me, you don't pretend not to." I was very moved by that because I knew I had failed him.'[12]

Tom subsequently returned to England and was looked after by Robert's friend, Ann Queensberry, who registered him at Port Regis school which was near her home in Dorset. Julie returned to the V&A and continued to work for Robert and Lean, conducting research into such arcane topics as the precise shape and size of ships' biscuits, the staple diet for eighteenth-century sailors.

Robert fell into a deep depression when Julie left him. There was no one he could talk to, no one he could have fun with, no one who appreciated the essential absurdity of the situation. 'Tom and Julie left yesterday, leaving me fairly desolate,' Robert told Ann Queensberry. 'However, a grim morning's work and a half bottle of hock followed by a sweaty afternoon sleep restored me to a more normal state of dejection. I am extremely touched by your maternal care for Tom. Touched be buggered. I was moved to the brink of tears; he's incredibly fortunate that his father has such a friend as you. And if he is appreciative of it then you've already done more for him than either of his parents. I find that I love him a lot, but I'm suspicious of that fondness which augments with absence. If he were here with me now I expect I'd be climbing round the walls.'[13]

Shortly after Christmas David Lean moved his team from Bora Bora to the main island of Tahiti. This not only made sense from a practical point of view – Bora Bora hardly boasted a telephone – but delighted Robert, since Papeete was filled with restaurants, bars and cinemas. Even though the weather was, if anything, more oppressive than Bora Bora, you could at least pretend you were in a tropical outpost of Europe.

To begin with everyone checked into the Beachcomber Hotel, a sprawling resort at the foot of the runway of Tahiti's international airport. 'The lagoon, when you can see it through the reeking rain, is strongly reminiscent of a reservoir in Lancashire,' Robert told Julie. 'I have met a couple of women in Papeete, neither of whom I want to see again but will because the alternative is tensely delicate conversation with David and Sandy or solitude which I don't like. I get on well with Dostoevsky who is at least mad but am sick to the teeth with Henry James who seems like a nasty old woman and full of shit on top of it. What I really need is a supply of pornographic detective novels.'[14]

Away from the tourists at the hotel, Robert thought the people in Papeete were indolent and arrogant: 'They are suffering from malnutrition because it's easier to buy muck at the supermarket than it is to fish and gather fruit,' he told his agent, Margaret Ramsay. 'The quality of life one senses to be dropping in direct ratio to the rise in the standard of living. Money is pouring into the country, partly as a bribe because the French have chosen hereabouts for testing their atomic bombs and pay the locals to keep mum about it.'[15]

Apart from his bulletins on Polynesian politics, Robert kept Ramsay fully appraised of his work and his relationship with Lean, which was deteriorating by the day. In particular, Robert was worried by Lean's apparent lack of interest in the deeper themes of the project.

> I'm almost sure that David's wonderful and fatal talent for exploiting 'directorial opportunities' will render the thing a shade juvenile [Robert told Ramsay]. He gets terribly restless if I try to fill out a character or heighten a theme, if only for a single page. Perhaps he's right; God knows, he's been uniquely successful. But it's a bit discouraging.
>
> If only he had a touch more literary interest what a marvellous artist he would be. He's much more intelligent than he allows himself to show; but what he does he does superlatively well and at the age of seventy I dare say he has the right to go on doing it. And I'd a million times rather work with a master craftsman

than with some vaguely aspirant avant-gardist. He's terribly sensitive about his standing with the intelligentsia and would be very hurt to think I had criticised him even so gently as this, so keep my doubts to yourself. But you see what I mean. It sort of blunts my mind a bit.[16]

January faded into February, then March, and it had never stopped raining. Tourists came and went and Robert noted that while they all looked sad, fat and ugly, they did at least have a plane ticket home. 'I have vowed not to visualise my return,' he wrote, 'but sometimes when I see across the lagoon the Air France Jumbo taking off for California *en route* for Europe I have a giddy foretaste of the day when I'll be on it and must suppress my feelings sternly and immediately lest I run laughing madly through the poolside restaurant upsetting canned pineapple over the dying tourists, or throw myself down gnashing at the plastic grass.'[17] Robert's dejection was not lifted by the approach of the dry season, an event heralded by a plague of snails and a cool, twenty-minute breeze each morning.

Lean and Robert had reached the point of the mutiny itself. Lean was quibbling over every dot and comma, only knowing what he wanted when Robert gave it to him, which was rarely. As Robert told Gillian Harrison, 'I simply couldn't get Bligh to get his arse into the longboat and Christian showed a maidenly reluctance to carry out the mutiny.'[18]

The problem was, no one could agree precisely why, on 28 April 1789, the most famous mutiny in British naval history had happened. While some historians put the blame on Tahiti, claiming that Christian and the other mutineers wanted to remain there with their native girl-friends, others felt that Christian's affair with a Tahitian girl appalled Bligh who, on the voyage home, vented all his sexual frustration on Christian. For his part, Robert wished he could simply blame the weather. 'My own guess', he wrote, 'is that Christian was a bit delinquent and Bligh a bit paranoid and that these effects were hypertrophied by the fact that the *Bounty* was here precisely in the season from which we are emerging: November to March. This is a fact which no one mentions (certainly the film won't mention it) and which effectively negates the usual theory that the crew wanted to stay here. Even the three-day tourists want to get away.'[19]

During his first months in Tahiti, Robert had been on the prowl for female company. Going out in public with Lean and Sandy made him feel like a gooseberry. Although he told Margaret Ramsay that 'sex is to be had as easily as a coconut', he needed a woman to talk to, someone to fill the vacuum left by Julie. By the end of March there were a couple of likely candidates. He told his friends, Roger and Liza Gard:

> I have met a number of young ladies, some of them physically pleasing but only one of real interest. She is a painter, nicely tainted with a modest success in Paris and New York and she has a quaint little house by the sea. But she regards all forms of feminine blandishment as a betrayal of the self; so *that's* no good.
>
> This evening however I am to dine intimately with a strikingly handsome little person of mixed extraction who is very Parisienne and goes in for feminine blandishment a good deal. On the telephone she says things like, 'I kiss you on my toes' in reference to my towering stature and herculean strength. I like this. Her name is Tiare and I suspect she is a flibbertigibbet. The name of the painter is Vaea. I like her a lot but she does have these hairy forearms.[20]

Robert met Vaea on 15 March 1978 at the Auberge du Pacifique, a smart restaurant near Papeete. It was David Lean's seventieth birthday and everyone wore traditional leis, and there was island music and dancing. Vaea caught Robert's eye and they began a halting conversation in his fractured French and her minimal English.

Vaea Sylvain was twenty-six, the daughter of a part-Tahitian mother and a part-Polish father who was a professional photographer. He had covered the filming of the Brando version of *Mutiny on the Bounty* for *Life* magazine, though most of his work was destroyed in a fire in 1968, a loss which devastated him and wrecked his health.

In Polynesian legend, Vaea is the goddess of comedy and it is also the name of the mountain on which Robert Louis Stevenson is buried in Samoa. Vaea was tall and slender with only subtle suggestions of Polynesian blood. Her left eye had a tiny blood spot near the iris, the result of a palm-frond piercing her eye when she was a child. Whereas most Tahitian girls lived in extended families and looked forward to marriage and children, Vaea was different, a perpetual outsider. She lived alone and felt stifled by Tahiti's enclosed society and by its isolation from the rest of the world. 'In

Tahiti,' she said, 'you would buy a newspaper and on the front page there would be a story about a ten kilo water melon and on the back page there would be a tiny announcement about the death of Brezhnev. I hated Tahiti and wanted to leave. Robert – I always called him Robert, never Bob – also wanted to leave. He missed the city, the people, his family and friends. He told me, "This is the last movie and I'm only doing it for David." Of course, he wanted to do it as well as he could, but he had so many plans for other projects, plays and books he wanted to write.'[21]

After a short while, Robert moved into Vaea's seaside cottage and commuted to the Beachcomber. As the relationship developed, so too did Robert's French and Vaea's English. 'We used a lot of dictionaries,' she said.

Although Lean seemed pleased that Robert had found himself a girl-friend, his own contact with Tahitians was largely confined to boatmen and waiters. Privately he thought that Robert – like Fletcher Christian – had gone native, if not mad, as evidenced by the way his appearance had slowly capitulated to tropical languor. His belly hung over the waistline of his frayed shorts, his beard was unruly, his shoes were filthy and his mode of transport was a battered Toyota truck. Lean wondered if Robert was losing his grip and Sandy thought his behaviour was 'delinquent'.

Robert had just moved in with Vaea when he learned that his thirty-year-old daughter, Sally, and Ann Queensberry's daughter, Tor, were coming out to see him. Sally was in the middle of an emotional crisis, having recently separated from her husband, Neil Simmons. Not wanting to upset or confuse Sally, Robert decided to move out of Vaea's cottage and into a large apartment in the Vaima Building, which is where Eddie Fowlie was living. On Sally's and Tor's arrival at the gloomy apartment, Robert became depressed when they took it over in 'a messily maternal manner'.[22] Tor said:

> Bob wanted to see Sally, but he didn't want her to go on her own because he knew she'd be bored. So I went with her and we took our babies with us, eighteen months and six months. Bob was hardly there. He'd tootle off every day to the Beachcomber to work from nine to nine. He kept Vaea under wraps for a bit because she was younger than us and he thought Sally would be shocked.
>
> Bob worried about Sally who always wanted to know if he loved her. And of course he did love her, but he got pretty fed up with being pushed and tested. She had to do it with

everybody and blamed herself for the split up with Neil, which was total rubbish. Because Bob was so busy, he sent us off to Bora Bora and Moorea, though we had one token meal with David Lean and Sandy which was hilarious because David couldn't cope with having two babies as well as us.[23]

As Robert tried to keep Sally and Tor amused, while at the same time entertaining Vaea and appeasing Lean, he had yet another person to attend to, the actress Mia Farrow, who had arrived in French Polynesia with eight children and two nannies. She was there to make *Hurricane* for De Laurentiis. Like Sally, Mia Farrow had just separated from her husband, André Previn, and was in need of reassurance. Robert had known Farrow for some years – her father, a film director, had once written a biography of Sir Thomas More – and he had occasionally advised her on which plays she might perform on stage. Robert adored her; like Sarah, she was intense, warm and as mad as a hatter.

With Sarah permanently on his mind, and Vaea and Farrow always within his sight, Robert could not avoid making comparisons between them. 'Vaea is a naïf egoist, if not quite in Sarah's class,' he told Margaret Ramsay. 'What *is* the matter with me? Mia Farrow is amongst us and comes on promisingly; but those huge blue eyes are clouded in a whirling chaos of emotional small print which Proust himself couldn't cut into clauses. I take it that she like me is just vulgarly lonely. What small and insufficient entities we are, when denied our customary social echo chambers and dumped down somewhere really alien.'[24]

Robert breathed a sigh of relief when, at the end of June, Sally and Tor returned to England with two of Mia Farrow's children who had complained of not having a piano in their rented bungalow. Farrow herself moved on to Bora Bora to make *Hurricane*. Only Vaea was left and he rapidly came to a decision about her, one which was coloured by Sally's incessant demands for confirmation that Robert loved her. He wrote:

> I have been restored to hope and working order, by allowing myself to become decently, I mean emotionally, involved with the young painter. . . . I decided I was messing her about and broke it off and was amazed by the intensity, the mingled anger and distress, of her reaction. This made me feel sufficiently trivial to take another look at my own motives which proved to be less nasty though more banal than I had imagined.
>
> I had more or less assumed that nobody any longer could

have me – though I credited myself with being widely liked – so that prudence dictated my not loving anybody. What I had to surmount was no shortcomings in Vaea but a hump of infantile fear of mistrust in myself. So here with incredulity are Vaea and myself, a locally recognised couple. I admit but do not dwell upon the improbabilities (age and culture differences) and am resolved to be grateful and not too far-sighted.[25]

As part of the purging of his system, Robert also stopped smoking. A sixty-a-day man for years, he quit through 'self disgust, the whole process taking about three minutes. It was a bit like cutting off a finger and I'm still suffering withdrawal symptoms after breakfast, upon commencement of work and after dinner, at which times I pace about a good deal, tearing the wallpaper and eating raw carrots.'[26]

Robert completed the script of *The Lawbreakers* on Sunday, 23 July 1978, ten months after his arrival in Tahiti. He did not rate it amongst his best work, describing it to Margaret Ramsay as 'Top Second if you know what I mean. Not really First Class. They are all saying "great". I don't think I've ever seen a great film. Not in the sense that Ludwig's 5th or Leo's W&P are great. In the improbable event of my surviving this experience I want: (a) a rest and (b) to write another play. Great plays I have seen. Written, no; seen, yes. It really is enormously demanding, this that I am doing. It's almost like a masochistic experiment, to see exactly what intensity of sheer hard graft for how long I can sustain. David and I have the same relationship as Dorian Gray and his portrait. David remains unlined and innocent.'[27]

However, the two DLs – David Lean and Dino De Laurentiis – were ecstatic about Robert's script, and with good reason, for it is a masterpiece that reads like a novel, no mean achievement considering the rigid format in which screenplays are written. Its quality also belies Robert's claim that he was only doing it for the money. Although *The Lawbreakers* ostensibly deals with the voyage out to Tahiti, culminating in the mutiny, Bligh's open boat voyage and the mutineers' arrival on Pitcairn, it weaves a particularly intricate structure that gives the story a remarkable set of perspectives.

The script begins with the mutiny itself, except that we are soon shocked to discover that what we are watching is not the mutiny at all but a theatrical rendition of it, performed on a London stage in 1790. Bligh is in the audience, shamed and quietly seething. He is next seen in Portsmouth, approaching a frigate called the *Pandora* whose captain, Edward Edwards, has been ordererd by the Admiralty to hunt down the mutineers and bring them back to England for justice. After a rather tense conversation, Bligh leaves Edwards with the *Bounty*'s log and as he reads it out aloud, we flash back to the preparations for the *Bounty*'s voyage. At key dramatic moments the screenplay flashes back to Edwards reading the log as the *Pandora* makes its way to Tahiti. As an evocation of life in the eighteenth-century navy and as an investigation into a popular myth, Robert's screenplay has no equals.

Lean was anxious to press on with the second script, *The Long Arm*, which would deal with the slaughter on Pitcairn, Edwards's harsh treatment of the mutineers who remained on Tahiti, his shipwreck off the Great Barrier Reef and his open-boat voyage to Coupang, which is where Bligh struggled ashore after his own journey. Bligh's second – and successful – breadfruit mission to Tahiti, the execution in London of three mutineers and the belated discovery of the sole surviving mutineer on Pitcairn would conclude the epic project.

Robert, though, insisted on taking a holiday. He desperately wished to return to the Old Manor in Devon and he wanted his family and his friends around him. But because the tax man would want his money, he went to Ann Queensberry's farmhouse at Cogolin in the South of France. His four children – Sally, Ben, Joanna and Tom – joined him there, as did Ann's three daughters, Tor, Emma and Alice. Robert also decided to take Vaea with him. They could all celebrate his fifty-fourth birthday together.

Although Robert revelled in his role as patriarch, his relationship with Vaea was strained, a fact which he ascribed not only to his own jumble of morals and motives but also to Sally's raw emotional state. Robert's interest in Vaea had made Sally resentful, if not jealous. Vaea, though, had her own perspective on the holiday: 'I saw how much he loved Ann,' she said, 'and I thought that he would probably marry her. Then I got depressed when I heard that my previous boyfriend had married and become a father. It was a difficult time for me, so I decided to leave for Paris and go back to Tahiti on my own.'[28]

'Vaea was quite a bit younger than Dad,' said Robert's son, Ben. 'Since there didn't seem to be any kind of intellectual marriage between them, I deduced she was not due for longevity in his life. She didn't seem to be in love with him or he in love with her. There wasn't any of the banter or fun in their relationship which I saw with women whom he did love. Otherwise, it was a great holiday. Dad had given up smoking, he'd swim for a mile a day, he'd drink wine and talk and he loved going out to all the restaurants. He seemed happy, un-neurotic and in very good nick.'[29]

As soon as Robert arrived back in Tahiti, he told Vaea that while they should live apart, he hoped they would remain friends. He urged her to leave Tahiti and live in Paris. Vaea took this badly; she felt as if she had been used, that Robert had been treating her like a child, a backward island girl. 'I do not know what went wrong when Sally was here and in France,' he told her. 'One does not love and cease to love for sensible reasons. It happens. I reproach myself. Believe me Vaea, I wanted to make it work very much. It gave me hope for my own future. I tried seriously; it was never a game or a pastime. It was a hard thing to accept that I did not want to, could not, ask you to share the rest of my life with me. And it was hard to tell you. I am not a monster, to enjoy giving pain, nor an idiot not to know that I am giving pain. I am in fact a coward and often lie or equivocate to avoid inflicting pain.'[30]

Having messily extricated himself from Vaea, Robert gathered his impressions of the holiday and wrote to Ann:

> That was, despite the various little handicaps, the best holiday of my adult life! I *liked* being with Tom. To you, who are so effortlessly and naturally loving, that will seem a curious circumstance to celebrate, but for me it was a revelation and relief. I have explained, point blank, the situation or lack of situation to Vaea and apologised for the error of my ways (her errors are not my business) and on the whole she has accepted it with good grace.
>
> One consequence of my brush with Vaea is the realization that I absolutely cannot judge of anything closely concerning myself while I am here. I am sufficiently an 'island hand' to be a bit potty. It was largely self-indulgent weakness on my part to pretend it was suitable, on her part largely strong-willed opportunism. Her fault lesser and more respectable than mine, my only credit being to have realized in time. So like I say it's the work, the whole work and nothing but the work. But that is a miserable diet.[31]

Robert also told Ann, in confidence, that since his return to Tahiti he had the distinct and uneasy impression that the films were falling apart, owing to a fundamental misunderstanding between Lean and Dino De Laurentiis. What he did not tell Ann, nor Sally, Ben nor Joanna, nor even Julie nor Margaret Ramsay, was that on the journey back to Tahiti he had suffered a heart attack.

FALLING DOWN

Biting my truant pen, beating myself for spite, 'Fool,' said my
Muse to me, 'look in thy heart and write.'

Sir Philip Sidney

After the twenty-hour flight from Paris, Robert had landed in
Papeete with a stinging pain in his chest. He staggered back to his
apartment and slept for thirty hours. When he woke up, the pain was
still there, so he took himself to hospital and saw a local doctor.

'He, an untrustworthy looking *pied noir* from Algeria with silver
sideburns, a pencil moustache and sad, bedroom eyes, ejected a hair
from his cardiogram and then said that a "piece of my heart is dead".
I liked the untutored poetry of the phrase but felt I should get a
scientifically more sophisticated opinion.'[1]

As soon as Robert told Lean that he had suffered a heart attack, he
was sent to see a specialist in Los Angeles.

There the doctors, for heavy cash consideration, subjected me
to various devices rejected by the Lubyanka as inhumane, and
confirmed the diagnosis. A piece of my heart is indeed dead and
the scar will not be complete until April when they want to see
me again. They are hoping to find it necessary to perform a
bypass operation but their expectation dwindled throughout my
sojourn in Los Angeles as my condition improved under the
medications which I am still imbibing.

The most distinguished and expensive of the three [doctors]
told me I had a very strong constitution. I am proud of the
strong constitution but a bit humiliated by the dotty self-
ignorance which can be unaware of a passing heart attack. It's
all very well to be absent-minded, but absent-bodied?[2]

Robert now felt able to tell his family and friends what had happened to him. From Los Angeles he wrote a bulletin to be circulated as widely as necessary. He made as light of it as possible: 'It seems that on Sep 2nd or 3rd, *en route* to Papeete, at the midway point of Los Angeles airport, deposits of rump steak, New Zealand butter and the sediments of moderately priced wines got together in one of the arteries of my heart and held a protest meeting. The pain continued and I found myself falling asleep over the typewriter more frequently than could be accounted for by the soporific qualities in my present subject matter. Hence my visit to the doctor in Papeete and subsequently here (the bill I imagine will bring on another heart attack).'[3]

Relieved he did not require heart surgery, Robert returned to Tahiti with a supply of pills and firm instructions to take more exercise, eat more healthily and cut out drinking. The work resumed.

Gillian Harrison said that Robert could not function without some sort of crisis going on, even if it meant that he had to invent one. In Tahiti he had several crises, some of which manifested themselves when he got there, the others he took with him. The pressure he was under was intense.

Working with Lean was an undoubted strain, though one senses a little bit of the prima donna in Robert's letters home. Lean did indeed drive Robert mad and it might be argued that he drove Lean mad as well.

The project was taking far longer than Robert had expected yet Lean seemed to conspire delays, even to the extent of initiating a documentary film for New Zealand Television after Eddie Fowlie discovered an anchor, believed to have belonged to Captain Cook, submerged in the sea off the village of Tautira. While Lean imported a camera crew and specialist divers and equipment, Robert was prevailed upon to write the script and to record part of the commentary. In London, even Robert's son, Ben, was called on to film a few shots of Admiralty Arch and the adjacent statue of Captain Cook. The whole enterprise took weeks out of the schedule and the documentary ends with Lean, Fowlie and Robert on the tarmac at Papeete Airport. 'Come on,' says a beaming Lean, putting his arm round Robert's shoulders, 'we've got a film to make.' Robert later thought that the forty-minute documentary, *Lost and Found*, was 'beneath contempt. . . . . The talk between David and myself is to make the flesh crawl but it's David's fillum and I wasn't prepared to argue because all I wanted to do was get back to the main project;

not because I'm enjoying the main project but because I long with a rending passion to get to the end of it.'[4]

While Robert always convinced himself that he was only writing the screenplays in Tahiti for the money, the evident depth of his interest in the project and the quality of his work tends to refute this. Nevertheless, Robert's letters home were becoming increasingly waspish about Lean: 'The bugger of writing for a brilliant film director', he told Julie, 'is that while you are certainly writing for a superior skill you may be writing for an inferior mind. You can't ponder the nature of Black Holes with a man who has never heard of gravity. I try to slip in my little contributions as I drive my pitons into the cliff face and work us along from one directorial opportunity (shipwreck, sacrilege, rape or sunset) to the next, but that's the most that I can do.'[5]

To Charlotte Taylor, who renovated the Old Manor, he wrote, 'If only David knew what he wanted I might be able to give it to him more quickly; he just knows he wants another Oscar and a blaze of glory. There's no artistic intention behind the films whatever. Except what I am able to smuggle in when he isn't looking. Anything even minimally over his head offends him. It's the acid test of a middle-brow that anything he understands is vital, anything he doesn't is highfalutin. There are for him three intellectual categories: the stupid, the pretentious, and himself.'[6]

Perhaps a greater strain than physically working with Lean was Robert's belief that the project was doomed. He blamed Lean for that and believed he would never be paid. And when it looked as if he was going to get paid, he was told that a significant amount might have to be deducted from his fee because Dino De Laurentiis had borrowed the money from Paramount, his distributors, and intended to charge Robert the interest on the loan. Since this was estimated to be as much as the income tax which Robert planned to avoid paying all along, the whole enterprise looked pointless, a sick joke at Robert's expense.

He also felt conned and resentful, having assumed all along that Lean was putting his own money into the project. This turned out to be far from the truth: 'I have learned, by chance and to my irritation,' Robert told Margaret Ramsay, 'that David intends putting in for past and present expenses at $1500 weekly. Just double what I have been getting. I had been led to suppose that David was magnificently meeting all his own expenses privately to unburden the budget.'[7]

Robert was also railing against Stella Richman who, he felt, still owed him money for *Augustus*. In Tahiti, though, he was powerless to do anything about it other than threaten lawsuits and write constant reminders to Margaret Ramsay. He also worried about the cost of maintaining the Old Manor; he worried about an arrangement with the National Trust which had some obscure claim to part of the property; he worried about his car insurance and his life insurance as well as his British driving licence which had expired and disqualified him from driving in Tahiti, and he worried about the ACTT of which he was president. His daughter Sally distressed him and the drama with Vaea was another crisis, this time entirely of his own making.

But one worry superseded all others: his son Tom and his former wife, Sarah Miles, who was living in Los Angeles trying to recover some emotional equilibrium after being accused of murder in Arizona. This left Tom in an emotional and geographical limbo and Robert knew well enough that he, too, was part of the problem. 'I am close to tears of helpless exasperation and pity (for Tom but for Sarah too and, doubtless, myself) whenever I think of his predicament,' he wrote to a colleague.

Sarah's problem was that everyone was against her and that whenever she and Tom were together, something happened to turn the occasion into an emotional thunderstorm. 'There is no question of your not seeing him,' Robert told her. 'You must see him as often as you can. The more often the better because the more often the less dramatic.'[8]

When Tom left Tahiti he was looked after by Ann Queensberry who enlisted him at a boarding school for which Robert paid all the fees. Having secured Tom in England, Robert found himself agreeing to let Sarah see him as little as possible and at one point Tom's passport was lodged with Robert's lawyer to prevent him from travelling abroad.

Since Robert himself was unable to visit England for tax reasons, he was receiving advice from friends who all said the same thing: Robert had to distance himself from Sarah. In particular, Robert's agent, Margaret Ramsay, disliked and distrusted Sarah with a passion and her letters to Robert such as this one which Sarah found in her files are injected with a particularly lethal venom: 'Sarah *wants* to put you in continuous anguish re Tom,' she wrote. 'This proves to her that she exists. She may take Tom temporarily but she will dump him back on you whenever she wants. In the end you will have both Tom and Sarah round your neck for the rest of their lives as no one else will want them. A lot is your own fault as you too *wallow* on these feelings and emotions. Sad and what a waste of genuinely *good* and productive emotions and energies. I despise her – she is dangerous.'[9]

As Robert's agent, Ramsay was overstepping the mark by involving herself in family matters and by acting on impulse and rumour. The fact is that Ramsay and Sarah hardly knew each other. But Ramsay was jealous of Sarah's influence over Robert's life and career, just as she was jealous of David Lean. 'I had to contend with all that,' she said.

Robert though, still cared deeply about Sarah, and he worried about her living in California where she was putting on a one-woman show called *SmileS*. Sarah opened the show in San Francisco and planned to take it to Los Angeles and London.

'Sarah does not lack spirit,' Robert told Ramsay. 'She's a stormy petrel that one. [Her show] seems to me a very chancy operation, demanding dazzling personality and expertise, to say nothing of phenomenal stamina. Mind you, she has more than her fair share of those qualities.'[10]

If Sarah and Tom were Robert's principal concern, another source of exasperation was Ramsay's constant moralising. What particularly upset Ramsay was that Robert had persuaded her that he was doing the *Bounty* scripts purely for the money and that they were killing him as a writer and as a person. And since Ramsay had a lifelong disdain for the cinema, she felt vindicated, even though ten percent of Robert's fee from De Laurentiis was worth much more to her than ten percent of his fee from *State of Revolution*.

When Robert gently reminded her about this apparent contradiction and asked that she cease writing about his lack of moral values, Ramsay fired off an extraordinary letter to Tahiti which threatened to bring their long relationship to an abrupt end:

'Your letter to me was appalling', wrote Ramsay. 'If you'd like to go you should do so, as you owe me nothing. I owe you far more for the years I've been associated with your extraordinary artistic development. Believe me, you haven't changed but there's a danger of a carapace of a kind where the hard water leaves its deposits on a kettle! They in the end prevent the kettle functioning properly. You don't know, quite, how all these problems and efforts are dangerous to you. . . a few people will tell you as few people remember you poor and unknown. They fear to offend you. I may be clumsy but I do want to tell you the truth.'[11]

Having got that off her chest, Ramsay spent the next three pages discussing contracts, VAT and income tax. It was guaranteed to produce a conciliatory reply:

I can hardly believe, [wrote Robert], that your suggested parting of our ways is seriously meant, but on rereading it I think it is. For me it is unthinkable. Dammit, Peggy, am I not allowed to react, or even over-react, without your levelling this biggest of guns at me?

I am terribly moved and grateful that you deliberately offend me. This is not the first time you have sounded a warning bell at exactly the right time. You must help me. Of course I can finally only help myself but do try to think of something I should do (I mean what rough direction you feel my work should take) against my return.

Au revoir, dear Peggy, I love, respect and rely on your – what shall I say? – let me say your love.[12]

Throughout his stay in Tahiti, Robert was being influenced if not bludgeoned by several women at once and there was not a single man in whom he could confide. There was only David Lean, who had no financial worries and no real life at all, except the film and his relationship with Sandy. And had Robert discussed his worries about Tom with Lean, all Lean could have said was, well, I abandoned my son and I haven't seen him for twenty years. Lean was obsessed only with the film and his own personal battle with his producer.

Dino De Laurentiis had brought in an expert to assess the film's budget and schedule. Bernie Williams was a no-nonsense Englishman, one of the sharpest associate producers in the business, and any worries Lean may have had about Williams's presence were partly dispelled by Robert. Williams had been the associate producer on *Lady Caroline Lamb* and he had Robert's friendship and confidence.

At first, Williams was thrilled to be working on a David Lean picture but before long he realised what a leviathan he had taken on. Although he was fascinated by the *Bounty* story and wanted to help Lean as much as he could, Williams's sympathies and loyalty belonged to De Laurentiis:

Apparently, David had said to Dino, 'Look, you may be the producer, but you don't get involved with the film, you keep out of the way, you have nothing to do with the casting, and I'll show you the picture when it's finished. Just send me the money.' And Dino says, 'I am not a cheque-book. I'm a film producer.'

I was caught between these two giants whose egos just

collided. I remember walking with David on the beach in Tahiti when he said, 'Bernie, we're going to charter a big ship and we're going to sail the Pacific. No one will know where we are. The cast and crew will live on the ship for a year and they'll work for nothing because they'll be delighted to work with me. I've told Dino that's the way it's going to be.' When David told me that I thought, have I got news for you . . .[13]

Because formal contracts had been exchanged, De Laurentiis had to find a legitimate way out of the deal. The only way to do this was to come up with a budget far in excess of the $25 million which had been agreed for the first film. Knowing only too well that Lean could not easily be fooled by such a ruse, Williams did his budget by all the rules. Meanwhile, De Laurentiis continued to pay the considerable overheads in Tahiti, which included Lean's expenses as well as Robert's, Eddie Fowlie's and the new art director's, Tony Pratt, who had his girl-friend and daughter with him.

I went off for two months with Eddie Fowlie, this prop man who was David's spokesman and who was like Mr Ignorant [said Williams]. We went looking for locations in the Cook Islands, Fiji and New Zealand, which were cheaper than Tahiti. Then Dino calls me back to Tahiti and we fly first class to Los Angeles with Dino eating vegetarian food as he won't eat meat on a plane for fear of food poisoning. He tells me he is intent on shutting the picture down. I tell him I'll do the budget in LA and he says, 'No, no, do it now! Pass me that sick-bag.' So I get this sick-bag and give him a pen.

He says, 'How many weeks to make the first movie?'

'About forty-four weeks.'

'How mucha week?'

'About half a million.'

'Twenty two million. . . . How mucha the ship?'

'Three million.'

'How mucha the sets?'

'Four million.'

'How mucha the costume?'

'A million.'

'How mucha the music?'

'Three million.'

So we go on, adding numbers to the sick-bag and I tally it all up and it comes to $42 million. Dino says, 'There!'

I said, 'Dino, you can't give David Lean a budget on a sick-bag!' So we did it properly and drew up a budget of about $42 million for the first film.

Lean flew over to LA, picked me up in the Rolls and took me to dinner at Trader Vic's where he buys me all these exotic drinks. He wanted to get me drunk and find out what was going on with Dino. I said, 'David, let me tell you something. Paramount have just made *Saturday Night Fever* for $9 million and it's taken $85 million at the box-office. Movies have changed, David. Making a film like *The Bounty* is not what's going on right now.'

He said, 'I totally disagree with you. I'm a visionary.'

I didn't want to argue with God so I said fine. When Lean gets the budget he goes hysterical. Dino sends me to see him at the Bel Air Hotel to explain why it costs so much. David said, 'How can you make me the world's most expensive director?'

I said, 'Because you are, sir.' Then Eddie Fowlie starts saying David this, David that and I'm talking to a prop man who's never produced a picture in his life. And then, through the corner of my eye, I see a man crouched in the shower with a tape recorder. I say, 'Mr Lean, who is that man in your bathroom with a tape recorder?'

Lean says, 'Oh, Marvin, get out you bloody fool.' It's David's lawyer, Marvin Mayer. It was like amateur night in Dixie.

There was a final, incredible meeting when Dino turned to David and said, 'David, I love this project, I love you as a film director. Bernie does the budget and I know you don't agree with Bernie so I take Bernie off the film.' Then Dino turns to his lawyer, Fred Sidewater, and says, 'Fred, write out a cheque for $25 million payable to David Lean.' Dino signs the cheque, hands it to David and says, 'David, here's the money for the film. Go and have a great time. Enjoy yourself, we are not involved.' So David goes, 'Thank you.' Then Dino says, 'Let me explain something to you very clearly. I give you this money. There is no more money. When and if you go over this money you put in your own money or you find it. But I no give you no more.' And that was the end of it.[14]

De Laurentiis put the project into turnaround and took Lean off the payroll. Shrewdly, he continued to pay Robert and he also owned the replica *Bounty* which was moored in New Zealand. This meant that if Lean found an alternative source of finance he would still have to negotiate with De Laurentiis over the rights to Robert's script and

the use of the ship. For Robert, this state of affairs only increased the
tension which already existed between him and Lean. Since Robert
was still under contract to De Laurentiis, Lean no longer had the
legal right to work with him on the script. Even by the standards of
the film industry, it was a ridiculous situation.

Lean was now rarely to be found in Tahiti. He flew to New
Zealand to try and raise finance from the fledgling film industry
there, and he was also hawking the project around Hollywood.
Whenever he was in Tahiti with Robert, he took the latest pages
apart and started again. 'I am scribbling away regularly, happily, and
I think quite well,' Robert told Julie Laird. 'It offends David's vanity
to think that I can manage much without his supervision (how he
supposes I write my plays I don't know) and if I do he always rejects
it and it can take as much as a month before he has forgotten what
he has rejected so that it can be reintroduced as his own contribution. I begin to feel intense sympathy with the subtle sycophants
who surrounded Oriental potentates.'[15]

Even though Robert and Lean disagreed violently over the first
scenes of the second script, United Artists were sufficiently impressed by them to send a representative to Tahiti. But any hopes
they might have had that UA would save the project were dashed
when the studio became embroiled in Michael Cimino's *Heaven's
Gate*, the escalating costs of which prohibited them from investing in
The Bounty.

On 7 March 1979, with the second screenplay still far from
completed, David Lean flew to Los Angeles in a last ditch effort to
save his project. Robert was far from optimistic about the outcome:
'David does not and will not understand or even consider as a
possibility the fact that in his old age his admirable self-reliance has
hypertrophied to the verges of megalomania,' he told Julie Laird.
'David is deeply convinced that he is the most unassuming and self-
effacing of men, almost culpably moderate in his demands. I'm
exhausted by the effort of trying to perfect something which in all
likelihood will not be seen.'[16]

Lean had heard that John Calley at Warner Bros was endeavouring to persuade several studios to form a consortium in order to get
the films made. Lean had also arranged a meeting with the movie
mogul Joseph E. Levine and, as a last resort, his old sparring partner,
Sam Spiegel. But all this was to no avail. Although Lean's status in
Hollywood was second to none, the new breed of executives were
looking for movies with an obvious appeal to young audiences.
Lean's stress on the youthfulness of Bligh and Christian, and his

intention to make the Tahitian scenes resemble a drugged, hippie commune, did little to persuade the studio executives. In Hollywood, Lean's great project had acquired a strangely melancholy subtitle. It was known as 'The Old Man and the Sea'.

While Lean remained in Los Angeles, things in Tahiti were winding down. Only Robert and Eddie Fowlie were left, the art director, Tony Pratt, having handed in his resignation. Instead of continuing to work on *The Long Arm*, Robert started to outline a reworking of *Gentle Jack* in the hope that his only real flop could be turned into a success. He told Ann Queensberry:

> I'm tired and fairly fed-up. It isn't possible indefinitely to give your best to something which you think will never happen and for which it seems increasingly you are in large part not going to be paid. I HATE CINEMA AND ALL ITS PERSONNEL with undying passion.
>
> Tony Pratt, his Israeli girl-friend and their infant daughter have left, very sensibly. David is in LA trying to find a backer for the films, also sensibly, but belatedly. I don't have much in common with the Property Master (actually David's nanny and Man Friday – all directors have one). I read Jung by candlelight and swat mosquitoes.[17]

Robert arrived in Los Angeles on Wednesday, 4 April 1979. He planned to stay for ten days, when he would undergo his medical tests, as well as see Sarah who had Tom with her for the Easter holiday. He planned to fly to London with Tom and then, if Lean or Sam Spiegel suddenly pulled off a deal, return to Tahiti to complete the second script. The vagueness of the immediate future obliged him to decline an invitation to serve as the President of the Jury at the Cannes Film Festival in May.

Robert was desperate to return to England and the Old Manor, even if it was only for a few weeks. The annoying thing was, he dared not arrive before 15 April for fear of being 'knocked down and stripped naked by the agents of the Inland Revenue'.[18]

After spending his first night in LA at the home of his friend Fernando Ghia, who had produced *Lady Caroline Lamb*, Robert went to stay with Michael and Shakira Caine at their home on Davies Drive in Beverly Hills. An added attraction for Robert was that Mia Farrow, having completed *Hurricane*, was also a house guest of the Caines. 'He was obviously tired and seemed to be on the verge of a breakdown of some kind,' wrote Caine. 'Romantically speaking, he was on his own. By chance, Mia Farrow had turned up, so Shakira and I tried to put these two obviously lonely and, we thought, compatible people together.'[19]

On the Friday, Robert went to St John's Hospital in Santa Monica for the first of his tests. The news was appalling. When the doctors told Robert he needed to have a heart bypass operation he said he would have the operation when he got back to London. But you don't understand, said the doctors, you need to have it immediately. Arrangements were made for Robert to enter hospital on Sunday and undergo surgery on Tuesday morning.

> He was absolutely devastated [said Ghia]. His shock was not only because he had to have an operation, it was because he knew he was not going home which is what he wanted most of all.
>
> On the Saturday I had lunch with Robert and Mia Farrow at Michael Caine's house. On the Sunday, Robert drove to see Sarah and he crashed his hire car. I mean, he really smashed it up.[20]

Sarah was living in Venice with the actor, Harris Yulin, with whom she had made a TV-movie called *Dynasty*. She had Tom with her as well as a school friend of his. When Robert arrived, shaken by his car wreck, Sarah was shocked by his haggard appearance. 'The strain of working daily with David Lean was enough to shrivel anyone up,' she wrote. 'David had a knack of vampiring the very life force from those around him, leaving his own countenance sparkling fresh.'[21]

After Robert gulped down a plateful of sushi, he took Sarah for a walk, arm in arm, along the beach. Physically and emotionally, Robert was a wreck and the sight of Sarah and Tom was almost too much for him. For the first time in eighteen months, he had his family again, even if it was a broken one. He kissed her tenderly and said, 'Come and live with me at the Old Manor where you belong.'[22]

'On the Sunday evening,' said Ghia, 'I took him to the hospital. He asked for paper and envelopes. Then, on the Monday, which was Oscar night, he gave me about fifteen letters he had written. He was terribly apprehensive.'

Robert wrote to his family and friends, as if he thought he might die on the operating table. Gillian Harrison was asked to investigate his medical insurance. He told Debbie Condon that he was watching 'a rather jejeune Academy Awards ceremonial and awaiting with querulous resignation a heart bypass scheduled for tomorrow'. Debbie was invited to lunch in England when they would share 'a glass of fat free whey and an organically grown lettuce'. Julie Laird was offered a share in a nut cutlet.

'Robert was very frightened,' said Ghia, 'and after I left him I went home to bed and set the alarm. I was woken at seven by a phone call from the doctor who told me that the surgery had gone well. I said, "But the operation isn't until eight thirty." Then the doctor told me that he'd had a heart attack at midnight and they decided to operate straight away. He had a triple bypass.'[23]

I was staying with my girl-friend Jo at my mother's house in Hampshire [said Ben Bolt]. The doctor in LA called and asked if I needed to come to the States. I said I didn't and he said fine, but if I did, now would be a good time. I'd never been to the States before, I'd never been further than Italy, so having put the phone down I thought what he said was extraordinary. As far as I knew there was never any warning that he was going to need a heart operation. I thought I might phone Dad and ask him if he wanted me to go out there and then I thought that would only worry him. I didn't know what to do. I just felt an overwhelming need to go over there. Although I never said it to anyone else, I thought he might die.

I borrowed some money from Charlotte Taylor and John Standing, who were an item at that time. She kept an emergency cash fund in her flat and we took John Standing's school fees out of a piggy bank. I went straight to the airport and took Freddie Laker's Skytrain to LA.

Dad was sitting up in bed having had the operation. He had this great dressing on his chest and tubes everywhere, but he seemed perfectly fine, totally articulate and not drugged in any way. He was very surprised and very pleased to see me. He insisted that I stayed with the Caines who were extremely accommodating.[24]

The next day, Wednesday, 11 April, Ben was having dinner with the Caines when a call came through from the hospital. 'We were told he'd had a stroke,' said Ben. 'I didn't know what a stroke was so they explained and said that damage had been done to his brain. I was so shocked and confused, I couldn't continue the conversation, so Michael took the phone. We went over to the hospital and Dad was unconscious. The doctor thought that some tissue had broken away during the operation and lodged itself in the base of the brain which caused the stroke. He was very upset and the prognosis seemed to be grave.'

When news reached London of Robert's stroke, there was shock and a desperate eagerness to help. Ann Queensberry flew out to Los

Angeles immediately and stayed at Sarah's house on Benedict Canyon, while Sarah herself remained with Harris Yulin in Venice. It was Ann's job to take Tom and his friend back to England for the new school term.

When Robert emerged from his coma he was unable to move or speak. 'After a week,' said Ben, 'Dad developed a quite clear method of communication. He could move his head or put on a mock pained expression on his face if he disapproved of something. So whenever someone asked if they could visit him I would check it out with him.'

Fernando Ghia, the Caines and Mia Farrow presented no problems. They visited him regularly and were instructed not just to sit there and behave compassionately; they had to occupy and stimulate his mind to prevent him lapsing into a vegetative state. Ghia talked about their work together, Caine used all his conversational brilliance and laconic humour, and Farrow sat close to Robert's bedside and read him short stories by Tolstoy.

David Lean, though, did present a problem. He had a terror of illness and could not bear to be near anyone who was remotely poorly. 'David Lean made one request to visit Dad,' said Ben, 'which was passed to me through the Caines. I never met Lean myself. I checked it out with Dad and he indicated that he didn't want David Lean to visit him. I can imagine that being hurtful but I don't think it's necessary to infer from that anything more than he didn't want such an esteemed colleague to see him in such a helpless state.'

Sarah, though, on one of her visits, bumped into Lean at the hospital which suggests that he was able to see Robert. But when she met him the atmosphere was decidedly frosty: 'Do you feel a little responsible?' she asked.

'No more than you must feel,' retorted Lean, 'for he never got over you, never.'

'Touché!' said Sarah.[25]

Sarah found her own visits to the hospital traumatic and she quickly sensed that she was regarded as an outsider by Robert's family, his friends and by his doctor. 'Sarah was made to feel unwelcome,' said Ben.

'I was still regarded by Robert's family and friends as the scarlet woman who had ruined his life,' said Sarah. 'I felt they all hated me so I never told them about our reconciliation on Venice Beach.'[26]

Robert possessed an active mind within an inert body. Words had been his life, his livelihood; everyone who knew him remembered the arguments, the piercing analysis, the wit, the way he'd wolf down his food at dinner parties and have the floor to himself while everybody carried on eating. That was now a thing of the past. Robert's first life had ended.

He had tried facing the wall, urging death on himself. But nothing happened; he was just looking at a blank wall. And then, one day, as Ben came into the room, Robert uttered his first word in a month. 'Bendi!' he cried.

And then he bellowed, 'Fucking hell!'

PART TWO

A MAN FOR ALL MEDIA

'Morality's not practical. Morality's a gesture. A complicated gesture learned from books.'

Sir Thomas More in *A Man For All Seasons*

'I have to tell you, Bob Bolt was a terrible disappointment. I thought he was going to be a really important dramatist but he preferred Sam Spiegel's yacht.'

Frith Banbury to author

FOUR

SALE

'It is the philosopher alone who can conceive the grandeur of Manchester and the immensity of its future.'

Benjamin Disraeli, *Coningsby*

Today, Sale is indistinguishable from the other towns that creep drably towards Manchester. But in 1924, the year of Robert's birth, it was a proud part of affluent north Cheshire. It was separate, if never completely individual. Often linked with Altrincham, its immediate and more attractive neighbour to the south, Sale's history can be traced back at least to the twelfth century, when a land document established the settlement as a proper town and not just a manor born out of the feudal system. Its name seems to have been derived from the Anglo-Saxon word, 'sealh', which meant a willow tree.

By the early nineteenth century Sale was still wholly rural, with a village green, scattered houses and outlying farms dedicated to quality meat and dairy produce. But with the coming of the Industrial Revolution and the expansion of Manchester into one of Britain's most important cities, Sale and its neighbours developed rapidly. A railway, which ran from Altrincham to Manchester, via Sale, was established in 1849, turning Sale into a residential suburb.

'The railways', wrote local historian N. V. Swain, 'enabled the middle class to move away from the manufacturing towns and have country homes built, usually within a short distance of a railway station. The wealthier of them in the Manchester area bought land and had villas built to the disgust of their hereditary landowning neighbours who referred to them as "Cottontots", a reference to the source of the wealth of the newcomers.'[1]

While Sale itself did not attract these wealthy industrialists – they preferred Wilmslow, Bowdon and Altrincham – it benefited from their proximity and their prosperity. 'Towards the end of the nineteenth century,' wrote Swain, 'the housing demands of the middle class in Sale having been largely met, smaller, semi-detached houses were built for the growing managerial class and yet smaller ones for artisans and the increasing army of clerks.'[2]

As the transformation of Sale was occurring – and similar transformations were happening all over Britain – Robert's antecedents were gathering in Lancashire from Devon and Wales.

> My father's family were very able [said Robert's older brother, Sydney]. My grandfather, William, was a rather interesting man. He was a liberal, deeply religious man with personal weaknesses like smoking which he could never give up. He also supported the Boers which got him into trouble at the start of the Great War. Because his name was Bolt, he was suspected of being pro-German so he went to Somerset House and got documents which proved his English heritage right back to the eighteenth century.
>
> Apparently, a remote ancestor was a ship's carpenter who had moved from Dartmouth in Devon to Liverpool, and from then on the Bolts were Lancashire people. This grandfather also took the entire family off to Canada but because he didn't know a thing about farming they came back within two years. My father, who was about five at the time, had vivid memories of the cold and knew that if you put a key in your mouth it would stick to your tongue. But William was obviously brilliant at business and made a go of things in the end.[3]

William Bolt had married a Lancashire girl, Ann Oxton, and they had eight children – John, Harold, Ada, Ethel, Sydney (a girl), Norman, Ralph and Stanley. It was Ralph who was to be Robert's father.

In due course, the Bolts became a relatively prosperous, lower-middle-class family, part of a generation which had benefited from the great wealth and industry of Manchester, whose citizens had steady jobs and a little money to spend on essentials, like household goods and furniture. William Bolt saw his opportunity and opened a shop, which made him and his family a tidy living.

In 1917, Ralph Bolt married Leah Binyon, a teacher who was a year older than him. She was also an accomplished water-colourist, having been taught by Joe Owen, a cousin of the poet, Wilfred Owen, as well as being qualified to teach the piano. 'They were both on holiday at a place called Norbreck Hydro, north of Blackpool,' said Sydney. 'They met playing tennis, among a group of office types of the kind you get in stories by H. G. Wells. They met in 1914, got engaged and married during the war.'

Leah's father was born in the workhouse of Shifnal, a Shropshire town, though his forebears were most likely Welsh. 'My maternal grandfather was a ne'er do well,' said Sydney, 'and he looked like someone in an Edwardian musical. He'd wear spats, a bowler hat and a waistcoat in a different pattern from his jacket. He was a rather splendid-looking character.'

Leah's family name was Fletcher. 'They were architects, sea captains, that sort of thing,' said Sydney. 'Highly respectable except for one brother, Arthur, who was a great hero to Bob and me. He ran away to sea when he was thirteen and got shanghaied. He was in mutinies, he was a hobo all over South America and in Australia he was wanted for manslaughter. He'd give Bob and me advice like, "If you're in Argentina, never go to jail because they treat you very badly. But if you're in Chile, especially in the winter, it's the best place to be." My parents didn't like us speaking to him but we thought he was the only relative we had that we could be proud of and boast about to the other boys at school. Because we only met him two or three times, he was able to remain mythical.'

When Ralph and Leah married, he was in the Army and had to return to the trenches in France. Leah continued with her teaching in Salford and hoped that Ralph would return home safely.

My father served in the war with some distinction [said Sydney]. He was offered a commission more than once but he didn't like officers with temporary commissions. He called them 'temporary gentlemen'. He was probably a bit of a snob. Anyway, he was a sergeant in charge of a Lewis gun and got extra money for being a crack shot. He was on the Somme and at Passchendaele, though he always thought Trônes Wood was the worst.

He ran into his brother, Norman, in France. When Norman got badly wounded at the Somme he said to my father, 'Hang on, Ralph, you may get wounded and we'll go home together.' My father was wounded, twice, though he stayed to the end of the war. Norman died of his wounds some years later.

I didn't know how good a soldier he was until 1928 when he took me to the Armistice Day celebrations. Because you never think much of your parents – at least, I didn't – I was amazed that as soon as he appeared and joined the other men of his battalion, they all began to cheer and called him Bolty. I realised then that he had been a good sergeant.

Just after the war, my grandmother was wandering through the streets and was asked by a friend about her sons, all just back from France. In every case, my grandmother replied, 'He's back and safe, he's got married and they're expecting a baby.' Then the friend said, 'Hey, the things these lads learned in France!' This story has nothing to do with Bob, except that he heard it a thousand times.

When the war ended, Ralph worked in his father's shop in Chorlton-cum-Hardy, which is where Sydney was born in 1920. A year or two later, and ready to set up on their own, Ralph and Leah moved to Sale and opened a small furniture shop at 13 Northenden Road, part of a short terrace of shops with houses above them, now a shabby ladies' hairdresser's named Hairline. It was just on the wrong side of the railway tracks, an extension of Sale's main shopping thoroughfare, School Road, a hundred yards beyond the canal and the railway station.

It was here that Robert was born on 15 August 1924. He was given the middle name of Oxton.

Robert described his father as 'a small man and the keeper of a small shop. It sold furniture, glass and china. It was new furniture later, but earlier there was second-hand furniture. Throughout my childhood, yes, this shop, and the sound of the shop bell, and the entrance, and three steps down to the shop from the house. These are very specific memories.'[4]

When Robert was four, his father moved to spacious new premises at 68 School Road, next to the bank and right in the heart of Sale's shopping area. Now sadly demolished and replaced by a spartan ladies' outfitters called Bon Marché, it was an outward display of prosperity. 'It had a big front garden and a big back garden,' said Sydney. 'My father built the shop out over the front garden. It was the largest furniture shop in the district. It was mortgaged, of course.'

If one thing is remembered from the Bolt household in School Road – an apt address for this family – it is the sound of argument. The Bolts debated and dissected everything. 'It was a strong nonconformist, quasi-revolutionary family,' said Sydney. 'My father took part in the 1911 demonstrations for the reform of the House of Lords and my mother was an ardent socialist, an early feminist, a romantic revolutionary.'

Ralph was also a Methodist, though his religious conviction was never as strong as Robert made out in some of his interviews. According to Sydney:

My father was born a Wesleyan but the war made him totally irreligious, in a religious way. He was so hostile to the war that he always talked about it like Brecht. If you asked him what he did, you never got an answer that you could swank about at school. He was also contemptuous of people who said their loved ones had survived the war because they had prayed. The idea that God was there, deflecting the bullets from those who had prayed, made him sick. He thought prayer was bogus and a form of self-congratulation. My mother, though, was a congregationalist which is a much more politically orientated form of protestant. Surprisingly, my father never went into politics, though my mother was very active in the League of Nations Union.

When Bob was about seven, and I was about eleven, they suddenly decided to take us to church, which they had never done before. We went to the Wesleyan chapel every Sunday for morning service, though my father would always pass comment on the sermons or the messages in the hymns which rather undermined their religious effect.

'I was brought up Methodist,' said Robert. 'I can remember my father saying to me when I was complaining about going to chapel, "When you're old enough, you can choose for yourself." So when I was sixteen I said, "Can I choose for myself whether to go to chapel or not?" and he said, "Yes, you can," and I've never been since. The interesting thing is that neither has he. I ought to be religious in the sense that I'm comfortable thinking in religious terms and altogether I seem naturally constituted to be religious. It is just my misfortune that I have no religion.'[5]

When Robert started school, Ralph and Leah hoped that he would do as well as his older brother. 'I always conformed,' said Sydney. 'I was good at everything and all my early childhood was really placid. I sort of sailed along, thinking everything was marvellous.

'My parents were very keen on education and they paid the fees for Bob and me to go to Sale Preparatory School which was a little private day school. Then I went on to Sale High School which was a preparatory school for Manchester Grammar where I won a scholarship. The intake into Manchester Grammar would have been about five hundred in those days and fifty of those were scholarships. I think I came about second.'

Everything came easily to Sydney and, in the beginning, it did for Robert as well. 'When I was about seven the whole business of school seemed laughably easy,' he said. 'I was more or less effortlessly the top of the class, the bright little boy. Then quite suddenly in one year – the year when I left the little preparatory school – I began to be a bad boy and that went on from bad to worse until round the age of fourteen or fifteen.'[6]

As he entered Sale High School, Robert changed into a monster and refused to learn anything. He did not so much resent his brother as hold him in awe and dared not compete with him. And when Robert started to fail at school, Ralph reminded him how much it was costing. 'I think my father took it out on Bob in this sense,' said Sydney. 'When he paid out a lot of money for Bob to go to the same schools, and when Bob didn't make the slightest effort to do well and on the whole spurned it, for fairly clear psychological motives, my father was pretty hostile. I think Bob always had this feeling that money didn't matter precisely because he was made to feel that money *did* matter.'

Robert fell in with a boy called Dick Puddephatt whose mother was a friend of Leah's and had attended the same teachers' college in Hereford. For some years Robert and Puddephatt were inseparable, egging each other on to commit acts of rebelliousness and even crime. They stole from shops and played truant from school, spending their illicit days messing about along the canal. If they found an advertising hoarding they would tear it from the wall and use it as an impromptu raft. Or they'd throw stones and smash things up. Sydney said:

We all stole in those days. I stole, though I must have been better at it than Bob because I wasn't caught. We always stole from Woolworths, sweets and little things you didn't really want, like batteries, flashlights, things of that sort. It was just a pastime.

Bob and Dick Puddephatt used to play private games together. I thought they were horrific because they were always imagining themselves as Roman emperors lashing their slaves. I'd hear Bob say, 'What are the slaves doing now?' and Dick would say, 'They're revolting!' Then Bob would scream at the top of his voice, 'Then lash them!' They'd just be sitting on the couch making this up. The Marquis de Sade would have approved totally, except there was no sex in it.

Although Robert did not make the grade at Sale High School,

Ralph nevertheless paid for him to attend Manchester Grammar, where Sydney was doing so well and seemed destined for university and a probable career in the Civil Service.

Manchester Grammar was the best school for miles around, boasting a history which stretched back to the fourteenth century when it was a chantry school attached to the collegiate church, later the cathedral. It prospered during the eighteenth century owing to its monopoly of malt milling, the vital ingredient for ale, though constant legal action by the brewers severely reduced its economic power by the mid-nineteenth century. In 1865, the school admitted fee-paying day boys for the first time, as well as 250 boys on scholarships. Throughout its long history the school maintained an impressive academic record. Robert's arrival, though, threatened to undermine it. 'The whole colour of my life as a child', he said, 'was a very dark one. Very gloomy, fraught, self-doubting, self-contemptuous, lots of petty delinquency, bad behaviour at school, cordially disliked by my teachers and a terrible worry to my parents. I used to steal things from shops and get into fights and was secretive and violent. I was bottom of the class, not just from time to time, but all the time. What all this was about I simply don't know. My parents were strict but not outrageously strict. My elder brother was very successful at school, which is a classic reason for a younger brother to be a bit of a failure.'[7]

Although Robert knew he was intelligent, the evidence was never to be found in his general conduct, much less in his examination results. Instead, he learned in private, at home with his imagination and around the dining table where the great issues of the day were thrashed out.

'There were always a lot of books at home,' said Sydney, 'and although Bob was hostile to school he never stopped reading. He had a tremendous ability to concentrate. He also started to write when he was very young. I remember a thing he wrote about knights in armour which was based on Sir Arthur Conan Doyle's *Sir Nigel* which is a book not many children of his age could have read.'

'I was always writing something,' said Robert. 'Exercise books full of stuff. And dreamed, read, mooned about the library. I used to write terrible historical novels, quasi pornographic, with long torture scenes, from the age of about nine onwards.'[8]

The Depression of the early Thirties, when Robert and Puddephatt were in their delinquent phase, had a significant impact on Ralph's business in School Road. People had no money to spend and the business was declining. To save money he dismissed his live-in shop assistant and asked Leah to run the crockery department. But in 1937 the economy had recovered sufficiently for a big Manchester furniture company to buy Ralph out. He sold the shop for enough money to buy a new house on Earlham Road and to retire. For two years he was a man of leisure, though when the Second World War broke out in 1939 he got himself a job with Turner's Asbestos and remained there until 1960, retiring as the company secretary.

By 1938 Sydney had achieved everything possible at Manchester Grammar and was becoming a star student at Cambridge. Robert was fast approaching the time when he would sit his matriculation examinations. He knew his chances of passing were slim, though he made a concerted effort to be a model pupil. The outcome of this perplexed him for years:

I remember my first experiment in being a good boy and a terrible wave of anger at the end of an English lesson. I was always very good at English. I don't mean the grammar and spelling but reading bits of poetry and stories and discussing them. I'd always got lots to say and could always interest not only the teacher but the class.

I remember the teacher saying something complimentary like, 'This is the way you should carry on all the time.' I almost wanted to cry because I felt the whole thing had been false, that if this was all that being good added up to, then it wasn't worth it. You know, a kind of precociously existential position overtook me for half an hour or so. I remember anger and a terrible sense of loss because I thought, 'My goodness, perhaps this is really all these good people are, they're just putting up with this ridiculous pretence.' And I suppose to some extent this is still my state of mind. I think these childhood preoccupations have never quite left me.[9]

At the end of my school career I ended up in a very pleasant form called Remove Beta, which is a kind of sump or appendix at the bottom of Manchester Grammar for draining off ineducable material. I had a couple of leisurely years taking School Certificate, took it twice and did rather worse the second time. My father said, 'You've made your bed, you must lie on it.' I was at panic stations. I didn't know what to do and drifted into an insurance office where I was a sort of office boy, running messages, looking after the boilers and so on. And such small clerical duties as I had to perform I did very badly.[10]

★

The Sun Assurance Company was in King Street, in the centre of Manchester. He found the place rather frightening since the older clerks, greying and dressed in suits that were shiny with age, gave him a glimpse of what he might become if he did nothing about it. Because of the war, there were no young or middle-aged men. There were just Robert, another male school leaver, and plenty of office girls, one of whom was Margaret Chapman. 'Everyone called him Bobby,' she said. 'He was always a character. He was different, no doubt about it, a very nice looking boy with a gorgeous complexion. I don't think he cared for the work, though he didn't let it show. He got on with his work and he was very keen on a girl called Joyce Whitaker but I don't think he got anywhere with her.'[11]

The work itself was sheer drudgery and every day all the files had to be taken down to the basement in case there was an overnight air raid. Robert could not decide if the work was beneath him or if he lacked the brains to do it. 'My head was full of rarefied nonsense,' he said, 'but I couldn't remember to post letters at the right time with the right stamps on them. This was the first time I ever consciously hated anything – I hated the office, I really hated it – I hated the life and was determined not to go on.'

Robert was in desperate need of a saviour, a way out, and he found one quite by chance, as Sydney explained:

> Bob Bunn was a humane and unique man. He was extra-ordinarily lucid, the sort of teacher you don't normally find. He was a brilliant man who taught me at Manchester Grammar and got me through to Cambridge. Now, it so happened that when war broke out, Manchester Grammar was moved to Blackpool to avoid possible bombing and as I'd volunteered at the beginning of the war, and was due to go to India, I thought I'd go to Blackpool to say goodbye to Bunn and to Bob. That was how they first met.
>
> When Bob came a total cropper at school and failed his matriculation, he was working in this office and bumped into Bob Bunn in the street. When Bunn discovered how unhappy my brother was he suggested he try for university and offered to give him private coaching. Bob also went to a private tutorial college and in a few months he sat the exam again and passed with flying colours. Bob Bunn was the making of Bob.

Manchester University had an impressive reputation, though it nearly closed soon after it had opened. In 1846, a local philanthropist, John Owens, gave around £96,000 for a new college which would educate male students. Within ten years there were only thirty-three students, causing the *Manchester Guardian* to report the 'mortifying failure of the enterprise'. But the college survived and eventually became a fully fledged university. In Robert's time there were nearly 5000 students, the majority housed in halls of residence which sprawled over a site of nearly 100 acres. Mirroring the image of Manchester itself, it became known as the University of the Future.

Bob Bunn had taught Robert the art of wanting to learn, of using his mind: 'I'd remained convinced that I was a highly intelligent person, though I was unique in this opinion,' he said. 'And then the first year at university was the opening of the gates of paradise for me. I was more or less drunk the whole year on freedom and ideas and new friends and, oh, everything.'[12]

Surprisingly, for his first year, Robert read economics. Not so surprisingly, he joined the Communist Party. Sydney had been a member, though he resigned his membership just as Robert was joining:

> My parents were hostile to communism and I remember being very shocked when I was about sixteen. My father said he thought that both fascism and communism were abominable but if you had to choose between them he would choose fascism because it had something spiritual about it. I was disgusted by that. This was in 1936, when no one knew about the horrors to come. But during the war, they were both pro-Russian.
>
> I joined the Party in 1938, after Munich, as an anti-fascist. Bob came in around 1943, with a general wave of people who saw Russia as the wonderful ally against Hitler. This was when I turned against Russia because I came to see what a bloody awful society it was to live in.

At university, Robert fell in with the McCabe clan. There were two brothers, Bernard and Herbert, and a sister, Eileen. The McCabes were Jesuits, intellectuals and competitive debaters. 'I first met Bob when I was pretending to be a law student,' said Bernard McCabe. 'He was bright, witty and very serious, too. At the time he was strongly interested in communism, which was very much the thing in those days. Some of the brightest people in Manchester were communists, though some of them were fairly sinister, of course. They recognised that Bob was very quick on his intellectual feet so they cultivated him.'[13]

Bernard McCabe's brother, Herbert, was at the university studying philosophy as preparation for becoming a monk. 'It was a time when students had no money to speak of,' he said, 'which in some ways made life easier. We were all very keen on Manchester and we thought we were at the only civilised university in England. Bob disapproved of my being a Catholic, though we were both in the socialist set-up. He had a primarily psychological account of faith which would be different from mine, like the difference between being in love and actually loving someone. I'm not sure, though, that he had any concept of faith, so we just argued a lot.'[14]

There was a permanent shadow lying across Robert's first year at University. Sometimes it would fall directly over his home in Sale, raining down German bombs, which devastated part of School Road. Robert always knew that he was liable for call-up and in the summer of 1943 he was directed by the War Office to report for duty and be received into the ranks of the Royal Air Force.

On 21 August Robert found himself with a thousand other young men in Regent's Park, London. It was the first time he had ever visited the capital. The men were enlisted at ACRC – Air Crew Reception Centre – and billeted at a block of flats called Stockley Hall on Prince Albert Road in St John's Wood. Robert regarded his fellow recruits as 'a lot of public schoolboys of whom I of course disapproved on principle but some of whom I liked enormously as individuals because they were so witty and their manners were so nice and so on. Some of them I hated because they were snobbish.'[15]

One of these public schoolboys was Anthony Quinton, now Lord Quinton, who had been educated at Stowe and Oxford. He said:

We were Britain's last throw. Our equipment was dished out to us, including some curious grey straps which one wore over one's shoulder. An experienced man, a Corporal Webb, said, 'Dis 'ere is the skellington webbing.' And to the person standing immediately beside me, who in fact was Robert, I said, 'Devised of course by the celebrated eighteenth-century sadist, the Marquis de Skellington.' He sort of got my number with that and a similar flow of absurd nonsense came out of him. We were pals from that moment onwards.

We went to the Seymour Hall baths where we stood with a thousand other naked Englishmen. We all walked like a fashionable society wedding of the Thirties through two columns of men bearing needles loaded with our shots for foreign assignment. Then we all went and had a swimming test.

Having been inducted and injected, and having proved that they could float if necessary, Robert and Tony Quinton were sent to an airbase near Stratford-upon-Avon to begin their training.

A respectable schoolmaster looked after our Flight, as it was called [said Quinton] and we learned elementary things like theory of flight and navigation. This lasted about a month. We lived in a hotel, ate rather heavily at a place called the Tudor Café which had the most magnificent sandwiches, and had a rather good time. We used to go to the Memorial Theatre but there wasn't a lot of Shakespeare on. It was mainly touring companies of light entertainment. The actors in these entertainments were rather peculiar because the men were very old who would stagger on stage and hope to give the impression they were gay young blades. Enchanting girls of about nineteen would be the objects of their pursuit. The process of conscription had weeded out all the others.

At Stratford I learned that Bob was a strong supporter of the Communist Party. I had come from Oxford and was fooling around being a Trotskyist, condemning the war as an imperialist war and saying the attack on Russia actually made no difference. This generated a terrific amount of argument between Bob and me and I think it fair to say that both of us were rather dressed up in our respective ideologies. I think he was more committed than I was. His brother Sydney had been a very dedicated member of the Communist Party and Bob was very much in awe of Sydney. I didn't think it was absurd to be in awe of him because he's an impressive and clever figure but if Bob's communism was truly deep-seated he would have spurned me altogether for being a Trotskyist.

After Stratford, we went to an elementary flying school at Elmdon, near Birmingham, and that was great fun. We had about a month there, flying tiger moths. By this time, we always worked it so that we shared the same room. Bob was a great laugh producer, enormously life-enhancing. He didn't just sit there glumly, complaining about everything. At that stage in our lives neither of us drank very much. Later, Bob had periods of severe over-drinking while I have just drunk steadily on without need of any medical attention. But during the war we didn't need much drink because we had a juvenile cheerfulness. We smoked a lot, though, incompetently, with bits of the paper adhering to the lip.[16]

From Birmingham, Robert and Quinton were transferred to Heaton Park in Manchester, a vast and perpetually damp assembly area from where the men were sent off to foreign parts to complete their training.

Quinton had been led to believe that Robert came from a rather impoverished background. Perhaps to justify his communism, Robert had drawn a picture of his life as being hard and unjust and that a lack of money had forced him to steal books in order to educate himself. Quinton remembered Robert saying to him, 'A bourgeois like you just doesn't know about need of this kind. You couldn't pilfer a book from a shop.' Not one to resist a challenge, Quinton went straight to the nearest branch of W. H. Smith and stole a copy of a Simenon novel. 'I don't feel very guilty about that,' he said. 'It was just to show him I could do it.'

As they were stationed so close to Robert's family home in Sale, Quinton was invited for Sunday lunch. 'And what do I find', said Quinton, 'but an extremely respectable household. Very nice father, slightly grim mother. I mean, she was a generous, good provider and all that, but there was a certain puritanical severity about her. The father was one of those easygoing, liberal-minded men. But the level of comfort was very considerable with no evidences of need whatever. It was just bravado on Bob's part.'[17]

Inevitably, the realities of wartime training meant that Robert and Quinton were separated, though they were reunited in the Fifties and would remain lifelong friends. Quinton was sent to Canada and Robert went to South Africa to complete his training, far from the dangers of enemy aircraft. One of the men he befriended there would later be instrumental in the progress of Robert's teaching career.

Like Robert, Len Smith was born in 1924. 'I came from Norwich,' he said, 'and after the local grammar school I went to Cambridge for a year, then into the RAF. I was sent out to Rhodesia for flying training. Towards the end of the war, about 1944, we were all sent down to a transit camp just outside Cape Town and it was there that I first met Bob. He suffered from air sickness and hated flying.'[18]

It remains uncertain if Robert had a genuine aversion to flying or if he was simply scared. 'Looking back on it,' he said, 'I'm not sure that this wasn't cowardice. Because I was good at it, at the elementary stages of flying. I was picked to be a pilot rather than a navigator. Anyway, I was too sick to be any use to them.'[19]

Cape Town is still my favourite place [said Len Smith]. I've been back three times since the fall of apartheid. It was British rule, of course, and the Afrikaners were against the British being there. I remember coming out of camp once and a car drew up. The door opened and this Afrikaner said, 'Want a lift into Cape Town?' I said, 'Yes please.' Then he said, 'Well, walk you bastard!'

Life was very relaxed in the camp. We were so lucky, on full pay, nothing to do, no war going on. It was just three months' holiday. We weren't let out until midday so we used to sit around, drink coffee and discuss things. None of us were officers, we were just ordinary irks. It was more of a university kind of life. There were a lot of ex-university people, like Bob and me, so we formed a sort of little group of what I suppose you would call intellectuals. A lot of us were left-wing, too. There was a left-wing group and there was also a very good artistic group, particularly the ballet club. A lot of musicians, too. This artistic and left-wing group sort of mixed up together. A lot of the people in the arts circle were Jewish because there were a lot of refugees there. It was such a lively place for music, the arts and politics. Bob loved it out there.[20]

'South Africa was absolutely marvellous,' said Robert. 'I met John Cranko and theatre people and artists. They made a great fuss of the RAF. Wonderful, oh . . . wine and peaches and all kinds of harmless junketings and girls at parties. The whole thing was madly glamorous to me and eroded this northern, nonconformist, completely moral and in any case Marxist view of right and wrong. It was beginning to dawn on me that life could be pleasurable without doing any harm to anybody.'[21]

Robert sailed for England aboard the *Andes*. 'It was direct voyage,' said Smith, 'with just a quick stop at Freetown in Sierra Leone. The *Andes* was a new liner and because it was such a fast ship we didn't have an escort. It wasn't luxurious, though, and we all slept in hammocks.'

The *Andes* docked in Liverpool on a freezing morning in January 1945. The men were transferred to Blackpool in a convoy of coaches. 'When we came back to England,' said Smith, 'we were offered a choice. We could either go into meteorology in the RAF, into the Army or into the mines. Bob went into the Army and I went into the mines. And there we rather lost contact for a while.'

Robert was given a few weeks of disembarkation leave and went home by train. Having arrived from the heat and beauty of the Cape, the scenery of Northern England was a shock. 'I remember grinding into Central Station in Manchester,' he said, 'through those industrial slums and factories which I knew like the back of my hand. You see, I'd never seen anything else. And looking out through the window, and like a physical blow in the chest, I was astonished and I thought, "My goodness, this is what people mean by ugliness." '[22]

Robert had hoped that his tutors at Manchester University might be able to persuade the War Office to grant him a release from active duty so that he could continue his studies. When this was not forthcoming, Robert obtained a transfer from the RAF to the Army. He also decided to get himself a commission and went to Sandhurst which, he said, 'partly repelled and partly seduced' him. Eventually, he passed out as a lieutenant, which gave him certain comforts and privileges denied the common soldier. 'I'd hated the awful discomforts of barracks life as a private,' he said. 'Bad food, chivvying, needless bullying by sergeants, but there was something respectable about being in the ranks, whereas being a young officer in a noncombatant unit at that stage in the war was really very humiliating. Most of my fellow officers seemed to me shabby and their preconceptions nasty. They were real fodder to my Marxism.'[23]

Even though hostilities ended in 1945, Robert was required to help build the peace and reconstruct Britain's Imperial trading interests. He was sent to the Gold Coast, one of Britain's most important possessions in West Africa which, in the seventeenth and eighteenth centuries, had been the centre of the slave trade. The Dutch, the Portuguese and the British had built a series of substantial forts and castles all along the coast, which had either fallen into ruin or served as prisons. At first, Robert was stationed at Cape Coast, where a magnificent castle lorded it over the fishing village. Then, in July 1946, he was transferred to the capital, Accra, where another castle, Osu, was the seat of government. Five years after Robert's stay in the Gold Coast these castles were subjected to a thorough archaeological study by a man who would become, briefly, a thorn in Robert's side: Professor A. W. Lawrence, the brother of Lawrence of Arabia.

Robert's job was to help renovate the country's telephone system. It was oppressively hot and would have been exotic were it not for the grinding poverty he saw all around him. The British gave orders; the Africans did all the manual work. 'I get on well with my signallers and I enjoy the work which is entirely practical,' he told his parents. 'The [unit] we have taken over from has very bad officers and is in a state of panic stricken disorder. Particularly with native troops' slackness in little things which seem futile at the time leads to a state of disorganisation which makes a lot of trouble, most of which is borne by the ranks. Life in a really badly run station is miserable.'[24]

Ralph had sent his son a leaflet, issued by the new Labour government, which explained how the state education system would be organised and funded. It urged graduates to seek a career as teachers. It was a crusade, not just a job, though Robert was not convinced. 'I don't agree that the prospects are so brilliant financially,' he said, 'but it would be a very satisfying job, exacting enough to keep my interest and provides comparatively long periods of free time in which to write and read and generally keep up with the times and enjoy myself. For some time to come there are going to be a lot of disheartening things about teaching, though, unless you go to an exceptional school.'[25]

In September 1946, Robert learned that Manchester University had secured his release from the armed services. Papers were dispatched to Accra informing Robert's commanding officer that his best interests would be served if he could resume his studies. 'The CO announced this,' said Robert, 'by asking, "Was I willing to leave the Army?" I said, "Yes." '

FIVE

SHOTGUN WEDDING

'The empires of the future are the empires of the mind.'

Winston Churchill

The Britain that Robert returned to after the war was ravaged. Vast swathes of its cities were in ruins, industry was shattered and food rationing was a part of everyday life. Nevertheless, there was a mood of optimism in the country and a belief that the newly elected Labour government would get things going again.

Robert returned to Manchester University and this time he read history. He was, of course, older than many of his fellow students for the war had created an interesting and sometimes tense mix of school leavers and men and women who had been in the armed services. Combat and service abroad had given the older students a deeper perspective and some of them were only two or three years younger than their tutors.

In late 1946 a new resident arrived at Robert's home at School Road. While he was in India, Sydney had met and fallen in love with an Indian beauty named Jaya. Although she was separated from her husband, Indian law prevented her from getting a divorce. Sydney suggested that she leave India and go to live in Sale and await his return. 'Sydney was very proud of Bob,' said Jaya, 'and in India he would show me his letters. I remember Bob sent him a little book of Henry Moore reproductions. Because I was a British citizen, I had no trouble going to live in England. I wanted a place at Manchester University but in 1946 they only wanted to take ex-service people. Fortunately, I had some army experience but the real reason I got in was because Bob was so well known in the faculty. Miss Collar, who was head of the sociology department, took me out of respect for Bob though there was a degree of hostility to people like myself who jumped the queue.'[1]

When Sydney returned to England he went straight to Cambridge, leaving Jaya in Manchester. 'There was always an incredible amount of argument at home,' he said, 'and when Jaya first stayed with us she was appalled. She thought we were going to cut each other's throats.'[2]

Taking advantage of a British law designed to protect women who impulsively married British sailors and were then left penniless, Jaya was able to obtain a divorce. She and Sydney married in 1950, when they returned to India to take up teaching posts. Until then, though, Jaya became one of Robert's companions at university and took part in the heated debates in the teashop. 'Bob was friendly with the brightest people,' she said, 'and fell in with the McCabes who published a magazine called *Humanitas*. There was also the lecturer, Walter Stein, and two other students, Bill Perceval and Eric John. They were all in a circle. I don't remember any women, though there was a painter called Iris who was quite close to Bob.'

'Bob was enormously witty,' said his friend and fellow history student Eric John, 'though I didn't think he was especially clever. A bit superficial, really. I never liked any of his plays and tried to avoid seeing them in order to avoid talking to him about them. When he was a student, he didn't make a huge mark in the history department but in our second year he and I did an optional course on the history of western philosophy. His essays, such as one on Locke and another on Gregory the Great and the Emperor Trajan, were superb.'[3]

Robert's ideas and his politics were changing and a year after he resumed his studies at university he decided to resign from the Communist Party. 'The Russians,' he said, 'were our gallant allies and just being a communist seemed to fill entire days of my life. Then gradually I found I was quarrelling with everything the Party stood for, it being still the time when Stalin was held up as all that was wonderful and nobody talked much about the invasions. So after asking a lot of naïve questions about freedom I resigned and lost a lot of friends in the process. A very difficult thing to do, of course, to leave the Party. You feel like a crab without a shell.'[4]

Resigning from the Party was a great relief. In a way, it was like being in the priesthood and made constant political and moral demands. You felt obliged to take a position on everything. But Robert's experiences in Africa, his disillusionment with the way that Russia had created an empire of its own and his excitement at the new course of politics in Britain made communism seem almost irrelevant, and stifling. He was simply enjoying life too much.

Enjoying life, though, was itself something of a riddle. If that was what he was doing, Robert wanted to find out why, what made it enjoyable, rather than simply bearable. It was not for him a question of religious yearning but a matter of analysis and scientific questioning. He told Ronald Hayman:

I've never been awfully good at enjoying myself. You see, come to think of it, it takes a puritan to make a duty out of enjoying yourself. Which is Lawrence's message. Blood and Sex and the Natural Impulses are Very Enjoyable and therefore you had better damn well Enjoy them. Your old classical writers took it for granted that sex was fun and said, 'Now what are we going to do about this?' But Lawrence discovered it like vegetarianism. My attitude to enjoyment has always been a bit like that.

When I left the Party, I was looking around for another absolute. I still hadn't got the message, which is that you've got to take life as it comes. I flirted with people like Martin Buber, the Jewish mystic, and Zen and Lao-Tse-Taoism and a little bit with the Christian mystics. Buber had an effect on the way I thought and a faint effect on the way I lived. What I was trying to say in the preface to *A Man For All Seasons* was not just that it's the individual that counts, but that the individual is all there is. For better or worse we are born individually, the unit of consciousness is the individual and whatever there is for good or bad comes in these penny packets. There's no way of uniting two of these penny packets together except possibly in the moment of love.[5]

At university, Robert did not have much time for girls. According to his friends, he would socialise with them, recommend books, give them his essays to read and generally help them with their studies, but romances were few and far between. 'I think perhaps there weren't enough animal spirits in the house,' Robert said of his early life in Sale. 'I think we must have been sparing in demonstrations of physical affection because for a long time, casual and promiscuous physical contact I found very disturbing.'[6]

'He had a deep, deep fear of women,' said a friend. 'At Manchester he was just out of the forces and was known as the "pretty virgin" because none of the girls chasing after him could get him.'[7] That changed when Robert met a slim girl who called herself Jo, though her real name was Celia Anne Roberts. Disliking the name Celia, she chose the name Jo from one of the characters in *Little Women*.

Jo came from Romiley, which lay to the east of Manchester, on the edge of the moors. Her father, Arthur, was an accountant. 'Arthur Roberts was a Victorian,' said Sydney. 'He had been an officer in the Great War and always reminded you he was.' Jo's mother, Hilda, came from a family who had been missionaries in India. Born on 26 December 1929, Jo was five years younger than Robert and had won a scholarship to the Manchester School of Art which was next door to the university, though not a part of it. In some ways, Robert and Jo proved the theory that opposites attract each other. If Robert was serious and could be solitary, Jo was light-hearted and gregarious.

'Jo came into the picture in late 1947,' said Jaya, 'and the following summer she came on holiday with us to Lyme Regis. She was clever and talented and had a marvellous way with anecdote and for imitating people.'[8]

'She was not a pretty girl,' said Eric John, 'but she was rather beautiful and even with rationing she always dressed well. People would look at her in the street. Bob was friendly with a girl called Iris Gillespie, who was a student at the art school, and I think she introduced them.'[9]

Because of her association with Robert, Jo quickly became an honorary member of the university's talking shops, meeting the McCabes, Eric John and Robert's other friends. And Jo's own friends, like Dora Harwood and Barbara McClelland, who had done her national service, had their own social circle at a café called the Britannia near the art school. 'We'd sit around a table, discussing, dissecting, talking about the world,' said Dora. 'Jo was going out with Bob and she introduced me to the group. Bob had a big voice and I can hear him now, saying, "Here comes Dai. With Cake." And whenever Jaya walked into the room, every single head turned in her direction. She was absolutely beautiful. Jo was a lovely girl, with a nice figure and very clear eyes. She'd been engaged to someone when she was sixteen but it hadn't worked out. Bob wasn't a sexy man. He had a natural charm and a natural politeness. He wasn't rough North Country and I remember my father always called him a gentleman.'[10]

In the summer of 1948, when Robert and Jo had been going out for some months, Jo suggested that they all went camping in North Wales, one of the most ruggedly beautiful and historic parts of Britain. Dora declined the invitation, though Barbara McClelland agreed to go with her. 'Bob and my boy-friend found out and followed us to Wales,' she said. 'This made it a difficult holiday because the Welsh were prudes who thought we were scandalous women. It all blew up in our faces, so I went back home while Jo stayed on with Bob.

'Jo was very keen on Bob, which was sad because they were mismatched. Bob had a flashing wit and was capable of such subtle thought. At the same time, he was down to earth, he understood ordinary people. I think when he first met Jo she probably thought he was sexier than he really was. He was an intellectual and very sensitive. Jo wasn't an intellectual at all. She was full of fun, very sexy, a bit volatile and reckless, not one to heed the consequences of what she did.'[11]

In the early autumn of 1948 Jo thought she might be pregnant and asked her friend, Dora Harwood, to go with her to the doctor. 'When Jo was told she was pregnant, she was horrified,' said Dora. 'Her mother found out quite early but I concealed it from my parents because they might have thought I had been playing around as well. When Jo's father found out she asked him for money to buy a wedding suit. He said she could buy a maternity dress so I lent her some of my clothing coupons to buy an outfit to get married in.'

'It was a disaster when Jo found out she was pregnant,' said Barbara. 'At least, I had the sense of a disaster because they were both trapped in a situation which neither of them wanted. That happened to a lot of people at the time and they probably wouldn't have got married if this hadn't happened. I think Bob married her out of a sense of obligation.'

Although Ralph and Leah were shocked, they gave Robert and Jo all the support they could. But Jo's father took the news badly, believing it had brought shame upon his family. 'Jo's parents were terrible people,' said Herbert McCabe. 'Her father thoroughly disapproved of her relationship with Bob. Then Bob started to go round saying, "Of course, we had to get married," which upset Jo. I think that was his way of coping with the guilt he felt about it. But I never had any sense that either of them felt they were trapped by it. They were funny together and clearly loved each other.'[12]

With Jo's baby due in May 1949, the wedding was arranged to take place on 6 November 1948 at a church in Moss Side. Because Robert's and Jo's parents did not get along – the Roberts believing that Jo was marrying beneath her station, to the son of a shopkeeper – it was never going to be a happy occasion. According to Dora:

> Jo's father didn't want anyone to know they were getting married, so he ordered us to wear our ordinary clothes to the church. I told my parents I was going to a drama rehearsal and

borrowed my mother's court shoes, which were two sizes too big, plus my mother's hat. Jo and I went to a restaurant in Piccadilly in Manchester where the reception was going to be held. We went downstairs to the toilets where I helped her change into the brown suit she had bought with my clothing coupons.

Then I said, 'Jo! You haven't got any flowers!' I found a shilling in my pocket and ran out of the restaurant. A lot of Manchester had cobbled streets in those days, so I staggered along in my mother's shoes and bought a single rose which Jo put in her prayer book.

The ceremony went smoothly but the meal afterwards was a terrible strain. There were both sets of parents who hardly spoke to each other. It was quite horrific, with that prudish attitude to everything. As for Bob and Jo, I think they felt they had trapped each other.[13]

Robert and Jo found a small flat in Sale, borrowing money from both sets of parents to make ends meet while Robert completed his studies at the university. 'Considering there was rationing,' said Eric John, 'Jo was terrific at providing spontaneous meals. I remember one of her specialities was date and onion sandwiches which sounds revolting but was really rather good. They seemed very much in love with each other and I don't feel they had trapped each other at all. But she believed in him rather too much, I thought, and years later, after he came out of prison, she was totally disgusted.'[14]

'I used to go round to their flat for tea,' said Dora, 'and took Jo these women's magazines. Bob picked them up, flipped through them and read the short stories. He said, "Do you actually read this mush?" I said, "No, I go for the knitting patterns." And he said, "Well, I could do better than this." '

'Bob was always writing,' said Eric John. 'His essays were good and then, to make some money, he tried writing romantic fiction for women's magazines. But because he always wrote them with his tongue in his cheek, they were all rejected with contumely.'

On 22 May 1949 Jo gave birth to a baby girl whom they named Sally Virginia. With a wife and a daughter to care for, Robert had to get himself a job as soon as possible. He graduated with a respectable 2/1 degree and although his principal history tutor, Professor Lewis Namier, urged him to remain in Manchester and become a lecturer, Robert decided to be a regular teacher at a regular state school. He also made up his mind to leave Manchester as far behind him as possible. He and Jo liked the idea of the country, with clean air and fields, a place where they were unknown, a place to make a fresh start as a family.

'When Bob and Jo started talking of moving to Devon,' said Jaya, 'you thought they were going thousands of miles away.'

SIX

A LIMITED AMOUNT OF GOOD

'At a pinch you might be able to do without Parliament. You could do without the Minister. You could certainly do without Civil Servants and almost as certainly without local education authorities. Without any or all of them the world might not seem much worse. But if there were no teachers the world would be back in barbarism within two generations.'

George Tomlinson, Labour Minister for Education[1]

In the autumn of 1949 Robert, Jo and six-month-old Sally moved to Exeter in Devon, where Robert was to take a teaching diploma at the university. Although they were leaving their friends and their cultural roots behind, they were delighted to escape grimy, rain-sodden Manchester and, for the first time, to encounter a rural way of life.

As a married couple and as parents they might have been expected to relish their freedom and independence from their own parents. But the next three years would be very difficult for Robert and Jo, principally due to a chronic shortage of money, persistent ill health and aspirations seemingly beyond their reach. And any freedom or self-sufficiency they might have sought soon evaporated, since both sets of parents were immediately obliged to subsidise them. This shaming experience of constantly running home in a figurative if not a literal sense (they could barely afford the train fare to Manchester), caused Robert and Jo feelings of bitterness and resentment. Yet the financial hardships, together with the constant surprises, delights, worries and frustrations of parenthood, would set the seal on a marriage that had been determined by the moral climate of the time.

Robert arrived in Exeter armed with some impressive testimonials from his tutors. Walter Stein, staff tutor in English Literature, wrote:

I have known Mr R. O. Bolt for about eight years. As an under-graduate Mr Bolt occupied a leading position in student life. Whether in academic discussion or public debate, or in the work of student societies, his outstanding combination of intellectual keenness, breadth and personal vigour could not help leaving their mark on his contemporaries.

Those who know him are agreed that Mr Bolt's distinction is of a very rare kind. It is difficult to define, since it owes at least as much to his general qualities as a person as to his specific scholarly gifts, impressive though these are. He is endowed with extraordinary funds of vitality and a correspondingly catholic range of enthusiasms and interests. With history as his subject, he is as at home with economic and political problems as with literature and the arts. . . . Above all, both in speech and writing, he has been brilliantly successful in infecting others with his insights and enthusiasms and the fertile wonder of seeing conventional problems in new and striking ways. . . . Such qualities as these promise a teacher of the very first rank.[2]

C. R. Cheney, Professor of Medieval History, wrote:

I am happy to write on behalf of Mr R. O. Bolt, whom I have known well since he returned to the University at the end of his war service in 1946. He entered the Department of History and distinguished himself at once by his energy and clarity of thought. He has continued to produce work for his teachers which is of real quality and he can hardly fail to secure a very good honours degree. He is a person of outstanding ability, possibly not the man to make a scholar of the deepest dye, but unquestionably far above the average of his year in intelligence. He is also a man of very pleasant manner with a gift for clear and telling expression, and a serious enthusiasm for the work of teaching. I do not know anyone more suitable to be entrusted with the task of teaching the young.[3]

Robert attended his first lectures on 10 October 1949. 'My tutor, Miss Mathias,' he wrote, 'gave a very stimulating and informative [talk] on the history of education in this country, and another person, a man whose name I have forgotten, gave an equally informative and less stimulating one on the history of science. He is very up to date in his jargon but I suspect very nineteenth century in his basic feeling on the subject. He was far more comfortable talking about the inevitable march of progress and enquiry than about the limitations and weakness of the scientific method.'⁴

Despite the march of scientific progress, life in Britain in 1949 was tough for all but a privileged few. The euphoria of victory over Germany and Japan had soon given way to a creeping apathy. War with the Soviet Union seemed inevitable – this was the time of the Berlin airlift – and the economic and social miracle promised by the Labour government, which had been elected in 1945, had failed to materialise. Only with American aid – the Marshall Plan – could Britain even hope to emerge from the ashes of war as a modern industrial nation.

There was the new National Health Service, to be sure, but bomb-sites scarred the urban landscape, incomes were pitifully low and rationing still ruled households: while bread, potatoes and clothing were no longer on the list, dairy products and meat were severely restricted. Fresh fruit and vegetables were hard to come by, unless you grew your own, and a prolonged dock strike put a stop to the importation of foreign provisions.

The greyness of life was hard to escape and when, on 17 November 1949, Robert was sent to Exeter Grammar School for some practical experience of teaching, he saw at first hand the dismal state of the English education system. The next day he wrote a full account for his father:

> . . . [the school] is fairly expensive, has most of the mannerisms of a really good school, and is fundamentally sloppy. The boys are like other grammar school boys, the little ones are very brisk and blasé, and the older ones either earnest or faintly hysterical with unused energy and waiting for jobs or conscription. The Common Room was awful, with an insidious atmosphere of comfort and mock responsibility. I can't describe them to you one by one but the young [teachers] seemed to be very cynical though with a core, half real and half make believe, of purpose. With only one or two exceptions they looked as though they were prematurely defeated. . . . The only happy ones were a couple of old timers who by reducing their awareness to a minimum had managed to bring themselves to a state of spinsterish bliss. . . . I can tell you the whole lot of them gave me a scare.⁵

A week after this disenchanting experience, Robert was sent to observe life in an infants' school. It proved to be a defining moment: 'Last week I went to a village school where the atmosphere of semi-unhappiness, both of pupils and teachers, was so strong that it really made me want to be a teacher, more strongly than I have since I entered the department here.'[6]

More than twenty years later, Robert was asked why, with all his obvious intelligence, interests and academic qualifications, he should have decided to teach at a village primary school. 'I had up till that point been a communist, a member of the Communist Party and extremely interested in politics,' he said. 'I sought a public solution for all life's difficulties. After the war I gradually became uncomfortable in the Party and hostile to it. I could get no sense out of the people I revered in the Party and no honest answers to the questions I was asking. So I left. I wanted a very private life in which I could do a limited amount of good, so I went to a village school.'[7]

When Robert decided to become a teacher at an infants' school, the profession itself was to some extent in its infancy; the notion of a teacher at a state funded school was quite new. Robert was one of many thousands who were in the vanguard, evangelists for a classless, articulate and motivated nation.

For centuries past, an education 'system' had scarcely existed; it was more of a pyramid of privilege. At its tip were the ancient public schools like Eton and Harrow, which bred and boarded the boys who would go on to Oxford or Cambridge and then, suitably equipped with Latin, Greek and moral righteousness, and inured against cold showers and scraps on the playing fields, would inherit the country's political, military and religious institutions, just as their fathers and *their* fathers had done before them. The overwhelming mass of the country's children had to make do with schools which were funded by private or church charities. Education was not a matter of great concern to governments because those who were born to lead did so and those who were not remained in their place.

So poor were the standards of education in Victorian England, even on the tip of the pyramid, that the Inspector of Schools, the poet Matthew Arnold, attributed the British defeat in the Crimean War to the 'ineffectiveness of our superior education'. But Arnold's words fell on deaf ears: fifty years later, at the turn of the century, the odds of pupils receiving a secondary education were 270 to 1 against and Britain could boast of having only seven universities.

Throughout the first half of the twentieth century funding for education remained extremely low. Apart from the handful of public schools, most children attended elementary school from the age of five to fourteen, whereupon the boys went straight down the mines, on to the farm, into the factories or the armed services. Girls married and raised families.

During the Second World War, the Conservative Minister for Education, R. A. Butler, announced sweeping reforms in his 1944 Education Act, much of which was adopted by the new Labour administration. In 1947 Labour raised the school leaving age to fifteen (an idea first proposed in 1926) and advocated a system of free primary and secondary education for all and the eventual introduction of comprehensive – or multilateral – schools which would dispense with the traditional grammar schools and their inbuilt notion of élitism. In the field of primary education no less than 928 new schools were built between 1945 and 1950 to cope with the anticipated rise in the birth-rate, the so-called 'baby-boomers'. An army of new teachers was needed and to recruit them Labour's Education Minister, Ellen Wilkinson, introduced the Emergency Training Scheme which drew on young men and women fresh from the services. Wilkinson's scheme was a huge success, producing some 35,000 new teachers within the space of five years. One of these was Robert.

Having recognised his mission in life – to be a village teacher, to do a limited amount of good, away from the internecine struggles of party politics or the groves of academe – Robert was unsure of where to practise it. While he loved the South Devonshire countryside – the grandeur of Dartmoor, the rugged coastal scenery, the estuarine bird-life, the quaint villages – he nevertheless felt isolated and sorely missed the intellectual stimulation of his friends from Manchester, many of whom had moved to London or, like Tony Quinton, to Oxford. Robert and Jo were also irritated by the necessity of sharing someone else's house.

When he was taking his diploma, Robert and Jo lived in the brief hinterland between Higher and Lower Shillingford, just west of Exeter. They rented a small flat in a substantial detached house – Crosslands – which boasted wooden window shutters, a wide glass conservatory at the front and mock-Tudor elements at the side. The house belonged to Mr and Mrs Nott, who had three daughters and a large, savage tomcat called Smokey, who lived on a diet of wild rabbits. Fortunately, after only a fortnight Smokey took kindly to the Bolts' cat, named Polly Flinders, and a feline truce was declared. The Notts were kindly if meddlesome people and far from the lively conversationalists Robert preferred for company. And, having moved away from his real parents, Robert was disturbed to find he had inherited a pair of surrogates: 'Mrs Nott', he wrote, 'is a very keen housekeeper [who] cannot really believe that there is more than one way of doing anything. Also she goes into our rooms when we are out, which is quite harmless no doubt, but discomforting. Mr Nott seems to have only quite a slender intercourse with his wife and daughters. When he comes home he goes straight into the garden and works there, chain-smoking, until it is too dark to see. He speaks very little and is very easy to get on with.'[8]

Perhaps because of a poor diet, Robert and Jo suffered from frequent colds. Jo was also quite seriously ill with a stomach complaint which was at first thought to be a grumbling appendix but was later diagnosed as a form of tuberculosis. Robert told his parents:

> Jo is about the same. That is to say, she has no positive pain, but is off her feed, and has only enough energy for half the day. She is full of penicillin but if the appendix has become involved she will have another sharp attack and will have to have it out. Jo is marvellously patient and cheerful about it. Her one worry is that she may slip into a permanently resigned attitude. Sometimes I know she is privately very depressed indeed but we both feel that if we can come out at the other end of this troublesome period with flags flying, so to speak, we are bound to have gained something from it.
>
> I simply can't say how good Jo has been. She is an absolute brick. When I think of my own mentality at the age of nineteen I am horrified. I think that she has set her teeth and has determined simply to go through this period without giving an inch of ground to whatever it is in life that seeks to defeat one. She finds it difficult to imagine what it will be like when she is alive again, and I think she is sometimes very cynical about it, but I feel that our relationship is becoming stronger each day and that when it is all over we shall have a splendid life together. Sally is in good health and increasingly charming, though still extremely plain. We had another parcel of baby clothes a few days ago which came in the nick of time as she has quite grown out of the first ones.
>
> The Notts are full of unspoken criticism as to the state of the flat, though how they expect us to cope, with Jo ill half the time and me with work to do and Sally filling nappies as fast as I can wash them, I don't know. They are superficially generous but inwardly cruel with the cruelty of mean-mindedness and would rather have Jo drop at the sink than have a visitor see into our untidy kitchen.[9]

When Ralph urged his son to be more understanding of Mrs Nott, he received a tart reply: 'Dad's remark that we must tolerate other people's idiosyncrasies simply doesn't apply. We are completely tolerant of any amount of either conventionality or eccentricity. They can go to church three times a week or they can play bagpipes in the bedroom so far as we are concerned. But we should not tolerate (though we do) their ceaseless and impertinent interference with *us*.'[10]

In order to placate Mrs Nott, Robert gave the kitchen a good coating of white distemper, rearranged the furniture and reduced the chaos to a single heap in the corner of a room. Accordingly, relations with their landlords improved to the extent that Robert and Jo asked Mrs Nott to baby-sit for them when they went out to the theatre or the pictures in Exeter. However, the experiment did not work out as they had hoped and they decided to make their own amusements.

To while away the evenings, Robert had taken an interest in weaving. He bought himself a loom and in no time presented Jo with a red scarf. Dismissing the new mechanised techniques of weaving on to canvas, Robert's work was organic and free-range, as staunchly traditional as anything produced by the local villagers. He planned to make a carpet for every room in their flat.

While Robert was busy teaching and studying by day and weaving in the evenings, Jo's illness and depression gave her little enthusiasm for painting; nor was it easy for her, as a Northerner, to enter into village life. She began to experience loneliness for the first time, a problem which would remain with her for many years and which would undermine the marriage. As Robert wrote to his parents: 'I see plenty of people during the day and when I get home I am ready to be quiet. But Jo, who rarely gets out of the house even to push the pram, has a pretty thin time. Our neighbours don't get home till four; I usually not till six.'[11]

Fortunately for Jo there were occasional visits from her friends in Manchester. When Dora Wigg brought her fiancé to stay with them she found an intensely serious couple: 'They dissected everything,' she said. 'We went house hunting with them and in the afternoon we sat in the garden. It was a hot day and Sally was playing with a bowl of water, wet through and grinning away. Jo said, "Oh, this is a happy afternoon." Then Bob and Jo started to analyse why it was happy, what made it happy, what it meant, and we all ended up feeling gloomy.'[12]

After six months at Crosslands, irritated by the Notts, Robert considered moving to Suffolk or Essex and applied for a teaching post in Colchester. He and Jo also thought seriously of quitting

Britain altogether and emigrating to the West Indies, an unusual idea since everyone in the West Indies wished to come to Britain while everyone in Britain dreamed of prosperity in America, Canada or Australia. No one, it seemed, was happy where they were for there was a widespread restlessness, born of idealism as much as economic factors. One thing, though, was absolutely vital: Robert had to find a job and a house which he and Jo could call their own. When his parents learned of the plan to move to the West Indies they both sent cautionary letters. Although Ralph's and Leah's letters are unavailable, it seems they were both anxious about Robert and Jo's tenuous hold on life and its implications for their granddaughter Sally. Ralph was also clearly worried by Robert's evident frustration and ascribed this to a lack of religious conviction. The West Indies idea was quickly abandoned, yet it produced from Robert a long and fascinating letter to his parents which reveals much about his emotional state, his ambition, his ideas about religion and, especially, his preoccupations with sexuality and manhood which he treats in metaphorical terms. It also shows that, when the mood took him, Robert worked hard on his letters to his father:

> Were there ever two generations with so much to divide them and so much to help them understand each other, as ours? On arriving back from Colchester I found two nice long letters from you both, for which many thanks.
>
> We have received long lists of reasons for not going to W Indies, from each of our parents, none of which include the fact that you won't want us, with Sally, to go so far away, and yet I am sure that this must in fact be a main consideration with you, as it is with us.
>
> Dad says he can't see why I should regard Truth as a kicking horse. Of course I don't mean that a Revelation of Truth would take the form of physical violence. But look: Dad says we can't find Truth but have to find a working hypothesis. Exactly – and since we don't know whether the hypothesis is true, truth might well upset our apple cart. It's like building a pyramid twelve inches off the ground. You might define the weakness of our generation as the inability to accept hypothesis, & this no doubt accounts for our exaggerated antagonism to your 'philosophy' which, since it is concerned to uphold Christian morality without the main Christian hypothesis, simply consists of a mass of hypotheses which don't appear as such to you and only because you have never stood *outside* your belief.

And once again Dad asks were Christ, Buddha, the Taoists and others (he doesn't include Mahomet because Mahomet is too alien to his own thought) like kicking horses? The answer seems to me quite clearly to be 'yes', & the fact that Dad (speaking for both of you as he does throughout the letter) so confidently expects the answer 'no' seems from my point of view sufficient proof that he has castrated them. Christ & the others each said a score of truths, each of which if followed would upset the apple cart of our civilisation. And in any case these great men were all speaking from great & original hypotheses. It seems to me that Truth may kick even harder & in even more unexpected directions than they did. The whole business of morality seems to me questionable.

What I meant when I coined my rather wild metaphor (it wasn't really wild but I sense that it offends you so I castrate it for you by saying 'my rather wild metaphor') is much better expressed in a phrase from the *Upanishads* which has stuck in my mind. 'Oh Lord they have put a golden stopper in the neck of the bottle. Take out the stopper. Let out life!' You know this to be true & so you set yourselves to pretend that the stopper isn't there, not really, not badly, only spiritually speaking (like Christ when he said that the rich could get to Heaven as easily as a camel through the eye of the needle), only in a rather wild metaphor.

We don't regard Sally as a 'self-incurred responsibility'. You may rely on us (as you would phrase it) to 'do our duty' by her. But to make a child the core & pivot of a family puts too great a weight on it, & is unnatural. I also 'incurred a responsibility' when I married Jo.

As for happiness lying within, not without, in external circumstances, of course it does, & some day I hope to be able to live exclusively by that truth. Until then, I have appetites for glamour (in a wider sense than the usual) which seem to me healthy. Nor does Dad wholly believe what he says since he 'can't see me being happy' in the external circumstance of a primary school. But this he would call 'only reasonable'. Thus he wishes to bring even the first elementary rung on the ladder of Truth down to the level of where he happens to be standing. This process is called 'not running to extremes' and 'being reasonable'. Jo and I can't ride the stallion & and know it, but you, it seems, creep under it with a pair of farrier's shears to render it 'reasonable'.

Anyway, as Dad says, one can't capture even one's own feelings in words. What matters is how one feels towards a person. And by that test it is clear that we very largely agree, however antagonistic our formulations may appear.

I didn't get the Colchester job. Love, Bob.[13]

Having decided that it would be foolish to leave Devon before he had completed his diploma, Robert and Jo did at least leave the Notts behind them. In March 1950 they signed a six-month lease on a flat in Exmouth which they rented for two guineas a week. While their flat, at 4 Alexandra Terrace, had only one bedroom and an outside lavatory, they were fully self-contained and ideally situated: the house faced the grandiose Imperial Hotel, complete with a garden and a mock Athenian temple. The sea was a hundred yards away. Life seemed better already and a model for existence was demonstrated by two new friends, an art master named Sam Avery and his brother, Wilfred. Robert's glowing account of them might also have been written about Robert himself a decade later: 'They live very well and graciously,' he wrote. 'They believe, as Dad does, that the artist must live in beautiful surroundings, including clean table linen and creased trousers. Since they can't, of course, afford a servant of any kind, they get up early and turn to themselves. Indeed they "turn to" with greater facility than any other people I have met, with the result that they have plenty of time for painting and talking. They are very jolly and positive about life, believing that one must detach oneself from evil and ugly things, and not put too much energy into reform.'[14]

With a more congenial place to live, and with the amiable Averys as near neighbours, Robert's spirits began to rise: 'I am trying hard for a job within travelling distance of Exeter,' he wrote. 'While the flat is very small we feel far more at home than we ever did at Crosslands which seems in retrospect incredibly unpleasant. We will never again go and live in the shadow of somebody else's domesticity. And I'll never again fall for the line that there is a mass of "ordinary nice people." Only the extraordinary people are nice – in England in 1950 at any rate.'[15]

Having passed his diploma and having been – as part of the course – a supply teacher at several local schools, Robert had gained an impressive reputation. So when, in August 1950, he was one of fifty-six applicants for a teaching job at a primary school he was not surprised to be hired on the spot. To celebrate, Robert and Jo opened a food parcel, which had recently arrived from Jo's parents, and they went to the local pub where they shared a pint of cider.

From 7 September 1950 Robert was to work at the primary school in the village of Bishopsteignton which lay on the north bank of the River Teign, three miles from the sea at Teignmouth. The river was heavily tidal, revealing vast sand banks at low tide, and it was rich in bird life. In many respects, it was an idyllic place to work and live. The village owed its name to a Bishop of Exeter who built a palace there in the twelfth century. It was in the middle of farming country and positioned half-way up an escarpment, affording fine views of the river and the south bank. The houses and cottages were chiefly clustered around Fore Street and there was also a large estate named Murley Grange.

Bishopsteignton Primary School dated back to the early eighteenth century, though its buildings were mid-Victorian. It was typically spartan – lofty ceilings made it freezing in winter and the boys, if not the girls, had to walk outside to find their lavatories. Now used as the community centre and the local museum, the school occupied an elevated position, on a curve in the road where, in Robert's day, a dozen oak trees, known locally as the Twelve Apostles, marched down towards the estuary.

The headmistress of the school, Miss Fanny Robinson, was a Northerner. To her pupils, she was the archetypal spinster teacher who ruled with a rod of iron, as a former pupil, Den Back, recalls: 'Although the Victorian era as we know it had passed, there was much of it still alive in teaching. Miss Robinson was one of the last Victorians. You went into class every day and you had to spell "Bishopsteignton." You did that every morning and then you did your two-times table, your three-times table and so on.' Miss Robinson also made it a rule that any child walking to school from the other side of the road should touch the post box which was built into the wall. This ensured that the children did not walk on or near the kerb. 'If you didn't touch the post box,' said Back, 'she'd give you a slap.'[16]

Another pupil, Sheila Robbins, was taught by Miss Robinson during the war and understood many of the reasons behind the headmistress's strict regime: 'Fanny Robinson was from Yorkshire who came to the school in the middle of the war when the village was alive with Bren gun carriers, tanks and servicemen all ready for D Day, so that's why the children had to cross the road that way. Also, the school was packed with evacuees. Miss Robinson took on a lot. I mean, if a child's parents were killed in London she'd get a letter and she would have to tell them what had happened. By the time that Mr Bolt arrived – and he was the very first male teacher she had hired –

she was nearing retirement and was very set in her ways.'[17]

Robert respected Miss Robinson and welcomed her help in trying to find him somewhere to live. For Robert had a problem: to get from Exmouth to Bishopsteignton each day – a mere eight miles as the seagull flies – he would have to take the ferry across the River Exe to Starcross, then a bus to Teignmouth and another to Bishopsteignton, at least an hour each way at a cost of a pound a week. Since they had to leave their flat in Exmouth by the end of August, Robert and Jo began a frantic search for another, preferably on the right side of the estuary and as near to the school as possible.

After a month of fruitless searching they gave in to the inevitable: they would have to live apart in distinctly penurious conditions. For Robert, a front line torch-bearer of Labour's new age of enlightenment and scientific progress, the world had never seemed so cruel or so unforgiving. He told his parents:

> I have the offer of a caravan in Bishopsteignton and Jo of free lodgings in a Nissen hut in Budleigh Salterton. In the past month we have spent almost fifteen pounds travelling and will have to sell something to last until my next cheque arrives. *Don't* tell me that we should have been more careful: we have had no pleasures of *any* kind; haven't even eaten properly. From *Picture Post* I learn that I earn only a few shillings per week more than a Billingsgate fish porter, and that the basic wage for a teacher is four shillings more than that for a builders' navvy. Tony Hodges [a friend from Manchester], who is simply an amiable nit wit, is now earning exactly twice what I shall be getting in five years time. My friends in London tell me I am a fool to be in this profession and I am very inclined to agree tonight. I feel that particularly intense anger which is called up by a situation for which one has only oneself to blame.[18]

For two months, Robert and Jo lived apart and only managed to make ends meet by Ralph's generosity. Ralph and Leah sent money, baby clothes, items of furniture and more money. Leah also sent Robert a pair of boots which delighted him – 'I love the feeling of being well shod,' he wrote, 'and we had just reluctantly come to the conclusion that I must buy a pair of shoes, which we needn't do now as the boots are a light pair and a village schoolmaster is not expected to be dapper.'

Fortunately, Robert did not have to endure the ignominy of a caravan; he rented a room in Radway Lodge, Bishopsteignton, and immersed himself in work:

I have a good deal of marking to do [he wrote], and when I've done that I don't feel like anything except a read or a stroll around. My feeling about teaching has not so far altered. I quite like it but am not enthusiastic. But then I didn't expect it to be. Miss Robinson is easy to work for in the personal sense though exacting from a professional point of view. I don't agree with her views on life; like so many Northerners she thinks that work and more work is the answer to all life's questions; but she is a good head. It (her philosophy I mean) has had a very narrowing effect on her personality – she has no sense of humour at all – so that I don't find her especially congenial socially. The position is simplified or complicated, I don't know which, by the fact that she has taken rather a fancy for me, and I know she would like me to be head when she retires in a few years' time . . .

The trouble is that until we can have some kind of home together we can't judge whether the various advantages of teaching really exist, as all these advantages have to do with domestic serenity and activity. . . . We'd rather live in a shed than go on living this scattered sort of life. . . . We're no longer finicky either, not only are we prepared to accept the romantic eccentricities of medieval cottages and ex-army huts, but also pink brick semis. . . . Oddly enough Jo and I are quite happy.[19]

In November, Robert and Jo moved into Murley Lodge which was originally the gatehouse to Murley Grange. Ralph paid all their moving expenses. Although they knew they could only live there for five months, when the rent would rise from two to five guineas a week, they were a family again. And it was a bungalow this time, not a flat, with a roof shaped like a pyramid and an eye-catching four-way chimney shaped like a ziggurat stuck on the top. 'School has seemed much more of an enjoyable proposition since Jo came to Bishopsteignton,' wrote Robert. 'I have lunch at home every day except when I am on dinner duty. . . . But I wish my work was more directly creative. I know that one has the possibility of doing some good with one's children, but sometimes the business of teaching seems very much a matter of drawing one's pay for going through certain motions rather than for producing anything – rather like the army. Still, my class is in much better shape than it was when I came, so I suppose I must have done something.'

The pupils found Mr Bolt a revelation, an extraordinary contrast to their previous teachers and to Miss Robinson. Den Back, then ten years old, who now makes a living by cultivating quality lawns in

Saudi Arabia and Kuwait, said:

> Mr Bolt was different. He would make funny jokes and we'd be able to laugh. He'd smile to himself and I remember that smile quite vividly. I'm not sure he was appreciated by the hierarchy but us pupils appreciated the fact that Mr Bolt relaxed the general principles of teaching. Before him, everything was taught parrot fashion. He was the sort of guy who, if you didn't understand something, he'd say, 'Ask me.'
>
> We had these desks with inkwells. I remember dipping my pen in the ink and seeing this big blot appearing on my exercise book. And all Mr Bolt did was to pick up the blotting paper. Miss Robinson would just hit you. Then we'd make the nibs of the dip pens into arrows and flick them across the room. Well, one boy did that, Mr Bolt noticed it and said, 'Now we are all going to write the word "Bishopsteignton" and one of you will have a problem!' That's all he said. Miss Robinson would have done her nut. But Mr Bolt never laid a hand on anyone.[20]

Another of Robert's pupils was Peter Wallis, now a retired Squadron Leader in the Royal Air Force. 'Mr Bolt was a very kind man who always wore leather patches on the elbows of his jackets,' said Wallis. 'He put up with a lot of trouble from us. He was very easygoing and I think we probably took advantage of him. But gradually we followed his line by example rather than by being driven. This was unusual in those days which tended to be more rod than carrot.'[21]

Despite the progress Robert was making with the pupils, he and Jo did not enter fully into village life, as one might have expected of a teacher who was, in some respects, as much a pillar of society as the local vicar and his wife. Instead, they regarded themselves as perennial outsiders, economically deprived and intellectually undernourished, and they viewed their neighbours with some scorn. Jo in particular found it difficult to mix with her neighbours and she is remembered as being a prototype hippie. 'She wore sandals, long skirts and long hair, which was unusual in those days,' said Sheila Robbins. 'She was a bit of a dreamer and never belonged to anything in the village.'[22]

'Mr Bolt ran the school sports single-handed,' said Peter Wallis. 'His daughter was toddling about and he was trying to look after her because his wife was, well, I remember her as a sort of hippie, a very artistic lady who spent her time at home painting. She wasn't into helping at school sports.'[23]

Robert was probably reflecting Jo's feelings as much as his own when he wrote:

Pictorially the village is lovely indeed but I don't like the people at all. After our experience at Shillingford we began to have doubts about village life, and Bishopsteignton, which has every reason to be a happy community, confirms them. Devonians are very different from Northerners. They are very heavy, and rather deceitful, but above all they are aggressively rude to strangers unless the strangers happen to have money. It finds expression in small ways – bills added up to a little more than the correct total, the silence that falls in shops when you go in, the failure of people of all kinds to do what they promise, and so on – it adds up to an unpleasant atmosphere. As Jo says, walking down Fore Street in Bishopsteignton is an ordeal by bad manners. By the way, we get a certain satisfaction that everybody here, high and low, is utterly and unquestioningly Tory.[24]

Robert, though, was questioning Labour Party policy and wrote to Prime Minister Attlee berating him for banning a full representation of the teachers' union at a party conference in Sheffield. He also sent letters to a number of newspapers about the threat of war in Korea and about Labour's apparent willingness to compete in the arms race. Inspired by a pacifist speech of India's prime minister, Nehru, Robert argued that the money spent on arms might be better used on developing nations such as India and Malaya. Years later, Bamber Gascoigne would describe Robert's position as advocating 'moral rearmament'.[25] In a single week Robert wrote letters to Attlee, *Picture Post*, the *Manchester Guardian*, a magazine called *Air Space* and the *Western Morning News*, and was delighted when the last published two letters from him, even though he had moderated his argument to avoid upsetting its Tory readership. 'We must make our voice heard,' he told his mother.

While letters came easily to him, fiction did not. Although he had begun to take seriously the idea of writing his way out of teaching, he lacked confidence in his abilities and had made many false starts. 'I don't seem able to settle to writing anything,' he told his parents. 'It is beginning to occur to me that I may not have the talent. But one must put up a fight. I feel I have certain possibilities in the creative way and I must try hard to actualise them. If the worst comes to the worst, I can always weave carpets I suppose.'

Robert's pupils, meanwhile, had been transformed from a rather unruly mob into a disciplined class. He achieved this purely by strength of character, dedication and experiment. In addition to the routine study and reading of books and the practicalities of spelling and elementary grammar which he demonstrated on his blackboard, he gave his pupils lessons in history, geography and drama, encouraging them to act out scenes from plays. He wanted them to appreciate education as a preparation for life.

'I have a suspicion that he didn't go down very well with the traditional ways of teaching,' said another former pupil, Terry Thomspon, who now works for the government's Health and Safety Executive with special responsibility for working conditions on North Sea oil rigs. 'I think Mr Bolt was way ahead of his time in his communication skills and the way he built up one's confidence. We used to dance to music in the playground but Mr Bolt started to teach us drama which was a very new thing. My job today requires a whole range of these skills which I believe date from the time when I put myself in front of an audience because of Robert Bolt.'[26]

Robert's first term was coming to an end and his efforts were paying off – the children were making tremendous progress, the headmistress was delighted and Robert's self-esteem had grown to the extent that he now saw a bright and fulfilling future ahead of him. He told his parents:

> I think I am beginning to like my work and today I had the satisfaction of hearing Miss Robinson say that the class was definitely much improved since the start of term. It is not so much the welding of a rather uncontrolled group of children into the rudiments of an organised class which gives a feeling of achievement, as the making active of the abilities of one or two of the children who were getting into slovenly and negative habits . . .
>
> It seems to me that the only reform which would really make a big improvement in education would be to halve the sizes of the classes, which would enable the teacher not only to bring the children on very fast so far as accomplishment goes but also to 'get at' them in all sorts of ways which are impossible when he has thirty or forty to cope with. At any rate, I feel fairly certain that even if I'm not a good teacher now, I could be, some day.[27]

SEVEN

DRAMA IN DAWLISH

'Words are wise men's counters; they do but reckon by them.'

Thomas Hobbes

It was in early December 1950 that Miss Robinson asked Robert to stage a Nativity play for the children of Bishopsteignton Primary. This annual ritual, as much a part of the British Christmas as carol singing, shopping in secret for presents and pulling crackers over a plump roast turkey, signalled the end of school and the start of the holidays. All across the country, children would drape themselves in sheets and dressing gowns and gaze at a cardboard star moving across the assembly hall. Teachers' favourites, a girl and boy, would be ordered to play Mary and Joseph while three other boys, wearing false beards and carrying boxes of gold, frankincense and myrrh, would lay them before a plastic doll in a makeshift manger lined with straw. As the rest of the pupils hung around the stage dressed as shepherds or angels, parents would look on with a mixture of pride and embarrassment, praying that their children would not get the windipops or forget their lines.

Robert took to his task with the emotional distance of an atheist, yet when it was finished it was a revelation.

The headmistress handed me a great batch of those little plays that are published for children to act. They were either unspeakably dull or unspeakably mawkish. There wasn't one I could bring myself to do and I thought, well, it shouldn't be too difficult with the St Luke Gospel or something. So I started to write one myself. Literally within about five lines of dialogue the penny dropped and I thought, this is what I want to do. It was an extraordinary sensation, realising that within five short speeches one had a situation of complexity, interest and discipline. It was like, almost like, the discipline of a poem.

It was a smash hit. It couldn't help but be with a source like that. Once you had got the Three Wise Kings on with a bit of argy-bargy, you could hurry on to the Angel Gabriel's speech and you were home and dry. With some fair-haired agricultural child dressed in white sheets reciting that stuff in front of a lot of blue crêpe, you couldn't miss.[1]

One of the leading actors in the Nativity play, which was performed in Miss Robinson's classroom, was Peter Wallis, who said:

I played a shepherd named Peter Lumby. All the cast, which really was the whole class, were given copies of the script which was typewritten. Mr Bolt rehearsed us all very carefully and I think his wife designed the costumes. I remember I had to take one of her drawings home and get my mother to make up my shepherd's costume.

The play ran for about half an hour and started off with three of us sitting round a fire. The shepherds were having an argument about the weather and I had to say, 'It's fine and sharp. This is the season for frost.' Then another shepherd said, 'Thank you for your lesson, Peter Lumby. The season for frost is it? I never knew that before.' These are the only lines I can remember. This was the first play that had ever been done at the school, and Mr Bolt started it all off. We thought it was marvellous.[2]

Writing now began to consume all of Robert's spare time. It also consumed much of his father's time, for until Robert could afford a typewriter it was Ralph who typed up the handwritten manuscripts. Robert was suddenly bursting with ideas, both for children and for adults, and he wrote with the passion of someone who has just discovered a new talent or a new lover. He knew he was a novice at these things and while he was quick to criticise himself he found it hard to accept criticism from others, as Bernard McCabe found out.

McCabe, who had not seen Robert since Manchester University, was himself teaching in Devon and, to his delight, discovered Robert and Jo living about ten miles away. Invited to Murley Lodge for the weekend, McCabe listened as Robert stood in the living room and acted out one of his plays. He was obviously very proud of his work; it was the best yet, he said. 'I didn't like it very much and said so,' McCabe recalled. 'I objected to an oratorical element in it, a sort of overblown quality which cropped up in his later writing. I realised at once that Bob and Jo were devastated by what I had said. I remember their jaws dropping and Jo putting her hand out to him. They had pinned their hopes on it and I felt like a total worm. But our friendship survived.'[3]

To place beside McCabe's criticisms, however, there was encouraging news from the BBC, where Robert had sent a short story for children, entitled *The Baron, The Miller and The Magic Trees*, as well as a play called *The Master*. A producer he knew slightly, Vivian Daniels, was impressed by them and was considering them for production by the radio drama department in Leeds. But Daniels was to consider them for far longer than Robert thought tolerable. Ralph had typed up *The Master* and had liked it. He asked what other subjects Robert had in mind. 'Another play for the radio is beginning to stir far down in my mind,' replied Robert, 'about the death of Sir Thomas More, a man who calmly, wisely, wittily and finally tragically, refused to go with the stream. A very good and relevant subject if I can do it.'[4]

At the end of February 1951, the lease on Murley Lodge ran out, obliging Robert and Jo to live apart again, he at a cottage in Bishopsteignton and she at a friend's house in Exmouth. His letters were still tainted by envy and resentment, the views of a man with a large chip on his shoulder. But now he bore an additional burden, the trappings of a fatalist: he had become convinced that atomic oblivion was inevitable. With his mind firmly focused on the worsening situation in Korea, he wrote:

> Now that we have accepted the situation, we feel all right again, though tending to take a very stern view of the selfishness of wealthy Devonians – as for example Deaconess Gould who lives in a colossal mansion and refuses to consider letting as a flat the old servants' quarters. . . . She has two old servants and the three of them must be occupying about 20 or 30 rooms. This is the worst case we know of but there are scores like it all round here. These moderately wealthy people are feeling the squeeze and are terribly frightened of losing their social position. And of course there is nothing like fear for driving out any generosity one may have.
>
> There is a man up at the Grange who has a pretty high position at the Foreign Office. Jo was up there and he was slightly drunk and began talking politics. Jo says that it was really frightening. His attitude was that we are virtually at war

already and that we should use the atom bomb. But what was really upsetting was his total lack of logic, principle and vital information. Jo was very depressed by the incident. And indeed our leaders are either Machiavellian or very ordinary men indeed. But we try not to take any notice of the news. If we have only a few years left then we will not load them down with anxiety. What we want is a house and some day a rowing boat. Not much to ask we would think but apparently unobtainable.[5]

On 22 March 1951 Robert and Jo were reunited again when they moved into a flat in the seaside resort of Dawlish. Dominated by its famous red cliffs, Dawlish was a creation of the Great Western Railway which transformed it from a sleepy fishing village into a fashionable resort for Victorian holiday-makers. The railway, that great engineering feat of Isambard Kingdom Brunel, ran down through the hills of Dorset and into south Devon, breaking through the cliffs and skimming the very edge of the surf. The platform at Dawlish station was more of a boardwalk, or a pleasure pier frightened of getting its feet wet, and from there the views along the coast were sensational, stretching from Lyme Regis in the east to the bizarre pinnacles of rock known as The Parson and The Clerk to the west.

Robert's and Jo's flat was up the hill at 10 Barton Crescent, now a quiet enclave of Victorian B&Bs and cruising learner drivers. The flat was smart and relatively spacious and had a real luxury: a purpose built bathroom. But Robert could barely afford the rent of four guineas which was over half his weekly take home pay. So Ralph and Leah, as well as Jo's parents, came to the rescue by each contributing eleven shillings and ninepence a week. As always, Ralph's business instincts and his innate Methodism demanded a precise accounting of Robert's debts. Not for him the cheque made out and rounded up. Robert sent his father the bill for their moving expenses, saying, 'I hate sending this bill but we can't pay it ourselves, so what can I do? My finances are not your concern, but your generosity makes them so. I do battle it.'[6]

While the BBC were still considering *The Baron* and *The Master*, Robert sent another play, called *The Dog*, to his father for typing. It was returned with some adverse comments about canine anatomy. What Ralph had not realised, perhaps, was that his son had not only become an artist – a suitably grumpy and impoverished one – he had also acquired all the artist's emotional baggage. In his terse reply, Robert said:

Dad was quite wrong in his criticisms. The script – and each word – had been gone over many times. 'Back haunches' was deliberate; of course, 'haunches' are always 'back' but in this case I wanted the 'backness' emphasising. Similarly 'thin front legs' means something other than 'thin forelegs' if only from the vocal aspect. A short story of that type is almost a poem in that the words are used to convey more than they 'mean'. Only the writer (even an inexperienced one like myself) can choose the words, often without knowing why, and often quite wrongly of course. I am not quarrelling with Dad's criticisms which were stimulating, still less with his right to criticise, but the grounds of his criticism were simply not valid.[7]

Five months after he staged the Nativity play, Robert entered his class in the Third Annual School Drama Festival at Dawlish. The competition was being promoted heavily that year as part of the nationwide Festival of Britain. The competition was open to all schools in the area and boasted entries from Teignmouth, High-week, Budleigh Salterton and Dawlish, as well as Bishopsteignton. Robert's entry was a fifteen minute historical comedy called *The King Who Tore His Trousers*.[8] 'I played a wizard in *The King Who Tore His Trousers*,' said Peter Wallis. 'The story was about this king who sits on a throne and won't get up to do anything. His courtiers think he's lazy but in fact he won't stand up because, much to his shame, he has torn his trousers.'[9]

Den Back played a herald who, much to his embarrassment, forgot to take his trumpet on stage and had to run off to fetch it. 'Mr Bolt rehearsed us for weeks, weeks, and he got us all word perfect,' said Back. 'Mind you, whatever Mr Bolt did for us as a dramatist when we were kids, somebody had to suffer. Money then was not as easy as it is today, even if you're on the dole. Everybody would chip in for the costumes knowing full well they couldn't afford it. But people just appreciated what he did for the community.'[10]

The star of *The King Who Tore His Trousers* was Peter Wallis's cousin, Terry Thompson. 'We all had to write down the parts we had to play which was a good way of learning the lines,' he said. 'Then we were taken to Dawlish where we were given lunch and a classroom where we got made up and changed into our costumes.'

Given the title role, Thompson was the first in a roster of stars which would later include Ralph Richardson, Michael Redgrave and Paul Scofield. But Thompson suddenly proved to be a temperamental actor. Just as Richardson a few years later worried about calling another character a 'little rat', Thompson thought that the climax to Robert's play was so shaming that he refused to play it. 'Things were rather conservative in those days and I remember being reluctant to present my backside to the audience,' he said. 'I refused to do it, so Mr Bolt agreed that we would tie a handkerchief to my trousers which would represent my underpants.'[11]

The adjudicator for the School Drama Festival was Keith Hamilton Price, an announcer for BBC West radio and a lecturer in drama at Exeter University whose 'practical constructive criticisms of each individual play and performer', reported the *Dawlish Gazette*, 'were carried out in a most amazing manner which will, no doubt, be long remembered with a smile by the children'.[12]

A week later, the *Gazette* carried a fuller account of the proceedings, even though the reporter got the title of Robert's play wrong: 'Mr Hamilton Price said that the festival was one of the best organised that he had ever attended. A play that received the appreciation of the adjudicator was *Cowslip Wine*, performed by the young pupils of Bishopsteignton Primary School and written specially for them by Mr R. O. Bolt who resides at Dawlish. Mr Price thought it an excellent choice of play and one which told a good fairy story with a great deal of humour.'[13]

Two months after Robert and Jo settled into Dawlish, they found a house they wanted to buy. They loved the place immediately they saw it and promptly lost it within minutes to a rival bidder. Fortunately, that deal fell through and they moved fast to secure it, hoping all the while that Ralph, recently promoted in his job with Turner's Asbestos, would raise the £200 needed for the deposit. The balance, to be mortgaged, was £1200. The address was 7 White Street in the seaside town of Topsham, on the broad estuary of the River Exe, just south of Exeter and only a couple of miles north of their first home in Exmouth. Topsham was – and remains – a pretty place with a colourful history dating back to Roman times and an ambience that suggests an old smugglers' haunt. Ralph raised the money over the weekend, enabling Robert and Jo to exchange contracts and move in by July 1951, the long school summer holiday having just begun. After a year of living in a succession of rented rooms in other people's homes and in converted flats, they had at last a place to call their own, with a garden which Robert thought big enough to support three home-grown cabbages.

Since the school at Bishopsteignton was too far away to contemplate travelling by public transport, Ralph was persuaded to send Robert enough money for a down payment on a motor-cycle. This was not an ordinary motor-cycle. It was an American-made Indian Brave with a powerful 250cc engine and a gear-shift like a car, operated by a free hand. Even at this early stage of his career Robert's tastes tended towards the opulent and the esoteric. Not for him a standard 50cc Triumph, or even a slightly racy Beezer, and before long the throaty sound of the exotic Indian Brave alerted the children at Bishopsteignton to their teacher's imminent arrival.

For the next six months Robert and Jo, with little Sally, were perhaps the happiest they had ever been. Topsham was in every way a nice place to live – too big for a village, too small to be regarded as a town, it was far more sociable than Bishopsteignton – and the waterfront was always busy with fishing boats and pleasure craft, giving Robert a love of the sea and a lifelong fondness for sailing.

Although the BBC were still dithering, Robert's confidence in his writing was growing and he felt it was surely only a matter of time before he would be 'on the air'. But before that happened there would be a major change in his teaching career which left the boys and girls at Bishopsteignton crestfallen. It also surprised his friends, for it took him away from classes of forty youngsters, the children of ordinary working people, into the world of millionaires and privilege. And it happened just after he crashed his motor-cycle on the way to school.

The injury to Robert's right arm was considerable, as was the compensation. Since the accident was not Robert's fault, he was awarded £1000 in damages, a massive amount in those days, considering the house in Topsham had cost £1400. But the money did not last long. Robert and Jo bought a pram, a boiler, a washing machine, a carpet, clothes and a new motor-cycle with a sidecar, using the balance to pay off some of the mortgage.

When news of Robert's accident reached Bishopsteignton Primary, everyone was devastated. 'I can remember Mrs Robinson standing and telling us that Mr Bolt had been hurt,' said Den Back. 'We all cried.'[14]

EIGHT

AVALON

'While we have sex in the mind, we truly have none in the body.'

D.H. Lawrence

'Remember, *Rashomon* . . .'

Naomi May to author

All the rural counties of the kingdom have their own traditions, their own dialects, customs, foods, and their own legends. None more so than the counties of the west – Cornwall, Devon and Somerset – and it was to the last that Robert and Jo moved in early 1952. There they encountered and fashioned a sort of life which enabled them, for a while, to live as the poets envisaged, close to the soil and water and to ancient myth and magic.

In the prehistoric past this slice of land, the shape of an anvil, had been a marsh, fed by the open sea, where Neolithic tribes built funerary monuments and mysterious circles of stone monoliths. The later Iron Age settlers fortified the tops of the highest peaks, the Quantocks and the Polden Hills, and established themselves as an island race within an island. And when the waters eventually retreated the sense of isolation did not; Somerset was always an island.

Legends abounded: huge hounds from hell were thought to patrol the moors and inside every cave like Wookey Hole a dragon lurked, breathing fire. Joseph of Arimathea was reputed to have founded an abbey at Glastonbury and when he knelt on the ground his stave immediately sprouted into the Glastonbury Thorn Tree, which flowers every Christmas. Then came King Arthur, bestriding the land from his castle at Camelot, that mythical place of idealism governed by steadfastness and steel.

Robert and Jo would live within sight of Glastonbury Tor, the legendary Isle of Avalon, a looming, perpetually green, breast-like mound with a nipple-like ruin on its peak which often rose above a blanket of mist. Beneath its earthy bulk was said to lie the Holy Grail, as well as the mortal remains of Arthur and Queen Guinevere. Rising more than five hundred feet above the plain, it is Britain's mausoleum to love and betrayal. Years later, the ashes of one of Robert's and Jo's children would be scattered there.

In the early Georgian era, Somerset was the setting for Henry Fielding's carnal comedy *Tom Jones*. The image in that novel – of fornicating rustics, lascivious clerics and English maidens waiting to be plucked – persisted through the centuries, aided by rumours of debauches at the great estates of Montacute and Barrington Court. Two centuries later, Brunel's Great Western Railway, known affectionately as 'God's Wonderful Railway', with its panting locomotives and chocolate-and-cream liveried coaches, was speeding through to places like Taunton, Westward Ho! and Minehead, carrying holidaymakers bound for the beaches and picturesque coves of the north coast. The hinterland of Somerset, though, remained a backwater of yokels, cheese and cider to make your head spin. Robert would later remember it as the best place of all, an earthly paradise.

Robert was in hospital, nursing his shattered right arm, when Jo brought him the *Times Educational Supplement*. An advertisement caught his eye: Millfield needed two English masters for January or April 1952 to teach 'Middle School upwards or downwards.' Applicants were also required to be 'interested in one or more of the following activities: games-coaching, scouting, canoeing, fishing, music'.[1]

Since Robert's injury made him unable to write, Jo sent off his application. Explaining his temporary incapacity, she wrote:

> [Robert] took his degree in 1949 and in the following year took a Teaching Diploma at the University of the South West, because he wished to teach at village schools and thought that this area would offer more opportunity for this kind of training. And since 1950 he has been teaching in a village school here. He took up this Primary School work against the advice of all

friends and instructors who warned him that the village school is not now a rustic idyll – if it ever was – and that the work would be totally unsympathetic to him.

He would like to be considered for either of the two English posts but would greatly prefer the upper school as this would enable him to harness his own literary enthusiasms more directly to his work. My husband has considerable experience of boating and fishing – hitherto on salt water – and would be willing to organise those activities.[2]

Millfield was a famously expensive school and its unorthodox teaching methods would have appealed to Robert. It offered none of the normal pressures of a state run primary or secondary modern school, nor did it correspond in any way to the popular image of the British public school. Millfield was located two miles from Glastonbury, on the outskirts of Street, a seventeenth-century village which, by Victorian times, had developed into a prosperous manufacturing town because of the Clark Brothers, Cyrus and James, both Quakers, who made sheepskin slippers, then leather shoes for virtually every adult and child in Britain.

Just as Street was a product of the Industrial Revolution, Millfield School could boast of no ancient traditions; nor were its students housed and taught in cloistered buildings dating back to the fifteenth century. When Robert joined its staff, the classrooms were Nissen huts, bought in bulk from Army surplus and laid out in two wide arcs in a cow field. In the winter they were freezing and in the summer they were like ovens. To begin with, Robert's desk was an upturned boat. The pupils wore no set uniform, much less the stiff collars and tailcoats of Eton or Harrow. Millfield was almost casual – boys were simply required to wear a jacket and tie – and from its inception, it was co-educational.

Millfield's founder, Rollo John Oliver Meyer, became a teacher by a quirk of fate. Born in 1905, Meyer was educated at Haileybury and Cambridge, where he won a Master of Arts degree. More crucial than any academic ability, however, was Meyer's sporting prowess: 'At university he was for three years a cricket Blue,' wrote his obituarist in 1991. 'He must at one stage have been very near an England cap because twice in his career he dismissed the Australian batsmen in their prime. He won a rackets Blue and once came within an ace or two of defeating an amateur champion. He was a fine golfer and would certainly have won a Blue if there had been ten days in a week instead of seven. He was capable of beating almost anyone in the land over eighteen holes, but would never have won a major event as he would probably have tried out several new swings in the course of a championship.'[3]

Instead of playing cricket for England, Meyer sought his fortune as a cotton broker in India. After his business in Bombay fell victim to the Depression he was employed as a tutor by the Maharaja of Limdi. Meyer had just one pupil in his charge, the Maharaja's grandson. Wanting a proper English education for the boy, the Maharaja sent Meyer back to England to start a school for the sons and grandsons of other Maharajas. Looking for somewhere to start his school, Meyer discovered that a large country house owned by the Clark family was for sale. Millfield House became Millfield School on 3 May 1935.

The early years were difficult. Millfield was exclusively the pre-serve of Indian princes and existed, like Somerset, in a world of its own. Its relationship to the English educational system would have been the same had Meyer's school been in the foothills of the Himalayas. But Meyer soon earned the school a distinctive reputa-tion: 'Millfield rapidly grew into a formidable coeducational school, one of the pioneers in this field,' wrote Meyer's obituarist. 'Meyer was one of the first teachers to recognise and treat dyslexia and to preach the value of very small classes. His cardinal belief was that every child had at least one talent whatever it might be, which must be unearthed and encouraged.'[4]

The future Kings of Saudi Arabia and Thailand arrived, as did the young Sir James Goldsmith and, later, the sons of Elizabeth Taylor and Sean Connery. The high fees demanded of these celebrities were spent on improving and expanding the facilities – a polo ground and a swimming pool joined the cricket, rugby and football pitches. Meyer also opened nearby Edgarley Hall as a prep school for Millfield itself.

There were no set rules for admission and no formal entrance examination. Meyer would take anyone, as long as he liked them and saw potential in them. And if a child wished to study a particularly arcane language or subject and no teacher on the staff was suitably qualified, Meyer would search for a teacher and engage him purely to teach just that one child. The ratio of teachers to those pupils taking A levels and Oxford entrance exams rarely exceeded one to six. As far as Meyer was concerned, success was equally a matter of brains and brawn. As he once said, 'We do not undertake to supply brains to pupils in cases where the Almighty has made other arrangements.'[5]

Meyer was proud of Millfield's record of producing great athletes – most notable in Robert's day were the Olympic gold medallists Mary Bignall-Rand and David Hemery, as well as the tennis player Mark Cox – and in order to achieve this he would accept for moderate fees boys and girls with evident sporting ability. On occasion, if he spotted a potential champion, he might waive the money altogether, knowing that the families of Arab or Oriental royals, diplomats and the English aristocracy would make up the deficit by paying fees which were high enough for Millfield to be listed regularly in the *Guinness Book of Records* as the most expensive school in England. 'His Robin Hood approach to school fees and scholarships,' wrote old boy Ian Baldwin, 'was done with such charm no parent or child whether giving or receiving was offended. His immense wisdom and keen sense of humour ensured a happiness amongst three hundred boys and thirty girls from over fifty nations at the school in my time there.'[6]

One boy, though, who did not gain admission to Millfield was the future drama critic, Sheridan Morley, whose father, the actor Robert Morley, met Meyer and said, 'I am told this is a very good school and that my son should do very well here. The trouble is that I did very badly at Wellington and have done very well since then. So you see, I really want a school where Sheridan can do badly.' Meyer replied, 'That could be arranged but I think it might cause disruption if others followed him down the primrose path. Goodbye.'[7]

When Robert's application arrived at Millfield it was read by none other than his Air Force friend in Cape Town, Len Smith, who was the Head of the English Department.

We never referred to Meyer as Meyer or as Mr Meyer [said Smith]. Everyone called him Boss. He went to the same college in Cambridge as I did – Pembroke – and I went to teach at Millfield in 1947. Teachers were known by their initials, so I was always L. E. W. Smith and Bob was always R. O. Bolt. Boss wasn't really political but he had to be right-wing in attitude. I mean, he was a very unorthodox man. I admired him enormously. He was an absolute genius the way he built up the school.

When we wanted a new English teacher we advertised and got a couple of score or more applications. Amongst those was one from R. O. Bolt. So I said to Boss, 'This is the man we want. He's lively, intellectual, sharp as anything and at the same time a man of great authority and integrity.' Well, when it came out that Bob was also left-wing, Boss was very doubtful if he would take him on. He didn't want a couple of communists. Boss was also doubtful because Bob had a History degree, not an English degree, but he was so articulate there was no question he would be a marvellous English teacher, which he was. Boss was impressed by him and took him on. I don't think anybody else came for an interview.

I think Millfield was one of the key things in Bob's development. The school in Devon was rather stressful, I think, having these young village kids around. Millfield was an easy place to teach, the classes were small, you had no pressures put upon you and all the children were willing to learn. You didn't have any homework to take with you. I think that was a great relief to him as he could write his plays in the evenings.[8]

Following his interview with Robert, Meyer wrote: 'He has vocation, he knows his stuff, he could adapt himself to higher work. He understands the Millfield philosophy.'[9] Robert was formally offered the post from 1 January 1952 at a salary of £540 a year. In his letter Meyer wrote:

I cannot precisely define your duties at this stage – every new term brings an unusually large crop of new problems which we try to solve as they present themselves – but generally speaking you will be expected to take over the English work of Mr A. A. Bulos. In those parts of the timetable where he was teaching Arabic and music you will be found work which I expect will be suited to your abilities and interests.

I am grateful to you for offering to take over the Sailing Club (Sundays in winter; Saturday afternoons in summer) and possibly the Canoeing Club and if you can help with the Army or Air Cadets on Fridays after tea I shall be still more grateful. I have not forgotten that you are interested in dramatics, which are run by Mr F. Ferguson Young, though I do not see how you could find time for them [though] of course your help would be welcome if time and opportunities are available.

During the course of his interview, Robert had suggested that Jo would be keen to teach art at Edgarley, the prep school. But Meyer had Jo's thin CV which, under 'Qualifications', listed only 'Matriculation (i.e., Nil)'. Meyer was therefore cautious about committing himself as far as Jo was concerned. 'I cannot, at the moment, promise Mrs Bolt any teaching of art,' he wrote, 'but I think it is probable that, in the event of your settling within range of Glastonbury, there would be a certain amount of part-time teaching to offer her later on.'[10]

Robert replied in a remarkably feisty way to Meyer's letter and seemed on the verge of offering to teach Swahili on Sundays:

> I shall keep my History furbished and shall be ready at any time to take it up to University Entry level. I doubt whether you will have any use for Economics or Philosophy, but I could bring my Geography, for example, up to scratch, if that would help.
>
> For the present I should prefer not to take on any work with the Cadets, partly because the other activities will take so much time but more because I have no aptitude for military matters. I am irretrievably civilian. I trust you will not think this unco-operative; I am most anxious not to undertake work which I am unfit to carry through.
>
> My wife asks me to say that she perfectly understands that the Art teaching, either at Edgarley or Millfield, is not now at issue, but that she would be more than willing to undertake it if it ever became so.[11]

Robert's and Jo's priority was to find somewhere to live. Selling their house in Topsham, though, proved to be difficult and they put it into the hands of an agent who offered it for rent at thirty-five shillings a week. It was eventually sold in October 1953, though hardly any of the rent, much less the sale price, found its way into the Bolts' bank account.

When Len Smith told them that the cottage adjoining his was available for rent, the Bolts moved in immediately. The address was 56 Butleigh, being in the village of Butleigh, some three miles south-east of the school. Smith's cottage, 55 Butleigh, and the one rented by Robert and Jo, were built in the sixteenth century. They were thatched and built sideways on to the narrow lane, so that the front doors were on the left as one entered the gate through the garden. Since the cottages were in a slight dip, their aspect was limited: 'From our garden', wrote Robert, 'you can only see two fields, but by walking half a mile up a gentle hill you can see right across the plain to the Mendips, and from the Polden Hills – three hundred feet high – you can see nearly twenty miles to the Bristol Channel.'[12]

While the rural setting could not have been more beautiful, the cottage was extremely primitive: heating was minimal and the lavatory was in the garden and had to be slopped out regularly, like an army latrine. But by far the most primitive aspect to the cottages was the lack of running water. 'There was electricity,' said Smith, 'but no running water so you had to go out to the well every morning and fill your bucket. Later on we had a washing machine but we still had to fill it with water from the well.' Taking a bath involved carrying buckets of water into the kitchen, boiling the water on the stove and a slosh down in the kitchen. 'It was a very romantic way of living,' said Smith.[13]

Butleigh and the surrounding farmland had once belonged to the Grembille family whose Gothic ancestral home, Butleigh Court, stood at the northern entrance to the village. As another teaching colleague of Robert's, Wyndham Bailey, recalled: 'Grembille had one of the first motor cars in Somerset and the whole village had to stand at attention and doff their caps as he drove by. When the Grembille line ended, the estate and Butleigh itself were sold off. Boss tried to buy the Court but he was outbid. Old Grembille started a Co-Op, which was an odd thing for a right-wing landowner to do. There was a post office, a baker, a blacksmith, a village school and a pub, the Rose and Portcullis. The church at that time had a minuscule congregation because the vicar drank cider. He was really a sad case. It was a close-knit community and we, as Millfield teachers, were the outsiders.'[14]

The Millfield teachers formed a social clique whose intellectual debates and political skirmishes were most often conducted over drinking sessions and endless games of skittles at the Rose and Portcullis.

> Bob and Jo were a very odd couple to live next door to [said Len Smith]. They were quite Bohemian. Bob nearly blew up the cottage a few days before my son was born. He arrived home from school, found the stove was out and threw a lot of paraffin on it. We had the fire brigade, everything, and the place very nearly burned to the ground.
>
> I think one of the reasons we eventually moved away was because my wife, Kurtuu, who was Finnish, could not stand their unorthodox life. Finns are very orderly and don't waste things but if Jo burned a saucepan she'd just chuck it out, even though they had no money. But Jo always felt Bob would make it as a writer and she made some sacrifices to help him.[15]

'Boss ran Millfield on a shoestring,' said Wyndham Bailey, 'and we all felt we were underpaid. You worked enormous hours, including weekends, so we sometimes felt very hard done by. They introduced pay differentials, so science teachers got paid more because there was a shortage of scientists. This caused some problems with the staff. Bob was a bit of a spendthrift – if he wanted a bottle of wine he'd buy one, or he'd eat prawns when the rest of us couldn't afford them – and they got into problems with money. You couldn't go to your bank for a loan and you couldn't run your credit card up because you didn't have credit cards.'[16]

Life as a pupil at Millfield was splendidly evoked by the writer, Victoria Glendinning:

> We were taught, brilliantly and intensively, in Nissen huts. In one Nissen hut, the future playwright Robert Bolt gave inspired English lessons. In another, an unrecognised genius, Miss Sawtell, taught essay-writing on principles I still use today, when I remember. In another, dapper Colonel Barter taught Urdu, Arabic, Spanish and Portuguese simultaneously to different groups, only occasionally getting them mixed up. In another, the Eeyore-like J. R. Bunbury dragged us mournfully, line by line, through Corneille and Racine, sitting on a high stool, his long legs tied in knots. We all passed our exams.
>
> There were not many girls at Millfield then. Boss called us the YLC – the Young Ladies Club. I broke one rule too many and was discovered in the orchard after dark with a boy – sniffed out by the Alsatian belonging to Amothe Sankey, Boss's secretary. I was summoned to Boss's study the next morning. In the presence of the inscrutable Miss Sankey, he told me that I would be expelled, but the boy would not, because 'it's always the woman's fault'. A harsh doctrine.[17]

The pupils looked up to Robert. He was young, passionate about his subjects and had a sense of humour. Just as the country boys and girls at Bishopsteignton were never intimidated by him, the peculiar mix of dim-witted aristocrats, budding athletes and intellectual marvels enjoyed his classes which very often bridged what in most schools was an unbridgeable gulf between master and student. Some pupils became friends and one in particular became rather more than that.

Naomi Keanie was an independent sort of girl. Dark and petite, she came from Scotland where her father's construction business employed 1000 people. Her mother was a magistrate, a pillar of society. They had maids, cooks, gardeners, a fine house, everything a post war family could dream of. Naomi was sent to a boarding school in Northamptonshire which she hated. Frustrated by the low level of education she was receiving, she wrote to Meyer and requested a prospectus which she forwarded to her parents who were on a skiing holiday in Switzerland. This initiative eventually led to her startled parents driving down to Street for an interview. Naomi's prospects were excellent: her parents could readily afford the annual fee of £300 and Boss admired her pluckiness in arranging her own education.

> Boss charmed my parents [said Naomi]. He talked about Churchill to my father and flirted with my mother. He went on and on about me being the ideal Millfield person because he liked enterprise. This enterprise thing at Millfield was interesting because the Labour government had nationalised everything and the Conservatives were bringing back private enterprise. The whole racket of Millfield was run on this. There were no servants. Instead, there was a thing called 'public works' which meant that the children did all the cleaning. Boss's philosophy was that if the boys were to run factories they should learn how people on the shop floor worked.
>
> A lot of boys had been expelled from other public schools and some were just ineducatably stupid, half-witted almost. There was the son of a Lord and Meyer just put him to work in the gardens. Meyer also got the parents of these problem children to pay extra. He did understand dyslexia. There was money in it. Not everyone passed their exams. In fact, I don't think the pass rate was better than elsewhere. Of the four girls who sat the Oxford entrance with me only one passed.[18]

Naomi joined Millfield in 1950, when she was sixteen, and began by studying for A level in History and English, which she passed with flying colours. 'Then we all heard about this new English teacher,' she said. 'I first saw Bob in a Nissen hut. He was a very bonny-looking young man wearing a brown corduroy jacket which was very dashing. I was supposed to be trying for Oxford in History but changed to English five weeks before the entrance exam. The head of the history department, an embittered old spinster called Miss Sawtell, was very angry that I did this. But I did it because I liked Bob and Len Smith.'

Naomi soon discovered that R. O. Bolt was not a conventional teacher and he, recognising that she was not a conventional student, began to monopolise her time by banishing the rest of the class to an empty Nissen with an essay to write or a poem to memorise. Naomi would be taught differently:

He'd tell me he hated the poets on the course and he'd read to me the poets he liked. He was very fond of Blake and as he read his blue eyes would fill with tears. I was supposed to be doing the Romantics, Keats and Shelley, but he thought they were rubbish. Luckily I'd done them for O level. But that was one of the things about Millfield. It was very open to abuses, so if a charismatic teacher tells you that the course is useless, that can cause very real problems for the student. Len Smith, though, was much more conscientious and he would just teach you the syllabus.

Bob would also talk about university at Manchester, his experience in the Air Force, and his political views. He used to say things that were most dissident. Practically all the children at Millfield came from rich backgrounds and Bob would rail against the capitalist parents of these children whose allowances were often greater than his salary. I knew it was naughty of him just to teach me and not the rest of the class, but Millfield was such a rackety place I didn't think anything of it. And nobody else thought anything of it either.[19]

Before long, Naomi was invited to the cottage at Butleigh, where she met Jo and young Sally. She was shocked to see how impoverished they were – the lack of running water and an outside lavatory were totally beyond her experience.

Everybody got around on bicycles and people started to notice a young woman in the garden of the cottage at Butleigh, Mrs Bolt, who always seemed to be alone. Jo was beautiful. She had long, rich brown hair, a high forehead, beautiful eyes and teeth and a nice smile. Her face sort of came to bits lower down but she moved like a dancer and when she wanted to be she could be enormously seductive.

I became very friendly with Jo who was terribly lonely. When Len Smith got married she had looked forward to some female company but she and Kurtuu did not get on well. I had come from a background with servants and wanted for nothing. I had eight horrible evening dresses, things like that, and Jo was pining for all these things. I was appalled by the way they lived and took on all their socialist views. My mother thought that something subversive was going on that might not do me much good in the long run. Eventually she met them and I was astonished how Bob and Jo bowed and crawled after her. Bob always wanted to know her opinion of everything he wrote and if she said anything critical he'd go away and amend it. That astounded me.

Naomi was also shocked by the way that Robert and Jo treated young Sally:

> They weren't very nice to this little girl and it's unlucky that she was such a sensitive and subtle child. Sally was the cause of all their troubles, the reason why they got married. As a result, Bob felt trapped as a grotty schoolteacher and Jo felt that Sally had ruined her figure and was very resentful of her. Both of them would pitch into this child. I remember when Sally broke a mirror, Jo turned on her and called her a bitch. Sally would whine a lot. They'd use North Country words and say she 'pratted' a lot and when Jo got pregnant she said she was 'in pig'. Things were better when Ben, or Bendi, was born. Bob could love him without complication; he was adored by both of them. Ben didn't cry. He didn't need to.[20]

Benedict was born on 3 May 1952 at Butleigh Hospital. Since Jo had miscarried an earlier pregnancy, the arrival of an apparently healthy boy delighted her. But within a fortnight, Ben was showing signs of extreme pain and he was rushed to hospital suffering from a strangulated hernia. An operation saved his life. By the time Ben was eighteen months old Robert wrote that he was 'still at the age when they can be treated like geraniums, fed, watered and forgotten. He seems to have a self-sufficient nature, too, but so did Sally at his age.'[21]

A month later Benedict had become 'a hulking child, very healthy and with lots of physical know-how. He is also jollier and more demonstratively affectionate than Sally. It is too early to say anything else though of course we detect signs of unusual intelligence every day.'[22]

Sally, though, was turning into a neurotic and unpredictable child. She tended to squint and had an operation at Bristol Hospital in an attempt to correct it, though it seems it was a nervous affliction. And as with many first-born children, she grew jealous of her parents' obvious affection for her little brother. Sometimes Robert and Jo would wake up to the sound of Sally chanting at Benedict, 'It's *my* mummy not yours. It's *my* mummy not yours!'

As Naomi spent more time with the Bolts, Jo began to confide in her, telling her the most intimate details about their courtship and their marriage. She said she was lonely because Robert would come home after school and immediately disappear upstairs to spend several hours at the typewriter; Jo often said she wanted to throw it into the River Brue. During the weekends, Robert was often away with the sailing club. But the solitude went hand in hand with a measure of chaos when friends, such as Tony Quinton or any number of McCabes, came to stay in the tiny cottage.

For Naomi, Jo was partly a surrogate mother, partly a surrogate older sister. 'Jo seemed pretty amazing to me,' she said. 'I had lived an extremely sheltered life at dreadful girls' boarding-schools but she had *lived*. Though she was only four years older than me, she'd had a shotgun wedding, she had two children, she lived in poverty which in a way had a kind of glamour, and she'd had lots of hard times, real life as it seemed to me. She told me all about her sex life, her babies and breast-feeding, all these things which at my age were fairly startling and fascinating.'[23]

Naomi was also besotted by the unconventional English master who taught and spoke so compellingly by day and who wrote plays by night. She felt captivated too by the way that Robert lived within the realms of the imagination: 'He'd spot a quite ordinary person in a lane or a farmer in a field, and would conjure a wonderful history for him. He'd be writing his plays and they were always filled with heroes and nobility. He was, though, very much a craftsman. He once said to me that writing was ninety-nine per cent drudgery and one per cent inspiration. He was totally caught up by the excitement of writing. This was Bob's and Jo's springtime, when they could have an impossible dream of success. They always grumbled and felt that life owed them more.'

For Naomi, there was something else: the place itself – the land, the river, the way the morning mists would engulf everything except the Tor, the buttercups that used to flower in vast honeyed drifts, the fusion of nature and Celtic legend. It was a world where Blake's burning gold, arrows of desire and chariots of fire seemed palpably real. There was also the reality of England in the post war years when food rationing and other privations led to a belief in the young that they were creating a new world, a new Jerusalem. Naomi said:

> It was very romantic. When it was chilly, we'd sit in the snug, just off the front parlour which was only used on special occasions, and talk for hours. In the summer, with its soft, soporific climate, we'd sit in the garden and Bob would read poetry or act out bits from his new play. We'd laugh a lot, eat

bacon or fried egg sandwiches, smoke cigarettes and drink cheap wine, which I would often bring.

We were all reading Freud and D. H. Lawrence, especially *Lady Chatterley's Lover*, which was like a Bible to Bob and Jo. They lived in the hope that they, too, would become Lawrentian. It's interesting that Jo would eventually go away with someone like Mellors . . .

At Butleigh, Bob was in the ascendant. He was writing his plays and he had this tremendous enthusiasm, a vividness, he could see his characters who were in another world. This probably helped him as a writer as his characters were better, more exciting, more Technicolored than real life, as it were, and more noble. There were always these ideas of nobility, of goodness, of beauty . . . as he'd always say, 'lovely. . . .'[24]

One evening at Butleigh, near the end of term, Naomi told Robert and Jo that she had been invited for an interview at Somerville College. If all went well she would be leaving Millfield and would return home to Scotland before starting her studies at Oxford. For her part, Jo told Naomi that Robert was depressed and that she had found him upstairs, crying on the bed. She was very worried about him. Indeed, Robert seemed uncommonly morose all evening and, later on, Naomi found out why. 'Bob took me home in the sidecar of his motor-cycle and as he was saying goodbye to me he said, "You're going back to Scotland. You come from a completely different social world from me and you will go to Oxford and live a completely different life. Our paths will never cross again." ' Robert then opened his heart and made a complete declaration of love, which left Naomi 'flabbergasted but also worried and overjoyed because I thought he was the most wonderful person I had ever met.'[25] He told her about his unhappy childhood, how he hated the army and how only at university had he seen light in the darkness. His life since then, he said, had become dark again. But Naomi, he said, had given him new hope.

Naomi felt that Robert was just 'thinking out loud. But I believed what he said – he made a point about honesty – and I was deeply affected. My imminent departure from Millfield was not so much a comfort as a resolution of a problem I could hardly cope with.'

After her interview at Oxford, Naomi met Jo in London and took her to dinner at L'Etoile, in Charlotte Street. Somehow it did not seem incongruous that she, an eighteen-year-old student, should take the teacher's wife to dinner in one of the most fashionable and expensive restaurants in London. 'Jo had never gone to a nice restaurant before and this was the dream place,' said Naomi. 'We had the best of everything, including liqueurs, and we got terribly tight. She told me that she longed for Bob to love her as Bernard McCabe loved her, or desired her. She was still the loving wife, though she probably knew that Robert was just teaching me alone which might have aroused her suspicions.' And that was where it might have ended, except that Naomi failed her interview at Somerville and was obliged to return to Millfield for further studies.

To begin with, life proceeded as normal. Robert would teach Naomi in the Nissen hut and she would spend the weekends at Butleigh. But gradually, as the term wore on, Robert's feelings towards Naomi rose to the surface again, and he would murmur things to her as they walked together to the Rose and Portcullis while Jo stayed behind putting the children to bed.

> Everything in those days was extremely inhibited [said Naomi] and if Bob had jumped on me I would have been scared out of my wits. That probably made him feel completely safe with me and that was probably why Jo felt she was safe as well. I thought Bob was terrified of women.
>
> Then one day he said to me, 'I have two children who are very little but if you could wait a while until I have more money to take care of them and Jo, would you consider marrying this poor schoolteacher?' That of course upped the whole thing. What had been manageable then became unmanageable. It was the beginning of adult life for me.
>
> Bob had been a father figure to me. In fact, he reminded me of my father who was right-wing where Bob was left-wing but they both felt passionately about things. I worshipped my father and was frightened of him because he had a terrible temper. He gave me my education by teaching me about Scottish history in the same way that Bob inspired me with English literature. They had a similar passion and charisma and they even looked rather alike. But when Bob asked me to marry him everything changed. My relationship with him was no longer chaste and trouble-free. The idea of breaking up a marriage was terrifying and, anyway, part of Bob's glamour was that he was married to Jo.

If a fourth person had been involved, the whole situation could have derived from D. H. Lawrence, with the characters seeing themselves living under a rainbow of animal passion and intellectual idealism. In fact, Naomi believes there was a fourth person – Bernard McCabe –

whom she saw as Robert's romantic rival and as a moral touchstone. But McCabe, who visited Butleigh on a few occasions, denies that this was so. 'I was never in love with Jo, not remotely so,' he said. 'There was a mutual attraction, occasionally talked about, more often joked about. But no secret trysts, letters, phone calls – *never* a shared bed. Nothing.'[26]

As far as Naomi's own romantic attachments were concerned, she sensed that Robert and Jo deliberately discouraged them. There was a boy at Millfield named Francis who came from Jamaica and who was one of the heirs to the sugar giant, Tate & Lyle. But Bob and Jo, acting as surrogate parents, urged Naomi not to continue her relationship with Francis whom they characterised as a 'callous capitalist and lounge lizard'. Not only did Robert want to monopolise her time at school, it seems they both wanted her alone at the cottage.

After some weeks of agonising over her dilemma Naomi decided to tell Jo everything about Robert's proposal to her. Instead of giving Naomi a good slap and throwing her out, as one might have expected, Jo confided in her more closely than ever before. 'From that moment Bob had had it,' said Naomi. 'There was a sort of counter-seduction when Jo appropriated me. It was the cleverest thing she could have done.'

There was a strange, soul-searching and eerily symbolic final weekend at Butleigh when Naomi, confused and shaken, launched a devastating attack on Robert. She denounced him in every way – as a man, as a father, as a husband and as a dramatist who feared to face reality and wrote only of the past. As Robert broke down in tears, Jo sat quietly in her chair. 'I keep trying to remember why I turned on him so mercilessly,' said Naomi. 'By then the counter-seduction was in place and I was doing it for Jo, as her mouth-piece. But I had a sense, too, of having been played with, invented, fobbed off. In particular I recall attacking him for his ideals of "goodness" and the contrast with his actual behaviour. I'm sure I never said this, but what really shocked me was that the author of *Baron Bolligrew*, beloved by children everywhere, should be so unkind to poor Sally.'[27] The tension in the tiny cottage had become unbearable so they all went up the hill for a drink at the Rose and Portcullis.

The next morning, Naomi awoke in a sleeping bag in the downstairs parlour and found Robert standing over her. Her mouth was wide open and she said that a spider had fallen into it. She remembers Robert saying to her, 'That will teach you not to abuse your moments of insight.'

'I had humiliated him dreadfully,' said Naomi. 'I hadn't set out to do this but over the course of several hours it all brewed up. He was mortified, very head-hung, and Jo became coldly vindictive, resentful and contemptuous. The humiliation Bob had suffered at my hands radically altered him. He lost his sweetness and warmth and became guarded, more ruthless and even more ambitious.'

Inevitably, the curious drama being played out in the cottage at Butleigh reached a wider audience. When Naomi skipped school to spend a day with Jo her absence from her lodgings at Wraxleigh was noted by Miss Sawtell. It was she who blew the final whistle by telling Boss that Robert and Naomi were lovers. Naomi was summoned to Boss's office and his secretary, Miss Sankey, with whom he was rumoured to be having an affair, was asked to leave.

I wasn't one of Boss's favourites because I wasn't sporty [said Naomi]. He was enormously tall and had a raddled handsomeness and long bony fingers which he used to crack. He stood me in front of the blazing fire, stroked my hand and started burbling on and on about brains and beauty.

Then he said, 'Now, about Mr Bolt. Are you having an affair with him, my child?' I said I wasn't but I was very friendly with both the Bolts. I told him I'd been ironing and sweeping and helping Jo. He gave me his profile and said, 'Millfield is partly a school and partly a training for life and you have had all the scandal of having an affair and none of the pleasure. That's incompetent and inept.' I thought that was funny and I told Bob and Jo what he had said. Neither of them thought it was funny.

Now that the headmaster had become involved in the situation, Jo felt compelled to write him a conciliatory letter: 'I want to say how much I regret that this little storm should have blown up over Naomi. . . . I hope that as little wrath as possible will be visited upon her as she has been most sweet and helpful. I had been hoping that she might get permission to come and see us for the last time this evening and hope you will feel able to grant it. But I appreciate that in view of what has happened you may feel it more politic not to. . . . Please accept my apologies for the anxiety you have been caused. I feel it is largely my fault.'[28]

'Part of the magic of that Age of Innocence', said Naomi, 'was not just the poetry, longings and dreams, but that we also had a great deal of fun together. Luckily, whatever else got lost, Bob kept his sense of humour which helped to sustain him during his harrowed later years.'[29]

Naomi left Millfield shortly afterwards, when Jo started to take an interest in another of Robert's pupils, a spotty boy who had the nickname of 'Brumas,' after a polar bear at London Zoo.

Naomi's second interview at Oxford – this time at St Anne's – was also a failure. 'Bob's cavalier approach to the syllabus,' she said, 'and his insistence that I should be honest at the interview certainly didn't help. But it would be wrong to blame him for my failing Oxford. His next student, Gillian Beer, did brilliantly. Besides, his inspired teaching no doubt influenced my better papers.'[30]

But Naomi was not to vanish from Robert's life and she was to wear the emotional scars for many years to come. Though she continued to visit the Bolts and regularly exchanged letters, she noticed that Robert was careful to maintain a formal, schoolmasterly distance from her. Naomi's relationship with Jo continued to be close and confessional, rather like the sisters, Ursula and Gudrun, in *Women in Love*. There was also a financial element in the relationship as when, a year or so later, Naomi loaned Robert £100 so that he and Jo could take a holiday in France. Shortly afterwards, Robert called her and asked for another £100 so that he could settle his debts with the Butleigh shopkeepers.

In September 1953 Naomi enrolled as a student at the Slade School of Art. There she met a talented sculptor, Mike Kellaway, and at their wedding a year later, Jo was Naomi's Matron of Honour. As for Robert, he was surprised and delighted that Naomi had married not a gormless stockbroker but an intellectual, an artist, with whom he could argue matters of importance. 'When I first met Bob,' said Kellaway, 'he was morally censorious, almost an intellectual sadist at times. He was very tough on Jo and not good with their daughter, Sally. Later on, after his marriage broke up, he changed from being a puritan into something of a libertine.'[31]

One of Naomi's strongest memories occurred just before she met Kellaway. She wrote to Robert to say how lonely she felt and received a reply which angered her and which demonstrated how Robert could subjugate real emotional problems into abstract philosophical concepts: 'He wrote and said that I was young and that when I matured I would realise that "the pain of loneliness would give way to the beauty of solitude". I thought, stuff him! What really annoyed me was being given Rilke's *Letter to a Young Poet* – you know, being fobbed off with a *book*!'[32]

NINE

ON THE AIR

'... that the people, inclining their ear to whatsoever things are lovely and honest, whatsoever things are of good report, may tread the path of virtue and wisdom.'

Inscription in the entrance hall of BBC Broadcasting House

Just outside Butleigh, [said Len Smith] there is a long avenue of cedar trees. Bob loved this avenue and he used to go there sometimes and sit under a tree and write. A wealthy old farmer on a cart-horse rode up to him and said, 'What yer doin' 'ere?' Bob said, 'Oh, I'm writing.' The farmer said, 'What do yer 'ope to get out of it?' And Bob said, 'Well, I hope to make enough money to buy up all the farmland.' And he did of course.

A lot of his early plays were locally inspired. There was a poster on a wall advertising fifty pigs for sale so he wrote a play called *Fifty Pigs*. That sort of thing. He was also writing the radio version of *A Man For All Seasons* and I used to hear little bits of it at the well every morning. One of the plays Bob went to see at that time was Miller's *The Crucible* at the Bristol Old Vic. Very similar play. Much later, I saw Bob after his play opened and he said, 'I'm earning as much in a week as I earned in a year as a teacher.'[1]

Within the space of five years, Robert wrote or reworked more than twenty plays. Most of them were designed principally for radio, which not only offered a well established forum for new playwrights but was the easiest means by which writers could achieve maximum exposure and the seeds of a reputation.

The BBC operated three national stations: the Home Service was devoted to talks, news and drama; the Third Programme specialised in classical music as well as drama; the Light Programme offered easy listening and comedy. The styles of presentation matched the programmes: the Light was jaunty and colloquial; the Home was severely formal and the Third was positively sepulchral, adopting an air of hushed reverence for its concerts.

While the Light and Third Programmes were national frequencies, the Home was broken down into regions, each with its own news, music and drama departments. As a result, plays which were regarded as parochial – perhaps a drama about Cornish tin miners – might never be heard on the national network. It was up to the regional producers to convince the Head of Drama in London that a new play was worthy of national exposure.

Television was on the verge of becoming a mass medium and the year in which Robert's first plays were broadcast – 1953 – was also that of the Coronation of Queen Elizabeth II, the live coverage of which is widely regarded as the moment when television arrived in many people's homes to usurp the radio as the principal source of home entertainment and information. But for most people, the radio remained the link with the outside world and with the world of culture. Families gathered around the wireless, often a box made from glossy bakelite, to listen to an extraordinarily diverse and stimulating range of programmes.

The nightly News – which in the Fifties dealt with the death of the King, the Korean War, the Festival of Britain, the Cold War, the Hungarian uprising and the Suez crisis – was intoned by men who were less journalists than the official voice of government. Alistair Cooke wrote and read a weekly *Letter From America*; Roy Plomley shipwrecked various celebrities and politicians and gently asked them for their *Desert Island Discs*; the Goons offered madcap comedy, Ted Ray a more traditional, music-hall variety; *Mrs Dale's Diary* soothed housewives and every weekday afternoon Julia Lang asked the nation's children, 'Are you sitting comfortably? Then I'll begin.'

The Home Service and the Third offered a constant flow of drama, ranging from mammoth serialisations of classic novels, such as *Nicholas Nickleby*, and the complete works of Shakespeare and Shaw, to new plays by Brecht and J. B. Priestley. The BBC also encouraged new dramatists and if they were paid relatively little money for their work the writers could be assured of a professional production and coverage in the BBC's magazines, *Radio Times* and *The Listener*.

The head of the BBC's Drama Department was Val Gielgud, the younger brother of John, and his deputy was a charismatic Scotsman named Donald McWhinnie, who not only commissioned and edited new plays, but often produced them himself. Beneath McWhinnie was a large team of script readers – nearly all women – whose job was to assess new work and advise on scheduling.

'Donald was a thin, haggard-looking Scots boy, a wonderful jazz pianist, who drank a great deal,' Nest Cleverdon told Humphrey Carpenter for his history of the Third. 'He had a great appreciation of modern writing and found himself in a Drama Department which was being run by Val Gielgud as if it were the days of Henry Irving. And he and Barbara Bray worked immensely hard to change things.'[2]

McWhinnie and his chief script reader, Barbara Bray, would have an enormous influence over Robert's career. But it would be a few months before Robert came into their sphere of influence since his first submissions to the BBC, when he was at Bishopsteignton, were sent to the drama department in Leeds. It took the BBC a full year to decide to broadcast them.

The Baron, the Miller and the Magic Trees was eventually adapted into a play by Vivian Daniels and was broadcast on *Children's Hour* in the North region on 8 October 1952 under the title, *The Thwarting of Baron Bolligrew*. Deryck Guyler played the Baron and halfway down the cast list was Peter Dews, later the director of the television version of *A Man For All Seasons* as well as *Vivat! Vivat Regina!* Sadly, because Robert lived in the west of England, he was unable to hear his very first broadcast, which earned him the sum of thirty guineas.

As for his other submission, *The Master*, Daniels had previously written to say that it had been accepted and would be recorded on 21 February for broadcast on 20 March 1952. Robert signed his contract on 6 February and awaited his payment of seventy guineas, this being calculated at the standard BBC rate of a guinea a minute. But the BBC's schedules were thrown into turmoil when, on the day that Robert signed his contract, the nation learned of the death of King George VI. Normal BBC programmes were cancelled, to be replaced by a week or more of solemn music, religious services and documentaries. When Robert was informed that the recording of *The Master* had been postponed, he waited a week and when no BBC cheque had arrived, he fired off a letter: 'I note that payment is made on acceptance,' he wrote, 'and I should be very grateful if you could let me know when I may expect to receive your cheque. No doubt you have been thrown into some confusion by the death of the late King. . . . The pressure of my finances emboldens me to say that I shall be happy to hear from you at your earliest convenience.'[3]

The BBC assured Robert that the cheque was on its way. Heartened by having had *The Master* accepted and also by having been paid, he next sent a copy of *A Man For All Seasons* to a producer in London who revelled in the name of Mr E. J. King Bull. Robert took care to say that he was not officially submitting the script; he just wanted Bull's private opinion as a producer of some distinction. In his covering letter Robert said, 'I am experiencing the usual desire to point out all the hidden beauties which I find in it, but I know that it must be left to speak for itself. However, there are two points of voice casting which I shall mention. The voice of More is high and sweet. Cromwell's voice has force but Wolsey's has force and charm, since Wolsey is large enough to be able to indulge his emotions.'[4]

Impressed by what he read, Bull sent the script to Val Gielgud. 'This man', wrote Bull, 'has taken the historical sequence of events, done a very good character sketch and given a picture in Tudor dress of a "purge" and how one man reacted to it. He is represented as a fine man, whether or not "Blessed", faced with the still topical conflict of private and political conscience. *Plus ça change*, etc. . . . It is perfectly well written [and] there is nothing which would rule it out for Monday night.'[5] Gielgud passed the script to McWhinnie who told Robert that he would accept it for broadcast if certain sections were rewritten. McWhinnie thought that Robert's opening scenes, which served to place the story within the European-Catholic context, were largely irrelevant. McWhinnie believed that the 'vitality of the play lies in the clash between More and Cromwell and we think that you might well have given us more of the actual trial'. He also suggested a shortening of the scene of More's execution: 'Once the trial is over we know what will follow, and dramatically the most important thing left is More's speech on the scaffold and the words of the executioner. If the trial scenes were to be lengthened with a very brief vivid execution scene, it could be highly effective in its dramatic irony.'[6]

Robert responded immediately, though not with the compliant tone of a novice writer anxious to please his potential producer and paymaster. Agreeing to cut the early scenes, he also consented to modify the execution scene: 'I could employ a few more minutes on the trial scene . . . the execution scene is not satisfactory as it stands because it is a mixture of naturalistic and ritualistic treatments. I propose to cut out all the crowd dialogue, thus leaving More's three wonderful statements, with their echo of Calvary, quite stark.'

However, Robert totally rejected McWhinnie's view of the play as a dramatic conflict between More and Cromwell:

I do *not* want it to be turned into a play of 'conflicts'. It is a play of one man, and its vitality no more depends on the clash you mention than the clash between Christ and Pilate. If it hadn't been Cromwell, it would have been someone else . . .

I greatly appreciate your interest and hope you will not think me uncooperative. As I have said, I will, if you wish it, rewrite the play exactly as you suggest, but in my mind this would be to destroy any individual merit the play might have. The play is not a whirlpool but a river running stiller and deeper until it plunges over a cliff. The last thing I envisaged was the 'conflict' with Cromwell. . . . I think there is ample drama in the beauty of More's behaviour, the tragedy of his position, the sordid violence of his end and the pathos of those who were left, so to speak, at the foot of the cross.[7]

The outcome of this exchange was something of a victory for Robert: he was asked to make only the changes he wanted to make and he did so, delivering his revised script in September, which met with McWhinnie's full approval. A contract was drawn up which Robert signed on 3 October 1952. He was to be paid a fee of ninety guineas.

In Leeds, meanwhile, Vivian Daniels still had *The Master* to record and he sent the script to London, proposing it for the national network. While one script reader, Cynthia Pughe, liked it, another, Helena Wood, found it 'sentimental, hackneyed and embarrassing. . . its values are sickly, a saccharine presentation of "life in the raw" with mawkish conclusion. Although not without a certain competence, it lacks even that bravura which might instil some dramatic vitality into it.'[8]

This play about 'life in the raw' was not some political rant about contemporary Britain, let alone an embryonic *Look Back in Anger*. *The Master* was set in the Middle Ages and dealt with the Golliards, a religious sect who wrote their own ballads and sought the pleasures of the flesh as much as the spirit. The hero was Peter Teignby, a young monk of St Edmund's whose determination to find a 'Master', a man of ultimate truth and learning, leads him to Paris. He quickly goes astray, indulging in wine and women, and develops tuberculosis. After five years of travelling in France and Italy, he returns home to St Edmund's, fatally ill, and on his deathbed he is asked if he found what he was looking for:

ABBOTT JEREMY
Well, Peter, did you find your Master?

PETER
Yesterday I thought not, but this morning
it occurred to me that if I have learnt
anything the road has taught it to me. The
road has been my master.

ABBOTT JEREMY
Do not say so, Peter. The road has been
your undoing.

PETER
That too.

The Master was a play which was inspired by many things: the endless
debates about faith with Bernard and Herbert McCabe, as well as
Robert's own love of poetry and his excited discovery of Helen
Waddell's anthology of Middle Age verse. Robert's frequent strolls
through the precincts of ruined Glastonbury Abbey must also have
fuelled his imagination.

Donald McWhinnie, admiring the play for its unusual subject
matter, was unable to decide which national network it was best
suited for. 'It falls into that awkward gap between Third Programme
and Monday night Home Service,' he wrote to Daniels, 'not really
quite distinguished enough for Third and with insufficient general
appeal for Home. However, Bolt is a writer worth following . . .'[9]

The result was that *The Master*, which starred Anthony Jacobs as
Peter Teignby, was broadcast in the North region only, on 15
February 1953 at 9.15 p.m. To accompany the play Robert wrote an
article for the *Radio Times*, which he thought was 'a little highbrow'
and which he feared might be spiked. Fortunately, the article was
published and it can stand today as Robert's dramatic manifesto, an
articulation of the Manichean themes which would subsequently
drive both his life and his work:

The lyric of the goliard was a beginning; it was the beginning of
the great humanist movement which has put Man in place of
God at the centre of the Universe, where he now so easily finds
himself. Perhaps the poignancy we feel in reading these poems
is akin to that of the elderly man who, in the multiplicity of his
cares, has a sudden recollection of some moment in his youth
when the way ahead seemed clear and joyful.

Not that the wandering scholars were pioneers of atheism. They maintained a vivid belief not only in God, but the whole teaching of the Church. The bulk of them were in fact churchmen, tonsured and gowned, claiming clerical privilege, and their pursuit of pleasure in this life was made urgent by their consciousness that damnation awaited them in the next.

Thus they were torn between two poles of Man's longing; his desire for a full cup here on Earth and his desire to serve a greater Being than himself . . .[10]

In what was Robert's first significant published article, one can already see the tensions which will bring his later characters to life. Very often the tension – we must be wary of calling it a 'conflict' – is explored by means of two or more characters who embody opposite sides of the argument, such as the abbott and the monk in *The Master*, Henry VIII and Sir Thomas More, the two Queens in *Vivat! Vivat Regina!*, the intricate Zhivago–Komarovsky–Strelnikov triangle, Lamb and Byron, Fletcher Christian and Captain Bligh, and the priest and the slave trader in *The Mission*, and Nostromo and Mr Gould.

For Robert, *The Master* was a traumatic experience. Daniels made many last-minute revisions to the text and the recording itself, attended by Robert, was often marred by deficiencies in performance and music. And there was also the nagging problem of length: Robert noticed that the play occupied a slot of eighty minutes, which was ten minutes longer than he had been paid for. A rather assertive letter brought a cheque for a further ten guineas.

The extent to which writing had taken over Robert's life is effectively described in a letter he wrote to his parents when *The Master* was broadcast:

Vivian seemed to get into a complete flap just before the production of *The Master* and sent streams of silly letters and telegrams; he also made a number of unwarranted alterations to the text, which of course he had no right to do. My opinion of his abilities as a producer fell somewhat during the final week and fell steeply during the actual performance, which I thought absolutely frightful. . . . I was rather upset by the first ten minutes, then alternately embarrassed and bored stiff . . . I honestly thought it was as bad as anything I have heard on the radio. But I think *A Man For All Seasons* should be a lot better as it is a better play . . .

I had a letter from London saying that they were accepting

Fifty Pigs and I have sent *The Banana Tree* to the West Region Children's Hour. I think there is a good chance of their taking it as it is good, certainly better than *Bolligrew*. If they do I shall have had all five plays accepted.

At the moment I am having a period of mental inactivity. Quite welcome, as writing seems to be obsessional. . . . *Caedwallon* is two-thirds done and I know what is to happen in the final third. After that I hope to complete *Dandelions*, a stage play of which, alas, only the first act is written. I should like to think that the day is not too many years distant when I can devote myself more fully to the plays . . .[11]

As with the broadcast of *The Thwarting of Baron Bolligrew*, Robert was unable to hear a live broadcast of *The Master*. A month later, though, he was in London to discuss with McWhinnie the possibilities of working for the BBC. But Robert was only offered part-time employment during the summer holidays and, as he told McWhinnie, he *needed* those holidays.

During the course of their meeting, Robert listened to the Leeds recording of *The Master* which helped McWhinnie explain why it failed to achieve a national broadcast. 'It is quite clear that he has learned a lot from this performance,' he said, 'and is fully aware of the deficiencies of the script – his ability for objective self-criticism was quite impressive. The production has in fact been a salutary experience for him and an interesting one from our angle, but we do not feel that it is really successful as a radio play.'[12]

If *The Master* was a troubled production, *Fifty Pigs* had an easy ride. This was a comedy based on the Ministry of Agriculture's strict laws regarding the ownership of livestock – the same laws which later inspired Alan Bennett's *A Private Function* (1984). To begin with, there are four pigs living without a permit and getting plumper as the MoA is bogged down by paperwork. Then an MoA official, who just happens to be the former fiancé of the farmer's daughter, arrives from London to sort things out. Love breaks out, as do the piglets.

McWhinnie received the script in January 1953 and sent it to Cynthia Pughe, who thought it 'amusing and natural' and recommended that instead of linking music, 'a snorting of pigs might be fun!' McWhinnie put the play into production and scheduled it as a matinée on 1 June 1953. Robert, who received forty guineas for the play – less than a guinea a pig – wondered if he should feel flattered to have it broadcast during a week of national importance. As he wrote to his script editor Charles Lefeaux: 'May I count it as a feather in my cap that it is to be produced during Coronation Week or is it a matter of chance?'[13]

Robert had now had three plays broadcast by the BBC and a fourth, *A Man For All Seasons*, still mired in script development. His children's comedy, *The Banana Tree*, which featured a boy named Benedict, would not be broadcast until 10 March 1955 and then only on the BBC West region. Instead of waiting patiently for *A Man For All Seasons*, he deluged the BBC with more scripts. He had become a workaholic, teaching by day and writing every night until bedtime.

Caedwallon, which he sent to McWhinnie on 12 May 1953, was his first taste of failure. Script reader Mollie Greenhalgh, who had recoiled from a serialisation of *Lord of the Flies*, found Robert's Dark Ages epic 'Neat, well-handled, lucid . . . the spiritual duel between the priest and the king is convincing and exciting . . . difficult to place but worth buying, I think.'[14] Charles Lefeaux overruled her, dismissed it as 'straggly' and turned it down. Agreeing with Lefeaux's criticisms, Robert said it was 'probably advisable for me to attempt a less enormous and profound subject in my next play.'[15]

Robert's forthcoming subjects, though, were hardly less enormous or profound. One of them, *The Last of the Wine*, the play that was to launch his reputation, dealt with the end of the world. The other was an adaptation of perhaps the most complex English language novel of the twentieth century, Joseph Conrad's *Nostromo*.

In addition to his original ideas for plays, Robert was encouraged to write adaptations of classic novels which formed a major part of the Home Service programme. Robert had been impressed by E. J. King Bull's production of Henry James's *The Portrait of a Lady* - 'Neither my wife nor I can remember anything else so enjoyable and complete' he told the producer – and the broadcast of *The Master* had followed the third episode of Charles Lefeaux's twelve-part adaptation of *Nicholas Nickleby* . Since the BBC was impressed by Robert's skill and needed a steady supply of serialisations, Lefeaux asked Robert for some ideas. The first of these was Conrad's sprawling saga of greed and revolution in South America.

In an ironic foretaste to his work on the same novel thirty-five years later with David Lean, Robert suddenly found that Conrad's tale had defeated him. 'I have been re-reading *Nostromo*,' he wrote to Lefeaux, 'with a view to making a serial out of it, as you suggested. I am most disappointed to say that it can't, to my mind, be done. It goes promisingly until the very end when the psychological action which has hitherto shared equal importance with the action suddenly becomes paramount. . . . It could be done but only by doing fatal violence to the book. It is a great shame as the rest of the book is most suitable. . . The difficulty of this kind of work is that novels proceed by analysed development whereas plays proceed by revealed climax . . .'[16]

There followed a month of bartering: famous titles and famous authors were held up for inspection and rejected for various reasons. Conrad's *Victory*, an easier prospect than *Nostromo*, had already been commissioned, while Jane Austen's *Emma* and *Persuasion*, as well as George Eliot's *Middlemarch*, had already been broadcast. The BBC suggested John Buchan's *Greenmantle* and Robert countered with *The Epic of Gilgamesh*. Returning to Conrad again, Robert and the BBC settled on *An Outcast of the Islands*, then changed their minds in favour of his short story, *The Arrow of Gold* which Robert proposed retitling *Passionate Adventure*. A first-draft script was written, never to be produced.

In November 1953 Robert completed his stage play, *Dandelions*, and sent it to Hugh Hunt at the Arts Club in London. When Robert and Jo learned that Hunt had sent it to Peter Ustinov they waited impatiently for the response, trying to suppress their hopes in order to diminish any disappointment. 'The garden went to pot while I was working on *Dandelions* as did the bits of housework for which I am responsible,' Robert told his parents. 'I seem to be chasing my tail all the time, and read very little. Just now we take half an hour each evening to read Dostoevsky's *The Possessed* aloud. When Benedict is of school age we will take stock and decide what is to be done. If I have had no success with my writing by then I think I may settle down to a life of rural pedagoguey, and Jo will stay at home, perhaps run a few hens and try to do some painting . . .'[17]

A Man For All Seasons was broadcast nationally on the Home Service at 9.15 p.m. on Monday, 26 July 1954. Produced by Wilfrid Grantham and starring Leon Quartermaine as Sir Thomas More, it was an enormous success, earning an especially high rating after the BBC had completed its audience research. 'I have heard that *A Man For All Seasons* was heard by two million people and got a result of seventy-seven,' Robert told his parents. 'Over the last five years only four plays have had a higher result than this; two of these were Shakespeare and one was by Pirandello and one by Anouilh. Not in living memory has a play written for radio specifically had such a mark. The great thing from my point of view is that the listeners were *moved* by the play; they did not sit back and criticise it objectively as they usually do. Several said that they were in tears. The audience, being so large, covered a wide range of types, from housewives to college lecturers.'[18]

Robert's next radio play was a much less auspicious occasion. *Ladies and Gentlemen* was originally a one-act play which he wrote the previous year for the Street Players – the Millfield Dramatic Society augmented by local civilians. Robert and Jo had sat through some unpromising rehearsals and spent many messy late-night hours making Chinese lanterns out of butter muslin and oil paint. The BBC's script reader was not enthusiastic about it: 'A ballroom, 1855. Lady Clare persuades her snobbish nephew, Randolph, to follow his heart and marry the young governess with whom he has been flirting ... An airy trifle that hardly seems strong enough to bear production. But the writing is intelligent and it might fill a corner somewhere.'[19] The BBC found a corner and broadcast the play on the Home Service on 22 September 1954.

As with *The Master*, Robert disputed the running time of twenty minutes and his fee of twenty guineas: 'I presume that the play has been timed to twenty minutes,' he wrote, 'and am surprised it should be so brief as a stage version, performed by our local amateurs, took thirty-five minutes . . .'[20]

The Romantic was drawn loosely from Robert's own experience as a teacher at Millfield. Delivered in August 1954, it was a study of an elderly Mr Chips-ish schoolmaster who was in love with teaching. Barbara Bray thought it 'remarkably true and delicate . . . well up to Monday night standard'.[21]

For *The Romantic* Robert decided to use the *nom de plume* of 'Jane Quentin'. He explained this in a letter to his producer, Mary Ellen: 'Can I ask you to be quite sure that my pen name, not my own, is used in announcing the play? None of the characters is drawn from life, but it might be difficult to prevent some of my colleagues at school doubting this.'[22] The play, which starred Martin Starkie, was broadcast nationally on 21 February 1955 and received a warm response from listeners. However, two significant changes were made just prior to the recording. The title was changed to *Fair Music* and Robert's *nom de plume* underwent a sex-change: 'Jane Quentin' metamorphosed into 'Sydney Brough'.

Mr Sampson's Sundays, broadcast on 16 July 1955, was about a vicar (Leon Quartermaine again), who faces the closure of his parish church. Aimed at what Robert called 'the middle of the middle-brows,' it earned him ninety guineas. 'I felt less as if I were listening to a play than as if I had been allowed to overhear a passage in Mr Sampson's life,' wrote the critic J. C. Trewin. 'This may be undramatic. Still, it is curiously compelling in its quiet way.'[23]

In less than three frenzied years Robert had acquired a reputation, and not only within the BBC. The new commercial television stations, which were to be launched on 22 September 1955, were approaching many playwrights and making them attractive financial offers: 'I am choked with work at the moment,' Robert wrote to Barbara Bray, 'having been asked to submit scripts for commercial TV. I don't want to write scripts for commercial TV but they are offering the sort of money which would enable me to leave teaching and devote myself altogether to writing which is what I want above all else.'[24]

Jo was becoming increasingly restless. Never less than supportive of Robert's work, she sometimes found his obsessional behaviour hard to deal with. While taking pride in his achievements, she also regretted the way that his work was isolating her. The smallness of the cottage meant that their bedroom, as well as their downstairs parlour, was also his office. Robert would arrive home from school and vanish upstairs and the sound of his clattering typewriter would begin. When it was time for bed, Robert's mind was still whirling, reviewing what he had written that evening, planning what he would write tomorrow and what he would rewrite the day after that. The physical side of their relationship, never entirely satisfactory, was putting a further strain on the marriage, so much so that Robert's failings in this regard made him think he should see a psychiatrist.

For her part, Jo had nothing to do during the day, except look after the children and cope with the hardships of the waterwell and the outside lavatory. And while guineas arrived from the BBC – a fee of ninety guineas representing nearly two months' salary at Millfield – there was still precious little money for indulgences. The extra money went on paying debts, the two children and Robert's travelling expenses to London.

Having failed at the outset to obtain work at Millfield, Jo continued to urge Boss Meyer to give her a teaching job. It was not only a question of money; it would give her a sense of her own worth. In June 1955, she wrote to Boss to propose that she replace an art teacher who was leaving. Boss, though, had forgotten about Jo's wishes and merely offered the possibility of part-time work.

By the autumn of 1956 their circumstances had changed significantly. Len Smith had left Millfield and Robert was appointed Head of the English Department, which increased his salary to around £800 a year. Jo had also persuaded Boss to employ her as a full-time art teacher at the prep school, Edgarley. She rapidly made it clear to the Bursar how unhappy she was with the arrangements:

> As you know, I came to Edgarley last term to start an Art Department and was given one half of the Nissen hut for it. I understood that this was a temporary expedient. But this term the Department has no premises at all and has been quartered in the Assembly Hall. Ordinary class teaching is difficult there; Art and Handicraft just about impossible. The physical inadequacy of the facilities, and still more the noise and disturbance caused by the unavoidable comings and goings, create an uneasy, makeshift atmosphere which has communicated itself strongly to the boys. . . I don't want this to be a personal complaint; what I have in mind is the reaction of the Ministry Inspector next term.[25]

Jo then quoted from Ministry of Education guidelines, a presumption which might be compared to prisoners-of-war in Burma alerting their Japanese captors to the Geneva Convention. Inevitably, her letter was shown to Boss who added, in his tiny, spidery hand, that Jo was just 'letting off steam' and was demanding more space than the size of the class warranted.

Although the radio version of *A Man For All Seasons* generated an overwhelming response from listeners, the play which really put Robert's career on the map was *The Last of the Wine*, first broadcast on the Third in April 1955 and repeated the following December on the Home as part of a festival of radio drama. Designed to mirror 'the very age and body of the time',[26] the festival also included Shaw's *Heartbreak House*, Huxley's *Antic Hay*, Forster's *A Passage to India*, Sartre's *Crime Passionel*, and Amis's *Lucky Jim*. Robert was in prestigious company.

Originally titled *Dandelions*, *The Last of the Wine* starred Fay Compton as the grandmother of a family who gather in the drawing-room of a terraced house in London. There are two brothers, Percy and Rupert, the former a Whitehall civil servant, the latter a potter; both are in love with Lucy, though it is Percy who has become engaged to her. Their constant bickering and romantic rivalry is set against a background of apparently impending disaster: mysterious pamphlets drop through the letter box warning that an atomic bomb is about to be dropped on London.

In one sense, the play seems both to pillory and to plagiarise the 'drawing-room comedy' ethos; in another, it warns against what had become Robert's principal obsession, the atomic bomb and the arms race. It was a mischievous fusion of a familiar form and a topical argument, a black comedy in which the family obstinately remain in London, revelling in their complacency. The play ends as Lucy rejects Percy in favour of Rupert and as they drink the last of the wine we hear the ominous drone of an airplane.

The process by which the play reached the air waves was long and convoluted. Robert submitted the script to Donald McWhinnie in June 1954 who sent it to his script readers. While Mollie Greenhalgh thought the characters were 'inhuman' and the overall message vague to the point of obscurity, a more favourable assessment came from Barbara Bray: 'This has a strange obsessional flavour. The "message" is pertinent and moving enough, the characters well defined and the dialogue excellent. But the play is far too long and shapeless as it stands and the author has made no attempt to make the critical situation – the bomb – at all convincing.'[27]

While all at the BBC thought the play was too long and rather scrappy, their main reservation concerned the ambiguity of the atomic threat – no one knows if the bomb is 'red' or 'black' and the family's radio conveniently conks out just as the BBC News is about to begin. Bray and McWhinnie felt that in the absence of any rational explanation, the climax – with the droning plane hinting at apocalypse minutes after the curtain falls – lacked credibility.

Robert responded to this in his customary manner, expounding on his theme so elaborately that chalk dust might have fallen out of the envelope. In discussing how the impending disaster might be conveyed, Robert was offering a peculiarly perverse English response to Orson Welles's radio production of *The War of the Worlds*. Whereas Welles's audience panicked and took to the streets for fear of a Martian invasion, Robert's characters remain at home, sort out their romantic problems, and calmly sip their wine.

> The only ways I can see to make the bomb dropping more realistic [he wrote] are either to have a war, or a hoax of some kind. The one would involve so much politics and patriotism that the play would be overbalanced, and the other would be an unmanageable anticlimax. The main point of the play is that the News tells us every day that our death is a day nearer, that we all know it and all refuse to know it. If a war were declared we should all admit it and the point of the play would vanish . . . the only purpose of the play is to say that this preposterous situation is the one that now obtains all over Europe: the facts that the

paper is delivered and that we have boiled eggs for tea does not alter the fact that, through our complacency, we are drifting towards the waterfall.[28]

After Robert had read Bray's reply – which advocated a BBC news bulletin in which 'the main item of news could be something else and the reference to the catastrophe tucked away in a corner where only the enlightened will notice it'[29] - he wrote another long letter saying he had decided not only to rewrite the play completely, but to set it in another epoch altogether. What Robert had in mind was to solve the BBC's problem by removing the contemporary context and leaving only a pure, Biblical metaphor: 'My proposal is that it should be placed, with stated flippancy, in the pre-Christian epoch. This "placing" not of course to be taken at all seriously but used as Giradoux uses the theme of *Amphitrion*. The City concerned would be recognisably London, the characters would be the same and the situation would be the same. The disaster would be a Punishment – like that of the Cities of the Plain – but with the difference that it was one self inflicted (like the atom bomb).'[30]

It seems likely that Robert, now a seasoned BBC writer, was playing games with Barbara Bray and that his idea was just another example of flippancy; and Bray, duly astonished, wrote to say that such radical revisions were unnecessary: 'The characters as they stand are, it seems to me, essentially and very satisfactorily contemporary, and if the play is reset in the pre-Christian epoch, their relevance may well be an oblique instead of an immediate one.'[31]

Having argued the point with Bray, Robert sought advice from Vivian Daniels in Leeds who suggested a mock BBC parliamentary report which Robert wrote with possibly less ambiguity than he might have wished but with a great deal of satirical humour.

Robert delivered his second draft in late August and changed the title from *Dandelions* to *News from Anywhere* which he misappropriated from William Morris. Script reader Cynthia Pughe thought this version 'pretentious and almost unintelligible. It seems to have fallen between the two stools of allegory and reality and the characters (who keep saying they are dead anyway) never come to life. Long tracts of it are dull. . . . I realise it is some sort of indictment against complacency but I doubt whether anyone would listen to all this about jugs and dandelions for long enough to find out what the author's driving at.'[32]

By December, Mary Allen was urging drastic cutting and perceptively compared Robert's theme to that of *Seven Days to Noon*, a British film of 1950 about a paranoid scientist who threatens to vaporise London if the government refuses to ban the bomb. Barbara Bray, meanwhile, still supported the play and she, in turn, was supported by Donald McWhinnie: 'I do feel that Bolt is one of the most interesting and original talents now writing specifically for radio,' he wrote, 'and I think it would be a pity, in spite of its weaknesses, to lose this particular piece.'[33]

By March 1955, the play had been thoroughly revised again and was ready for rehearsal. Robert changed the title again – to *The Last of the Wine*. The process of rewriting had all but exhausted him and the BBC's prevarications exasperated him, as he told his parents: 'I don't yet know if the BBC is going to accept the third version – if they don't I shall never attempt anything original for them again but will stick to the cliché-ridden routine which they seem to prefer.'[34]

Robert's fleeting hostility towards McWhinnie and his team was misguided – after all, they were at the time starting to promote Samuel Beckett – and it says much for their admiration of the play that they cast Fay Compton in the leading role. A veteran stage and screen actress, Compton was a star whose presence would guarantee the play more attention than usual.

As *The Last of the Wine* went into rehearsal, word of its quality and topicality quickly began to leak out amongst the theatre community. One of those who heard about the play was a theatrical agent named Margaret Ramsay, who operated from a cramped former brothel off St Martin's Lane, right in the heart of London's theatre district. Ramsay wrote to Barbara Bray asking if 'Mr Bold's' [sic] play was also available in a stage version': '. . . obviously this kind of play has to have an immediate transfer,' wrote Ramsay, 'linked to the actual reaction from the production on the air. . . . Please don't think I'm interfering, or that I want to "take over" the author. I'm only too happy to help any newcomer or talent and with this opportunity, he shouldn't miss it from lack of foresight! I never think plays based on important topical issues have a very long life, and therefore it's necessary to act fast – all the same I hear something important is being said . . .' Ramsay added a curious postscript, wondering if 'Mr Bold' was in fact a pseudonym: 'Is Mr Bold any chance Mr Gielgud?! I know his penchant for topical themes.'[35]

Barbara Bray met Ramsay and gave her a copy of the script. Ramsay was so impressed by the first few pages that she immediately wrote to Murray Macdonald at the Royal Court Theatre: 'The BBC are absolutely crazy about this play,' she wrote, 'even taking me out to dinner to say would I represent it and help the author. Having glanced at it, I see the dialogue has a quite exceptional high standard of wit and style. I wonder if, as you are a friend of Fay Compton, you could get her opinion and if she would repeat the performance on the stage. . . . The play is fearfully topical [and] the cast say that once it is broadcast it is going to create a considerable stir. I have seldom heard a script praised as highly as this . . .'[36]

The Last of the Wine went out on the Third Programme at 6.40 p.m. on 3 April 1955 and was repeated four days later at 9.35 p.m. Its success was undeniable and Margaret Ramsay moved swiftly to secure Robert as her client.

Margaret Ramsay was not then an important agent; in fact, she was just starting out and was hungry for talent. But her obvious intelligence, her enthusiasm and her total confidence in herself and in her judgement led one to believe that she was the most vibrant force in British theatre. Inevitably, she became just that and it was Robert, her first client, who made it possible.

Born in Australia in 1908, Ramsay spent most of her childhood in South Africa where her father was a doctor and an ostrich farmer, though that business went bankrupt when ladies of fashion preferred the remnants of other animals draped over their shoulders. At university at Grahamstown Ramsay was seduced by a professor of psychology, who took her off to Europe. Their marriage was short lived. She had hopes of being an actress or an opera singer though her real talent lay in her ability to assess a script, a gift which was recognised by the theatrical agency, Christies, who employed her, initially on a freelance basis and then as a permanent member of staff. In due course, Christies made her a loan which enabled her to set up her own agency.

Her timing was propitious, for the English theatre was about to undergo a revolution. The West End stage – like the British cinema – was creatively exhausted and existed on a diet of predictable thrillers, drawing-room comedies and historical pageants. The rusting keys to the kingdom – owned by Terence Rattigan, Noël Coward and a few others – would soon change hands.

'Although [Ramsay] had the manners and appearance of any upper-middle-class lady of colonial origins,' wrote James Pettifer, 'her instincts were radical and despite her enormous personal and financial success in later years she remained something of an outsider. This gave her an instinctive sympathy with the sort of new talents, many from working class backgrounds, who were appearing on the scene at the time.'[37]

While Robert was not working class, he was impoverished. And he had a gentle North Country accent, as Ramsay was soon to discover. But another agent, also impressed by *The Last of the Wine*, had beaten Ramsay to it. Robert wrote:

> The first time I struck Peggy Ramsay – or rather was struck by her – was when I was about thirty. I was a schoolmaster and could see no way out of my present impasse except by writing plays. I had had half a dozen of them on the BBC. One was paid ninety guineas for a ninety-minute play, a sum which went far to settling up our outstanding accounts at the greengrocers and the baby linen and so on. One simply never thought of writing for the stage. One's name was Rattigan or it was not.
>
> The post brought a formal letter signifying that the signatory had heard my plays and decided that it was about time that I thought of trying my hand at a real play; to be acted by well known actors on the West End stage.
>
> The letter was carried about by me like a talisman for a couple of days to be shown to anyone who would look at it and hadn't already been shown it a couple of times before. This letter promised high finance and fame. A couple of days and I was ready to answer it. Then the post decanted a much less proper letter, written by a certain Margaret Ramsay, on a typewriter, though barely decipherable through the ink, indentations and brackets. It breathed a sort of half-commitment to my plays, which, if they got a great deal better, might be fit to pass on to one of the West End managements. She would be pleased to act as my agent. I don't know why it was but I answered the second letter, sending a fulsomely polite refusal to the first.
>
> I drew on my pocket money and stood the fare to London. I found the airless court, reeking of coffee which poured from the coffee shop below, and found myself in the office, about twelve foot square, comfortable but not too comfortable. She had a staff of one. This was a secretary enclosed in an even smaller room. Since then she has expanded upwards and downwards, yet always I think of the smell of roasting coffee as the authentic smell of the West End theatre.
>
> She was entrancing. The full untrammelled flower of the theatre. She was full of advice. I must write. I must write without ceasing and with enjoyment. I stumbled down the stairs and back to Somerset with my ears ringing with names like H.M. Tennent.[38]

Within six months, Robert sent Ramsay a new play which she

dismissed out of hand. The next play, and the next, met with a similar fate and Robert began to wonder what agents were for. Ramsay seemed less a guiding light than one of those savage drama critics: 'The little figure over the coffee shop had become a pillar of fire,' he said.[39]

Ramsay had, though, loaned Robert some money, a sure indication of her confidence in him. He continued writing furiously in the hope that he might just conceivably produce something that she liked. This happened when he presented her with a play called *The Critic and the Heart*. He completed it by November 1955 and described its theme and atmosphere to his parents:

> My last play *The Critic and the Heart* is a very sad one full of tender pessimism which I am far from feeling but which is fortunately fashionable. Its theme is something about selfishness and pity and in it I have an exhilarating bang at critics and all those 'in the know' middlemen who in their hearts despise creativity and fear the untidiness of life. It is intended to wring the heart of the audience and provoke tearful enthusiasm on the opening night. Sydney, who told me that humour was the only worthy aim for a contemporary artist, would disapprove of it. I know what he means; but I should like to move my audience beyond itself, and am willing to risk revealing myself in the process.[40]

Set in a town called Budmouth (Thomas Hardy's Weymouth), *The Critic and the Heart* is as 'revealing' about Robert and his personal circumstances as we would like it to be. Although Robert was quite ready to admit that he appropriated Somerset Maugham's *The Circle* for his dramatic structure, his play can also be related to Samuel Beckett's *Waiting For Godot* – which Margaret Ramsey represented – since the principal character, the instigator of the action, never appears.

In the first act, William Brazier is upstairs in bed, unmistakably if invisibly approaching death's door. In the second act he is dead. Brazier is a wealthy artist whose eldest sister, Winifred, has sacrificed her entire life to him. She is, as Robert wrote, 'one of society's, not one of nature's spinsters.' In his will (a familiar theatrical pretext for drama), Brazier leaves Winifred the house but denies her his money since 'the function of money is the enlargement of life and she has demonstrated that she has no capacity for life'.

Entering into this gloomy portrait of sibling resentment are a doctor, a solicitor, a friend of the family named Muriel who is pregnant and her husband, Pat, an aspiring artist himself. But most crucially there is an art critic named Newton Reeves who appears on the scene with the aim of writing Brazier's biography. Not only does Reeves have the power to promote an exhibition of Pat's paintings, he also manages to obtain a collection of love letters written by Brazier. These are published in a Sunday newspaper and reveal that Brazier was sexually impotent and that he courted young women only with words.

The Third Act charts the emotional upset of the will and the ambition of Pat who has inherited a portfolio of portraits of Winifred which he proposes to sell, splitting the money with her. The play is a sustained debate about the monetary and intellectual value of art and the human pain and cost in its creation. None of the characters is especially sympathetic, some are thoroughly detestable.

Here at last was a play which Margaret Ramsay thought should be staged. From her cramped offices in Goodwin's Court came a flurry of letters alerting theatre managements that a new talent had been discovered. She wrote to H. M. Tennent, the Theatre Arts Club and the Royal Court, where Robert's script was passed on to one of their readers, John Osborne, who was taking home some thirty or forty scripts for two pounds a week. Osborne had just had a new play accepted by the English Stage Company which was based at the Royal Court: it was called *Look Back in Anger*. He wrote:

> The plays sent in at that time could be divided into a few recognizable categories. A number of them were written by clergymen's wives. Almost every post brought a play about Mary Queen of Scots, the Virgin Queen, Queen Victoria and Lady Jane Grey. Then there were the plays about literary figures like D. H. Lawrence or Henry James; Loamshire plays; plays set in the past and plays set in the future where lone survivors of the Atomic Holocaust addressed themselves but not each other. Schoolteachers were almost as prolific as clergymen's wives. I read what was probably Robert Bolt's first play, *A Critic on the Hearth* [sic], and recommended it. Tony [Richardson] made it clear that for someone who had written the best play since the war I had a lamentable critical intelligence.[41]

John Perry of the all-powerful Tennent Productions was initially enthusiastic and Ramsay believed they would buy the play. But Perry soon turned it down:

> I am afraid I did not like it as much the second time. I find one weakness is that it is difficult to know exactly what it is about. I

suppose Mr Bolt is putting the case for the questionable theory that artists as a breed are selfish, unreliable and wholly lacking in moral scruples and that people who devote their lives to them must have a wretched time.

On the credit side, I think Winifred is an excitingly drawn character and so are the characters of the Doctor and the Solicitor. I am not quite sure about Newton Reeves. I think his motives are obscure. To sum up. I think the play would not do in its present form, but Mr Bolt undoubtedly has a talent for creating characters and I would be very glad to read anything else he writes.[42]

By March 1956 Ramsay had succeeded in selling the play to the producer Jack Minster, who took a three month option knowing full well that Ramsay was determined to have it staged at the Arts or the Royal Court. But when Minster failed to renew his option, Ramsay was sorely disappointed: 'Could I have the scripts back when you have the time. As you realise, I desperately want to try and get the play on this autumn, and I have no script at all.'[43]

While Ramsay was trying hard to sell *The Critic and the Heart*, Robert continued to write for the BBC. With his plays for 'adults' proving to be so difficult, he thought he could enjoy himself and earn some easy money by writing for children again. He wrote a new *Bolligrew* story, *Sir Oblong Fitz Oblong and Baron Bolligrew*, for BBC West which was broadcast on 22 January 1956. Such was its success, Robert wrote six further *Bolligrew* plays at thirty-six guineas a piece.

The Window was a more serious affair, arguably the most overtly political play that Robert ever wrote, in which he attempted to dramatise his growing contempt for Soviet communism, especially after the Hungarian uprising, a dismaying event which was hotly debated by the teachers and mature students at Millfield. His main character, Dr Bernstein, is blind – always a heavy symbol – and he lives in a fascist dictatorship threatened by communist insurrectionists. Bernstein is courted by both factions, though he prefers to remain uncommitted to everyone except the innocent refugees. His daughter is in love with a communist and with communism itself, while his wife is having an affair with a playboy named Farrar. When his daughter is arrested, Bernstein at first agrees to work for the fascists but faced by their tyranny he becomes an outspoken opponent. He flees the country only to return to his wife who, moved by her husband's political stand, breaks off her relationship with Farrar. Now reconciled and very much in love, Bernstein and his wife go to prison together.

When Margaret Ramsay turned it down, Robert entered it in a competition in Leeds. He also sent it to the BBC whose script reader, Helena Wood, thought it 'Novelettish and rather worn, the characterisation is flattened by subjection to thesis. I do not find this as good as the author's other plays.'[44]

Much to Robert's chagrin, the play was rejected for a national broadcast and it went out – as *The Master* had done – only in the North region on 20 December 1956 as a distinctly unseasonal offering. Nevertheless, Robert's fee of one hundred and five guineas was his biggest to date.

With no positive news about *The Critic and the Heart*, Robert began to have doubts about Margaret Ramsay's abilities as well as the entire theatre world. As he told his parents:

> I am naturally a bit browned off about the shilly shally and delay. I feel I could have done better myself if only I had the contacts, but I haven't, and that is what one pays an agent for. Agents are nothing but a sort of clot floating in a soup of contacts. They create nothing and don't really do anything but they get round all the right bars and parties and see all the right shows, and a nightmarish existence it must be. I think it will all come out right for this play in the end and I am a third of the way through another, but after this one is finished I am going to turn my attention to Sound Radio and TV where I have a pretty assured market until the West End appreciates me in terms of cash. At present they tell me I am very good and obviously couldn't care less. They are the most weird bunch of characters I have ever met. My acquaintance with them at least serves to show the personnel of the BBC in a more favourable light.[45]

That despondent letter was written on 1 April 1956, exactly a year before *The Critic and the Heart* received its first public performance at the Oxford Playhouse. It was not the West End, nor the Arts Club, but it was the next best thing and, if it proved a success, a transfer to the West End could never be ruled out.

The play was staged by Jack Minster and starred Margaret Vines, Pat Keen, Nicholas Grimshaw, Christopher Banks, Ian Hendry and, as Newton Reeves, Robert Eddison. Ramsay and the Playhouse's General Manager, Elizabeth Sweeting, haggled for months over the financial arrangements – which ultimately gave Ramsay ten per cent of nothing – and Robert worried that the critics would bypass Oxford on their way to the opening of the new season at Stratford: 'I am doubtful they will allot much space to a provincial performance of an unknown play by an unknown author . . . It is tightly written and well characterized, but it has no gimmick to strike the jaded sensibilities of a newspaper critic.'[46]

The first night, as Robert predicted, was attended by only a few of the important critics, as well as Robert's parents, Tony Quinton and Bernard McCabe. Ralph had urged Robert to go on stage to make a speech, an idea which alarmed his son: 'As for the few words you urge me to have ready, I think it very unlikely indeed that they will be called for, and in any case am increasingly of the opinion that authors should not be public except through their work. And if the demand for a gracious phrase or two is irresistible, well, a few words is possibly the one thing I have never been short of.'[47]

The reviews were mixed, the most favourable written by Patrick Gibbs of the *Daily Telegraph* who called it 'the most promising first play seen for many a month. . . . If the conclusion that the way of artists is hard and ministering to them even worse was not very original, at least it was engagingly illustrated, with excellent touches of humour and much depth of feeling.'[48]

The anonymous critic of *The Times* was more critical, saying that its structural weakness – the non-appearance of the main protagonist – was only compensated for by the convincing performance of Robert Eddison. 'We are content to remain in ignorance about the painter's character; but it is a pity that the author does not satisfy our curiosity – with one exception – about the characters we do see.'[49]

T. C. Worsley, writing in the *New Statesman*, was far more positive: 'I have space only briefly to record a most interesting new play by Robert Bolt. The theme – not an easy one – is the world of art. In his handling of the critic and of a young artist, cousin germane to Jimmy Porter, Mr Bolt shows a very promising talent.'[50]

The Critic and the Heart ran for just two weeks, drawing modest audiences and earning for Robert nothing except a considerably enhanced reputation. He had successfully negotiated the first hurdle in becoming an established playwright, even though, at the age of thirty-three, he might have been regarded as middle-aged by the standards of the twenty-seven-year-old John Osborne whose *Look Back in Anger* had caused a sensation at the Royal Court the year before. But Robert's arrival on the scene could not have been better timed: audiences and critics were hungry for new ideas and Robert already had one safely delivered to Margaret Ramsay.

TEN

HIS NAME IN LIGHTS

'Success is relative: it is what we can make of the mess we have made of things.'

T. S. Eliot

Robert invented a dull man named Jim Cherry who has worked for twenty years in a city insurance office and dreams of buying an orchard in his native Somerset. The dream, which would be his hero's undoing, gave Robert a satisfyingly ironic and Chekhovian title, *Flowering Cherry*.

Every day of his working life, Cherry goes to the office and paces the rubber carpet which makes him feel as if he's 'walking on corpses'. At home, he has a sexless marriage with Isobel who barely tolerates him. When she discovers that he has in fact lost his job and has been pilfering from her purse and drinking gin and cider in secret, she decides to leave him. Their son, Tom, meanwhile, who has been blamed for his father's pilfering, is about to do his National Service and their daughter, Judy, an art student, is threatening to leave home and set up in a flat with her friend Carol. The Cherrys are not a happy family.

Robert put a measure of his personal experience into the play. His memories of working for the Manchester insurance firm certainly coloured his principal character, for Robert understood only too well Cherry's 'mad longing to be out of this environment'.[1] Robert's own entrapment as a teacher and his dream of becoming a famous playwright might also in some way have mirrored his hero's emotional state. And there was, of course, Somerset. Even the long avenue of cedars where Robert often sat and wrote found its way into Cherry's big set speech in Act Two: 'From our big field you looked right over the Plain of Somerset; nothing but pasture and orchards, it's too wet for crops, it's not much above sea level; green and blue as far as you could see. The men were a rough lot and I wasn't much better than the men, but the place was something all right. . . . The way those old-time squires planted trees – there was an avenue of elm trees two miles long that didn't go anywhere; it's still there, I'll bet . . .'

If Cherry looked for an escape route from drab suburbia, Robert himself, writing under the influence of Brecht, searched for ways to escape the straitjacket of naturalistic, drawing-room drama. He devised a remarkable ending which took the audience abruptly away from Cherry's dreary home and into his fantasy. When Cherry's dream has collapsed and Isobel has packed her bags and has left the house, he grabs an iron poker – which has been an insistent and obvious symbol of his sexual weakness – and tries to bend it over the back of his neck. Although the poker starts to bend, the effort is too much for him and he falls to the floor, stricken by a stroke or a heart attack. As he lies dying, his vision of the blooming cherry orchard appears on a cyclorama backcloth.

Robert's friend and teaching colleague, Anthony Rossiter, remembered the play being written: 'I would listen as Bob read the next few pages of his play *Flowering Cherry*. His voice, with its beautiful touch of Northern accent, would bring his evocative theme and words right into one's mind, where they lingered long after-wards. When I saw it in London a year or so later, I really could not hear the famous actor speak the familiar lines. I could hear only the voice of their author, as he slumped in a wicker chair before a blazing fire, surrounded by his cottage furniture, his dogs, half a dozen beer bottles, and Jo, listening quietly too.'[2]

Ramsay despatched it to Frith Banbury, one of the West End's best directors. She also sent it to Elizabeth Sweeting at the Oxford Playhouse and to Jack Minster, who was about to stage *The Critic and the Heart*. Banbury responded at once, offering to option the play for £200 and Ramsay was at once startled and embarrassed, for she had given Minster the impression that he was her first and only choice. When Minster discovered that he had lost the play before he'd had a chance to read it, he was understandably peeved and rather shocked by Ramsay's cavalier behaviour. 'Yes, I *do* feel I have behaved "ruth-lessly" and I don't like myself very much,' she wrote to Minster. 'All I ask is that you won't "take it out" on Bolt. . . . I did what I did because I wanted to give him peace of mind and also to earn him some money. Over Bolt I suppose I am a bit emotional – I have such belief in him. . . . One of the reasons I sent the play to Banbury is that, frankly, I don't like it nearly as much as *Critic* regarding subject-matter, and I definitely think it's off-beat. So does he.'[3]

'Off-beat?' said Banbury, when he saw this letter some forty years later. 'Off-beat? I thought it was less off-beat than *The Critic and the Heart* because it dealt with family and the middle-class audience likes families. I liked it because it wasn't cosy and it told truths that middle-class audiences don't like to hear. It was a moving, funny and clever play.'[4]

Banbury immediately thought of Celia Johnson in the role of Isobel and he sent her the script.

'You have found a fascinating new play,' Johnson replied. 'He can certainly write, Mr Bolt. Have you met him – what's he like? I think the vision at the end is a mistake and I don't like the Judy-Carol set-up. I imagine that's simply put in in the hopes that the Lord Chamberlain will ban it. Do you agree? Can we meet and talk about it? I'd like to play it if you don't want to do it too soon.'[5]

Having secured Celia Johnson's agreement, Banbury had the clever idea of casting Trevor Howard as Cherry, which would have reprised their partnership in David Lean's 1946 film, *Brief Encounter*. Robert revealed to Banbury that he had never seen Lean's film which, in 1957, had a dismal reputation and Howard's own reputation as a drunkard finally deterred Banbury from offering him the role.

On 22 March, the script was sent to Ralph Richardson, who was starring in the Broadway production of *The Waltz of the Toreadors*. Richardson also committed himself to it immediately and urged Banbury to produce the play in partnership with H. M. Tennent, the powerful West End company run by the legendary Hugh 'Binkie' Beaumont. Confronted by Banbury, Richardson, Johnson and a script they all liked, Beaumont readily agreed to put up half the production budget of £4000. Richardson's and Johnson's contracts earned them both £322.18s.5d per week for the duration of the run.

Robert was naturally jubilant when he learned that Binkie Beaumont was his producer and that his play was to be performed at the Haymarket Theatre with Ralph Richardson and Celia Johnson. His name was finally in lights, not in Oxford, but in the heart of London and on the marquee of what most people regarded as the West End's most beautiful theatre. 'I shall not forget the main placard announcing my play,' he said, 'with my name in bold type, stuck outside the Haymarket Theatre about four weeks before the opening. I crossed and recrossed the street a half a dozen times to get the full flavour of it.'[6]

Frith Banbury was just as excited as Robert. 'Only twice in my life have things fallen into place exactly as they should,' he said. 'The first was a play of Wynyard Browne's called *A Question of Fact* where Paul Scofield and Gladys Cooper said yes, just like that. The second was *Flowering Cherry* where we got Ralph and Celia immediately. Of course, this gave Bob the feeling that it was much easier than it really was. He was this jolly, apple-cheeked fellow who hadn't got any money, naïve with people and naïve in his assumptions about the theatre.'[7]

While one might have expected Margaret Ramsay to be as thrilled as Robert and Banbury, she sounded many notes of caution, worrying that Robert might feel he had triumphed with what she regarded as a rather modest work. Ramsay also foresaw some unflattering comparisons with *Death of a Salesman* even though Robert had never read Arthur Miller's play, much less seen a production of it. Ramsay had already discussed these concerns with Barbara Bray at the BBC:

> Yes, indeed I do fear that there will be comments about *Cherry* and *Death of a Salesman*. One worry about this is that the Miller play was so much more for your money! (Four rooms instead of one and a flower-bed, more scenes, more sex, and a juggling with time.) This play is not so depressing – no funeral – and the 'transfiguration' at the end will cheer us all up (though what it means, if anything, I don't know. . . .!) Really this play is the lowbrow *Johnson Over Jordan* (which anyway was the British *Salesman*) only that too had more scenes, more sex, and Benjamin Britten too!
>
> Personally I think this play is just another step in the career of Robert Bolt, and I am rather alarmed that with the stars and the grand theatre and management, people will imagine that this is the peak of a career, instead of a beginning.[8]

When *Flowering Cherry* went into rehearsal in September 1957 – everyone had to wait until Richardson had completed his New York engagement – Robert made it known that he could ill afford the train fare to London. Banbury thought this was a ridiculous situation, though he managed to persuade Beaumont to give Robert an advance against royalties.

Robert's attendance at the rehearsals was a salutary experience, for he soon became aware of the aura and the not always benign influence of a major star. Richardson's innate humour and his natural fondness for little bits of business were rendering Cherry less dull than cheery. While everyone recognised that Robert's delicate balance was being slightly – if spectacularly – upset, no one saw any reason to scale Richardson down a notch or two. 'I had to give Bob a lecture,' said Banbury. 'Ralph was all over the place, but it was his place. Bob had made a rhythm of the speech but Ralph wanted his own rhythm. He would take a speech and chop it up. So Bob came to me and said, "He's driving me mad! Why can't he do it as I wrote it?" So I said, "Look, I'm here to tell you, it's no use. Ralph is not keen on directors and if you want him to sit down you tell him to stand up. It's no good going to his dressing room with a notebook. All you get is a large Scotch which means fucking well shut up." Bob didn't understand this, so I told him that Ralph would make hay with his speeches and he just had to settle for that. And he did.'[9]

Ramsay, who saw a great performance in the making, worried about the advance publicity emanating from Tennents and about Banbury, who seemed not to understand the play at all. She fired off a letter to the director: 'As an agent I want to be seen and heard only when I can be of use. . . . I hope you will not be annoyed if I say how very depressed I am by the preliminary announcements of the play I have read in the *Telegraph* and *The Stage*. Dare I tell you that if I read these descriptions about another play, I would give that play a miss. . . .'

'That was Vivienne Byerly at Tennents,' said Banbury. 'She was never any good at publicity. Go on. . .'

'The particular point stressed in the publicity,' continued Ramsay, 'is that the play is about the incompatibility of two people married during the 1914–1918 war. Now this to me means a play of my parents' generation and obviously the children of such a couple would have been born about 1920 which means they are over thirty-seven apiece . . . in fact, two old people. If I feel like this, and I am middle-aged, what will everyone under forty feel?'[10]

A less antagonistic letter from Ramsay followed the next day:

Surely the play's theme is far far deeper than a mere inspection of incompatibility between husband and wife? Cherry seems to me to be the prototype of a million ordinary men who work for their living in the city but who have their roots in the country. His dreams are the extension of every office worker who cultivates a small garden and this longing for something to "grow" is deep in the English character.

Cherry's dilemma is that he has lost his self-respect. . . his masculinity is shaken and his sex-life has gone wrong and with it his relationship as head of the family. It is because he wants them to be proud of him that he escapes from his mediocrity into dreams, and then into lies and into petty theft. Harold Hobson and I were talking about Richardson the other day and he was saying that he was the greatest actor in England. I said that his genius lay in making the ordinary seem extraordinary and that when Richardson plays the 'average man in the street' he transforms him into something deeply moving and mysterious. Surely this play depicts the contemporary predicament of the average man and the incompatibility with his wife is only a small part of the total human condition . . .

PS: I hear that even Mr Beaumont himself (the un-average man) has taken to growing roses![11]

After Ramsay attended the first public performance at the Royal Court Theatre in Liverpool, she wrote to Beaumont, whom she hardly knew:

Naturally I know you by sight but I specially did not ask to be introduced as I saw you were looking after Lady Richardson and I know stars' wives are dynamite . . .

I will not write about the first performance except to say that I was glad a lot of things did not go properly, because these mistakes and *longueurs* lead everybody to improve everything.

Bolt does not make it easy for actors . . . and he has no technical skill in contrasting his scenes. Bolt never says to himself (like Rattigan), does this hold, 'does this *finally* entertain?' He gives a particularly awful problem with his ending, relying as he does on the scenic effect to lift the play emotionally and poetically. How odd it is that Sir Ralph brings all sorts of miraculous things of his own while not being at his best in Bolt's best scenes – that simple speech about the country and the men under the trees and the church is meaningless at the moment because it is so elaborately broken up but perhaps this speech is anyway too literary and does not work off the page . . .

Meanwhile it is an immense comfort to think that Bolt's play is in your hands. I am sure he has a 'future' and can only hope, for all your sakes, that he has a 'present' too.[12]

Five days later, by which time the company had transferred to Oxford, Ramsay conveyed to Beaumont her criticisms of the music and the cyclorama of cherry trees which she thought lacked impact:

What we need emotionally is blossom, a drift of pale blossoms.

I don't know much about Somerset but I lived in Japan as a child and the cherry blossom there is something I can never, never forget – it filled the universe. And Cherry's dream is, after all, based on childhood memories . . . it must overwhelm us emotionally and we should be anguished when it fades and we are left with a man in a kitchen. (By the way, both 'curtains' were badly mistimed last night.)

I hope you don't mind my writing like this – the play seems to be getting better all the time.[13]

For Robert, the out-of-town engagements were both an education and an agonising experience. While he found the constant reshaping and adjustments a fulfilling challenge, he had to endure a roller-coaster ride on the backs of the regional theatre critics: 'In Liverpool,' he later told *The Times*, 'we had the most shattering notices I have ever read in my life. Someone called it "morbid and melodramatic". The next week, in Oxford, they praised it. Leeds damned it, Edinburgh praised it, Glasgow hated it. By that time I did not know what would happen in town. A great deal of newspaper criticism is of an ineptitude that has to be seen to be believed. And yet there is no criticism that you cannot learn something from.'[14]

Ralph Richardson's performance was also giving him cause for concern: 'The play opened in Liverpool last Monday,' he wrote. 'Sir Ralph had a sort of spastic cramp for the occasion, spreading panic throughout the cast. . . . The dear Knight pulled himself together on the Tuesday and for the rest of the week I am told it went well. At least the theatre is pretty well full.'[15]

With the London opening less than a month away, Margaret Ramsay decided to inject Frith Banbury with an overdose of her own adrenalin. She sent him an extraordinary four-page letter – her typing never able to keep pace with her thoughts – and invoked, *inter alia*, Tennessee Williams, Havelock-Ellis, Ovid, Marlowe, Pirandello, Gide, *Faust* and *Phaedra*. She wrote parts of it in French and parts of it in Latin; she wrote all of it with passion:

As agent for Bolt, it's his career I care about, not just this one play. If I thought this play as it stood would be an artistic success and a commercial failure, I would think your money well lost! But it *cannot* be an artistic success – the play is a straightforward play of emotion and relationship. The set is in the tradition of the modern American play and breaks no new ground, the music doesn't startle in its originality, it isn't as angry as Osborne, or as poetic as Fry and Tennessee Williams, or avant garde as Ionesco. It has the problem of being a realistic play with what seem to be unrealistic moments. But are these moments unrealistic? Not really. Cherry dreams and we have decided to illustrate his dreams, that's all. It's a commercial success in embryo.[16]

It now appeared to Banbury that it was Ramsay who was misunderstanding the play. But she was incorrigible, writing once again to Beaumont in terms that might well have expressed a desire to see Banbury fired. 'That was her prerogative as an agent,' said Banbury. 'She wasn't ever a nuisance. . . well, she was a nuisance. She fussed a lot and she overstated all the time. She overstated life. But she was brighter than anybody else. There was no other agent like her. I had great regard for Peggy Ramsay.'[17]

Despite Ramsay's passion and her obvious commitment to Robert, her problems with the cyclorama effect, which she saw as undermining a naturalistic drama, were wholly wrong-headed. Such effects were hardly unfamiliar to audiences and had *Flowering Cherry* been a film and not a play there would have been no question about its artistic validity. However, this debate about naturalism and non-naturalism would have a lasting impact on Robert and led to a creative impasse with Banbury and his only resounding flop, *Gentle Jack*.

During rehearsals Richardson had severe problems with one particular line – when he was to call his successor at the office 'a little rat' – though a long letter from Robert and assurances from Celia Johnson made him give way.[18] Banbury, Beaumont and Johnson also knew that Richardson's fondness for overacting was less apparent on the evenings which followed a matinee. Accordingly, on the day of the first night in London, they suddenly announced a run-through at three-thirty in the afternoon as a way of calming him down.

Flowering Cherry opened at the Haymarket on 21 November 1957. Prior to the opening, the Lord Chamberlain – confirming Celia Johnson's initial doubts – ordered the word 'bugger' and the phrase 'screw you, Judy' to be changed.

Hearing that it was the custom for playwrights to spread first-night gifts among the cast, Robert spent some of his advance against royalties, lugged a large hold-all from Butleigh and opened it in Banbury's house, hoping that his gifts for Richardson, Johnson, Andrew Ray and the others would meet with his director's approval.

Jo attended the first night with Robert's proud parents, as well as friends such as Ann and David Queensberry and Mike and Naomi

Kellaway. Robert also sent Boss Meyer a pair of tickets and with them went an amusing covering note: 'Here are the tickets for next Thursday. I do hope you will be able to make use of them. But don't expect very much – it's an odd kind of play and of its kind, not specially good. But the acting ought to be enjoyable – unless Sir Ralph has one of his Falstaf attacks.'[19]

Backstage, after the performance, there was a clamour, so many people, and so many strangers, that Robert hardly knew whose hand he was shaking or if that hand was attached to someone important or not. He found himself embracing strangers and shunning colleagues, as he wrote later to the BBC's Head of Drama, Val Gielgud: 'I learned recently that you were backstage and as soon as I was told it, realised that I had in fact seen you on the backstage chairs. I hope you didn't recognise me either, for if you did, my behaviour must have seemed exceedingly odd, considering how much I owe to your Department.'

The reviews were wonderful, especially for Richardson, and Ramsay might have felt chagrined that none of the major critics made an issue out of the cyclorama. All of them, though, mentioned Miller's *Death of a Salesman* as well as Chekhov and, naturally, John Osborne whose name cropped up everywhere. Plays were either quite unlike Osborne's or they were rather similar. Robert was to find that being unlike John Osborne was a heavy cross to bear. 'No doubt about it,' wrote Kenneth Tynan, 'Sir Ralph Richardson gave an amazing performance of *something* at the Haymarket. No actor in England is more interesting to watch. Even when he plays a dull man, that dull man is never permitted a dull moment. What is the word for that voice? Something between bland and grandiose: blandiose perhaps.'

Tynan's view was not all laudatory, though; he felt Robert 'never goes to the roots of the neurosis whose surface symptoms he reproduces so brilliantly.' In comparing *Flowering Cherry* with *Death of a Salesman*, Tynan noted that 'Mr Miller, the sociologist, attributes Willy Loman's downfall to social forces outside himself; Bolt, the psychologist, looks inside Jim Cherry for the seeds of his failure'. And as far as Robert's ending was concerned, Tynan thought it 'abject melodrama. By a single stroke the play moves down from alpha minus to beta plus. All the same, in a desert of gammas it is a considerable oasis.'[20]

The critic of *The Times* spoke of Banbury's 'firm and imaginative direction' and Richardson's way of 'showing some unsuspected quality of humour or goodness shining through a quite commonplace being . . . the play suggests by its character drawing and by its dialogue that the London theatre has come by a new dramatist.'[21]

Robert's principal supporter was Harold Hobson of the *Sunday Times* who was to see *Flowering Cherry* on two further occasions and write glowingly about it each time. 'This play by Robert Bolt,' he wrote, first time round, 'brings into the London theatre a man who, if attempts to read the future have any validity at all, is plainly destined to become a distinguished dramatist. . . . In an aesthetically similar situation, in *The Entertainer*, when the myth of Archie Rice's indifference to what the world thinks of him is exploded, Mr Osborne's heart fills with a compassion which I would call Christian if Mr Osborne did not regard that term as an insult; but in Mr Bolt's attitude towards Cherry there is no gleam of pity, no hint of mercy. Mr Bolt looks on the writhing misery, the complete self-contempt with the cold eye of a surgeon and with the analytic, relentless perceptiveness of a Proust.'

Such was the success of *Flowering Cherry* that members of the Royal Family wanted to see it. Beaumont decided to hold a charity performance in the presence of Princess Margaret, a prospect which filled Robert with mixed feelings: '*The Times* Court Circular says HRH P Margaret is to attend the charity performance, but as you see, it gives a funny date,' Robert wrote to Banbury. 'I think someone ought to get in touch with the British Museum or wherever it is they live to straighten this out. We can't lose such publicity just because some pin headed equerry can't keep his diary in order. Also, I personally want this; in the Headmaster's social spectrum, Bolt is permanently situated at the infra-red extreme while Royalty is ultra, but ultra violet, and to have the two brought thus markedly together might with luck bring on a brainstorm.'[22]

Two months into the run, Robert started to worry about Richardson all over again. He had travelled up to London from Butleigh on several occasions to monitor the production and each time Richardson seemed to be getting bigger. He wrote to Banbury:

I'd be happy if you went to see *Cherry* because he's swollen to the dimensions of a good sized Victorian plum – in the First Act anyway. That is so ungrateful and flippant that I must qualify at once. My difficulty in assessing Ralph is that there are two sorts of sheer size on the stage, one more rare and valuable than pieces of the True Cross, the other deplorable, and Ralph has them both. If one were permitted to say only one thing about this performance then one would obviously choose to say that it is great (with a greatness that Olivier's *Entertainer* misses to my mind). But if a second thing were permitted then I would say that in places where the part won't hold greatness Ralph goes on giving a great performance so that one has the painful spectacle of the elixir spilling over, where it becomes as merely messy as if it were mere beef tea.[23]

As *Flowering Cherry* settled into a long and profitable run at the Haymarket, Robert resumed work on a radio play called *The Drunken Sailor*. A year before, Val Gielgud had written to commission a new full-length play for the Home Service, on a subject of Robert's own choosing, for which he would receive a fee of £500. Robert replied soon enough to say that he thought the naval press gangs of the eighteenth century – a foretaste of the *Bounty* project, as well as an earlier brush with Captain Cook – might be an exciting subject. Gielgud readily agreed with him.

The play, about a servant boy's misadventures, took Robert a year to write, partly because *Flowering Cherry* and his Millfield duties took up so much of his time, partly because he found it difficult to convert his historical research into the confines and conventions of a ninety-minute radio drama. By the time he delivered the script to Gielgud in February 1958, he was far from happy with it:

> You will, I fear, find it a hard script to read. This is because I have tried to make it *depend* on radio effects, not merely to use them as background. Thus the action is hard to follow unless the effects are imagined as one reads.
>
> It is a play without a hero, not only in the sense that none of the characters is either totally sympathetic or totally unsympathetic, but also in the sense that none of the characters has the lion's share of the lines. In short, if this is anything at all, it is a Producer's play, and very much a radio play.[24]

The BBC put *The Drunken Sailor* into production without delay. Perhaps Robert's reputation was now sufficiently impressive to persuade his producer, Donald McWhinnie, to take the play as written and not search for ways of improving it. In any case, McWhinnie was concurrently going through that tortuous process with a new writer for radio named Harold Pinter whose script, *Something in Common*, had been sent back for a rewrite.

The Drunken Sailor was broadcast on Monday, 10 March 1958. When Len Smith wrote to say how much he was looking forward to hearing it, Robert dismissed it as 'at best a plain tale, at worst a pretentious farago weighed down by cliché. I am not at all happy about it but when I accepted the commission I needed the money.'[25] The critics did not share his view. The *Sunday Times* found it 'deeply experienced, deeply imagined. . . . This play is as durable an entertainment as radio has offered.' *The Listener* thought it 'may well be Mr Robert Bolt's best play to date . . . a likeable and entirely satisfying experience. I implore Mr Bolt to volunteer for further duty.'[26]

The Drunken Sailor proved to be the last of Robert's radio plays. All subsequent approaches from the BBC – the last of them made by the producer Michael Blakewell in 1962 – were firmly if politely declined, blaming pressure of work. But the BBC had benefited enormously from Robert's contributions and he, in turn, would look back on that period as one of invaluable experience and close collaboration. Perhaps, at the very end of his life, Robert noted an ironic symmetry in the fact that his first work was for the BBC and so was his last, his television adaptation of *Wild Swans*.

Two months after the first night of *Flowering Cherry*, the *Evening Standard* Drama Awards were presented at a banquet at the Savoy Hotel. The judges were John Fernald of RADA, the novelist Rosamond Lehmann, the film producer Sir Michael Balcon, the conductor Sir Malcolm Sargent and the critics Milton Shulman and Harold Hobson.

When they came to consider the Best Play of the Year, there were three major contenders: *Flowering Cherry*, Osborne's *The Entertainer* and Ray Lawler's *The Summer of the Seventeenth Doll*. The judges were undecided – Sargent favoured a light comedy, Lesley Storm's *Roar Like a Dove*, because it cheered him up and because he disliked the characters in Osborne's play who merely moaned and got drunk. Shulman voted for Osborne because the play 'was a mirror of what is now going on in this country – a study in social dry rot.' Hobson initially voted for *Flowering Cherry*, then sided with Shulman. Balcon, who favoured *Flowering Cherry*, was reluctant to vote for Osborne because 'he is a very considerable figure with a lot to say . . . but in *The Entertainer* he tries to say too much.' In the end, though, the anti-Osborne group won the day and Robert, too, was squeezed out. Balcon and Sargent sided with Lehmann and voted for Lawler who won the award. But when it came to the award for Most Promising Playwright there was total agreement: all the judges voted for Robert.[27]

Robert and Jo took the train to London and headed for the Savoy.

He wore a tight-fitting dinner suit and she clutched a daffodil. By any standard, they had arrived.

Because *Flowering Cherry* was such a success in London – it would run for more than a year – a Broadway production inevitably followed. Robert had deep misgivings about this, knowing that the spectre of *Death of a Salesman* (though not 'Death of a Sale Man') would be raised again. As he wrote to his friend Bernard McCabe: 'The play has a swiftly diminishing prospect of a production on Broadway with Eric Portman, though I'm not sure that I want this as several people here said I'd pinched it from *Death of a Salesman* and this suspicion would be sharper and more indignantly felt over there and I don't want a flop just now. I shouldn't mind it so much if *Death of a Salesman* wasn't so very good, just the play I would pinch from if I could.'[28]

The Broadway production, starring Eric Portman and Wendy Hiller, went ahead in the autumn of 1959. By this time Banbury had noticed that Robert was a changed man: 'He'd had this incredible success and became a completely different person. He started to throw his weight around, oh yes. He didn't like Reece Pemberton's set and insisted on a totally new design. So I said, all right, let's get somebody else. So we got this American, Boris Aronson, whom I had worked with on *The Diary of Anne Frank*.'[29] Aronson was taken on a tour of South London suburbia to get an idea of what ordinary middle class houses looked like. This research, together with his reading of the play, merely reinforced his view that the play should be staged in an entirely naturalistic manner. On Broadway, *Flowering Cherry* would become decidedly 'Mrs Minivery' and would dispense entirely with the cyclorama blossom.

Robert decided against his better judgement to accompany Banbury to America and see the play through its out-of-town engagements in Baltimore and Washington DC. Because his past associations with the Communist Party worried the US Immigration Service, his visa was delayed and was only obtained after he had enlisted the support of Hugh Beaumont and Lord Rothermere, the proprietor of the *Evening Standard*.

Robert's first visit to the United States was marred by many things: his father was taken ill and the play was causing several problems, most of which were attributable to Portman's drinking binges. In Baltimore, Portman was drunk throughout the first night and insulted a journalist who had come to interview him. Robert dutifully reported everything to his parents:

I have come to the conclusion that the principle advantage of visiting America is the increased appreciation of England which it affords. I wouldn't live in New York for all the tea in China. It is dirty, rapid, exhausted, frigid, and feels dangerous; the main impression is one of brutality very near the surface. It looks impressive, if not beautiful, seen from a distance, particularly at night, but in detail it is mostly very ugly indeed – quite as bad as Manchester.

Baltimore is the 'South' and really a bit frightening. The people look nervous and aggressive and have that over sweet sing-song in their voices. The police in particular, with a rather threatening swagger in their walk, and hung about with pistols, clubs, handcuffs and so on, are not unlike my conception of the German SS. Nor do I think they would be offended by the comparison but rather tickled by it. There is a big proportion of negroes in the population, mostly rather poor and timid looking and whatever the law may say there is complete segregation.

The theatre is an old one, with two balconies in big sweeping curves, like a Mississippi riverboat. It's a bit tatty but remains handsome. Inside that is; outside, it's almost a ruin. There seems to be no civic pride here . . . this combination of neon lighting, filthy streets and peeling paintwork, all under a hot moist sky, is very disturbing to an inhibited Englishman like myself.[30]

As they inched towards the New York opening, Robert's fear of failure was increasing. Portman and Wendy Hiller did not get on, partly because the probability of a flop created an infectious atmosphere of tension. 'I don't myself feel we have much chance of a success,' wrote Robert, 'and I rather fear an outright flop. The audiences here are only interested in climaxes, not the path by which you arrive at them, and they like jokes, not humour. And then we are getting a very erratic performance from Eric Portman, good in places bad in others, and never the same places two nights running. Partly as a result of this, but partly too because it is her natural style, Wendy Hiller is "pushing" her part somewhat . . . straining after effects and the result is a performance that is in places strident and so tends to repel rather than attract the audience. But we have all worked extremely hard and have a show which we need not be ashamed of and there is a fighting chance that we shall pull it off.'[31]

Flowering Cherry opened at the Lyceum Theatre on Wednesday, 21 October, the same week that Frank Lloyd Wright's Guggenheim

Museum of Modern Art was officially opened to the public. Although Portman's drunken behaviour at a press conference had dismayed the New York journalists, the reviews the next day were not as scathing as Robert feared. 'Although the scale is small, the workmanship is fine in Robert Bolt's *Flowering Cherry*,' said the *New York Times*. 'Mr Bolt, a new British playwright, has drawn the character portrait of a minor suburban charlatan: and he has also woven a cheerless drama of family life out of the same material. . . . Since Eric Portman gives a superb performance as the disintegrating charlatan, since Wendy Hiller gives a superb performance in contrasting colours as a wife and mother, *Flowering Cherry* has considerable distinction in the quality of its workmanship. But when the curtain falls on the disaster that concludes this domestic drama, the scale still seems unhappily small and *Flowering Cherry* seems rather old-fashioned in style for a new dramatist.'[32]

Robert's worry that *Death of a Salesman* might be used as a sledgehammer to crack a nut turned out to be unfounded; and if a transatlantic war between the two plays had broken out it might have been beneficial, for the New York critics, cautious in their praise, inflicted a lethal wound by making *Flowering Cherry* seem irredeemably dull and parochial. The play closed the following Saturday after only five performances.

'Bob did not show himself at his best in America,' said Frith Banbury. 'He was not difficult with me because he saw what a problem I had with Eric Portman who was drunk all the time. But Bob left us to face the music. The morning after we opened, Wendy Hiller rang and said, "Bob has run away. I rang him to ask what he thought of the notices and he'd already gone to the airport. That's a black mark, isn't it?" And I must say I thought so myself.'[33]

For Robert, the fabled Great White Way had proved the rockiest of roads, even though his total American royalty payment amounted to over seven hundred pounds, more than a year's salary at Millfield. He vowed that his next time on Broadway would be different.

A stream of visitors now came down to deepest Somerset: sleek Daimlers and Rolls-Royces negotiated the narrow lanes to decant the likes of Ralph Richardson and Celia Johnson for tea. Margaret Ramsay arrived to discuss new ideas and journalists, too, beat a path to 56 Butleigh.

Robert and Jo made a 'good story' because the way they lived seemed more interesting than the plays he wrote. Without exception, the journalists drew a picture of quaint rusticity – the tiny cottage without running water and Jo serving coffee as Robert held forth on the price of fame and the problems of the modern world. All the journalists wondered how Robert was going to cope with an income of £300 a week; it was if he had won the football pools.

One feature was headlined 'The New Hit Playwright Promises I'm Committed, I Won't Change, I Won't Be Decorative'.[34] A profile in the *Evening Standard*, entitled 'Mr Bolt is afraid of earning £300 a week', was illustrated by an eerily prophetic cartoon of two images of Robert: one as a yokel, drawing water from the well, the other as a dandy, posing in tail coat beside a Rolls-Royce outside the Savoy Hotel. 'Their rustic idyll has now been dramatically shattered,' wrote the *Standard*'s Thomas Wiseman. 'It is a success story *par excellence* but one with unusual ramifications. For Mr and Mrs Bolt are as fearful about success as most people are about failure.' Robert was quoted as saying: 'I have no doubt that success can corrupt and though I hope and believe it will not corrupt us I am perfectly aware of the subtle and insidious way in which it can eat into one's life. It would be naive to think that one can go from being an unknown schoolmaster earning £20 a week to being a playwright earning £300 without it having some effect. The danger is that one loses one's human values which are essential to a writer and substitutes them for money values.'

Wiseman also reported that Robert was anxious to distance himself from the other playwrights whom the press had called 'angry young men'. 'What seems to be wrong with all these furious chaps,' said Robert, 'is that although they are all furious about different things, they have this in common: they are identified by their hates, by what they are against.

'I am for my family, which is the most important thing of all to me; writing, though I sometimes hate my own; England, because I like living here; the writing of George Orwell; some of Tennessee Williams; Rossini; Handel; fish and chips; the left wing of the Labour Party.'[35]

An unlikely visitor to Butleigh at this time was the American novelist, John Steinbeck. In June 1958 Robert was wandering in Glastonbury Abbey when he noticed two American tourists. Perhaps he recognised Steinbeck or maybe they struck up a casual conversation and discovered a common bond. As writers, one was at the beginning of his career, the other nearly at the end.

Steinbeck was travelling with his wife, Elaine, and Robert took them straight off to Butleigh to watch an hour's cricket, followed by cider and skittles at the Rose and Portcullis. Steinbeck told Robert that he was hoping to write a modern version of Sir Thomas Malory's *Morte d'Arthur* and planned to live in Somerset for a year, writing the book and drawing inspiration from the nearby sites of Arthurian legend – Glastonbury and Cadbury which is thought to be the site of the mythical Camelot. Robert offered to help the Steinbecks find a suitable house and within a few months, after the Steinbecks had returned to America, he wrote to them to say he had found an ideal cottage for them in nearby Bruton.

They arrived back in England in February 1959 and would stay at Discove Cottage for ten months. Elaine Steinbeck said:

> We were just enchanted with all of it. We saw Bob and Jo a lot and John and Bob became close friends. We fell in love with their children, Sally and Ben. They were very funny and we'd baby-sit when Bob and Jo went to London. It was our first taste of country family life, rather primitive but we were being rather primitive ourselves in Discove Cottage.
>
> After Bob and Jo separated we rather lost touch with them, but we did see Bob again just the once and he gave us rather a shock. It was in London in early January 1965. We had just arrived in London from spending Christmas in Ireland with John Huston and Bob came to see us at the Dorchester. He was a big writer then and, I tell you, he was very, very grand, with a handkerchief hanging from his cuff. He wasn't at all like the man we knew in Somerset.

Although Steinbeck never fully realised his dream of rewriting Malory – a failure which depressed him greatly – he and Elaine would always cherish their time in Somerset. 'On the day John died, in 1968,' said Elaine, 'he asked me where we had been happiest during our twenty years together. I said "you first" and he said, "No, I'm dying and you'll just agree with me." So I suggested that I wrote it down, which I did, and handed him the piece of paper. Then John said "Somerset" and he looked at the piece of paper. And I had written Somerset. And the Bolts were part of our lives there.'[36]

In gratitude to Robert for finding Discove Cottage, Steinbeck gave him a gift of the thirteen-volume Oxford English Dictionary. In Volume One he wrote:

> Dear Bob, I wish you joy of these noble books and I can think of no more precious gift for a writer. For here is the whole structure and life story of the most glorious of languages –

sensitive, subtle, strong, catholic, intuitive and formidable. It can truly roar like a lion or sing sweetly like a dove.

These books make me feel very humble against the giant architecture of our speech, astonished at its size and multiplicity, but, looking closer, the life story of each word makes me also feel that it is close and dear, for they are my family and yours. And words are truly people, magic people, having birth, growth and destiny.

May you, in your writing life, add to this glittering tower which was made, added to and kept alive by people like you and me. Good luck and looting and with thanks to you and Jo.[37]

Robert and Jo did not fully share the Steinbecks' delight at the quaintness of it all, a delight that only many years of luxuriance can inspire. Instead, Robert's new success and comparative wealth made his surroundings appear almost wilfully perverse. The little cottage at Butleigh seemed increasingly small, especially when, on 3 May 1958, Jo gave birth to their third child, a girl whom they named Joanna, though she soon became known as JoJo. Eight months after the birth Robert reported that 'Joanna is incredible, ceaselessly active, a clear personality, terribly wilful, a tyrant. We are inordinately proud of her.'[38]

The time had come for Robert to hand in his resignation at Millfield. For two years, Boss Meyer, to his great credit, was indulging Robert to a degree, allowing him fairly regular absences in London. However, Robert still had pupils to teach, pupils whose very lives and futures depended on him and it is entirely characteristic that he never allowed his success or his mounting workload to undermine his duties as a teacher. 'I always thought that I could go back to teaching if things didn't work out,' Robert later told Malcolm Muggeridge. 'I liked teaching clever children, that is, children who really didn't need teaching. And I liked teaching simple things to fairly stupid children. But I was no good at teaching mediocre children.'[39]

One of Robert's cleverest pupils at this time was seventeen-year-old John Dunn who had been at Winchester, which depressed him, and was in a hurry to pass his A-levels. Although Dunn was not taking English, a friend of his named Christopher Stein, who was one of Anthony Rossiter's most promising art students, recommended that Dunn speak to Robert and ask if he might give him advice in writing papers. Dunn said:

Bob was one of the four men I've met in my life who I felt very close to, who I really felt I could talk to about important things. He was very unpushy in the way he dealt with his pupils and I think that was what first impressed me about him, the combination of very considerable ability, patience, and a respect for what he was trying to teach. There was a real human grace about him. He had a rather simple way of thinking about most things. I always thought that his gift was illuminating simplification and I found that very stimulating because I have too many thoughts for my own good. Bob didn't gain from having too many thoughts; he managed to think the thoughts he did have with a lot of vigour and clarity.

He'd say, 'Write me an argument about something that seems to be of some importance' so I went away and did it. He tried to persuade me to write more simply and clearly. He loved writing and I began to see how you could come to love writing. It was quite addictive.[40]

Taking Robert's advice, Dunn wrote a paper about the history of twentieth-century art and on the strength of it he won a scholarship to Cambridge, where he now lectures on political theory.

Another of Robert's pupils at this time was thirteen-year-old John Sergeant, now the BBC's Chief Political Correspondent. Sergeant's father taught languages – no less than thirty of them – as well as divinity at Millfield and because the father was brilliant, Boss thought the son was genetically bound to be the same. Young Sergeant was taught mathematics by Mr Glasspool, who had been a headmaster before the First World War and was in his eighties. Since Mr Glasspool did not have a Nissen hut and was listed on the bulletin board as being 'peripatetic', Sergeant found himself being taught calculus in Mr Glasspool's car. His Latin teacher, Mr Salisbury, was even stranger: he had been a judge in India whose legal career ended dramatically when he was convicted of manslaughter. Every day for a year, Sergeant made his way to Robert's Nissen Hut for his lessons in English and English Literature:

It was at the far end of the camp, corrugated iron with brick at one end and a coke stove in the middle. There was a blackboard but he didn't use it very much. Bolt was remarkably serious about what he was doing, even though this was the year that his whole life changed. He gave very little hint of this. Occasionally lessons were cancelled when he went to London but broadly speaking the course of our year and the course of his year were kept completely separate.

We had three books to go through, two of which were conventional. There was the prologue to *The Canterbury Tales* and *Henry IV Part 1*. The third book was Thor Heyerdahl's *Kon-Tiki Expedition*. Bolt made no reference as to why we were doing a Norwegian book for English Literature and he would pronounce 'Kon-Tiki' very carefully, as if it was Chinese. There were a few jokes, but not many, and no subversion because he wanted us to respect the books. He was also very thorough and organised and he had this idea that a working man is a good man. That certainly affected me.

As the year went on he got more prosperous and he bought a brand-new red estate car. The reviews for *Flowering Cherry* came out and he was obviously a tremendous success. Two years after he left Millfield he came back to judge the drama competition. I was producing and appearing in a show about a prisoner-of-war camp in the Far East. I'd got a real Japanese boy to play the guard and I played the Japanese colonel. It was a clash of values piece and Bolt, to my surprise, gave us a very poor review because he said it was communist propaganda. I was taken aback by that because I thought it was a play about ideas.

Before Sergeant went up to Oxford, he travelled in America and worked briefly as an accountant at a cement factory near Washington. A rich friend invited him to New York where he encountered an unfamiliar world of suites at the Sherry Netherland and parties at 21 where people would order platefuls of caviar and mashed potato. He even met Sam Spiegel. But when, back at the Sherry Netherland, his friend produced a line of call girls to choose from, Sergeant recoiled from the world of show business and its sybarites. 'I saw then', he said, 'what an evil world it could be.'

At Oxford, Sergeant saw his future in comedy and subsequently wrote scripts for Alan Bennett and appeared in Bennett's TV series, *On the Margin*. But he finally decided to abandon acting and writing. It was the memory of Robert which was partially responsible for his change of direction. 'The reason why Bolt was so important in my life was because I had respected him and had followed his career intently. I saw how his life had fallen apart and how out of his depth he was when he married Sarah Miles. He obviously had great unhappiness and had failed to write the great play he thought he should. Instead, his life was a morality play. It was a sad thing to see.'[41]

As Robert's and Jo's time at Millfield ran out, they began to sense

that their colleagues were treating them differently, that their success
– which Robert had not been shy of boasting about – had made them
the objects of envy: 'Apart from two or three of our closer friends,'
wrote Robert, 'people have subtly altered towards us this last year.
There is a queer mixture of sneering and flattery, a constant
reference to our success and untold wealth, which doesn't add up to
much but it is uncomfortable. We find ourselves falling into attitudes
of defence. If you bring your success with you into a new district, it
is taken to be a natural attribute, but if your success comes to you
among your friends it is thought to be freakish, a matter of luck,
possibly stolen. Not many people have enough self-respect to think
that an equal of theirs could deserve success. The majority react by
placing you above or below themselves; in either case you are in
some measure rejected.'[42]

Anneka and Anthony Rossiter also noticed a shift in the way that
the Bolts were treated after *Flowering Cherry*. 'Bob was really kicked
around at Millfield,' Rossiter recalled. 'He had to run the boating
club and other things because he was a nobody to them, just a
Manchester schoolboy. But when he became famous, Boss asked
him to be a visiting lecturer at a thousand pounds a week and Bob
turned him down. He just came down occasionally to adjudicate play
competitions.'[43]

If Robert felt that people were treating him differently, his friends
were correspondingly alarmed by the change in his character, as
Frith Banbury had already noticed. On one of his frequent trips to
London Robert stayed at the Highgate flat rented by Mike and
Naomi Kellaway. Naomi said:

> After *Flowering Cherry*, Bob was always up in London and he'd
> stay with us and tell us all the marvellous things that had
> happened to him. And of course we were delighted for him. But
> then he started to become rather arrogant. One night he came
> back from a dinner with a stinking bundle of fish and chips
> wrapped in a newspaper. He had been to some smart restaurant
> and said, 'I've brought you some supper.' We said we had
> already eaten and didn't want any supper. Then he laid out this
> awful fish and these greasy chips on the floor and shouted, 'Eat
> it!' Then he sat down and ate it himself, throwing bones all over
> the carpet. This was a symbolic insult aimed at Mike who hadn't
> fulfilled his promise as a sculptor. I then demanded the hundred
> pounds which I had loaned Bob to pay off his debts and it came
> in dribs and drabs.[44]

Robert himself sought to make a joke about the money and explained how his new found wealth had yet to reach his bank account: 'Here is £50 of yours,' he wrote to Mike and Naomi. 'This should have been sent before Christmas, and the second fifty now. It is depressing that the Bolts, so extremely efficient at borrowing money, should be a shade dilatory at paying it back. But for various reasons we haven't seen any of this money ourselves yet; and if the situation is pressing please say so and I will find the next £50 at once (it would cause us no hardship at all, merely a small inconvenience). Can you come and see us here? If you come I'll promise to get, if necessary, drunk.'[45]

Success would indeed change Robert, as it does everybody, even imperceptibly, though in Robert's case the changes were dramatic. While his material circumstances had improved to an astonishing degree, there were also serious sexual and psychological problems. The strains it put on his marriage finally led him to seek psychiatric help. 'Bob was seeing a psychiatrist, Dr Armstrong Harris,' said Frith Banbury. 'I can't say this definitively because I have no proof . . . and Bob never talked to me about it . . . but I thought he was seeing Harris because he wasn't able to "get it up" as far as Jo was concerned. I can't remember why I felt this, I just did. Of course, Peggy Ramsay used to say the most tactless things about her clients. I always remember her saying, "Bolt is money mad! money mad!" The neurosis was enormous, the jolly Farmer Giles and, inside, screaming hysterics.'[46]

The melodrama with Naomi had a lot to do with this. She had exposed a vulnerability or a flaw in Robert's psychology, a portent of his future life with Jo and, later, with Sarah: there was something in his nature which invited, if not welcomed, sexual humiliation and the periodically impotent Jim Cherry was the first of many protagonists to reflect this. 'Years later,' said Naomi, 'Bob told me he had been analysed, then had suddenly walked out, deciding it had all been a waste of time. This was hardly fair since Dr Harris's confidence in Bob as a writer helped him overcome his mortification at not being "a good bull".'[47]

Naomi's husband, Mike Kellaway, believed that Robert underestimated Harris's importance. 'Harris had started out as a doctor in the Merchant Navy,' he said, 'so he'd had experience of rough and tumble. He was a big, solid character and I think he helped Bob enormously. I remember Bob telling me that Harris had told him, "Your mind is heavy with sex and your balls are heavy with thought." That's a very Boltian opposition.'[48]

Although Robert had decided to end his career as a teacher he was never able to shake the chalk dust from his jackets; he was always a teacher and there were many who felt that he tended to lecture on subjects rather than just discuss things. And if he and Jo had decided to quit the countryside for the city it was to prove a brief acquaintance, for he was always, like Jim Cherry, a countryman at heart: he had a fantasy of an old manor house, with trees and lawns. Most of all he wanted a conservatory, a room which would bring the garden into the home, just like the cyclorama of cherry blossom.

But in early 1959, the lure of London, even one of its leafier outposts, was hard to resist. As he wrote to Bernard McCabe: 'It's just that I'm chocekered, or, alternatively, chockered, with shambling up and down the railway line from Castle Carey to Paddington and back. We have strong hopes of a big bugger of a Victorian house on Richmond Green which would be less oppressive for the children than the cobbled alleyways of the Old Town itself.'

As if to retain a grip on reality, Robert ended the letter on a rather plaintive note: 'We have three children. I am 34 years of age and was born in Cheshire, Great Britain.'[49]

ELEVEN

BURNING BRIGHT

'Radioactivity stimulates mutation; and the chances are astronomically against a mutation being favourable. In other words, it produces monsters.'

The Tiger and the Horse

The Royal Borough of Richmond-upon-Thames had been the hunting ground of kings since the twelfth century. Situated two miles upstream from Hampton Court, above a broad bend of the river, it afforded sweeping vistas of the surrounding countryside, as far as Windsor Castle to the west and the City of London to the east. A vast expanse of heathland had been a royal chase for centuries until Charles I enclosed it in 1637, creating Richmond Park. By the Fifties it was still a haven for deer, badgers, foxes, wildfowl as well as minor Royals and Bertrand Russell who grew up in Pembroke Lodge. At the heart of Richmond was its Green. Occupying one side of the Green was Richmond Palace, originally built by Henry VII, who bestowed upon the site his Yorkshire title of Earl of Richmond. His son, Henry VIII, spent much of his reign there and it was the favourite residence of his daughter, Elizabeth I, who died in the palace in 1603. Later on, rows of immaculate Georgian houses were built around the Green to create one of London's most congenial urban settings. The author of *A Man For All Seasons* could not have chosen a more appropriate or evocative place to live.

Robert and Jo found a house which lay on the north-eastern corner of the Green. The house cost around £5000, a hefty amount considering it came with a lease of only fourteen years. As soon as Robert moved in he started to wonder how he might maintain it as well as his family. He found it difficult to believe that he could make a proper living out of writing plays; even with a major hit behind him, it did not seem like a real profession, offering only passing riches and permanent insecurity. 'When we got here from Somerset,' he wrote, 'with the children tired and fractious, we were horrified and angry to find the previous occupant still here, several rooms half full of his extraordinary rubbish, the whole house filthy from floor to ceiling, and himself half drunk. We had to go to the shops and buy detergent, disinfectant and mops there and then even before the pantry was clean enough to use. I washed it thoroughly, walls and floor, while the Pickfords men filled up the dirty rooms with our lumber. We have been doing the same thing room by room ever since, and only now is it possible to see what a very comfortable home this is going to be.'[1]

It was a large Victorian house, with three lofty reception rooms on the ground floor, one of which Robert used as his study, a kitchen, breakfast room and pantry. Upstairs were five bedrooms, the largest of which was destined to become a playroom for the children, and over the garage were three further rooms which Robert planned to refurbish for guests when, and if, his next plays made a profit. 'Our greatest compensation for the rural pleasures of Butleigh is the river,' he wrote, 'which is reached by a quiet walk of about five minutes through back lanes without traffic. There are large parks on both sides of it hereabouts, so that it is pastoral, not industrial as it is further down, nor suburban as it is further up. There are tremendous trees on both banks, swarms of ducks, swans and even heron. The children have established a claim to a boat trip every weekend.'[2]

Sally and Ben were sent to a nearby school, the Vineyard, which was state run, though later on, when Ben was nine, Robert and Jo thought of sending him to Eton. 'I was given a choice,' said Ben, 'and because the Vineyard seemed to be a good school I thought, why should I go to this place called Eton, so I said no, thank you very much. It wasn't discussed again.'

As soon as the house was in a semblance of order, with cans of paint stacked in the hallway, Robert vanished into his study. 'My recollection until I was six', said Ben, 'was of a normal father–son relationship. It was the same with my sister Sally. He would take us for walks, he'd tell us how haystacks were built, all the stuff that dads do. When we moved to Richmond, when he became very successful, he had his own study and that was a place we were not allowed to go during the day. His working day would be very long, so I saw less and less of him.'[3]

In his final year at Butleigh Robert wrote a play which in some respects was an elaboration of *The Last of the Wine*. It was a study of a family – this time a distinctly bookish one – whose emotional conflicts are crystallised by the hydrogen bomb, which becomes a fully fledged, albeit off-stage character, Robert's favoured catalyst for all reasons. His original title was *Forests of the Night*, borrowed from Blake's *Songs of Experience*, though he soon changed it to *The Tiger and the Horse*, having in mind a phrase from Blake's *Proverbs from Hell*: 'The tygers of wrath are wiser than the horses of instruction.' It was another drama which pondered the nature of love, conscience and commitment. Robert told Mike Kellaway:

> But will they like it? No. Even if it is thoroughly competent they won't like it, because it isn't what is anticipated from 'the new, exciting school of rebellious young British playwrights' and if they show people (particularly critics) something they didn't anticipate being shown, they mostly conclude you've not shown them anything. The reason why the critics are now as indiscriminately favourable towards the work of this new school is that they have now seen enough of it to have evolved the stock response to it. They expect untidiness overall, and within they expect alternate slices of arrogance and timidity, cruelty and 'compassion'.
>
> Now this play of *mine* is intended to be, not a mood or invitation or plea, but something existing objectively, 'over there' so to speak, like a piece of heavy furniture against which these lightweights may break their toes if they wish. And if they don't use their heads (and they don't) it won't be intelligible. And the key word above is 'intended' in any case – I haven't brought off this classic intention; it's a large play but still cramped in places, in places aggressive and elsewhere tentatively lyrical. It will be easy for the bastards to damn if they want, and I expect they will . . .[4]

The early stages of writing were agonising. Robert had the idea and the overall theme, though not the story that went with it. He wrote the first act three times and each time he destroyed it. Then Frith Banbury called him up to ask how it was going.

'I've just burned the first act again,' said Robert.

'It doesn't have to be a masterpiece, you know,' said Banbury.[5]

Banbury's advice rang true. 'When I started to write *The Tiger and the Horse*,' Robert later told the *Daily Mail*, 'I filled large notebooks with the first act. I got to the stage of behaving like a romantic young artist. Then I found out what was wrong: I was expecting to write a success. I was expecting every line to sparkle and shine. I had been corrupted unawares by believing that everything I wrote needed a surface gloss. The moment I realised my mistake I discovered I could get on with it.'[6]

The Tiger and the Horse evolved into a drawing-room drama about a family, the Deans, who live surrounded by books and fine furniture in an ancient university town – Oxford or Cambridge, Robert does not specify which. Jack Dean is the Master of the College and a former astronomer who now writes mediocre books on philosophy. His marriage to Gwendoline is one of mutual indifference – he spends most of his time in his study, poring over his books while she pours all her creative energies into her garden. Gwendoline has convinced herself that Jack's lack of interest in her is a symptom of his deep intellect and almost saintly disposition; she believes she is unworthy of him.

So far, so Ibsen. But Jack and Gwendoline have a daughter, Stella, who is clever, vibrant and romantically attached to Louis, a socialist Research Fellow whose studies take second place to his activities with CND. Another daughter, Mary, is wilder, a flirt, the victim of few repressions. After some awkward scene-setting, the real drama begins when Louis asks Jack to sign a petition for CND. Jack refuses, fearing that endorsing something so radical might destroy his chances in the forthcoming elections for vice-chancellor of the university. Gwendoline, who has read about the horrors of nuclear tests and the effects of radiation on innocent children, is shocked by Jack's weakness but she, too, is persuaded not to sign by the incumbent vice-chancellor.

It is a painting by Holbein which brings matters to a head. The canvas, owned by the College and hanging in Dean's drawing room, is of the founder of the College, his wife and his eleven children. When the painting is cleaned and restored, one of the founder's children is revealed to be a hunchback. This revelation hardens Gwendoline's resolve, who sees in the sixteenth-century painting not only a terrifying prescience but also a reflection of her inadequacies as a mother. And when Stella announces that she has become pregnant by Louis after a single night of weakness and passion, the prospect of a baby born into an irradiated world makes Gwendoline lose all reason.

By the final act, Stella's baby – Nicholas – has been born and she has moved into a flat on her own, having refused to marry Louis. Off stage, Gwendoline suffers a mental breakdown and destroys the valuable Holbein with a pair of garden secateurs. Louis's petition is pinned to the torn canvas.

Jack now realises that his aloofness, his lack of emotional, political or moral commitment, has precipitated the crisis. He signs the petition and sacrifices his chances of being vice-chancellor. He signs, though, not for any commitment to nuclear disarmament but to save his wife and himself from the stigma of insanity. Stella and Louis, meanwhile, decide to marry, each overcoming a lack of emotional commitment.

The Tiger and the Horse is the most schematic of Robert's plays. While it never preaches, every line and every scene drives the metaphor. Everything in it was close to Robert's heart and his experience: he and Jo were both members of CND and believed that they and their children were doomed to be vaporised in a nuclear war. On a less apocalyptic level, the marriage in the play echoed Robert's obsession with his work, while Stella's refusal to marry the working class Louis may well have reflected Robert's perception of how the moral climate had changed since his own marriage: illegitimacy was beginning to lose its stigma.

Despite its connections with CND, the play's debate about commitment is timeless and in the symbol of the Holbein painting Robert not only found a way of suggesting the evolution of ideas but made a direct, if subtle, connection with *A Man For All Seasons*. It was Holbein who painted the most famous portrait of Sir Thomas More and by defacing Holbein with a CND petition Robert brought the sixteenth century's philosophies crashing into those of the twentieth.

'I have read *The Tiger and the Horse*,' Frith Banbury wrote to Robert, 'am fascinated by it and will have a hell of a lot to say about it when I have had time to study it further. This may take several days so you will have to be patient. All I would say at this point is that I want to buy it.'[7]

'You should buy this play,' replied Robert, 'not because it fascinates you, or out of any kind of regard for me, but only if you adore it and itch to find big actors for it at once.'[8]

The actor whom Robert had in mind to play Jack Dean was Michael Redgrave, recently knighted, very grand, personally complex and an undoubted box-office draw. The script was sent to Redgrave with the suggestion that his own daughter, Vanessa, might be perfect in the role of Stella. Redgrave, who was staying at his country home in Somerset, loved the play and wrote Banbury an extraordinary letter:

As luck would have it a bloody pigeon settled outside my

window among the wistaria branches (and my last memory of my dreams was that a baby was crying!). I'd have got up and shot it if I hadn't feared waking the household and also if there had been a gun. This was at seven this morning – so I went down and had a cup of tea – and then the post arrived! I groaned at the sight of another script, because I'd wanted to write, all day if necessary, to get my beastly book rewritten and finished. But it was early, so I propped myself up in bed and started to read.

After Act I, I went down for more tea and started on Act II. I noticed that by the end of that act I hadn't drunk my tea. When I was starting Act III, 'Nicholas' started to cry, and the pigeon started mewling and puking again. I blessed it for having woken me.

I have been laughing and crying by turns all through the play. I shall read it again, many times, I hope, but I don't need to read it again to know that (if Mr Bolt will pardon the expression for it is only meant in affection) it is 'my' play. For I truly love it – so much that if I could think of anyone who I thought might be better suited for Dean than I am (and I don't know that I *am* – but as you know I never know that till I find I can do it) I would say, 'Get him! Forget me!'

Of course you are right about Vanessa. She has the vulnerability and also the essential youthfulness which should – as the author observes – 'carry' the change of façade in Act III. Also she has a conscience, like her mother's, the size of Grand Central Station.

Whether it is wise for her sake that the two of us should play again together so soon in her career is another matter and I shan't tell her anything about it until you and I have met. But that Stella is a part in which a girl can 'make her name. . . .' There can be no doubt of that.

They are all wonderful parts and I long to hear what casting you have in mind. It's slightly unfortunate – I feel – that Gwen Ff-D had such a notable hit in *Long Day's Journey* (with its 'mad scene') for surely she'd be perfect casting for Gwendoline? I long to write on and on but I must get to work. This, though, I have to say: Louis *must* surely, be very attractive physically. His is the most difficult part. No? (I don't of course mean 'good looking.') Louis also, I feel, should be 'vulnerable' – and look not a day over the specified age of 30.

If we decide on Vanessa, or whether we do or not, the rough outline of what are only 'plans' include a film in Ireland (six weeks) and possibly a limited season of my own adaptation of *The Aspern Papers*. So if we wait till the end of Stratford I have plenty to do if you and Mr B are really prepared to wait.

OH! but suddenly, and out of the blue, what of *Flora* for Gwen? I must stop!!! Yours ever, Michael.

PS: I hear that Mr Bolt lives not far from here in Somerset. Perhaps he sent that pigeon. The pigeons of disturbance are wiser than the owls of slumber?[9]

Robert was jubilant when Banbury told him of Redgrave's response. Although he was nervous of approaching Redgrave direct, Jo met a friend at Millfield who gave her his address at nearby Batcombe. 'I am writing to say how happy the news from Frith has made me,' Robert wrote to Redgrave. 'I don't know where else we should have found anyone to embody the difficult combination of the potent scholar, red-blooded man consumed by elegance of mind. Thieves, kings, coalmen are comparatively easy.

'By a rare coincidence, I lost a pair of pigeons about a week ago. I wondered where they had gone and had supposed they were merely wasting time somewhere. I'm glad to hear they have been occupying themselves usefully.'[10]

Redgrave knew of Robert's life as a schoolmaster and how he lived in a cottage without running water. Unable to resist dropping by, he went to Butleigh three days later and stayed for just three minutes, long enough for Jo to be charmed off her feet and for Robert to form a scholarly opinion of him: 'How extraordinary to find a man who can both act and think,' he told Banbury.[11]

The script was also sent to Dorothy Tutin, then Peggy Ashcroft, both of whom turned down the role of Gwendoline. While this was a major disappointment, Vanessa Redgrave readily agreed to play Stella. Within the space of two weeks, Robert had Banbury, Redgrave and Vanessa Redgrave committing themselves; he thought the play would be on in no time.

Almost at once, Redgrave demanded rewrites. Aware of his status and wanting to be loved by his audience, he felt that Jack Dean needed to be made more sympathetic and one way of doing this was to rewrite Gwendoline's role so her madness appears to be a sudden collapse rather than a gradual process for which Dean is largely to blame. Robert readily complied with this, though not to Redgrave's satisfaction: 'Although I think the rewrite of the Bolt play is on the whole a great improvement,' he wrote to Beaumont, 'I am not so happy about the rewrite of the wife in relationship to my own part, for she now appears to be so plainly dotty from the start (an opinion that I think is shared by Peggy) that it makes the husband unbelievably obtuse.'[12] In the midst of Redgrave's demands on the script, he told Banbury and Robert that if they wanted him, they would have to wait for a year or more before he was available for what was expected to be a long West End run.

'God in heaven what a rat race it all is,' Robert told Banbury. 'I hear from Doris Lessing, whom I met recently, [that] Peggy Ashcroft is to take part in a play of hers – the part of a lady with nervous and sexual troubles who is interested in the question of nuclear disarmament. If that goes on while we are marching and countermarching up and down Shaftesbury Avenue, I shall doubtless be told I have borrowed from her as I borrowed *Cherry* from *Salesman*. That's the way it goes, but who'd be a bloody playwright if he could get a steady job as a tightrope walker, space monkey or looking after lepers?'[13] But Robert and Banbury decided to wait for Redgrave, knowing how crucial to success was the presence of a major star. It was a full seventeen months before *The Tiger and the Horse* went into rehearsal.

As Robert impatiently hung about for Redgrave he enjoyed the social round of a world into which success had given him an entrée. He made friends quickly and gave frequent parties at Richmond – food, drink and conversation were usually rounded off with a fireworks display. Regular guests were Michael Caine, Sean Connery and Diane Cilento, Peter Hall and Leslie Caron, Kenneth Williams and Ralph Richardson.

If Robert's old friends, such as Mike Kellaway and Herbert McCabe, noticed a dramatic change in his personality and circumstances, Robert himself found it hard to come to terms with the way that other people lived. What he saw perplexed him and perhaps he recognised, too, both the pitfalls and the pleasures which would come his way in less than a year's time.

I went to Redgrave's last Sunday evening (by myself, Jo being down with flu) and was puzzled by the plushy atmosphere which successful people of the theatre seem to drift into. I had the impression that Redgrave was puzzled by it too, as though he had woken one morning to find it all grown up around him without his own volition. Presumably one first feels that one must have a good carpet, then good furniture to go with the carpet, then good pictures to go with the furniture, then a better carpet to live up to the pictures and so on. Anyway, there he was in the thick of it, like a second line Oxford don with private means, or a youngish stockbroker with a subscription to *Encounter*, not at all my idea of an artist who can't afford so much lumber it seems to me.

An artist must always be precarious I think – not financially precarious, but spiritually, and so he must be a bit of a moral athlete to put up with his situation, and this plushness I speak of, however harmless in other respects, is the opposite of morally athletic. Picasso is a millionaire and lives in a castle, but I have seen many pictures of it and it is wild and workable. The more I see of other actors the more I realise how lucky I was to get Richardson; he too lives in a very sumptuous manner, but it doesn't affect him; he is still delighted and surprised by the power of his Bentley, the softness of his carpets and the stripes on his manservant's waistcoat and obviously feels that it may at any moment vanish. He seems to have retained his innocence – which of course makes him exasperating, too.[14]

Shortly after Robert moved to Richmond Margaret Ramsay suggested that he prepare a stage version of *A Man For All Seasons*. Although he had no way of knowing it at the time, Robert would have the rare experience of seeing two of his plays performed next door to each other on Shaftesbury Avenue. A quirk of fate – Redgrave's schedule – would ultimately work to Robert's advantage: two major plays, opening within a month of each other, turned him into the most conspicuously successful playwright in London.

There had already been a television production of *A Man For All Seasons*, for which Robert was paid one hundred and twenty guineas. Transmitted by the BBC on New Year's Day 1957, it was recorded by the Midlands drama department and produced by Peter Dews, who had been in the radio production of *Baron Bolligrew*. Starring Bernard Hepton as Sir Thomas More, it was, as many of the reviews pointed out, a slightly static production with little to distinguish it from the earlier radio version.

In order to start work on the stage version, Robert had to ask the BBC to send him a copy of the script because he had given away all his own copies. But since Robert was searching for a way to present his historical research and his moral argument with as much stylisation as possible, much of his original version was destined to be discarded. Brecht posed many of the formalistic questions and provided many of the answers too. For Robert, who described his approach as 'bastardised Brecht', the key to the play was the nature and importance of integrity, ideas which were central to Brecht's

Galileo. As if to acknowledge one of his inspirations, Robert borrowed Brecht's speech for Galileo by deliberately misquoting it for More's thoughts on the Apostolic Succession in Act Two, Scene One: 'What matters to me is not whether it's true or not but whether I believe it to be true, or rather not that I *believe* it but that *I* believe it. I trust I make myself obscure?' More wanted to avoid transparency for fear it might cost him his life. His position is that he takes no position, until the very end. Robert's admiration for More was obvious, as he told a reporter just before the first night:

> There are plenty of people who are courageous, and noisy but there are not many who are active, and quiet. They interest me. More was not a man who set out to be a saint. He was a worldly man; that is, in the world of society and politics. He never regarded himself as martyr material. But he kept one small area of integrity within himself. And once the powers-that-be found out, they could not rest until they got at it. So he became a martyr against his desires, because he would not do what the authorities wanted. They assumed he must be in with the Catholics. In fact, he was fond of the King, as they all were at the beginning, and scrupulously loyal. When he was attacked, the Catholics thought he must be on their side. He was not. Both sides had the wrong end of the stick throughout. I think there are many parallels in our own day.

Asked about the play's stylistic approach – the most pressing theatrical issue of the day – Robert expressed some scepticism:

> Experimental theatre? If 'experimental' means 'expendable' then it is a waste of time. Of course one tries to do something new. I think there was something new about the way *Flowering Cherry* was put together, whether or not anyone noticed. In *The Tiger and the Horse* I have tried to break away from naturalism without breaking away from reality.
>
> The Jacobeans were the last to break away successfully in relation to their own times. I have tried to do this in my studies of Sir Thomas More – possibly choosing the historical form because it gave me the courage to drive away from the naturalistic form, a courage I lacked when dealing with my own times.[15]

On 3 February 1960 Robert sent his mother and father a copy of his completed script with a covering letter:

> I have been unfortunate in my timing. Anouilh and Fry have

each just completed a play on the theme of Thomas a'Beckett. The situation between Beckett and Henry II was not altogether dissimilar from that between More and Henry VIII and the plays are certain to come in for comparison. Anouilh and Fry, being very established writers, don't have to worry about that and may even benefit by it, but I must get my play on quickly if I am to avoid the dusty rear.

Quite apart from ordinary impatience, I cannot risk such a delay financially. I shan't know anything further until Binkie Beaumont returns from holiday. A complication is that he is also managing the Fry and Anouilh and might just try to hold my play back until these more important productions are established. I am not going to let him do this unless he can offer me some quite dazzling recompense, but I shall have to bear the possibility in mind, as he is a very astute and persuasive man.[16]

The praise that flowed back from Robert's parents delighted him: 'It has had a lot of bouquets from various sources,' he wrote, 'but none has given me such pleasure as yours. The great Binkie Beaumont is enthusiastic about it – he phoned his manager from N Africa to say so and to instruct him to pass the message on to me. This is not the way in which he normally responds and when due allowance is made for flannel, it bodes well for the production. There is just a glimmering possibility that I might get Olivier for it.'[17]

Beaumont decided to stage *A Man For All Seasons* in the summer. Frith Banbury, who was preoccupied with *The Tiger and the Horse*, would have loved to have directed *A Man For All Seasons* as well; not only did he think it was the better play, he worried that Beaumont was going to open the plays in the wrong order, to the disadvantage of *The Tiger and the Horse*. He told Beaumont:

I have reread *A Man For All Seasons*. I am now ready to burn my boats and say there has been no play in this genre written in English to compare with it since Shaw wrote *St Joan*. It demonstrates what I have always suspected, that Bolt has nothing to fear from Messrs Anouilh, Fry, let alone the Osbornes and the Mortimers. The man who wrote it will be able to make his own terms with the theatre and the rest of us will have to like it or lump it.

You do see now, don't you, why I am more keen than ever that *The Tiger and the Horse* should be seen first! I have come to love that play, but it will have a hard row to hoe if it has to follow *A Man For All Seasons*.[18]

Although Banbury could easily have taken on both plays, it was Robert's rather obsessive interest in freeing himself from naturalism that led him to seek another director for *A Man For All Seasons*, one less staunchly traditional than Banbury. According to Robert, he took the disappointment, 'like a gentleman. His reaction was lovely, superb.'[19] Banbury also took a financial interest in the play which, over the years, has been something of a nest-egg.

Robert found his director in Noel Willman, a hard-drinking forty-two-year-old Ulsterman and melancholic homosexual. As an actor, Willman had made his professional stage début in John Gielgud's 1939 production of *Hamlet* but scored his biggest success in 1954 in Bridget Boland's *The Prisoner*, playing the interrogator opposite Alec Guinness. As a director, Willman took the Old Vic on tour and seemed equally at home with Shakespeare or Rattigan. When Willman was brought in for *A Man For All Seasons* things started to move quickly. Having directed Paul Scofield in Christopher Fry's first play, *A Phoenix Too Frequent*, Willman suggested that Scofield was the ideal actor to play Sir Thomas More. Eight years younger than Alec Guinness, Scofield had the same intensity, quietude and diffidence. He said:

> When I first read the play I saw at once the danger of More being played over-piously, but it was not written that way; Robert gave him humour and severity and obstinacy as well as goodness. As always, my final guide was the writer. I agreed at once to do it.
>
> The first time I met Robert must have been at the first reading. He had a smiling, rosy, clumping and always friendly manner. I use the word clumping because he walked like a farmer. Robert attended some of the rehearsals though the director's policy was, I think, to debar an author from directly talking to the actors or making suggestions or criticisms to us – a wise stricture because a production can only be co-ordinated by one person. I think Robert's experience of actors was limited. At that time he seemed instinctively to mistrust us – he once complained of my 'insouciance' at rehearsal which I hope was merely a pretence of light-heartedness on my part, which covered a multitude of anxieties! I think that at that time he truly didn't understand the way an actor works. The one actor in whom he had complete faith was Leo McKern. And rightly so.[20]

McKern had been cast as the Common Man, a role which was the most significant departure from the radio and television versions.

The Common Man was a specifically theatrical device, a character who confides in, alienates and finally shocks the audience. He pops up in a variety of guises: as a steward, a boatman, a gaoler, the foreman of the jury who seals More's fate and finally he is More's executioner. There is in him Brecht's concern for taking the audience out of the play and into the broader argument, though there is just as much Greek chorus and Mystery Player in him as well. If Robert's story was set in the sixteenth century, he was using all the devices which were held to be modern, including a stark, unadorned set which not only shunned the conventions of the 'historical play', it physically mirrored More's asceticism.

Andrew Keir was Thomas Cromwell, though Robert had initially tried to persuade Willman himself to take the part. Wolsey was played by the portly Willoughby Goddard, Henry VIII by Richard Leech and More's wife, Alice, by Wynne Clark.

The first night was on 1 July 1960. For Scofield it was 'a grey occasion. I had then, and perhaps even now, a sense of resentment at the distorted atmosphere of first nights, the imposed need to impress, the feeling of "now or never", the pretence of total fruition when we all knew that we still had a long way to go. We were not at our best that night. In the middle of the first act I heard from the stalls a loud whisper, "Oh, get on with it." I'll swear it was Robert's voice. Ah well!'[21]

The reviews the next morning were generally favourable, though by no means consistent in what they praised or criticised. While Kenneth Tynan mocked Motley's stark set as 'impenitently Swedish-modern', T. C. Worsley admired its 'suggestive economy for we are not in the least interested in the pageantry of Henry VIII's life and times. Sir Thomas More was not a pageant man.' For Tynan, Robert's play was a conscious attempt to:

> do for More what Brecht did for Galileo. In both cases, the theme is persecution, and the author's purpose is to demon-strate how authority enforces its claims on the individual conscience. . . . According to Brecht, Galileo was disloyal to the new science, and is therefore to be rebuked; according to Mr Bolt, More was loyal to the old religion and is therefore to be applauded.

It is hereabouts that the two playwrights part company. I have no idea whether Mr Bolt himself is a religious man, but I am perfectly sure that if someone presented him with irrefutable evidence that every tenet of Catholicism was a palpable falsehood, his admiration for More would not be diminished in the smallest degree. . . . If Brecht had suddenly learned that his protagonist's hypotheses were totally untrue, he would either have torn up the manuscript or revised it from start to finish. From Mr Bolt's point of view, it matters little whether More's beliefs were right or wrong; all that matters is that he held them, and refused to disclose them under questioning. For Mr Bolt, truth is subjective; for Brecht, it is objective; and therein lies the difference between two plays . . .[22]

All the reviews mattered to Robert, though perhaps Tynan's mattered more. For one thing, it was the longest, the most argued; for another, Tynan was more important than any other critic. He was not the London equivalent of 'the Butcher of Broadway', able to close a play with one stroke of his pen. Rather, he had positioned himself, like Petronius, as the ultimate arbiter of taste and fashion whose judgements were backed up by a formidable intellectual rigour. Robert felt compelled to respond with an essay which was just as long and considered as Tynan's review. The subject under discussion was the nature of truth:

Mr Tynan's certainly fair and probably generous notice of my play raises incidentally a philosophic question of practical importance [wrote Robert, claiming he only roughly understood the term, 'Objective Truth' and questioning how Tynan knew that Brecht might have torn up his play]. Is this Mr Tynan's guess, or did Brecht himself say he would? For what it means is that the worth of his play is conditional upon the correctness of Galileo's hypotheses. I don't believe this, and I don't think Mr Tynan does, really. Thus:

The difference between the hypotheses of modern cosmology and the hypotheses of Galilean cosmology is already quite as sharp as the difference between the Galilean and the Aristotelian. If the Galilean hypotheses were 'true' and showed the Aristotelian to be 'untrue' then by the same token the Galilean are now shown to be untrue. If the Galilean hypotheses are untrue, then, according to Mr Tynan, *Galileo* should be torn up or rewritten. In fact, Mr Tynan and I both think it's a great play.

Or, if this comparative view of the truthfulness of comparative hypotheses is insufficiently 'objective' for Mr Tynan, let us anticipate the dawning of that day when every feature of the Galilean cosmology has been discarded in favour of others. If that day is tomorrow, will Brecht's absorbing profound and illuminating play at once become boring, superficial and dull? It will continue to be as absorbing, profound and illuminating as it in fact is. But where can these virtues now reside? What is left when the 'objective' truth of Galileo's beliefs is removed from the play *Galileo*? Just Galileo. And that is what Brecht's play is about, as mine is about More.

There are many differences between the two plays (apart from the obvious one in sheer stature) but the *basic* difference is this. Both men were passionately and to their core convinced. Both were required by Authority to deny themselves. One complied; the other refused.[23]

It was Tynan, naturally, who had the last word. Calling Robert's 'dissenting gloss on my review a healthy phenomenon', he showed he was no slouch when it came to discussing the tenets of Galilean hypotheses. But what still perplexed Tynan was the ambiguity of More's belief system: 'We are expected to sympathise with him simply and solely because he declines to reveal his convictions.' Tynan ended his own essay with a vicious barb: 'I concede that people like Mr Bolt might easily behave, in comparable circumstances, as corruptly and as boorishly as the character played by Leo McKern. What is rude and tendentious is that a character who is the essence of boorish corruption should be labelled "The Common Man." '[24]

Beyond this arcane argument, most critics focused on Paul Scofield's performance. T. C. Worsley thought Scofield had, 'an unmatchable dignity and a kind of humble grandeur. It is a magnificent piece of acting, so tranquil, so composed, so controlled.' Other critics, though, were less admiring. A. Alvarez, writing in the *New Statesman*, thought Scofield had 'thrown all his habitual panache to the winds and emerged as a gentle, restrained, ironic More, looking for all the world like a rather ill and donnish Fred Astaire'. And while admiring Robert's dialogue, Bernard Levin in the *Daily Express* rounded on Scofield, describing his performance as 'so bad that it obscures the play's merits. His face is frozen, his voice dull and he makes every line sound like a platitude and extinguishes every spark of fire that Mr Bolt manages to blow into brightness. Towards the end, when he is bowed and greyed but unbroken, Mr Scofield comes into his own, for greyness is then needed. But until then his playing bores the doublet and hose off me.'[25]

Scofield's performance was designed to build towards the great and terrible scene of More's execution, the moment when he finally abandons protocol and speaks the truth about the King and the church. 'Up to this moment,' wrote Harold Hobson in a rather grudging review, 'Mr Scofield has been a bowed and stooping man. For the first time when hope is finally lost, and no means exist any longer for escaping the declaration of what truly is in him, he straightens his back and lifts his voice. The effect is very great [but] it is disconcerting that *A Man For All Seasons* is not more theatrically gripping than it is. Perhaps Mr Scofield's performance is too grey. In Mr Scofield there are the unwearied mind and the unflagging caution, but only at the end the blaze of excitement. Scofield looks as if the Fellows of All Souls had pooled their brains and put them inside his skull.'[26]

Even though the play had been tried out in Oxford and Brighton, it was far from ready by the time of the first night at the Globe. But it improved night by night, week by week and Scofield in particular grew into the role as he found his understanding of More undergoing subtle shifts. He said:

I think I was only half-way there when we opened. By the time we finished we could, I think, be counted as a success. All performances grow with repetition and with the gathering certainty of simply doing it and thinking it, my understanding of More and his predicament and his inflexible faith and purpose grew beyond any initial visualisation. In the early stages of rehearsal and for some time I was stuck with his rigour, his zeal, his intractability, all qualities vital to the unfolding of the story. His humanity came to me after I had established those qualities firmly for myself. It came to me bit by bit, facet by facet, and slowly. I liked More, finally, after I had found the sweetness in him, his love for his family, his loyalty to friends, his deep, impartial lawyer's wisdom.

The whole production developed like a forest fire during the run. I received a letter from Bob, which was intended for John Perry of H. M. Tennent and John Perry got the one intended for me. The one that I opened in my dressing room said, 'I think Paul was a bit better last night, but perhaps that was because the Duke of Edinburgh was in front.[27]

Considering the way that *A Man For All Seasons* has outlasted not only Brecht's *Galileo* but *Look Back in Anger* and *The Caretaker* – it quickly became a 'set play' for English GCE students and has never been out of print – it is perhaps surprising that the British critics did not herald a masterpiece. Nor did the public immediately go in throngs to the Globe; Binkie Beaumont was always on the brink of taking it off. In London, *A Man For All Seasons* became a hit by stealth and perseverance.

It was another story on Broadway when the play opened at the American National Theatre Academy (ANTA) on 23 November 1961. And in the nearly two dozen laudatory American reviews pasted into Robert's scrapbooks, Brecht's name does not appear even once.

'The Broadway production was necessarily different from London because nearly all the actors were American,' said Scofield. 'Noel's approach was the same as before and we used the same scenery and costumes. The play was hugely successful in America. Audiences seemed to view it from a moral and spiritual standpoint whereas, broadly speaking, London audiences enjoyed it more as a story about England, as a historical play.'[28]

If anything threatened the New York production it was Leo McKern, who proved to be as difficult as Eric Portman in *Flowering Cherry*. For Robert, who went to New York accompanied by Jo, this was a difficult time for he had become extremely fond of McKern. In his memoirs, McKern wrote:

I had agreed to go against my better judgement for I was extremely tired after what had been a long run in London; but a sense of responsibility to both the author and director, both of whom wanted me in the play, decided me. I had also agreed to change roles, relinquishing the Common Man for the part of Cromwell which I later played in the film. I was deeply attached to the Common Man which was one of the best parts I have ever had. I was not altogether happy with his loss, even though Cromwell is an important and powerful part; and I was also conscious of the fact that whether I liked it or not, the whole of my day is generally affected by the personality of the character that I am playing, and Cromwell is not exactly a bundle of fun . . .

In the scene of Cromwell's moral and political seduction of Richard Rich (I think on the opening night, but I can't be sure), I became aware of a quite alien sound. It sounded rather like gas escaping somewhere, but then it suddenly struck me; I was being hissed from the front stalls. Not by one or two individuals, but in fact by the majority. It is quite possible that they were hissing the performance, but, self-conceit or not, I do not believe it; I am positive that they were hissing the villain of the piece, and immediately following the initial shock came a feeling of enormous satisfaction, for it was of course an immense compliment. The beastly Cromwell had become unbearable.[29]

New York terrified McKern who imprisoned himself in his room at the Algonquin Hotel. He also became extremely depressed when he learned that his pet dog had been killed in England. Breaking his golden rule not to drink before or after a performance, he drank to 'induce a narcotic blanket and deep, escaping sleep'.[30] Although Robert, Willman and Scofield gave him all the support and encouragement they could, it was hopeless. As soon as a replacement was found, McKern left the production and returned home.

The Tiger and the Horse was tried out at Manchester, Leeds, Edinburgh, Brighton and Oxford. Catherine Lacey had been cast as Gwendoline, Jennifer Wright was playing Stella's sister, Mary, and Alan Dobie Louis, after Ian Bannen and Peter O'Toole had been unsuccessfully sought. The play was capitalised at £8000, with Redgrave and Banbury making significant investments. Robert himself reinvested his modest advance in the production. The tour, though, was traumatic and very nearly delayed the London opening. Right from the start, in Manchester, Redgrave was drinking heavily, he didn't know his lines and, as a result, the play ran much longer than it should have. 'When he'd had a few,' said Banbury, 'Michael was capable of putting a quarter of an hour on the running time.'[31]

When Robert decided that Banbury was not having any noticeable effect on Redgrave's performance or behaviour, he persuaded the director to return to London, leaving Robert to direct the production in Leeds. But Robert found himself getting nowhere with Redgrave, so Banbury was recalled. 'I can't do anything,' Robert told Banbury. 'Every time I say, "Can we have a session? Can we go for a walk?" it's always, "I must lie down," always some excuse.'[32]

After the experience of staging *Flowering Cherry* in New York, Banbury was prepared for Robert's wilfulness. 'Right from the start, Bob told me he wanted Sam Avery to do the sets. He said, "Sam knows what I want, nothing too naturalistic." So poor Sam did it and he's never done anything again. It was bloody awful. The moment Bob saw it, he was awful to Sam and on the first night he cut him dead. Bob could be very ruthless.'[33]

Robert's main pleasure was to see Vanessa Redgrave visibly maturing as an actress as the tour progressed; here was a great performance and the arrival of a major new actress. While Redgrave was receptive to Banbury's direction, Robert's discreet coaching and general conversation inspired her to become involved in politics. '*The Tiger and the Horse*, and Robert Bolt himself, influenced me immensely,' she wrote. 'He attended all the rehearsals, never intervening in the direction of the play but talking seriously and deliberately about its ideas. He was a socialist. I started reading a newspaper every day again, where everything indicated an increasing threat of nuclear war.'[34]

At one point, though, Robert did intervene in the direction of the play and his ideas went a little too far. 'The play opened', said Banbury, 'with Vanessa standing on the stage, talking. Bob said to me, "She shouldn't just stand there. She should be like Rodin's *Thinker*." And he showed me what he meant. Of course, it was ridiculous but we did it one afternoon and it was quite appalling and Bob knew it. Had I been left on my own and not been niggled at, which Bob did all through that production, I could have done it to his satisfaction. As it was it had its faults, and Michael Redgrave fucked it up.'[35]

Somehow, the production arrived in London on time, opening on 24 August 1960. Redgrave himself, though, was not on time; he was still stretching the play by acting in slow motion. The floor staff at the Queen's Theatre, foreseeing trouble ahead, asked for and were given an allowance for taxi fares home, since by the time that Redgrave left the stage their last trains home would have left long before him.

The play gave the press much to write about: Robert was still the village schoolmaster hitting the big time, with two plays running simultaneously, and the theme of nuclear disarmament was highly topical; but most interesting to the press was the sight of Michael and Vanessa Redgrave on stage together. That, above all, was the play's trump card, the element which guaranteed its success with the public.

Bernard Levin was so besotted with Vanessa – he called her performance 'shiningly perfect' – that he went back to see the play again, just to marvel at her and write another panegyric with the promise of a separate article devoted to her. 'There is a kind of play that is known as a talk-all-nighter,' wrote Levin after his first viewing. 'If I get a wink of sleep between now and Saturday – the first opportunity I have to see Mr Robert Bolt's new play again – I shall be surprised. Mr Bolt's dialogue . . . is so astounding it gave me hiccups: it is deeper and finer than ordinary speech. In other words, it is poetry. . . . And now to talk all night. What a play! What a play!'[36]

While all the critics were united in their praise of Vanessa Redgrave, her father's performance received decidedly mixed reviews. Some found the play too wordy and strident in its arguments; others thought it a pale pastiche of Ibsen, too content to remain in its ivory tower. There was no debate this time with Kenneth Tynan, who was on holiday, nor did Robert benefit from the wisdom of Harold Hobson who was also away, though Hobson caught up with it later and hailed Robert's 'interest in intellectual matters, his capacity to combine Pascal with nuclear disarmament, his knowledge that the lawns of Cambridge are among the pleasantest things in life, but are not the whole of life, give *The Tiger and the Horse* a rare distinction'.[37]

With his two plays running next door to each other, Robert spent many evenings in Shaftesbury Avenue, hopping from one foyer to the other, listening to the comments of the audiences and monitoring the performances which led him to send the cast letters of encouragement and advice. If there was a competition between the plays, *The Tiger and the Horse* was winning in terms of box-office performance and Robert thought he knew why: it was the difference between having a knighted actor in the cast rather than a knighted character on the stage. '*The Tiger and the Horse* is doing very good business indeed, much better than *A Man For All Seasons*,' he told his parents. 'I don't complain of this but *A Man For All Seasons* is much the better play. A phenomenon which does alarm me is that the takings of *Man* fell off rapidly the week after *Tiger* opened. It looks as though if you're going to see a Bolt play, you go to see the later one next door with a Knight in the cast. That's all right provided they like it, as in that case they will sooner or later go to see the earlier one. But not everyone does like it, whereas everyone seems to like Sir Thomas.'[38]

Although the knighted actor was drawing the crowds, Robert was still worried about Redgrave's performance: 'I simply feel terribly glad that it's over and thankful that we have such a substantial measure of success, an outcome that seemed most improbable two months ago,' Robert told Banbury. 'I am unable to shake off an aftertaste of something shoddy and unlikable which has been swallowed and has not yet worked its way through the system. We are not yet out of the wood because if Michael returns to his Manchester style we shan't have much of a show. Between us, we must make pretty regular visits I fear, and must keep up a constant eye on running times.'[39]

By the close of 1960, Robert's plays were earning him nearly

£1000 a week. Journalists arrived at Park Gates to write profiles of him, while Robert in turn wrote long articles on nuclear disarmament and took part in public debates about the state of British drama. Although he was credited, along with Pinter, Osborne, Arden and Wesker, with revolutionising the British theatre – 'a man who's bringing the sixties to the boil,' as the *News Chronicle* had it[40] – he was something of an outsider. He would turn up with John Mortimer to debate at the Royal Court, both of them wearing grey suits and ties and find the 'home team' of Lindsay Anderson and Arnold Wesker in duffel coats and jerseys. 'It was the progressive theatre versus the West End, the committed versus the uncommitted, the lean artists versus the fleshy money-makers, the new versus the old,' reported Bamber Gascoigne. 'These distinctions soon crashed to the ground. It was noticeably the West End dramatists who talked about human beings and theatre, while the home team could hardly keep off box-office returns and subsidies. When the visitors had clearly won the day, the contest turned out to have been between the inarticulate and the articulate, the outdated and the undated.'[41]

With *A Man For All Seasons* and *The Tiger and the Horse* still running, Robert started preliminary work on another play. He had spent much of the autumn talking and thinking, enjoying the riches that had come his way, and analysing his success and its effect on his life. He told his parents:

Jo and I exist in a kind of fatigued dream. We sometimes remember ruefully how peaceful we thought a writer's life would be, and how peaceful a schoolmaster's life by comparison was. If one did the requisite norm of work with reasonable efficiency, conscience was satisfied and one's time was really one's own. But now it seems that I owe every waking (and some sleeping) hour to my work; even my leisure is regarded as a necessary preparation for more work. But it's an exciting way to live and full of privileges and we wouldn't change it, and after what they've seen it's doubtful if our children will have any romantic illusions about it. Perhaps they'll settle down to earn their livings in some sensible manner, quite as if they already knew their tables, which alas they don't.[42]

No one, least of all Robert, would have guessed that the opening night of *The Tiger and the Horse* brought to a close his glory days as a playwright. Although there would be four further plays, stretched over seventeen years, he had in some ways outgrown the medium.

The Tiger and the Horse, especially, shows all the virtues and all the drawbacks of the stage; it seems too contrived, too schematic, too claustrophobic. Scenes take place on sets – irredeemably phoney ones – that should be set somewhere else but cannot be because of technical considerations. Because of this, the most important scene in the play – Gwendoline's destruction of the Holbein – happens off stage, a weakness from which the play never recovers.

For a while it seemed there might be a film version, produced by the team of Muriel and Sydney Box. The prospect of a film thrilled Robert, for it was the answer to his concern with naturalism. In the cinema anything was possible: we could see Gwendoline's garden, we could see her slash at the Holbein: 'Bob specially likes the idea of *using* a university town and breaking up the whole play,' wrote Margaret Ramsay to Banbury.[43] Perhaps we can be grateful that Muriel Box never filmed *The Tiger and the Horse* for in her hands it would have surely been that most dreaded of things, the filmed play. What Robert needed was someone who was a born movie-maker, someone who could combine the essence of the theatre – as a medium of ideas and acting – with that of the cinema, a medium in which ideas are expressed as action. And he soon found exactly what he was looking for.

TWELVE

MAD DOGS AND ENGLISHMEN

'I know you've been well educated, Lawrence. It says so in your dossier.'

Lord Allenby in *Lawrence of Arabia*

Until 1960 Robert regarded the cinema as little more than a diversion, a night out and, with luck, an amusing one. Much to his friend Mike Kellaway's dismay, Robert was as deeply suspicious of the arty waves breaking across European cinema – Bergman, Godard, Antonioni and so on – as he was about experimental theatre in Britain. As far as movies were concerned, he preferred traditional entertainment pictures from Britain and Hollywood. In 1972, having just completed his first film as a director, Robert was asked if he thought the cinema was an inferior art to the theatre. He told an audience of movie buffs in London:

> To my shame I did. There is a kind of sloppy and unthought feeling in theatre that film is a lesser medium, less artistic. It's not quite so silly as it sounds because for a play to succeed it's got to be fairly good. There's only the dialogue to listen to and the acting. Plays flop much more frequently than films. People went to the cinema more or less automatically because it's effortless, the thing is so vivid, like a daydream with things put into your mind. You have so little to do. The verisimilitude is so total, the things they can show you are so exciting. I think everybody has had the experience of thinking quite happily, 'this is rubbish'. You cannot sit through a three-act play thinking this is rubbish, happily. They won't boo in the cinema. They will in the theatre.[1]

When his first plays were enjoying success in London and earning him more money than he ever believed possible, Robert gave scarcely any thought to becoming a screenwriter. He knew, though, that a film version of *A Man For All Seasons* was a vague possibility, if only because popular and critically acclaimed plays, like novels, tended to be snapped up by film-makers. He also knew that few film directors had the talent or inclination to originate stories of their own. Because of this, and in order to earn their high fees, screenwriters needed to be as thick skinned as a rhinoceros.

Horror stories about serious writers who had been destroyed by Hollywood were legion – William Faulkner, F. Scott Fitzgerald, Raymond Chandler and others were little more than highly paid serfs, enslaved to directors, producers and studios as well as the bottle into which they poured their compromises. In Britain, only Noël Coward and Terence Rattigan seemed to commute between the stage and the screen without getting hurt too much.

Rattigan, though, had recently had a bruising experience: his play about Lawrence of Arabia, *Ross*, began in 1952 as a screenplay for David Lean. After Lean withdrew from the project Rattigan joined forces with director Anthony Asquith and planned a film to star Richard Burton, which was cancelled because of the Suez Crisis. Three years later Rattigan and Asquith revived the idea and cast Dirk Bogarde as Lawrence but this, too, was cancelled just weeks before it was due to start shooting in Iraq. Giving up the idea of a film about Lawrence, Rattigan converted his screenplay into a play. In 1960, when the play was about to open, Rattigan learned that Lawrence's brother and literary executor, Professor A. W. Lawrence, was threatening a lawsuit, claiming an infringement of the copyright to *Seven Pillars of Wisdom*. Not only was the Professor distressed by Rattigan's script, which implied that his brother was a homosexual, he was also in league with the film producer Sam Spiegel, who was also planning a film about Lawrence with David Lean. But *Ross* went ahead with Alec Guinness and it proved to be a huge success.

Rattigan's vicissitudes, which were well documented in the press, would not have escaped Robert's attention. And when he looked at the 'Angry Brigade' at the Royal Court, their experience of the cinema was not an encouraging sight. After having directed the stage production of Osborne's *Look Back in Anger*, Tony Richardson was able to secure finance for a film version only after Richard Burton agreed to play Jimmy Porter for a fee of around £30,000, far less than he could command in Hollywood. A 'professional' screenwriter, Nigel Kneale, was brought in to write the screenplay when

Osborne – who, like Richardson, was only being paid expenses – said he was too weary to bother. The film cost £220,000, received some excellent reviews and was a box-office flop.

The film version of Osborne's *The Entertainer* fared no better. Nigel Kneale was again brought in to write the script, Osborne contributing less to the dialogue than to the debate about how the play might be opened up. As with *Look Back in Anger*, Tony Richardson was anxious to avoid shooting in a studio and wanted to film on real locations, thereby placing a stylised play – and a stylised performance by Laurence Olivier, who did the film for next to nothing – within a realistic context. The result was a botched job, with technical problems delaying its release until July 1960, when it flopped just as spectacularly as *Look Back in Anger*.

For a relatively new playwright like Robert, seeing Osborne's glittering career in the theatre rewritten for the cinema would have sounded resounding notes of caution. There were other examples at hand: Shelagh Delaney's *A Taste of Honey* was filmed by Richardson for £120,000; Pinter's *The Caretaker* was privately funded and filmed for £30,000; Arnold Wesker's *The Kitchen* was filmed for rather less than £20,000 and funded by the film technicians' union, the ACTT, of which Robert would later become President. No one seemed to be making any money.

Robert had already received a few offers from film producers. He told his parents:

> I've had two offers to write films. One from the great Walter Wanger of 20th Century-Fox who offers me about £10,000 for writing a film of Camus's *The Fall*. It's a book I admire, but I don't at all see how it could be filmed. Nor I think does Wanger. He's a liberal minded tycoon who expects a high style of thinking from himself but hasn't I suspect any real passion for a high style of thought. The money is enormous but I don't think I'll do it; the set-up looks very plushy and extravagant, and everyone tells me that these big film corporations regard their writers as their property body and soul when once they have them under contract.
>
> The other, which I find rather more attractive, is from a new, much smaller Company, also American but working in this country; much younger men, a much less streamlined style. They want to do a very small, quiet, black-and-white film of the arrest and trial of Christ. What attracts me is that they seem willing to let me have artistic control (or some of it); that it's an

idea I have sometimes considered myself, and above all that it would be started at once as they want to forstall three huge epics which are to be made on the subject this coming year. I dare say I'll go along with it – provided they pay well.[2]

The film about the trial of Christ, which Robert could surely have turned into a gripping political thriller, never happened and his brief skirmish with the film industry seemed to be over. He settled down in his Richmond study and started work on what eventually became *Gentle Jack*, a largely experimental and symbolic work which took him from the world of naturalism into fantasy.

As he started work on the play, an offer arrived which would utterly transform his life: Sam Spiegel asked him to work on the screenplay of *Lawrence of Arabia*, though at the time the film was called *Seven Pillars of Wisdom*, after Lawrence's own literary epic. Spiegel had a serious problem. An enormous film crew was assembled in Jordan and everything was ready to go but David Lean was unhappy with the screenplay that had been written by an American, Michael Wilson, who had resigned after a year's work. Lean would not shoot a foot of film until the script was modified to his satisfaction. Spiegel wanted someone to apply a quick polish, some minor structural surgery and some rewriting of dialogue. He was willing to pay for seven weeks' work – 'a week, one assumes, for each pillar,' joked the *Guardian*. In any case, that was when they had to start shooting.

Robert sat in Spiegel's office smoking cigars and drinking malt whisky from a bottle which, the label said, had been 'Specially Bottled in the Highlands of Scotland for Mr Sam Spiegel'. Robert protested to Spiegel that he was a serious playwright and not a Hollywood rewrite man. Spiegel then mentioned a fee – £7000 – and Robert left Spiegel's office with Wilson's bulky script under his arm. He began to read it on the Tube home to Richmond. 'I couldn't understand what was being said or what they were trying to say. I got home and rang Sam and said I couldn't understand the script and couldn't therefore rewrite the dialogue. So then Sam said start from scratch. At the end of my seven weeks David was called in and both he and Sam were very pleased. Sam said they would now find another writer and carry on.'[3]

Lean was so impressed by Robert's dialogue he insisted he be hired to rewrite the entire screenplay and be flown out to Jordan as soon as possible. It was a defining moment in Robert's career: he had walked unwittingly into a whirlpool of love, hate and clashing egos.

Robert on the balcony of his apartment in Tahiti in 1978.

The cottages at Butleigh, near Millfield School, where Robert's first plays were written.

Robert with Jo and young Sally, c.1952. (*Courtesy Dora Wigg*).

Staff and pupils at Millfield, 1955. Second row (seated) are Boss Meyer (second from left), Robert (fourth from right) and his friend L.E.W Smith (eighth from right). (*Courtesy Millfield Society*).

Robert's first wife, Jo, with baby Sally, photographed in Devon, c1950. (*Courtesy Dora Wigg*).

On the Great Wall of China in 1966:
Hugh Trevor-Roper, Robert, Mary Adams and Ernie Roberts.

Opposite page: Robert and Sarah, a 60s couple,
pose in the garden of Mill House, Byfleet.

ROBERT BOLT—a rustic idyll has been shattered.

The cartoonist Keith Mackenzie captures the rags to riches success of the new playwright. (*Courtesy Evening Standard*).

Robert and David Lean fly in a DeHavilland Dove to one of the remote desert locations for *Lawrence of Arabia*. (*Courtesy Kevin Brownlow*).

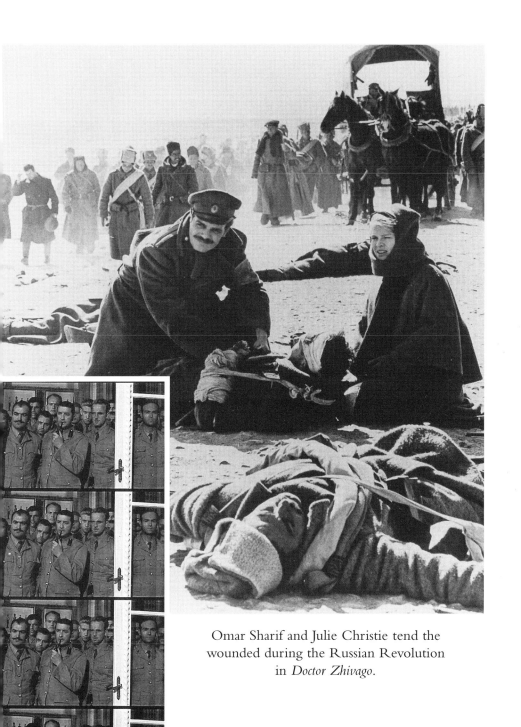

Omar Sharif and Julie Christie tend the wounded during the Russian Revolution in *Doctor Zhivago*.

Robert, with pipe, makes a brief appearance as a British officer in *Lawrence of Arabia*.

Robert Shaw as Henry
VIII and Paul Scofield
as Sir Thomas More
in the film version of
A Man For All Seasons.

Robert confers with
Fred Zinnemann on
the set of *A Man For
All Seasons*.

And not only that, by working for Lean and Spiegel he was to be introduced to a world of unlimited wealth and resources. But whatever Robert wrote, for the first time in his life he was writing to order. If Lean or Spiegel did not like it he would have to rewrite it and rewrite it again or it would not be shot. Robert learned quickly that in a myriad ways a playwright's life is very different from that of a screenwriter. He had a choice to make: *Gentle Jack*, which he loved, or *Lawrence of Arabia* which paid well. For Robert's friends and colleagues, this was a critical decision. 'I have to tell you,' said Frith Banbury, 'Bob Bolt was a terrible disappointment to me. I thought he was going to be a really important dramatist but he preferred Sam Spiegel's yacht.'[4]

Sam Spiegel and David Lean made for a brilliant if unlikely partnership. Lean was handsome, shy and meticulous, embarrassed and haunted by his drab Quaker upbringing in suburban Croydon. Spiegel, an ugly barrel of a man, was highly cultured and used his money to collect art, antiques and young women.

Like Robert, Lean was a dunce at school; unlike Robert, this was not a matter of childhood rebellion but a genuine resistance to academic disciplines. As a result, Lean was never less than insecure and had a lifelong suspicion of 'intellectuals'. By the time that Robert began working on *Lawrence*, Lean's reputation among the intelligentsia was at an all-time low. *Kwai* was disliked by the serious critics and Lean was thought to have sold out to Hollywood and become a cold technician with no discernible personal style. By deciding to work with Lean Robert earned no kudos at all, only envy at the money he was making.

Like Robert, Lean had wasted a year in an office before he got a job in the late Twenties as a general dogsbody at a film studio. He worked his way up the ladder, becoming Britain's most talented and highest paid editor, before Noël Coward offered him the chance to direct *In Which We Serve*. After three collaborations with Coward, including the classic *Brief Encounter*, Lean's reputation soared when he made his two adaptations of Charles Dickens: *Great Expectations* and *Oliver Twist*.

In 1947 Lean was married for the third time, to the English actress Ann Todd, though the three films he made with her were widely regarded as failures. He separated from Todd and began a more nomadic existence, refusing to live in England because he felt humiliated by the failure of his marriage to Todd and because he refused to pay tax. He had a Rolls-Royce, a suitcase and a son, Peter, whom he ignored. When Peter went on holiday to Venice with his girlfriend, he had no idea that the film crew in St Mark's Square was headed by his own father who was making *Summertime* with Katharine Hepburn. It was after *Summertime* that Sam Spiegel offered Lean *The Bridge on the River Kwai* and the rest, as they say, is history.

Sam Spiegel was born in 1901 in Galicia, Poland, which was then part of the Austro-Hungarian Empire. His early life is shrouded in mystery – he somehow managed to escape the pogroms, settled in Palestine after World War One and arrived in Hollywood in 1927. Through sheer chutzpah, he was hired by Universal Pictures, a haven for Jewish émigrés, and was promptly sent to Berlin as the studio's general manager. When the Nazis came to power in 1933 Spiegel fled to London, where his attempts to become a film producer earned him a short term in prison for financial misdemeanours. On his release he went to Mexico and entered the United States under an alias, S. P. Eagle. Within five years he was a minor producer at 20th Century-Fox.

Despite the fact that many people in Hollywood treated with derision the man called Eagle, Spiegel managed to ingratiate himself with Harry Cohn, the legendary boss of Columbia Pictures. When Spiegel went into partnership with John Huston, Columbia gave them virtual carte blanche. After a few commercial failures they struck gold in 1951 with *The African Queen*, starring Humphrey Bogart and Katharine Hepburn. When Spiegel joined forces with Elia Kazan for *On the Waterfront* in 1954, Spiegel sensed an artistic and commercial triumph and dropped his alias. People no longer laughed at him. *The African Queen* and *On the Waterfront*, for which he won an Oscar, made him rich and famous; his independence was something to admire and envy. He decided to base himself in London and promptly hijacked a project called *The Bridge on the River Kwai* which Alexander Korda had turned down. This, then, was the man with whom Robert had signed a contract, a man as far from Binkie Beaumont as it is possible to imagine, though both possessed a high degree of charm.

Spiegel's great gift as a producer was bringing together various talents – the best actors, directors, cameramen – but he regarded the writer with some scorn. He genuinely believed that Robert could work for seven weeks and then happily hand over to another writer. *Kwai* had been written like this and because two of the writers, Carl Foreman and Michael Wilson, were blacklisted by the McCarthy witch-hunts – and therefore cheap and disposable – Spiegel blithely gave sole screen credit to Pierre Boulle, author of the novel on which the film was based. Boulle then won an Oscar for a screenplay which contained not a single word he could call his own. It is doubtful if Robert knew of this at the time, though his experience on *Lawrence* would end with a bitter dispute over screen credit.

When Robert was offered *Lawrence of Arabia*, he was spending a lot of time at Stratford where Peter Hall had recently been appointed Director of the Royal Shakespeare Company. 'I was always trying to get Bob to write a play for us,' said Hall. 'I wanted him to write two plays about the English Civil War which would have been an ace subject for him. He was such a wordsmith, a dramatic architect. He was intrigued and messed about with the idea but he spent a colossal amount of time on those films.'[5]

At this time, Hall was married to Leslie Caron and for some years they were close friends with Robert and Jo, even to the extent of each couple becoming executor for the other's will and guardians of each other's children should either couple perish in a car or plane crash. Like most people, Hall was impressed by Robert's charm and his knowledge. He also felt a kinship in that both of them had a similar background. According to Hall:

We were both Richard Hoggart boys, scholarship boys who'd had a state education and believed in the welfare state. We were postwar socialists. One of the problems of the Richard Hoggart boys is that they are very surprised to find they've made it, surprised they've got a Rolls-Royce, surprised they are invited to Buckingham Palace and worried lest they be found out.

In my experience, most artists are deeply insecure and always feel they are about to be found out. They feel that their success, such as it is, is a matter of luck. Then you meet a few people who have a complete certainty that they are who they are. I would instance Benjamin Britten, Michael Tippett, Harrison Birtwistle, Harold Pinter and Samuel Beckett. None of those people, even if they'd had no success at all, would have stopped writing. They'd have just gone on doing it. That kind of possessed confidence is quite rare and is almost a definition of genius. Bob didn't have it.

What's interesting about Bob is not so much what he wrote but that he was a product of the times. He was a working class boy who made good and was destroyed by market forces. He loved money, much more than I did. I mean, he really loved it. It was a measure of his status.[6]

Robert's friendship with Peter Hall was put under some strain by *Lawrence of Arabia* and it was all due to Peter O'Toole, whom Robert already knew well and had tried to persuade to play Louis in *The Tiger and the Horse*. But O'Toole turned Robert down because of his commitment to Peter Hall. Lean and Spiegel had first thought of Marlon Brando as Lawrence but when Brando opted instead for *Mutiny on the Bounty* Albert Finney was offered the part and, much to Lean and Spiegel's dismay, he turned them down, explaining that he did not want to become a movie star. After Lean saw O'Toole on stage at Stratford, he gave him a brief screen test and hired him on the spot. The problem was O'Toole was drawing rave notices as Shylock at Stratford and Hall was depending on him to launch the RSC's forthcoming season in London. Although O'Toole had already scored a notable success in London in the stage production of *The Long and the Short and the Tall*, in which he had replaced Albert Finney, it was his performances at Stratford, playing opposite Peggy Ashcroft, that fully established him as one of the leading actors of his generation.

'The *Lawrence of Arabia* time was terribly difficult for us,' said Hall, 'because O'Toole was under contract to the RSC. When Sam Spiegel said to him, "Walk and let them sue you," he walked. We didn't have the resources to sue him so he nearly wrecked the start of the RSC. Peter was one of the staunchest people to commit to the Company and suddenly he was gone. Peggy Ashcroft was absolutely furious because she was Dame Integrity. Bob was spending a lot of time at Stratford and he was caught in the middle of all that and very distressed by it. We remained friends, though it was acrimonious at times.'[7]

At home in Richmond, Robert faced the prospect of rewriting a film which was planned to run for more than three hours. He began by reading *Seven Pillars of Wisdom*, a book he had taught at Millfield and which the previous screenwriter, Michael Wilson, had initially been unable to use as the screen rights were controlled by Lawrence's younger brother, the shy academic Professor Arnold Lawrence. This was a major hurdle for Spiegel, who wanted to call the film *Seven Pillars of Wisdom*, or at the very least claim it was based on Lawrence's book.

Wilson's early draft derived from *With Lawrence in Arabia*, a pot boiler about Lawrence's exploits by the American journalist and documentarist Lowell Thomas. Wilson began work with a considerable handicap: he was writing a screenplay about a historical personage without reference to that person's first hand account of events. Wilson had grappled with this dilemma in a memo entitled, 'Problems of Infringement. Example: The incident in the Damascus Hospital when a British medical officer slaps Lawrence's face. Lawrence is the sole original source, because he and the major were the only witnesses to what happened. Lowell Thomas does not report this at all. The Problem: Are we denied the use of this significant scene because it does not appear in Thomas's book? Can we use the incident, even without the rights to *Seven Pillars*? If we cannot use the actual incident at all, can we invent an incident related to it?'[8]

Fortunately, Professor Lawrence was so impressed by Wilson's treatment that he relented and sold Spiegel the screen rights to *Seven Pillars* for £22,500. Spiegel had a bargain and knew it, though the Professor shrewdly retained ownership of the title, *Seven Pillars of Wisdom*: if he disapproved of the finished film he could prevent Spiegel from using the title on condition that £5000 of the fee was forfeited. Wilson's initial inability to use *Seven Pillars* was the cause of many of his screenplay's problems – his reliance on the Thomas book had established an approach to the story which was hard to shake off. Nevertheless, the narrative structure which Wilson devised, its clever blend of fact and fiction and its smooth tele-scoping of characters and of history, was to remain in the finished film.

Wilson had been paid $200,000 – about £72,000 – for his screenplay. After Robert's seven weeks were up he was offered a new twenty-week contract worth £15,000, to be paid in weekly instal-ments. Clause 2(B) of the contract stated, 'If the company requests it and the Writer agrees (which he shall not be under any legal liability to do) the Writer shall render further services after the said period without any further payment.'[9] In the end, Robert would work for more than a year on *Lawrence*, about the same length of time as Wilson.

When Spiegel first hired Robert to work on the screenplay David Lean, who was in Jordan, was kept in the dark. As far as Lean was concerned, Spiegel had already replaced Wilson with two other writers. One was David Garnett, who had edited a collection of T. E. Lawrence's letters, and the other was the playwright Beverley Cross, who had been sent out to Jordan and spent most of his time playing nursemaid to Peter O'Toole who was learning to ride a camel and was soothing his sores in the fleshpots of Beirut. Lean's ignorance of the real position, as well as his sense of frustration and isolation, can be judged from his letter to Spiegel which persistently misspells Robert's name:

> Do you realise what a dreadfully frustrating situation I am in out here? You left over two weeks ago, Mike has walked off the picture in circumstances partially beyond my comprehension, the script is nowhere near right and I sit here with the physical preparations going ahead with little or no information about what is happening on the rewrite.
>
> I have never been kept so far away from a script, and now it's happening all over again with Boult. You know as well as I do that no top-rank director will work in this way. As far as Boult is concerned he is taking his briefing from you direct, and you know as well as I do that the first briefing sets the stage and style more than anything else. Once he starts thinking along those lines it will be very hard to get him off them . . .
>
> The method of the past God knows how many months has ended us up with a near disaster script. There's barely a scrap of my particular style, bloom, call-it-what-you-will in the three hundred pages, and again work is being started without my having said a word to the men concerned. I not only feel miles away out in the cold, but the whole film is gradually drifting away from me. It's a very dangerous situation as I'm not Mike Curtiz who can take over a script Saturday and start shooting Monday. For both our good I've got to get back into the swim of it and have got to talk to Boult by myself.
>
> I hope you realise how *very* far off we are. The character of Lawrence which was what fascinated us in the first place hardly peeps through at all – and I don't think it ever can with the present way of telling the story. I've been doing some very hard thinking and see a glint of light in the distance, but oh God do I need help. . . For the love of God bring Boult out here quick.[10]

In late March 1961, more than two months after Lean wrote this letter, Robert finally flew to the Jordanian capital, Amman, and then by private plane to Aqaba, the old garrison town which Lawrence had captured from the Turks in 1917.

On the beach, the film crew had set up a busy bar and a restaurant where the unit's caterer, Phil Hobbs, served roast beef and Yorkshire pud and apple pie smothered with thick, smooth custard. There was beer and whisky, table tennis and a 16mm movie presentation two evenings a week. It was just like home, except there was a sort of madness in the air, an element of 'Mad Dogs and Englishmen', which for Robert was summed up by the sight of David Lean tooling around the desert in his Rolls-Royce. Lean justified the expense of shipping the Rolls because it had air conditioning. Lean's civilian army lived like soldiers in two rows of Nissen huts. But Robert, who might have felt perfectly at ease in a Nissen hut, was allotted a stateroom aboard Spiegel's yacht, the *Mulahne*, which was anchored in the bay. No sooner was Robert aboard than Spiegel worried that the rocking of the yacht might disturb his concentration. But Robert, who loved boats and was never seasick, insisted that it wouldn't. Spiegel, though, was looking for a way to install stabilisers at some-one else's expense. He dismissed Robert's seaworthiness, had the stabilisers installed and charged it to the production.

Spiegel himself hardly ever visited the location – as a Jew, he was terrified of spending time in an Arab state. Because Lean was living in a caravan in the desert, and Peter O'Toole was going through a self-immolation phase, living as rough as Lawrence had done, Robert often had the yacht to himself. He could write and, whenever he liked, he could slip over the side and swim in the warm waters of the gulf. Spiegel's chefs and butlers were there to serve him French food and fine wines, and attend to his well-being.

As he set to work, Robert could hardly have known that many of the people there would become a sort of second family. Apart from Lean, there was the production designer John Box, a quizzical man of unusual talent and a military bearing; Freddie Young, the veteran director of photography, who would contribute so much to *Lawrence of Arabia*; the prop man and Lean's friend, Eddie Fowlie; and Barbara Cole, the continuity girl who, shortly after filming began, became Lean's lover. And there was Peter O'Toole, drunk most evenings and laughing with Robert over their good fortune.

The holiday mood continued when Jo visited Akaba. They swam in the sea, drank with O'Toole and toured the ancient Nabatean ruins of Petra, where Lean had decided to stage a battle between Lawrence's Arab army and the Turks. But as the start of shooting drew closer Robert's work intensified. For two or three days a week, Lean would closet himself with Robert and Barbara Cole, going over the script line by line. When he listened to Robert reading the scenes aloud Lean realised what a good actor and mimic he was and asked him to make a tape recording of the entire script. While Lean, Peter O'Toole and Omar Sharif would make frequent use of it, seasoned actors like Alec Guinness never went near it.

Robert and Lean established a way of working, a way of discover-ing each other. It was tricky at first, due to Lean's insecurity with anyone with a university degree. But just as Robert always felt intimidated by the intellect of his brother Sydney, Lean had a similar relationship with his brother Edward, who was a brilliant linguist and head of the BBC's European Service. Lean also found Robert's attitudes to the cinema quite similar to Edward's and deeply suspect: 'I was absolutely terrified of him,' he said. 'He reminded me of my brother who used to say, "David, you really just cannot do that sort of thing, but I suppose you can in the movies." Robert had this sort of thing you know, every now and then. He was very superior in those days.'[11]

For his part, Robert seemed intimidated by Lean and was reluctant to suggest anything too extreme. He still felt that the cinema was less suited to overstatement and innovation than the theatre. 'There's a scene', said Robert, 'where Lawrence has just executed Gasim and he's talking to Allenby, saying how guilty he feels and then mentions, "there's something else." "What is something else, Robert?" asked David. "Well," I said, "he sort of enjoyed it." David's script went up into the air. "For heaven's sake, why don't you put it in?" '[12]

If Lean was trying to shape the film into an adventure story, with a charismatic if enigmatic hero at its centre, the Rt Hon. Anthony Nutting was endeavouring to keep the film as close to historical fact as possible. Nutting had been hired by Spiegel as the film's 'Oriental Counsellor'. A landowning British diplomat who had resigned from his post at the Foreign Office over the 1956 Suez crisis, Nutting had a peerless reputation in the Middle East and successfully negotiated with King Hussein over the use of Jordan as the main location. Although Lean was initially suspicious of this Establishment gentleman, Nutting's charm, his knowledge and his enthusiasm for the project quickly won him over. At a dinner Lean asked Nutting what he liked about the desert and Nutting replied, 'It's clean,' a line that quickly found its way into Robert's screenplay. Later on, when Nutting visited the location and saw Lean covered in sand and behaving like a schoolboy he thought, 'Oh God, here's another Englishman going potty in this bloody desert.'[13]

Some of the ideas in the screenplay began to bother Nutting, especially the sequence in which Sherif Ali emerges from a mirage to shoot Lawrence's guide, Tafas, dead. Nutting knew that this sequence of events, already present in Michael Wilson's script, could never have happened in real life and might upset Arab sensibilities. 'I don't know why Omar agreed to do that,' said Nutting. 'An Arab would never shoot another Arab at a well. I realised that Bolt and

Lean wanted to get rid of the character of Tafas and I tried to persuade them to do it another way. But the scene stayed and it makes me sad to see it.'[14]

One of Robert's improvements to the Wilson script had been the introduction of the desert. Lean had told him that the audience's first sight of it must make an unusual impact, an unforgettable image of sunlight and sand. Although it would have been easy just to have cut simply to the desert, Robert came up with a brilliant idea, not only intensely cinematic but also richly symbolic:

> I invented a little trick he did with matches, which is ostentatious, which is masochistic but which takes a little courage. But it's finally a party trick. In the scene with Dryden, the civilised evil genius who exploits Lawrence's neuroses and feels rather guilty about doing so, Lawrence says it's going to be fun, the campaign in the desert. Dryden says no, only two kinds of people get fun from the desert, Bedouins and Gods, and you're neither. And of course the whole story of Lawrence is a man trying to find an identity for himself – Aircraftsman Shaw, Sheik this, Colonel Lawrence of the secret service. Lawrence strikes a match and is about to do his trick. He says, no Dryden, it is going to be fun. Dryden says, it is recognised you have a funny sense of fun. Lawrence then blows out the match and we cut from that to the rising sun, which was supposed to look like a great big flame he couldn't blow out. It was a little thematic message.[15]

Along with the mirage, this is the most famous scene in the film. Not only was Lean happy to take all the credit for it – later on, Robert never lost an opportunity to remind him whose idea it was – he never realised its full potential. After viewing the rushes in London, Robert and Spiegel ordered a retake. Even after shooting it again, Lean still messed it up: 'I should have gone much further,' he said. 'I should have arranged Peter in such a position that he had a bloody great sun-god plaque right behind his close-up, so that when he stood on top of the train, the sun behind him, the audience would subconsciously connect it with the "warning" in the office. I should have had Claude speak the lines with due appreciation for his intuition that this sort of danger existed for this young man. I think it would have been most effective and would have sounded a drumbeat of things to come. Over the top. You're always terrified of going over the top.'[16]

On 15 May 1961, almost two months after Robert arrived in

Jordan, shooting began at Jebel Tubeiq on the border with Saudi Arabia, an area of ochre dunes and black basalt rocks and pinnacles. To begin with it was just two men on camels – Peter O'Toole and Zia Moyeddhin, who was playing Lawrence's guide, Tafas. For Moyeddhin's first line of dialogue – 'Here you may drink. One cup' – Lean demanded take after take and then abandoned it. Moyheddin said later it was a form of sadism.

If Moyheddin had a bad time, the French actor Maurice Ronet had a nightmare. After a German actor, Horst Buchholz, and a French actor, Alain Delon, had proved unavailable, Ronet had been hired to play Sherif Ali. To get his work permit from the British government all manner of cartwheels had been performed. But as soon as Ronet arrived in Jordan Lean knew he was wrong for the part and that his French accent could only be disguised by dubbing his voice with that of another actor. Ronet also refused to wear contact lenses to disguise his bright blue eyes. So a dirty trick was done to Ronet: Spiegel and Lean had discovered a likely Egyptian actor, Omar Sharif, and had him flown from Cairo to Jordan. Sharif was put into a costume and asked to take a test alongside Ronet. Ronet believed that Sharif was testing for another role; in fact, Lean just wanted to compare the two actors side by side. After the phoney test Ronet was sent back to Paris and only when the carpets he had bought in Jordan arrived a week later – together with a bill for the freight charges – did Ronet realise he had been fired. Ronet received $50,000 for not playing the role, while Sharif received $20,000 for playing it and later had to pay his own fare to attend the première in London.

While Lean's ruthlessness might have come as a shock to Robert, an even greater shock was to see the colossal amount of money, time and effort spent on making a major picture on location. Only three years earlier, Robert had agonised over a cyclorama of cherry blossom on a stage. Now he was watching Lean issuing orders to alter the topography of the Jordanian desert: 'David, looking like a far-flung character from out of his July days in the better-off provinces – everybody else was in bush shirts – collected me in his aeroplane. After half an hour's flight I was in Wadi Rumm. I never saw David, then or elsewhere, cease to be full of romance for a place once he had chosen it. "Look," he would say, "Auda's heavy cavalry can come out of here at the gallop, full pelt!" I objected, pointing out the cliff-high boulders scattered there. "Blow them out of the way!" David replied, "I think it would be terrific." '[17]

Lean was a general commanding a vast army in a battle against the elements and against time. There was a technical crew of about a hundred people and to achieve even a straightforward tracking shot of two men on camels required many days' work – the track had to be laid perfectly level on the undulating desert floor; no trace of foot or hoof prints was allowed to be seen within the range of a wide-screen lens; the light would have to match the previous shot and the camels would have to hit their marks. The huge 65mm cameras and the sound equipment had to be protected from the sand, the film kept within certain levels of humidity, and sandstorms could blow up without a moment's notice. All this in searingly hot temperatures with a crew requiring tea- and lunch-breaks, toilet facilities and fresh water, which had to be bowsered in on trucks from 300 miles away.

Lean was also fighting another, internal battle, against his own nerves and lack of confidence, and against Sam Spiegel, whom he had cast in the role of stage villain. Lean was convinced that Spiegel planned to swindle him out of his money and that there was a conspiracy to close the film down and shoot it elsewhere, where Spiegel's Jewishness would not be an issue. Robert's departure only added to Lean's worries for he knew that, in London, Robert would have direct contact with Spiegel. Perhaps an even greater worry for Lean was the sight of his writer disappearing when only half the script had been written.

On his return to London Robert gave a brief interview to 'Atticus' on the *Sunday Times*, who quoted him as saying that movie-making was 'A continuous clash of egomaniacal monsters, wasting more energy than the dinosaurs and pouring rivers of money into the sand.'[18] This did not go down well with Spiegel, who worried that Columbia might take Robert's comments literally and attempt to exercise tighter control on the production. Realising he had made a blunder which might jeopardise his future film career, Robert was compelled to publish a denial: 'The status of the makers of *Lawrence of Arabia* is secure by reason of their known achievements,' he wrote. 'They need no defence but are owed an apology. The conspicuous waste and hectic atmosphere of film-making afford an easy theme to would-be wits, myself among them. But Atticus misrepresents me. I was the more distressed because, as I told him, I have myself been treated with every kind of generosity . . .'[19]

In London, Robert was working on the second half of the screenplay, as well as attending screenings of the rushes from Jordan. With him at these screenings were Spiegel and the film's editor, Anne Coates. This procedure only made Lean feel more isolated, a fact which Spiegel exploited by sending Lean regular cables which criticised the footage and urged him to get a move on. And rather than deal with Lean over the screenplay, Robert's pages were being scrutinised by Spiegel. It was not the best way of working.

Frith Banbury, who had not heard from Robert in months, wrote to ask why he had taken on this film. Robert seemed to be wondering the same thing:

> Nice to hear from you. You say it would be interesting to hear exactly why I am doing this film. It would be nice to know. As you know, I suddenly received a number of offers from the film people. Peggy thought I should do one, if I could find an idea I liked, partly to see if it was congenial, partly as an insurance policy in case of financial lean periods in the theatre. Spiegel asked me to do seven weeks' work on *Seven Pillars*. I did; got interested, undertook to complete it and am still at it. I live in a state of mingled fury and excitement. The first rushes of film seem very beautiful. Nevertheless I wish I had never embarked on it. I don't expect I'll have another play ready by this time next year.[20]

By September, Lean was running out of scenes to shoot. Robert had still to complete the second half of the script and Lean had had no opportunity to discuss it with him. Since a good portion of the second half of the film was to take place in the British Army's bases in Cairo and Jerusalem there was no way – beyond building vast sets – that they could be filmed in Jordan.

Spiegel was getting increasingly restless. With Robert and Anne Coates, he sat in London viewing hours of material which seemed to consist solely of men riding camels across the desert. Robert's comments to the *Sunday Times* seemed to be entirely accurate when Spiegel watched the screen. Millions of dollars were being poured into the production and into an Arab country. Finally, in September 1961, after four months' shooting, Spiegel ordered the film to shut down. Lean was furious, especially since leaving Jordan would prevent him filming in Petra. The decision was made to move the production to Spain. But before that Lean could view his footage in London, then travel to Madrid to resume work on the script with Robert.

There was only one problem. Robert was in prison.

THIRTEEN

THE DRAKE HALL ONE

'Every man is encompassed by a cloud of comforting convictions, which move with him like flies on a summer day.'

Bertrand Russell

Robert and Jo were active supporters of the Campaign for Nuclear Disarmament. From its birth within the religious and cultural élite, CND had grown into a mass movement which organised demonstrations outside military bases which housed nuclear weapons. To begin with CND's annual Easter march went from London to the base at Aldermaston, where the demonstration fizzled out in a field. It took a few years before the leaders realised they were marching in the wrong direction. Once they were properly organised, the movement grew to a size that had not been seen in Britain since the suffragettes.

'Still at the head of the movement', wrote Christopher Booker, 'were the old faithfuls, Canon Collins, the Rev. Donald Soper, Bertrand Russell, Michael Foot, Mervyn Stockwood. But behind them were not only the leavening of earnest idealists, but also a strange and growing assortment of adolescents, beatniks, students and ravers, many of whom were confessedly stringing along with the CND "just for a giggle" and because it was becoming a teenage craze to wear the badge and "belong." '[1]

In early 1961, CND's leader, Canon Collins, faced a breach in solidarity when Bertrand Russell formed a more militant breakaway group called the Committee of 100. Robert, one of the Committee's founder members, said:

I am absolutely opposed to the possession and making of atomic weapons. People say, 'Well, you don't object to little bombs, why do you object to big bombs?' This is logical but it isn't common sense. I was talking to Bertrand Russell about this and he said, 'Yes, it's astonishing how people hate the intrusion of common sense into morality.' Anyway, I had this letter from Russell saying he wanted this 'Committee of a Hundred' formed and that the idea was to make some token breach of the law and court imprisonment, because legitimate means seemed to be having no impression at all on the politicians. I wrote back and said I hated the idea of breaking the law, which I do, as you'll have gathered from *A Man For All Seasons*. I have respect for the law because I think that the human being is a potentially chaotic and destructive creature, and society and the law are infinitely valuable, but I said I would be one of his Hundred.[2]

Robert did his duty by the Committee and rarely let an opportunity pass without warning of humanity's rush to self-destruction. In January 1961, for instance, he responded to a series of articles which Noël Coward had written for the *Sunday Times*. Lamenting the loss of traditional entertainment values in the theatre, the substitution of polemics for eloquence and dubious innovation for solid crafts-manship, Coward launched an assault on the 'New Movement in the Theatre' – the playwrights and the critics who encouraged them. Coward's articles caused quite a stir.

Readers expecting a cultural broadside from Robert, the self-proclaimed representative of the new playwrights, were treated at first to a homily on the bomb, an indulgence which only served to prove how right Coward was. The title for his *Sunday Times* article was 'The Last of the Wine,' a sly reference to the theme of his radio drama:

We think that Theatre is a human activity – not by a long chalk the most important, but important enough. And we think that the human situation today is unique, and uniquely perilous. . . . If, as seems probable, Man destroys himself, it will be because, on balance, Man prefers to; because his hatred of life is stronger than his love of life, because his greed, aggression and fear are stronger than his self-denial, charity and courage. Because, in short, of his nature.

We are aware that the question of Man's nature is an old one, that it has been moving up on Man ever since the Renaissance when Man began to move away from God. But because the bomb enables Man for the first time to realise irreversibly whatever fantasies of evil he may have, we think we are the first generation which cannot dodge the question behind Empire-building, mathematics, social welfare, or whatever it may be.

It's a great question, for the great world to answer. In the little world of Theatre one response to it is to provide entertainment to pass away the dangerous days. Of all the things a play may do – instruct, provoke, illuminate, move, entertain – the last is the only absolutely necessary requirement, though of course a very great play will do them all . . .

And as for craftsmanship, it isn't to be expected we should have the finish Mr Coward has. . . . We are truly sorry our first effort at a vintage of our own should taste so nasty to a cultivated palate. It doesn't taste so good to us. But it can't be helped. We think that other bottle is quite, quite empty. It was Mr Coward who had the last of the wine.[3]

As a result of this article Robert was invited to deliver a lecture at Exeter University on 'Theatre in the Sixties'. Again, his thoughts focused on the purpose of artistic endeavour in the nuclear age:

This title presupposes a gift of clairvoyance, and if I had this I would be able to know not only about theatre in the Sixties, but also whether, at the end of the decade, there will be any theatres standing, or any other buildings. I am referring, of course, to the possibility of atomic war. If your heart sinks at this portentous opening, may I say how much I sympathise with you. Let me hasten to reassure you that I am hostile to the view which maintains that the theatre is a branch of sociology or of politics, but I am equally hostile to the view which flies in the face of common sense and seems almost to deny that theatre, or any other art, is a human activity at all.

We speak of the bomb as though it had some volition of its own, but it will not go off unless we make it, and if we do this, it can only be because on balance we want to. I refer, of course, to humanity and not to Britain, Russia or America. Thus if an atomic war happens, it happens because we want it to.

Art is the most distinctly human of all activities – it is the activity in which the nature of the human animal is not only demonstrated but also explored. We know that one of the conditions to which the human animal is prone is rage. You can demonstrate rage either by writing one of the speeches from *King Lear* or by hurling a brick through a plate-glass window. I would say that the brick is the more effective method, but it does not in any way illuminate or explore the nature of human rage but merely demonstrates it, and this is why I say that art is a method of exploring the human condition. And that, if you have followed me, is why I dragged the bomb in at all.[4]

Despite these public assertions, Robert had little sympathy for the Committee's principal policy of forcing by violent demonstration Britain's abandonment of its nuclear deterrent. As he wrote to his father:

I have no mania but on the contrary a strong and increasing distaste for associating. I believe this Ctte of 100 is the first thing I have ever done out of a sense of mere duty, and a drab motive I find that to be. I drag myself unwillingly to one meeting in three and sit longing for it to finish. I was asked to speak in Trafalgar Square but explained to them that I didn't feel so sure of either the Unilateral position, nor Civil Disobedience of strengthening it, that I could persuade anybody other than myself to embrace it. All I feel I can contribute is my own individual bodily presence at the demonstrations, and that most dubiously. And if they started getting excited and indignant and began to stage the sort of demonstration that courts martyrdom at the hands of the police, I have my letter of resignation already composed in my head.[5]

'He found it distasteful but felt it had to be supported,' said Robert's brother, Sydney. 'Bob was reluctant to take an all-out position, which is the same as More in *A Man For All Seasons*. He knew that truth was intricate, not simple, and I think his position is summed up by that poem of Day-Lewis, who said, "That we who lived by honest dreams, Defend the bad against the worse." '[6]

The intended confrontation with the state machinery happened in early September. At a rally in Hyde Park Russell called for a mass mobilisation of protesters at Trafalgar Square on 17 September. The police moved to stop this by arresting a third of the Committee's membership, charging them with incitement to commit a breach of the peace.

On 12 September 1961, at Bow Street Magistrate's Court, Robert, along with Lord and Lady Russell, Arnold Wesker and other members of the Committee, refused to be bound over to keep the peace and were duly convicted. In consideration of their age and infirmity, Lord and Lady Russell were sentenced to seven days' imprisonment; everyone else to one month. After sentencing, they all went straight to Brixton prison in Black Marias and underwent the standard induction process for all convicted criminals: a strip search and the issue of prison uniform of grey trousers and a blue-and-white striped shirt.

Robert's imprisonment shocked many of his friends, including Kenneth Williams who, in a fit of indignation, cancelled his subscriptions to the *Daily Telegraph* and the *Sunday Telegraph*. In his diary, Williams wrote: 'When a country sends a man like Robert Bolt to prison for one month, for a token civil disobedience act done on a Sunday & incurring no harm it seems the kind of savagery one connects with fascist regimes. The issue here is whether one can, in all conscience, be a party to the manufacture & acquiescence in the usage of something as horrible as H-bombs. For any honest person the answer can only be *no*. . . . I have to join the demonstration on Sunday and run the risk of being arrested.'[7]

Support came, too, from the management of the Globe Theatre where two leaflets were inserted into the programmes for *A Man For All Seasons*. The first stated, 'Your playwright, Robert Bolt, is a fervent supporter of the Committee of 100. Together with Lord Russell he has been imprisoned for his connection with the demonstration on Sunday, September 17.' The second leaflet, issued by the Committee of 100, was an exhortation to join the demonstration which went ahead, willy-nilly. On a wet and chilly day, over 100,000 people brought the centre of London to a standstill. One thousand people were arrested, including John Osborne and Vanessa Redgrave. It was the largest mass arrest in British history.

Robert and the other Committee members endured the Victorian iron fist of Brixton for two days before they were transferred to Drake Hall Open Prison which would be Robert's home for a month. 'I was nine when Dad went to jail,' said Ben Bolt. 'We were told that he hadn't committed any crime though some of the children at school said some pretty nasty things. And the press photographers were always there trying to get a photograph of us.'[8]

Drake Hall was – and remains – in pleasant countryside a couple of miles north of Eccleshall in Staffordshire. On the road to the prison, as far from the sea as it is possible to be in England, there is a Raleigh Hall and then, half a mile further on, there is Drake. In the reception office a notice is displayed which lists the birthdays of every member of the Royal Family. On those days the Union Jack is to be flown from the flag-pole. Drake Hall was put up during the early years of the war as accommodation for labourers who were building a munitions factory at nearby Swynnerton. As many as 1000 workers lived here, in H-blocks with walls a foot thick in case of an attack by German bombers.

After the war, Drake Hall became a refugee camp, then a teachers' training college. It was converted into an open prison for male offenders in the late Fifties, closed in the mid-Sixties and reopened in 1970 as an open prison for women, a motley collection of drug addicts, fine defaulters, prostitutes and violent criminals nearing the end of long sentences. Three of the original H-blocks still stand in the neat gardens. It was in one of these that Robert and Christopher Logue, the poet, shared a room. Arnold Wesker has written of the 'cosiness' of the rooms – they were emphatically not referred to as 'cells' – which measured about ten feet by six and at each end, filling its width, was a narrow single bed. Above each bed there were two perfunctory shelves. Seen today, the rooms have the time-lapse quality of a museum exhibit.

Drake Hall was not a high-security prison; there was no high wall, nor were there scores of guards. The prisoners were not locked up at night, but certain restrictions inevitably applied: prisoners were allowed only two letters a week and personal visits from friends and family were allowed once a week. The men had access to the prison library, they were given regular exercise and were encouraged to hoe the gardens. In the evenings Christopher Logue gave poetry recitals. 'When I broke the law and the police put me in prison,' said Robert, 'I was deeply shocked. Although I blush to confess it, I think that throughout my communist and Marxist period, I had always had the feeling that policemen were there to look after me and would not do anything *really* nasty to a nice person like myself. And there I was with rough warders and tin plates and a jerry in the cell.'[9]

'I read more books in open prison than in the previous six months of the year,' wrote Arnold Wesker, 'and besides, it was such an utterly puny incarceration when measured alongside the imprison-ment of a Mandela or a Solzhenitzen, to say nothing of the millions who languished whole lives away and died in the gulags of the world. And we could all have signed an order to keep the peace and been released on the spot at any time . . .'[10]

While his fellow inmates could idle the time away by reading or writing poetry, Robert had *Lawrence of Arabia* to finish. To the prison officials, writing a poem was not considered work; Robert, though, was earning money, a great deal of it, and he was singled out for special treatment. As Vanessa Redgrave wrote to her father: 'Bob Bolt is in an open prison with the rest, Wesker, Michael Randle, Christopher Logue among others. And they are treated extremely well. But the prison authorities refuse to allow Bob, alone of all the others, to write, and I hear he is very het-up and worried as he must finish the *Lawrence of Arabia* script by tomorrow or probably be sued by Spiegel who is furious. He even applied to the Home Office and all he can get out of them is that if he would sign an agreement to keep the peace then he could write or leave prison or anything.'[11]

Sam Spiegel had become so exasperated by what he regarded as Robert's sanctimonious behaviour that he went to see Jo in Richmond. Spiegel told her that Robert's little show of principle was costing a great deal of money and that if Robert refused to be bound over to keep the peace he would make sure he never worked again. Jo was appalled by Spiegel's arrogance and indifference to principle. Having got nowhere with her, Spiegel decided to make a personal visit to Drake Hall. He would appeal to Robert's clearly well developed conscience and tell him that while he languished in prison the entire film crew, more than 100 men, were going without pay and that the whole film, in which millions had been invested, was in jeopardy. At least, that was Spiegel's story and he took it to Drake Hall on Wednesday, 27 September.

'And then all hell broke loose,' said Robert. 'Sam Spiegel just went absolutely mad – "So have these people got to lose their jobs and lose thousands of dollars just so that you can go to heaven when you die?" was his line. So after a fortnight I bound myself over and came out. I felt that although there were very good reasons why I should, I knew that ultimately I should *not* have come out and it was simply because Sam had built up the pressure to such an extent that I couldn't hold out.'[12] When the release formalities were completed, Robert was driven away in Spiegel's Rolls-Royce to a celebratory lunch at the Berkeley Hotel. Robert suddenly became aware that if he had served his full sentence – another two weeks – nothing would have happened. The picture had been shut down anyway, not because he was in jail but because Lean had run out of scenes to shoot and Spiegel had decided to quit Jordan. Nor was it a question of Lean moving from Jordan to another location and starting again immediately; Lean would not shoot a foot of film unless he was happy with the script and that meant spending many weeks with Robert, going over every scene and every line of dialogue. Lean and Spiegel knew they would not resume shooting until Christmas and the appropriate budgetary allowances had been made for that.

Robert had been conned. He was seduced by the importance of the enterprise and by his part in it, and intimidated by Spiegel's exercise of power for power's sake. Within hours of his release from Drake Hall he knew that he could quite easily have served his full sentence and avoided what was, for him, 'the most shameful moment of my life'.[13] 'For six months,' he said, 'I found it very hard to look at myself in the mirror because it seemed to me, however it was wrapped up, almost pure weakness. I gave the money away – that is the money I earned as a result of coming out of prison, gave it oddly enough to Arnold's Centre 42.'[14]

A few weeks after release from jail, Robert wrote to his father:

> My spell in prison opened my eyes to a lot I hadn't known about society and about myself. My coming out of prison more so. It was an experience as raw as the experiences of childhood and as formative. Exactly what it's taught me I don't know, but something fundamental; I feel as though the world had tipped a little. What a fuss I seem to be making of such a small event! In short I feel that the difficulties facing us are much greater and our own strength weaker than I had dreamed. I never had much faith in the wisdom of wise men but now I have none. I don't mean that there are not men greatly wiser than I but that their wisdom doesn't cast much illumination beyond the limits of their own individual lives. Most of us, and taken in bulk all of us, are stupid and lazy beyond calculation.
>
> The CND want me to speak in the Albert Hall, the Ctte of 100 want me to speak in Trafalgar Square; I have with an effort refused them both and feel unusually happy with the decision. The job needs doing beyond question, but I can't do it; and what is really frightening, there doesn't seem to be a better man on the scene at the moment. There's a big movement of hope beginning in the People and apparently no one to give it shape, so I suppose we shall relapse back into the steady tide of our appetites which seem to be flowing unmistakably towards destruction. I really must get off the subject.
>
> I finish work on the script of *Lawrence* on December 18th, whether it's finished or not. I've had all I can take of that set-up. Then I have ideas for two plays and, between them, a book.[15]

The Committee of 100 was disbanded in January 1963 after Bertrand Russell resigned. The new leader of the Committee, Michael Randle, served a further prison term while another prominent member, Helen Anagransa, took her own life after serving eight months in Holloway jail. As for Robert, he had signed a Home Office statement which barred him from taking part in any further demonstrations. It would be ten years before he engaged again in overt political activity, when he became President of the film technicians' union, the ACTT.

Arnold Wesker claimed that CND 'gave courage to the students of America showing them that peaceful demonstrations could make an impact, produce results. CND inspired the civil rights movement which succoured the anti-Vietnam War campaign which surely must have taught Solidarity something about collective action which led to the toppled Berlin Wall and brought about the collapse of Soviet tyranny. From four hundred marchers to Aldermaston to the end of an empire.'[16] Except that CND's impact in Britain was minimal. The Cold War and Britain's nuclear deterrent continued, oblivious to oblivion. When the present writer asked Robert about his CND activities and his imprisonment he said, 'God, do we have to go through all that again?' He said this, still pained by the experience, when the Berlin Wall no longer existed, when the USSR had been dismantled and when communism had been thoroughly discredited. The bomb had finally reaped the peace dividend and those voices of dissent, however honourable, now seem as fleeting as confetti in a storm.

Three weeks after he was released from prison Robert left Jo and the children, and flew to Spain to resume work on *Lawrence of Arabia*. His relationship with Jo was already strained by his absences and, when he was at home, by his compulsion to be rich and famous. But Jo, who had visited him in prison, was shattered by the way he had compromised his principles, the ease with which he had signed that piece of paper: despite the force of his published articles, his homilies on commitment, Robert had shown a sudden and shocking weakness of character. Jo seemed to be made of stronger stuff, even though it was not her career which was on the line. Peter Hall said about her:

> I liked Jo very much. She had a fearsome integrity. Bob's tragedy was that he also had a fearsome integrity together with a pragmatism which made him suffer a great deal. He was Mr Everyman crossed with Mr Worldlywise, quite a difficult combination. He knew he was being seduced by Hollywood. He wanted to be seduced yet he didn't want to be seduced. Perhaps if he'd been more certain of himself, more certain of his talent, I think that like Pinter or Stoppard he could have done both. But he always seemed to be getting into choices, like coming out of prison to keep the film going.
> The consuming of Bob, the consuming of his talent and his principles by David and Sam was monumental, beyond normal

practice I would say. I was worried about that because it seemed
to me that Bob was ill equipped to withstand it.[17]

'The CND thing really went very deep,' said Robert and Jo's friend
Sian Phillips. 'It upset him dreadfully and he never felt the same way
about Sam Spiegel again. Robert was a terribly honourable person
and in the film world he was like an infant surrounded by sharks. It
came as a terrible shock to him that anyone could be so devious. He
felt he'd been manipulated and wondered how he could have been
so stupid. Jo thought he had sold out and that made their relationship very difficult. Robert was in another world and Jo didn't want
to enter it. That happens a lot in our business.'[18]

Robert stayed in Spain with Lean for three months, even making a
brief appearance in the film as a British officer, puffing on a pipe,
gazing through a window as Lawrence persuades Allenby to support
the Arab Revolt.

The second half of the film was far more intricate than the first,
which was essentially the story of one military action – the assault on
Akaba. Lean was thrilled by Robert's grasp of narrative and his way
with dialogue. Whereas Wilson's screenplay was an often turgid
account of tribal politics and imperial imperatives, Robert stripped
the story to its essentials, dispensed with speeches and arrived at a
tone which frequently borders on satire.

Robert also found his favourite thematic device, a dualism, as
expressed by the romanticism of Lawrence and the stoicism of
Allenby, the father figure. It is this relationship that gives the second
half of the film much of its richness, even though the key scene
between these two characters was subsequently cut by Lean soon
after the film's première.

Another scene mystified Lean and offended Sam Spiegel. After
Lawrence has been shot by a Turk during the raid on the train, he
falls to the ground and appears to gurgle. Robert's script had
Lawrence say, 'Good, Good, Good,' then get to his feet and say, 'Oh
dear, oh poor Neddy Lawrence, oh poor Neddy.' Robert claimed
that Lean never understood the scene and encouraged O'Toole to
fluff the line, 'Good, Good, Good.' When Spiegel viewed the rushes
in London, he ordered the second line to be cut for fear that
Professor Lawrence would assume it revealed his brother's homo-
sexuality. Robert was furious. 'I miss that line, "Neddy", like a
hand,' he wrote to Lean. 'Sam utterly misunderstood the weight (or
weightlessness) of that line, with his vulgar apprehensions of vul-

garity. Delicacy is *not* effeminacy. Beauty is *not* prettiness. Heroism is *not* brutishness. Sam would agree in principle, but in practice, never.'[19]

When his work in Spain was over Robert returned to his family in Richmond and resumed work on *Gentle Jack*. Lean continued in Spain for another three months, then transferred the unit to Morocco and afterwards to England for the remaining sequences. All Robert had to do was to wait for the film to come out and enjoy the acclaim.

On 10 December 1962 Robert Bolt, until quite recently a reluctant guest of Her Majesty Queen Elizabeth II at Drake Hall, was introduced to Her Majesty at the Odeon Leicester Square. During the previous week, a thick, freezing fog had descended upon southern England, causing the deaths of more than 300 people and severely disrupting public transport. But nearly 2000 guests gathered for the Royal World Premiere of *Lawrence of Arabia*. As Her Majesty the Queen and the Duke of Edinburgh arrived at the cinema, the Royal Horse Guards sounded a fanfare and inside the art-deco auditorium the Welsh Guards played the National Anthem. Following the performance, Spiegel and Lean hosted a midnight party for 500 guests at the Grosvenor House Hotel in Park Lane. Robert's parents had turned down their invitation, claiming they were too elderly (they were in their early sixties), though Sydney and Jaya attended. 'We weren't in the middle of things,' said Sydney, 'rather on the sidelines and seated with the captain of Sam Spiegel's yacht. I recognised Kenneth More and in all his films he always said, "Come on, chaps!" When I looked up there he was, with a bunch of friends, and I heard him say, "Come on, chaps! Champers!" '

There was plenty of reason to celebrate. Those fourteen months of shooting in inhospitable conditions and the frantic dash to get the film ready faded in the memory as the praise flowed in from critics and public alike. But there were a few dark shadows as well. Just as the real T. E. Lawrence was a controversial figure, so the film caused some controversies of its own. One of them was the cutting of twenty minutes from the running time within five weeks of the World Première. To his dying day Lean always claimed that Spiegel cut the film behind his back, though documentary evidence has since come to light which proves conclusively that Lean himself decided on the cuts.

Variety quoted Spiegel as saying, 'When the press heard that we were doing some editing the *Evening News* accused us of bowing to commercialism and we got a stream of letters protesting it would be sacrilege to cut it. We don't want any more trouble in England . . .'[20] The 'trouble' that Spiegel was referring to was the campaign against the film by people with history on their side, with personal axes to grind and grievances to make public. In the forefront of this was Professor Lawrence whose contract with Spiegel included a clause which allowed Lawrence a period of four weeks following his receipt of the final script in which to approve the use of the title *Seven Pillars of Wisdom*. Lawrence had sold the screen rights on the basis of Michael Wilson's treatment and while Lawrence obviously knew that Wilson had been replaced by Robert, he did not see a single page of Robert's script until July 1962, when only the so-called 'blood-bath', the motor-cycle accident and the St Paul's Cathedral exteriors remained to be filmed.

Lawrence read the script and was appalled by its distortions. On 7 August 1962 his lawyer, Richard Henniker-Major, told his client that Spiegel was still anxious to use the title *Seven Pillars of Wisdom* and that if he, Lawrence, exercised his veto, the remaining £5000 of the contract would be forfeited. By 16 August 1962 Lawrence had indeed exercised his veto and the money was repaid to Horizon Pictures. Spiegel asked Lawrence to reconsider and invited him to view a rough-cut of the film. At first Lawrence refused, only to be persuaded by his publisher that it would be unwise to criticise a film without having seen it. Lawrence saw the wisdom of this and went with his wife, Barbara, to the cutting rooms in South Audley Street on 5 September 1962. For an academic like Lawrence, who hardly ever visited the cinema, viewing a film at this stage of post-production must have been especially bewildering. There would have been no music, no effects tracks and no real narrative continuity.

'Lawrence was furious,' said Lean. 'You felt the seats were heaving about five minutes before the end. He stood up and shouted at Sam, "I should never have trusted you!" There was a horrendous row and he stormed out with his wife in pursuit, trying to placate him.'[21] Lawrence started his campaign by recruiting the historian, Basil Liddell-Hart, who had tried unsuccessfully to get himself a job as a consultant to the film and had peevishly turned down an invitation to the première. Liddell-Hart wrote to the newspapers and to Robert, beginning a long and tortuous correspondence which both Robert and Liddell-Hart seemed reluctant to finish.

The most significant attack on the film was Professor Lawrence's article, 'The Fiction and the Fact', published on Sunday, 16 December 1962 in *The Observer*:

Perhaps no film can ever be true to a character from life, especially a life as remarkable and a character as complex as my brother's. And certainly no film, however good, can be true to a book, especially a long and complicated book such as *Seven Pillars of Wisdom*.

The American author [Michael Wilson] of a preliminary film-synopsis, which followed *Seven Pillars* with extraordinary fidelity, wrote of his adaptation three years ago: 'I had to take considerable liberties with the text – not only rearranging and telescoping events, but inventing scenes which never actually occurred.' The film that has eventually been made – from a script of a very different nature by Robert Bolt – is, I think, far less closely related to the book, the rights of which I sold for the purpose, than was the play *Ross* which Terence Rattigan wrote without needing or acquiring any rights.

Neither the play nor the film could have been produced without knowledge of the book, but each is an imaginative reconstruction of the story to suit a personal interpretation of the main character. The film, though, is above all a spectacle in which skilful directing, visual splendour and music sugar-coat the script's bitter treatment of character and events. I had reserved the power to prohibit use of the title and exercised it when I saw how widely and consistently the final script diverged from the book. . .

The film Lawrence has more than any one man's share of psychological aberrations, which are displayed by episodes that do not appear in the book and by distorted versions of some that do. . . The real key to the hero is sadism – a trait which a good many Englishmen could have observed in T. E. Lawrence if it had existed . . .

I do not want to give the impression that I consider the Lawrence of the film entirely untrue. So far especially as determination, courage and endurance are concerned, he is comparable, in Mr O'Toole's rendering, with the man he purports to represent. How much else is right or wrong, and how much of the truth, both good and bad, is missing, I must leave to people who are familiar with the relevant books. I need only say that I should not have recognised my brother.[22]

Lawrence's article was published in America on the day the film opened in New York. In an interview for the *New York Times*, Lawrence said he thought that Robert had written the script as anti-war propaganda, since his CND affiliations were well known. According to the *New York Times*, Robert 'denied the film reflected his own disarmament beliefs by portraying a military leader as a maniac willing to sacrifice helpless and innocent people'. Robert was also quoted as saying, 'I sympathise with Lawrence's relatives, but no film could hope to satisfy them.'

Lawrence's article adequately summarised many of the liberties taken by the film. But when he said that the key to the film's hero is 'sadism' he knew that the real word was in fact the reverse – namely, 'masochism'. Indeed, Robert and Liddell-Hart had argued over this in their exchange of letters which largely focused on Lawrence's role in the massacre of the retreating Turkish column.

Professor Lawrence knew that the film would create a revival of interest in his brother which might bring to light the more disturbing aspects of T.E's later life, in particular the way he was ritualistically flogged by a Tank Corps private named John Bruce. Although the Professor believed that only members of the immediate family knew about the floggings, it was in fact known to several outsiders, including Anthony Nutting, who made the information available to Lean and Robert. While they could not portray this in the film for any number of reasons – their screen Lawrence was tortured enough as it was without having him order up a beating on room service – their knowledge of it went into their psychological portrayal. Professor Lawrence's objections to *Lawrence of Arabia* in 1962, six years before the floggings became public knowledge, were in fact an extremely effective exercise in damage limitation.

While his campaign against the film was fought in public, other disputes were conducted in private. The Allenby family complained formally to Columbia about the portrayal of their ancestor and the descendants of the Arab chiefs, Auda Abu Tayi and Sherif Ali, initiated legal action. A descendant of Ali, a Saudi diplomat, was especially upset by the mirage sequence – vindicating Sir Anthony Nutting's original worries – which portrayed his ancestor as a murderer. Only when Columbia's attorneys suggested that Ali had fired in self defence was the legal action dropped. Auda's son argued that his father was portrayed as a thief, a man open to bribes and only interested in financial gain. The case rumbled on until the Seventies and seemed to fall down when Columbia argued that since the film had been banned in most Arab countries it could not have caused damage to anyone's reputation.

Distressed by these controversies, Robert sought to find a way to justify his approach and, at the same time, placate Professor

Lawrence. When Robert's regular publisher, Heinemann, proposed publishing the screenplay, Robert thought his problem was solved.

All Robert's plays had been published by Heinemann Educational Books and he had struck up a close friendship with his editor, Edward Thompson. Although the financial rewards for published plays were small, except for *A Man For All Seasons*, Robert always wrote a special introduction for them and was consulted on the design and covers. For the screenplay of *Lawrence of Arabia*, Thompson proposed a more lavish edition than usual, with colour photographs and an introductory essay by David Lean.

Robert called his own introduction an 'Apologia' (see Appendix II) which summarised his approach to the story and attempted to answer the criticisms of the Professor, Basil Liddell-Hart and others. But sadly, the essay was never published. Nor was the screenplay. Robert delivered the Apologia to Edward Thompson on 21 January 1963 and withdrew it four days later. The idea of an Apologia infuriated Lean, who didn't think that anyone, least of all Professor Lawrence, deserved any kind of apology.

'Thanks for your letter,' Robert wrote to Lean, 'and as for its principal burden, then fine – I'll not print the Apologia. I don't *really* care much about the opinion of these people; it's just that I wanted to make clear that we do have a properly considered case, are not being irresponsibly sensational or even didactic in our film, and this very restrained, pseudo-scholarly style is the particular poison I like to administer to that kind of antagonist. But your straightforward indignation at the mere idea of our explaining ourselves is so much better a response that I fall in with it happily.'[23] Robert then told Edward Thompson: 'Heard from David Lean. He hates passionately the idea of an Apologia. On reflection I agree with him. The script is what I have to say about T.E.L., in my chosen form, and the rest should be silence. Will you let me have the Apologia back however? I will file it, in case it ever seems necessary.'[24]

Without the Apologia, which might have given the published screenplay additional authority and historical legitimacy, Heinemann became rather nervous about the whole enterprise and contacted Jonathan Cape Ltd, the publishers of *Seven Pillars of Wisdom*. Cape's chairman, G. Wren Howard, indicated that there might possibly be a breach of copyright, since the events depicted in Robert's screenplay belonged to the T. E. Lawrence estate which was controlled by the Professor. Wren Howard, acting on behalf of Professor Lawrence, handed it over to Cape's lawyers. In June, Robert's lawyer, Laurence Harbottle, wrote to Edward Thompson:

'Horizon were granted film rights and limited synopsis rights in *Seven Pillars* but no publication rights. Mr Bolt granted Horizon copyright in his screenplay but of course could not include copyright in material taken from *Seven Pillars* as he did not own that material. Even if Mr Bolt's screenplay were wholly original or based on fact and therefore in the public domain he would in my view be in great danger of granting new publication rights to you.'[25]

When Professor Lawrence was fully apprised of the situation he wrote to Wren Howard: 'It occurs to me that Heinemann may be unaware of the very strong feeling against the film – which, in fact, means Mr Bolt's screenplay – shared by everybody who has personal knowledge of my brother, or of the campaign, or of Arab affairs. One and all (so far as I am aware) regard the work as an unpleasant travesty wherever it impinges on their own experience. . . . No special knowledge is required to perceive its falsity. . . . Such is the work that has been proposed for an Educational Book!!'[26]

In September an exasperated Robert wrote to Thompson: 'I don't know what to say about this Lawrence business. I'm reluctant to abandon it if only because I put a good deal of precious time into preparing it for publication. I have never really understood the situation. Exactly what is it we are threatened by? A law suit by the Prof? Against whom – my publishers or me? On what grounds – misrepresentation of TE, or infringement of copyright? I'll abandon the project if I must, but I should like to know why.'[27]

The veiled threat of a lawsuit frightened Heinemann, especially since they could not have any support from Spiegel's Horizon Pictures or Columbia since this was to have been a separate enterprise. It was a case of censorship conducted by intimidation. In November, a year after the picture was released, Heinemann's chairman formally capitulated to Wren Howard: 'This business of Robert Bolt's screenplay has been dragging on for some time. In view of A. W. Lawrence's views, which he holds very strongly, we have decided not to proceed with the book.'[28]

As if the verbal and legal contest with Professor Lawrence was not enough, Robert was also fighting another and potentially more damaging battle over *Lawrence of Arabia*. When he was first offered *Lawrence*, he knew he was replacing another writer, Michael Wilson. He would also have known that Wilson had been blacklisted after he refused to testify at a hearing of the House Un-American Activities Committee. When Wilson started work on *Lawrence* Spiegel asked him to sign a statement to the effect that he was not, nor ever had been, a communist. Spiegel, who never asked Robert for a similar statement, claimed he needed this in order to mollify American distributors who feared the film might be picketed by right-wing groups. But Wilson refused to sign anything.

Eighteen months after he had resigned from the picture, Wilson began to take an active interest in Robert's screenplay, which he had not read. In June 1962 he wrote to his friend and fellow blacklisted writer Adrian Scott who was living in London. Wilson told Scott that he was trying to obtain a copy of Robert's script and he sought Scott's advice as to how to approach the union of British screenwriters if he decided to take the matter to arbitration. 'In due time I will address myself to Robert Bolt himself,' wrote Wilson, 'but I don't want to do so until I have made the preliminary moves. It goes without saying that I don't want the news of my campaign of self-defense to reach Spiegel ears at this time.'[29]

Wilson's brother-in-law, Paul Jarrico, was also staying in London and somehow he and Scott managed to procure a copy of Robert's screenplay on an overnight loan. Jarrico then called Wilson in Los Angeles and told him that a considerable amount of his work had been retained. Jarrico's estimate was ninety per cent of the dramatic structure and ten per cent of the dialogue.

In early November, a month before the picture opened, Spiegel honoured his legal obligations to Wilson by sending him a copy of the shooting script.

> It is clear at once that little of my dialogue remains [Wilson wrote to Spiegel], certainly less than ten per cent. I assume that the dialogue was written by Robert Bolt, and through you I must congratulate him on a job well done. He is a gifted man. If screen credit were determined on the basis of dialogue alone, I could not claim recognition for this picture . . . the overall structure of the shooting script is mine. . . . The continuity – by which I mean plot detail and the progression of scenes – remains my continuity . . .
>
> Most of my *inventions* have been retained – incidents which are not to be found in *Seven Pillars of Wisdom* or any other work about Lawrence. . . There isn't one chance in a thousand that another writer could have independently created the same fictions. . . . It might be argued that some of the contributions I claim as my own were first advanced by David Lean or by you. . . . It is difficult to say in retrospect who had which idea first. It makes no difference. In determining a writer's

contribution, those ideas *executed* by him and transformed into written drama must be attributed to him.[30]

When Spiegel's lawyers dismissed Wilson's request for joint credit, he took the matter to arbitration, a procedure involving a small committee of screenwriters governed by rules laid down by the Producers' Association and the Writers' Guild of Great Britain. These rules stipulated that a writer who is deemed to have contributed at least one third of a script is entitled to a credit. This proportion could be calculated in terms of dramatic structure and continuity, as well as in dialogue or a combination of both.

With the film's première less than two weeks away, Wilson obviously realised that his chances of initiating an arbitration hearing and securing a screen credit were remote. But he knew that the planned release pattern of *Lawrence of Arabia* was such that he might possibly secure a credit for himself in time for the general 35mm release.

In his letter to Jim Johnson, General Secretary of the Guild, Wilson outlined his involvement with *Lawrence* and described fourteen incidents which he claimed to have invented and which had been retained by Robert:

1   Lawrence's first meeting with Ali, in which the stranger, later to become his closest friend, kills Lawrence's guide. This is sheer invention – mine.

2   Lawrence meets a British officer (Brighton) in the desert who tells him to keep his mouth shut about Arab affairs. When they arrive at Feisal's camp, a Turkish plane is attacking the Bedouins. My fictions, these.

3   At his first conference with Feisal, Lawrence takes issue with the official British viewpoint. This did not happen in life.

4   After learning of Feisal's intention of retreat to the coast, Lawrence persuades Ali to join him in a Bedouin raid on Akaba. This is not at all the way it happened in *Seven Pillars*. I altered the events to suit dramatic purposes.

5   While crossing the desert, one of the raiders is lost and forsaken, and Lawrence turns back to rescue him. A few days later Lawrence executes the man he has saved. Both these events are recorded in *SPW* but at different times, different places, different persons. I conjoined them in order to dramatize (my invention) the key conflict between Ali and Lawrence – predestination vs free will etc.

6   Lawrence persuades Auda to join the raid by swearing that the

Turks hoard gold in Akaba; and when no gold is found, gives Auda a personal IOU for five thousand guineas. This is invention. '

7   Lawrence crosses the Sinai with only Farraj and Daud as companions, and Daud dies in a quicksand. This is plain fiction. Check my screenplay.

8   Lawrence takes Farraj into the Officers Bar in Cairo and is insulted there. (Only this idea is mine, not the scene that follows.)

9   The American journalist Lowell Thomas is nowhere mentioned in *Seven Pillars*. In my screenplay there is such a character, and his is a special role in the story. The name and the dialogue have been changed in the shooting script, but the journalist's function remains the same.

10   When the Revolt is at a low ebb, Lawrence persuades Ali to come with him to the Turkish garrison town of Deraa. Lawrence is arrested, Ali is not. (Here I altered the facts to keep alive the Ali–Lawrence relationship.)

11   Lawrence's decision to return to Jerusalem and throw in his hand is a direct consequence of his experience with the Turkish bey. This motivation is my invention, for it did not happen that way in life.

12   [The] key scene between Lawrence and Allenby has been thoroughly rewritten, but my idea (an invention) remains the point of the scene – that Allenby in effect challenges Lawrence and his Arabs to race the British army to Damascus.

13   When Lawrence returns to the desert, there is a subtle change in his relationship to Ali. The destinies of the two men have crossed: Ali, once the feudal tribesman, is becoming the nationalist zealot; Lawrence, once the civilised Englishman, is becoming the primitive Messiah. Thus, in the massacre of the Turkish regiment, it is Lawrence who is swept away by the blood bath and Ali who tries to stop the slaughter. All this is my own contribution to the storyline.

14   Superficially, this scene [in the town hall of Damascus] bears little resemblance to mine, but the basic personal solutions are mine: Auda returns to the desert; Ali remains in Damascus to learn politics; while Lawrence can neither stay nor go back to the desert.[31]

All Wilson's claims were fully justified. The odd thing is that Wilson never once claimed authorship of the underlying flashback structure of the film which begins with Lawrence's fatal motor cycle crash and Memorial Service and ends, as does *Seven Pillars of Wisdom*, with his departure from the desert.

The next day, Wilson wrote a cordial if determined letter to Robert: 'I am your predecessor,' he wrote. 'Unhappily, we have never met; yet when I threw in my hand my sole gratification was the knowledge that the writer to follow me was the author of *A Man For All Seasons*. Yes, I threw in my hand. I felt I had gone about as far as I could go, that if I lived to be a hundred I could not fully satisfy David Lean.'

Wilson outlined to Robert his involvement with the project but stopped short of listing those sequences which he felt were his creations. However, Wilson left Robert with no doubt that he would pursue the matter of screen credit right to the wire. He also – as one writer to another and as one former communist to another – unleashed all his frustrations that the blacklist imposed, referring again to *A Man For All Seasons* which, for a blacklisted writer, would have been a significant text. As Kenneth Tynan had written in his review of the play: 'I have no doubt that we are meant to draw an analogy between More and those witnesses who appear before the Un-American Activities Committee and take the Fifth Amendment.'

'I have just begun to emerge from that shadowy realm,' wrote Wilson, 'not through any abandonment of principle on my part, but because at long last I have found an American producer [Martin Ransohoff] who has the courage to give credit to a writer he engages, and the witch-hunters be damned. The men in control of *Lawrence of Arabia* lack that courage. If I were "clean" my name would already be alongside yours as co-author of this picture. I implore you to believe this is not a paranoid assertion. I am not a man for all seasons.'[32]

Wilson, who knew of Robert's imprisonment and that Spiegel had persuaded him to sign a recantation, was cleverly exploiting Robert's weakness. And Robert himself knew of this strange connection between them so that his resistance to Wilson receiving credit might have gone, even subconsciously, beyond a simple matter of assessing one man's contribution over another's. While Robert's political compromise had furthered his career, Wilson's refusal to compromise had wrecked his. Wilson seemed to be occupying the higher moral ground.

Robert's reply to Wilson was equally forthright:

Your letter came this morning as a bombshell. I had no idea that there was any question of my sharing credit with anybody. I was under the impression that the script as shot was my own work utterly.

Here is what I think: We seem to agree that there is nothing but my work in the actual writing – I mean both dialogue and descriptive. Your claim is made on the basis of story. The line of the story, with two exceptions, is taken from *Seven Pillars*: his stays in Cairo, his journey to Feisal, his raid on Akaba, support by Allenby, campaign against the railway, loss of men through looting, death of Farraj, torture in Deraa, desire to escape the desert, sending back by Allenby, blood-bath, failure in Damascus culminating with the hospital. I don't know of *any* account of Lawrence's life which does not follow that storyline. I will look again at your script if Sam will give me one and see how closely you follow it yourself. But I really can't admit to have taken it from any other source than *Seven Pillars*, like everyone else.

The exceptions are: the death of Daud by quicksand rather than by illness, and the collapsing of the two characters (the one whose life he saved in the Nefud and the one whose life he took to avoid tribal bloodfeud) into one. I can't quite remember, but I know Sam and David told me that one of these ideas was theirs, not yours, and I think they said both. In any event I can't agree that even both of these ideas would entitle you to equal billing as against the entire bulk of the script. I cannot tell you how hard I have worked on this film. Some of it I have written five times over to meet the requirements of Sam and David. It has been back-breaking and the target, for me, has been that it should be my script that is shot, and I think it is.

I wish you well; I have heard nothing but good things of you from people I respect; I am particularly sympathetic because of your particular political predicament; I have myself no objection to your receiving credit for 'preliminary work' or 'ideas' which are yours. But I'm damned if the screenplay is by anyone but Robert Bolt and that is what the Credit ought to say.[33]

The Writers' Guild set up an arbitration committee of three writers: Leigh Vance, who would later contribute to the *Avengers* TV series, Bryan Forbes and Howard Clewes who had co-written *The Day They Robbed the Bank of England*, the film in which Lean had first seen Peter O'Toole. They reached their decision in June 1963 and voted unanimously in support of Michael Wilson.

Robert was appalled by the verdict, describing the affair as a 'disgusting mess'. Refusing to speak to the press, Robert prepared a statement which he gave to Margaret Ramsay and Mike Frankovich at Columbia:

> There are three elements in a film script: (1) The dialogue and camera directions, which embody (2) the psychological and moral interpretation of the storyline and (3) the storyline itself. (1) Of the dialogue and camera directions in the script about one per cent is Mr Wilson's. (2) The interpretation is my own entirely. Professor Lawrence, T.E's brother and executive, publicly rejected my interpretation on the ground that it was radically different from that of Mr Wilson which he had previously approved. (3) The essential events of the story line are drawn from *Seven Pillars of Wisdom* and any account of T. E. Lawrence must follow the same line. Of the half-dozen incidents which are wholly or in part fictitious, one or two are mine and one or two are Mr Wilson's. So far as I can see these comprise the whole of his contribution. I have never met Mr Wilson but wish to say that if this Award were to credit him for preliminary work or such fragments of it as remain in my script, then I should warmly welcome it. It must be a bitter experience for a writer to have his work passed over and his place taken by another, but the suggestion that he is equally responsible with myself for the script that was shot is absurd.[34]

Robert's main point would seem to be the fact that A. W. Lawrence had publicly repudiated Bolt's interpretation of Lawrence, having previously approved of Wilson's. Indeed, Robert's portrayal of Lawrence was substantially different from Wilson's but on the matter of dramatic structure, Robert's case was built on sand and by any standards of judgement Wilson deserved some form of recognition. And, after a fashion, he got it.

On 18 December 1963, more than a year after *Lawrence of Arabia* had opened, the Writers' Guild presented Wilson with their Award for the Best Screenplay of 1962. Robert had himself collected the Award a year earlier and gave an acceptance speech which lasted more than twenty minutes. One screenwriter who attended the ceremony recalled it as a 'pontificating harangue [which] did appear to establish Bolt as sole author to which he was not really entitled. Frankly, I was bored silly by the verbosity which held up the presentation of other Awards that night.'[35]

The matter lay dormant until *Lawrence of Arabia* was restored and re-released by Columbia in 1989. As Wilson had died in 1965, his brother-in-law, Paul Jarrico, took up Wilson's cause and wrote to the Screen Writers' Guild of America in the hope they might persuade Columbia to have Wilson's name incorporated into the credits of the restored version. But since Lean and Robert were active in the promotion of the restored *Lawrence*, as well as collaborating on *Nostromo*, which they hoped Columbia might finance, Jarrico's efforts were in vain.

But Jarrico never gave up. After Lean's death in 1991, Jarrico's campaign gained momentum and six months after Robert's death the Writers' Guild of America declared that Michael Wilson was to be officially acknowledged as the co-author of the screenplay of *Lawrence of Arabia*.

Following the Guild's statement the Academy of Motion Picture Arts and Sciences gave Wilson a posthumous nomination for *Lawrence*, though the controversy had almost certainly prevented Robert from winning the Oscar for which he alone had been originally nominated. Jarrico's fight finally ended when Columbia Pictures undertook to amend the credit titles on all future prints of the film to 'Screenplay by Robert Bolt and Michael Wilson.'

FOURTEEN

NOT A FRIENDLY PLAY

'I don't know if this is the Forest or the dark inside of my own skull.'

Jacko in *Gentle Jack*

Despite the altercations with Professor Lawrence and Michael Wilson, *Lawrence of Arabia* propelled Robert into a different sphere. Hollywood besieged him with offers, none of which appealed to him, even though he knew he could make a lucrative living by concocting screenplays which would pay for the occasional indulgence, like a play. But Robert chose a different path; he still regarded himself first and foremost as a playwright, and he wanted to work again with David Lean on another major picture.

The next three years, though, would consume a vast amount of creative energy and destroy the thing most precious to him: there would be two films, two Academy Awards, a disastrous play and a wrecked marriage. While the work would make him rich beyond his wildest dreams, the price was loneliness and despair.

As David Lean was in Los Angeles for the première of *Lawrence*, he began to think about his next project. He also wrote his very first letter to Robert and began with the kind of praise that screenwriters can only dream of:

I have thought about you such a lot these last couple of weeks and have wished so much you could have been here... You have had as much acknowledgement here as you had in England, so you can double eat those words of yours! As I told you right at the beginning, the reason that most film writers don't get credit is that they don't deserve it. Most so-called script writers are adapters and 'added dialogue' writers. The movies don't possess a dramatist. For that reason this film of ours has knocked the top film-makers sideways.

In short, they all say they have never seen anything like it. The top American movie-makers are more generous than anyone in the world, and they have given us their praise on a plate. Don't quite know how to describe it to you at this distance but among the real ravers are Willy Wyler, Billy Wilder, Fred Zinnemann, Richard Brooks, Joe Mankiewicz and the great old-timer, King Vidor. They are all so bloody generous that every one of them has said words to the effect, 'It's out of our class' and really mean it . . .

This film has put me into a fantastic position and that a team consisting of you and I would be backed up to the hilt – bigger than anyone in this so-called industry. We could really call the tune and if money is of interest to you, you wouldn't have to worry about it for the rest of your life if we hit the jackpot. The more I see the reactions to *Lawrence* the more I realise we have something *very* out of the ordinary as a joint team. I won't say why. I know it's so. I'm just mad keen to work with you again . . .[1]

Robert had already suggested two possible ideas to Lean – Joseph Conrad's *Nostromo* and a film of Cecil Woodham-Smith's vivid account of the Charge of the Light Brigade, *The Reason Why*. But Lean swatted them both as one would a fly. He felt that adapting a major novel like Conrad's would be, for him, a regression, a sort of running for cover, a return to the days of his success in the Forties with *Oliver Twist* and *Great Expectations*. 'Robert,' he wrote, 'it would be really lazy to do an already written novel. If that was all we could find you should write a play. That wouldn't be the point of working together. The *Lawrence* type of biography is as near as we should get to an already written subject. Perhaps one of us might hit on a short story or even a *bad* novel as a *basis* but unless everything deserts us – no further.'[2]

Buoyed up by the success of *Lawrence*, Lean groped for a new project. He wanted to create an original, lasting piece of art, a movie that might qualify for a Nobel Prize, much less an Oscar. His ideas were vague, garbled and pretentious:

Robert. I have an idea. It's so frail I don't know how I'm going to convey it you, but at the same time it's enormous if only it could be given a shape. Maybe you'll stare at this page deadpan and think I'm loopy. I can only explain it in a very roundabout way.

I think one of the great modern-day problems for the average
man and woman in the street is a thing I can only describe as a
general lack of pride and self-respect. Added to this they have
no real faith in anything. I continually ask myself, 'What am I?
Who am I?' We people are damned lucky. We travel and we are
in a continual process of exploration in the imaginative sense.
Most people travel up on the same damned train day after day
and sit at the same damned desk. They are cogs.

I remember reading somewhere about the problem of factory
workers who spend their days tightening two kinds of bolts on a
car chassis or others that bang half completed tennis balls up
and down on a bench. None of these people can have any pride
in the finished article because they have contributed such a
small part to it unlike the old days when a man made a chair and
could take pride in the finished result . . . what, I suppose, I am
trying to say is that the average human being of today has no real
sense of purpose except in the narrowest sense of trying to earn
more money in order to buy a flat, a car or a TV. Their greatest
adventure is their two week yearly holiday. Cogs.

I was walking down Curzon Street from the cutting-rooms
one evening. There was the roar of a jet engine and I looked up
to see the great silver fish whooshing down towards London
Airport. I remember saying 'Bloody marvellous!' It is bloody
marvellous! I also remember standing in the starlit garden of the
Cecil Hotel in Old Delhi and seeing a bright star which I soon
realised was not a star because it was travelling at speed across
the heavens. I watched it until it suddenly went out as it entered
the shadow of our earth. It was of course a satellite and next day
I read in the paper that it had been launched from Cape
Canaveral and realised that I had seen it on its first trip around
the earth. Bloody bloody marvellous!!

Now, Robert. Where did all this begin? Where did we begin?
If H. G. Wells was right in his *Outline of History* we began as a
microscopic piece of jelly in a sunlit pool. We got out of that
pool. We developed lungs, legs and a brain. Then, as Wells says,
one tremendous evening one of us looked at a sunset and dimly
thought it beautiful.

Now, having explored our earth we are going outwards once
again. My silver fish over Curzon Street is taken as a matter of
course because no-one has put a frame round it. The Sputnik is
called a Russian achievement, and the fantastic Venus 'probe'
an American. They are not. They are us. Us, the jelly in the

sunlit pool. We are a part of the whole human race and I think it's the biggest success story within our knowledge.

If we could make a movie which said, 'This is the story of you. You sitting there looking up at the screen,' I think people would go out with their heads a little higher. Yes, that's just about it. Their heads a little higher. I won't go on about it because if you see at all where I am floundering you will see much further than me. I can only see rather dimly that such a movie – and I think the film medium is the only medium in which it could be done properly – could be an enormous power for peace. It would be anti race-pride, anti suburban mentality – but there I go.[3]

Robert's reply was just as long and just as flattering. It was also full of plans and ideas:

We won't bandy compliments David. You want to work with me again. Good. I want to work with you again. I admire your craft and artistry very much indeed. . . . Now, my immediate future is all occupied. There's no point in presenting the situation as other than it is. I don't just mean this present play. I'll think aloud, on paper for you:

I'll finish writing this play, God willing, pray for me, this March. Let's say it's set up immediately, in April. Rehearse May, Out of Town June, Open London July.

I'm then, if Columbia mean what they say, to write and direct a little film of *Man For All Seasons*, pray for me again. I don't think that having helped with *Lawrence* I am now a director but there are one or two ideas I want to try. I'll write it in the Autumn, shoot it in the Spring, cut it in the Summer, say complete by the early Autumn. Then (and here's the bitter bit, David) write another play. Yes, I must, there's no 'I think' about it. That will take 1964.

Then I would be ready to do another big film . . . the idea you throw out in your letter is very exciting. Almost too exciting. I smell a great, great danger in the terms you use: The greater the 'theme' the more specific must be the circumstances in which you trap it. I mean the story. The story is the frame, and it's the frame that makes the picture. Without the frame even the greatest picture would be a doodle (by frame I mean the hard rectangular, arbitrary shape of the picture). The more ambitious and imaginative the doodle is, the more sickening. *Lear* is the most thematically ambitious work in our language and look how absurdly specific is the *story*.

But this concept of the tired, lost, self-doubting, self-disgusted man we have all come to be, confronted by and responsible for the marvellous beauty and glamour of (for instance) those giant silver planes that come into London Airport in the gloaming, so meekly and gently like mysterious moths, or those shattering rockets that rip through the firmament like calico, this is a very exciting concept indeed. A warning bell is telling me that I'm not yet able to think of this in the right way. We've got to find a beautiful story to contain all this, and you can't find a beautiful story just for wanting it, but the idea of a hard, critical, unsentimental look at our present squalid predicament which shall yet be finally a message of congratulation to that sun-warmed bit of protoplasm, this is an enormous concept and one that will work on me. If you're still interested that is. I should imagine you could turn your attention elsewhere before 1965 . . .

We each have our own souls to save, David, and I know that I need lots of quiet, and solitary work, before I can embark on such an undertaking, which would be either all or nothing.[4]

Beneath the carefully gauged flattery, Robert's letter reveals a man in a state of euphoria about his career, yet deeply concerned about his private life. He faced a choice of writing plays, which would keep him at home, or writing for the cinema, which would take him away for months on end. And the two most influential women in his life were pulling in the same direction: Margaret Ramsay was urging him to commit himself to the theatre and Jo was urging him to commit himself to her and their children.

Robert and Jo had decided to move away from London. Despite the obvious attractions of the house on Richmond Green, they were unhappy there. Jo in particular disliked London and was shocked by the way that Robert's success was changing him for the worse. Whereas, back in the Butleigh days, he was gauche or easily humbled in the company of contemporaries or older people, he sometimes seemed arrogant and pompous, forever ready for an argument, forever playing the font of all wisdom.

Robert was revelling in his fame. Barely a week went by without his views – on educational issues, on nuclear disarmament, contemporary theatre, the existence of God, the fate of Mankind – being spread across one newspaper or another. He lectured at many universities around the country and was a regular panellist on the BBC-TV programme *The Brains Trust*, a peak-time ghetto for punditry. On ITV's rival programme, *Dinner Party*, he locked horns with host Malcolm Muggeridge and fellow guest Hugh Trevor-Roper when they debated the Profumo scandal which was rocking the Conservative government. While Trevor-Roper thought that John Profumo might be forgiven for keeping a mistress but not for lying in Parliament, Robert was much harsher on the philandering Minister and condemned the government for its moral bankruptcy.

Park Gates was open house to anyone in the arts. There were lavish parties at which Jo often felt excluded and insecure. Peter O'Toole and Sian Phillips, Michael Caine, Sean Connery, the Redgraves, Ralph Richardson, Peter Hall and Leslie Caron, Lindsay Anderson, Sean Kenny, Bertrand Russell, Kenneth Williams and others made their way to the Bolt residence. Richmond, surely, had not seen a greater mingling of minds since Sir Thomas More dined alone in the palace across the Green.

At one of these parties at Richmond, Robert's brother Sydney remembered seeing Arnold Wesker and Vanessa Redgrave leaning against a door frame for what seemed like hours, locked in conversation and oblivious to everyone else. 'Wesker was on a humanitarian mission', said Sydney, 'to persuade Redgrave that she had the potential to energise people and every time I passed them he was saying the same thing.'[5]

At another party, or perhaps it was the same one, Mike Kellaway saw a drunken Peter O'Toole take Ben's sound-track recording of *Lawrence of Arabia* and throw it into the fire. Sean Connery and his wife, Diane Cilento, were also among the guests. Cilento was wearing a startling miniskirt and when Jo saw her she said to Robert, 'I'm not having someone dressed like that in my house.' Unfortunately, her remark was overheard by Connery and led to a few awkward moments.

'Jo wrote and painted,' said Kellaway's wife, Liz, 'but I think she found it hard trying to compete with him or just being the wife. I remember her sitting by the fire at Richmond looking out of focus out of the window while everyone at the party talked.'[6] One way of salvaging the marriage was to move to the country. There, Robert could write in peace and Jo could paint and raise the children in more congenial surroundings. Life, surely, would be simpler there. They could be themselves again and have their closest friends down for the weekends.

Robert's parents, Ralph and Leah, had moved to Everton in Hampshire, so Robert and Jo looked for a house nearby. They quickly found what they wanted near Lymington, close to the sea and on the edge of the New Forest. Pylewell Home Farm was a sprawling farmhouse of early-Georgian origin that overlooked open pasture and, if one stood on tiptoe in the attic, you could catch the shimmer of the Solent and the hills of the Isle of Wight.

The lane to Pylewell was often carpeted with slithery cowpats as dairy cattle passed the Bolts' front door on their way to the milking shed. It was similar in its bucolic pleasures to Devon and Somerset, except that Robert was no longer the ambitious, penurious teacher who could barely afford a glass of cider. In Richmond they lived like wealthy Bohemians; in Hampshire they lived as the Lord and Lady of the Manor, with Jo dispensing wages every Friday to the domestic staff and Robert wearing silk smoking jackets.

Robert had always loved boats and being so close to the sea meant that he could indulge his passion for sailing. In Topsham he used to watch the fishing fleets and the weekend sailors, and long to be out on the water with them. In Butleigh he took the Millfield boys out sailing and in Richmond Robert finally acquired a boat of his own. In Hampshire he could sail in the Solent, towards Spithead, from where the great Captain Cook and, later, William Bligh, sailed for the South Seas.

> When I think of my childhood relationship with Dad [said Ben], the best bits involve boats. When we were sailing he seemed to be more *there*, alive to the present moment rather than preoccupied as he so often was. If I try to remember Dad simply happy, nothing comes more vividly to mind than him sitting at the tiller of a sailing boat, studying the sail for any evidence that the course or the sheet needed adjustment. He would catch me looking at him and he would smile with such an uncomplicated love of life, which in that moment would include me. It was wonderful.
>
> The first boat I remember was an eighteen-foot clinker-built sailing boat with an inboard diesel engine. She was called *Dandelion* and Dad bought her when we were at Richmond. She was moored on the Thames, just downstream of Richmond Lock on the Middlesex side, and one afternoon we christened her with champagne. When we moved to Hampshire, *Dandelion* was moored off the mud flats near our house and we used to sail her in the Solent. He also bought me a British Moth dinghy and taught me to sail it.
>
> We never planned trips, a destination, we'd just sail around for fun. He didn't regard sailing as educative, a way of learning

hard but necessary lessons about life, which was so often his way with me. Even the healthy respect for the sea which he taught me wasn't designed to make me ponder my own shortcomings. It was part of the enjoyment. He loved telling me about tides, sailing rigs, the comparative merits of hull shapes. He loved yacht chandlers more, I think, than he loved art galleries.[7]

As they settled into Pylewell, Robert was completing his play, which he called *Gentle Jack*. He told David Lean that the work was inching 'forward painfully like a wounded snake, speech by speech, day by day. . . . Oh Lord I hate writing. It's so very solitary. Of course I'd hate even worse anything that wasn't. But we've started choosing baths and sinks and things for the house in Hampshire and that's a simultaneous solace and stimulant.'[8]

Gentle Jack was not only Robert's attempt to break free of the strait-jacket of naturalism, but also his bid to be regarded as an artist, a poet of the stage. In 1960 he had told his father that Peter Hall had asked him to write a play for the RSC to star Edith Evans. Hall himself cannot remember making the suggestion and can only recall asking Robert to write two plays about the Civil War. 'But if he had come to me with *Gentle Jack*,' said Hall, 'I have to say politely that I would have turned it down.'[9]

If *Gentle Jack* had been performed at a fringe theatre, or the Royal Court or what became the National Theatre, its fate might have been different. But as a West End production from H. M. Tennent, starring Edith Evans and Kenneth Williams, it was doomed. Promoted as a 'new play from the author of *A Man For All Seasons*' its departure from traditional drama was startling and its pessimism overwhelming. This was emphatically not a 'well-made play'. *Gentle Jack* was a pagan rite in modern dress, always a risky undertaking, and its effects were so abstract and its subject so insistently symbolic that it was a failure from the first night at the Queen's Theatre on 28 November 1963. Audiences sat in silence and in a state of bewilderment: 'I think my best play was *Gentle Jack*,' Robert told *Plays and Players* magazine in 1977. 'But there was obviously something violently wrong with it because audiences sat like mice, actively hating it. I like writing in a big, grand manner [and] that's why I liked *Gentle Jack*. It was an attempt to write in what I regard as a theatrical manner without taking refuge in historical costume.'[10]

By juxtaposing the world of big business with bucolic myth, Robert was developing his central idea in *Flowering Cherry*. But where the earlier play was staunchly traditional, *Gentle Jack* was experimental, leaving the audience convinced that life offers only impossible moral choices, only the dualisms which Robert found so intriguing. Accordingly, there were two Jacks, or at least a Jack and a Jacko. The gentle one, Jacko, is an oppressed accounts clerk who works for Violet Lazara, an empress of industry who rules from a palatial City office and from Attis Abbey, deep in the forest. Although he is treated like a doormat, Jacko is attracted to the power and to the *status quo* as represented by Miss Lazara. But in the forest resides the fallen god Pan, whose survival rests on his ability to invade another's personality and compel him into acts of evil. In midsummer, Jacko inherits Jack's baleful power for a week. It ends brutally with two murders, including Jacko's own. 'Thematically it is very ambiguous and difficult,' said Robert. 'It is the life of the mind, and morality, and social order, and control, which implies repression; against the life of the body, and spontaneity, and immorality, the natural order against the social order, which implies release.'

Robert was thrilled when Dame Edith agreed to play Violet, even though, at seventy-five, she was some twenty-five years older than the character which Robert had originally conceived. While Dame Edith was known only to him as a great actress and a legend, Robert wanted his friends, especially Kenneth Williams as Jack, and Sian Phillips as Penelope, a seductress, to play other major roles. Another old friend, Noel Willman, directed the production, though Robert was so visible and active during rehearsals that he can be regarded as a co-director.

The part of Jacko went to Michael Bryant. 'I'm probably stupid,' he said, 'but I think it's a great play. But it was done appallingly badly in the West End. I mean, the glamorous woman in her forties was played by Edith Evans at the end of her career. The god Pan, the god of lust, was played by Kenneth Williams . . . it was ludicrous. And Noel Willman didn't know how to handle it at all. For instance, we had two rustics, the Brackets, who were supposed to be funny, the light relief. But Willman told them if they got a laugh he would go mad.'[11]

When Kenneth Williams was offered the role of Jack, he writhed and squirmed like a snail with salt on its head. He turned it down, then thought maybe, then said yes, and thereafter blamed himself for the play's failure. Starting in January 1963, Robert conducted a difficult six-month courtship of Williams. It proved to be an emotional minefield. In his praise of his friend's talent, and of the role, Robert suddenly realised he had not stimulated Williams's ego, only his inferiority complex: 'It is isn't vital to either you or me that you play the part,' wrote Robert in February. 'It would be agreeable, very agreeable, but it's nothing to be agonised about. . . . One gets a bit obsessed here, day after day, you know. Dear Kenny, I write no masterpiece. If you did decide to play that part I want you to take it and use it, freely and critically. To have presented it to you in the light of something to be "lived up to" is rank lunacy on my part. What I love to feel is that I've made something for an actor to have some fun with. And that's my pride.'[12]

Williams read the letter and called Robert immediately: 'He said it was a good part but obviously I would have to go under Edie Evans. But how far under? I don't know. After all, it will be me that is being a draw, not her. Why should I have to prop up these sort of ruins?'[13]

Two months later, Williams was in full flounce, resisting Robert's appeals, as he recorded in his diary for 30 April: 'One of the things I resent most of all about B. is his patronage of me. The last thing he said to me was, One thing I am certain of is that the part doesn't need you any more, "it's strong enough on its own now." No part is ever strong on its own.'[14] That did it as far as Williams was concerned. He agreed to play Jack and went to stay with Robert and Jo, where he met Noel Willman.

'We took the play to Brighton,' said Michael Bryant, 'and it was when we were all staying at the Albion Hotel that we heard the news that Kennedy had been shot. We weren't well received in Brighton. They like nice Agatha Christie plays. I opened in *Look Back in Anger* there and we were booed and hissed. They thought we were disgusting. Williams was an amiable chap, though. He used to tell filthy jokes in the Kardomah café and make the old ladies of Brighton laugh. They all knew who he was and if it was anyone else they would have walked out in a state of shock.'[15]

After two and a half weeks at the Theatre Royal, Brighton, the company moved to the Queen's in Shaftesbury Avenue to prepare for the first night and the critics.

Edith took the part without reading it [said Sian Phillips]. Her script was pristine clean except for the pages that she was on stage. She dressed herself in Hardy Amies evening gowns to play a tycoon at ten o'clock in the morning. She was completely wrong in the part but I just worshipped her and loved watching her work.

Some years later, I happened to be with Robert on the day she died. I said, 'Oh, Robert! Dame Edith has died!' He said, 'Well, I'm not sorry.' I said, 'Robert, how can you say that?' And he said, 'Well, she was no good for me.' He kind of resented the way she didn't take the play on board.

Kenneth Williams started with the best will in the world. He had to speak a lot of old Welsh in the play and he learned it from me. But his public just dragged him back into a Kenneth Williams mould. I've seen that happen to other actors. It happened slowly and imperceptibly but it wasn't what he wanted to do.[16]

Robert's friends attended the first night in force: 'We went to a supper party hosted by Binkie Beaumont,' said Mike Kellaway. 'Tony Quinton was there and reprimanded us for being overly enthusiastic about the play. Bob knew this famous psychiatrist, Masud Khan, who behaved outrageously. He went out, hijacked a van and took everyone away from the party to his big apartment in Hans Crescent. I felt very sorry for Beaumont because Bob went as well which was very bad of him. Beaumont himself wasn't even invited.'[17]

The critics were forthright in their condemnation: the play was wordy, obscure, depressing, miscast and pretentious. The only remotely kind words came from the critics of the *Daily Mail* and *The Times*. Even Harold Hobson, Robert's staunchest supporter, found it hard to disguise his disappointment. His review, with its sly reference to Robert's articles for Hobson's own paper, the *Sunday Times*, must have hurt Robert deeply: 'The story of *Gentle Jack* is confused where *Waiting for Godot* was clear: its meaning, like Mr Beckett's, is obscure; this obscurity is not lightened by any unusual eloquence; we miss the controlled and glittering wit of Christopher Fry. Mr Bolt does not seem to be equipped to be a Fry or a Beckett. He is equipped to be himself, that is, a dramatist whose new wine tastes delectably when poured out of old bottles.'[18]

Robert's Air Force friend and colleague at Millfield, Len Smith, wrote to say how much he had liked the play and how much he felt for Robert after the critical onslaught.

It is a terrible disappointment to me [replied Robert] and there is no disguising the fact that this constitutes a real failure. I do think that a playwright must write for his available audience. If a writer feels that the theatre audience is so stupid that it will not accept anything good, then he should write for some other medium. But the corollary of this is that the verdict of the audience must in some sense be accepted not only as final, but as correct. There must be something arid or arrogant or aggressive in the play which upsets people. Also, I suspect that

I tried too hard. There was I think an element of intellectual conceit in the writing. It was not a friendly play. It took a sort of God's-eye view of humanity, which is not a suitable view for any human to take. Anyway, there it is, least said soonest mended. But I thought that stylistically it did represent, here and there, an advance on my previous work.[19]

Gentle Jack was taken off in early February 1964, after only seventy-five performances. It was Robert's first taste of failure and he hated it and felt confused by it. He felt especially sad about Kenneth Williams and wrote him a touching note:

I confess that the chorus of sneers from the Press and the incomprehension of the public were so vilely uncomfortable to me ... what I regret as much as anything is that I should have involved of all people you in a failure. You are, to Jo and me, a hardy spirit of fun-in-adversity and I hate to see you tramelled with this dull thing. Doubly and trebly since I so nakedly beseeched you into it against your better judgment. Of your performance and your general behaviour throughout you already know my opinion and I won't embarrass you with repetition. My agent too, Noel, and other people were deeply struck by your preternatural discipline and the altitude of your criteria.

Well, well, let it go. Can you come and stay for a day or two in March? For the rest of this month I shall be busy on this film, and part of it abroad. Jo sends with me, Love.[20]

Robert had reached a turning point in his professional life, which was recognised and acutely analysed by his friend, John Dunn:

I think Bob wanted to be a great playwright but hadn't turned out as one. That feeling was a process, it wasn't a single moment in time. We talked a lot about *Gentle Jack* and why it hadn't worked. I think he was trying for something metaphorically grand, really. What was good about *A Man For All Seasons* was its illuminating simplification. *Gentle Jack* wasn't an effort at simplicity and he knew it didn't work. He was a bit wounded by that.

The period between *A Man For All Seasons* and *Gentle Jack* is very important in his relation to the theatre. His talent for the theatre turned out to be more humdrum while his discovery that he could reach out to the immense audience of the cinema, and as long as you weren't too pretentious about it, was something that he could do very well.[21]

FIFTEEN

LARA'S THEME

'It is amazing how complete is the delusion that beauty is goodness.'

Leo Tolstoy

Robert's commitment to the cinema was undoubtedly reinforced by the failure of *Gentle Jack*. The play had taken a full year's work and from it Robert received critical sneers and no financial return. He badly needed to make some real money.

His main preoccupation – to direct a film of *A Man For All Seasons* – was mired in studio politics. Columbia's executives were not persuaded by Robert's insistence on doing it cheaply in black and white; they wanted something with more popular appeal and hoped that a major director might want to make it. With some bravado, Robert tossed this crumb to David Lean, knowing that if Lean showed interest, so would Columbia.

Would you be interested to Direct a film of *Man For All Seasons*? I haven't breathed a word of this to anyone (except Jo) so please don't you. And no false motives, David; don't touch it if you don't want it. I know you like epic and this would be small . . .

I've decided (think I've decided, seem to have decided) that I don't want to Direct. I think I *could* or could learn to, and I want to. But I find I have one life with a limited number of years in it; so many months, days, hours in each year and it's not enough for two careers and my family and a little ordinary citizenship, too.[1]

Lean had no desire to inherit a project from Robert; he was still hoping to find something completely original. But as Lean left America by ocean liner in April 1963 – his stay in Hollywood being prolonged after he agreed to direct some scenes for *The Greatest Story Ever Told* – his agent, Phil Kellogg, handed him a novel. Lean groaned when he saw how heavy it was: 'I looked at it with its five hundred and something pages and I thought, "Oh, God." We were crossing the Atlantic and I realised I had to get down to this bloody book. So I propped myself up and I read and read the first night and became more interested. The next night I thought, "I'll finish it tonight," and ended up with a box of Kleenex, wiping the tears away. I thought if I can be touched like this, sitting in a liner, I must be able to make a good, touching film of it. As soon as I landed I contacted my agent and said, "Yes, I'll do *Doctor Zhivago*." '[2]

There was a certain irony to this decision. Lean had backed away from *Nostromo* or anything that had 'classic novel' written on the dust wrapper. His vague idea about the story of man's emergence from the primordial ooze came to nothing and it fell to Stanley Kubrick and Arthur C. Clarke to tell that story in *2001: A Space Odyssey*, a film which Robert detested. But in mid Atlantic, Lean found himself gripped by just the sort of novel he wanted to avoid. As far as Hollywood was concerned, Boris Pasternak's *Doctor Zhivago* was the *War and Peace* or the *Gone With the Wind* of the age. It had been banned in the Soviet Union, it had won a Nobel Prize, it had the Russian Revolution and it had a marvellous love story. The screen rights were already owned by the Italian producer, Carlo Ponti.

Robert, of course, had already read it and he was thrilled by the idea of turning *Doctor Zhivago* into a film; not only that, he already knew in his mind's eye what the film would look like and how much it might earn him.

> I am perfectly mesmerised by the idea of *Zhivago* [he told Lean]. I love the book and it would be an honour to work on it with you . . .
>
> How much money would I get? A percentage? Could I have a quite substantial chunk of it on signature of the contract? Would Ponti accept me as writer? Would he pay me the fantastic sort of figure the Yanks have been offering? I'd like that. Could we get effective artistic control?
>
> I'm sure we could do a good thing on *Zhivago*. If the whole film could be made atmospheric in substance but clean and athletic in story. Snow – beautiful in landscapes, downright dreary sometimes around the house, settling affectionately or like death's fingertips on a man's clothing, but best expressed by

a single crystal photographed by microcamera – why not? Are wolves to be seen anywhere these days? No, better just to hear them – have you heard that howl? My God, there's the sound of brutal nature if you like, and of the purest beauty too, it makes your scalp flap on your skull like a flag. A snow crystal to look at and a howl on the sound track – that sort of thing.

A daffodil. An ocean of daffodils. A man, tiny, stands in it. What's he doing? We hold the 'meaningless' shot long enough to raise the question. Close shot the man; what is he doing then? Just standing. We move round to his face: crying perhaps? No, just standing, and looking. His POV: the daffodils again, the birch leaves, the white birch branches, we hurl the camera through them, we race, we are drunk, we soar, we return, we skim the daffodils and settle at the man's broken-booted feet, ascend slowly to his face. He is as before; but we have been the poet's *mind* for a minute. That kind of thing, David? Risky, but oh worth *trying*.[3]

Once Lean had committed himself to making *Zhivago* there was no doubt that the film would be made or that Robert would write the screenplay. The problem arose as to which studio would finance it. Because Columbia had financed *The Bridge on the River Kwai* and *Lawrence of Arabia*, they naturally were anxious to produce Lean's next film. Ponti, though, was hoping to make a deal with MGM. The studios jousted with each other for a month or so, until Ponti had his way, selling MGM the rights to Pasternak's novel for $450,000. For Robert, this was good news: he feared that if the film were made for Columbia, Sam Spiegel would somehow become involved in it and Robert had sworn never to work for Spiegel again. The only draw-back to this arrangement was that Robert's plans to direct *A Man For All Seasons* for Columbia fell by the wayside, a casualty of the fight for *Zhivago*.

As far as Lean was concerned the arrangement could not have been better. Free from any interference from Spiegel, he quickly made friends with MGM's boss, a feisty Irish-American named Robert O'Brien, and he achieved a world record fee of $500,000 plus thirty-three per cent of the net profits. But for Lean the best part of the deal was that Ponti had decided to take a back seat: Lean claimed he met him only once before the film's première. To all intents and purposes, Lean was the film's producer as well as its director.

Robert's contract was not drawn up by Margaret Ramsay but by Irving Paul Lazar, the diminutive literary agent known to everyone in Hollywood as 'Swifty'. Because Lazar represented Pasternak's novel in America, Ramsay allowed him to negotiate with MGM on Robert's behalf. He told Lean:

> Irving has the bit between his teeth. He says [the contract] will be simple because at every dubious point I simply pass the buck to you. Thus: 'As agreed between the author and David Lean', 'If so requested by David Lean'. You'll have the legal authority to use my skin for lampshades so far as I can see.
>
> Irving says there's only one thing which is liable to be a source of deep and lasting trouble, and that is the precise basis on which I get my percentage. He said that if I want a quick conclusion to the deal I would be well advised to waive the percentage and take a larger lump sum. He says they'll pay $200,000 which I know is not as much as I'd make from a percentage of a successful film, David, but is a thumping sum of money all the same.[4]

Robert was eager to conclude the deal and receive the first tranche of his money and with Ramsay's agreement he accepted the flat fee of $200,000. If Robert had been more patient, or if Lazar and Ramsay had been shrewder and pressed for a percentage, he would have been several million dollars the richer. But Robert's decision was also influenced by Lean, who liked to tell stories of how Spiegel had swindled him out of his profit participation on both *Kwai* and *Lawrence*. For years Lean claimed he never saw a cent from *Lawrence*, though documentary evidence has since come to light to disprove this. But at the time, Lean's stories about crooked producers would have made Robert highly sceptical of promises of money further down the road. 'Oh dear oh dear,' Robert wrote to Margaret Ramsay, after the deal was concluded. 'How harsh and suspicious become the movements of the mind in this world of Big Films. I can't begin to tell you the chicanery and brutal impudence of these promoters; they leave you with your mouth open. Did you know that their principal source of income is straightforward embezzlement?'[5]

To begin with, and to put it crudely, Robert wanted to make a film about humanity in the grip of the Russian Revolution, while David Lean wanted to make a film about fucking. Robert thought the central thread of the story – that of the woman falling for the artist, the poet Zhivago, not the man – rather clichéd. This provoked an extraordinary response from Lean whose earlier love stories – *Brief*

Encounter and *The Passionate Friends* – had been about sexual repression. But behind Lean's response also lay his four failed marriages, his excitement over his relationship with Barbara Cole and his own status as an artist. In the background, too, lies Robert's own standing as an artist and as a man. While Robert was drawn to Zhivago's nobility and sensitivity, Lean invested him with great sensuality:

> I'm fascinated by what you call 'the old story of woman falling not for the man but the artist, not realising that only the man and not the artist can return their love'. Artist and man. If you agree with me that the artist is the man with the hatches off, let me try and defend him. I won't accept that only the man and not the artist can return a woman's love. The artist's woman also takes his hatches off. Don't tell me that Anne Hathaway didn't experience a full Cape Canaveral countdown (forgive the vulgarity) which she could never have experienced with an uncreative Mr Jones. Shakespeare *must* be different from Mr Jones in bed. He's just got more life force than Mr Jones (You may tell me that WS was impotent and that his tragedy was that Anne went popping off with a Sugar Ray Robinson – but in that case they were exceptions handicapped by psychological or physical kinks).
>
> Isn't love making one of the greatest forms of self-expression known to man? (It certainly is to a woman.) Isn't it therefore an art? Doesn't imagination, power, lyricism and the ability to disclose form the basis of both love and art? I'm not talking here about promiscuous fucking . . .
>
> I have a feeling that women, real women, are fathomless. A man will rise only to his own limitations, but a woman will go right on up the scale alongside the man until *he* can go no further. The imaginative lover must surely take her further up the scale than Mr Jones. Mr Jones likes to fuck but he probably calls it an overrated pastime. What I'm trying like mad to explain is that the woman who has been an orchestra with a Beethoven is in a perilous emotional situation if he should leave her. . . . I don't mean that he physically has to leave the woman, but that he may have to leave her emotionally. . . . She once had the man and the artist – now the artist has gone off to hack away at some marble and is putting all his force into that. Perhaps sex has left him altogether. I think he will be equally dismayed. One of the prices that has to be paid for the heights.[6]

Lean left Robert with little doubt that they had a love story on their hands, which was uncharted territory for Robert. His reply to Lean was especially revealing:

I can't imagine what I can have meant by saying that Zhivago's attitude to the Revolution is more important than the love story. The love story is more important than anything else. If the love story isn't powerful then the film isn't powerful . . .

I don't think I agree with you about the artist and the man. But this is metaphysics. I think artists are bound to be deplorable men unless they take special and rather artificial steps not to be. I think there's finally something wrong with being an artist. I do not for a moment accept the dictum that the artist is a self-cured neurotic, which I think is a Freudian recrudescence of the old Romantic wild-eyed dreamer thing. But I do think that a lot of deep energies which by nature go into sex, concern, money-making and other more or less animal activities are put by the artist into the creation of fictions, and there's something wrong about this. It no longer worries me for myself, I'm committed to it, but I notice that it is so.

My fictions absorb me as though they were people; I brood over them, love and resent them, tend them, and it's potty. The only possible excuse would be if they were so beautiful and potent that they could affect others too as though they were people, and that's probably a forlorn and misguided aspiration. But what I mean is that artists are so horrible that the only chance they would have of getting into Heaven would be if there were a mansion there for honest workmen. In every other respect, they are a sort of feeble demon. That's why they've always been at once greatly honoured and subtly despised.

How soon do you think we'll get round to signing contracts?[7]

This, then, was the start of *Doctor Zhivago*. From the outset Lean wanted Robert to work alongside him and since Lean, for tax reasons, was unable to stay in England, Robert would have to go abroad. Robert resisted this: he was still working on *Gentle Jack* and Jo made it clear that, having moved into their new house, she did not relish the prospect of Robert vanishing for months at a time.

A compromise was reached when Robert flew to Venice where Lean had moved with his wife, Leila, to stay at the Bauer Grunwald Hotel. It was Robert's first visit to Venice and Lean delighted in showing him the city where he had shot *Summertime* ten years earlier. Once Lean and Robert had decided on the best way to proceed with the screenplay, Robert returned to Pylewell with the intention of producing a treatment, a breakdown of the novel which would clarify their narrative line.

Before he started work in earnest, Robert needed to satisfy himself that the published English translation of *Doctor Zhivago* – by Hayward and Harari – was authentic. MGM agreed to finance an exhaustive analysis, engaging an Oxford Don, Richard Freeborn, and a Berkeley Professor, Gleb Struve, who was living in London. Freeborn's favourable report made everyone breathe a sigh of relief: without his endorsement, MGM would have had to commission a fresh translation, which would have taken months if not years.

Robert soon realised that Pasternak's novel might have been written specifically to frustrate any attempt to turn it into a film. Robert found the problems of unravelling the novel's time shifts and multiplicity of interconnecting stories a daunting task. 'That *bugger* Pasternak!' he told Lean, 'it's like "straightening cobwebs." '8

When he was writing *Lawrence of Arabia*, Robert used Lawrence's *Seven Pillars of Wisdom* as a guide to a historical event and as an insight into a character. But *Doctor Zhivago* was a totally new experience for him, a novel whose author had to be respected. Taking an axe to that exquisitely phrased prose and stripping that intricate web of chapters down to its essentials, made Robert feel like a barbarian. When the screenplay was published he wrote:

> *Doctor Zhivago* covers a great span of time. And this time is not covered flowingly but in sudden leaps. At the end of Chapter 14 Lara and Yuri have parted, Strelnikov has shot himself; the main story is over. Chapter 15 commences, 'It remains to tell the brief story of the last eight or ten years of Yuri's life . . .' and finishes with the reported death of Lara. At the start of Chapter 16 another gulf of years has been jumped; we learn of the existence of Yuri and Lara's daughter, now grown-up, and hear from her the story of her childhood, which is at least as poignant as anything in the story of her parents. As if this were not enough, the last section of this chapter begins, Five or ten years later . . .' and reflects upon the possible place of Yuri's poetry in the post-Stalinist thaw.
>
> Now, the reader of a novel can accept these very vigorously wagging tails to the main story as a pleasurable bonus. But in the film, with its overriding need for continuity, we felt that it would be hard to keep the audience in the cinema when the main story had ended and ended so tragically – and that to interest them in

the emergence and the story of an entirely new character (the daughter) so late in the evening would be very difficult indeed. But we felt that it had to be done if we were not to betray the book. The device we employed was the well-tried one of the narrator. Following a hint of Pasternak's, we promoted the shadowy figure of Yevgraf, Yuri's half brother, to this post, and still following Pasternak, we placed him half in and half out of the story.

Because of Robert's work on his play, *Gentle Jack*, and because of Lean's equivocations, it was not until March 1964, nearly a year after they agreed to make the film, that they sent their treatment – which they called 'An Account of the Intended Script' – to MGM. Robert O'Brien handed it to Russell Thacher, the studio's executive story editor and final arbiter of any commissioned screenplay. Robert, who was used to writing purely for himself, was furious when he read MGM's response: 'I am bridled to read that "in general Bolt and Lean are to be commended". Who in Hell is Russell Thacher? There's something about these letters from MGM which infuriates me. What possible value can they attach to their own opinions when nine-tenths of what they like turns out to be palpable muck? Let them ask us. We'll tell them whether it's good, bad or indifferent . . . they are passengers and should not disturb the engineers and drivers with their childish chatter.'[9]

Having scouted locations in Yugoslavia, and dismissing the idea of ever filming in the Soviet Union, Lean decided to make the film in Spain. He left his wife in Italy and moved with Barbara to the Hotel Richmond in Madrid where preparations were being made to construct Tsarist Moscow in a field outside the city. Lean insisted that Robert join him in Madrid but Robert resisted this. Not only did he want to work at home, he also felt that his presence at Pylewell was vital.

Robert locked himself away in his study for hours on end, poring over Pasternak's novel and his own independent historical research. And while he was working, the house was being renovated and embellished around him. Jo had got to know a local carpenter and handyman named Gordon Riddett who was in the house all the time, fixing cupboards and shelving units, hammering and drilling, drinking cups of tea and chatting and playing with the children. Before long, Robert started to wonder if Jo and Riddett were getting rather too friendly with each other. Then he convinced himself that they were, in fact, having an affair right under his nose.

Lean and Barbara believed that Robert's concern about his marriage was having an impact on the way he was writing *Doctor Zhivago*, especially his treatment of the two women in the film – Zhivago's loyal and devoted wife, Tonya, and Lara, who betrays her husband, Pasha, by having affairs with the lecherous opportunist, Komarovsky and then Zhivago himself. For Lean, Lara was the ultimate woman; what appalled him was that Robert was turning her into a slut and Tonya into the film's heroine. 'I find it difficult to get a really clear picture of Tonya,' a confused Lean told Barbara. 'I don't see why Robert thinks she's such a wonderful character. Maybe Robert is really saying, "Jo is a wonderful character." '

Telling Robert this was not a task which Lean relished and his closely typed, eleven-page letter to Robert took him three days to write. Rather than confront the problem head-on, Lean approached it with stealth and subtlety, each point and paragraph building up to a conclusion which Robert would have found personally shocking and dramatically sound:

> Do you realise that Lara has become quite a different woman from the Lara of the book? I find her so 'chippy'. I find Tonya *infinitely* more feminine, attractive, a really marvellous girl . . . *You* know Lara but you introduce her to me in a keyed-up state of mind which I automatically believe to be her normal self. She becomes more and more dramatic where, to put it mildly, I find her very tiresome.
>
> I beg, beg, beg you, Robert not to be offended. You can hardly help be because in this rum job of ours I'm in the position of having to do something I'd never do in real life. I'm being personal and critical about a woman you're in love with. After the first shock and affront please endeavour to stand back and see her through other eyes – as represented by mine. . . . You have got to write a Lara who has a 'certain something' that Tonya hasn't got.[10]

Robert thought Lean's letter was 'marvellous. . . . I agree with every damn thing you say about what Lara ought to be. . . . Jesus, what a mess. . . . I don't think I have some special corner in knowledge of the female; it's like claiming special knowledge of existence, just batty. Oh dear, oh dear, I'm getting really scared by this. I thought I'd done her marvellously, you know. I thought I'd written a mature woman stirred by grief and love to the very depths. I do think she should be stirred to the very depths you know, not with that old mysterious citadel of womanhood where all is calm as a secret pond.'[11]

When this crisis passed, and having completed his first draft screenplay, Robert could no longer avoid going to Madrid. But before leaving he had the most pleasant and unexpected of diversions. Robert was asked by the BBC if he might present a television documentary on Bertrand Russell, who was about to celebrate his ninety-second birthday. Even though Russell's books and philosophical treatises were hardly best-seller material, he was as famous as a film star. Consequently, Russell's gaunt features, and his shock of white hair, were a common sight on television. As he wrote in his autobiography, 'Those who wish to make up their own minds as to whether or not I am senile or, even, sillier than they had formerly believed me to be, have been given ample opportunity to do so . . .'[12]

The producer of the documentary was Malcolm Brown. 'It wasn't really my cup of tea,' he said, 'though I knew the only way to do it was to obtain a major new interview. We just had to find the right interlocutor.' When Brown proposed a number of seasoned television interviewers, Russell and his adviser, Ralph Schoenman, turned them down. Instead, they suggested Robert. 'I knew of Robert Bolt of course,' said Brown. 'I knew he had been arrested with Russell, so he qualified because he had a whiff of martyrdom. When we put the idea to him, he accepted at once but with considerable diffidence. He felt terribly honoured to be invited to interview Russell. I suspect he felt as if he would be talking to St Paul!'

Brown went to Pylewell to discuss tactics and to prepare with Robert 'a scenario of intelligent and muscular questions'. The next day, as they drove to Russell's home near Portmeirion in North Wales, they worried about Russell's advanced age. 'I thought he was a great volcano that might have gone extinct,' said Brown, 'but Robert slowly lit the flame.'

Brown had shrewdly decided to dispense with the traditional method of filming an interview with ten-minute reels: instead of using one camera, and then, once the interview was complete, turning the camera around to film the questions, he used two, loaded with thirty-minute reels. This made it possible for Brown to capture the entire interview exactly as it happened and enabled Russell to get into his conversational stride without having to break off every few minutes while the camera was reloaded.

'Although Robert and Russell didn't seem to know each other

well, there was an obvious rapport,' said Brown. 'Russell was a bit slow to start but Robert's gentle, affectionate and penetrating questions finally elicited some remarkable answers. Robert's approach was extremely modest. He didn't want to appear too clever, nor did he want to seem a fool beside that great mind. He struck the perfect balance. It was soon clear we had the makings of a fine documentary.'

Once the programme was edited to its allotted length of fifty minutes Robert had to write and record his commentary which linked his own interview with the recollections of others, including Lord and Lady Huxley, Michael Foot, Leonard Woolf and A. J. Ayer. Although Robert had never done this sort of work before, Brown was impressed by the ease with which it came to him: 'He asked me to list for him how long he had between sequences,' he said, 'and to note down the gist of what needed to be said. When he came to the recording studio he gave a flawless performance. He had timed his commentary to the second and was a dream to work with, utterly professional. It was a remarkably satisfying collaboration between a producer and a presenter and we parted the best of colleagues though our paths never crossed again.'[13]

The Life and Times of Bertrand Russell was transmitted on 19 May 1964. The reviews were nothing less than ecstatic: 'Nobody toadied,' said the *Observer*. 'Robert Bolt as narrator had a touch of natural diffidence that made a fresh change from the experienced telly interviewer's professional self-assurance.'[14]

The Times thought that 'Mr Bolt proved to be just the right man to get the best out of the great humanist with whom he has such deep and evident sympathies. It was his skill which revealed the many facets of Russell's character and belief – which projected the whole man instead of a rapid and random selection of his attributes.'[15]

The critic of the *Daily Herald* was a playwright manqué named Dennis Potter: 'Bertrand Russell', he wrote, 'could long since have subsided into the respectable oblivion of an ancient monument. But the parchment dry voice still rasps, the pen still bites into the page, the passion of a great intellect still passes out in sane and necessary rebellion. Last night's tribute did not have to take on the hushed tones of a premature obituary. The wispy figure in a windy Trafalgar Square needs no such impertinence. . . . Malcolm Brown's film was the best kind of tribute.'[16]

The only dissenting voice came from T. C. Worsely in the *Financial Times*: 'The Birthday Tribute to Bertrand Russell showed a splendid upright incorruptible old philosopher being jumped through the hoop by a moist-eyed idealist, Robert Bolt. Well, it was a birthday tribute, so fulsomeness was presumably the order of the day.'[17]

Robert left for Madrid on 29 June 1964, intending to stay for only two months, the idea being to produce the final draft with Lean and to discuss the casting. He asked Jo to accompany him, if only for the first couple of weeks, but she preferred to stay at home. Margaret Ramsay, who knew of Robert's suspicions about Jo and Riddett, warned him of trouble ahead. She knew that the film world and its attendant luxuries held little appeal for Jo and that the ease with which Robert had come out of prison had put the marriage under greater strain. 'For God's sake remember the Corruption of the Grand Hotels,' she warned him as he headed for the opulence of the Hotel Richmond.

The work was no easier than before; if anything, it was harder as Lean questioned every single dot and comma: it became a case of not being able to see the silver birch trees for the wood. While Robert had been in England, massively detailed letters were sent back and forth. Surprisingly, the letters did not stop in Madrid, when Robert and Lean were living down the corridor from each other. They would work all day, have dinner together, then send each other twenty-page memos about what they had written and discussed that day. One of Lean's missives, dated 5 October 1964 – dealing with Yuri's journey from Varykino to Yuriatin, where he meets Lara again – ran to thirty-six single-spaced pages.

Robert's contract with MGM had expired even before he left for Madrid. But his slowness in writing and Lean's equivocations were worrying MGM and Ponti, who were anxious for the film to get underway. Robert's fee was also worrying the studio since, having been paid his $200,000, he was now on a weekly rate of $1666.66 plus his living expenses. While this made him the highest paid screenwriter in the world, he was earning every cent: the work was agonising, for even if he and Lean had the story, Lean's fastidiousness meant spending days over the tiniest details, the sort of thing which most directors would leave until they were on the set with the cameraman and the actors.

If the writing created problems, the casting was no easier. Lean thought that an actress would have to be 'in the Olivier class' to play Lara. The producer, Carlo Ponti, was married to Sophia Loren who, at the time, was rivalled only by Elizabeth Taylor and Audrey Hepburn as a leading lady. Lean was terrified that Ponti might insist that Loren played Lara. 'Ponti has behaved with the utmost correctness,' he told Robert O'Brien, 'and never once has her name been mentioned to me by him, but at the same time the atmosphere is such that I would be an insensitive clot if I didn't realise what was in his mind and I find it a great unspoken embarrassment.'

Lean's objection to Loren was simple: 'I arrive at casting by trying to imagine an actor playing specific key scenes. Most actresses will be able to cope with the introductory scenes. The real test begins from the moment Komarovsky starts his seduction. The key to this scene is the girl's genuine aura of youthful innocence. . . . This is why I want a young actress. Innocence cannot be acted except on a superficial level. I would not believe this was Miss Loren's first encounter with sex and, if I don't believe it, I'd think she was a bitch.'[18]

After Loren was discreetly shunted aside, MGM proposed Yvette Mimieux and afterwards Jane Fonda, whose American accent and romance with Roger Vadim led Lean to discount her. Lean then suggested a young British actress named Sarah Miles, who had scored a big success in *The Servant*. It was Robert this time who swept that suggestion aside. 'No, no,' he told Lean, 'she's just a North Country slut.'

Julie Christie, though, had caught Lean's eye right from the start and she, together with Alec Guinness who was playing Yevgraf, was on his original 'wish list'. Like many film-makers and critics, Lean had been beguiled by Christie in *Billy Liar*, as the free-spirited girl who turns her back on the North by taking the train to London. 'She has extraordinary screen presence,' wrote Lean.

To play Yuri Zhivago himself, Lean and Robert required an actor capable of projecting romantic appeal and artistic intensity, without ever being given any conventionally heroic scenes. Throughout the film Zhivago is a rather passive figure, a man who is tossed around by history like a cork on a waterfall. MGM wanted Paul Newman.

'Oh dear,' Lean wrote to O'Brien, 'I do hate to disagree, not about his star name, but about his aura as an actor. I can only see him as a very practical young man who would be able to arrive at a decision without difficulty. I can discover nothing of the dreamer in him. . . . Zhivago is exactly the opposite; he is deeply impractical and he finds it, in the very best sense, hard to make decisions. He sees far too deeply and all the big crises in his life are taken out of his hands by fate. I hate going on like this because it makes our Zhivago sound a dreaming bore, which he is not.'[19]

Both Lean and Robert wanted Peter O'Toole to play Zhivago,

though Lean had some reservations. He had been dismayed by O'Toole's irresponsible, drunken behaviour when they were both in New York for the opening of *Lawrence of Arabia*. 'O'Toole is in fact much too extrovert for ideal casting,' wrote Lean, 'but I would rather suppress his exhibitionism than attempt to cope strength out of a lily. Unfortunately, Zhivagos do not become actors.'[20]

Robert and O'Toole had become close friends and saw a great deal of each other in London. But O'Toole had seen an early script of *Zhivago* and let it be known he thought it was terrible. Although the final draft caused him to change his mind, Lean was deeply hurt by O'Toole's initial response and did not speak to him for more than twenty years. Lean now asked Omar Sharif to play Zhivago, having previously cast him as Pasha.

Pasha was the idealistic young bolshevik who marries Lara and then metamorphoses into the tyrant Strelnikov. Robert favoured Albert Finney and wrote him a long letter explaining that the role was by far the most dramatic, even if it was not the main role. Lean, though, could never forgive Finney for turning down *Lawrence of Arabia*. Tom Courtenay was eventually cast, possibly because Lean had seen him play opposite Julie Christie in *Billy Liar*. For Komarovsky Lean had wanted Marlon Brando, then James Mason, before Rod Steiger was cast.

This left just three principal roles: Lara's mother, Zhivago's wife, Tonya, and his father. When Jeanne Moreau turned down the role of the mother because she thought she was too young, the part went to the Irish actress, Siobhan McKenna. Robert was delighted when his friend Ralph Richardson was cast as a distinctly Home Counties patriarch. For Tonya, Lean had initially thought of Audrey Hepburn but in what turned out to be an inspired choice, he cast Charlie Chaplin's daughter, Geraldine.

By late September 1964 Robert had finished the screenplay and was no longer being paid. Instead of feeling surplus to requirements, he decided to remain in Madrid, refining some sequences and contributing to the discussions about the sets and the casting. If he had been somewhat on the periphery during the making of *Lawrence of Arabia*, Robert felt wholly committed to *Doctor Zhivago* and the experience of living at a grand hotel, dealing with Hollywood studios, shuffling stars like playing cards, filled him with excitement. Initially he had found it hard to tear himself away from home; now he found it equally hard to leave Madrid. But there was something else as well, the fear of what he might find when he returned home.

Robert's reluctance to depart perplexed his two agents because no one in the film industry worked for nothing – Lean, for instance, charged the studio for every meal he ate and every cigarette he smoked. For Ramsay and Lazar, Robert was setting a dangerous and costly precedent. 'I happen to know that both Swifty and Margaret Ramsay have been "upset" because of Robert's generosity,' Lean wrote to MGM's lawyer, 'and as they split commission it must be like drinking vinegar every morning for breakfast. Joking apart, they may press for one extra week of coverage because Robert records the whole script on tape and I would not like to be without it. Whether or not Robert, Miss Ramsay or Swifty put in a bill for this I cannot tell, but if they do I suggest we pay it without quibble because I think you will agree Robert has been very generous with the overage period that in fact I believe could have stung us for quite a lot.'[21]

When Lean suggested that Robert might like to be present during the shooting Ramsay put her foot down as firmly as possible, warning Robert of the financial implications as well as the consequences for his family:

> ... all next year will be spent at the heels of David Lean. A THOUSAND TIMES NO. Other writers do a script and are let off the hook – why not you? You aren't being paid to produce, or cast, or being offered a profit-royalty. Why should you even consider this matter? It seems that David Lean is dominating you by these months under the same roof and the sooner you are under your own the better. I am prepared to be an absolute dragon on your behalf ...
>
> Now: about when you start writing your play. I beg you, really beg you, to go into this as if you are about to dedicate yourself to some religious festival! The word in the Bolt household must be SACRIFICE – and this goes for you, Jo and the kids. They are all beginning to get a little bit out of touch.
>
> You shouldn't allow yourself any of the indulgences that success and money have brought you – no living it up, no escapes to grand hotels, no special benefits. You must live as your audience lives. . . . Make 1965 an extended Lent. Try and let it be as it was while you were writing *Man*. Everyone must go into a state of siege – I will, too, if it helps.[22]

Robert left Madrid for London on 23 October 1964. He had been away from home for four months. When he got back to Pylewell, he had no alternative but to leave at once.

SIXTEEN

A WEIRD VOMITING OF THE HEART

'He that hath wife and children hath given hostages to fortune; for they are impediments to great enterprises, either of virtue or mischief.'

Francis Bacon

When Robert returned to Pylewell Home Farm, he found Jo with Gordon Riddett. Jo told Robert that their marriage was over, that she was having an affair and that she had decided to make a new life with the children and her lover. During Robert's prolonged absence in Madrid, she had continued to modernise and renovate the house. Riddett was employed to do much of the work and friends who visited Pylewell around this time noticed that an unusually large number of secondary doors and shelves were under construction.

A kindly, ordinary man, with a craftsman's methodical calmness and a countryman's modest outlook and wit, Riddett was living with his wife and child in a nearby cottage. His character was as far from Robert's as could be imagined, but since Jo regarded herself as very much alone and shared Margaret Ramsay's view that Robert's success had changed him for the worse, she found Riddett's uncomplicated dedication to her difficult to resist. Robert might conceivably have been able to cope with Jo's betrayal, were it not for the fact that Riddett was on the verge of moving into the house and seemed to be as permanent a fixture as one of his cupboard units. To Robert, it must have seemed like one of the worst clichés of romantic fiction come to life. Wasn't it a truism that so many lonely women fell for the man with mud on his boots, or wood shavings in his hair, the man who comes to fix the boiler or to build the tennis court or swimming pool? Except this was not a joke.

Robert chose the only course open to him: he left the house immediately and went to stay with his parents, who lived nearby in Everton. For two or three nights he endured his own humiliation and heartache – and that of his mother and father – before finding temporary digs at Noel Willman's flat at 33 Elizabeth Street, Chelsea. In gratitude to Willman, Robert secured him a small role in *Doctor Zhivago*, then objected to his fee of £1500 which he thought was a paltry sum.

Robert badly needed a shoulder to cry on and his friend, Ann Queensberry, not only offered hers, she needed his shoulder to cry on as well, for her husband had walked out on her, even though they had just celebrated the birth of a new baby.

Ann Queensberry and Robert had met some twenty years before in Somerset, when Ann had visited her sister-in-law at Barton St David. By chance, the Bolts were invited to dinner and they became friends that very evening: 'You can meet some people and you know instantly that you will be friends for life,' said Ann.[1]

She came from a theatrical family. Her parents were singers and she spent much of her childhood accompanying them on tour. As a result, her education was somewhat chaotic: she attended no fewer than eighteen schools. As soon as she was old enough, Ann became an actress, calling herself Ann Zane, after her great grandfather who was a Dane with a taste for drink. She married an actor, George Radford, who was the son of Basil Radford, a much loved British character actor best known for his screen partnership with Naunton Wayne. As soon as Ann gave birth to a daughter, Victoria, Radford deserted her and emigrated to Canada.

When Ann married David Queensberry she became the Marchioness of Queensberry, a grand sounding title which belied the fact that they led a simple life.

> Dave's father [said Ann] lost all his money and left him a gold watch and a burial ground in Scotland, which was already full. Dave absolutely adored my daughter, whom we called Tor, and readily adopted her. Then we had Emma.
>
> Dave was a potter and we lived in a tiny cottage in Staffordshire. I found it very difficult living in the country. I think I stuck out like a sore thumb. I wore all the wrong clothes and would go to a women's lunch thinking it was jeans and eggs on toast and they would all be wearing hats. It was also hard being an actress living in Staffordshire. Later on, though, we moved to Richmond when Dave got a job as a professor of

ceramics at the Royal College of Art.[2]

Ann and David Queensberry would have dinner with the Bolts at least once a week. They would discuss politics, marriage, children and the theatre. Their friendship was not in the least damaged when Ann auditioned unsuccessfully for both *The Tiger and the Horse* and *A Man For All Seasons*. And when the Bolts moved to Hampshire, the Queensberrys were frequent house guests. Not only had they the bond of friendship and common artistic interests, but both marriages were less than ideal. When Ann's husband disappeared for six months, Robert and Jo gave her a home away from home whenever she wanted it. Their daughters, Sally and Tor, became inseparable, and Ben and Joanna looked upon Ann as a member of the family.

On David Queensberry's return from wherever he went, Ann soon found herself pregnant again. Their problems started immediately the baby was born. According to Ann:

We had just had Alice. When she was a couple of months old, Dave told me he was going to leave me and he left that night. He rang Bob and Jo and said he was very worried about me and would they ring me and make sure I was all right. We had a long, long talk, the three of us on separate telephones. I knew that their marriage was going to end because Jo had confided in me. I think Jo is convinced that Bob left her. But it wasn't really like that. He was devastated by it.

I think Bob and Jo were determined to stay the same people. I could recognise that because when I married Dave it was a different world from the one I had been used to. With Bob, when he became successful, there was part of him that was attracted and excited by the new world he was introduced to and another part of him that didn't want to change his roots. He was away a lot and certainly Jo wasn't happy in London. Bob wasn't either, but he had his work. Jo used to paint but I think it was really tough on her. It's hard to have two stars in the same family. They had people to help, cooks and cleaners, but that's difficult to handle, too, if you've never had that before.

Bob and I met virtually daily after that as we were the perfect audience for each other. We just listened to each other for hour after hour. We were both determined that our marriages were going to come together again. We would cry and he'd get very angry, too. It was very tricky because I was still seeing Jo and it was like walking a tightrope, trying not to say anything that she had said to me that was going to hurt him. It sounds ridiculous, but we behaved like a couple of girl guides.[3]

For the next year or so, Robert and Ann were soul mates. Although she admits to falling in love with him at this time, they were more like twin brother and sister, both convinced that their marriages would be restored to them.

Robert had swiftly to reorganise his life. He needed to find a house or flat, he had to move his things, and he had to make sure that his children were safe and as happy as possible. He also had to tell David Lean what had happened; the prospect of making final adjustments to the script of *Doctor Zhivago* and recording it on to tape filled him with dread. Nevertheless, he was loath to give Lean the impression that he was incapable of work and sent him the briefest of letters: 'This is my fourth attempt to write this letter. My landmarks have gone and I don't know what style to affect. I will be factual. Jo and the children are leaving me. I think they are not only justified but right. I shall be grateful if you will keep secret to Barr and yourself my personal news for the time being.'[4]

Lean and Barbara thought that the best thing for Robert to do was to leave the wreckage behind him. They urged him not to blame himself and hoped he would join them in Spain for the start of shooting, on 14 December, when Lean could show Robert exactly how movies were made. Robert replied immediately:

David, I take your point about this built-in self-accusatory thing; what you say is true. Believe me I am not hugging my grief nor savouring my humiliation. I am exploiting the odd minutes of gaiety which come my way. But as yet they are few and far between.

I am camping out at Noel Willman's flat, he being in America. I think I must find something here in London before he gets back in a week or two. Your urging very nearly took me straight to London airport. But I should be a death's-head to you if I came out now. Can I come later? You could teach me the rudiments of your craft, and as you say I could perhaps take off from there. But for the moment I just don't know. I think I ought to write something soon, if only to have something on which to centre my self-respect.

Another thing which bothers me: I'm going to be pretty broke. If you invite me out will MGM pay my fares and my living allowance? I don't see why they should, but don't see otherwise how to afford it. The children take absolute precedence and I have to see that Jo herself is secure. Thanks for your warning about the Lawyers. I don't think the question arises. If they or anyone can embroil Jo and me in a financial wrangle then I really do give up. . . . It's all too bloody for words.[5]

Lean and Barbara offered to pay Robert's fare to Madrid, a typically generous gesture which only pierced his enormous sense of pride and plunged him into deeper despair. He wrote to Barbara:

I'm not *that* unselfish and I'm not going to be so broke that I could allow you to pay my fare to Spain. But I'm going to have to watch my expenses carefully because I want to be able to write what I want to write, for fun, for the next eighteen months, which may mean no income. What to do about Christmas is an approaching nightmare. The idea of spending it away from my children and the idea of my 'dropping in' on them in some civilised and light-footed manner are equally nauseating to me. Wherever I turn I seem to see an infinite black void with a howling wind of loneliness in it . . .

I've been to the Pickwick Club, a stamping ground of the younger theatrical set, with some vague idea of finding female solace, but at the sight of all those bright, cheap, pretty faces wreathed in cigarette smoke, their uneasy, predatory eyes, I experience a weird vomiting of the heart. Everyone and everything appears nasty. I think I appear pretty nasty myself; I have that bad smell of sadness on me than which nothing more rapidly arouses contempt . . .

The thing is (sorry to go on but it's good to talk to anyone who knows me and will listen) that I'm not yet utterly certain that this has really happened. Maybe the wish is father to the thought and it's just that I can't take it. But I can't quite believe that anything is worth the destruction of what Jo and I had, or I thought we had. She's coming to see me on Monday and perhaps I'll get a new look at her and at myself then. I know that if I am to break free and live again, then I shall have to hate her for a period at least, and the plain fact is that except for some feeble flashes of petulant resentment I am very far from hating her . . .

If this letter represents me as broken, then I've exaggerated my plight. I love your kindness to me but I'm not washed up yet.[6]

By the end of November, Robert's plight had circulated amongst his friends in London. Tony Quinton was one of those to whom Robert turned for solace and explication. 'There was that awful business of why Jo went off with that younger chap,' said Quinton. 'A lot of time was spent on analysis as to why that should have occurred. I suppose it was because he was so completely eaten up by the other things he was doing. I don't think he provoked it by any wandering around at that stage in his career; later the environment of the film industry led to a certain amount of wandering about. In fact, Bob said to me that he was completely domesticated and was so committed that he felt he paid no attention to her whatever. David Lean completely absorbed him.'[7]

Kenneth Williams noted in his diary: 'It transpired that Bob Bolt is living at Noel Willman's flat because he's left Jo Bolt. Apparently she's fallen for some carpenter or other and he is actually living in the house. It's very extraordinary, but the bogus nature of their marriage always made me suspicious. There was far too much of the "we are all so happy" stuff to be convincing.'[8]

Robert asked Mike Kellaway to intervene on his behalf by going to see Jo to try and persuade her to think again. Kellaway's own marriage to Naomi had broken up some years earlier, leaving Naomi to find herself a flat and live off tinned sardines. But no sooner had Robert asked Kellaway for this favour than he changed his mind: 'I enjoyed our faintly lugubrious evening,' he wrote, '[and] find on waking this morning a saner mood and I feel a bit of confidence. I also have a twinge of guilt. I did, despite my protestations to the contrary, ask you to see Jo. And that is nonsense. I don't mean nonsense for you to see her, but nonsense for me to ask you, or for you to see her *because* I ask you to. So if you can, regard what I said as unsaid, will you? Whatever happens between Jo and me must happen between Jo and me. I do have a terror of her getting isolated, but it's impure: I can't help hoping that our friends can do something for us; and they can't.'[9]

Robert quickly found somewhere to live – Flat 6 in a block at 15 Chelsea Embankment. There was a view of the Thames, the houseboats which were trendy Bohemian residences in the mid Sixties and, across the water, the trees of Battersea Park and that monolithic symbol of the Industrial Revolution, Battersea Power Station. Just a few hundred yards to the west, on fashionable Cheyne Walk, was Lindsey House, an impeccable seventeenth-century town house which was built on the site of Sir Thomas More's London residence.

It was comfortable, of course [said Robert's friend and former pupil, John Dunn], but it was an extremely bleak habitat. He was walking on eggshells but there was nothing feeble about him. He still had a lot of vitality. He had suffered a lot, though. First of all he had been humiliated and I think he felt he had done badly.

Jo was attractive, warm and nice to be with. But she wasn't very interesting really, whereas Bob *was* very interesting. He was one of those people who drew your thoughts and feelings out of you. It must have been very trying for her as he'd disappear for these huge spans of time, even though impressive streams of cash flowed back. I remember I went down to the house in Hampshire and Gordon Riddett was there as a very un-Dirk Bogarde sort of servant. He wasn't a force at all, he was just pleasant. But the thought that someone could have chosen him rather than Bob was an odd thought and what it suggested to me was that he was 'not' Bob rather than himself. I thought what Jo did was an act of anger and I sensed that was how Bob saw it as well.[10]

No sooner had Robert moved into his new flat than he accepted Lean's invitation and flew to Madrid. He hoped he might learn something by studying Lean's techniques and he would be able to make a tape recording of the script. His main worry was that his melancholic state might make a dismal Christmas for everyone else, though at the dinner which Lean hosted, Robert found himself sitting next to a beautiful twenty-five-year-old American girl named Carolyn Pfeiffer, who had the glamorous job of being Omar Sharif's secretary. When the film got under way, Carolyn also co-ordinated the deluge of press demands for interviews with Julie Christie and Geraldine Chaplin. 'Robert was a wonderful teacher who genuinely enjoyed expanding one's mind,' said Carolyn, who now runs a frozen yogurt business in Jamaica. 'I was like a sponge. He couldn't recommend enough books for me. We had a great friendship, and an affair. He was smarting from the break-up with his wife and was very depressed about it. I was coming off another relationship and was also a little bit vulnerable. I think that vulnerability was the magnet between us in the beginning. We had a nice time together but since I was in Spain and he was back in England, it was a long distance relationship.'[11]

Robert's fortnight in Spain sped past and on 5 January he returned to the gloom of London, still confident that Jo would come to her senses and change her mind about Riddett. Awaiting him at the empty flat on Chelsea Embankment was a letter of sympathy from Kenneth Williams and an invitation to lunch at L'Etoile in Charlotte Street where Jo and Naomi had exchanged confidences ten years earlier. Williams duly recorded the occasion in his diary: 'Met Robert Bolt at L'Etoile and we had an excellent meal, and he talked v. sensibly about the domestic upheaval. He says the impulse to start again must come from Jo and it must be genuine. I think he is absolutely right. Then we were joined by Sian and Peter O'Toole and we all went off to a place called Tiberio where the drink was flowing like mad.'[12]

Williams awoke the next morning with a serious hangover and Robert, too, felt distinctly jaded: 'Evenings with Peter always extend into the early morning don't they?' he wrote to Williams. 'It's this quality in him which you diagnosed of making every occasion a holiday. I wonder if it feels like that to him. It must be lovely if it is so.'[13]

Robert continued to send weekly letters to Lean and Barbara and received from them news of the film, which was progressing slowly, mainly due to the refusal of the Spanish mountains to produce the desired amount of snow, a problem which was solved only when Lean took a reduced crew to Finland.

In London Robert took his son, Ben, to see Peter O'Toole in *Lord Jim* and sent Lean a long critique in which he expressed admiration for the film and sympathy for its director, Richard Brooks, whose ambition to adapt Joseph Conrad brought the inevitable drubbing from the critics. Robert hoped that the same fate would not befall their adaptation of Pasternak.

Robert looked forward to these visits from his children, who would stay for a couple of nights in his flat. One immovable date in the diary was the annual Boat Show at Earls Court. 'We went to the Boat Show every year,' said Ben. 'He would entertain vague plans of buying a boat and we'd be shown over them by the salesmen. He never bought one, though while we were talking at length about this boat or that we'd sort of be doing it, enjoying a rare and fleeting relaxed intimacy. When I was staying with him in his flat in Chelsea, the two of us would just sit silently and happily reading yachting magazines while the traffic roared past outside. He had become a "Weekend Father" and he'd try and cram all paternal strictures into an impossibly short space of time, with the result that he forgot the more easygoing, instinctive side of being a dad.'[14]

In his weekly bulletins to Lean, Robert started to dwell less on his personal problems, perhaps realising that Lean and Barbara had more than enough on their hands, driving their army of extras across the Spanish 'steppes', to play father and mother confessor for much longer. 'I'm coming soon to the end of this tunnel of uncertainty. I had Ben here this last weekend and went back with him to Hampshire to see JoJo who was asking for me; she says the most heart-rending things. Between Jo and me it's awful; face to face we look at one another helplessly and feel nothing. But when we turn our backs there's a wrench from all that accumulated tenderness and respect which feels as though it will pull our heart and liver out. However, I can feel it coming to an end. . . People tell me that I've changed and I can't quite tell whether they mean for the worse or not. Not my concern anyway; the watchword is get-on-with-it.'[15]

By this time, in late February, four months after his separation from Jo, Robert had something to be getting on with. He had started to remodel his earlier radio plays, *The Thwarting of Baron Bolligrew* and its sequels. Those plays were written for children; now, though, he wrote specifically for *his* children, a bedtime story about dragons to be told in his absence. And he also returned to his very first performed play, *The Critic and the Heart*, with a view to thoroughly revising its story about the sacrifices people make for artistic endeavour. He now called it *Brother and Sister*. His new writing projects were, in fact, not attempts to forge a new life, they strove to recapture the shattered remnants of an old one.

Friends continued to rally round, though one wonders if some of Robert's principal confidantes – Ann Queensberry, Kenneth Williams and David Lean – were the ideal marriage guidance counsellors, being, in turn, emotionally traumatised because of a separation, a tormented homosexual, and a philanderer who had abandoned his son.

There were cheering dinners, too, with Ralph Richardson and Margaret Ramsay, and Robert also spent an enjoyable week at Rex Harrison's villa in Portofino. Harrison, himself no stranger to love affairs and divorces, asked Robert if he might write a screenplay about Charles II and the Restoration. Even Sam Spiegel took pity on Robert and offered not only his yacht for the summer, but also two lucrative chores of rewriting the screenplays for *The Chase* and *The Night of the Generals*.

Robert lapped up the sympathy and turned down the offers of work. Instead, he immersed himself in his plays and made several visits to Spain: 'I madly enjoy Carolyn,' he wrote to Lean, 'but it frightens me to be taking so much from someone without offering myself utterly in return. I can't offer myself utterly to anyone just now yet I can't forego the happiness she gives me. I did well to stick so rigidly to marriage: in that difficult because restricted form it was possible to behave according to my principles; now the principles don't quite fit, and I'm scared of losing principle altogether and degeneration. I see you grimace. But the Ethiope can't change his skin. You can give him a good scrub, though.'[16]

Robert continued to empty his heart and fill the ashtrays in Kenneth Williams's flat: 'Bob's conversation is as Johnsonian as ever,' Williams recorded in his diary. 'There is no sign that his conceit has lessened. I don't think that the collapse of his marriage has really harmed him. His jokes remain heavily laboured and the quotes (Thomas More etc.) are as schoolmasterian as ever . . . We talked about Jo. He is still willing to take her back but said there was a mountain of deceit standing in her way. I said that her voice was always too contrivedly modulated for my taste. I feel everything vocally.'[17]

By September 1965 Jo made it clear that she wanted a divorce and intended to marry Gordon Riddett who was himself in the process of getting one. 'Bob and Jo have now had their showdown and Jo has opted for the carpenter,' Williams recorded in his diary. 'There is a great irony here somewhere. . . . RB said he found the decision a great relief. But all his behaviour is a denial of this. There is no relief. Again & again his thoughts come back to her, and his children. He seems to have been most wickedly torn from his way of life. He said he liked & valued me & added "it is good to have friends, but especially when they have probity – that is very good". When I related this to Noel Willman he said, "Probity? It sounds like an insurance agent or something. Probity! Indeed! What a ridiculous word." '[18]

The divorce proceedings were conducted as painlessly as possible; that is to say, they hurt a great deal. The children, robbed of the everyday dull security on which all children depend and thrive, were never fully to recover from it: as with many children in these circumstances, they all believed their father did not love them any more. To ensure that Sally, Ben and Joanna were at least financially secure, Robert established a trust fund in which the children were to receive the royalties from all future stage productions of *A Man For All Seasons*. Pylewell Home Farm was sold – to the director Stuart Burge – and a new house for Jo and the children, Cuckoo Hill in Fordingbridge, was bought with money from the trust.

Just as Robert was worrying about his financial prospects, *A Man For*

All Seasons was sold to Columbia Pictures. Because he had carefully excluded any film deal from the trust fund for his children, Robert would receive $100,000 for the screen rights, £50,000 for the screenplay plus twenty-four per cent of the net profits. By any standards, it was a most lucrative deal.

The film was to be directed by Fred Zinnemann, a Hollywood veteran whose reputation was founded on *High Noon* and *From Here to Eternity*. Like his friend David Lean, Zinnemann was a perfectionist, intensely serious and socially rather shy; and like William Wyler, he was very deaf, an affliction which could be used to his tactical advantage on the set. Zinnemann said:

> I saw the play during its first run and found it a very moving experience, though I didn't think it would make a film because of the enormous amount of dialogue. Later on, when I was having difficulty in finding material, Mike Frankovich of Columbia, who was a great friend of mine, called to suggest I do it. They had bought the rights to the play, even though Bob was having misgivings because he felt he was being pushed around by the studio. He feared he would lose control of it but Peggy Ramsay persuaded him to stick with it.
>
> Columbia at the time were involved with some very expensive productions based in Britain. They wanted this made cheaply, for around two million dollars. I accepted a low, but not abnormally low fee in return for total control, though I knew that Bob was the real creator of the story. I was an interpreter, not a conductor.[19]

Having told the story of Sir Thomas More for radio, television and the stage, Robert now reinvented him for the cinema; Sir Thomas had indeed become a man for all media.

The principal problem was how to adapt what Robert himself described as 'bastardised Brecht' for the more naturalistic terrain of film. While Zinnemann had a natural sympathy for the play's principal theme of individual conscience, he didn't want to stint on the pageantry of royal palaces, stately homes, sixteenth-century gardens and barges on the Thames. The film was to be as lavish as the budget allowed and the climactic inquisition scene in the Palace of Westminster, so stylised and minimalist on the stage, would become a set piece, with scores of costumed extras and a huge interior set. The art director John Box, who had conjured up Akaba and Tsarist Russia in Spain for *Lawrence of Arabia* and *Doctor Zhivago*, was to perform similar miracles by rebuilding the façade of

Hampton Court on the studio back lot for £5000.

The only casualty in the transposition to the screen was the Common Man. Robert failed to see how this character could translate into filmic terms; after all, neither he nor Zinnemann was a cinematic innovator like Jean-Luc Godard or Alain Resnais and *A Man For All Seasons* was for mainstream cinemas, not the art houses. Zinnemann, though, hoped that the Common Man might be retained and virtually all their early discussions centred on this problem. 'I asked him to try and keep the character, the all-time opportunist who winds up as the executioner,' said Zinnemann. 'I thought he was just marvellous. But it just didn't work for a film. I was astonished that Bob would so eagerly change things and cut characters himself.'[20]

Although Leo McKern had caused problems with the Broadway production, Robert felt a loyalty to him and asked him to play the odious Thomas Cromwell once again. But McKern still mourned the loss of his beloved Common Man: 'Robert Bolt's play made a highly successful film,' he wrote, 'but it is not as good a film as the play is a play because the limitations of the cinema (and this seems a paradox, for one would expect the cinema's possibilities to be greater) could not encompass the licence that the play enjoyed – mainly, the character of the Common Man. Because of his exclusion from the film, a highly important facet of the play was lost, even though the author attempted to retain him. The conventions of theatre, so readily accepted by audiences through suspension of disbelief, proved unworkable in this film.'[21]

Once the problem of the Common Man was resolved, Robert found that the work came easily: 'It's coming faster than I can write it down,' he wrote to Barbara Cole. 'I know the material backwards of course, and all I've learned from working with David seems to be available to me. It's wonderful and I'm grateful to him.'[22]

Robert was doubly relieved that he was writing the script in record time because he was desperate to be involved with the editing of *Doctor Zhivago*, which he felt was just as much his creation as David Lean's. Shooting on *Doctor Zhivago* ended on 7 October 1965, when Lean, Barbara Cole and the editor, Norman Savage, flew to the MGM studios in Hollywood. MGM insisted that the picture be ready for release by Christmas in order to qualify for the Academy Awards and to reap the potential harvest of festive cinema-goers. While a mere three months to cut, dub and score a three-hour picture would seem impossible to most film directors, especially in the days before computerised techniques, Lean relished the task.

Robert searched for a way to honour his commitments to Zinnemann, who he knew would want to pick over the script in minute detail, and still be able to join Lean in Los Angeles.

This dilemma escalated into what might be termed a 'trilemma' when, out of the blue, he was invited to China. Since China was then rarely visited by Westerners, Robert had little hesitation in accepting. In separate letters to Lean and Barbara he said, 'I am invited to China for three weeks as a guest of the Red Government, together with three other persons of known Left-Wing sympathies. . . . I suppose they hope to convert us or make us instruments of propaganda, but there can't be any harm in looking and it's an opportunity not to be missed isn't it? I feel a bit guilty because Freddie's mad to get the first draft of *Man* (Incidentally, what a decent, gentle, tough little man that is). But partly because I'd half said I'd go some time ago, if they couldn't find anyone else, and partly because I feel a need to crack out of London and this bloody bloody flat, I'm looking forward to it. It's quite an adventure by my modest standards of travel.'[23, 24]

'I was eager for the script,' said Zinnemann, 'and when Bob said he was going to China he thought I would just sit and wait for it. But I didn't. I went mountain climbing.'[25]

Robert was a sponsor of the Society for Anglo-Chinese Understanding, known by its acronym SACU. Like CND, its upper echelons comprised the usual suspects of artists, intellectuals, union officials, labour politicians and members of the House of Lords. With the Soviet Union, under Krushchev, having momentarily opened up to the West, China became the great unknown, the last frontier, the most desirable place on earth to see, and be seen in. While some SACU members had a genuine interest in China and Chinese history, others enlisted merely in the hope of an exotic freebie. But by publicly supporting SACU, members were announcing their allegiance to Chinese communism and left themselves, and their reputations, open to exploitation.

On 24 September 1965 Robert reported at Heathrow Airport and met his three fellow travellers, among them the distinguished historian Hugh Trevor-Roper, now Lord Dacre, with whom Robert had already exchanged views on the television programme *Dinner Party* in 1963. Robert was a substitute for Vanessa Redgrave who had decided, at the last possible moment, to abandon the trip and return to Rome, where her marriage to Tony Richardson was in difficulty. Trevor-Roper was a substitute for Maurice Bowra, the

warden of Wadham College, who had declined the invitation for
health reasons.

> It was a party of four [said Trevor-Roper]. The other two were
> Mary Adams and Ernest Roberts. Mary Adams was one of the
> silliest women I've ever met. She was a professional joiner, she
> was vice-president of the telephone users' society, the patients'
> society, this society, that society and, of course, SACU. She had
> no mind at all. Ernie Roberts was a frightful character, the
> assistant general secretary of the engineering union, the AUEW.
> He was a trades union hack, an *apparatchik*. He was very
> dapper, with smart shirts and ties, and his hands had obviously
> never touched a machine. He was a total blind bigot.
> At the airport, Ernie Roberts appeared with the *Daily Worker*
> ostentatiously protruding from his pocket. Derek Bryan, the
> secretary of SACU, told him to conceal that because we might
> be photographed. This was the first admission to me that we
> were crypto-communists.[26]

The four delegates were each to examine a different aspect of
Chinese society. Robert was to meet Chinese playwrights and see as
much Chinese theatre as possible; Trevor-Roper was to visit universities; Mary Adams, who was also on the board of the Independent
Broadcasting Authority, was to watch television, visit the studios, as
well as study developments in social welfare; Ernie Roberts was to
hold discussions with Chinese trades union leaders. But the mission
did not work out quite as SACU expected. As Derek Bryan said,
'SACU was launched at a very bad moment because the next year
the Cultural Revolution started. That gave us lots of difficulties, of
which Trevor-Roper was one.'[27]

As David Lean was recreating Russia in Spain, Robert flew over
the real thing. The journey was arduous, subject to bureaucratic
delays and unscheduled stops, but the party eventually arrived at the
Chien Men Hotel in Peking. 'Robert Bolt started complaining,'
recalled Trevor-Roper. 'He said, "We are not being treated in
accordance with my status." He was very status-minded and not
satisfied at all. He was quite right in a way because we were obviously
regarded as a very low form of life, what Lenin called "useful
idiots." '[28]

Robert and Trevor-Roper soon realised they would never be able
to meet the people they expected to see. While Robert was taken to
see many examples of contemporary Chinese theatre and opera,
which were staged in miners' clubs and workers' halls as well as

conventional theatres, he was denied access to any playwright. In fact, he soon discovered that the traditional idea of the single playwright, beavering away in a Peking garret, simply did not exist in Revolutionary China. In this respect the Great Leap Forward was more of a step backwards; Robert simply took heart in the fact that whatever production he saw drew huge audiences of ordinary working people. He said:

> On the whole, these plays were committee pieces, rather like American films with three or four scriptwriters. There is also, I gather, a watching brief held by the party as the play is written, to make sure that nothing untoward is said. It is difficult to say anything about the quality of the writing, as I don't speak Chinese, but the plays I saw I read in translation and the lyric bits, the songs, struck me as distinctly poetic. This committee producing has great strengths ... there is certainly a tremendous feeling of team spirit on the stage. You never see an actor slacking, however tiny his part, with the result that the play is one long explosion of energy ...
>
> It is going to be very interesting to see if they can hold on to their conventions when they've stopped making these totally black and white plays, wherein the good triumph and the wicked, after seeming to triumph, are cast into outer darkness. When they begin to attack the more subtle and difficult modern problems then they will have a theatre which will be adaptable all over the world, certainly a kind of theatre which I myself would like to see.[29]

By the end of their first week in the People's Republic, Robert's and Trevor-Roper's frustration with the bureaucracy was giving their hosts cause for concern.

> Our guides were morons [said Trevor-Roper], and their table manners were awful. There was an exaggerated emphasis on proletarianism, as if certain forms of civility were regarded as bourgeois deviation. So they advertised their peasant heritage when eating. One of the guides would throw bits of food on the floor. There was something repulsive about them. They were barbarians really. Robert described one of them as the archetypal Peking Man.
>
> Robert also accused me of making a great mistake. At the airport in London, Derek Bryan said we had to choose a leader of our delegation since the Chinese would expect it. I proposed

that Mary Adams should be our leader on the grounds that she was the oldest and on the grounds that she was a woman. As a consequence of this, Mrs Adams was presented to Chairman Mao on National Day when there was a vast ceremony. Mao shuffled in and had to be helped on to the dais. He looked as if he'd had a stroke. The speech was delivered by Chou En-Lai. We were seated as far as possible from the balcony but we watched as Mrs Adams was taken up to meet the great man. This gave her ego an unnecessary boost.[30]

When Robert and Trevor-Roper began to abscond and took to walking on their own, their guides decided to restore discipline by moving the delegation out of Peking. The problem was, they had no idea where to take them. 'I was the only one who knew anything about China,' said Trevor-Roper, 'so I said firmly that we should go to Luoyang and Xi'an which were the historic capitals. This made Ernie Roberts rather cross because I don't think he wanted to see anything. He just wanted to say that he'd been to China.'

The gang of four inspected Luoyang and Xi'an (which did not then have a terracotta army on display) and were then invited to visit Shanghai. While Mary Adams and Ernie Roberts readily agreed, Robert and Trevor-Roper dissented and announced their premature return to London. 'Robert and I were very frustrated,' said Trevor-Roper, 'I think we saved each other from going mad. At the end we broke away. We'd had enough. I told the Chinese I wanted to return home on the Trans-Siberian express. I wanted to show them that I wasn't in a hurry to get home. I was just in a hurry to get away from them.'[31]

Robert arrived home exhausted on 8 October 1965 and, a month later, had the dismal prospect of addressing the full SACU membership. Hugh Trevor-Roper had already caused a stir by his article in the *Sunday Times* in which he castigated China for everything except its scenery and ancient history. The article was headlined 'The Sick Mind of China', a title which, he hastened to point out, was not his responsibility. The SACU members held their breath.

Mary Adams, who spoke first, said she was unable to watch much television but had been impressed by the 'happy, well-fed and clothed people'. She approved of the country's birth control programme and forgave the relentless propaganda because it reflected a 'consistent philosophy'. Trevor-Roper said he had been subjected to a 'horse drench of propaganda and was expected to evacuate it in this country'. Ernie Roberts said he saw everything he wanted to see and was impressed by the 'atmosphere of freedom and security'. Robert, who spoke last, said he had been 'deeply impressed by the egalitarianism he had encountered, such as finding a factory director sharing identical housing with his workers'.[32]

A little less than three months after Robert's visit China closed its borders and embarked upon its genocidal Cultural Revolution. In the light of that, Robert might subsequently have regretted many of the things he said – regretted even mere ambivalence – for he was, to some extent, blinded by the propaganda. As he wrote to David Lean, 'What the Red Government is doing is overwhelmingly good, but oh my stars the impacted self-righteous narrowmindedness and superiority.' He added a piquant afterthought about *Doctor Zhivago*: 'Oh, Siberia really is covered with silver birches, and very extraordinary they are.' [33]

Inevitably, Robert failed to deliver his script to Zinnemann on time, which prevented him from joining Lean in Los Angeles.

> I've been trying to cram the first draft of *Man* into the space before November 1st and haven't managed it [he wrote to Lean]. When I spoke to Freddie about coming out to be with you he pulled a very long face indeed and I dropped it at once. So short of his accepting the first draft in its entirety as a Final Version, which is in the last degree improbable, I don't see how to be with you until it will be too late . . .
>
> It maddens me not to be with you, partly because I should just like on principle to see you cutting, and particularly since you seem to contemplate some pretty radical alterations in the story-telling. I know you'll improve it by what you do, but I feel as though something were being done to me while I was asleep. I'm horribly anxious for the film to be a big success and look forward to seeing it with a nauseous mixture of fear and expectation – Fear, not because I fear anything *you* may have done, but in case what we did together proves less good than it seemed to us at the time. It was difficult, wasn't it?
>
> Is it *moving?* Oh Lord, I wish the premiere over and done with. . . . What *you* must feel like on such occasions I don't know . . .[34]

As Robert predicted, Zinnemann took a microscope to the first draft and within a month Robert had completed a second draft. 'I'm liking work with Freddie very much,' he wrote to Lean. 'He's tough but not stubborn and doesn't care who "wins" so long as something good emerges. His weakness, for this project in particular, is exactly as you predicted: he's more in love with the play than I am, so that the comic situation arises of him wanting to retain things for their "beauty" which I want to pitch out in favour of speed. But I think it'll be good, though I can't see it making a penny.'[35]

Having shown loyalty to Leo McKern, Robert and Zinnemann were both convinced that Paul Scofield should repeat his stage role and that all attempts by Hollywood to cast an established star should be resisted. But Scofield had appeared in only two films since his screen début in 1954 and was not regarded by Hollywood as an actor likely to draw an audience. Columbia's preferred casting was Laurence Olivier as More, Alec Guinness as Cardinal Wolsey and Peter O'Toole as the King.

Since it was widely known that Laurence Olivier coveted the role, Robert and Zinnemann went through the motions of a meeting, though Zinnemann knew that Olivier's assertive style of acting was seriously at odds with the character. Richard Burton was also a contender, having recently starred in the screen version of *Becket*, though his crowded schedule, as well as his normal fee of $1 million, quickly put paid to his chances.

Columbia finally relented and agreed to Scofield starring in the film. He was paid the peculiarly precise fee of £26,785.14s.3d, plus a respectable ten per cent of the net profits. It was Scofield who transformed the production when it started shooting the following March: 'On the first two days of shooting,' said Zinnemann, 'the crew behaved as if it was just another movie. On the third day Scofield had a speech to make and then it became a mission rather than a movie.'[36]

'I was surprised and honoured to be chosen for the film,' said Scofield, 'being almost unknown in the movie world. I missed the Common Man as a potent link between More and the working man, but accepted that a film is not a play. My own task was unaltered except that I now focused my thought on to a camera instead of an audience.'[37]

Scofield's performance won him an Academy Award and a fame which he habitually shunned. 'I can't come to California for the awards presentations,' he told Zinnemann. 'It will come as no surprise to you that I am not sorry at the prospect of missing the occasion, but it does cause me a sense of real regret in that I know you would like me to go. I would hate above all to cause in you any sense of disappointment in my course of action. I am wiring full regrets and explanation to the Academy people.'[38]

Thirty years later, Scofield is able to look back on *A Man For All Seasons* and the role with which he became so closely identified:

> I was lucky. I'd done a lot of work in the theatre; at Stratford and for H. M. Tennent in London. I'd even done a musical, but being asked to play Sir Thomas More was an unexpected gift. I would have imagined that, let's say, Sir Ralph Richardson had more qualifications for the role and that a film star would be chosen for the movie.
>
> It is hard to know one's own strengths or weaknesses, but certainly I felt I could play it, and the character and the play became a defining cornerstone or milestone for me, though less so than *King Lear*. The hazard of being part of the kind of success enjoyed by all of us who took part in *A Man For All Seasons* is that one is subsequently only thought of in terms of the character one played. Thus many saintly roles came my way in the immediate thereafter and were not interesting for that reason.[39]

Richard Harris and Peter O'Toole were in the running to play Henry VIII before Robert Shaw was hired for £10,000 compared with the $350,000 he had been paid for his last film, the Second World War epic, *Battle of the Bulge*. It was, though, a decent fee for what was little more than an exuberant cameo. Shaw, who was a fiery, intensely competitive actor, as well as a playwright of some distinction, would become a close friend of Robert's and his saviour when the press pursued him in Los Angeles some seven years later.

After Vanessa Redgrave regretfully turned down the role of More's daughter, Margaret, preferring to film Antonioni's *Blowup* by day and play in *The Prime of Miss Jean Brodie* by night, the part went to Susannah York, for a fee of £12,000. Wendy Hiller – a personal favourite of Zinnemann's – received £8000 for playing More's devoted wife and for his screen début as the scheming Robert Rich, John Hurt was signed for £3000. Zinnemann then pulled off a coup by casting Orson Welles as Cardinal Wolsey for a fee which, doubtless, was as vast as his bulk and talent.[40]

Robert was enjoying himself: he was exerting a genuine influence over the casting of the picture and could legitimately regard himself as more than just a screenwriter. But *A Man For All Seasons* was only one of three babies requiring his constant attention: the RSC had decided to stage *Bolligrew* while in America MGM was preparing for the world première of *Doctor Zhivago*. Robert, realising he had no way of seeing it before the première, deluged Lean with letters about the film:

> Marvellous that you find Julie so good. If you're right in thinking she'll soon be where Peter was after *Lawrence* I hope she isn't exploited, or doesn't exploits herself, so hard. He seems to be in a bit of a pickle. *Why* do films destroy so much young talent?
>
> How splendid that Omar is appearing so finely as you cut. If we've got a quietly impressive Yuri I think we may be all right. I've been sweating a bit on that score ever since you told me how strongly Lara and Komarovsky assert themselves. I'm, perversely, a bit pleased that you now have reservations about Rod's performance. Just as a big English actor (like Ralphie) *will* wear his heart on his sleeve, so these Americans (like Quinn) will wear their balls on their sleeve – where to my mind they look most unsightly and distract attention from the performance.[41]

Margaret Ramsay had sent Robert's script of *The Thwarting of Baron Bolligrew* to Peter Hall at the Royal Shakespeare Company. Hall's stewardship of the RSC was never less than controversial: his autocratic management style attracted as many brickbats as his creative flair drew plaudits. His Shakespeare productions were often radical and in Harold Pinter, who had become his 'house playwright', he had steered the RSC into a position of equality if not supremacy over the National Theatre.

If Hall's interpretations of Shakespeare and Pinter's minimalist essays in pessimism sometimes constituted an aesthetic challenge to the RSC audience, Hall's Co-Director Peter Brook's interest in the 'Theatre of Cruelty' courted the attention of the censor, the Lord Chamberlain. Brook's productions of *The Marat-Sade*, starring Glenda Jackson, and *US*, an obscenity-ridden tirade against the Vietnam war, outraged many of the RSCs supporters and board members. Peter Cadbury, who ran the powerful Keith Prowse ticket agency, hit the headlines when he denounced the RSC's plays as bordering on the obscene. There were calls in the tabloid press for the West End to be 'cleaned up'.

As a result of these artistic and managerial tensions the RSC was always having to justify its Arts Council grant which, for 1965–6, was £90,000, a figure which left the Company with a runaway deficit. The RSC was accused of being defamatory, élitist and expensive; most important, there were many who felt that the National Theatre should be the sole beneficiary of taxpayers' subsidy. Hall now demanded a rise in the grant to £247,000 per year.

In order to deflect many of the criticisms, Hall looked for ways to broaden the RSC's appeal. He wanted a family audience to dispel the belief that the RSC catered only to intellectuals with a taste for sadism and other *outré* delights. He also wanted as many children in his audience as possible, and not just school parties for *Romeo and Juliet* or *A Midsummer Night's Dream*. 'We were trying to get children into the Aldwych,' he said. 'It's a task which the theatre still has, but I think all theatre people who have children want to do children's plays. We all want to feed our children. It's a kind of therapy.'[42]

Although Hall and Robert had seen relatively little of each other in the last two or three years – their careers had gone in different directions and their divorces had effectively ended their socialising – they remained firm friends. Hall had no hesitation in staging *Bolligrew*, for it was the very thing he was looking for: a new work by a major playwright which would appeal to children.

He decided to present the play over the Christmas period, a bold and politically shrewd move which would nudge the Aldwych Theatre and the RSC towards the highly competitive Christmas Panto market. *Bolligrew* would not, though, have a 'first night', rather a 'first matinée' on the afternoon of 11 December. The run, which was to end on 15 January 1966, would include only three evening performances. Hall handed over the production to the most favoured young director on his staff, Trevor Nunn, who said:

> It was during a probationary period I had at the RSC. Peter Hall wanted me to be the next Associate Director but he wanted me to begin as an assistant. The first thing I did was one half of one evening of one-act plays. The second thing was *Bolligrew* and of course it was a coup as far as I was concerned to be offered a play by Robert Bolt. It had to be cast with existing RSC players and designed to fit within the programme of plays being performed in the evenings.
>
> It was a play that exemplified language, wit and the power of the imagination. Its laconic tone, ironies and slapstick exaggeration were designed to amuse the parents as much as the children. In Sir Oblong Fitz-Oblong, I felt Robert was seeing himself as being schoolmasterly, innocent, dogged, to some extent gullible. I sensed there was some self-amusement in it.[43]

Like so many of Robert's plays, *Bolligrew* began as a radio production which proved so popular with listeners that Robert was encouraged to write several more yarns about the curmudgeonly Baron and his arch-nemesis, the pedantic Sir Oblong Fitz-Oblong. What Robert regarded as an archetypal story about moral imperatives, children could see as a ripping yarn of dragons, noble knights, hissable villains, rhubarbing peasants and a pair of talking magpies, all costumed up to the nines. And there was a veritable feast of funny words such as 'mulligrubs', and weird names such as Obidiah Bobblenob. To reinforce the idea of the play as a 'story', there was a formal Story-teller, a Common Man, who not only stood on stage to explain and introduce the action, but also occasionally engaged the characters in conversation. There was a minimum of scenery since any recreation of caves, castles and forests would have been expensive and unavoidably phoney; instead, there were scores of props, off-stage musical effects and a bogus ruin which could be moved around on castors and on top of which the magpies made their nest. Nunn's production was as stylised as anything the London stage had ever seen and Ann Curtis's costumes celebrated the incongruous: the Story-teller wore glasses, a modern suit and bow-tie; Bolligrew wore a handlebar moustache, a garish check jacket, pantaloons and a cheese-cutter hat; Sir Oblong might have just shopped at the Camelot branch of Burton's.

Robert's old friend, Leo McKern, took little persuading to play Bolligrew and he fitted Robert's description precisely: 'Small but burly; red face, black whiskers, choleric and selfish but with the fascination of childish greed.' At rehearsals McKern said, 'Kids are the most rewarding audience in the world. Once you've got them laughing, well, it's the greatest sound an actor ever heard.'[44]

RSC regulars John Normington and Michael Jayston took the parts of Sir Oblong and the Story-teller. The dragon was also a character, whose voice was recorded on tape. Although Robert claimed that he played the dragon – and he is listed in the cast of the original programme – it seems that Paul Scofield also made a recording of the dragon's lines. Nunn is positive that it was Scofield's recording which was used, though Scofield himself is unsure. 'How odd,' he said. 'I'm quite sure that Robert did a recording because I have a distinct recollection of actually hearing it. This was perhaps when I did my recording, as some sort of illustration for me.'[45]

Trevor Nunn cannot recall Robert attending any of the rehearsals. 'He was uncontactable, detained somewhere,' he said. This absence worried Nunn who was introducing many changes to the script, notably some musical sequences. 'I thought the play would be enhanced and expanded,' he said. 'I thought we could offer more. So I wrote some songs and Guy Wolfenden wrote the music. When I finally got Robert on the phone he said, "What's this I hear? What's going on?" Finally he came to see it at the dress rehearsal. He concluded that he didn't find anything sufficiently offensive to want it removed. However, he was absolutely clear that the music should not be part of the published text.'[46]

To help publicise the play the RSC launched a competition for the best review written by anyone under the age of sixteen. The prize was a visit backstage and a tea party with the cast. The genuine newspaper reviews, coming at the end of a dreadful year for Robert, were heartening, even if the majority of critics tended to base their judgements on those of their children, grandchildren and anything in pigtails or short trousers they could persuade to accompany them to the Aldwych.

Milton Shulman's young advisers had a few reservations. Accordingly, so did Shulman: 'Mr Bolt introduced too many sophisticated qualifications in his characters when in this kind of play children can only really understand simple and stark goodies and baddies. Yet there were some exciting scenes with lots of dragon's breath and romping and sword fights that kept the audience noisily amused even if they only vaguely understood what was going on.'[47]

'There is some comic sword-play and some polychromatic magic,' wrote B. A. Young in the *Financial Times*, without reference to anyone under ten. 'There are no girls whatever, which simplifies Mr Bolt's task of suffusing the whole proceedings with a sturdy middle-class moral atmosphere that, like the general tone of the dialogue, put me in mind of T. H. White.' Young then succumbed and asked a twelve-year-old if he preferred knights and dragons on stage or *Dr Who and the Daleks*, who were on television every week. 'After an inner struggle with his better nature, he said Daleks. But parents with conservative ideas about the literary and moral quality of their children's entertainment may well prefer *Bolligrew*.'[48]

The anonymous critic of *The Times* took no child to the Aldwych, merely his critical faculties:

It may seem a backhanded compliment to describe this children's entertainment as Robert Bolt's best play to date, but it is certainly the best constructed. Mr Bolt's talent is one that thrives on the traditional conventions and his big problem in the past has been to find a workable dramatic form at a time when such conventions have largely broken down. This problem does not arise in writing for children, for here the old rules of story telling remain intact: and in *The Thwarting of Baron Bolligrew* he has given up his losing battle against naturalism and spun a tale of magic and talking animals with a good strong plot line and a firm moral. . . . It is an irresistible entertainment for anyone over the age of eight.[49]

Robert's brother, Sydney, has a particularly high regard for *Bolligrew*:

The reasons why I have always thought *Bolligrew* to be Bob's best play are long-standing. In one way they are technical. It is truly 'epic', in Brecht's sense: the detachment from the action, the sense that the actors are not identifying with characters but telling a story about them adds the necessary salt to the work of a writer whose interest is so ethical . . .

This results in an irony missing from the More play, which is also about a good man. More may have difficulty making a choice, but he has none about being morally superior to everyone around him. A good man is bound to know that he is better than other people, unless he is a fool. How does he handle the knowledge? Humility, the virtue on which the wicked magician operates, is particularly tricky in this connection. And yet everything is obvious – on the stage. The wicked magician is the only complete villain who, significantly, is an academic.

There is a good joke about realism towards the end of the first act which is typical of the tone of the whole play. Exeunt Oblong and Blackheart fighting desperately, and the narrator warns the audience that it is not the best man but the best fighter who wins a fight. They re-enter. Oblong has won.[50]

'After finishing the script for *Doctor Zhivago* I was deeply tired,' said Robert. 'I wanted to write something which was less demanding, something with a straight narrative line. Of course, that was nonsense. *Bolligrew* turned out to be as much of a salt mine as anything else. . . . Of all the plays I've written, this is the one that has given me the greatest pleasure.'[51] For Robert, writing *Bolligrew* was a purgatory experience, a memory of the myth and magic of Devon and Somerset and a present to his children. When *The Thwarting of Baron Bolligrew* was published by Heinemann, the dedication page read 'For Joanna'.

Doctor Zhivago opened at the Capitol Theatre in New York on 22 December 1965. By a strange irony, it was not Robert's commitment to Fred Zinnemann which prevented him from attending, it was his visit to China. The American Embassy viewed with the deepest suspicion his links with Chinese communism and turned down his application for a visa. Robert also had a criminal record, thanks to his CND activities, and since he was one of many signatories to an advertisement in the *New York Times* which protested the Vietnam War, he epitomised the undesirable alien: intelligent, outspoken, dangerous. Even the combined forces of Margaret Ramsay and MGM could not persuade the US Immigration Service to let him in.

Not only was Robert denied the thrill of seeing the picture with Lean at the world première, he was not to see it for three months. In addition to an invitation to New York, he had also received one to a dinner party in London. Robert had been to many such parties and in the weeks preceding Christmas he often had a choice of two or three. Usually they were uninteresting, a few hours of pleasant theatre gossip, perhaps an opportunity to lecture his fellow guests on a matter that concerned him, followed by vague promises to meet next month for a drink to discuss a possible script. As this party was hosted by a close friend, Leslie Caron, he accepted readily. The evening was to transform his life.

SEVENTEEN

SARAH

'Mad, bad and dangerous to know.'

Lady Caroline Lamb on Lord Byron

It was a chilly evening in November 1965 when Robert arrived at 31 Montpelier Square, one of many elegant, wistaria-clad town houses just a wallet's throw from Harrods. He rang the bell and was ushered up to the impeccably decorated first-floor drawing room where he met his hosts, the actress Leslie Caron and the actor Warren Beatty.

Caron and Peter Hall had recently divorced and because the settlement required that their children remain in Britain, Beatty had moved his career from Hollywood to Europe, a sure sign of his devotion to Caron. Beatty and Caron had just made a film together called *Promise Her Anything*, a piece of romantic fluff set in Paris which was made in London. Now Beatty was preparing to make *Kaleidoscope*, a comedy-thriller which would have drugs, gambling clubs and Swinging London as its trendy background.

Before the guests sat down for dinner, Robert rolled up his shirt-sleeves, parked himself on a sofa and lit his pipe. A young woman sat next to him. She had not wanted to go to the party and had been frog-marched to Montpelier Square by her agent. Dressed in a miniskirt and high-heeled shoes, the young woman was every slender inch the Sixties 'dolly bird'.

Robert turned to her and said, 'You look like a debauched Alice in Wonderland.'

'Since I didn't dress myself, I cannot be held responsible.'

'It wasn't your clothes I was looking at.'[1]

The young woman's name was Sarah Miles and their dialogue, recalled by Sarah, might have come from a Bogart and Bacall picture of the Forties.

Beatty had two actresses in mind to co-star with him in *Kaleidoscope*: Sarah, who had already turned the part down, and Susannah York. In order to avoid the formality of an audition at the studio, Beatty asked Caron to organise a dinner party so that he could study Sarah in more congenial surroundings. Caron also invited Robert as a friend and as intellectual ballast. Conversation never flagged when Robert was present.

'My table was round,' said Caron. 'Bob and Sarah were sitting across from each other and very early in the dinner party repartee started flying from one to the other like a fast ping-pong match. Pretty soon, everyone stopped talking, aware that we were witnessing the most intense interest or hate for each other. Bob drove Sarah home after the party and we soon learned without surprise that they were living together, had, in fact, not left each other since that dinner party. During the evening everyone thought that she was beautiful and scintillating and obviously Bob thought so too.'[2]

If Robert remembered his dismissal of Sarah to David Lean as a 'North Country slut' he gave no sign of it. Instead, he saw someone who was gorgeous, lively and distinctly Home Counties posh, far removed from the Mancunian-accented actress he had seen in *The Servant*. He was instantly attracted to her and summoned all his conversational brilliance to impress her. 'Robert on that first evening entertained us all triumphantly,' said Sarah. 'He had the most wonderful stories. He was also very dapper, clean and sparkly, with amazing eyes. He just made Warren Beatty look like a non-starter.'[3]

When Sarah decided to leave the party, Robert jumped to his feet and offered to escort her home. 'Have you transport?' she asked. Indeed Robert had; he hailed a taxi and took her to the Pickwick Club where she watched him resume his verbal fireworks display in the company of cronies. Later, Robert returned Sarah to her home in Hasker Street, Chelsea, and kissed her good night. He walked back to his flat on Chelsea Embankment knowing he had found his ideal woman.

Kaleidoscope went ahead with Susannah York.

Sarah Elizabeth Miles was twenty-four when she met Robert. Born to a wealthy family in Ingatestone, Essex, she was named after Sarah Bernhardt and, like many girls at the time, after the young princess and later Queen. But everyone called her Pusscat. Wide-eyed, with a shock of hair and ears like Dumbo's, she was nothing but trouble as a child. There was a history of pranks, lies, misadventures and general rebelliousness. She attended several schools, including

Roedean from where she was expelled. Her next school, Crofton Grange in Hertfordshire, also decided to dispense with her talent for disruption and general indolence. School, as Sarah found out, was not an endless St Trinian's romp. It was bloody awful. Suffering from dyslexia and a stammer, her independent spirit and propensity for self-expression made her a natural for the Royal Academy of Dramatic Art.

Sarah was one of many young aspiring actresses at the time. Just as she secured her first professional engagement, in *Dazzling Prospect* in 1961,[4] contemporaries such as Vanessa Redgrave, Julie Christie, Susannah York and Rita Tushingham were making their first appearances on stage, television and in films. There was also a new breed of actors emerging from RADA, provincial repertory theatres and B-movies – Albert Finney, Peter O'Toole, Tom Courtenay, Terence Stamp, Richard Harris, Michael Caine, Sean Connery and James Fox, a handsome young guards officer with whom Sarah had her first significant love affair. Since many of the new playwrights and screenwriters – though not Robert – wrote for the young, these new actors found themselves much in demand. Most of them came from the working classes and boasted strong regional accents. Many would become stars in their first major films.

Although Sarah had made a fleeting appearance in the film version of Tennessee Williams's *The Roman Spring of Mrs Stone*, which starred Warren Beatty and Vivien Leigh, her real screen début was in *Term of Trial*, a story of a middle-aged schoolmaster's infatuation with one of his pupils. As the girl, Sarah had one of the best parts of the year, since she would be playing the Lolita-like temptress of Laurence Olivier, the most famous actor in the world. Olivier was attempting to follow up his previous stage and film performance as Archie Rice in John Osborne's *The Entertainer* by burying his heroic, classical image and reinventing his career in the scrubby half-light of 'social realist' drama. However, *Term of Trial* was old-fashioned enough to cast a French actress, Simone Signoret, as Olivier's tormented wife. Signoret had previously appeared in *Room at the Top*, as the adulterous lover of Laurence Harvey, and since she was French she overcame the producers' reticence to cast an English actress – Celia Johnson? Joyce Grenfell? – in such a seedy role.

The main interest of *Term of Trial*, otherwise a rather leery, obvious melodrama, was in the way that the young, represented by Sarah and Terence Stamp, are portrayed as liberating if threatening influences.

As expected, *Term of Trial* brought Sarah rapidly into the

limelight. It also brought her something entirely unexpected: a love affair with Olivier, whom she had idolised ever since her parents had taken her to see a revival of *Wuthering Heights* during her school holidays. The affair, which began on location in Paris, was conducted clandestinely in Sarah's house in Hasker Street, Chelsea, and at various anonymous hotels on England's south coast. Sarah called Olivier 'Lionel Kerr' – a conflation of Richard the Lionheart and Olivier's middle name – and he called her 'Dame Sarah'. Amazingly, their affair, which lasted for four years and then resumed in the Seventies, was to remain unknown to the press until Sarah chose to reveal it after Olivier's death.

Sarah was in demand. After a brief run in Shaw's *St Joan* at Worthing Rep, she went to Spain for Laurence Harvey's film *The Ceremony*, which was a flop. But *The Servant* was another matter. Directed by Joseph Losey and scripted by Harold Pinter, it was one of the key British films of the Sixties, its sultry decadence and withering satire on class turning it into a box-office hit. Sarah's role, as another 'North Country slut,' the sexual catalyst who comes between James Fox's master and Dirk Bogarde's seedy servant, won her rave reviews; as the critic David Thomson wrote later, 'As Vera from Manchester, she shattered the stereotype and thrust sexual appetite into British films.'[5]

But Sarah's career lost momentum. Under contract to Beaumont, she was at the Royal Court in *Kelly's Eye* with Nicol Williamson, with whom she had a brief affair and co-starred in a short film, *The Six-Sided Triangle*, directed by her brother Christopher. She did some television, a big-budget comedy, *Those Magnificent Men in Their Flying Machines*; then Noël Coward's *Hay Fever* at the National and a low-budget film set in Ireland, *I Was Happy Here*. When she was cast opposite Terence Stamp in *The Collector*, to be directed by William Wyler from John Fowles's first novel, she was jubilant, then deeply distressed when the producer, Mike Frankovich, changed his mind and cast his own discovery, Samantha Eggar, instead.

'I was in a bit of a muddle about where my career was going and the muddle was all mine,' said Sarah. 'I turned down the chance to play with Ralph Richardson and did *I Was Happy Here* in Ireland. I turned down Charlotte Rampling's part in *Georgy Girl*, I was offered a sex girl part in a Bond film. I made some huge errors at that time. But I would never go abroad because of my dogs. What I regretted most was that I never played comedy and became a sex symbol instead.'[6]

When Robert met Sarah she had just signed to appear in

Michelangelo Antonioni's *Blowup* with Vanessa Redgrave and David Hemmings, who had suddenly replaced Terence Stamp. London at the time was a mecca for foreign film-makers – François Truffaut was filming *Fahrenheit 451* with Julie Christie, Jean-Luc Godard was filming *One Plus One* with the Rolling Stones and any number of Americans were on location in 'Swinging London' to make what Richard Lester defined as 'Double-Decker Bus pictures'.

Antonioni had been sent a play called *The Photographer*. Written by Robert's friend, Kenneth Jupp, it had been staged in 1963 and was based on the life and career of the fashion photographer David Bailey. Although he rejected Jupp's story, Antonioni thought a photographer would make an interesting hero. This idea eventually turned into *Blowup*, which was to be the ultimate statement on London's vibrant cultural scene.

In the early Sixties, Antonioni could do no wrong and his dramas about urban alienation were adored by the critics and filled the art houses. 'Bob thought Antonioni was a poseur,' said Mike Kellaway. 'I thought his *L'Avventura* was a fascinating film but Bob thought it was nonsense. I think Bob encouraged Sarah to misbehave on *Blowup* which was naughty of him because he helped her to discredit herself.'[7]

Blowup was the coolest, hippest picture in town when it opened in March 1967. But Sarah was totally mystified by her part, which involved nothing more than lying and sighing beneath a naked John Castle. Having little time for Antonioni's pretensions, she walked out on the film, leaving her character in an even deeper orgasmic limbo. She did not make another film until Robert wrote one for her. Egged on by Robert, Sarah's behaviour on the set of *Blowup* earned her a reputation for being difficult.

After the party at Leslie Caron's house, Robert had laid romantic siege to Sarah, deluging her with invitations, notes and constant phone calls. 'He didn't half do some chasing,' said Sarah. 'Of course, that's fun on an egotistical level, though I want my man to play a more subtle game. But Robert made me laugh and I like that most of all in a man. I have a catchy laugh and I remember we went to see Paul Scofield in *The Government Inspector* and he did a scene with such brilliance that it made me laugh. Not out loud, just a constant chuckle that made my eyes water. Robert caught the laugh as well and we were soon both bursting and had to leave the theatre.'[8]

On one occasion she turned down Robert's dinner invitation, claiming she was having a dinner party of her own at Hasker Street.

In fact she was lying, as only Olivier was expected that night. But Olivier cancelled at the last moment and Robert showed up on her doorstep anyway and discovered her deceit. As far as Robert was concerned, he felt he had to be totally open and honest with Sarah, especially about sexual matters which were, at first, a distressing problem for him. 'Whatever sexual problems he had at that time were certainly sorted out,' said Sarah. 'He was very frightened when I met him, frightened of freeing himself. Robert had a very low esteem of himself sexually which I actually have to dump on Jo because he came pretty much fresh from that, except for Carolyn Pfeiffer. He wasn't a hugely sensual person. You had to guide him into the joys of sexuality. But often people with pent up, frozen fear blossom into wonderful new beings. And Robert was an example of that. But I have to say he wasn't much cop at the beginning. His passion was his work.'[9]

By February 1966, following a holiday in the Canaries, Robert and Sarah decided to live together. They both wanted to live in the country and soon found what they were looking for: a spectacular early-Georgian house in Byfleet, Surrey. The asking price of £40,000 was divided equally between them.

Mill House was an idyll, with vast grounds, ancient trees, a delightful river, a stable block with a clock tower and the old wooden watermill itself, which Sarah decided should be turned into Robert's study. At the back of the main house a lavish conservatory was soon built which provided a bright and airy living space, as well as an atmospheric venue for dinner parties. There was a tennis court and plans were made to build a swimming pool. And to take advantage of its waterside setting, Robert bought an inflatable dinghy with a powerful Mercury outboard engine which sent the ducks flying in all directions. Robert later decided to build his own boat, a sleak vessel made of timber, though when the hull had been laid down he realised it was too big ever to escape the ground floor of the mill. The boat was destined to be in dry-dock for all its life.

Staff were subsequently hired to manage the property, including the stables which Sarah wanted to turn into a profitable stud farm. Never especially fond of horses, Robert told his friend Kenneth Jupp that the expense of buying and breeding them was like 'standing under a cold shower and tearing up twenty pound notes over your head'.[10]

Apart from the house, the most conspicuous symbol of Robert's wealth was his new car, a maroon Rolls-Royce, just like David Lean's. In terms of material possessions, this former communist and village schoolmaster had changed beyond recognition, though in a curious way some of the puritanism of the Manchester Methodist still remained. However much he loved Sarah and rejoiced in their lavish surroundings, the fact that they were unmarried worried him. He hoped that by living with her he wasn't giving the impression that she was a loose woman. 'I have moved to this new house out of London,' he told Lean, 'where I'm living very happily with Sarah. She is slowly teaching me to take what life offers without too much concern for the morrow and too meticulous an examination of the state of my soul. As you may imagine, I'm disconcerted to find myself Living in Sin but each day seems very liveable (it's a couple of years since that was so) and I can't see that I'm doing anyone any harm, if I'm not harming Sarah, which she says I'm not. It's a lovely house; I wish we could see you here.'[11]

Robert's tone astonished Lean. 'I'm struck anew by his naïve streak,' he wrote to Barbara. 'Doing Miss M damage! He must be a much more complicated man than even we know.'[12]

Following his divorce from Jo, Robert saw his children separately, usually at weekends, so that Sally, Ben and Joanna could feel individually loved and wanted. Inevitably, Sarah had to be introduced to each of them in turn and the chosen venue for this potentially hazardous social ritual was the King's Road branch of the Soho restaurant, the Trattoria Terrazza.

Dad hadn't indicated to me that Sarah was his girl-friend [said Ben]. I remember that during the course of the meal they had a mock fight, throwing sugar lumps at each other with increasing delight. I suddenly realised that this woman was something special to him. I'd never seen him behave that way before and it was obvious this wasn't the first time they'd done this sort of playful thing together. It delighted me, too, because it went against all notions of good behaviour which Dad was rather relentless about with his kids.

I called Sarah 'sis'. It wasn't so much an expression of brotherly acceptance as a way of twitting Dad that she was so much younger than him. There was also an element of claiming this exciting creature as being more suitable for someone of my age than his. Not in any spirit of disapproval, it was rather that I enjoyed playing with the ludicrous fantasy of being able to compete with my own father for this gorgeous, wild girl. I knew I couldn't really, it was just fun. Sarah brought fun back into my relationship with Dad, as long as they were happy together.[13]

EIGHTEEN

GREAT SOUL

'If only Bapu knew the cost of setting him up in poverty!'

Sarojini Naidu

During Robert's courtship of Sarah, *Doctor Zhivago* opened in America. Greeted sniffily by the critics of the serious newspapers, more enthusiastically by the popular ones, it turned into a goldmine for Lean, if not for Robert who had been persuaded to take a higher than usual fee in lieu of any profit participation.

As he was unable to attend the premières in New York and Los Angeles, Robert sent a barrage of congratulatory messages to Lean who was already repeating his tactic on *Lawerence of Arabia* by reducing the film's running time. Marooned in London, Robert was desperate to see the picture. He wrote to Lean:

> I'm longing to hear from you what the film is really like. The notices are so contradictory. However, I'd rather the highbrows sneer and the lowbrows rave than vice versa. But what do *you* think? Peggy says she read in *Variety* that you'd already taken 17 minutes out. Is that so? Freddie [Zinnemann] said the first half was perfect but that the second needed stiffer cutting. I wish, oh how I wish, that I'd seen it; it's infuriating. The visa mess was just silliness I'm sure, nothing sinister.
>
> How is everybody? Is morale good? Among the cast I mean – particularly Omar, who really went out on a limb, didn't he? And how about MGM? How is the thing doing at the Box Office and what's the word of mouth? Please write, dear man.[1]

Within a few months *Doctor Zhivago* became MGM's biggest money-maker since *Gone With the Wind*. For even if some of the critics disliked it, the public adored it. There were Omar Sharif and Julie

Christie, and it was hard to tell who was the more beautiful. And for several freezing American and European winters the Sixties trendies dressed in the height of *Zhivago* fashion – heavy long skirts, leather boots and fur hats. But most of all there was that balalaika music, 'Lara's Theme', destined to play in every bar, elevator and hotel lobby in the world.

When MGM held its first screening in London, on 11 February 1966, Robert could not attend since he was in Bristol, judging some new plays for the BBC. It seems strange that Lean could not have arranged a screening for him – he would have needed only to pick up the phone – but another month passed before Robert finally saw it for himself. The day after he and Sarah arrived home from the Canaries he fully expected to see Lean, as well as the picture. But Lean had left London for Paris the night before, an especially unfriendly thing to have done, though it seems that he was anxious to avoid meeting Robert. Lean was convinced – wrongly, as it turned out – that Robert blamed him for the collapse of his marriage to Jo.

> I wanted to see you very much (wouldn't have come back from the Canaries otherwise; was depressed to find you gone earlier than you'd said) but had a weird indifference to actually seeing our film. When I did get to see it, I understood the mechanism of the indifference ('Freud for the Under-Twelves' page 9). The adverse notices effected me more than I knew. I went into the cinema in a state of fear . . .
>
> It is a *tremendously* good film, and anyone who doesn't like it condemns himself. It's moving, powerful, beautiful, serious and continuously held my wrapt attention; Peggy and I sat like a pair of housemaids and ended with sodden handkerchiefs. I can't tell you how proud I am to be your lieutenant in the enterprise. It's in a different street from *Lawrence* and that's saying a lot . . .
>
> If I have to select any one thing to congratulate you on, it's Omar. I believed in him utterly. It is, or looks like, a performance of great depth and stunning restraint. He almost never seemed in the slightest degree inadequate. Not so Julie, I thought. It's a lovely performance, that goes without saying, and sometimes remarkable but once or twice I thought the King's Road Chelsea nearer than the Nevsky Prospect. That's a criticism of perfection, mind you. She's lovely.[2]

On 14 April 1966, Robert's reputation was considerably enhanced when his screenplay won the Academy Award. Unable to attend the ceremony himself, Robert's Oscar was collected by David Lean, who was considerably peeved that he had just lost as Best Director to Robert Wise, who had made *The Sound of Music*. And at the end of the year Fred Zinnemann's film of *A Man For All Seasons* opened to rave reviews and packed audiences. A second Oscar followed in April 1967, which Robert collected in person.

In Hollywood, Robert could do no wrong. Columbia was courting him and MGM, flush with the profits from *Doctor Zhivago*, invited him to write a screenplay about Charlemagne, as well as an adaptation of André Malraux's epic novel of China, *Man's Fate*. Robert turned them both down, though the Malraux project was eventually taken up by Zinnemann, who worked on the script with Malraux himself until the production was cancelled by the new cost-cutting management of MGM three weeks before shooting was due to start.

Seeing how the directors of his screenplays – Lean and Zinnemann – received most of the credit and most of the money, Robert started to think again about directing, or at least becoming a co-producer.

When Zinnemann was preparing *A Man For All Seasons* he had initially cast John Huston as the Duke of Norfolk. Huston was a buccaneering figure who had settled on an Irish estate, St Clerans, where he could indulge his passion for fox hunting and escape the remittance men. As a director, he was an outstanding if wayward talent who survived in the Hollywood mainstream by juggling purely commercial enterprises with more personal projects. Huston, who possessed a fireside voice and a constant chuckle at his own pompous pronouncements, had also started to act in films, though he turned down Zinnemann at the last moment, preferring instead to make the James Bond spoof, *Casino Royale*, a decision he soon came to regret. 'We were on holiday at my parents' house in Cornwall when the phone rang,' said Sarah. 'It was John Huston. He said, "I'm doing *Casino Royale* and I want Robert to rewrite the Scottish section. It's a terrible mess and there's a great part for you in it. Why don't you drive up to London?" We left immediately and Robert took this meeting with Huston. Robert read the stuff and said, "It's just crap." They were offering a lot of money but there was nothing he could do as they were so near to shooting.'³

Out of this, though, came the idea of a movie about Queen Nefertiti which Robert would produce as well as write for Huston. While he could expect to find resistance from Hollywood, which was still smarting over *Cleopatra* and now worrying about a Middle East war, the international excitement generated by the Tutankhamun exhibition was certainly in Robert's favour. It was also one of the first projects that he devised as a starring vehicle for Sarah. 'Robert saw me running across our field in my altogethers,' said Sarah. 'I had a rather slim body in those days and I think Robert thought of Nefertiti. She used to hunt naked and Robert thought I had her spirit. My face was about as far as you could get from hers, but they could put a nose on me. He got completely locked into that for a while.'[4]

Huston, though, had bitter memories of Egypt. Two years earlier he had gone there to film part of his epic *The Bible* and had watched helplessly as his army of five thousand extras rioted. Huston noted later that 'corruption ran rampant. . . . Egypt was an experience I'd like to forget.'[5]

Through Omar Sharif, Robert had met an Egyptian businessman of reputedly stupendous wealth who fancied himself as a movie mogul. 'The finances,' he told Huston, 'will be made available. In fact I know they will; I have been told so point blank.' Then Robert, in his schoolmasterly way, gave Huston a primer in Egyptology: 'I think from what Peter O'T has told me that you are a bit of an antiquarian which I am not so that in what immediately follows I am probably teaching my grandmother to suck eggs. But that can't be helped; in order to give you the "smell" of the film I envisage I must sketch my sketchy understanding of ancient Egypt for you – I mean I must sketch for you why I find it so passionately interesting. If what follows seems insultingly elementary, don't put it down to an insulting desire to instruct but, please, to my own elementary understanding of the period and my anxiety to take you with me . . .'

After two full and fustian pages of history, Robert wrote, 'I don't see this film in terms of (say) Liz Taylor with two hundred well-trained chorous girls in titillating costumes, against glittering plastic sphynxes and breath-taking colossi, but in terms of sand, sky, mud, bare skin, quiet. The figures not delicately powdered but gleaming with sweat, not nubile and tactile, but flat and hieratic. The colours not opulent but bleached, floating in blinding light. It hope it doesn't sound pretentious or vague – I see it so clearly . . .'

Robert outlined the momentous drama which would culminate in a dramatic climax:

Now Aye will return to Thebes, the proper ancient capital, the old ways, the old religion. Nefertiti acquiesces. The whole lot leaves in an armada of dhows with coloured sails, swimming into the camera like butterflies in close-up, horns blaring, drums bashing. The royal barge will go at last. But no, Nefertiti will not go with Aye. 'That bloke of yours was a good bloke but a bit of a charlie when you come right down to it.' 'You bloody nit,' she tells him. 'We're the charlies, he was a right guy and what's more he had the right end of the stick. I've done what needed doing but so far as I'm concerned you can all fuck off – Me, I'm staying here.' And Aye goes and Nefertiti wanders with a few attendants through the deserted streets of the doomed pretty city with the sand already silting. . . . The End.

Robert was evidently adopting a style which he thought might amuse Huston; Lean would have been distressed by the frivolity, while Zinnemann would have found the frivolity, as well as the crudity, offensive. Perhaps Robert also feared that his close association with Lean's perfectionism and open-ended schedules might give Huston cause for concern, especially if Robert, as the source of the finance, ended up as the producer as well. Huston was a man who finished a picture as quickly as possible – he had better things to do with his life, like gambling, hunting and women. So Robert concluded with a curious disclaimer: 'I loathe epics,' he wrote. 'I think our film should aim at two hours flat. I also loathe runaway budgets – they lead to flabbiness and uncertainty of story. Do you agree? There's something sharply distasteful about those mindlessly expended millions.'[6]

Three months later, Robert was obliged to write to Huston to say that the project was off: 'By now you must have given up expecting to hear from me at all! But it is only now that I have been able to come to a definite conclusion about Nefertiti.' The project itself I am as keen about as ever. I am quite convinced it could make a very good film indeed – and a rather unusual one if done properly. But the set-up which I had "secured" turned out to be so insecure as not to be a set-up at all . . . the only backing was from a rather shadowy Egyptian businessman. . . . But I hope we can revive this project at a later date.'[7]

As Queen Nefertiti was abandoned to the silting sands of the Nile, Robert launched himself into another project, a film biography of Mahatma Gandhi. Robert's involvement with *Gandhi* had begun in early 1963 when he was approached by Motilal Kothari, a diminutive diplomat with the Indian High Commission in London. Following Gandhi's assassination in 1948, Kothari had dedicated his life to promoting the Mahatma's philosophy to the world at large, eventually realising that the most effective means of doing this would be somehow to initiate a feature film. Although the Indian director, Satyajit Ray, had an international reputation by the early Sixties, the

Indian cinema was ill-equipped to produce a film on the scale which Kothari thought necessary. So he looked to Britain, the old colonial power, to find a writer and director to realise his dream.

With *Lawrence of Arabia* in release, Kothari approached Robert to write the script for the Gandhi Foundation, an organisation with the slenderest of resources and the deepest of principles. But Robert turned him down. Kothari also approached Richard Attenborough as a possible director. At the time this was a peculiar choice, since Attenborough had yet to direct a film. However, the baby-faced, Toblerone-scoffing, emotionally charged Attenborough had already become a producer through his partnership with Bryan Forbes. Called 'Richard' by strangers, 'Dickie' by people in the industry, 'Dick' by his close friends and 'Bunter' by Forbes, Attenborough was on the first rung of a ladder which would elevate him to the peerage and make him the chairman of a number of British film industry institutions.

Perhaps Kothari had done some research into Attenborough's impeccably liberal background; anyway, he found a sympathetic ear when he spoke to him of Gandhi's policies of racial tolerance and non-violence. And after Attenborough read Louis Fischer's 1952 biography of Gandhi, which Kothari had given him, his heroic twenty-year quest to get the film made had begun. Attenborough's first step was to meet Robert; by chance, they both lived on Richmond Green. 'Bob seemed to me to be the one person who ought to write the screenplay,' said Attenborough. 'One of the reasons why Bob felt unable to do it was because of his marriage. But I think also he may have thought, why the hell should he write for me? He would have been quite entitled to say, "Look, forgive me, but I write for David Lean and you've never directed a film and why should I assume you can? You're obviously not going to pay me a fortune because you don't have a fortune, I'd be writing for you on spec, and this is something that needs a mammoth amount of research. . . ." I'm making this up but this could have been the unwritten scenario.'[8]

Robert and Attenborough then went their separate ways, Robert going straight into *Doctor Zhivago* and Attenborough continuing to act in movies in order to make enough money to subsidise his growing obsession with Gandhi. Some of this money went into a screenplay by Gerald Hanley which, though far too long and diffuse, at least served a purpose in turning a dream into a scripted reality. Hanley's script also met with the approval of the Indian government whose co-operation was vital.

In July 1964 Attenborough met the American producer, Joseph E. Levine, a flamboyant figure who had made his name by buying an Italian epic, *Hercules Unchained*, and spending more on promoting it than the film had cost to make. By this single and immensely profitable act of showmanship, Levine became one of the world's top independent producers, a rival to Sam Spiegel in both charm and chicanery. Levine agreed to finance the Gandhi project if the Hanley script was rewritten. Robert was contacted again and the answer was still no because, Attenborough believes, Robert would still not write for 'a mere actor'. Disappointed but characteristically unperturbed, Attenborough offered it to Bryan Forbes and, after he declined, went to Donald Ogden Stewart, an Oscar winner in 1940 for *The Philadelphia Story* who had been living in London since he was blacklisted by the McCarthy hearings.

With Stewart rewriting Hanley's screenplay and Levine as his producer, Attenborough felt sufficiently confident to fly to Madrid to make a courtesy call on David Lean who, it was well known, had worked on his own Gandhi project before abandoning it for *Lawrence of Arabia*. Attenborough's aim was to elicit from Lean a statement of intent: if Lean still expressed a strong desire to make the film Attenborough was quite prepared to stand aside. To his delight and surprise, Attenborough found Lean lacking any real interest in the subject matter.

I said to him, 'Now David, you are unquestionably a great movie director. I've never directed, I don't know if I can, but it seems to me that the most important thing is not who makes this movie but that the movie should be made. I passionately believe in what Gandhi stood for and I think that is the prerequisite for making the film.' And David told me he was not going to make it. My instinct is that for a period of time David was fascinated with India, because of his relationship with his wife, Leila. If you are going to tell stories of India, unless you go back to classics, you are going to talk about Nehru, the freedom of India, about Gandhi. I don't think David was interested in that sort of thing at all, not even interested! I remember flying back thinking that my meeting with David was infinitely less painful than it might have been. He was quite able to discard it without apparently any emotion.[9]

Lean's flirtation with *Gandhi* is worth examining for it reveals much about his personality and the sort of films that he and Robert made together. Lean first went to India in 1953, ostensibly to research a film about the building of the Taj Mahal. It seems likely, though, that his trip was engineered by Alexander Korda as a way of cooling the temperature between Lean and his then wife, Ann Todd, both of whom Korda had under contract. Although the Taj Mahal project never got much further than a treatment, written by Emeric Pressburger, Lean was intoxicated by India, the remnants of the Raj and by a married Indian woman named Leila Maktar, with whom he had an affair and whom he later married.

Lean returned to India in 1955 to research a film called *The Wind Cannot Read*, based on a melodramatic World War Two novel by Richard Hughes. By the time the screenplay had been written and a Japanese actress had arrived in London for English lessons, Lean abruptly abandoned the project and made *The Bridge on the River Kwai* instead. But Lean's love of things Indian can be detected in what is perhaps the greatest scene in the film, when Alec Guinness, leaning against the railing of his completed bridge, reflects on his life and says, 'I love India. . .' The film, made in 1956, can be regarded as a reflection on the role of Britain in the post-Suez, post-colonial world, a world in which Englishmen are nostalgic for Empire and regard themselves as foreigners in their native land. Certainly, Lean felt that way. By the time he made *Kwai*, he was himself an exile. As he wrote later to Barbara Cole:

I was knocked over by the first impact of the East. I suppose it was really the first time I realised the world was mine and that I needn't be fenced in. . . . Curious thing but in ways I can't yet fathom it's all to do with my ex-wife Ann [Todd]. She treated me *so* horribly that I think I was far more deeply hurt than I've ever acknowledged even to myself. It's bad enough to be used as a kind of inanimate tool for the sex gratification of someone who doesn't really give a damn for you as a human being. But what was worse is that I had to leave my country in order to pay this woman for the harm I was supposed to have done her – like a fool I resisted pressures to make her the guilty party when I had every opportunity – and I ran. I think I substituted England for her. I remember how I tried to avoid all English people for months and months. I was unknown and able to start again with only an occasional whiff of my English shame. Perhaps shame is too strong but it's not far off. She had talked such a lot and told everyone I was impotent. Even saying I was fond of young boys and insinuating that my relationship with her young son was unhealthy. I suppose I thought that everyone knew and everyone believed. So I was waiting for an attack or a look of disapproval whenever I met an English person. I can see this reads like a fabricated nightmare – and it is of course. I suppose that's why I'm so touchy about being recognised by those that matter in England – even to the extent of half wanting to tell them all to jump in the lake if they ever went so far as to offer me a knighthood. I hope you can be as childish as this. I suppose that's why I used to call you my English Love out there at Jebel Tubeiq. It was the beginning of coming home again.[10]

Lean's affair with Leila and his long drives across the sub-Continent in an Aston Martin had a profound impact on him. Everything he saw, he associated with her. He loved the scenery, the hotels with their cool drinks on the veranda, their obsequious staff and silent punkah-wallahs. He felt inspired by the visual opportunities offered by the villages, the spice markets, the people washing in rivers, worshipping in temples, walking with their loaded camels through the suffocating heat, the immediacy of life lived on the streets. Everything he saw was just waiting for CinemaScope and the only story he felt qualified to make was the loss of Britain's 'Jewel in the Crown' and the independence movement.

Having decided to make *Gandhi*, which he hoped would star Alec Guinness, Lean returned to India in 1959 with Sam Spiegel and Emeric Pressburger. They met all the important politicians and went on a long recce for locations. Pressburger's draft screenplay, though, did not meet with Lean's approval and the project was abruptly dropped for *Lawrence of Arabia*. After *Doctor Zhivago*, Lean gave *Gandhi* little thought, filing it away with many other unrealised projects. For one thing, his marriage to Leila had all but ended and her mental instability – she was undergoing electro-shock-therapy and later had a partial lobotomy – was causing him considerable anguish. For Lean, the romance of India had vanished along with his marriage.

If the collapse of Lean's marriage finished his interest in making *Gandhi*, the end of Robert's marriage had the reverse effect. By January 1966 Robert had apparently changed his mind and was willing to write the screenplay, knowing that a prolonged stay in India would not undermine his marriage. But it was Motilal Kothari's passion and persistence which brought about this change of heart, even though Kothari evidently failed to teach Robert how to spell Gandhi's name correctly. Dismissing Attenborough from the equation, Robert urged Lean to direct the film: 'I'll come right out with it and tell you,' he wrote, 'I'm more and more attracted to the Ghandi thing. Are you absolutely off it? I'm not asking for an answer here and now, but is it even on the cards for you, so that we could talk about it and I could go on brooding over it? I see it, tentatively, in black and white, but that's a detail; but I think you could put something universal and visually terrible, beautiful and reassuring by turns on to the screen with it. . . . . I think we ought to tackle something important enough in theme to move and humble and demand everything from us.'[11]

A month later Robert urged Lean to meet Kothari. 'He's a very ordinary looking little Indian and is a man of great distinction unless I am the world's idiot. He's a follower of Ghandi, knows all sorts of very distinguished people in that ambience (Mountbatten, Mrs Indira Ghandi and so on) but more importantly is a sort of walking advertisement for Ghandi's influence. He's dedicated to the idea of getting a film on Ghandi made, but isn't a pusher nor remotely on the make. Anyway, see him and judge for yourself.'[12]

It was Fred Zinnemann though, not Lean, who met Kothari and, for a short while at least, Zinnemann looked like bringing *Gandhi* to the screen. Attenborough was just as prepared to make way for Zinnemann as he was for David Lean: 'At this particular time,' he wrote, 'I had abdicated my right to the film in favour of Moti, Bob Bolt and Fred Zinnemann or David Lean.'[13]

Although Zinnemann denies he was ever seriously interested in making the film – 'It was not really my kind of subject,' he said, 'and the problems of filming in India were enormous'[14] – he nevertheless contacted his Los Angeles agent, Phil Kellogg, about it, if only to satisfy himself, like Attenborough before him, that he was not poaching a project from his friend, David Lean, who was also Kellogg's client. As Lean wrote to Barbara Cole: 'I want to tell you about a conversation I had with Phil last night. He said, "I have a mission from Fred Zinnemann." Then proceeded to tell me Fred felt guilty and wanted to know my reaction before proceeding with a film on Gandhi with Robert Bolt. (They seem to have overlooked the film of the same subject which Richard Attenborough is doing according to Attenborough in an interview I heard on the BBC.)'[15]

With Lean dithering, Zinnemann non-committal and Attenborough passionate yet inexperienced, the enthusiastic corporal in a world of seasoned generals, Robert formed an even stronger alliance with Kothari and aimed to produce the film himself. Because of the success of *Doctor Zhivago*, Robert went to MGM whose Chairman, Robert O'Brien, was immediately sympathetic to the idea and requested a complete history of the project. Robert's lawyer, Laurence Harbottle, responded with a letter to Ben Melniker, a senior MGM executive in New York:

> I understand that Robert Bolt and Bob O'Brien had a meeting in New York last week and that Bob O'Brien asked that all the facts regarding the proposed Gandhi film should be sent to you as soon as possible.
>
> I act for Motilal Kothari who originated the idea and was later joined by Richard Attenborough and with him formed an English company called Indo-British Films Ltd. Robert Bolt is now interested in the project and he is also a client of mine. He and Mr Kothari have discussed the project with Fred Zinnemann and he is also interested in the project subject to Robert Bolt preparing a treatment but he has no commitment until he has seen and approved that treatment and decided to go ahead.
>
> Indo-British's assets relating to the production are: 1. The film rights to two books by Louis Fischer entitled *The Life of Mahatma Gandhi* and *The Essential Gandhi* subject to certain payments if the film rights are used and an agreement to pay 5% of the Indo-British profit from such film to Mr Fischer. 2. The copyright in a screenplay by Gerald Hanley. 3. Indian Government approval of the project and the Hanley screenplay. 4. 1500 feet of film in Technicolor of crowd scenes in India shot last year.

These assets, wrote Harbottle, were the property of Joseph E. Levine's company, Embassy Pictures, and amounted to $97,000. There were additional monies, including £6739 which Attenborough had expended personally on the project. If MGM decided to proceed, these would be its immediate costs. Harbottle also urged MGM to underwrite the cost of Robert going on a research trip to India in January 1967 since Nehru's daughter, Mrs Indira Gandhi, had indicated she would be available for a meeting at that time. 'If his journey to India can take place,' wrote Harbottle, 'he would be able to deliver the treatment by 30 September 1967 and deliver a screenplay by 31 December 1967. The intention would be to allow for first exhibition of the film in September 1969, the centenary year of Gandhi's birth.'[16]

Robert's fee for the screenplay would be $210,000 plus $40,000 for the treatment, the figures which Robert and O'Brien had already discussed in New York and which represented a twenty-five per cent increase on his fee for *Zhivago*. While MGM decided to consider the fees, they approved two research trips for Robert. In early December Robert taped an interview he conducted with Lord Mountbatten, then flew to Vienna to meet Mrs Madeleine Slade, who was Gandhi's principal British associate and known in Gandhi circles as Mirabehn. She and Gandhi had been constant companions, utterly inseparable, and it seemed to many that Gandhi simply could not function without her friendship and guidance. As Robert had anticipated, Mirabehn made a considerable impact on him and he left her, wondering if she and Gandhi had ever been lovers.

On 11 January 1967 Robert and Sarah joined Kothari in New Delhi. By now, India's politicians were accustomed to meeting film-makers from Britain and America: in 1959 there had been Lean, Spiegel and Pressburger; Otto Preminger, who also planned a film on Gandhi, had been there in 1962 and so too had the crew of *Nine Hours to Rama*; a thriller about Gandhi's assassination. And, since 1963, Richard Attenborough's visits were so frequent that he was almost regarded as a house guest.

Robert and Sarah made what had become a well-trodden Gandhi tour – a meeting with Indira Gandhi was followed by discussions with other senior politicians who had known the great man. There were formal dinners and visits to Gandhi's various houses and prison cells, and his ashram. When Robert and Kothari attended their meetings, Sarah often went out on her own, determined to discover – like Adela Quested – the real India. 'It changed me a lot, India,' she said. 'I wasn't sure why or what it was because I was very ignorant of all that. But as soon as I arrived I felt very secure and I met some extraordinary people. We also sat at a Moviola and watched hours and hours of footage of Gandhi. That was fantastic. You've got to understand what a wily little fox he was, just like Donald Pleasence.'[17]

When their official engagements were over, Robert and Sarah turned into regular tourists and drove down to Agra to see the Taj Mahal. In those days there was only one place for people of means and discernment to stay: Laurie's Hotel, a pleasant cluster of colonial-style buildings with beautiful gardens, tennis courts and a swimming pool. And there, sitting in the restaurant, was David Lean. Robert and Lean had not met for nearly two years and they embraced warmly. Any worries Lean may have had about wrecking Robert's marriage soon vanished when he saw how happy he was with Sarah. While Sarah could not take her eyes off Lean's enormous ears, Lean playfully reminded Robert about his dismissal of Sarah as a 'North Country slut'. 'David was like a prep-school boy,' said Sarah. 'He told us he had fallen in love with the tea girl. That tickled his fancy and he said she brought his tea every morning and that she worked at the hotel. Later, he added that her parents owned the hotel.'[18]

The 'tea girl' was Sandy Hotz, a twenty-year-old blonde whose parents owned the Hotz Hotel Group. 'She was bright and clean and fresh,' wrote Lean to Barbara Cole. 'I was about to write that she was just the sort of girl I'd love to have as a daughter. I found her like a bright light shining through the mist of my lifelessness. I wasn't carrying on a flirtation. It was just a sudden return of life – and I didn't even feel the danger ahead.'[19]

A month later, Lean told Barbara that their relationship was over: 'I have fallen in love with a young girl. In my bloody arrogance I used to say I could never understand such a thing, that I was immune, above the common crowd . . .'[20] All Lean could think of was *Doctor Zhivago* and that by some magic Boris Pasternak was determining events in his life. He saw himself as Zhivago, a character who 'sees far too deeply and all the big crises in his life are taken out of his hands by fate', as Lean once wrote. In particular, he remembered the scene when Zhivago goes to get some medication for his pregnant wife and, by chance, meets Lara again. On the way home Zhivago is kidnapped by Red guerrillas and never sees his wife again.

'I keep thinking of Pasternak,' Lean told Barbara. 'For the first time I've come up against what almost amounts to a game carefully laid out by fate. I wasn't looking for anything. I only wanted to get back to you. Perhaps I'm making an effort to make fate and not me responsible for this hurt to you. I suppose I am trying to tell you I have schemed nothing. I cannot even find guilt or badness within me. Forgive, if you can, this terrible mess.'[21]

Just as Lean had virtually abandoned Leila as soon as they were married, he now dropped Barbara. Lean had found – perhaps he was fated to find – what he had been obsessed with for more than three years, for in the youthful, Nordic-looking Sandy, Lean had discovered his own Lara. He was fifty-seven, some thirty-seven years older than Sandy. And Robert was seventeen years older than Sarah. Out of this eventually came *Ryan's Daughter*, a story of the fear older men have that their young and sensual wives will betray them. But when they met in Agra Robert had *Gandhi* on his mind, though Lean's ears were not entirely receptive to Robert's ambitious plans. 'Lean felt a bit uncomfortable,' said Sarah, 'and started crossing his legs, because by that time he'd made it clear to Robert that he wasn't going to do it because of Leila. We always assumed that was his reason.'[22] Robert and Sarah left Lean at Laurie's where he would remain for three more months. Only when Sandy reached her twenty-first birthday was he able to whisk her away to Europe and a tour of the *Zhivago* locations in Spain.

As soon as Robert and Sarah returned to Byfleet, on 11 February 1967, he presented MGM with an expense account for £2165.4s.11d and plunged straight into writing his treatment. If MGM approved it he would be paid $40,000. But Robert knew that MGM would be reluctant to invest large sums without a director committed to the project. With only Robert, a mere writer, and Kothari, a minor diplomat, driving the engine, *Gandhi* seemed a doubtful proposition. Robert added to these problems by making creative demands and by his steadfast loyalty to Kothari, who was already on the MGM payroll at $500 a month. Robert now insisted that Kothari serve as the film's executive producer for a fee of £90,000.

On 9 June 1967, Laurence Harbottle wrote to Frank Rosenfelt, General Counsel of MGM in New York and a future Chairman of the Board: 'The important question is the selection of the Director and Producer over which Mr Bolt would like absolute control if he is not to have final control over casting and the ultimate form of the screenplay. This approval was a means whereby the difficulties of script and cast approval were avoided for *A Man For All Seasons* and I think is the only practical method of preventing difficulties later. Mr Bolt would like to retain the possibility of ultimately writing a play about Gandhi.'[23]

Robert's preliminary treatment, entitled *Gandhiji*, was delivered to MGM in the late summer and met with an encouraging response from two of the studio's production executives, David Karr and Arthur Lewis, who wrote to Robert O'Brien on 14 September 1967: 'We believe that many aspects of this deal should be handled quickly. . . . We think the new trend toward examining non violence now gripping ever larger segments of the world (as witness the Beatles' coming trip to India) adds timelessness and commercial value to the project.'[24]

Although Karr and Lewis were right in trying to find contemporary parallels in Gandhi's story, so vital to box-office interests, they might perhaps have emphasised Martin Luther King's advocacy of non-violence, often thought to have been inspired by Gandhi, rather than the Beatles' dalliance with the Maharishi. Even so, with the Vietnam War raging and peace protests taking place in major American and European cities, a film about Gandhi would indeed have been timely. MGM, though, still worried about the lack of a director and it seems that no one was being approached; the studio merely hoped that a director of the calibre of Zinnemann or Lean would take charge and only then would they purchase the full rights to the project from Joseph E. Levine. Attenborough, meanwhile, was left dangling.

Robert had no option but to write the full screenplay on spec. He did it in something of a rush, leaving Sarah to her own devices, which were mainly her horses, and to discover what it was like living with a writer. At times she felt as if she was living alone:

> I think Robert felt *Gandhi* was bringing out the 'noble' in him. Gandhi was for peace and Robert was for peace, so all his motivations were from the right part of his nature. But he was pretty miserable writing *Gandhi*, he wasn't getting off on it because we left India with him thinking it's a bit tedious writing about a saint.
>
> I wasn't allowed in to his study. Not for fire, flood or theft. He was locked in there from eight to six at night. I was quite lonely, living in the country without ever seeing my man. I climbed up a ladder to see what the hell he was doing all day. There was coffee, bits of paper, chip butties, thick white bread, masses of butter and chipped potatoes. That's how he lived. Completely manic.
>
> He just wanted to be finished with it so he could get on with something that I could be in. Then he would show me scenes he had done. He didn't want me to comment, really, he just wanted me to say, 'That's brilliant.'[25]

'With luck I shall have *Gandhi* lodged with MGM by Christmas,' Robert told Fred Zinnemann. 'It's either very good or very bad, it's certainly unusual. The story presents lots of opportunity for "epic" but its real interest lies in the really rather subtle moral position which Gandhi occupied. By "subtle" I don't mean complicated or prevaricating. On the contrary, subtlety and simplicity are nearly always found together, as in a Chinese vase which is absolutely simple and yet ungraspably subtle. Whereas a Victorian clock is ungraspably complicated and unbearably crude. The difficulty is, of course, that most film producers have a natural sympathy with Victorian clocks and couldn't tell a Chinese vase from a jam jar.'[26]

Two weeks later another letter to Zinnemann revealed two crucial points: the sort of film that Robert had in mind and the fact that

David Lean had called him to Rome to work on something entirely different: 'I have today come to the end of the *Gandhi* film. Sometimes it seems very good; sometimes I just don't know; it is certainly very unusual and I think will be possible to make. I've managed to exclude all the historical characters with the exception of Gandhi himself. In about a fortnight's time I expect to be working with David again on an "original". It will be loosely based on the *Bovary* idea, but very loosely, bearing about the same relationship to Flaubert as *Stagecoach* did to Maupassant.'[27]

When Robert and Sarah arrived in Rome, they handed Lean the *Gandhiji* script. In Hollywood, Robert O'Brien had already read it and liked it very much. Because Lean's involvement with India had now resumed its original romanticism, thanks to his relationship with Sandy, Robert was able to write to O'Brien with exciting news: 'Thank you for your kind telephone call telling me of your satisfaction with the *Gandhiji* Treatment. David has now read it and his response was enthusiastic – so enthusiastic, in fact, that it would be immodest to repeat what he said. He definitely wants to do it. It would make me very happy if we could agree upon and clinch a definite deal now, so that Mr Kothari, who put this project and the necessary materials into my hands and has incurred a lot of personal expenses in pursuit of the project over the last five years, could be made comfortable.'[28]

Lean committed himself to making *Gandhiji* after his next picture, which would eventually be titled *Ryan's Daughter*, on which he and Robert had just started work. But just as *Gandhiji* looked as if it was about to happen, the project quickly fell apart. While Lean often stated that he decided against making the film because he was dissatisfied with the screenplay, Robert's letter to MGM suggests that this was not the case. In fact, the MGM files indicate that the undoing of *Gandhi* was money.

Everyone believed that *Gandhiji* would be a major film, an Oscar winner and, hopefully, as big a box-office hit as *Doctor Zhivago*. There was a large cake and when Lean joined the feast, large portions of the cake vanished quickly. He demanded a fee of $1 million dollars to direct the film, plus a hefty percentage. Robert therefore increased his asking price to $400,000, plus ten per cent of the net profits. This proposal, forwarded to MGM by Margaret Ramsay and Laurence Harbottle, met with a frosty response from MGM who had previously agreed a figure of $250,000 for the treatment and the screenplay. Then Robert, growing steadily more impatient with MGM, wrote an extraordinary memo:

I still accept that a 50% share of profits properly belongs to MGM, leaving 50% to be divided between Director, Producer, myself and Mr Kothari. However, David has now asked for 35% and 5% for the producer. I regard David's participation in this project as very desirable indeed if not essential. However, since David and the Producer are to take 40% of the profits, there only remains 10% to be divided between myself and Mr Kothari. I am firmly resolved that Mr Kothari shall receive no lesser percentage than myself. This is a subjective decision for which I can offer no objective arguments but I am sure it is correct. Now, if Mr Kothari and I are to split 10% we shall get 5% each. I am not interested in 5%. I therefore wish to relinquish any share of the profits. . . .[29]

Robert then demanded a deferred payment of $500,000, additional to his $400,000 fee, guaranteeing him $900,000 whether the film was profitable or not. Although Margaret Ramsay quickly issued a disclaimer, saying that Robert would accept $400,000 and five per cent, these financial demands undoubtedly led to MGM's tactical retreat. This left Richard Attenborough as the sole keeper of the flame.

By the time he embarked on *Gandhiji*, Robert had finished *Brother and Sister*, which was his reworking of *The Critic and the Heart*. Writing it had been pure drudgery, as Robert explained to David Lean: 'Hell how slowly it creeps forward. About five pages of rewrite to one page of real script. You'd be amazed how much you've taught me. Film (meaning you), not Theatre has made me properly conscious of the audience, that dangerous beast out there in the dark of the auditorium.' The project had not pleased Margaret Ramsay, who felt that Robert should be originating new material and, when it was first performed in May 1967 in Brighton, Robert had serious doubts about it too, describing it to Mike Kellaway as 'dreadfully "interesting"'.[30]

Directed by Noel Willman for H. M. Tennent, the play starred Flora Robson as Winifred Brazier, the sister of the late artist she has devoted her life to. After its Brighton run the play went on tour to Liverpool, Manchester, Birmingham, Oxford and Bournemouth, collecting some decidedly mixed reviews. While most critics found it relentlessly contrived and old-fashioned, others admired it for the nobility of its ideas and its stylised setting.

It's only when you come up against a playwright who can pour forth fresh new ideas like a mountain stream [wrote a gushingly nascent Jack Tinker] that you realise what damnably thirsty work theatre going can be. And in the desert wasteland of meagre showmanship in which middlebrow theatre languishes today, Robert Bolt stands as an oasis.

Dame Flora manages the changing moods as she sweeps her way through the confusion of argument in the most masterly fashion. It is a performance of such intense humanity that it transcends all the improbabilities with which the part is burdened.[31]

Three weeks into the tour, as the play reached Oxford, where *The Critic and the Heart* had opened ten years before, Robert shocked everyone by announcing that it would be withdrawn, denying London critics and audiences the opportunity to see it. 'I began to feel uneasy about the play while it was in rehearsal,' Robert told the *Oxford Mail*. 'While the cast were doing all they could, it remained interesting rather than gripping. I thought I could get around my difficulties by some substantial cobbling while the play was on tour. But as time went on it became obvious to me that something very radical was wrong. So I went to Binkie Beaumont and Dame Flora and they generously agreed that the play should come off. It was very brave of them.'[32]

'This setback for Mr Bolt,' reported the *Guardian*, 'comes at a particularly fruitful phase in his career. *A Man For All Seasons*, the film based on his play, won five Oscars, one of them for Mr Bolt's screenplay, and a new stage play would have been a major West End event.'[33]

Robert, though, did not regard it as a setback at all. He thought his decision was eminently sensible and he was supported by Binkie Beaumont and Margaret Ramsay. And when Frith Banbury wrote to say he thought the play should continue, that 'everyone concerned should summon up a bit of courage and at least go down with flags flying', he got a swift reply from Ramsay: 'Surely to decide to pull the play and start all over again is even more courageous,' she wrote. 'I don't see why it's brave to go down with flags flying. Is it brave to risk doing something which both the management and the author think could be done better? Personally I am full of admiration for the courage of this decision and I think that all the good things you recognise in the play will, everyone hopes, be reinforced by Bob working on its weaknesses.'[34]

Six months later Robert was ready to try again. This time he decided that the character of Brazier, the artist, should make a brief appearance at the beginning, grunting and growling before he dies and establishing a character rather than a rumour. Robert also injected some topicality into the scenes with the art critic, not only to bring the play up to date, but to intensify its arguments. Ramsay, though, took the opposite view: 'This play is immeasurably better,' she wrote. 'It's not just a rewrite, but a different play. There are tiny flaws: naming Harold Wilson is dating to the play and somehow unworthy. It's so easy to crucify someone . . . he isn't worse than the rest of the government. By the time the play is produced he might be a god – you admired him once, why not again? I find this somehow distasteful and it stops me from being interested in the larger issues.'[35]

Because Robert's principal reservations about the first run concerned the production design, he decided that he wanted to take complete control and direct the play himself. Ramsay counselled him against doing this: 'Regarding Directing: I'm still a bit unsure whether you will get the best out of the play without the tension of another person asking you questions. I feel it's terribly important for us to get a really super production and make no mistakes.'[36]

Brother and Sister was relaunched on 29 May 1968 at the Theatre Royal in Bristol. Finding a theatre and a cast had been difficult since, even with Robert's name attached to the play, it was slightly stigmatised by having been withdrawn the year before. Consequently, Wendy Hiller, who was offered the role of Winifred, turned it down, unsure of which version she was being offered. The part finally went to Sonia Dresdel. Basil Henson played the invasive critic and Brazier himself was played by William Hartnell, famous for his role as Dr Who on television. Because of his film commitments, and possibly taking Ramsay's advice, Robert decided against directing the play himself. Val May became the director and Robin Archer designed a totally new multi-level set, which enabled the audience to see into Brazier's upstairs bedroom.

Since Robert worried that the play still needed some work, Ramsay bombarded Val May with impossible questions and demands. 'Is there any chance of not inviting the critics in the first week, and if the play doesn't work, would you be prepared to hold them off? I know, dear Val, one is asking the most from you. We are grateful at your wanting to do it, but Bob and I are frankly scared stiff because of his reputation, and all the critics know that it was performed and withdrawn, and they probably have no idea that it is entirely rewritten.'[37]

The reviews this time were less kind and the play was withdrawn again after a brief run. Robert was able to shrug it off, as he usually did, though for Ramsay the experience of *Brother and Sister* was a salutary one. She felt that Robert's career was on the slide, that he had become lazy, seduced by money and by Sarah. What Ramsay feared most of all, though, was that Robert no longer had any need for her. Ramsay was beginning to behave like a jilted lover.

In India, Sarah had learned that she was pregnant. There was only one course of action open to Robert: he had to get married, as he had done with Jo. 'It was hard to know what Robert really thought about Tom's oncoming arrival,' wrote Sarah, 'for he never mentioned him unless I did, his mind always being elsewhere. When I'd given him the news that I was pregnant he took it in his stride, made all the right noises, but I never felt that wonderment of having created a new life together . . .'[38]

Before marrying Sarah, Robert sought the advice of his closest friends: 'When Bob met Sarah I remember him ringing and telling me,' said Ann Queensberry. 'And then I met her. I thought she was very good for him because she laughed at him, she was light-hearted, while Bob and Jo were both intensely serious. I felt that he could really do with someone who wouldn't let him be too serious. I think that worked, for quite a bit, because he had become pretty gloomy. Then he took me out to dinner and asked me if he should get married to Sarah. He'd always want my opinion.'[39] Robert and Sarah were not a happy couple on 25 February 1967. What had been planned as a quiet family affair turned into a circus, with the press gathered outside Woking Registry Office.

In August, with Sarah's belly becoming almost as large as Robert's, they went sailing in the Mediterranean. It was a holiday for children, with Sally and Ben joined by Sarah's younger sister, Vanessa, on whom Ben had 'quite a heavy adolescent crush' .

'The boat was a blue Dutch barge called the *Leiden*, converted to a yawl rig,' said Ben. 'We sailed out of San Remo and went west to Iles d'Hyeres, off the Côte d'Azur. There was a crew of two, the Captain, Barry, and his wife, Millie, who was a superb cook. Dad learned to aqualung and water-ski and in the evenings we'd wander round whatever harbour we were in and admire the sailing boats and pour scorn on the plastic gin palaces, the huge motor yachts. It was a fabulous holiday.'[40]

Robert was immensely proud of Sarah and equally so of Mill House. Everyone he knew was invited to stay for the weekend for conversation, wine, food, tennis, ping pong, croquet and canoeing. The house was filled with animals. Sarah had a horse named Daisy, a gentle name for a towering beast which everyone regarded as unstable, and a Pyrenean mountain dog named Addo which was as big as, well, as big as a mountain.

On 20 October 1967 Sarah gave birth to a son whom she and Robert named Thomas, after Sir Thomas More. On the very same day Jo and Gordon Riddett were married.

Baby Thomas was almost immediately known by Robert as Tom and by Sarah as Tomcat. Even though the world into which Tom was born was unusually privileged, blessed with bright and wealthy parents, the first two decades of his life would prove to be traumatic in the extreme. Sarah wrote:

> Robert, not caring to participate in 'baby' issues, must have felt subconscious twinges of guilt because he took his love for me into his study, where he began writing the screenplay for *Madame Bovary.* . . . Robert compensated for his lack of attention by writing what he thought was a great part for me. How could I tell him that I'd rather be sharing a few hours of the day with him than receiving the writer's gift of a great role? I've always thought life much more important than a career. Besides, all through those first years of having to cope while Robert was forever up in his study, I remembered that day in Hasker Street when I fell down the stairs and he simply continued typing. That's what drew me to him, made marriage with him a possibility – that he would never suffocate me.[41]

NINETEEN

REMARKABLE WOMEN

'I feel I am about to make an ass of myself and of Sarah and that I am asking you to risk your enormous reputation on some highly personal spree of my own.'

Robert Bolt to David Lean

As soon as he fell in love with Sarah, Robert wanted most of all to write something for her, a play or a film which would stretch her talent and make her shine. For five years, apart from *Brother and Sister* and *Gandhi*, little passed through his typewriter without Sarah being its inspiration. 'I never asked him to do a damn thing for me,' said Sarah, 'but he only seemed to be happy when he was writing for me. He used to take "me" into his study. That turned him on. He really believed in me as an actress and was always dumbfounded that I was so different from my North Country slut films.'[1]

Being married to a sex symbol appealed to Robert's ego, as it would to any man's. Perhaps unwittingly, Robert and Sarah presented an image of the scholarly writer and the sexy, vibrant actress in much the same way that Arthur Miller and Marilyn Monroe had done a decade earlier. The press rarely left them alone and photographs at the time show a glamorous couple, with Robert wreathed in dinner jacket and a cloud of tobacco smoke, and Sarah in a succession of exotic evening gowns, clinging to his arm. But whenever Robert made the news, he invariably found himself referred to as 'Robert Bolt, playwright husband of Sarah Miles'.

Bob's attitude towards Sarah was indulgent [said Robert's brother, Sydney]. I don't mean to say that he wasn't very attached to her, for he was very deeply attached, but in the sense that she could be forgiven or allowed almost anything because she was only a child. He thought she was madly amusing. She'd say the most ridiculous things and Bob's shoulders would heave and he'd say, 'There she goes again! Isn't she marvellous!' She was Rousseauesque, a child of nature, not a Pygmalion figure since he wasn't trying to fashion her into something else.

Peggy Ramsay said he sold out, but this wasn't due to some selling out of artistic standards. It was due to Bob having more of an ethical than an aesthetic commitment. He had a communication theory of art rather than an aesthetic theory of art. He thought that certain truths were important and this came from our nonconformist background. He thought he had to make people see certain things and it might have been, as in *A Man For All Seasons*, to show the difficulties in taking an ethical position. I don't believe Bob was an artist, he was a communicator.[2]

Many friends noticed a distinct change in Robert's writing after he married Sarah. To begin with, he started to write major parts for women, something he had not done before. A more subtle change was the way that Robert's interest in the ethical and political dilemmas of the time was now realised in period melodramas about the perfidy of women. John Dunn, his former pupil, said:

My experience was that Bob had remained much the same when he was in Hampshire. Things became very different when he was with Sarah Miles in that grand house in Byfleet. I didn't like Sarah Miles. Perhaps later on I would have liked her a lot more, considering what happened, but at that time she struck me as being a fantastically spoilt bitch, really. But for Bob, Sarah was an exhilarating salve to a wound.

Bob was a very serious person and when he was talking to me, he was deeply engaged in trying to understand things that were important. I felt that Sarah represented very different values. She could be extraordinarily charming, but it seemed a more superficial and ultimately pointless orientation than what I had felt to be true at Millfield and after he left Millfield. A lot of it was to do with sex, of course, but there were other things too. I don't think Sarah suspended the things Bob cared about but she did shift his attention quite a lot. And those three things they did together, that Irish thing and *Lady Caroline Lamb* and *Vivat! Vivat Regina!* , they weren't very good, were they?[3]

Bernard McCabe was struck by the way that Robert's life had

changed after he married Sarah. 'Bob asked us to dinner at the White Tower,' said McCabe. 'Seeing him and Sarah was not like seeing Bob and Jo. They made us feel almost country-bumpkinish. After the meal a waiter came over and said, "Mr Bolt, your car has arrived," and outside was this huge red Rolls-Royce with a chauffeur. We both sat in the back with our cigars and I said to Bob, "This is ridiculous, you can't live like this." I prodded and prodded him but he wouldn't respond. He took it very seriously and I began to feel uneasy with his work.'[4]

'I remember that dinner,' said Sarah, 'and we all made fun of the chauffeur. Robert thought it was healthy to give the high life a bash but Bernard didn't think that at all. Robert said afterwards, "Poor old Bernard, he's become so dull. Did you notice his contrived dirty finger nails? Done especially for me, no doubt." Robert was simply acknowledging the little boy within, going bananas in the tuck shop. Everyone wants to taste the high life, just once. Show me someone who doesn't and I'll show you a liar.'[5]

Margaret Ramsay was never one to hold back an opinion and the more bluntly it was expressed the better. Ramsay took an immediate dislike to Sarah, underrating her talent and ignoring the liberating effect she was having on Robert's personality. For Ramsay, Sarah represented an even greater threat than David Lean to her custody over Robert's talent and career. Ramsay disliked Robert's weakness for money and his laziness in not writing a brilliant new play. Unlike her latest clients, notably Joe Orton and Christopher Hampton, she felt Robert was abandoning the theatre and abandoning her. As *Brother and Sister* was going through its painful development, Ramsay wrote a stinging letter to Robert:

> My feeling is that you are still at the beginning of a very big career with many new plays and films still to be written, yet our attitude (and yours) is rather as if you're the grand old man who can do whatever he wishes. I don't think this is true at all. I think we need to work and fight for your career, *as never before*. The couple of Oscars are not in the least helpful: I spit on them.
>
> I shan't hide my worries because I want to spur you to take this business incredibly seriously. I feel sometimes as if I'm trying to talk to some kind of sybarite who had eluded me. Why do I feel this? It's not just puritanism, it's based on some area of fact!!!
>
> Of course I'd really like you back to no running water and the lavatory a bog at the end of the garden. No, I don't wish this,

but I'm always aware that a career can turn full circle. So, Bob, let's pull the collars of our overcoats up over our ears, and let's pull our hats over our heads and grimly *go forward*. If we don't do this, we might go *back*.[6]

'I'd only met Peggy Ramsay at one meal,' said Sarah. 'She did all the talking and I never got a word in edgeways. As I sat down, she had already formed her opinion of me and nothing I could say would have changed that. So I didn't try to butt in and prove my worth. Life's too short. I just sat there, watching her overly zealous mouth move.'[7]

When Robert and Sarah went on holiday to the Canaries he gave her a copy of Jane Austen's *Emma*. 'Go on, try her, she's an easy read, witty, too,' he said. Sarah later claimed it was one of the first major novels she had ever read. 'The reason I had read so little', said Sarah, 'was due to being 87 per cent dyslexic. Try to imagine the enormous effort that goes into reading when you can't. Robert recognised the hell I was going through and it's one of the reasons I had such compassion when he had his stroke. I had been there all my life, knowing what I had inside but lacking the ability to get it out.'[8]

Robert started work on a screenplay, thinking that Sarah could play Austen's heroine to perfection. Austen had written of her creation, 'I am going to take a heroine whom no one but myself will much like. . . I like her with all her faults; nay, I like her for her faults . . .' Emma's relationship with the dull, intelligent and highly principled Mr Knightley contained the personal, dramatic element Robert was looking for and the age difference between Emma and Knightley – seventeen years – was precisely the same as that between himself and Sarah. But after six months' work, Robert abandoned it. He told Len Smith:

The film of *Emma* never materialised. You must agree that it would be difficult to present the relationship between Emma and Harriette with all the moral tensions invested in it by Jane Austen without Emma and Mr Nitely seeming to be a pair of ludicrous and disagreeable snobs. Readers of Jane Austen accept her social form of reference all at a blow but a cinema audience would not. They would judge the characters by the standards of today. And if one commenced the film with some sort of dramatised exposition of Regency society the audience would think that one was inviting them to laugh at that society. The other alternative, of course, would be to present it simply as a light romantic tale but that would not be worth doing and, indeed, ought not to be done.[9]

From Jane Austen's *Emma*, Robert turned to another, Gustave Flaubert's Emma Bovary. Here the story was more conducive to modern taste and the part for Sarah even more attractive and dramatic. Robert was so excited by the prospect that he immediately contacted David Lean about it: 'I'm going to do a script of *Madame Bovary*. Do you know it? Besides being a "classic", it's an immensely disturbing account of frustrated passion and romantic longing. Very intimate, dramatic to the verge of melodrama, and yet implacably realistic. Marvellous parts. Sarah for Madame Bovary of course. It would have to be shot in France. Does it interest you? You're the perfect director for it. If not, can you suggest who would be second best?'[10]

Robert's letter reached Lean in India. 'Isn't it a *bugger* darling?' he wrote to Barbara Cole. 'I don't know the book but I bet it's good. Dear old Robert must be in a temporary madness. Aren't we all, from time to time. I can't believe that Miss M has the weight for such a character, and unless he gets someone like me I don't think a distributor will back her little known name in such a huge title role. . . . I'm afraid he must write the part for her and *her* character. I can also imagine what rehearsals would be like with Miss M knowing more about Robert's intentions than anyone else, including me.'[11]

Unperturbed, Robert spent a year writing *Madame Bovary* and sent it to Lean who, by then, was living in Italy with Sandy Hotz. The script reached them in Naples, where Lean was planning to show Sandy the splendours of Capri across the bay. As Sarah – and before her, Jo – had had to learn how to live with a man who disappeared for days on end to write, Sandy found the same problem with one who vanished at intervals to read. She told Kevin Brownlow:

> David read it with a terrible concentration and when he finished it he wrote Robert a ten-page letter explaining why he couldn't possibly make the film. When he got to the end of the letter, he tore it up and began another, much longer letter, saying that given changes, major changes, he would be willing, in fact excited, to work on it.
>
> I remember sitting in that gloomy mausoleum of a suite at the Excelsior for almost a month while David slaved over his portable typewriter, never going out, eating in the hotel dining room night after night. In the end, I found a bookstore and read *Gargantua and Pantagruel* over a weekend, not something I

would willingly do again. So I never got to Capri. But that was the beginning of *Ryan's Daughter*.[12]

Lean's change of mind is not hard to understand. Just as Robert suddenly found himself drawn to stories about love affairs between younger women and older men, Lean discovered that his new relationship with Sandy was effectively mirrored in Flaubert's novel. And there was something else. . . . In his recent letters to Lean, Robert was arguing that their next collaboration should be on a smaller scale than *Lawrence of Arabia* or *Doctor Zhivago*. 'I'd like our next to be . . . what? I don't quite know,' he said. 'But something simpler in its mechanics, with more emphasis on atmosphere (like *Brief Encounter* if you like), less sheer strained ingenuity of story-telling. A simple but grand theme that could be told in lesser length.'[13]

And a month later: 'I forget exactly what I said in my last, but I don't mean another *Brief Encounter* in the sense of anything as "small" as that. . . . It ought to be a simple story with an important or exciting theme. Simple so as to give us *room*, important or exciting so as to give us impulse and energy. We want something we can expand instead of compress. I don't mean something we can be leisurely – that's *never* possible in drama – but something that gives us room to manoeuvre.'[14] This idea of Robert's undoubtedly stuck in Lean's mind. The thought of returning to the small-scale, intimate drama of *Brief Encounter* appealed to him, even though he wanted to set the story against a rather grander landscape than suburban England. Known for making huge, international epics, Lean made it known that his next film would be a simple love story, 'a little gem', he said.

Because *Doctor Zhivago* had been such a colossal hit, Lean and Robert were confident that MGM would agree to whatever terms they proposed. The result for both of them was a deal which, at the time, was potentially the most lucrative ever achieved by film-makers. Lean would receive $1 million dollars plus thirty-five per cent of the net profits and a generous living allowance. Robert would get $400,000 in instalments, plus ten per cent of the net profits and a similar living allowance. In rather tortuous English, Robert's contract described the screenplay as 'A love story about a passionate young girl against a continental background in the early twentieth century who becomes involved in a hasty marriage which is neither psychologically or emotionally satisfying and therefore seeks fulfilment with more sympathetic men.'[15]

When this deal was signed, on 23 January 1968, Robert was the highest paid screenwriter in the world. By way of contrast, Harold Pinter received $75,000 for *The Go-Between*, which was financed jointly by MGM and EMI. Tennessee Williams could command about $100,000 for a screenplay such as *Boom!*, while Paddy Chayevsky's asking price was around $200,000. Only William Goldman, who wrote *Butch Cassidy and the Sundance Kid*, was remotely in Robert's league and even in the late Seventies fees for screenplays rarely exceeded $300,000. With adjustments for inflation, Robert's fee of $400,000 would be in the region of $3 million in today's money and to command that sort of figure a writer must produce something of the brilliance and originality of *Lethal Weapon III* or *Showgirls*.

Robert was earning these impressive sums when the Labour government's taxation levels meant that anyone earning £100,000 a year would keep just £14,337. Although he had no intention of leaving England for good, he knew that he could avoid paying a substantial amount of tax if he spent a year away from home. Lean's own obsessive flight from the remittance man made this possible: by spending several months in Rome and six months on location, Robert could combine a maximum of socialist integrity with the maximum of income.

Robert, Sarah and Tom flew to Rome and checked into the Parco dei Principi, the newly opened luxury hotel where Lean and Sandy had taken over most of the top floor.

To begin with, we were all in the Parco dei Principi [said Sarah]. It was a strange set-up, a bit oppressive really, but it worked for David. I loved David who had lots of little fetishes. He'd use his soap, even the hotel soap, until it was paper thin. He couldn't bear to throw it away. So strange! He had this balcony with all his plants, so if you were in the swimming pool you could look up and see where David was because that part of the austere building was covered in greenery.

After a month we moved to an apartment which meant we could be together and Robert could go to the hotel to work. Those were good times. They worked all day, and I didn't interrupt them. Sandy used to take me shopping. It staggered me what Sandy used to buy and just to see someone with limitless resources was gob smacking. In the evenings we'd all go out together. Sandy was learning Italian and practising all her wonderful lilting Italiano. 'Isn't she clever?' David would say.

David couldn't speak a word of Italian, it was beneath him. He had to have his marmalade, his sausages and the BBC wherever he was.[16]

Sarah was wandering in Rome one day when something in a shop caught her eye. It was a blue Lamborghini which she thought was the most beautiful car she had ever seen. When Robert had admired it too, he told Lean about this superb piece of Italian engineering and design. The next day Lean presented the Lamborghini to Robert and Sarah as a belated wedding present. It was second hand but it still cost a fortune. 'It isn't a sensible conveyance,' Robert told Lean, 'but it is a delight.' But Lean's generosity brought its own problems, for Robert knew that if he took the car to England the taxman would be lying in wait for it. 'I have to pay 40 per cent of its value, which in view of the princely nature of your gift would be more than I would normally want to pay for a car outright!'[17]

With nothing to do except see the sights, and thrash the Lamborghini along the autostradas, Sarah left Robert and Lean in their smoke-filled suite and returned to her horses and dogs in Byfleet. When she came back to Rome a month later, limping because of a badly twisted ankle, the result of a riding accident, Robert failed to notice. 'He said, "Hello darling, can you get me a whisky?" He didn't notice my leg. Then David comes in and says, "What have you done to your leg?" A few days later David forced me to go to his doctor who found my ankle was broken. That was the difference in their personalities. Even though Robert was a much more caring man in many ways, David had the power of observation. Robert didn't really see anything except his work.'[18]

Every day was the same. Robert would walk to the Parco dei Principi and find Lean ready with his criticisms of what they had done the day before. Robert would sip the first of dozens of espressos, place his cigarettes and tobacco on the table, light up his pipe and put another sheet of paper into the typewriter.

The story they knew. They didn't know yet where it would take place and once they did know it would change. Preserving only the core theme of *Madame Bovary* – a young woman married to an older man – they decided they needed an outside conflict, 'something over the hill to come in and affect the characters,' said Lean. They considered various locations, including India, and finally settled on Ireland. 'The 1916 Irish situation suited us rather well,' said Lean, 'and in fact the Troubles come into the village and go out again.'[19]

Robert and Lean devised a screenplay populated less by characters than by universally recognised archetypes: the sexually innocent, dreamily impressionable girl, Rosy Ryan; the scholarly yet emotionally frigid teacher, Charles O'Shaughnessy, whom she marries; the Byronic, shell-shocked, crippled war hero, Major Randolph Doryan, whom she has an affair with; a grizzled village priest with eyes in the back of his head; and Michael, a deformed village idiot. Add to this a charismatic IRA gun-runner and Rosy's father, a publican posing as a Republican who betrays his daughter to save his own skin, and you have a full-blown Gothic melodrama. The final ingredient was the weather, which would erupt on cue and introduce a pantheistic note, underlining human frailty and implying that greater forces were at work.

In fact, Robert began by writing a storm sequence, and not just a storm. This was to be a meteorological convulsion on a Biblical scale. As the priest, Father Collins, says, gazing at the fuming clouds and heaving waves, 'You'd think they were announcing the coming of Christ.'

'The theme', Robert told the American critic, Joseph Gelmis, 'is about control and duty and loyalty as against impulse, greed and self-expression and one wanted radiating from this a number of characters with different degrees of consciousness, awareness and spontaneity. The idiot is the existential hero. To my mind, he remains merely pitiable. You have a priest who is highly conscious but whose view of the spontaneous is almost entirely punitive. You have a schoolmaster who is very upright, conscious, sympathetic, but whose self-abnegation, whose selflessness is to some extent a disguised kind of cowardice. Above all you have the girl who is abnormally conscious of the dichotomy as well as suffering from it.' When Gelmis asked if the girl's behaviour was specifically female or just an example of human nature, Robert gave an extraordinary reply:

> What one does is draw on the feminine in oneself. The difficulty about this is not that there is insufficient feminine in oneself but that one is reluctant to admit how much there is in oneself. So when your feminine character begins to be involved in a specifically feminine situation, like let us say rape, your subconscious begins to panic. It doesn't want to know. It doesn't want to know because it can't know, but because it can probably know too easily the strange ambivalence of a woman who is undergoing rape – the horror, the shock and the delight, the pleasure, the abandonment. There is probably sufficient of a

woman in every man to understand this and, of course, it's slightly disagreeable.[20]

As the screenplay took shape, Robert and Lean had every reason to be pleased. They had escaped the restrictions of literary adaptation. Flaubert was a mere ghost. They had at long last created an original. The 'little gem' which Lean had planned was due to run considerably more than three hours.

Lean and Robert delivered their screenplay to MGM on 14 October 1968. It was called *Michael's Day*, after the character of the village idiot, though Robert wanted the title changed to *The Back of Beyond*. MGM authorised a budget of $9.4 million and a shooting schedule of 162 days. The only reservation they had over Robert's screenplay was the ending in which Major Doryan commits suicide by blowing himself up with some of the arms which have been sent by Germany to assist the IRA. MGM's Russell Thacher thought this ending much too downbeat and suggested that Doryan should die during a struggle with the IRA man. His death would then amount to something. Robert politely said no:

> The manner and circumstances of Randolph's death are in themselves exciting, I think. What I sense behind your criticism is your feeling that his death is arbitrary and a shade convenient for David and myself . . . but that arbitrary death was very much what we wanted. Our point about Randolph is that he belongs to death from the moment of his first appearance. The First World War was not (we wish to say) an act of mass murder but something worse: a worldwide suicide pact. Randolph is meant to be a paradigm of this condition. He hates and fears the Front but is sexually and emotionally incapacitated away from it. His affair with Rosy, so improbable, unsuitable and in every way impractical, is a last blaze of natural life which he and she and, we hope, the audience, understands to be foredoomed.[21]

While Robert was in Rome writing the screenplay he received a message from an Italian producer named Fernando Ghia whose current production was in serious trouble.

> I knew of Robert before I met him because my background is in the theatre [said Ghia]. In 1967 I was working for Franco Cristaldi and we were shooting the first Italo-Soviet production, *The Red Tent*. There was an Italian screenplay, a Russian screenplay and an English screenplay. The Russians wanted to go one

way, we wanted to go another and there was a lot of trouble. It was a sixteen month schedule and we were half-way through. When you were dealing with the Russians, the actors and technicians were paid by the State and when they were shooting they were paid a bonus, so they shot for ever.

The Russians planned a four-and-a-half hour film, so we had a big crisis with our American producer. He said we needed someone to write some new linking material which could be shot and made into a shorter film. He said, 'You need someone like Robert Bolt.'

When I found out that Robert was at the Parco dei Principi, two blocks from our office, Cristaldi said he would pay him anything to get us out of trouble. I went to see him, we talked and I took him to Franco's house to see two hours of material. Robert said, 'This is fantastic, who wrote the script?' I explained our problem and he said, 'Look, I'm very sympathetic to your situation but I have to finish this script with David. If you still need me in three months I might be able to help.'

One evening he took me to dinner with David. Robert was taking the piss out of him. Now, David was living in Rome for years and he would not say a word of Italian. And he went to one restaurant only, Celestina, because he knew how to drive his Rolls-Royce from the hotel. It was quite funny.

Robert was fed up with David. He was working around the clock trying to be rid of the script and the intensity. Then he tells me he has five weeks free, that he could help and that he was the most expensive screenwriter in the world. He said, 'Make me an offer.' I knew that whatever I said he was going to double it so I said a hundred thousand dollars. He said, 'Lovely figure, but it's wrong. Seventy-five, that's about right.' I couldn't bloody believe it! It had never happened in my life before and it will never happen again. But Robert knew how much work was involved. There was a sense of justice about him. He would never take you for a ride. He said to me, 'You have to understand that I can't take credit for my work but if anyone asks me I will always confirm that I worked on it.'

He wrote around our existing material and added a new character, the explorer Roald Amundsen, who was played by Sean Connery. And it was through Robert that we got him. Sean worked on the film for five weeks while Peter Finch worked for over a year.

Robert was brilliant and more than willing to cut his own

dialogue. He said, 'You never fall in love with lines.' I asked him if he had ever thought of directing and he said, 'If I ever make the decision to direct, I would like you to produce it.' In this business, these things are said every day to everybody. But Robert kept his word.[22]

Lean's friend, Eddie Fowlie, had found the ideal location for what was then called *Michael's Day* on the Dingle Peninsula in County Kerry. The scenery was wild and rugged, with towering cliffs and sweeping sandy beaches. It was remote and virtually uninhabited, apart from the village of Dingle itself, which offered scores of bars, one or two fish restaurants and an ugly barracks of a modern motel, the Skeilig. A few miles west of Dingle, near Dunquin, Lean's production designer, Stephen Grimes, constructed the fictional village of Kirrary, complete with fully functional cottages, pub, police station, schoolhouse and army encampment. While it stood, Kirrary was the westernmost village in Europe.

Casting the picture had been relatively easy. Sarah was always part of the package, even if she did not realise it herself. She was signed for $150,000 plus a living allowance of $600 a week. All she had to do was wait until production started. 'Don't know how we'll survive till February,' Robert told Lean. 'Sarah alternates between a sort of soaring excitement and gloomy convictions that it's too good to be real, won't happen, or that she'll act badly, look awful etc. etc. Thomas however absorbs any surplus energies anyone has to offer.'[23]

In Rome, Lean had met his old chum John Mills and offered him what was then the title role of the village idiot, Michael. Mills, who was signed for $250,000, thought he had been typecast. Also for $250,000, Trevor Howard was cast in the role of the priest after Alec Guinness turned down the part. Robert persuaded Lean to offer the part of Ryan, the publican, to Leo McKern who also happened to be in Rome when Robert was writing the script. McKern accepted immediately, a decision he later came to regret.

For the role of Major Doryan, the crippled war hero, Lean wanted Marlon Brando who at first agreed, then changed his mind, having failed to master the crippled leg. Lean then considered Steve McQueen but settled on Christopher Jones because he liked the way he looked. Jones was a James Dean figure, slim, with haunted eyes, though in watching him in *The Looking-Glass War*, Lean failed to realise that Jones's American voice had been dubbed by another actor.

Casting the role of the village schoolmaster, O'Shaughnessy, was critical. The way the part was written, it might have been played by a physically slight and sensitive actor, like Leslie Howard in his heyday. O'Shaughnessy had to convince the audience of his love of Byron and Beethoven – 'though I'm not one of those fellas meself' – his fondness for pressed wild flowers and his inadequacy in bed. If he did that, an audience would accept him wandering along a beach in his nightshirt after he discovers that Rosy has been sleeping with someone else. And at the end, they would accept his nobility in taking Rosy back and protecting her from the baying mob of villagers who have accused her of betraying the Republican cause by fornicating with a British soldier.

'He's a jolly good, dull character,' said Lean. 'Now, if you get a jolly good, dull actor and play him in that part, the audience will be yawning their heads off in five minutes flat.' Having decided to cast against type, Robert and Lean thought initially of Patrick McGoohan, then Paul Scofield who declined, as did George C. Scott. It was then that Robert suggested Robert Mitchum, whom he had seen interviewed on television and was struck by the actor's 'dignity and mildness as against his swaggering tough-guy image'.

Robert Mitchum was arguably the most sexually charged and masculine star in the world. He also had a singular reputation: he was said to be lazy, reading scripts only to discover how many days he had off and where he might spend them. He was reputed to be a womaniser, a drunkard and a junkie, and he hated directors who thought that every shot had to be a Van Gogh. Yet he had collaborated willingly in Charles Laughton's *The Night of the Hunter* and Joseph Losey's *Secret Ceremony*, two of the strangest films ever made. Apparently, he wrote poetry. He was a legend. When Robert called Mitchum to offer him the part, the latter told him that he was unable to accept it because he had decided to commit suicide. 'Oh,' stammered Robert, 'if you would just do this wretched little film of ours and then do yourself in, I'd be happy to stand the expenses of your burial.' Mitchum appreciated Robert's wittiness as much as MGM's generosity and signed a contract for $800,000 for twenty-six weeks' work.

A month before shooting started, MGM urged Robert and Lean to change their title. *Michael's Day* meant nothing to the studio executives, who submitted a list of alternatives, including *Circle of Gulls*, *The Storm*, *Wind of the Sea* and *Rising Tide*. It was not a sea story, though, and Robert and Lean cast aside those suggestions, proposing *Coming of Age* instead. On 11 April 1969, when the film had been in production for two months, MGM announced the final title as *Ryan's Daughter*. The cast and crew gathered in Dingle in February. While Lean and Sandy billeted at the grim Skeilig Hotel, Trevor Howard, John Mills and Robert Mitchum were allotted cottages in the village. Robert and Sarah, though, were given Fermoyle House, a handsome Georgian residence on the far side of the peninsula. Although Sarah could never understand why they had been singled out for exile, the isolation suited Robert who planned to spend the whole of his Irish sojourn writing a new play about Elizabeth I and Mary Queen of Scots. And when he wasn't writing the play or revising the script for Lean, he sailed a boat in the bay, dodging dolphins and sudden squalls.

Shooting on *Ryan's Daughter* started on 24 February 1969 and by 11 June the film was forty days over schedule and $940,000 over budget. It seems that no one had foreseen the consequences of the Irish weather. It rained for days on end and when the sun came out it was not the same sort of sun or the same sort of cloud as before, making it impossible for the cinematographer, Freddie Young, to match the previous shots. And if it re-emerged it went in again by the time the crew had arrived on the location and set up their equipment.

Lean was getting testy and Mitchum, Howard and McKern were getting drunk, which made Lean get even testier – and because he refused to allow them to go to London or Dublin, in case the sun came out, the actors got even drunker. Robert, meanwhile, sat in remote Fermoyle House, lost in the faraway world of the Tudors.

By 15 July the film was sixty days behind schedule and $1.5 million over budget. By 14 October, when the film was eight-seven days and $2.5 million over budget, MGM had been bought by a Las Vegas businessman, Kirk Kerkorian, who installed James Aubrey as the new President and CEO at the studio. Immediately, he flew to Ireland in the hope of speeding things up, cutting costs, or both. When Aubrey arrived on the set Lean called a halt to the shooting and sat calmly in his director's chair, awaiting Aubrey's comments. Every minute that Lean was not working was costing MGM thousands of dollars, so Aubrey left without solving anything. The weather did not improve.

Robert Mitchum later said that making a film with David Lean was 'like building the Taj Mahal out of matchsticks'. Mitchum used to goad him continually and send him up. If Mitchum had done an especially good take and had received praise from Lean, he would say, 'Thank you. David. You don't think it was a little too Jewish?' Since Lean lacked a sense of humour, especially when he was on a film set, he mistook Mitchum's mischievousness for blatant rudeness and disrespect.

> Theirs was the funniest relationship [said Sarah]. Our three caravans were all in a row and I was pig in the middle, and also the go-between, because the mountain would not go to Mohammed, nor would Mohammed go to the mountain. So there was me trailing notes between these two great men.
> 'Tell Robert he's got to wear his shirt out of his trousers.'
> 'Tell David I'm fucking not going to wear my shirt out.'
> 'Tell him he's got to!'
> So I'm running back and forth, holding the collar of a shirt.[24]

There is an industry legend that Robert Mitchum and Sarah had an affair during the making of *Ryan's Daughter*. The fact that Mitchum's wife, Dorothy, and Sarah's husband were always at Dingle makes this rather hard to credit. And Sarah denies it vehemently. But Sarah did find Mitchum unusually attractive and in the long periods between set-ups, when the weather was misbehaving or when Lean was staring out to sea, thinking, she spent many hours in Mitchum's caravan. That is how the rumour started and before long Robert knew about it as well.

The irony was bizarre. Robert had written a story about a schoolteacher who believes his wife is having an affair and even before he substantiates the rumour he becomes the victim of village gossip and is branded a cuckold. O'Shaughnessy is deeply humiliated, yet redeemed by his nobility, even when he discovers that his wife had lied to him and that the rumours were true. 'Robert Mitchum and I were soul mates,' said Sarah. 'We were very close, but we weren't doing it. People always assume you're doing it and we both knew that everyone was thinking that and I find that a bit tacky. But I knew the truth and Robert knew the truth. People also thought I had an affair with Robert Shaw on *The Hireling* but if I got uptight about everyone who lied about me, I'd be dead. The whole film set was abuzz. I'd go in Mitch's caravan and they thought, "Well, they must be doing it." I find that very distasteful.'[25]

All the actors were having a miserable time. 'Except Johnnie Mills,' said Sarah. 'He was with his wife, Mary, and always seemed to be enjoying himself, even though he was nearly drowned once when David sent him and Trevor out in a boat in a rough sea. Poor old Trevor Howard was bored out of his mind and desperate to get home to his wife but David wouldn't let him.'

Christopher Jones had his own problems, many of them stemming from the fact that Lean made it clear that casting him had been a mistake. Jones's American accent meant that his entire part would have to be dubbed later by another actor. And because Jones was incapable of performing the love scene with Sarah, Lean called a halt and decided to reshoot the entire sequence. When Robert learned that the scene would have to be reshot, he rewrote it completely. Then he wondered how Sarah might respond to his idea that she play the scene naked. He wrote to Lean: 'We see Rosy in the first stage of love-making shy and inexpert and then, as you say, "swimming in her own water". Here we would see what Randolph had done for her. I haven't mentioned the idea to Sarah who might take off and hit the roof; but then again she might not. If she's feeling pretty and liked I think that secretly she doesn't really mind being photographed *au naturelle*. Whether she'd relish it with Christopher Jones is another matter.'[26]

The Irish weather put paid to reshooting the scene in the bluebell wood near Killarney and for a while it looked as if Lean might have to go to Italy or even New Zealand. Then Eddie Fowlie came to the rescue and created his own bluebell wood in a local dance hall, complete with butterflies and twittering birds. The scene was reshot with Sarah and Jones discreetly naked.

'Leo McKern had a bad time as well,' said Sarah. 'David's direction of him during the storm sequence lacked any kind of care. I was there when Leo said, "David, when my hand goes up that means I'm in trouble, real trouble, and you've got to get me out." I remember seeing that hand go up and the divers in their black suits saying, "His hand's gone up," and David hissing, "Leave it, leave it." And when Leo was fished out of the sea he'd lost his glass eye. That was the day that Leo lost respect for David and lost his respect for the whole business because he pissed off back to Australia, gave up acting and played around with boats.'[27]

After a year, David Lean was finally forced to come to terms with the fact that the Irish weather was beyond his control. No matter that he had outmanoeuvred the MGM executives, his power did not extend to directing the scudding clouds, the Gulf Stream or the Atlantic tides. Although Eddie Fowlie had faked the bluebell wood, there was no way he could recreate the beaches and cliffs in a studio. The answer was to find another location and hope no one would notice the join.

Fowlie got on a plane to South Africa. Finding suitable west-facing beaches south of Cape Town at Chapman's Bay, near Noordhoek, he took photographs, gathered up a handful of sand and was back in Dingle so quickly that Lean was unaware he had been away. 'The Cape Town beaches looked just like the Irish beaches. We just had to spray the white rocks black,' said Lean, in a masterpiece of ecological understatement. 'And I'll tell you, if you showed me the film now, I'd have to think hard which beach was Ireland and which was South Africa.'[28]

While a second unit was left behind in Dingle to shoot the storm sequence, Lean and a reduced crew, plus Sarah, John Mills and Christopher Jones, flew to Cape Town on 27 December 1969. By this time the film was 100 days and $3,270,264 over budget. The plan was to shoot the remaining beach scenes, when Mills discovers the explosives which leads to Jones's suicide at sunset. But because Cape Town's weather proved to be just as fickle as Dingle's the two-week schedule was extended to four weeks.

Robert flew out to Cape Town with Sarah, eager to renew his acquaintance with the city that he had fallen in love with during the war. But the South Africa of 1970 was a very different country from that of 1945. Following independence from Britain in 1960, the country had been expelled from the Commonwealth and banned from participating in any international cultural or sporting events. A trade embargo in respect of military equipment was also in force.

Sarah fell foul of the apartheid regime almost at once, when she held the hand of a black photographer who helped her find her balance when she slipped on a sand dune. 'I had no idea who he was,' she said, 'and it was clear that he was only escorting me over rough ground, but I was taken to the police station. I felt great outrage at what was happening there.'[29]

A few years before Robert went to South Africa a group of playwrights had decided to prevent their work being performed to segregated audiences. Robert's name joined those of John Arden, Samuel Beckett, John Mortimer, Harold Pinter and Arnold Wesker. Their stance was widely reported by the press and produced a flurry of correspondence, most notably from Laurens van der Post, who argued that the ideas expressed in, say, *A Man For All Seasons* could only be of value to the divided culture of South Africa. While Robert agreed that *A Man For All Seasons* would be acceptable to the South African government, he said that 'the play's central character, Sir Thomas More, were he alive in South Africa today, would be in prison. He was an actively good man, and active goodness is never acceptable to evil Governments. Art sometimes is . . . An artist may become well known. Then he can express political opinions not only in the polling booth but also in a more resounding forum . . . since he has the privilege it is probably his duty to exercise it on occasion. The most effective way in which a playwright can declare his disapproval of racial segregation is to refuse to have his play performed for segregated audiences.'[30]

Another South African who opposed the ban was Athol Fugard, a prominent playwright and anti-apartheid activist. Fugard had already met Robert in London and argued that a cultural boycott served little purpose other than appealing to the British playwrights' moral righteousness. Fugard thought that if plays by Arden, Pinter or Bolt were presented in South Africa, even to segregated audiences, the broader dissemination of their ideas could only be of benefit to his blighted country. Fugard also criticised Robert for allowing his films, which earned him considerably more money than his plays, to be shown in South Africa.

Robert could easily have decided against visiting South Africa; instead, he flew straight into a moral quagmire. Fugard told a local newspaper: '[Bolt] doesn't allow his plays to be performed here but writes a film that is not only free to be shown here to segregated audiences but is made on the unhallowed soil of the country, with his wife in a leading role and with himself in attendance.'

Robert hastily flew back to London, pursued by a Cape Town journalist who sent Robert a letter via Margaret Ramsay. In response, Robert wrote:

You ask why I 'allowed' *Ryan's Daughter* to be shot in South Africa. The answer is quite simple: the choice of location does not rest with the writer. The film is set in Ireland and it was only our extreme ill luck in the matter of weather which forced the producer and director to find a few days of sea and sunshine elsewhere. Had the decision been mine, I should have tried to find somewhere other than South Africa.

You are quite right in supposing that the financial sacrifices involved in disallowing stage presentations is slight. No moral kudos accrues from it, and indeed one is open to the charge that one is seeking moral kudos at very little cost. Many respected people, such as Laurens van der Post, take the view that more would be achieved by allowing stage presentations in South Africa than by the embargo. However, the South African citizens, both Black and White who are actively opposed to apartheid, are overwhelmingly in favour of the embargo.

My visit to South Africa did not change my views fundamentally but it heightened my sense of the poignancy of the situation there. The choice before a liberal-minded South African seems to be either to toe the line and go along with Government policy quite passively or else to invite trouble and even ruin and imprisonment. I do not blame anybody for making the less heroic choice. If I were myself a South African, not being made of heroic stuff yet unable to stomach the continuous injustice which subsumes South African society, I suppose that I would take the decision to exile myself from my homeland. The potential of South Africa and its peoples seems to me enormous. It could be a country for the human race to boast about instead of being as it is a country from which most of us feel we must turn away in embarrassment.[31]

Shooting on *Ryan's Daughter* was completed on 19 March 1970, 135 days over schedule and $3,549,833 over budget. The total production cost was $13,015,877, by no means the most expensive film ever made but a high price to pay for what had begun as a small-scale romance. As Lean and his editor, Norman Savage, settled into the Great Southern Hotel in Killarney to edit the picture, Robert and Sarah prepared for their début as a creative partnership: the première of *Vivat! Vivat Regina!* at the Chichester Festival on 20 May.

The play was causing problems, and so was the title. Robert's working titles were *The Caged Falcons* and *Prisoners of State*, which Margaret Ramsay dismissed as titles for costume plays of the Twenties. Ramsay herself suggested *Extraordinary Women* which Robert changed to *Remarkable Women*. 'This is a costume play,' wrote Ramsay, 'but at least *Remarkable Women* is something you don't forget, and if it doesn't sound like a conventional title, so much the better. *Remarkable Women* will soon be known as a play about Elizabeth and Mary. I don't think the title of *The Tiger and the Horse* told us anything at all about that particular play, but that didn't stop it running for over a year.'[32]

After agreeing on *Remarkable Women*, Robert changed the title again. Asked by a television interviewer about the new title Eileen Atkins, who had been cast as Elizabeth, said, 'It's called *Vivat! Vivat Regina!*. Spoonerism that and you're in trouble.' The prospect of seeing *Vivat! Vivat Regina!* on theatre marquees did not impress Ramsay at all. 'I want to add RAH RAH RAH to the title,' she wrote, 'because to my mind it is public school amateur dramatics.'[33]

By this time Ramsay had become a living legend and knew it. She was growing into a character not far removed from Edith Evans in *Gentle Jack*. She would counsel her writers by sending them Urdu poetry, leaves from Balzac's grave, or offer stern advice such as, 'Burn it, dear, and start again,' or, 'Have a wank and get on with it.' To Ramsay, Robert was a playwright who was setting a bad example and whose enslavement to Sarah and to box-office success could be held aloft as a warning. At least, that was what she told her younger clients, such as Christopher Hampton. On the other hand, Robert's fees were turning Ramsay into a rich woman and the promise of a major hit with *Vivat!* made her briefly consider producing it herself.

In a sense, *Vivat! Vivat Regina!* is a distaff version of *A Man For All Seasons* in which matters of state are personalised and simplified, and lead inexorably to the gallows. As Irving Wardle wrote in *The Times*, 'It is a parade of famous names with the monarchs at the head of the procession. We are to take personal interest in them because they were born to greatness: saints or villains, their lives count for more than that of the common man. Given the two figures in question here, it is still possible to get away with this approach.'[34]

Robert could not help but make Elizabeth the dominant character – she was, after all, the one with the most power. This concerned him deeply because Sarah was to play Mary and he did not want her to be overshadowed. 'Robert really understood Elizabeth,' said Sarah. 'He got the toughness, the masculinity, the wit, the core of the woman. He'd had a passion for Elizabeth ever since I first met him, but for some reason he saw me as Mary who was this ethereal, mysterious thing that no one can get hold of. It troubled me that Robert couldn't trap her in his butterfly net.'[35]

Sarah was not given the script to read. Instead, when Robert had finished writing it in Ireland, he recorded it on tape and played it for her. Despite the brilliance of Robert's acting, Sarah knew at once that playing Mary would prove to be an invidious task and a reading of Antonia Fraser's biography of Mary, then selling in tens of thousands, did nothing to change her mind. Robert, though, was adamant that Sarah should play Mary; she had the same sensuality, the same mystery. Although they never met, Mary and Elizabeth were obsessed with each other and this obsession gave Robert another of his trademark dualisms, between the Romantic and the Classical, between what John Knox in the play calls 'the virgin and the whore'. There could even be an entirely different dualism, between Sarah and Jo, between the woman who will sacrifice principle for love and the one for whom principle is everything. If Sarah found the key to Mary elusive, she had to bear an even greater burden: she was the writer's wife, a position which invariably attracts more scorn than envy. But rather than try to persuade Robert that she should play Elizabeth, or play no Queen at all, Sarah did nothing and prepared for the worst.

Vivat! Vivat Regina! reached the stage at Chichester by a curious route. The script was sent to Binkie Beaumont, who thought it too expensive to be produced by a regular commercial company. Robert then suggested to Beaumont that a solution might be to offer the play to Peter Hall at the RSC and later, if it was successful, transfer to the West End. Robert had been delighted by the way that the RSC had handled *The Thwarting of Baron Bolligrew*, which was revived for Christmas 1967 starring Roy Kinnear in a production which Trevor Nunn regarded as better than the original. When Beaumont convened a meeting with Hall to discuss *Vivat!* Robert was pleased to see that Hall was accompanied by Nunn, now the RSC's associate director. 'The meeting was a rarity,' said Nunn, 'and I felt like an impostor in the presence of these giants. It was held in Beaumont's office which was panelled in dark wood, low lighting, highly perfumed.'

The play was formally offered to Peter Hall and with it came Robert's request that it be staged during the summer of 1970. When Hall explained that he could not undertake it for at least a year, it was offered to Nunn.

> It was not a very truthful meeting [said Nunn] because it went from point to point with the assumption that we were dealing with a masterpiece. I didn't think that. I thought it was a flawed project and I think my lack of enthusiasm came over to the other people there.
>
> It was at the meeting that I heard Sarah's name mentioned in connection with it. I thought, were we really talking about the best possible casting or were we talking about an infatuation or an emotional necessity that lay outside the life of the play? I should have said that I would have no doubts about casting Sarah in the film version – she would have been without equal at that stage in her career – but she had never been part of the RSC.[36]

Beaumont's and Robert's plans to have the play subsidised by taxpayers' money at the RSC broke down because Robert was in a hurry and on account of his insistence that Sarah was to be the star of the show. From the RSC's point of view, casting Sarah would not only smack of nepotism, which worried Trevor Nunn, but would unsettle the many equally fine actresses who were an established part of the RSC and who regarded the great queens of the realm as their personal domain. If Sarah starred as Mary it would look like an expensive vanity project funded by the RSC. And Hall and Nunn felt that the play itself, irrespective of who starred in it, was just not good enough to deflect those criticisms.

Frustrated by the impasse, Robert risked a breach with Beaumont when he offered the play to Chichester, the annual festival financed by private subscription and box-office revenue. Peter Dews, who had directed the television version of *A Man For All Seasons*, came in as the director and managed to persuade Robert to abandon his original idea to present the play as a revue in the style of *Oh! What A Lovely War*. Dews had nightmares of the play becoming known as *Oh! What A Lovely Whore*. Having settled on a more traditional style, Carl Toms was hired as the designer, creating sets which were pitched midway between the abstract aesthetism of the stage production of *A Man For All Seasons* and the full-blown Tudor pageantry of the film version. Eileen Atkins was cast as Elizabeth I and, as Sarah predicted, she walked away with the best reviews.

For Sarah, the Chichester season was an agonising experience and when it was over she dreaded the inevitable transfer to the West End. 'Binkie Beaumont and Robert went to every famous actress there was,' she said, 'but they all wanted to play Elizabeth. This only confirmed to me how unplayable the part of Mary really was. So I soldiered on, for I loved Robert too much to let him down, though I did stipulate that I wouldn't play the role on Broadway.'[37]

Vivat! Vivat Regina! opened at the Piccadilly Theatre on 8 October 1970 to thin newspaper coverage since the critics, knowing it was the Chichester production, saw little reason to see it again. The public, though, filled every seat, night after night. Sarah and Eileen Atkins signed contracts for a six month run, during which time Sarah never reconciled herself to her part and became ill with worry. She lost weight and had to have injections of vitamins to keep up her strength. The fact that she was on stage six nights a week was enough for Robert; the problems which went with it were of little concern to him. While Sarah felt lost and abandoned, Robert again took 'her' into his study at Byfleet to write *Lady Caroline Lamb*. 'That was a very dark period for me,' said Sarah. 'I was grateful when it was all over.'

Because she was on stage when *Ryan's Daughter* opened in London on 9 December 1970, Sarah was unable to attend the première, an event which was ruined by a power failure during the screening at the Empire, Leicester Square. The film had been preceded by the American reviews which were unusually vicious and derisory. The British press followed suit, not so much roasting the film as incinerating it. It hardly matters that there are sequences in *Ryan's*

Daughter which surpass anything in *Lawrence of Arabia* or *Doctor Zhivago*. The early scene between Christopher Jones and Gerald Sim, who is leaving for the trenches in Europe, is a little masterpiece, a short story tucked into an epic, while the scene in the pub, when Doryan imagines he is back at the front and suddenly finds himself and Rosy embracing, is a startling break with naturalism. But the critics loathed it and held it up to ridicule. The American critic, Pauline Kael, summed up the overall response by saying, 'Ryan's *Daughter* is an expensive movie, but it's a cheap romance. Lean and Bolt are probably the leading exponents of bourgeois romanticism – gush made respectable by millions of dollars tastefully wasted.'[38]

In the era of *The Graduate*, *Bonnie and Clyde* and *Easy Rider*, *Ryan's Daughter* had all the characteristics of a movie dinosaur – an extinct species with an enormous body and a tiny brain. Although its box-office performance was far from what MGM had hoped, it ran for more than a year at the Empire and was nominated for several Oscars. For Lean the critical onslaught was so shattering that he lost his confidence. After being humiliated at a dinner organised by the New York film critics, he virtually retired from film-making. As for Robert, he was able to shrug it off. 'He knew it was a better film than that,' said Sarah, 'and that he and David didn't deserve that sort of attack.'

Sarah and Eileen Atkins ended their run in *Vivat! Vivat Regina!* during the first week of April 1971, when they were replaced by Judy Parfitt and Margaret Tyzack, who went on to do 442 performances, the longest run enjoyed by any of Robert's plays. Instead of taking a well-earned break, Sarah flew immediately to Los Angeles to attend the Academy Awards, having been nominated as Best Actress for *Ryan's Daughter*.

For the Oscar ceremony, which was held on 15 April, Sarah decided to wear her costume from *Vivat! Vivat Regina!* Disappointed though not surprised at losing – ironically to Glenda Jackson who was playing Elizabeth I in a BBC series – Sarah did go on stage twice, to collect the award for Freddie Young and to present the award for Best Original Screenplay. Since Robert had not been nominated he had decided against attending the ceremony and remained in London, where he was completing *Lady Caroline Lamb*. 'I pleaded with Robert to come with me to LA,' said Sarah, 'because to go to the Oscars without a man on my arm, was too much to bear. He promised he would and then he let me down at the last minute, which is something he did regularly. But if Robert had come with me to Hollywood our destinies might have been very different. Instead, in walked David Whiting.'

TWENTY

LAMB

'Show me a hero and I will write you a tragedy'

F. Scott Fitzgerald

Sarah was staying in the secluded Bungalow 14 at the Beverly Hills Hotel when David Whiting walked into her life. To help her during her stay in Los Angeles Sarah had hired Robert's former girl-friend, Carolyn Pfeiffer, as her personal assistant and publicist.

Whiting arrived to interview Sarah for *Time* magazine, for which he was a show-business writer. Instead of simply getting down to work he talked about himself and he noticed a fierce boil on Sarah's face which had erupted just in time for the Academy Awards ceremony the next day. Whiting examined the boil closely and said he had just the remedy. After two hours, he returned with pills and cream and the boil duly vanished. This journalist, thought Sarah, not only came armed with his personal cocktail mixture in a hip flask, he also offered instant miracle cures. And not only that, he was young, charming, immaculately groomed and seemed to know a lot about everything. And he made it clear from the outset that he was a fan of hers who loved *Ryan's Daughter* and Sarah's performance.

Sarah and Pfeiffer were sufficiently intrigued by Whiting to invite him to dinner that evening. But when they flew to New York, they were amazed to find Whiting occupying the next room in the Sherry Netherland Hotel. Whiting was excited because he had persuaded his editors at *Time* to run a cover story on Sarah, not just an interview. Making the cover of *Time* was in some respects more prestigious than winning an Oscar, for it was normally the preserve of presidents, prime ministers, Nobel Prize winners and cultural icons like the Beatles or Andy Warhol. Any suspicions that Pfeiffer may have had were forgotten when she checked with the magazine and received a glowing endorsement of their reporter.

When Pfeiffer returned to Los Angeles Sarah stayed on at the Sherry Netherland and allowed Whiting to take her into her walk-in closet to smoke marijuana. Sarah had first smoked dope with Robert Mitchum, when they were making *Ryan's Daughter*, though Whiting told her that the effects of the narcotic were greater if it was smoked in a confined space. One joint led to another, then another, after which Sarah allowed Whiting to make love to her. That was a big mistake. The next morning, filled with remorse, Sarah told Whiting she didn't want to see him again, even though this would cost her the cover story. When Whiting waved her off at Kennedy Airport, she thought she had seen the last of him.

By the time Sarah arrived back at Byfleet, Whiting was already there, beaming with triumph, having told Robert that he was to do a cover story about Mr and Mrs Bolt. This would take a lot of research, he said, as *Time* journalists were accustomed to shadowing their subjects for months, watching them at work and at home, and generally being a fly on the wall. Whiting, though, would prove to be the fly in the ointment. Robert invited Whiting to stay overnight at Byfleet, then for the next night, and suggested he stay for a week. He ended up living there for over a year.

> My dad was always suggestible [said Ben]. When my parents broke up and he started to date a lot of beautiful women, I always thought that was the David Lean influence. Lean always advocated that great artists should fuck a lot of women because that would make you a greater artist. That happened to Dad because he happened to be with David Lean. And because Lean had a Rolls-Royce, Dad had to have one too. When he was working on *Gandhi* with Moti Kothari he liked Moti's calm and economy, and thought that was the way to go. And when he was with Robert Shaw he was this marvellous raconteur. I don't think this was a weakness. He just had an enthusiasm for all sorts of people and different ways of life. If he saw that someone was on to something he was going to give it a go.[1]

Whiting manipulated Robert just as easily as he had manipulated Sarah. He told Robert how much his plays and films had meant to him, and what a wonderful, loving and talented wife he had. He said he loved the house and that he was at their service. At first, Robert found him irresistible. He wrote:

> He bowled me over at the first meeting. He was witty and

sardonic, shrewd and well-informed. I had just set up my own company to make *Lady Caroline Lamb* and was floundering among the businessmen. Sarah had recently left her agent and her affairs were in a mess.

David suggested he could be useful to us both. And he was, both as my director of publicity and Sarah's business manager. He would sing my praises to my face in a way that was a bit unnerving. He would run needless errands for me, more like an adoring son than an equal friend. While his emotional dependence upon me seemed to deepen, he revealed by degrees an attitude to Sarah which was both protective and possessive.[2]

It was as if two recent films were being enacted at Byfleet. In Pier Paolo Pasolini's *Theorem*, Terence Stamp had played a gorgeous if mysterious stranger who invades a bourgeois family, seduces everyone and destroys their lives. And there were also rather eerie echoes of Losey's *The Servant*, in which Sarah herself had played the catalyst who uses sex and flattery to upset the *status quo*. One can see how Losey would have treated the situation: a close shot of Whiting, a smile on his face, closing the front door of Mill House, leaving the camera outside to contemplate the door, then track away, slowly and ominously, as the house takes the measure of its new inhabitant.

David Andrew Whiting was born in New York City in 1947. His mother, Mrs Louise Campbell, could not remember if he was born on 25 or 26 August. 'I'm not sure which is the right one,' she told *Esquire* journalist Ron Rosenbaum, 'but I remember we used to celebrate it on the wrong day.'[3] The puzzle over his birthday would have appealed to Whiting, for he cultivated a sense of mystery about himself. This meant lying about everything: his school, his college and his family background. He told his mother that he had never been married, though an air hostess would later come forward and prove that she had married Whiting on 29 January 1970. They divorced within a year.

Whiting's bible was F. Scott Fitzgerald's *The Great Gatsby* and he had a dog-eared copy with him at all times. He liked the society in which the characters moved, the elegance and the money, but most of all he liked the hero, whose past history is a secret to everyone except himself.

Whiting's parents separated when he was a young boy and his mother soon remarried. His father was an executive for PanAm which enabled him, he said, to travel around the world first class and for free, which was also one of the perks in marrying an air hostess. He could fix tickets, hotels, anything, even boils. The fact that he arrived in Byfleet before Sarah, after having waved her off at JFK, proved to her that he could.

Whiting seemed destined for Harvard but never made the grade. Instead, he went to modest Haverford and claimed he was at Princeton. While he was studying to be a lawyer he went to Libya for a holiday and inveigled his way on to a film set. Seduced by the glamour and finding that movie people were not as smart as he was, he transformed himself into a film buff and claimed to know every star and director in Hollywood. He was going to be a producer, he said.

Instead, he started to write features for magazines like *Time* and *Cosmopolitan*, sometimes adopting the pseudonym of 'Anthony Blaine,' a combination of two Fitzgerald characters – Amory Blaine in *This Side of Paradise* and Anthony Patch in *The Beautiful and Damned*. He profiled Candice Bergen, pursuing her to Spain, then showed up at her home in Beverly Hills. He wrote about Paula Prentiss and her husband, Richard Benjamin, who he thought had the ideal show-business marriage. 'He needed something from us,' said Prentiss, 'he wouldn't come out and say it, but we could tell. He'd sit and drink martinis and pop pills all the time. But we did have some good moments with him.'[4]

Whiting did finally publish a piece about Sarah, though not in *Time*. His article, which appeared in the December 1971 issue of *Cosmopolitan*, described Sarah as 'the greatest dame since Eve . . . perplexing, outrageous, provocative and, inevitably, misunderstood'. The article is a typical piece of show-business journalism, with none of the expected hints of Whiting's obsession and sexual involvement with his subject.

Whiting never published another article. Instead, he found what he had always wanted: a surrogate family, a nice house and a job in the movie industry. He was prepared to devote every minute of the day to Sarah's comfort and career; in fact, he was completely obsessed by her and had an armory of psychological weapons at his disposal if he was ever asked to leave. Robert, locked away in his study and immersed in the preparations for *Lady Caroline Lamb*, did not realise what was happening until it was too late.

At first the film was called, simply, *Lamb*. Robert was fascinated by William Lamb, the future Prime Minister, Lord Melbourne, and his marriage to Caroline Ponsonby, who had a celebrated affair with

Lord Byron. Everyone had affairs in Regency society: Caroline's mother – in the words of Robert's screenplay – was 'the most notorious trollop in the country', while Lamb's mother, Lady Melbourne, committed adultery with at least three men, including the Prince of Wales. Caroline's mistake was to conduct her affair with Byron in public, almost wrecking her husband's political career in the process.

In Robert's eyes William Lamb was a hero, though a 1997 biography by L. G. Mitchell revealed that he abused his children and that, like T. E. Lawrence, he was a flagellant. But for Robert, Lamb was a man of high principle and intellect who cannot abandon the woman he loves, no matter how much she humiliates him. It was exactly the same story as *Ryan's Daughter*, but in this case the unfaithful wife falls for the real Byron, not just a Byronic figure. 'It's a sort of simplified exploitation of the Romantic and Classical impulses,' Robert told John Dunn. 'It isn't a shapeless heap of unrelieved hokum which at certain points along the way I thought it was going to be.'[5]

In writing the screenplay Robert showed far less respect for history than he did with *A Man For All Seasons* and *Vivat! Vivat Regina!* It was half a travesty which made it seem that Caroline began her affair with Byron immediately after her honeymoon and died of a broken heart only months after Byron walked out on her. In fact, Lamb and Caroline were married for twenty-three years and Robert totally ignores Caroline's scandalous and apparently awful literary endeavour, *Glenarvon*, which dramatised her affair with Byron as a *roman-à-clef*.

Robert asked David Whiting to prepare a synopsis of the script which would be circulated for publicity purposes. It has been argued that what Whiting produced was not so much a synopsis of *Lamb* than a reflection of his new domestic arrangements. Of Lady Caroline he said she was 'On fire for the dramatic, the picturesque, a creature of impulse, intense sensibility and bewitching unexpectedness. On those for whom it worked she cast a spell which could not be resisted. . . Such a character was bound finally to make a bad wife.' Of William Lamb Whiting said he had a 'capacity for compromising agreeably with circumstance. . . . When Caroline threw herself into her notorious affair with Byron, William refused to take it seriously. . . he was not jealous but his spirit was wounded.' When he came to describing Byron, who was the same age as Whiting, the adjectives went into orbit: 'He was a raw, nerve-ridden boy of genius, a kind of embodied fantasy . . . . Divine fire gleamed fitfully forth through a turmoil of suspicion and awkwardness. . . His sophistication was a mask for shyness. At the most elementary level he was a poseur.'

David Lean had been urging Robert for years to direct a film and half-way through writing *Lamb* Robert felt ready to take the plunge. It was a big film, though not on the scale of *Doctor Zhivago* or *Ryan's Daughter*, and he could not think of anyone who could do it better than himself. Having made the decision to direct, the question was how? The answer seemed to be: with the best help available.

Remembering his promise, Robert sent the screenplay to Fernando Ghia and asked him to produce it. In the process of making *Lamb* Ghia would be taught English by one of the best ex-schoolmasters in Britain. He said:

> The script was beautifully written, though a lot of things were alien to me, because they were not belonging to my culture. I also had some reservations about the male characters who were too clean-cut, too black and white.
>
> Robert had decided to direct because there was something disappointing to him about *Ryan's Daughter*, about what Sarah was in the film. The concept was that she was a jewel and had this fantastic treasure inside but she was not capable of handling it or showing it. Robert felt that she hadn't come across in *Ryan's Daughter* so in *Lamb* he wanted the substance to take over the appearance.[6]

In the screenplay of *Lady Caroline Lamb* Robert wrote a scene between Caroline and her mother, Lady Bessborough, which summarised his personal view of Sarah, if not himself:

> LADY BESSBOROUGH
> Your Mr Lamb is probably the most superior young man I have ever met. But there is nothing at his centre.
>
> CAROLINE
> Nothing? Wh . . .
>
> LADY BESSBOROUGH
> Shssh. Nothing whatever. He is pure decency. And solid good behaviour through and through. Now you are mostly nonsense. And your behaviour is mostly bad. But at your centre is a diamond . . .

William will find it and when he found it
you will give it him, if he can take it. And it
will make him some kind of great man I
think. And you a happy woman. For that is
called requited love.

CAROLINE

Huh!

Casting his reservations aside, Ghia set about raising the finance.
Because the film was to be a co-production between Britain and
Italy, it would have to be shot in both countries. Ghia and his
partner, Franco Cristaldi, finally put together a complex deal: the
film would be funded by Cristaldi, EMI in London and General
Electric in America, with MGM as their American distributor. The
budget was set at less than $4 million, a third of what Lean had spent
on *Ryan's Daughter*. To keep the costs down Robert and Ghia
deferred their salaries and hoped to see some cash if the film made a
profit. But they still needed someone, an associate producer, who
could cut corners without anyone noticing, someone who could
bully the production along at a fast pace without sacrificing quality
or exhausting the crew.

When Ghia asked me to work on *Lamb* [said Bernie Williams]
I'd just finished *A Clockwork Orange*. Stanley Kubrick had gone
from a twelve-million-dollar *2001* to a one-million-dollar
Clockwork Orange, so they thought, get Bernie and he'll help us
make the movie for the least amount of money.

I met Robert in Byfleet and learned very quickly that he had
written this script for Sarah Miles. I was always confused about
Robert because he spoke as a socialist and drove a capitalist
Rolls-Royce. But we felt the same way about things and we both
wanted the good things in life. But as the writer and a first-time
director, he was under a lot of pressure. It was a big movie with
a big cast but he was smart enough to know about budgetary
problems. He said to me, 'Bernie, it's not written in stone. If I
write something in a huge ballroom and you tell me you can't
find the location, I'll change it to a cup of tea in the breakfast
room. The integrity of the scene will be in tact.'

There was no proper payroll and we were all a bit suspicious.
We had to go every week to the Dorchester and get cash out of
a suitcase. Norman Savage, the editor, had a very strong voice
and he said, 'I'm not taking Mafia money! I want to be paid

properly.' And we said, 'Well, we just want to get paid.' Actually, it was all very clean, it was just the way it worked on that movie. Robert said everything was all right and, indeed, they were very nice people. Cristaldi was a real gentleman and Ghia was charming, a delightful man.[7]

On *Doctor Zhivago* and, to a lesser extent, *A Man For All Seasons* and *Ryan's Daughter*, Robert had seen at first hand how difficult and how critical casting could be. But he already had his leading lady and that was the greatest hurdle of all. Sarah was handed one of the juiciest roles of the decade which required her to be funny and sad, often at the same time. It was as difficult a role as Mary, though without the strain of performing it every night on stage. And she knew, this time, that she could do it.

Margaret Leighton agreed to play Lady Melbourne and Robert knew he had an actress who could effectively mirror and weather Caroline's tempest. And when Ralph Richardson, John Mills and Laurence Olivier were recruited as George IV, George Canning and the Duke of Wellington, Robert not only knew he had a class production, but also that they were so professional that he would not need to embarrass them by his inexperience.

Looking for an actor to play William Lamb, Robert had selected Timothy Dalton, whom he had seen in *The Lion in Winter* as well as on stage. 'Robert interviewed Timothy Dalton in our kitchen,' said Sarah. 'When he went for a pee, Robert said, "What d'you think?" I said, "I think he'd be good." When Timothy reappeared Robert offered him the part and Timothy accepted. Later on, Robert cast Jon Finch, who I thought lacked the charisma shown by Timothy. I told Robert this and he said, "Lamb had little charisma, that's why Caroline was unfaithful." ' When Timothy Dalton heard that he had lost the role after signing a contract, he went to court and won undisclosed damages.

'I had just finished *Macbeth* for Polanski,' said Jon Finch. 'I'd also done *Frenzy* for Hitchcock who was a fat, selfish bastard, a sort of Robert Maxwell of the cinema. When Robert offered me the part of Lamb I said thank you very much but I'd much rather play Byron. Robert told me that Richard Chamberlain was playing it. I said, "Richard Chamberlain? He's six foot two and incredibly slim. Byron was short, enormously fat and had a clubfoot. He can't possibly play Byron." And Robert said, "Yes, I know, but Richard looks like people's imagination of Byron." '[8]

Historical films often look or sound more like the period in which they are made than that in which they are set. While Tony Richardson's *Tom Jones* brazenly transferred the pop art and sexual liberation of 1963 to the early Georgian era, John Schlesinger's adaptation of Thomas Hardy's *Far From the Madding Crowd* had perhaps more Sergeant Pepper in it than Sergeant Troy. Richard Harris and Vanessa Redgrave in *Camelot* were clearly peaceniks, hippies with flowers in their hair, and Robert himself detected a King's Road element to *Doctor Zhivago*.

Lady Caroline Lamb applied an early Seventies interest in Women's Lib to the Regency era. Sarah's costumes, however closely researched they may have been, would not have looked out of place on the hangers at Biba, the trendy emporium on Kensington High Street. And Lord Byron, as played by Richard Chamberlain, was conceived as the Regency equivalent of Mick Jagger, pouting and strutting, and fawned on by an army of female admirers.

'Robert called it *Lamb* at first because he was really a Melbourne character,' said Jon Finch. 'It would have been a bit too near the knuckle if he'd said it was about him and Sarah who was a pretty wild chick. Nobody could really imagine Robert and Sarah together. Most people I knew thought, "Well, lucky bastard, good for him." '9

On the first day of shooting Robert was handed a viewfinder and looked through it the wrong way round. He himself often used to tell this story and always got a laugh at his own expense. It is one which is easy to dismiss as apocryphal, though in Robert's case it is true. What is uncertain is whether he took the wrong end of the viewfinder on purpose, in order to break the ice, to show the crew that he needed them more than they needed him.

When David Lean heard that Robert was about to embark on his first film he sent a letter of encouragement, which also contained a lot of advice about actors, cameramen and producers. Although Robert was grateful for Lean's interest, he decided against having Lean's team around him, which meant no John Box, no Eddie Fowlie and definitely no Freddie Young. It was not because Robert disliked these people or thought they lacked talent; on the contrary, they were too talented and the last thing he wanted was to make an ass of himself in front of Freddie Young.

He did make one exception by hiring Norman Savage as his editor. Savage, who always wore a sharp suit and tie, had been an assistant on *Lawrence of Arabia* and was promoted to full editor on *Doctor Zhivago* and *Ryan's Daughter*. Not only would he edit *Lamb*, he co-authored the shooting script with Robert and was present for much of the shooting, a fact which upset the cameraman, Ossie Morris.

Morris was a true professional and Robert was lucky to get him. Once David Lean's operator on *Oliver Twist*, he had shot *Moby Dick* and *Reflections in a Golden Eye* for John Huston, *Look Back in Anger* and *The Entertainer* for Tony Richardson, *Lolita* for Stanley Kubrick, *The Taming of the Shrew* for Franco Zeffirelli and *Oliver!* for Carol Reed. Morris was immensely versatile, happy to experiment or adapt to any director's preferred style. Unfortunately, Robert's inexperience resulted in a lack of rapport with Morris, which led Robert to feel that the film's routinely lustrous imagery detracted from its thematic ideas. 'I think perhaps the academic opulence made the sense obscure,' he wrote to Mike Kellaway after the film was completed. 'Now what do I do about that? I could get a camera and try to teach myself . . . but I hate the bloody things. A better bet would be to find a cameraman whose work had the style I'm after. I'd like a rather flat and two dimensional, iconlike style, rather still and formally composed. Have you seen any films like that recently which I could study?'[10]

Three years later, Robert might have seen in Stanley Kubrick's *Barry Lyndon* the formal approach he was looking for. But the odd thing is that while Robert clearly knew what he wanted, he felt unable to communicate it to Morris.

> I didn't have any lead from Robert about the way the film should look [said Morris]. He never complained at the rushes because he was just looking at the actors and listening to the dialogue. So *Lady Caroline Lamb* was just photographed, not badly, just ordinarily. Because of the subject matter and because of Robert himself, I'd include it in my favourites but on a purely technical level I wouldn't say it was one of my best. Robert seemed so close to Norman Savage that I didn't feel I could interfere, which meant that I copped it from Fernando Ghia.
>
> Half-way through the film Fernando called me to his office and said, 'Ossie, this is confidential, but we're very worried. You don't seem to be helping Robert as much as we expected you to.' I said, 'Hang on, you have an editor who Robert calls to the set when he's worried about a scene. No two people can direct a movie and certainly three people can't and I'm not prepared to intervene if Robert wants Norman to give him advice.' I put all this down to Robert's nerves, you know, but he improved tremendously as we went on.[11]

Despite the small budget, Ghia had assembled a first-class crew and a prestigious cast. Although David Whiting's presence on the set rather puzzled Ghia, he tolerated it. Bernie Williams's only worry was that the film's star and director were married: 'You don't have your wife as the leading lady. You're with her all day and night, there's no relief, no separation. To go independently financed, on a co-production with Italian producers, which was rare in those days, without that much technical knowledge, with a very strong and opinionated editor, who was David Lean's watchdog in a way, and with Sarah Miles, who was very hard to control, was a huge undertaking. I love Sarah but she was a wild lady in those days, a drama queen, the highest-ranking extrovert you can imagine.'

In playing Lady Caroline, Sarah lived the part both on and off the set, which is why her performance is so good and why it is hard to imagine another actress in the role. She went at it pell-mell.

> One day we were shooting up on the moors, near Chatsworth [said Williams]. Sarah had this crazy horse called Daisy which should have been put in a glue factory. I said to her, 'You're not going to ride that horse in the movie.' She said, 'I am, I am, I love my Daisy.' I said, 'That horse is insane, it's going to kill you.' It was huge and she was this little thing on the back of it.[12]

Sarah, though, was an excellent horsewoman. She mounted up and went at a full gallop until she approached the green baize lawns of Chatsworth. Knowing that Daisy would reduce the lawns to a ploughed field, as a worried Duke and Duchess looked on, she bailed out, falling to the ground and ending up in hospital with an injured back. 'And that was just to shoot the credit titles,' said Williams.

> Sarah always knew her lines and laughed a lot [said Ossie Morris]. She seemed to know exactly what she wanted to do and Robert didn't interfere with her. I assumed they just discussed it all at home. I'd already done a couple of films with Sarah, *Term of Trial* with Olivier, and *The Ceremony* with Larry Harvey. I liked her a lot but she could be very vulgar and that embarrassed Robert. We did a shot where she walks the length of the set and goes through a door when Robert called 'Cut!' She comes back and shouts to Robert, 'How was that?' He says, 'Oh, very good.' Then she shouts, 'I farted. Did you hear it?' Robert cringed and I felt very sorry for him on that occasion.
>
> Sarah had to wear all these incredible costumes. She was naked, really, and we wetted the front of her dress because Robert said it was the style of the period, that women wore this thin material and wetted it to show their breasts and nipples. We

all thought this was shocking and daring, though no one bats an eye these days. But it was a daring thing to do in 1972 and most actresses would have balked at it. But not Sarah.[13]

The scene with the wet dress, and another in which Sarah appeared topless, were shot but later cut owing to pressure from the censors and the need to avoid an 'adults only' certificate which would have halved the film's potential audience. But even without these sequences the picture captures Caroline's outrageousness when she accompanies Byron to lavish parties. Carrying an enormous fan of feathers, which is used to cool the Byronic brow, Caroline is made up as a blackamoor, naked above the waist apart from a heavy necklace. Systematically humiliated by Byron, she throws a tray of drinks into the air and storms out of the party. The sequence is a triumph for Sarah: she is by turns ridiculous, hilarious and desperately sad.

> Sarah was a lot of fun to work with [said Jon Finch]. She giggled a lot and the camera was very fond of her. I remember at the beginning I said to my stand-in and a couple of other guys, 'The rule on this picture is that nobody gets hold of Sarah. She's right out.' And they said no, no, of course. I didn't say this for any altruistic reason. I did it because I liked Robert so much. This sounds a bit presumptuous but in film terms, if someone got hold of that bird it would have made for a terrible atmosphere. David Whiting, though, was obviously besotted by her. Like most publicity people he just sat around being oily and greasy. He'd been to an American business school and got a degree in creepy.[14]

> Michael Cimino told me a story which I've never forgotten [said Bernie Williams]. Cimino was ghosting all of Clint Eastwood's scripts and Clint said to him, 'Michael, I've got a hundred million dollars in the bank, I've got a multi-picture deal at Warner Bros, I call my own shots, direct and star in anything I want, I am at the height of my career, I have all the power I want and every time I make a movie I hand pick the cast and the crew. And on every movie there's always one bad apple who turns up and spoils it.' And that went for *Lady Caroline Lamb*. We had a great set-up and unfortunately David Whiting came against the grain. He was working against Fernando, he was obviously Robert's adversary and he was basically sucking up to Sarah. He was highly strung, neurotic, totally dysfunctional.

It was a very sad experience for me because, well, I can only speak about what I saw rather than gossip . . . I got thrown into all that. Whiting was brought in to promote Sarah's career and I got the impression that he and Sarah were having a relationship which was very sad. I don't know how Robert coped but I had to deal a lot with Robert not talking to Sarah and Sarah not talking to Robert. That was almost from the start. And if I mentioned anything to Robert he would just say, 'Bernie, I can't deal with this. I can't get involved.[15]

David Whiting always hovered at the edge of the set, ready to run errands for Sarah, making plans for her career. His obsession with her was obvious to the entire crew. What was less obvious was that Whiting's manipulation of Robert and Sarah had reached the stage when he had cut himself off from all his family and friends in America. He just lived for his work, his ambition and for Sarah. And when Robert decided to throw him out of Byfleet Whiting took an overdose.

Whiting had stuck like glue and the last thing that Robert and Sarah needed was the scandal of a suicide. In fact, a third suicide. A girl named Thelma who had lodged at Sarah's house in Hasker Street had killed herself. Sarah had known her slightly at RADA and she seemed in such an emotional state that she allowed her to stay in the basement flat. What followed was a nightmare of overdoses, LSD, strange men in the house and Thelma's young son, who seemed to make her condition worse. When Robert, who was courting Sarah at the time, saw how she was being manipulated, he told Thelma that she should leave Hasker Street at once and if she was serious about suicide, well, why didn't she just jump? Thelma left the next day and jumped.

The second suicide was Johnnie Windeatt, a debonair homosexual who rented Hasker Street when Sarah and Robert were at Byfleet. He claimed to be a landscape gardener and to be wealthy. When he failed to come up with the rent and was on the verge of being evicted, he put his head in Sarah's gas oven.

On 2 March 1972, just weeks before the start of shooting on *Lady Caroline Lamb*, David Whiting was having his stomach pumped out at St George's Hospital. 'Each time we asked David to leave,' said Sarah, 'he didn't threaten suicide, he simply took an overdose. Because of our history with Thelma and Johnnie Windeatt, we had to treat him with kid gloves. We were both terrified.'

A compromise was reached when Whiting moved to Hasker

Street, where he entertained a succession of women, as well as Sarah on occasion. While Robert hoped he might just fade away, Sarah was being blackmailed, because Whiting had stolen Laurence Olivier's letters to her. Hoping to get them back, she allowed him to sleep with her. 'He smelt of disinfectant, potions, strange chemical creams,' she said. 'There was nothing erotic about him, he repulsed me deeply. He turned me into a numb, fear-ridden alien. That's what was terrifying Robert, the fact that I was teetering on the edge. So was he, but he had to direct a bloody film on top of it.'[16]

When Whiting saw Sarah on the set, wearing those revealing costumes, he became jealous, unpredictable and seemed capable of violence. He was unable to cope with the fact that Rosy Ryan, the demure Irish village girl, was just a shadow on a screen; Whiting now had to deal with Lady Caroline.

The first major clash between Whiting and Ghia came when the former applied his sharp lawyer's mind to Sarah's contract and found that she was being underpaid; the second came when Whiting decided to initiate a documentary about Sarah and the making of the film. Today, this is a key component of any film's publicity campaign and is built into the budget. But Robert's film was being made as cheaply as possible and no such documentary had been planned. 'Whiting was very arrogant,' said Ghia, 'though he would never interfere with Robert. I was the one who suffered him. When he decided to make a documentary he went straight to Nat Cohen at EMI, a lovely man, and somehow got the money to do it. When Nat told me what had happened I literally exploded. I went back to the studio and fired Whiting on the spot. The next thing I knew he had been made a director of the company set up by Bob, Sarah and her lawyer.'[17]

Having successfully outmanoeuvred Ghia, Whiting hired the documentary director, Jack Hazan, to make the publicity film. Hazan said:

> Whiting was very sweaty and later on I realised he was on speed. He couldn't stop talking, always hyper, and arranging our contracts with him was awful. We were working for him but we thought he was going to sue us. He told us we had no rights to anything and told us redundant things in a vicious way.
>
> No one was supposed to know what was going on between Whiting and Sarah but it was clear to everyone. He was madly in love with her. Bolt's attitude towards Whiting seemed permissive and tolerant, as if he was an errant son, not a rival.

Bolt was pretty green as a director and he'd always have Norman Savage to tell him where to put the camera. He was good with the actors and he gave us a quite complicated interview at his house. My lasting impression of him is smoking these bloody Benson & Hedges, constantly lighting one from the other. They had a huge power over him, just as Whiting was always drugged up to his eyeballs.[18]

After shooting at Chatsworth and at Wilton House, the film continued at Pinewood Studios until Christmas. After a hiatus of a month or two the unit moved to Italy to film in the Roman amphitheatre at Pompeii where Caroline tosses money to some beggars, unwittingly causing the murder of one of them. It is a romantic gesture set within the classical context of the Roman building where death and degradation are still the order of the day.

Because the film was a co-production, the interiors of various Italian palaces stood in for English stately homes in order to increase the quota of Italian locations. Months before the film started production Robert went to Italy with Williams for a recce.

We went to Caserta to look around [said Williams] and when I got out of the car a guy in a white raincoat came up behind me and said, 'You're Bernie Williams.' I was amazed and said, 'Yes?' He said, 'My name is Mario Bussi and I'm from the film section of the Mafia.' I said, 'Excuse me?' I thought this guy was a joke so I asked if there was a hotel rep and an airport rep. He said there was.

Bussi said, 'Are you going to film here?' I said, 'Well, I don't know, we're just sightseeing.' Bussi said, 'Well, without me you can't film here.' So I said to Robert, 'Don't like it, please don't like it.' We go into the palace and Robert walks around like an eighteenth century artist, with his cigarette and long hair. If he had had a cape it would have been flying. And of course he loved this huge gold room – 'This is where Wellington should be. I love it!' Bussi said it would be five thousand dollars, no paperwork, in cash. I left at once and of course I came back two months later cap in hand to negotiate.[19]

Because Norman Savage did not go to Italy Ossie Morris found Robert unusually friendly and keen to have the benefit of the great cameraman's advice. But Morris also felt that Robert was desperately lonely. 'When we were in Caserta,' he said, 'Robert would have lunch with my wife and me and pour his heart out to us.

He ate his food tremendously quickly, he was like a Hoover, and I asked him if he had eaten like that all his life. He said, "Ever since I was at school because if you didn't eat your food quickly the other boys grabbed it." He'd talk about the movie, what hard work it was. We knew something was going on between Sarah and this American chap, Whiting, and Robert became more and more isolated.'[20]

'The shooting in Italy went well at first,' said Ghia. 'Then a strange thing happened. Sarah came to me with a piece of paper which she asked me to sign. It said that she was not happy with the Italian still photographer and that she wanted approval of any pictures taken of her on the set. This was ridiculous because that was in her contract anyway, but she insisted I sign it. As I was about to sign, she opened the door to the room and in rushed Whiting with his camera crew. He shouted, "Film him signing, film him signing!" It was one of the crazy things that happened.'[21]

Because some pictures had been released without Sarah's approval, Whiting planned his revenge carefully, knowing that Ghia would be upset and not forewarning the director of the documentary, Jack Hazan. 'I didn't know what was going on,' said Hazan. 'Whiting told us to have the camera ready when we went on the set. He walked up to Fernando and started insulting him. Fernando looked dismissive and then spat at him. I pointed the camera down in dismay, not knowing what we'd walked into. We looked really compromised, just a tool of Whiting.'[22]

When the satirical magazine, *Private Eye*, learned of this story, they wrote: 'The producer, volatile Italian Fernando Ghia, spat in Mr Whiting's left eye and ran screaming from the set. As always, faithful, rock-like, left-wing millionaire Robert Bolt smiled tolerantly and did nothing about it.'[23]

David Whiting was out of control in Italy and nearly killed himself. 'In Rome we stayed at Claridge's Hotel,' said Bernie Williams, 'and Whiting locked himself in his room for days. When we broke the door down there were thousands of pills everywhere. I've never seen so many pills in my life. He'd passed out.'[24]

If Whiting had not been around the time in Italy would have been a happier memory for everyone. Laurence Olivier arrived, with a large false nose, to play the Duke of Wellington who sleeps with Caroline for one night, then promptly gets rid of her, precipitating the final stages of her emotional collapse. Their scene together is one of the highlights of the picture, a cleverly written and wittily acted bedroom comedy with the darker edges of tragedy. At the time, Robert was wholly unaware of Sarah's previous involvement with

Olivier. He simply welcomed Olivier's presence in the picture and let him get on with it.

'I can't remember Robert giving Olivier, Ralph Richardson or Johnnie Mills a lot of direction,' said Ossie Morris. 'It was all in the script and they came beautifully prepared. John Huston always said to me, "If you cast correctly, seventy-five per cent of your work is already done." There's a lot of truth in that and maybe Robert thought the same as Huston.'[25]

Shooting on *Lady Caroline Lamb* was completed on schedule, leaving Robert with mixed emotions. 'I thought I could gauge the bulk of activity involved from having been so close to it before,' he wrote, 'but I far underestimated it. It's nearly two years since I started to write it, nearly ten months since I started the directorial phase, and in that time I have been so densely occupied that I hardly belong to the human race. It's no wonder that so many films have such tenuous and quirky connections with life. Film directors are surrounded by an invisible field of vibrating resentment and self-pity which makes it impossible for life to approach.'[26]

As soon as Sarah returned to England she went straight into her next film, an adaptation of L. P. Hartley's *The Hireling*, in which she played a wealthy widow who is briefly brought out of her depression by her chauffeur, played by Robert Shaw.

Robert saw little of either Sarah or Whiting at this time, because both were involved with *The Hireling*. Robert thought he was well rid of Whiting, since there had been an incident at Byfleet which ended with him losing his temper and knocking him to the ground. What added insult to injury was that this altercation occurred in the presence of his youngest daughter, Joanna.

Robert now employed a new secretary, Gillian Harrison, a mother of two who had worked in television and who lived near Byfleet. She said:

Robert was doing post-production on the film when I started working for him. I did the usual secretarial work and I also went out and bought his child's shoes, got his clothes cleaned, anything that came to hand. In a way, I was a supernumerary part of the family.

Sarah wasn't around very much since she was making *The Hireling* and I didn't see much of David Whiting either. But I remember when Robert gave a birthday party for Sally he ordered a lot of wine which stood in the hallway. Whiting was

on his way to Hasker Street and I saw him take three bottles
from one of the boxes. I thought, 'You shit.' So I rang up the
off-licence and got them to send replacements before Bob
noticed they were missing.[27]

Robert's trusted editor, Norman Savage, was pulling *Lady
Caroline Lamb* into shape. To reduce the running time, almost the
entire first thirty pages of the script were cut, including the scene
between Caroline and her mother which, for Robert, had lost its
emotional appeal and truth. While this was being done, Richard
Rodney Bennett was composing the music. 'With the music added,'
Robert told John Dunn, 'it is really irresistibly moving. To me,
anyway, and though easily moved in general I am so sick of every
moment of this film that I didn't think it could ever move me again
to anything but disgust.'[28]

By the time the film was shown, though, Robert had second
thoughts about the effect of the music, especially at the film's climax,
when Caroline expires in a classical rotunda, one of the adornments
of her family estate. He told Dunn:

> The stuff at the end was deliberately over the top. I explained
> what I wanted and why and when we had it sufficiently flatulent
> the orchestra put down their instruments and fell about. The
> idea was to inflate the Romantic bubble – 'She died of a broken
> heart' – and then burst the bubble with the line, 'Well, *wouldn't*
> she?' I don't mean that the Romantic aspect of the film was
> *entirely* tongue-in-cheek. It's what we refer to in the trade as a
> fruitful ambiguity.
>
> In Dublin [a critic] came and complained that he didn't know
> at the end whether I approved of Caroline or William; and when
> I told him that was the point of the film and congratulated him
> on his unique percipience he thought I was making excuses. He
> was no doubt the motor-cycling correspondent of the *Limerick
> Gazette*, a decent and humble man . . . but it is very irritating to
> be pooh-poohed by one's inferiors.[29]

The final stages of *Lady Caroline Lamb* were made intolerably sad
when Robert's editor, Norman Savage, discovered he was dying
from leukaemia. But Savage was so devoted to Robert that he even
had a cutting room installed at his hospital. Sarah recalled that no
one on the ward died while Savage was there, though he himself
passed away shortly after the film had its première. 'He was one of
the two or three people I have ever known, completely without

malice,' wrote Robert. 'It made him invincible. I have seen him take to task some famous monsters of our industry and seen their astonishment turn to respect. You instinctively wanted him to think well of you.'[30]

Savage's untimely death put Robert into a strange frame of mind. He liked Savage so much that he began to analyse the differences between his relationships with men, which seemed simple, and women, which were not. 'Apropos Norman,' Robert told David Lean, 'I wonder if I'm not a bit queer. So far as I know I'm not a bit attracted by men physically and I'm sometimes violently attracted by girls. But the only woman I trust is Peggy Ramsay who for me at any rate is sexless though I suspect she's very far from that. And I'm hopeless with ladies, as you know, lacking both that easygoing contempt which they find irresistible and also lacking a real instinctive trust in them. I present them I suppose with the worst of both worlds – a limited respect. No wonder they always end by pissing in my chips.'[31]

When *Lady Caroline Lamb* was ready, there was a private screening at the Empire, Leicester Square, for the producers, the crew, and for Margaret Ramsay. Robert recorded Ramsay's response in an article he wrote for the *Sunday Times*:

'It's a lovely film, dear, lovely,' she said. 'It's going to be a big success.'

'All right, but what did *you* think?'

'I think it's *extraordinary*!'

'It isn't. Whatever it is, it isn't that.'

'But of course it is. It's so utterly *you*. Don't you think it's you?'

'I don't even know what you're talking about.'

'But the whole style of it, dear, and what you're saying. It has all your strengths, all. And of course it has your weaknesses, too.'[32]

Lady Caroline Lamb had its world première at the Empire on 21 November 1972. At the reception afterwards Robert said, 'I don't think I can feel anything now. All I want to do is read the notices and see what the first four weeks' business is like.'[33]

The critics had much to consider. In one sense the film was a traditional costume romance, such as might have been made in the Fifties; in another, it was entirely modern, with Sarah's role a beacon for the burgeoning women's movement. On the whole, the reviews were encouraging.

George Melly, writing in the *Observer*, found much to praise, even if he felt slightly guilty at doing so. 'As Lady Caroline, Sarah Miles manages not to drive one mad,' he wrote. 'This is quite an accomplishment in itself. Bolt's heroine, a well-heeled madcap, more sinned against than sinning, either rushing about or exaggeratedly still is potentially an important bore. Miss Miles succeeds in giving her some real pathos; no one can do the caged spirit bruising its wings against the bars of convention better than she.'[34]

Alexander Walker's review was almost a rave. 'The passions are not allowed to run riot,' he wrote. 'It's not an orchestral film sweeping you off your feet, more an experience in emotional chamber music. Bolt has been bold with history [and] eschews cheap inflation. Oswald Morris's camerawork is breath-takingly effective . . . perfectly in tune with its world of court and society.' As for Sarah's performance, Walker said this depended on whether you were 'allergic to this actress's style in smothered hysteria. The likelihood is that she is nearer historical fact than anyone else in the film but truth is not always true-seeming and I can't help feeling the film needs a bigger centre than Sarah Miles supplies. On the other hand, perhaps no one could succeed in involving us deeply with a woman whose only means of self-expression was self-destruction.'[35]

Almost all the critics compared Robert's film with David Lean, noting a similar style and lavishness and coming out with puns like 'A Lean piece of Lamb'. Having now directed a film himself, Robert decided not to repeat the experience. He was exhausted.

In February 1973 Robert and Sarah were both in America. He was in Los Angeles for the première of *Lady Caroline Lamb*, she in Arizona, making a Western for MGM. The continued presence of David Whiting in their lives meant that their marriage was hanging by a thread and if Sarah had gone to Arizona without Whiting things might have been very different.

On the morning of 11 February 1973 Robert awoke in Bungalow 14 at the Beverly Hills Hotel. Since it was a Sunday he had a day off from the gruelling round of promotional interviews and could relax until the evening, when his film was to be shown at the Directors' Guild. At around eleven he was joined by Fernando Ghia and, a little later, by Carolyn Pfeiffer, who was to have lunch with him. When Carolyn arrived at the hotel she was surprised to see that the bungalow was the very same one where David Whiting had first met Sarah two years earlier.

Robert, Ghia and Carolyn were having a drink and chatting when the phone rang. Robert answered it and immediately turned pale. He had obviously been given some distressing news. 'David Whiting is dead,' he told Ghia and Carolyn. 'Sarah found him in her bathroom.'

TWENTY-ONE

THE RIDDLE OF THE STAR-SHAPED WOUND

'It serves me right for putting all my eggs in one bastard.'

Dorothy Parker

For years, Gila Bend in southern Arizona was famous as the hottest place in America. Summer temperatures regularly reached 120 degrees, putting all other contenders for the coveted title into the shade. But in 1965, when the United States Weather Bureau discovered that someone had been taking a hair dryer to the thermometer, Gila Bend promptly lost its status and sank back into its former oblivion as a pit-stop on the long road from Tucson to Yuma. It was David Whiting who made Gila Bend briefly famous again.

Sarah had gone to Gila Bend to make a Western called *The Man Who Loved Cat Dancing*. Although it was not as prestigious as *Ryan's Daughter* or *Lady Caroline Lamb*, it was Sarah's first Hollywood picture and was a big break for her. Robert, though, was decidedly snooty about the film. 'A distinguished cast and a mediocre script, the usual story,' he told David Lean. 'Why won't they learn? They must waste hundreds of millions of dollars every year on scripts which are only half worked out.'[1]

Financed by MGM, *The Man Who Loved Cat Dancing* also starred Burt Reynolds, one of the world's most popular leading men, and Lee J. Cobb, one of the most respected actors in America. Sarah would get to ride horses across some dramatic scenery and, since Westerns were still in vogue, a box-office success seemed assured. And because making a Western would be fun, if physically demanding, Sarah wanted Tom to be with her as well; for most boys of five being part of a Western would be a dream come true.

Throughout the making of *Lady Caroline Lamb* David Whiting had been actively promoting Sarah's career. Despite his own emotional imbalance and the problems he gave Robert and Sarah, he obviously did a good job since it was Whiting, not Sarah's agent, who persuaded MGM to cast her in the picture. This meant that he also insisted on going on location. On Monday, 29 January 1973 Sarah and Whiting checked in to the Travelodge Motel at the east end of town. It was a typical American motel, consisting of a two-storey block of rooms placed at right angles to a separate single-storey block. Each block had two rows of rooms, those at the rear facing the mountains and those at the front facing the parking lot and the highway. There were a coffee shop, a pool, some ornamental dwarf yucca plants and a lot of dust and scrubby cactus. It was reasonably comfortable and wholly charmless.

Sarah was given room 127 in the single-storey block. It had a separate dressing-room area and a door which linked it to room 126, initially occupied by Whiting. But on Friday, 2 February, Whiting moved out when Tom arrived with his nanny, Janie Evans, who was also Whiting's current girl-friend. With Evans at the motel, Sarah thought that Whiting would leave her alone. Whiting moved into room 119, on the ground floor of the two-storey block. A broad wrought-iron stairway rose directly in front of his room to the first floor. This fire escape was perfect for Whiting: while he could easily monitor anyone entering or leaving Sarah's room in the block opposite, the fire escape made it difficult for him to be seen looking out of his window.

Whiting was behaving badly and, as usual, he was jealous of anyone whom Sarah befriended, notably her co-star, Burt Reynolds, and the cowboys and wranglers attached to the picture who liked to drink beer, talk horses and dance in the motel's restaurant and bar. Although Sarah often invited Whiting to have dinner with her and Tom in the restaurant, he rarely did. Instead, he would have a meal by himself and returned to his room to stare out of his window, checking on when Sarah returned to her room. He had got her the part, he had turned her into a Hollywood star, and she just chatted and danced with the wranglers. Whiting was seething.

'When I'm on a picture,' Sarah later told the inquest, 'I'm – see, he had known me as a girl who lived in the country, who loved horses and who lived a quiet life. When I get on a film I like to get to know everybody. The wranglers – I never met wranglers before. Christ, they're marvellous people, you know. I mean I want to spend all my time with cowboys.'[2]

Work on the picture, though, began smoothly, even if the famously short-tempered Reynolds clashed occasionally with his director, Richard A. Sarafian, who got the job after a young tyro named Steven Spielberg had turned it down and when the first director left in pre-production. Sarafian said:

> I came on replacing Brian Hutton. I had a month to prepare this thing and had a meeting with MGM's boss, James Aubrey, who said, 'She's a cunt, he's a son-of-a-bitch and I don't want to see any horses riding back and forth. That's it.' Those were his instructions to me.
>
> I liked Sarah. She was a very gutsy woman and much smarter than any of the men. She was like a piece of ripe fruit, a very seductive lady, who enjoyed manipulating all the men around her. I said to Burt, 'Flirt with her, because that would be good for your character, but whatever you do, don't jump in the sack.' And he swore to me afterwards that he never did jump on her, so to speak. He held to that. I've not spoken to Burt since the picture.
>
> I thought Whiting was a really gentle man. He was young and obsessed with Sarah. A night or two before the tragedy he said to me, 'I just want you to know, Richard, that I won't get in your way.' I thought that was strange because he was welcome on the set. He was a film buff and had an extraordinary knowledge of movies, much more so than kids today who don't know anything beyond the last two years. He was a very fastidious kind of guy, well groomed and a bit of an anachronism, like he came out of a Scott Fitzgerald novel.[3]

On the evening of Saturday, 10 February there was a birthday party for Burt Reynolds at the Pink Palomino Inn, a bar in the mining town of Ajo, some forty miles south of Gila Bend. The party had been arranged by the American TV talk show host, Merv Griffin, who was covering the production for two days. Sarah's role at the party, for the benefit of the TV show, was to play Reynolds's official date.

In his autobiography Reynolds claims he was driven to the Pink Palomino in Lee J. Cobb's Citroën-Maserati, a sleek hybrid of a sports saloon. He also claims that Cobb drove him back to Gila Bend, that he went straight to bed and was unaware of anything unusual until 2 a.m. when he was woken by a pounding at his door: 'It was Sarah,' he wrote. 'She had a bloody nose and was crying. "David beat me up," she said. I stupidly took my chivalrous

Southern self outside and looked for him, but I couldn't find him anyplace. Nowhere. Back in my room, Sarah asked if she could spend the night. As God is my witness, there was nothing going on between us. She just wanted to feel safe. No problem. But I woke up very early and told her to get her ass back to her own room before anyone saw her. A minute later she knocked on my door again. "He's laying on the floor," she cried. "Dead." '[4] Reynolds's account is simple and to the point, allowing for no missing minutes, no ambiguity, no suspicion. It is not quite what he later told the inquest.

Sarah's account is completely different. Because Whiting had not been invited to the party, he was jealous of Reynolds having Sarah as his companion for the evening. Sarah says that she, not Reynolds, was driven home by Cobb, though it is quite possible that Cobb went back to Ajo to fetch Reynolds in order to give his new car an extra run. When Sarah returned to the motel she went to the restaurant and bar where the wranglers were drinking and dancing. She danced with one of her co-stars, Beau Hopkins, who told her that she should not have abandoned Reynolds at the party and that she should apologise. Surprised, Sarah nevertheless went to room 135, in the same block as her own room, to apologise to the star. 'He preened as if it really mattered to him,' wrote Sarah. 'I'd done the right thing obviously.'[5]

Reynolds invited Sarah into his room and told her that he was expecting a masseuse any moment. According to the masseuse, a Japanese-American named Letsgo, who had been hired to massage Sarah because she was doing her own stunts, Sarah remained in the room, turned on the TV, ate some fruit and fell asleep. The masseuse left Reynolds's room at 2 a.m. An hour or so later Sarah also left Reynolds's room and walked alone to her own. Whiting was waiting for her. 'He was dribbling with mad uncontrollable jealousy. . . . It was so foul I honestly thought he was having a fit and – who knows – perhaps he was,' she said.[6]

Whiting demanded to know why Sarah was out so late and when she told him it was none of his business he attacked her. Sarah fell to the floor, instinctively protected her face with her arms and screamed for help. Janie Evans ran in and tried unsuccessfully to pull Whiting away. Sarah shouted to her, 'Get Burt!' and as soon as Whiting heard that name he fled from the room. Evans immediately dialled Reynolds's room.

It was here, as Whiting left Sarah's room and headed for his own and as Reynolds was on his way to Sarah's, that their paths might possibly have crossed. Reynolds stated to the police and to the inquest that he saw someone approach the two-storey block of rooms. 'It was on my left as I came around,' he said. 'I saw someone going in the door and the door slammed very hard behind him. Later I found out, the next day, that that was David Whiting's room.'[7]

When he reached Sarah, Reynolds insisted she put some ice on her face and return to his room where she would be safe. According to Sarah, though not to Reynolds, the star left the room for a minute or two, then returned to take Sarah back with him. It was then, Sarah told the inquest, that Reynolds said, 'If I was not as mature as I am now, I would have laid him out.'

Once Sarah was safely inside Reynolds's room she said she wanted to call Whiting to see if he was all right. 'Whenever he has hit me,' she told the inquest, 'he has always been so ashamed afterwards, so remorseful.' But Reynolds, she said, advised against it and urged her to deal with Whiting in the morning. He gave her a sleeping pill and she went out like a light.

Reynolds claimed that he woke early and sent Sarah straight back to her room. He said she returned a few moments later with the news that Whiting was lying on the floor, dead. 'I went back to my room,' said Sarah, 'and saw David lying on the floor of my bathroom. There were pills all over the place. He seemed quite dead. I took Tom out of his room and saw Merv Griffin's TV crew lining up to be ready when Burt came out of his room on his birthday. The next room to mine was occupied by Leigh Poll, the wife of the producer, Martin Poll, and she came out and said, "Sarah, you look like you've just seen a ghost." I went into Leigh's room and when I told her what had happened, she said, "We've got to tell Burt." Some time later, I can't remember how long, I went back to my room and that was when I saw all the blood.'[8]

The Gila Bend police were not notified about Whiting's death until midday. Sergeant Forrest Hinderliter had already dealt with one cadaver that day: a black man had been shot dead, either by a woman he was making love to and who claimed not to know him, or by another man who arrived unexpectedly. It might have been an accident or a murder.

Ten hours later, at 12.30 p.m., Sergeant Hinderliter looked down on another body. David Whiting was lying on the floor of room 127, his nose touching the metal strip which divided the carpeted dressing area from the tiled floor of the bathroom. His arms were clenched around a waste basket and there were a dozen or so red pills scattered on the floor. Hinderliter observed all this professionally, noting that the man had died several hours before, that it looked like an overdose and that the room belonged to a woman – the bathroom was filled with cosmetics, bottles of pills and there was a large hair-piece draped over a suitcase.

A man from MGM appeared. 'He'd been drinking,' he told Hinderliter. 'He swallowed a lot of pills, he took a bunch of pills and he was dead. He took an overdose. He was Miss Miles's business manager. It was Miss Miles who found him.'[9]

When the coroner arrived Hinderliter went to interview Sarah in Martin Poll's room. Hinderliter took detailed notes, then returned to Sarah's room. Something else was now on the floor: blood was seeping from Whiting's head. It seems that in moving the body the coroner had caused a hitherto undetected wound on Whiting's head to start bleeding. A search of Whiting's clothing rendered only a key to Sarah's room. A search of his own room – 119 – revealed bloodstains on a pillow, on a towel which lay at the foot of the bed, on wads of toilet paper in the bathroom and on a key to room 126 – Janie Evans's room. All this blood came from the back of Whiting's head. Thus began the riddle of the star-shaped wound. '[This] stellate or star-shaped contused laceration', said a doctor at the inquest, 'is the kind of injury we frequently see in people who fall on the back of the head. . . . This, of course, does not preclude the possibility of the decedent having been pushed . . .'

Whiting's body also revealed several scratches to the abdomen and on the hands, and bruises to his chest and left shoulder. The doctor who performed the first of the three autopsies confirmed that these marks were consistent with someone having been involved in a fight.

There was another story to be found inside Whiting's body. The police discovered a total of twelve different kinds of medication or drugs at the Travelodge. While the majority – cough mixture, vitamin pills, antibiotics, tranquillisers – were entirely legitimate, given a star's need to avoid colds and steady the nerves, there were also some tablets of Methaqualone called Mandrax, otherwise known as Quaalude, a drug which produces a relaxation of the muscles, feelings of contentment and general drowsiness.

At the time, the medical world was in disagreement over the number of Quaaludes needed to kill the average man. The first autopsy suggested that Whiting had taken two, and no more than three, plus a modest amount of alcohol and other chemical substances, mainly anti-depressants. But those pills, together with the blow to the head, might have been enough to put him into a coma and eventually to kill him. No one knew for sure.

'These uncertainties', wrote Ron Rosenbaum, 'placed David

Whiting's final Mandrax dose in a disputed netherland between therapy and poison, leaving unanswered the questions of whether he took the tablets to calm down or to kill himself, or whether he killed himself trying to calm down.'[10]

Whiting's personal effects, found in his room, were hardly revelatory: a Nikon camera and fifty-nine photographs of Sarah, which Whiting had taken on the set; a copy of *Playboy*, two bottles of whisky, a typewriter with the ribbon torn out, a novel called *The Mistress* which Whiting had optioned for Sarah, and a script called *The Capri Numbers*. There was no suicide note.

At Gila Bend attention turned to the precise circumstances of the discovery of Whiting's body, and how and when he might have received the star-shaped wound. It could have been during his assault on Sarah; he might have received it during his fight with Sarah and Janie Evans or after he fled from Sarah's room, on the way to his own room, or actually in his room. He might have been hit or simply have fallen over. But at some point Whiting's head was injured and he had clearly spent some time bleeding on his own bed and had tried to staunch the flow of blood with toilet tissue before returning to Sarah's room, which is where his body was found.

At first, the Gila Bend police suspected that the wound might have been caused by a blow from a cowboy spur. This theory led to everyone who wore spurs – including all the wranglers as well as Lee J. Cobb, Burt Reynolds and Reynolds's stuntman and buddy, Hal Needham – having their fingerprints taken.

The testimony of Janie Evans corroborated much of Sarah's account by stating that she found Whiting beating Sarah, that she had telephoned Reynolds and that he arrived within minutes. When Reynolds and Sarah left the room, Evans said she returned to her own room, where Tom was sleeping peacefully, and went back to bed and quickly fell asleep.

Twenty minutes later, Evans testified, she heard noises in room 127 and a voice calling Sarah's name, as if Whiting had returned either to see if Sarah was all right or to continue the argument. 'I was scared,' Evans told the police. 'I mean, he had been violent. I didn't want to see him so I didn't say anything more.' Evans claimed she went back to sleep again, woke up at 7.30 a.m. and went into Sarah's room and saw nothing. The fact that the lights were still on and that Whiting's body was lying close to the door which connected the two rooms created another mystery. Either the body was not there, or Evans did not see it, or she did and failed to report it.

Then the police asked her a question: 'Did you hit David Whiting over the head with anything?' Evans replied that she had not.

'We were trying to figure out how he might have gotten that star-shaped wound,' said Sarah's attorney, Benjamin Lazarow, 'and we figured it may have happened when the nanny was trying to pull Whiting off Sarah during the fight, but both she and Sarah said no.'[11]

In his autobiography, Reynolds claims that the nanny did indeed hit Whiting. 'Years later,' he wrote, 'I found out what really happened. Apparently, when I'd gone out to look for Whiting, Sarah had gone back to her room to get the nanny. I'd already been there and found nothing. But then he walked in and started attacking Sarah again. Just like in the movies, the nanny grabbed a large lamp and hit him over the head. It stunned him long enough for them to flee in separate directions.'[12]

The police, faced with a contradictory series of statements, were never convinced that Whiting had been hit over the head by anyone. If he had been beaten up on his way from Sarah's room to his own, his body might have shown more evidence than the scratches and bruising which Sarah inflicted on him during their tussle in her room. The police also considered the possibility that Whiting may have been drugged and had fallen on his own, though nothing in any of the rooms suggested this was the case. There was one final possibility: that Whiting had stumbled outside and hit his head on the fire escape or on the asphalt. But it had rained heavily in Gila Bend that night and any bloodstains would have been washed away.

What no one seems to have considered is that Whiting's body might have been moved to Sarah's room so that she would discover it and narrow the possibilities. If anyone was to take the blame for what had happened, Sarah was the most expendable person on the set. After all, Whiting was her business manager.

On Monday, 12 February, the day after Whiting's death, Richard Sarafian filmed a scene in which Reynolds caked Sarah's face with mud. By the time the scene was in the can, Sarafian had been warned that an army of journalists was about to descend on Gila Bend. 'We had the head of the Teamsters Union show up,' he said, 'and Barry Goldwater was informed about what had happened. I told everyone, "It's Walter Cronkite time" and we got out of there that afternoon.'[13]

The entire crew left Gila Bend for Nogales, 200 miles away on the Mexican border, and resumed filming the next day.

Robert's immediate response to the news from Arizona was to be with Tom and Sarah. When he arrived at the Rio Rico Inn, Nogales, accompanied by a team of MGM executives and lawyers, he could have chosen to take Tom away with him and leave Sarah to face the crisis alone. But Robert elected to remain in Arizona and not only that, he reread Eleanor Perry's script for *The Man Who Loved Cat Dancing* and started to rewrite it. This astonished Sarafian. 'When Robert read the script, he said, "Richard, you don't have a fucking chance. It needs so much work." So I said, "Robert, help me." I'd never met a man like him before. He had so much energy. He started to rewrite the scenes and would act them out for me. I knew I had at my disposal one of the greatest writers in the world but when I read his scenes they were so far removed from what we wanted I told him it wasn't going to work. Robert stayed for about a week and then he went home. Later on, I got a nice letter from him saying there could only be one captain on the ship.'[14]

The situation was truly bizarre. 'We'd had David Whiting dead in my bathroom and the police and the press were everywhere,' said Sarah. 'Then Robert arrived and instead of wanting to take me and Tom away, he wanted to stay and take over the film. He'd brought his portable typewriter with him and he took Burt through all the new scenes he'd written. It was . . . surreal.'[15]

Robert left for Los Angeles and successfully eluded the press by staying at the home of Robert Shaw, before returning to England on 24 February. 'I'm in disagreeably good shape,' he told David Lean. 'It seems that there is after all some limit to my moral self importance and appetite for guilt. Whiting, the suicide, was a genuine split personality. One of the personalities was profoundly unpleasant, the other only superficially agreeable. I feel a kind of horror when I think of his state of mind at the time of the deed – unhappy, vindictive and silly – but that is all. No better outcome was at all probable and worse were quite likely. The shit-eating Press gathered joyfully around but seem for the moment to have lost interest.'[16]

Sarah was left behind with Tom and Janie Evans to continue work on the film and await the inquest, which had been convened for 27 February. 'I didn't want a lawyer,' said Sarah. 'I never needed a lawyer when Thelma and Johnnie Windeatt killed themselves and I didn't think I needed one at Gila Bend. But when Robert arrived he said I needed one and the head of MGM, James Aubrey, forced one on me. I was told exactly what to say and so was Burt, who had his own lawyer.'

On Thursday, 15 February Whiting's mother, Mrs Louise Campbell, arrived in Arizona and went straight to Ganley's Funeral Parlor in Phoenix. When Whiting's body was brought to her for identification she asked the mortician to prove to her that all her son's internal organs were in place following the autopsy. As Whiting's body was opened up for his mother's inspection, she found the wound on her son's head and asked why it had stitches in it.

'To keep it from leaking all over the table,' said Mr Ganley. 'And she said, "Don't do anything else to it." And then she'd probe up there with her finger.'

'She actually put her finger in it?' asked the reporter, Rosenbaum.

'Oh yeah,' said Ganley. 'She never expressed one bit of grief except when I first saw her and she sobbed and said poor David or something.'[17]

MGM's lawyers had arranged for the Arizona State Police to interview Sarah, Reynolds, Evans and others at the Rio Rico Inn on 22 February. Their interviews, which were tape recorded, were offered as unsworn testimony at the inquest, making their personal appearances unnecessary. At least, this is what MGM wanted. But Gila Bend's Justice of the Peace, Mulford Winsor, was not one to be pushed around by a Hollywood studio. He issued subpoenas to Sarah, Reynolds, Evans and Lee J. Cobb, compelling them to attend in person.

On the day of the inquest, 27 February, MGM's lawyers appeared in court and asked that the subpoenas be nullified so as to avoid what they called 'adverse publicity and public display'. Justice Winsor himself was served with a restraining order, barring him from calling witnesses. The inquest went ahead with Sergeant Hinderliter's testimony. During the hearing Whiting's mother distributed to the assembled journalists photocopies of a letter her son had written to her. The letter proved, she said, that Whiting was not in a suicidal frame of mind. Whiting's mother was clearly implying that her son had been murdered and that a verdict of suicide would constitute a libel on the deceased.

By mid afternoon, as Justice Winsor was about to send the jury out to consider their verdict, Mrs Campbell's lawyer, John Frank, scored a notable victory. Accusing MGM of using their power and money to pervert the cause of justice, Frank convinced Justice Winsor that a proper verdict was impossible to reach without the testimony of Sarah, Reynolds and Evans. Winsor, who was himself outraged by the absence of the three principal witnesses, announced that a second inquest would be held on 14 March.

At Byfleet Robert agonised over whether he should attend or not. 'I'm damned if I go back, I'm damned if I don't,' he said. 'If I go back to be with Sarah, I'm the husband showing up and that puts us rather on the defensive, doesn't it? And if I don't go, they'll all say we're separated. Sarah is quite capable of holding her own. She does want me to go back, but I don't know. My work here is terribly important, so to leave that . . .'[18]

Sarah faced the inquest alone. It was always going to be a traumatic experience, though the press and television coverage turned it into a circus. She ended her sometimes tearful testimony by submitting two statements. She told the court she had never tried to avoid giving evidence. 'I was bulldozed by my husband, producers, Burt Reynolds, MGM,' she said, 'and for this I feel a grudge.' Sarah also offered to bury David Whiting's body since no one else appeared willing to do so. After that, she ran from the courtroom.

Sarah was never asked any difficult questions and neither were Janie Evans nor Burt Reynolds, whose testimony was constantly interrupted by Whiting's mother, who pointed at him and cried 'Murderer!'. The obvious contradictions in the testimonies were left hanging in the hot desert air and the star-shaped wound was ignored. The verdict was inevitable: David Whiting died from a self-administered drugs overdose. He had committed suicide.

Janie Evans and young Tom arrived in London on 17 March and were met at the airport by Robert and an army of reporters and photographers. After a brief and unseemly scuffle, Robert was quoted as saying, 'My wife is being pilloried. They have autopsied this wretched boy half a dozen times and they keep coming up with the same result – a self-inflicted overdose. For God's sake, it's like the old days of Lana Turner.'

Robert had done as much as he could to protect and support Sarah without ever being seen at her side in Arizona. In an attempt to dampen down the press speculation, he even agreed to write a personal account of what had happened for the *Daily Mail*. Robert's article, a necessarily selective account, was published on 13 March 1973, the day before the inquest. He portrayed Whiting as sad and lonely and said that while he and Sarah offered him all the help and understanding they could, he seemed set on a path of self-delusion and self-destruction. While Whiting's death was a tragedy, said Robert, its aftermath was sickening.

There have been some pretty evil innuendoes in the Press, hints even at homicide. They are quite baseless. . . . Why is speculation in the Press nearly always ugly? I blame you, the reader.

The gentlemen of the Press write as you want them to write.

Tragedies big and little pile up daily on their desks, reduced to words; they are probably unaware of the distress their words are causing. They say they write as you want them to write. I wish I could think they were wrong.[19]

Sarah returned to London on 22 April and, again, Robert and most of Fleet Street were at the airport to meet her. Robert had hoped that his article and the verdict of the inquest might have discouraged further speculation, but one night in Byfleet Robert and Sarah were woken by noises below. Fearing that a burglary was in progress, Robert crept downstairs and found that a freelance reporter had broken into the house. There was a scuffle and the reporter fled as quickly as possible. And throughout the day photographers with long lenses could be glimpsed through the trees.

Sarah never managed to overcome the suspicion that she might have murdered Whiting and the few interviews she gave were ample proof of what Robert feared and detested in the press. Everything she said, or was quoted as saying, seemed sensational and incriminating. Perhaps she would have been better off saying nothing, but she was in a state of shock and was badly advised in Arizona. At times, she looked like a fall-guy. 'I was accused of murder,' she said, 'and I've had to live with that ever since.'[20]

Robert's scrapbooks of this period are a jumble of reviews for *Lady Caroline Lamb* and articles about Gila Bend. Headlines such as 'A Marriage That Ran Downhill' or 'The Scandal of the Age' might have applied equally to real life or Regency fiction. Robert had been forced into a situation very much like his hero, William Lamb, though Caroline was never accused of murdering anything except the English language.

Robert's and Sarah's marriage was over; they both knew that and agreed that a separation was inevitable. 'Sarah and I are parting,' Robert told Lean at the end of 1973. 'I've known this clearly for six months or more, known it intermittently for a year, suspected it for two. It's been grim and unnatural keeping it to myself. All passion is now spent; all that remains are the grizzly mechanics of it. I've tried so hard to keep the thing alive and am so thoroughly emptied of any further impulse to try any longer that I'm emptied also of guilt. Feel a gain and a loss, on balance. Both lighter and harder hearted. It's a matter of survival I suppose; when you know your essential self is threatened you get very sensitive to other people's discomfort.'[21]

Two months later he told Lean: 'As for my parting with Sarah –

when I said it was a matter of survival all I meant was that I'd come to the bottom of my barrel. I'd have to start cutting into myself to continue, diminish myself permanently, that is. Which I won't do and, come to that, don't think I ought to. In myself I'm feeling fine. I'm anxious about Sarah's future because she's so drawn to disaster but it's a pretty detached anxiety because I've done all I practically can. When I know what she's going to do about Tom I want to sell up here and lighten the boat radically.'[22] The thing which Robert and Sarah most wanted to avoid was a messy divorce and a custody battle. This was finally settled when Robert was granted legal custody over Tom, Sarah having decided to live in Los Angeles.

In May 1973 Sarah attended the première of *The Hireling* at the Cannes Film Festival where she gathered some marvellous reviews and the film itself shared the major prize, the Palme d'Or. Immediately after Cannes she flew to America for dubbing sessions of *The Man Who Loved Cat Dancing*, which MGM was rushing into cinemas. At first, the film was released with an advertising campaign which said, 'Two women loved him. One died for him. One killed for him.' When that failed to attract audiences, MGM's publicity machine countered with 'The first Women's Lib Western' and when that didn't boost attendances, MGM hit rock bottom with 'Burt and Sarah in the torrid love story that shocked the country!' Nonetheless, *The Man Who Loved Cat Dancing* flopped.

While Burt Reynolds's career went from strength to strength, Sarah soon realised that she had been unofficially blacklisted. Virtually banished from the screen, she threw herself into stage work, prepared a one-woman show and announced that she would be playing Shaw's St Joan in a stage production in Los Angeles. Robert flew over to LA to assist her, coaching her in the role and performing some minor surgery to Shaw's text. After a tour of Australia, where he promoted *Lady Caroline Lamb*, he flew to Rome for a holiday with David Lean and Sandy Hotz.

There was one outstanding screenplay which Robert had written for Sarah, an adaptation of D. H. Lawrence's *The Plumed Serpent*. It would be filmed in Mexico, Argentina or Spain and would be directed by Sarah's brother, Christopher, who had already filmed an impressive adaptation of Lawrence's *The Virgin and the Gypsy*. Sarah could have played the role of Kate Leslie to perfection. A widow, Kate travels to Mexico hoping to find spiritual renewal and becomes involved with a sensuous and charismatic soldier, Don Cipriano, who introduces her to a revolutionary and mystic, Don Ramon Carrasco, who has revived the ancient Aztec cult of Quetzalcoatl, the plumed serpent. It is a story of considerable power, violence and eroticism, a risky undertaking.

With Robert and Sarah both away, it was decided to rent the house at Byfleet to Robert Redford who was in Britain making a picture with Mia Farrow. At least David Whiting would have appreciated the irony for the film Redford was making was *The Great Gatsby*.

TWENTY-TWO

STATE OF THE UNION

'One step forward, two steps back.'

Lev Davidovich Trotsky

Robert threw himself into work, living on drink and tobacco and writing all day and all night in the Mill. Because the house now held some bitter memories he put it on the market and watched anxiously as potential buyers were escorted around the grounds. Although the asking price of £150,000 was not unreasonable, there was a problem in that London's proposed orbital motorway, the M25, would in due course form the garden's southern boundary and shatter the rural idyll.

One day two attractive young women showed up to view the house. One of them was representing the Hollywood actor Jack Palance, who was thinking of moving to England. The other came along because she already knew Robert slightly through her ex-husband, the playwright Kenneth Jupp. Her name was Debbie and she was the daughter of Richard Condon, the American author of *The Manchurian Candidate* and *Prizzi's Honor*.

In the Sixties, Debbie had been one of London's most successful models, often adorning the pages of *Vogue, Harpers & Queen* and *Tatler*. She was tall, slim and beautiful, with a great sense of fun and, like Sarah, an obsessive love of horses. Robert often used to rib Debbie about her horses, which he described as 'a uniquely demanding and unrewarding animal. If people hunted horses with packs of foxes I might well join in.'[1]

Robert asked Debbie out to lunch and they soon became lovers, commuting between Mill House and Debbie's home, a racing yard in Hampshire. Debbie quickly realised that having a father and an ex-husband who were writers was ideal training for life with Robert.

She deliberately chose to call him Robert, even though many people called him Bob:

> I took a priggish pleasure in calling him Robert which stood for the side of him I liked best. I knew what writers were like so I took him cups of coffee and made him lunch and left him to it. During my father's last illness he'd seemed distant at times and when I mentioned this to him he said, 'I have an inner life.' When I told my mother this she said, 'Does he now? Well, he can carry on with it!'
>
> I think all creative people have inner lives and when everyday life intrudes it can be very difficult for them. Even so, Robert always made an effort to make time for me. One day I decided that fresh air and exercise would do him good – he'd been working and smoking for nine hours – so we tacked up two horses and went for a late ride. He was still immersed in his inner life and his physical co-ordination hadn't clicked in. His horse stumbled, they went over and Robert was pinned underneath it.
>
> We were in the middle of nowhere. I got the horse to its feet but Robert couldn't move. Because I knew that people in shock had to be kept warm, I threw my shirt over him and set off to raise the alarm. He ended up in hospital with broken ribs. The first thing he said when he saw me was, 'What are you doing here, darling? I thought you were having dinner with your father at the Savoy. You mustn't miss that.'
>
> Everything about the episode reflects the man's unerring talent for gallantry. Never once, in all the time I knew him, did he ever try to put me down. We had a mystical line of communication. Just after he'd had his stroke, when that beautiful voice was so severely impaired, I always knew what he was trying to say.[2]

Since Robert knew that Debbie's previous boyfriend was a Greek tycoon, he assumed that she was used to the best of everything. Debbie said:

> Robert wanted to be as good as he was so we always travelled first class. But what Robert didn't know was that my Greek friend always flew economy because he was convinced that the tail section of the plane was safer.
>
> Bob was very greedy, with large appetites, bordering on the Rabelaisian. Though he liked to dress up and do smart things,

he was just as capable of having his dinner in an undershirt beneath a naked light bulb. If we were going to the theatre he always wanted to eat before the play so we'd meet at six o'clock in empty restaurants. His food was gone the minute it was put before him. He was like a Hoover and not the ideal dining companion because you were left eating by yourself.

To Robert's relief, the sexual problems which had plagued him in earlier years, did not recur. According to Debbie: 'Robert was quite cerebral about sex. I would say that it wasn't his best area. I don't mean he was impotent, he was . . . slightly hysterical. He was also rather feminine, with dainty hands, small feet, fine skin and you thought of him as being small boned. Yet he had a sort of navvy appeal.'[3]

Although Robert had just come through the agonies of Gila Bend and his separation from Sarah, he told Debbie very little about what had happened, preferring to keep the pain to himself. 'Robert didn't talk about Sarah much,' said Debbie. 'I think he was afraid of her but he liked the danger of her as well. What he wanted was a middle-of-the-road life-style with a few big outings. And I liked that, too.'[4]

Debbie was falling in love with Robert and hoped that he might ask her to marry him. As she awaited the proposal which never materialised, she was more successful in introducing a friend of hers to a friend of Robert's.

Debbie's friend was Liza Dietz, whose father, Howard Dietz, was the legendary publicity director of MGM who is believed to have created the studio's motto, *Ars Gratia Artis*. Dietz was also an important lyricist who wrote *The Band Wagon* and many other evergreens of Broadway and Hollywood. Liza remembers the dinner as two parallel conversations: one between the men and the other between herself and Debbie. However, she ended up marrying the man opposite her.

Robert's friend was Roger Gard, a Cambridge don and combative intellectual who taught English and specialised in Henry James and Jane Austen. Robert had met Gard in Cambridge in the Sixties when he was staying with Sydney and Jaya. Like Mike Kellaway, Tony Quinton and Sydney himself, Gard was an important figure in Robert's life on account of his impeccable academic credentials and because he was never shy of an argument, even if the object of dispute was one of Robert's plays or films. Robert respected them all because they had remained faithful to their academic ideals. Gard said:

I was a snob but I had a certain prestige with Robert which was given to me by Sydney who has an irrationally high opinion of me and who is one of the cleverest men in England. Sydney classes me as an Exquisite, an elegant Cambridge intellectual. So Robert saw me like this as well.

I had an attitude towards Robert which we both liked. I used to tease him about his work which I didn't despise but put down as middlebrow. I said it wasn't real art. I said he was a craftsman and he liked that. Looking back, I think I was rather rough on him, though I did admire *A Man For All Seasons* and still do. But I thought *Flowering Cherry* was banal and told him so. Robert wrote about themes . . . here's a problem and we are going to dramatise it. The problem of conscience, duty and so forth. What I feel limited his work was the lack of unpredictability. You know it's going to go that way, that there aren't going to be any surprises, that nothing is going to get out of hand.[5]

Two major projects were preoccupying Robert at this time and both of them are perfect illustrations of Gard's analysis. One was the screenplay for *Gandhi*, the other was completely new: a play about the Russian Revolution.

Robert's mentor in the *Gandhi* project, Motilal Kothari, had died on 15 January 1970, when Robert was in Ireland for *Ryan's Daughter*. By coincidence, Louis Fischer, on whose book Robert's screenplay was based, died the very same day. The *Gandhi* project might have expired with them were it not for Richard Attenborough who was still backed by Joseph E. Levine.

Robert's previous reservations about Attenborough – his inexperience and lowly status as a mere actor – no longer applied since Attenborough was now a director of some stature, having made *Oh! What a Lovely War* and *Young Winston*. To Attenborough's delight, Robert agreed to resume the work he had started with David Lean and a contract between Robert and Attenborough was signed on 29 March 1973. The deal that Robert struck was startling: 'Out of veneration for the principles of Mahatma Gandhi the Writer has agreed to render his said services for a nominal consideration subject only to the payment of the Writer's expenses as hereinafter specified.'[6]

Robert agreed to deliver his screenplay by June 1973. His expenses were to be ten pounds per week, or seventy pounds if he went abroad, and he could claim secretarial and stationery expenses. For the completed screenplay he would be paid one pound only. Stated in letters, though not in the contract, was a 'gentleman's agreement' that if the film went into production and made a profit, Robert would waive his rights to any residuals and instead nominate three charities which would be beneficiaries of his ten per cent. The charities which Robert nominated in advance were Kothari's widow, Mrs Dorothy Kothari, the pacifist politician, Jayaprakash Narayan, and the housing charity, Shelter.

'[Levine] seemed thrilled that a writer of Bob's eminence was prepared to commit himself to the production,' wrote Attenborough, 'and I remember exchanging a series of euphoric telegrams with Joe, conveying the bubbling enthusiasm that I felt. . . . Bob and I spent a great deal of time together, planning the film sequence by sequence. This manner of working was very productive, and the whole of the Southern African segment worked out very smoothly.'[7]

In late June 1973 Robert delivered *Gandhiji* to Attenborough, who immediately sent a copy to Levine. To Robert's astonishment, Levine disliked it, though Attenborough believes that Levine was looking for any excuse to withdraw from the project because of the Indian government's alliance with the Arabs over their war with Israel. This led Robert to write several angry letters to Levine, who he thought had reneged on a solid deal.

Attenborough also sent Margaret Ramsay a copy of Robert's screenplay and a cheque for one pound. In his covering letter he wrote:

Laurence [Harbottle] has a copy of Bob's Contract, together with all the correspondence [with] regard to the arrangements for the ten per cent share to go to the Charities nominated by Bob. The major concern on everyone's part is that this percentage should, if possible, be received by the Charities free of tax. . . . In any event, do please be assured that I, personally, am prepared to guarantee that ten per cent of the profits will go to the Charities.

I am enclosing a copy of the script. . . . I do hope you will think it as good as I do. . . Bob's achievement in containing the story within this length, of making one perpetually anxious to know what happens next and to give the feeling by the time you have reached the end, that one has really come to know this extraordinary man, is a feat which I am sure few writers in the world could have accomplished.

Perhaps I might add finally that I don't think I could possibly have enjoyed the association – which will undoubtedly continue

– any more than I have done. He really is a smashing bloke.[8]

In fact, Attenborough, in his characteristic way, was merely being polite for, like Levine, he too was disappointed by the script:

> Robert wrote an extremely efficient screenplay which veered unquestionably towards the academic. If you wanted to make a docudrama for university library shelves, you would have made Bob's script. I was greatly in awe of Robert but I remember reading his script for the first time and, as you know, I'm an emotional character, I work and live on my emotions rather than cerebral matters, and I remember being devastatingly disappointed in that I was not drenched with tears having read it. Whether it was Bob's style or whether he adapted his style to what he perceived the subject merited I don't know. What I do know is that nobody I went to for money felt any attraction for the project.[9]

Robert's carelessly typed, 176-page screenplay begins in South Africa with Gandhi being ejected from a first class train compartment. As he lies on the station platform, various images pass through his mind – his childhood, the death of his father and his education in England, a scene which Robert fleshes out with some rather crude caricatures of the Victorian working classes.

While Robert adheres very much to the story told in Fischer's biography, he diminishes the Indian characters, such as Nehru, and places a surprising emphasis on the British characters, including a 'Common Man' figure named Jones. There is also a British official named Turton, who comes into contact with an Indian mystic teacher named Godbole, as if Robert had in mind some bizarre connection with E. M. Forster's *A Passage to India*. And, most contentiously, during a key scene between Gandhi and the British Viceroy Robert contrives images of the atomic bomb attack on Hiroshima, a concept, if not a conceit, which astonished Attenborough.

GANDHI
One undivided Independent India, now.
And war without weapons.

VICEROY
(sitting back, appalled)
Oh, Mr Gandhi, *please!* Be realistic!

CUT: Realism takes over in the form of the atomic bomb

expanding in Lucipheran splendour over Hiroshima. As the too familiar but still terrifying image follows its predestined mutations we hear:

GANDHI
(sound over)
War is not evil under these conditions. War
is always, unconditionally evil. And every
war is followed by more evil and another
war. What else would we expect? Effect
follows cause –

CLOSE SHOT GANDHI, his face expressionless, his eyes intent, his utterance deliberate and expository:
– in an unbroken chain, evil effects from
evil causes. Afterwards, our statesmen will
arrange the chain in complicated patterns,
hard to follow –

THE BOMB again, the mushroom developed and beginning to drift:
– but cause and effects are not confused.
Link follows link through all their winding.
No arrangement of evil can issue in good.
The chain must be broken. Someone at
one point must suffer evil and give back
good –

OVER SHOULDER shot of Gandhi; he is addressing a silent multitude:
– Some nation at some point must suffer
violence and not retaliate. That will be a
heavy effort but it is not superhuman. The
name of that effort –

THE SILENT desolation of Hiroshima, after the Bomb:
– is love which is the human name for God
within us, waiting. God can wait for ever,
but can we? Perhaps this effort must be
made quite soon or not at all. Perhaps by
our own generation. Here, in India.[10]

In writing the screenplay, Robert would have recognised some striking similarities between the stories of Gandhi and T. E. Lawrence: just as Lean's film began with Lawrence's death and memorial service, Fischer's biography began with the assassination and the funeral; both stories describe the hero's attempts at racial unification in the face of a common enemy – Gandhi's efforts to reconcile Hindus and Moslems, Lawrence's determination to unite the warring tribes of Arabia; both Gandhi and Lawrence were accorded honorary names, 'Mahatma' and 'El Aurens' respectively, and both stories are illuminated by American journalists, Fischer and Lowell Thomas, who are renamed Walker and Jackson Bentley in the finished films. Robert also faced a problem by transferring the project from Lean – whose sympathies for the colonial powers are undoubted – to the more liberal-minded Attenborough who was anxious to please an Indian government which would donate much political and logistical support.

Attenborough was consequently obliged to buy back from Levine the rights to his cherished project and look elsewhere for finance. By the time he was finally ready to make the film, Robert was in Tahiti, though it seems unlikely that Attenborough would have called on him. Robert's screenplay, together with Gerald Hanley's, was handed over to a new writer, John Briley, who subsequently won an Oscar for it.

Although Robert sometimes claimed that sections of his screenplay were used in the finished film, a detailed comparison reveals few similarities and where they occur they correspond to key passages in Fischer's biography. For example, when General Dyer gives evidence at the enquiry into the Amritsar massacre, he speaks of being prepared to treat the wounded children, 'if they applied'. Dyer is asked, 'and how does a child apply?' The scenes in Robert's and Briley's scripts are almost identical and both are lifted straight from the pages of Fischer, who had the official transcript of the hearing to draw on.

Two years before the film was finally made, Robert decided not to press Attenborough about his obligations to the charities which Robert had nominated. 'I know I'm in the rights of it just as I know there's nothing I can do about it if Dickie chooses to forget his undertakings regarding Mrs K, Jayaprakash and Shelter,' Robert wrote to Margaret Ramsay. 'It's much easier for me personally to let it drop and now I will and hereby do.'[11]

Nor did Robert pursue the matter of screen credit. Finding himself in a similar position to Michael Wilson's over *Lawrence of Arabia*, Robert declined the indignities of a Writers' Guild arbitration. In any case, he knew that Attenborough had been unhappy with the script when he delivered it nine years earlier. For a man who had suffered a severe stroke and was trying to maintain a career and a reputation, the prospect of losing an arbitration fight was a dismal one indeed.

By chance, however, Robert got his revenge. In 1983 he was invited by the British Academy of Film and Television Arts to serve on a committee to judge that year's BAFTA award for Best Screenplay. At the time, Attenborough was the Vice-President of BAFTA and *Gandhi* was expected to win all the major awards. But Robert greatly admired the film *Missing*, and decided to vote for Costa-Gavras and Donald Stewart for their screenplay. The passion of his argument swung the jury, denying John Briley the BAFTA award, which everyone had assumed would be his.

The whole *Gandhi* experience had been exhausting and frustrating for Robert and his campaign against the picture seemed rather churlish for not only did Attenborough quietly give Mrs Kothari a percentage of the film's profits – which were considerable – he also gave Robert a percentage as well. But perhaps Robert never came to terms with the fact that *Gandhi* had been his first experience of rejection. Sadly, it would not be the last.

After completing *Gandhi* in June 1973, Robert immersed himself in his play about the Russian Revolution. To begin with it was called *Lenin's Testament*, which was later changed to *State of Revolution* when Peter Hall and Christopher Morahan thought Robert's original title lacked popular appeal.

Robert had begun work on the play during a holiday with Debbie at Rossenarra, Richard Condon's Palladian manse near Kilkenny in Ireland. He soon realised that this was by far the most complex play he had undertaken and the research alone, the fruits of which occupied every inch of wall space in his study and accounted for every day and every momentous event in revolutionary Russia, took two years. But if the age of Stalin, Lenin and Trotsky should have seemed somewhat remote, Robert was surprised to find himself in the thick of it. In the autumn of 1973 he was flattered to be asked if he would stand in the forthcoming election for the presidency of the film-maker's union, the ACTT.

This would prove to be a time-consuming, frequently laborious yet stimulating and restorative experience, since it enabled Robert to renew his overt political activity which had virtually ceased after his release from Drake Hall prison a dozen years earlier. Because the ACTT was in a state of virtual civil war, he turned his experience to advantage: much of the charged atmosphere of *State of Revolution* derived from his union experience.

The General Secretary of the Union at the time was Alan Sapper:

I started off being antagonistic towards Robert because *Lady Caroline Lamb* was made outside the Union agreement. I told him the Union wouldn't agree to that sort of set-up and he said he'd sue me. He didn't think much of me until he became President of the ACTT and then we got on very well.

He'd been a member of the Communist Party and was very proud of it. He took on the presidency, I think, because he felt that collective action was better than individual action. He was a wonderful chairperson of meetings. We were under attack by the Workers Revolutionary Party, which merged with the militant feminist movement which was even worse. But the broader membership recognised what was happening and we defeated them. Robert always gave the impression of being above the battle and that he only had the best interests of the union at heart.[12]

The ACTT – the Association of Cinematographic and Television Technicians – was in turmoil, as indeed was trades unionism right across the country. The Conservative government, led by Edward Heath, had come to power in 1970 and was soon plunged into an energy crisis: Middle East oil prices were dramatically increased and the British coal miners, sensing an opportunity to exert their muscle, went on strike. In the hope of lessening the impact of both, Heath imposed a three-day week and power rationing across the country. People began to live a strange existence by erratic working hours and evenings spent in candlelight; statisticians later recorded a rise in the birth-rate. There was a general air of disquiet and militancy, and although the Labour Party would resume power in 1974 – the Heath government having been brought down by public sympathy for the striking miners – several political groups were advocating a more extreme form of social change.

The upheavals within the ACTT were in part a reflection of the crisis then affecting the British film industry. Cinema attendance in Britain had shrunk by seventy-five per cent in twenty-five years and the Hollywood studios, which in the Sixties had invested heavily in British films, were going home. *Easy Rider* and *The Graduate* had shown American studio executives that films made for the youth market did not need to be set in 'Swinging London' nor feature an army of dolly birds in miniskirts or Minicars.

For the British film industry, this retreat was catastrophic: when Robert was elected as the ACTT president, only six films were in production, as against sixteen a year before. MGM closed down its studios at Borehamwood, EMI cut its Elstree Studio work force in half and British Lion faced collapse. To add to these problems, the newly elected Labour government imposed punitive levels of taxation, which obliged resident film-makers to move abroad, and deterred foreign directors and stars from working in Britain. The closed shop was almost literally that. And, as with the newspaper industry, technological change was transforming the television industry, making large film crews, especially news crews, unnecessary. Union activists considered themselves at war.

'There was a powerful move by the Socialist Labour League to put together a base for revolutionary Trotskyism inside the entertainment industry,' said Roy Lockett, now Deputy General Secretary of BECTU, the successor to the ACTT. 'So, very cleverly, leading people in film and television were drawn into the SLL. There were some very bright people – Roy Battersby, Tony Garnett, Ken Trodd – and the pinnacle of their success was when the Union adopted the policy of nationalising the film industry. This meant all the studios, television companies, distributors and cinemas would come under state control.'[13]

Things came to an ugly head when the Union, heavily infiltrated by the SLL, wanted to close down an independent film to be made by non-union members in a studio which had been 'four walled' – rented outright by the film-makers themselves. Although commendable in many respects, and routine practice nowadays, this was totally against union policy at the time. The Union's worry was legitimate: if the film went ahead, the BBC and ITV would regard the union as having lost its power and influence.

> We were running the freelance shop [said SLL member Roy Battersby], but there came a point when the right wing, based around Michael Winner and Ken Russell, decided this had to end. They organised a vote of no confidence and a big meeting was called. Anyway, the right wing and the Stalinists came out together and defeated us. After that, Robert Bolt was brought in.[14]

Alan Sapper's deputy, Roy Lockett, said:

> Robert got elected on a wave of anger and revulsion. Stuart Hood, who was a Trot, stood against him and lost. People felt the Union had drifted into this revolutionary chaos and that someone of Bolt's stature and standing would bring new authority. He was very assiduous, a tough cookie, nobody's

patsy and could be very fierce. I don't think he had much time for Sapper, nor for the Trots because they were not his constituency, but because he was once a communist, he understood the language.

He'd always invite me down to his house in Byfleet. I was reluctant to go because he was very famous and for some reason I didn't want to be thought of as a star fucker. But he said, 'Oh, for God's sake, come down.' So I went and we drank a lot and talked through the night. And the next morning, through a terrible hangover, he put on the Albinoni. I always think of Robert when I hear that.[15]

Robert was the chosen candidate of a pragmatic alliance between the right wing of the Union – represented by the successful film-makers – and the old-style, Stalinist executive. But if he found both sides uncongenial, his real adversary was Battersby whose party, the SLL, had been reborn as the Workers Revolutionary Party.

The WRP, led by Gerald Healy, was by far the most prominent of the dozens of British left-wing political parties, if only because of the publicity generated by two of its principal supporters, Vanessa and Corin Redgrave, both of whom were members of the actors' union, Equity. Just as Battersby had virtually taken over the ACTT, the Redgraves were active in the executive of Equity, where they campaigned for a state take-over of all theatres and television stations. Their biggest fear was that the Establishment would form an alliance with the military and stage a *coup d'état*. 'The WRP genuinely believed that the revolution was about to happen,' said Lockett. 'They thought troops were being mobilised and were taking over airports. I remember Waterloo Bridge was closed for repairs and this was believed to be the first move to seal off London. It was crazy, barmy, barmy. Then there was Gerald Healy, their charismatic leader, who was shagging all the young Trotsky women. He told the girls it was their revolutionary duty and they said, "I understand that, Gerry, but why dog fashion?" A lot of people, like Battersby, paid a very high price because Trotskyism burns people out.'[16]

Although Robert and Battersby often found themselves on opposite sides of an argument, they respected and liked each other. They also knew each other slightly, since Battersby's first job had been to stage the first out-of-town production of *The Tiger and the Horse*. 'Bob was comfortable in the working class movement,' said Battersby. 'He'd got a bit of form in the past. But he went through hell. I know we went too far on some things but we had an accurate historical perspective and he understood that. I have memories of him at the end of his tether, looking like shit, worn out with this struggle, but he stood up to all this for about four years.'

Robert was trying to maintain an even balance between the two factions of the Union and, in his public pronouncements, convey a sense of radicalism without being condemned as a WRP toady or as a wishy-washy liberal who drove a Rolls-Royce and lived in manorial splendour. In every sense he was a humanist, a moderate, a Yuri Zhivago figure surrounded by Strelnikovs, and the fact that he had written *Doctor Zhivago*, hardly a paean to revolutionary socialism, did not incur Battersby's scorn:

> It's this whole English thing, that if you're a revolutionary activist you're also a kind of ideologue with narrow cultural views. On the contrary, the position of Trotskyism always had the widest perspective culturally and was supportive of all forms of artistic activity. This goes back to the Twenties when there was a tradition of defending the rights of writers and eventually film-makers against Stalin. So for us, we had only respect for Bob and what he had done. And one of the ground rules at the ACTT was that you never drew distinctions over questions of quality. One technician is the same as another when it comes to the fight.
>
> I remember that Stuart Hood hosted a lunch for Bob. It wasn't a matter of trying to recruit him, though we would have been delighted if he'd joined. It was more a matter of finding out what his position was. For instance, he'd never taken a public stance on the policy of nationalising the film industry.
>
> Stuart asked him, 'Bob, how do you see the near to medium future politically, here in Britain?' And Bob said, 'Well, I sometimes think that what I should do is get a big house with a big wall around it and have a flag-pole and every now and then have a look over the wall, see who's winning and run up the appropriate flag.' We fell about laughing as we understood that only too well.[17]

By the autumn of 1976 the future of the British film industry had become a political matter. The Prime Minister, Harold Wilson, set up a working party filled with producers and television executives. Wilson's representative was his recently ennobled personal assistant, Lady Falkender, and the Union was represented by Alan Sapper. After more than two years of deliberation the working party issued a list of thirty-nine recommendations – inevitably dubbed 'The 39

Steps' – which prompted Wilson's successor, James Callaghan, to set up another talking shop, the Interim Action Committee, shortly to be known as the 'In-Action Committee'.

All this debate required Robert, as the President of the ACTT, to make up his mind about nationalisation. His dilemma was that his own career ran counter to union policy; by nationalising the film industry, Hollywood would inevitably be squeezed out of Britain altogether and budgets would drop to a level which would only please independent film-makers, such as Derek Jarman or Mike Leigh, who were just beginning their careers. Because Robert knew he could never adapt to making films for less than half a million dollars – the sort of budget that was regarded as feasible if the government were to foot the bill – he never advocated full nationalisation.

He finally outlined his views for BBC television in November 1976. Citing the success of *Jaws* and *The Godfather*, he said, 'You cannot make piratical profits by pursuing a prudent policy. . . . I think there ought to be at least one government studio and arising out of that a government distribution system, even with a government owned chain of cinemas. . . . I am not a full-scale supporter of nationalisation. . . . I want to keep my demands moderate. . . . I don't see the private sector as wicked. I see it, in this country at any rate, as proven to be inadequate.'[18]

Robert fought hard on the Union's behalf for the rights of British film-makers and technicians. But when it came to fighting for himself, Robert turned his back on England and took the battle to Hollywood, where the money was and where, to a large extent, his reputation was too.

Although *Lady Caroline Lamb* had been a commercial disappointment in America, it had sufficient prestige to convince Hollywood executives that Robert's partnership with Fernando Ghia should be taken seriously. Realising that Britain or Italy could never be a source of major funding, Robert and Ghia formed a company called – none too elegantly – Filmit Inc. and set up shop in an office on North Roxbury Drive in Beverly Hills. In one of those strange coincidences, the office building was the West Coast headquarters of *Time* magazine, where David Whiting had once worked.

Throughout 1975 and 1976 Robert commuted between Byfleet and Los Angeles, postponing work on *State of Revolution* in order to concentrate on his partnership with Ghia. By agreeing to move to Los Angeles for prolonged periods he hoped to avoid paying the punitive levels of British taxation. But he would miss Debbie's company and he disliked Los Angeles and had few friends there. Los Angeles also meant that Robert would be seeing Tom and Sarah, who were living in a beach house in Malibu with a young actor named Bruce Davison. Sarah's days seemed to consist of hanging out, smoking the occasional spliff, swimming in the ocean and listening to Davison strum on his guitar. If Robert was depressed by the way people lived in Los Angeles, he was at least relieved to find that Tom appeared to be happy. As he wrote in one of his weekly reports to Debbie:

> Jet lagged I am my mind out of. My Harrods haircut excites approval from the senior citizens, mistrustful glances from Sarah's friends. Actually, she seems to know a nice bunch. I can't remember their names except Sally Kellerman, very ravishing and ravished but hopelessly potty. . . . Assisted Sarah to purchase evening meal for guests at a really colossal supermarket and ended traumatised. . . . At least sixty sorts of cheese, all identical except in packaging. I bought a Morzarella which tastes and handles like an ingenious substance for cleaning the bath. . .
>
> Tom is in fine shape physically, mentally and emotionally. I've been to his school . . . small but with a respectable emphasis on work despite the family atmosphere. He looks entirely charming and fragile accoutred in his American Rugby Football gear . . .
>
> I wonder what is the suicide rate hereabouts? They all seem friendly and friendless. Something wrong somewhere. Most of the natives have a precise and heavy quota of heroin, cocaine or other chemical to get through between Friday evening and Monday morning and are badly in need of rest by office opening. Additionally there is an elaborately patterned ritual of wife and girl swapping, loaning and leasing of husbands and boy-friends, with consequent arrangements for meeting and sleeping, avoiding and gathering, the whole of a complexity which makes Mah Jong look like noughts and crosses and takes a heavy intellectual toll of the drug-bemused participants.[19]

Soon after he arrived in Los Angeles Robert checked out of his hotel – the Beverly Wilshire – and went to live on the beach near Sarah, which meant enduring two hours on the traffic-choked freeways every day as he drove to the office and back. After two weeks he began to have worries about Tom living in the drugged, sub-tropical torpor of Malibu. 'I'm not sure whether I feel better about Tom or not,' he wrote to Debbie. 'He's fit enough certainly and seems OK altogether, but it's not a place I'd choose to bring a child up. Californians seem to live in a daze of abstract dreamy aspirations shot through with rods of low greed. I met this girl at the weekend, very good-looking and full of vitality – at twenty-one she ought to be – but Jesus, one meal with her and I was so bored I was almost angry.'[20]

Although Robert had been given custody over Tom, he did not wish to prevent Sarah from seeing him if that was what she wanted. But after several meetings with lawyers in Los Angeles they decided that Tom would return to England for his schooling.

'We had a deal with Paramount who financed us for maybe three years,' said Fernando Ghia. 'Robert was like the Artistic Director. The idea was to find a number of projects of quality and ambition.'

Among Filmit's first projects, to be written by Robert, was *Minamata*, about a Japanese fishing village which had effectively been destroyed by industrial pollution. Filmit also owned the rights to a European heist movie, *Big Deal on Madonna Street*, which they were thinking of remaking, and there was also *Megalopolis*, a big-budget project about inner city decay which had been scripted by Dalton Trumbo, a former blacklistee and the writer of *Spartacus* and *Exodus*. In some respects Trumbo was Hollywood's version of Robert: big stories and big themes were common to both of them.

Another project was handed to Ghia just as he was about to catch a plane from New York to Los Angeles: 'A friend of mine told me about this guy she knew who was dying to write movies,' said Ghia. 'She told me he had a treatment and he wanted me to read it. The next day as I was checking out of my hotel there was this guy standing by the door. Long hair, a face like an Indian and incredibly powerful-looking. He gave me the treatment and because all my bags were packed I had nothing else to read on the plane to Los Angeles. The writing was rough and incredibly generous, I mean, much too much. But we paid him $10,000 and got him over to LA to meet Robert.'[21]

The treatment was called *The Baker File*. The writer, not thirty years old, was a Vietnam veteran. He was fiercely intelligent, spoke fluent French and had taken advantage of the GI Bill to get himself enrolled on a film studies course at New York University, where one of his tutors was Martin Scorsese. To make some money to pay for his rent and dope he was driving a New York cab. By the time Robert met him, he had already directed a feature film, a low-budget thriller called *Seizure*, but that had done nothing for his career. The writer's name was Oliver Stone.

I had written many screenplays in New York [said Stone, sitting in his seventh floor office in Santa Monica]. *The Baker File* was about the kidnapping of Patty Hearst, my version of it, which imputed that government informants may have been involved. The concept behind it was the state using terrorism for their own ends.

Bolt had this company. Franco Cristaldi was the money man and Fernando Ghia was the juice, the brains, the producer. Ghia brought me out to LA where I met Robert, who had just been through a divorce with Sarah Miles which had made him broken-hearted. But I met a man in great spirits who was very sweet to me. I had dinner with him a few times and felt very much like a kid around a great man. I was a little embarrassed, I didn't want to be aggressive or pushy and I didn't want to be the fan. I was very respectful, so maybe I had less a personality than a motive.

For two weeks I went to his office and he would tape our conversations. That led to my writing the first draft which was called *The Cover Up*. Sometimes he would rewrite a page and make it more his. The resulting screenplay was really excellent and had a lot of Robert's dryness and wit in it. I really got grilled by him on my pages and he'd sometimes tear them out and do them himself. The Kissinger scene at the end is pure Bolt. Fernando wanted me to direct the movie but I was willing to waive that and I did. Then Fernando went out to all the top directors at that time and they all passed. Unfortunately it never got made.

The most important thing that Robert gave me was confidence, a way of thinking, a way of writing screenplays. He had a very distinct, English view of America that was pretty clipped and very socialist, not in touch with the American way. Not superior, but easily dismissive. A lot of labelling goes on. I found that later with Alan Parker and David Puttnam on *Midnight Express* – a lot of anti-Americanism, that Americans were crude, all that British thing. I only say that because in some ways Robert was not entirely in touch with *The Cover Up* story but it was good because of his technical proficiency. He also taught me the concept of doing less, believe it or not.

When *The Cover Up* went down the tubes I was obviously very disappointed. But through Robert's intervention Stan Kamen, who was the most powerful agent, took me under the aegis of William Morris. So I got an agent and wrote *Platoon* the following year, incorporating many of the thinking processes that Robert had given me.[22]

Although Stone's script of *Platoon* would not be filmed for ten years, the quality and force of the writing got him noticed and led to him being hired to write *Midnight Express* for director Alan Parker and producer David Puttnam. 'Stan Kamen had recommended Oliver to write the script,' said Ghia, 'and Alan Parker called me to ask if he could be trusted. I said, "Sure he can," and Oliver went on to get the Oscar. Now his hair is properly cut. . . . I mean, he's mad – but he covers his emotional fragility with arrogance and power. But the man is incredibly fragile, like a piece of paper, with a stream of talent, like a river, and when he turns on it's terrific.'[23]

Three years later, on 9 April 1979, as Robert lay in hospital awaiting his heart bypass operation, he switched on the TV to watch the Oscars. It was the night Oliver Stone won for *Midnight Express*. 'Funny, how I was a protégé of his and how I prospered that night,' said Stone.

By far the most important of Filmit's projects was *The Mission*, then known under the title, *Guarani*. Ghia had come across the story in the Fifties when he saw a play by Fritz Hochwalder called *The Holy Experiment*, which dealt with the spread of Christianity in South America. When he started work with Cristaldi, Ghia was startled to discover that Cristaldi owned the screen rights to the play: 'I found some of the research, some books and copies of original documents, letters between the Pope and the King of Spain. Then I realised that this story about the confrontation between the priests and the Indians was not a play, it was a movie.'

Among the books in the file was one written in German called *The Secret Powers of the Jesuits*. 'That's where I learned that the Jesuits used music to communicate with the Guarani Indians,' said Ghia. 'The music hypnotised them because although they only had drums, they had an extraordinary musical sensibility.'

In 1970, after further research, Ghia took the idea to Robert, who was then in Ireland for *Ryan's Daughter*. 'I'd prepared a speech because if I failed to interest Robert in it I had nowhere to go. The size of the project demanded it be made in English. So I told Robert this story about four Jesuits who had a lute and a flute. . . . I was also careful to emphasise the great integrity of the Jesuits which I knew would appeal to him. I said to him, "You wrote *A Man For All Seasons* about Sir Thomas More and Sir Thomas More wrote *Utopia*. Well, this *is* Utopia." '[24]

Instead of seizing the idea immediately, Robert asked Ghia to wait until he was freer to put his mind to it. Three years later, after *Lady Caroline Lamb*, he was ready and summoned Ghia to Mill House. 'It was pouring with rain,' said Ghia, 'and Robert came out to greet me. He wasn't wearing socks or shoes, just a shirt and pants. He took me straight into his sitting room and he put on some music by Thomas Tallis who I had never heard of. There came this fantastic choir, incredibly sophisticated. As the music was playing, Robert said, "A huge river, crocodiles, gigantic trees. On the river is a boat with important dignitaries and they come to a pier and start to hear this music. There are a thousand Indians singing on the riverbank." That was how he saw the opening of the movie.'

Paramount agreed to finance a treatment for $100,000. Ghia then proposed that he and Robert visit South America to see the countryside and the ruins of the Jesuit missions. 'Robert was not keen to go,' said Ghia, 'but I was strong on it because I thought we had to avoid any scenes with the Pope or the European courts because those characters are killers. The play I had seen, *The Holy Experiment*, had been set in Europe but I felt the film had to be set in the jungle.' In February 1975 Ghia went on his own to South America to put together an itinerary. Three weeks later Robert arrived in the sweltering heat, wearing a fur coat. He had not realised that February in Argentina was high summer. Ghia took him to the Buenos Aires branch of Harrods, bought him a tropical outfit and off they went.

Ghia had persuaded the Argentine navy to ferry them along the coiling Parana river. They toured the missions on the Argentine side of the river and slipped across the border into Paraguay, which was then one of the world's least visited and most oppressive countries, ruled by a crackpot named General Stroessner whose portrait loomed large at every turn of the river. 'I organised the tour so that Robert saw everything and then ended up at the Iguassu Falls,' said Ghia. 'The falls made an enormous impact on him, as they had on me. Then I took him for a long walk through the jungle, which frightened him. He said, "Why are you doing this to me? Why do I have to do this penance?" and out of that came Robert de Niro's penance in the movie.'[25]

On his return to Mill House Robert needed to get his professional life in order. His play, *State of Revolution*, seemed to be the priority, even if it would earn him relatively little money. And in addition to *Guarani* there were two attractive and lucrative offers from Hollywood.

Robert and Sarah attend a reception in 1973.
Their marriage was already over.

Robert at work on *Gandhi* in his study at Mill House.

Mill House, a waterside idyll, with Georgian house, watermill and Robert's trademark conservatory.

(*Above*) Robert, Sarah and baby Tom on location on the Dingle Peninsula for *Ryan's Daughter* in 1969. (*Below*) Robert and David Lean wait for the sun to come out for *Ryan's Daughter*.

Sarah poses for a publicity shot with David Whiting.

Robert and the only woman he ever trusted, his agent Margaret Ramsay.

Robert plays film director, Sarah plays Lady Caroline Lamb and Laurence Olivier plays the Duke of Wellington.

Robert with his son Tom, a heroin addict by the age of twenty, photographed at Sussex House in 1986.

Robert and Ann Queensberry on their wedding day. To Ann's left is her daughter Alice and Robert's son, Tom. (*Courtesy Ann Queensberry*).

(*Opposite page, above*) Robert at Cannes for the world premiere of *The Mission*, seen here with Roland Joffé and Jeremy Irons.

(*Opposite page, below*) David Puttnam and Fernando Ghia on location for *The Mission*. Robert loved them both and tried to remain detached from their disputes.

Robert and Sarah at
Chithurst Manor.

Before committing himself to any of them he decided to write to David Lean, who was living in French Polynesia. If Lean had a project in mind Robert wanted to know about it and he wanted Lean to be kept fully informed of his own prospects:

> Incredibly I still have not finished the play and incredibly it seems to me that I am writing well even though I am writing so laboriously. It is not that the various personal upsets of the recent past have put me off my stroke, I think. It is mainly that the subject itself is enormously complicated. . . . I have never done so much rewriting. Of course the uncertainty of my personal plans (house, divorce etc.) doesn't help; and the Union is taking a lot of unrewarding labour also.
>
> I have to come to a decision about what to do next. . . . I need – not urgently but quite definitely – to earn a lump of money. There are three projects the sponsors of which assure me that they can give me $400,000 plus fifteen per cent, one of which I am in love with, one of which I would very much like to do, and one of which I wouldn't mind doing. The first is an original about a very strange and significant historical episode which took place in South America in the seventeenth century. A strange mixture of barbarity and sophisticated beauty and a deeply moving theme. The sponsor is Fernando Ghia though I don't know whether he can raise the money but he says he can and I have told him that I am not doing any more work on spec (*Gandhi* has taught me that lesson) . . .[26]

The other projects were an adaptation of Mary Renault's novel, *The King Must Die*, and a film about Brigham Young and the Mormons which had been proposed by Al Ruddy, the producer of *The Godfather*. Then a fourth project materialised from nowhere.

For ten years, the film director George Englund had been trying to make a film about Captain James Cook. Having already commissioned a screenplay from James Poe, Englund met Robert socially and asked him if he would write a treatment. In a curious foretaste of his work on *The Bounty*, and revisiting the world he created for his final radio play, *The Drunken Sailor*, Robert drew on his love of sailing, quickly researched the life of Cook and sent Englund an elaborate nineteen-page treatment which he called *The Pathfinder*.

Despite Robert's determination not to write on spec, he did the treatment for Englund for nothing. 'He wrote it out of his enthusiasm,' said Englund, 'without an army of agents, which was very rare. Paul Newman and I were partners at the time and the idea was that he would play Cook. Anyway, I didn't think Bob's work was his best. He wrote it in a burst, it lacked structure and I didn't feel able to show it around. So I sat with it, as if it was a piece of cobalt, and then I told him we couldn't run with it.'[27]

Cook's three Pacific voyages may have been momentous – too momentous for a three-hour film – but he was also a rather one-dimensional figure, a nuts-and-bolts seaman rather than a romantic or obsessive hero. The fact that his widow had burned all his private correspondence made his character all the more elusive.

When *The King Must Die* and the Mormon project also came to nothing, Robert decided to put *State of Revolution* aside yet again and write *Guarani*. He loved the story and, more important, he loved Ghia and felt a deep commitment to him. Robert completed his screenplay for *Guarani* in 1976. Taking just four months to write it, he contrived a dramatic story – the conflict between an elderly Jesuit priest (modelled partly on Herbert McCabe) and a virile slave trader – in which to tackle the broader theme of the conversion of the Indians to Christianity.

The screenplay received a bewildered response from Paramount, whose executives were involved in one of those perpetual power struggles which make Hollywood so interesting and – because the men involved are rarely cultured or especially intelligent – so ridiculous. 'This is a weird town,' Robert wrote to Ghia. 'The reaction seems to be: "This is a masterpiece; we don't want to make it." They have two reasons for their doubts of the film's commercial potential, one silly, one sound. The silly reason is – how can I put it? – well, that it has no sharks, sunken ships or possessed children. True, we have a good deal of blood-letting and a little rape, but only towards the end. I think this is a silly reason because (a) we have spectacle and action aplenty in addition to the moral themes, and (b) the themes themselves are of urgent interest to everyone everywhere. The theme of personal integrity in *A Man For All Seasons* was evidently felt urgently by people all over the world.'[28]

The second reason, which Robert thought was reasonably sound, was a matter of emotional distance: the Paramount executives found the subject alien and daunting. The problem was, Robert found the Hollywood jungle just as strange as Paraguay's and he viewed the studio executives with amused contempt, as he wittily described in a letter to Ben:

I'm not sure what's happening with my picture. Met with the

heads of Paramount, Barry Diller, David Picker (in that order) and their artistic adviser or underling Richard Silbert[29] who is able to read and on good days to construct simple sentences and commit them to paper unaided. David Picker confines himself to big game fishing for the most part but for relaxation will occasionally drop in at the studio and bugger up whatever happens to be going forward. Barry Diller remains incarcerated in the Presidential office without light or air, gibbering quietly to himself.

They find my script 'distinguished, moving and thought provoking'. They offered me a modest sum to prepare a second draft clarifying such obscure points as clerical celibacy and the status of the Pope in the Catholic hierarchy but we declined. I'm already preparing a second draft but if I take more money from them they'll want to extend their option and Fernando and I would rather it ended, freeing us to take it elsewhere. Actually, some of the points they made or tried to make were good and valid . . .

The position at Paramount is a bit complicated. Barry Diller was appointed President by the man who owns Paramount, one Charlie Bludhorn. He is on the way out it seems. It is widely assumed that David Picker has been appointed as his number two to take over when the time comes for Barry's defenestration. So, because it was Barry who bought the option on our property it is in David's interest to devalue it. On the other hand, suppose our property turns out to be valuable and is acquired by some other studio? Mr Bludhorn would be displeased. It's all impenetrably mysterious, like trying to guess what's going on in the Kremlin.[30]

After Paramount allowed its option to expire, Robert made some revisions to the screenplay, which quickened the pace and simplified the political strategies of the Vatican. He also gave it a new title: *The Mission.* Everyone in Hollywood turned it down. 'It was a European film with the framework of a Hollywood movie,' said Ghia. 'They were fascinated by the whole thing but also frightened because it was really foreign to them.'[31]

Throughout his stays in Los Angles Robert had Debbie Condon on his mind. By a strange coincidence, he also had Debbie's ex-husband, the playwright Kenneth Jupp, on the payroll. Jupp had become fascinated by the story of George Sand, the mistress of

Chopin, and had written a script for the BBC. When Jupp's deal with the BBC fell through he took the idea to Robert, who was enthusiastic about it, as was Fernando Ghia. After several intensive meetings at Byfleet, Jupp was suddenly invited to work on the screenplay in Los Angeles.

> Robert was insistent the script would be one hundred per cent mine [said Jupp]. He would confine himself to advising and editing. The system worked very well and I learned an enormous amount from him. Then one day it suddenly dawned on me that what I was really learning was pure David Lean. That Robert had got it all from Lean, and was passing it on to me. To confirm this I took another look at *The Bridge on the River Kwai* and sure enough there they all were, all those great movie rules, years before Lean had met Robert. If Robert were sitting here now, I'm sure he would agree.
>
> Anyhow, as well as all the work with me, he was also writing *The Mission* and simultaneously taking on two or three rewrite jobs. At that time he would do anything for money – three weeks' work, a hundred thousand dollars in cash – providing it didn't have his name on it. I thought he was killing himself, and I told him so.
>
> Our office opened at nine and Robert would always be there, waiting for the door to be unlocked, having been to a party the night before, having smoked his usual seventy-five cigarettes and drunk his usual bottle. He had this phenomenal energy, but he seemed to be a driven, crazy person.[32]

While Robert was advising Jupp on the screenplay, he sought Jupp's advice in the matter of romancing his ex-wife, Debbie. This went on for some months, in London as well as Los Angeles. According to Jupp:

> Robert decided he was in love with her. Debbie and I had broken up in 1968 but we had stayed good friends. We also had a daughter, Jemma, and I was very keen for Robert to become the man in Debbie's life because of my concern for my daughter. I wanted Jemma to have a stepfather I got on with, because it's a difficult situation if your ex-wife marries some oaf and your daughter is brought up by him.
>
> So Robert asked me to coach him. He'd say, 'You know Debbie better than anyone, what should I do? What does she like? What do you think of this sweater?' It was a strange

situation, but I was so fond of him I was doing everything I could to promote him. And then Debbie would call me and say Robert had taken her to the South of France to stay with Rex Harrison or that she'd been knocking around with David Lean in Rome. And I'd say, 'That all sounds very nice, Debs, are you having a good time?' But it just didn't work out.[33]

Debbie said:

You see the colour snapshots in your album years later and think how fabulous it looked – Rex Harrison's villa, Liz Taylor's suite at the Hotel de Paris to watch the Monaco Grand Prix, but I think you have to want it to enjoy it.

Rex Harrison was cross about his current marriage and an overall spoiler of our fun. He might not always have been like that but on that trip he was and I won't forgive him for it. He wouldn't let us burn candles at the dinner table so we endured the glare of wall brackets on May evenings at Cap Ferrat. Because he was unhappy, I suppose he couldn't stand for it to be romantic.

David Lean in Rome was better because we stayed in a hotel. But these *séjours* failed for me on two counts – I was blinkered by my obsession with my horses, which can't have been attractive, and I don't think either David or Rex saw the point of me as far as Robert was concerned. I know Lean was desperate that his boy shouldn't be hurt again and he couldn't imagine that an American divorcee, horse-mad model and mother of one was destined to be otherwise.[34]

Robert, though, had fallen deeply in love with Debbie Condon, whom he called Dibbles or, sometimes, Dibbling. He also called her the cleverest and stupidest woman he'd ever met. Even her fondness for horses did not disqualify her from his affections and he doted on Debbie's daughter. But when he finally asked her to marry him she turned him down. 'She had found someone else,' said Debbie's friend, Liza Gard. 'Then Bob decided that the only thing he wanted to do was marry Debbie. But it was too late. So I became his shoulder to cry on.'[35]

Robert and I took a holiday from each other, with enthusiastic mutual consent [said Debbie]. I was in love with this horseman who had a house on the same farm as I did. But he turned out to be a manipulative shit so I went to look at another house which belonged to the man who became my second husband.

Then Robert came back to see me and when I told him about this man he was gutted because he said he wanted to marry me.

He made a tremendous performance over his feelings for me. He asked Lee Remick to pretend she was having an affair with him so it would get into the papers and upset me. But Lee Remick said it would just upset her husband . . .[36]

'Lee Remick was a rather shrewd move on Robert's part' said Jupp, 'because Remick had been at Debbie's school and she even looked like her when she was twenty. But Robert was heavy-handed with women. It's strange, he was such a clever and sensitive man, yet he had this huge blank space about women. He seemed to lack confidence. When I arranged for him to meet a girl in Los Angeles he said, "Do you think she'll let me do it?" which was the sort of thing a schoolboy would say. When he was having problems with Debbie he said, "Well, if I can't get her any other way, I'll buy the bitch."'[37]

'I think he bought the flat in the Barbican and the house in Totnes just to impress me,' said Debbie. 'He'd got it all worked out, how we would live in the country and have the occasional weekend in town, seeing plays and going to restaurants. When I said my favourite car was a two seater Mercedes he went straight out and bought one.'[38]

'Robert got it all wrong, he really did' said Jupp. 'I told him it didn't work that way, that two tickets to *Traviata* and a rose would get him much further with Debbie than a Mercedes.'[39]

TWENTY-THREE

STATE OF APATHY

'Most revolutionaries are potential Tories.'

George Orwell

It took two years to sell the house at Byfleet; the projected M25 motorway, which would run just beyond the end of the garden, discouraged potential purchasers and today, as one stands in the sadly overgrown garden of Mill House, near the rotting conservatory, the muffled roar of the traffic is inescapable.

Robert was anxious to return to the West Country. Ann Queensberry lived in Dorset, near Shaftesbury, which Robert had rather mystical misgivings about: 'I've always adored Dorset,' he wrote, 'but it's never seemed *quite* West enough to be magic. But it's West enough to be not too far East of Devon.'[1]

But it was to Devon itself that Robert went house hunting, back to the countryside in which he and Jo had started married life and where he had taught at the primary school. In time he found what he wanted, a ramshackle manor house, snugly thatched, that claimed to be in the village of Littlehempston but lay hidden, like Merlin's grotto, in a small valley beyond the reaches of the ancient town of Totnes. 'I'm not sure exactly that I've found what I want in Totnes,' he wrote to Ann, 'but I've found something to which I could usefully give something. Sad that it should be a place and not a person. . . . The realisation that London is all those miles away invests the deep West Country with a sort of dotty magic, like being taken to another place in Time, with today a distant rumour. This is a highly reprehensible thing to desire of course but I seem almost to *need* it. And Totnes is so blessedly small and the house so hidden. I shall feel like Mr Badger in *Wind in the Willows*, dispensing security and hot pork pies to wayfaring friends. That's my story anyway and I'm sticking to it.'[2]

The Old Manor, which cost Robert £60,000, consisted of the main house, a guest cottage, a lofty, chapel-like building, two inner courtyards and a great deal of surrounding land. The entire property needed renovating and, as luck would have it, Robert knew someone who could do the work for him.

Charlotte Taylor first met Robert when he arrived with Debbie at Rex Harrison's villa at Cap Ferrat. She was then living with Robert's friend, John Standing, and one evening started to bemoan the fact that she didn't have a career of her own. When Robert visited Charlotte's rented cottage in Hampshire he liked it so much that he asked her to supervise the renovation and design of the Old Manor. 'It was an amazing thing to ask somebody,' said Charlotte, 'but he gave me an enormous cheque, around £40,000, and told me to do it. I put in central heating, had the roof fixed and went out and bought all the furniture and paintings, everything, down to the last ashtray. When Robert went to Michael Caine's house he saw his big screen telly, so he had to have one of those as well. I went straight to Harrods and bought it for him. He was a tremendous possessions man.'3

Robert was still seeing Debbie, though by now his interest in her had turned somewhat paternal. Having been rejected as a husband, he was busy assessing her fiancé. He also kept her fully informed about his impending move: 'I feel increasingly waves of timidity dragging at my knees as the date for my removal to the solitudes of South Devonshire approaches,' he wrote to Debbie. 'But it's the house I've always dreamed of so I'd better go and see if I'm brave enough to live as I dream. And Charlotte is doing a really loving and thoughtful job on it, nicely pitched between stately home and farmhouse. I absorb her care and affection with unbridled greed like an alcoholic in a brewery.'4

Robert moved into the Old Manor in the spring of 1976 which soon turned into one of the hottest and driest summers on record. 'When the house was ready,' said Charlotte, 'he came down on the train and was very tired and irritable. We'd got everything going, the fires, candles, lilies everywhere. He dropped his suitcases on the floor and said, "Darling, who does all this stuff belong to?" I told him it was all his. He hadn't seen the sofas or anything. Then we opened a bottle of champagne.'5

For the first time in his life, Robert found himself with full responsibility for Tom; the Old Manor was their home.

Although Sarah was one of the earliest house guests she was still based in Los Angeles, leaving Robert and Tom alone together. Robert found his son alarming in many ways and he worried about the boy's apparent disdain for any kind of education: 'Tom paints, reads, thinks or is anything sedentary only at pistol point,' wrote Robert. 'His bent is athletic, with obtaining money under false pretences as a profitable sideline. His unconditional virtue is physical courage. But he's much more like a member of the human race and less like a raider from the land of the faery now that he has a genuine home. I'm getting to love him quite a lot; which is good for us both.'[6]

Robert soon indulged his love of the water by buying himself a Drascombe long boat which he had moored on the river in Totnes. 'My boat is being re-rigged by a man called Lance who looks as if he might have sailed with Drake,' Robert told Mia Farrow. 'It is a very small, open boat and the rig is to enable me to sail it single-handed. Alas. One large brown sail instead of three small ones, quickly raised so that Tom doesn't get tired of waiting. Not the least unpleasant thing about children is their tedious impatience.'[7]

Having equipped himself for the water, Robert needed something to negotiate the narrow country lanes. The answer was a Range Rover, and a high-powered Japanese motor-cycle and the full black leather toggings to go with it. At the age of fifty-one, Robert was learning to live like an affluent bachelor with an expensive toy for every excursion. Tom was given his own machine, a miniature motor-cycle which followed in Robert's exhaust fumes.

Having voluntarily cut himself off by living in Devon, Robert beseeched all his friends to come and visit him and enjoy nature's spectacle. He told Mia Farrow:

> It's very lovely here. It's been a foul spring but quite suddenly the sun began to shine (I ought to have known you were back) and the sodden primroses in my personal wood were suddenly replaced by bluebells. They are unbelievably blue, like an optical illusion or a fragment of sky. There are badgers and I have bantam cocks and hens. They don't do anything; they just stamp about looking medieval . . .
>
> This is a magic place, both the house and the environs. Could I prevail upon the Previns to spend a weekend (or week) with me? It's a stiff journey but worth it when you get here. Honestly.[8]

After Debbie turned down his offer of marriage, Robert embarked on two affairs, the first with an actress, the other with a woman named Brenda Beardsall. Neither turned out as well as he had hoped. But while his London friends rarely made the journey to Devon, Robert made some new friends living locally. The first couple were David and Sarah Salmon who were friends of Charlotte Taylor and owned a magnificent Georgian house in the middle of Dartmoor. From their garden the view extended for miles without a building in sight. David Salmon was a dealer in oriental antiques, especially those from Tibet, Nepal and Bhutan; Sarah was the former wife of Noel Harrison, the son of Rex Harrison. 'We used to see him once or twice a week,' said David Salmon. 'He was quite lonely when he moved in and wanted company. He had an enormous cascade of words and stories. He was also a bon viveur, he loved food and wine, going out to restaurants. We used to go to a place called the Hungry Horse in Littlehempston but generally we went to each other's houses. He had a nice Australian housekeeper who always cooked the same meal.'[9]

It was at one of these regular dinner parties that Robert met Mary Siepmann, an extremely clever woman who was about to reinvent herself as the novelist Mary Wesley. She said:

> I was very broke and was knitting cardigans for friends. I'd charge them according to how much money they had. I knitted a sweater for Robert and asked Sarah Salmon if Robert was rich. She said he was so I charged him a lot.
>
> The first time he came to see me I was absolutely terrified. He had this enormous motor cycle and he was dressed in black leather, like a knight on a charger. He was a non-stop smoker and a non-stop talker. No one could get a word in edgeways.
>
> He had Tom with him who was going to Dartington School. Tom was being naughty and wasn't eating. It was just a way of getting attention. But Robert was treating him all wrong by sticking notices all over the house – 'Tom Must Eat His Breakfast' and so on. Sadly, he hadn't a clue how to bring up a child.[10]

Robert thought that if he was on his own, he would lock himself away and try and enjoy the solitude. By doing this, he could write as writers liked to write – alone and in congenial surroundings. Whenever he got tired or stuck, he could revive himself by wandering around his grounds, like Yuri Zhivago, and enjoy the flowers, the trickling stream and the bird song. Even the daily coughing of the Dartmouth to Totnes steam railway, which ran at the end of the garden, was a pleasantly reassuring sound. It was the perfect place to get down to what Margaret Ramsay had been imploring Robert to do for years: write a major new play.

This archetypal image of the obsessive playwright living in a sort of languid paradise found a strange echo in John Fowles's novel *Daniel Martin*, which was published just as Robert moved to Devon. The book is a long and penetrating study of a British screenwriter whose creative compromises are as numerous as his love affairs. Eventually the hero, who lives in Devon, decides to write the 'great novel'. Since so many episodes in *Daniel Martin* – such as an extended journey to the Arabian desert – suggested parallels with Robert's own life, several of his friends believed the main character was based on him. Robert believed it too, an assumption which Fowles tried to dispel. 'Just before *Daniel Martin* was published,' he said, 'I heard that Bolt had moved to Littlehempston, near Totnes, a village only a few miles from where I set my own book, Ipplepen. I did write to him saying I realised that confusion was likely, but it was all totally unmeant on my side and all the incidents in the book were autobiographical.'[11]

Robert wasn't fully persuaded by Fowles's disclaimer: 'John Fowles had written a book called *Daniel Martin* which people say is about me,' Robert told Julie Laird. 'Just before it was published he wrote to me to say that it wasn't. So I suppose it must be. It's about a corrupted playwright (not very good but good enough to be corrupted) who has taken to writing filmscripts and has a farm near Totnes. Warner Brothers have just asked me to write a script of it and I have had the satisfaction of excusing myself on the grounds that I want to write another play.'[12]

If Robert appreciated the irony – of declining the script in the same way that his presumed alter ego, Martin, declined further easy money in favour of a great work of creative genius – he nevertheless went to see Fowles at his home in Lyme Regis. 'He spent quite a long time trying to persuade me that the novel was unfilmable and that was why he had rejected it,' said Fowles. 'Although not knowing him well, I liked him and respected his views. I can remember him arguing almost fiercely that the novel could never make a movie. I respected him for his vehemence [and] cannot deny that he may have been perfectly right. Negotiations over it still drag on in Hollywood.'[13]

Robert was working on *Augustus* and he was completing *State of Revolution* which he had never abandoned, only postponed because of his work in Hollywood. It was a brute to write, a great sweep of history with many characters. By the end of it he had amassed

3000 pages of research, all of them pinned to the walls of the Old Manor.

> I got totally obsessive about having to read everything ever written about the revolution [he told Sheridan Morley], and the more I studied it the more I began to see terrifying parallels with the way we live now.
>
> The event was so terrible, the personalities so strenuous, the endeavour so total and the outcome so tragically far short of what was intended, that to think about it steadily is to be overwhelmed by primitive pity and awe. I began to wonder why nobody had ever written this play before. Then I began to write it myself and realised why they hadn't.
>
> You simply cannot sit down and start off Act One Scene One: 'Morning Lenin, where's Trotsky? Just popped out with Gorky, has he?' You have to get away from all that and deal with the ideas as much as the people. My first draft took three years to write and ran four hours with a cast of nearly thirty. The running time is now down to less than three hours but the cast is all there, thanks to the National. I knew this play had to come to them because of the size of it.[14]

When the play was finished, Robert thought its contemporary parallels might create some controversy; England, after all, was going mad, caught up in union strife, violent demonstrations, soaring inflation and a Labour government reduced to doing whatever the International Monetary Fund told it to do. Mountains of uncollected rubbish festered on the city streets, the trains didn't run and Robert himself was embroiled in the guerrilla warfare of the ACTT. The great British public rekindled the 'Blitz Spirit' and simply put up with it. The nation state was being readied for Margaret Thatcher's revolution. For Robert, *State of Revolution* was partly a historical panorama, along the lines of *A Man For All Seasons* and *Vivat! Vivat Regina!* and partly a personal exorcism of his own communist affiliations. He intended it as an epic of disillusionment.

The script was delivered to Peter Hall, who had commissioned it for the new National Theatre on the South Bank which had opened to thunderous fanfares the previous autumn. Designed by Denys Lasdun in a starkly geometrical, neo-Stalinist style, the NT's concrete enormity would not have looked out of place in Bucharest or Ulan Bator.

State of Revolution was but a part of Hall's grand plan. To celebrate the opening of the National he had commissioned new plays by

Britain's leading playwrights: John Osborne, Harold Pinter, Alan Ayckbourn, Stephen Poliakoff, Howard Brenton and Robert. A mixture of controversy and delight was confidently expected.

Hall read Robert's script and liked it very much. Although it had a large cast, which would be expensive, the sets were minimalist and suggestive: a desk and chair here, a door there, darkness everywhere. After Hall assigned the experienced Christopher Morahan to direct it the cast was finalised: Michael Bryant, who had played in *Gentle Jack*, as Lenin, Terence Rigby as Stalin and Michael Kitchen as Trotsky. 'We didn't see much of Robert at rehearsals,' said Bryant. 'Unlike Pinter who says, "Do the play or leave it," Robert wasn't hard and fast about what he wrote and he approved the little changes we made. Morahan was marvellous, he knew what it was all about. I'd worked with him in television and he was the reason I agreed to do Lenin. *State of Revolution* was my first play at the National and I'm still there, twenty years later.'

The play was tried out in Birmingham, where it opened only two weeks before the first night at the Lyttelton. Bryant remembers the Birmingham run going smoothly except for one performance: 'One evening we were half-way through when a poor demented girl climbed up on the stage. She said, "Somebody help me find my boyfriend. He's gone away. Will someone in the audience help me." Eventually she was led off but we'd stopped the play.'[15]

On 4 May 1977 Peter Hall went to see a performance in Birmingham and noted in his diary: 'It is brilliantly acted, captures well the turbulent lives of the Russian revolutionaries, and will certainly establish Christopher Morahan as a major director with the company. But I am worried. What I read was an anti-Marxist play. Yet in performance it seems to be too soft, too fair, too reasonable, too liberal in its understanding of the extremists' point of view. I understand that it needs to be objective, but it mustn't be cosy. All this was said after the performance to Chris and to Bob, who were receptive and very open. I am glad I went, for they needed to be challenged.'[16]

The director, Christopher Morahan, believes Peter Hall's doubts might have been due to a misreading of the play. 'It was written to present rounded, human portraits of the characters,' he said. 'Things change in performance, so Lenin became more sympathetic and Stalin became more implacable. Robert was in Birmingham for the two weeks there and he changed a lot of it, dashing off new pages. He was very practically fine-tuning his play. This could pose problems for the actors and one of them came up to me and said, "If he changes anything else, I'm going home." It was a fascinating experience because there were a lot of dedicated Trotskyists about at that time. We did a question and answer session after one of the performances and the questions were very hostile.'[17]

The first night, on 25 May, was very nearly a non-event since the National was threatened by a strike. 'I walked into the stalls with my wife,' said Morahan, 'and a stage manager came up to me and said, "The prop men have locked up the rifles and the blanks." It was my first production at the National and I sat with my heart in my mouth, wondering what was going to happen. Then I heard that some of the actors had broken into the prop room. There was quite a revolutionary feeling about the place.'

Peter Hall's second viewing of the play did nothing to dispel the worries he had had in Birmingham. He wrote:

> It's better but still too fair. I wish it was more passionate in its condemnations. If you're going to write a play taking Marx, Lenin and Stalin apart, then do it. You can't have it both ways.
>
> I met an angry Jennie Lee [Labour's Minister for the Arts] who said Bob Bolt had falsified history; what about the Cordon Sanitaire the West threw around Russia at the end of the war? I said I didn't think that was Bob's main concern. But she wouldn't have it. Her eyes glowed with romantic fire and she spoke of her communist father and of her visits to Russia in the twenties and thirties.[18]

The temperate climate of Robert's play seemed calculated to offend the red hot socialists of Britain's government at the time. And how peculiarly ironic it was that the theatre itself, which was staging a play about communism written by a former communist who was currently president of a trades union, should fall victim to its militant workers. Somehow the drama on the stage seemed less powerful, less pertinent than the drama behind the scenes.

The dispute started when a plumber named Ralph Cooper was fired. The *Sunday Times* examined the issues and concluded that Cooper had been dismissed for refusing to mend a couple of sinks. 'Two Wash Basins Halt National Theatre', ran the headline. Because Cooper also happened to be a shop steward, the strike call gained momentum and a picket line soon appeared at the stage door. The second night of *State of Revolution* was cancelled and there was a real sense of chaos at the National, affecting the casts, the management and the public. The real state of revolution seemed to be Britain itself.

The reviews astonished Peter Hall. 'I never remember a play getting such mixed reviews,' he wrote. 'Normally "mixed" is a euphemism in the theatre for bad notices. But these are genuinely mixed: some brilliant, some terrible.'[19] Hall would have agreed with Irving Wardle of *The Times*, whose review appeared beneath a particularly damning headline, 'Nothing Definite To Say'. Although Wardle greatly admired Terence Rigby's Stalin, calling it a 'performance of nightmare clarity,' he took issue with Robert's structural approach and Morahan's solution to it. 'Despite the speed of the action and the rapid scenic transformations of Christopher Morahan's production, one is mainly conscious of the sheer weight the piece has to carry. For every event that appears, one is aware of how many have been omitted: a feeling that would not arise in a piece fired with something definite to say.'[20]

Colin Chambers, the critic of the communist daily, the *Morning Star*, laid into the play not because of its ideological stance but because it failed to communicate the excitement of the times in which it was set: 'Bolt opts for a series of debates between the same half-dozen characters in a succession of dismally similar settings. The overall impact is diffuse and dull, mainly because the play has no drive, no focus, no guts.'[21]

Robert could take heart from Bernard Levin, who had written the most enthusiastic review of *The Tiger and the Horse*. Confronted by *State of Revolution*, Levin went into euphoric overdrive:

> The plays seeks to do two mighty things, either of which alone would, in the contemplation, make falter the boldest spirit: to explain the course of the Russian Revolution and the thrice-heated hell that its promise of heaven produced, and to put credibly upon the stage the protagonists of that stupendous drama. In both of these extraordinary endeavours Mr Bolt has succeeded beyond the dearest hopes of those who wish him well and who regard the seven years that have elapsed since his last play as seven lean years indeed . . .
>
> All this is couched in language with the strength of carved oak and wrought iron, the malleability of fine gold. Again and again Mr Bolt uses declamation without declaiming, offers sermons without preaching, tells the truth and shames the devil. . . . Robert Bolt has come back to the theatre, which is his true home as an artist, after far too long away.[22]

Far too long away . . . Robert was in Tahiti, enduring another one of his 'lean years', when he learned that Peter Hall had removed *State of Revolution* from the National's repertory. Despite the fact that it had been running for seven months, Robert was appalled by the news. He would have been equally appalled if anyone had told him that *State of Revolution* would be his final play. He told Ben:

They're taking my play off. Yet another wrong decision. Have you met anyone who's seen the bloody thing? I had confidently anticipated sitting at the well-paid centre of a political uproar. I'm going to write a play for three characters, in the nude, without sets but taking place in an abandoned public lavatory. Aimed at small repertory companies and amateur societies, particularly schools.

I tell you, it's a rum world. Here, except when as now it is like skuba diving in a drain, it is so lovely and inconsequent that the people are reduced to inertia. In England we're reduced to inertia by all those myriads of misguided tiny energies colliding. The country is going to the dogs.[23]

PART THREE

FUCKING HELL

'Do write on any case. I shan't be I proper letter until about the centre of Jerusalem. But see how I am longing to.'

Robert Bolt to Vaea Sylvain

TWENTY-FOUR

DEADLINES AND LIFELINES

'As a decrepit father takes delight,
To see his active child do deeds of youth,
So I, made lame by fortune's dearest spite,
Take all my comfort of thy worth and truth.'

William Shakespeare

Robert Bolt's second life began on 18 May 1979, when he arrived back in London from Los Angeles. Many of his friends thought it was a miracle he was still alive: the heart surgery and the ensuing stroke would surely have killed anyone with a less sturdy constitution. But the surprising thing is not Robert's capacity for self-preservation, it is the fact that his second life, although shorter than the first, was just as busy. His compulsion to work, evident since he wrote his first plays, would progress beyond a means of making a living; it was now literally a matter of living. For Robert, deadlines became lifelines. From Los Angeles, Robert went straight to the National Hospital for Nervous Diseases in Queen's Square, where he would remain for two months. Speech therapy and physiotherapy began at once.

Robert had decided to fight and he did so largely because of his love for his son, Ben, who was the last person he saw before his stroke and the first after it. His first word had been 'Bendi' and for a week or so it was his only word, apart from expletives. 'Everyone and everything was Bendi,' said Ben's wife, Jo. 'Cats, dogs, lampshades, anything.'

'It was very difficult to understand exactly what he was thinking because his speech was so impaired,' said Robert's secretary, Gillian Harrison. 'He was tailoring his thoughts to what he thought he could say, so what came out was very simple. He found "yes" difficult, so he'd say, "of course" which has overtones to it. You had to keep thinking, he doesn't really mean that. He kept saying to a doctor that he had to tell Phil Hurricane something. No one knew who Phil Hurricane was. So the doctor asked him to write it down and Phil Hurricane became Gill Harrison. That sort of confusion happened a lot.'[1]

One of Robert's regular visitors was Julie Laird who, after returning from Tahiti, had resumed her job with the Victoria and Albert Museum. Before going to see Robert in hospital, Julie called on Margaret Ramsay. 'She poured me the biggest whisky I had ever seen and told me what she felt about Robert and where it had all gone wrong,' said Julie. 'She said, "Give me a writer and once they earn more than ten thousand a year you've lost them. They've gone. Just don't get fond of him, dear, that's all." '[2]

Julie, though, was already deeply fond of Robert and the scratchy, garbled postcards he sent her from hospital were heart-breaking: 'I am on you can see making myself rather ill. You didn't know that my writing was still so much word than my speaking did you? See you soon?'[3]

Like everyone else, Julie was relieved to find that visiting Robert in hospital sometimes had its amusing moments. 'He was pretty miserable,' she said. 'They were giving him speech therapy and asking him to say words like "violet." The sister came up to me and said, "You come to visit Mr Bolt quite often. I wonder if you have any influence over him?" I said, no, I didn't. So she said, "Well, if you do have any influence over him could you persuade him to say 'Bugger' instead of 'Fuck'? We want to make him practice his Bs." So from then on, every time I went to see him, we had to say "bugger" about four times.'[4]

Ben had some tough decisions to make regarding his father's imminent discharge from hospital. Because the Old Manor in Devon was too remote for Robert's therapy to be conducted, as planned, by friends and professional therapists based in London, it was put on the market. The reason why Robert had bought the property – for its seclusion – was no longer in its favour. A house in London seemed to be the only answer.

Ben decided to take a year off work and dedicate himself to his father's recovery. His girlfriend, Jo Ross, readily fell in with the plan and put her own acting career on hold. It was a peculiar time for everybody, but especially for Ben. Not only was it emotionally draining for him, the problems seemed daunting and wholly beyond his experience. But there was more than this, something more bewildering than the year of therapy and personal sacrifice which lay ahead. Even in Los Angeles, Ben had become aware of a startling and profound shift in his relationship with his father: 'Because he hadn't been around much as my father, I was now in the position of being a father to him. He had become like a son. That was an enormous adjustment to make. I didn't have children, I wasn't married, I didn't have dependants. I just felt I had total responsibility for my father without any practice to draw on.'[5]

Another vital decision was made by Ann Queensberry, who had brought Tom back to England and had enrolled him at a boarding school in Dorset. She found a house in Doneraile Street, Fulham, an attractive row of immaculate terraced Victorian houses with elaborately tiled front paths and beautiful stained glass panels in their front doors. Keeping her own London house in Ashlone Street, Putney, Ann suggested that they rent the house in Doneraile Street and live there together as an *ad hoc* family. Ben saw nothing strange in this offer: 'The whole thing was bizarre and unnatural,' he said. 'Ann is an extraordinarily caring and nurturing person. Now, I couldn't have predicted that she would move in for months but when she did, it just seemed to be part of the extraordinary things that were going on.'[6]

The house had a large garden and was close to the River Thames, a location which delighted Robert who always liked having the river or the sea close by. 'We took him out in a wheelchair for walks along the towpath,' said Ann. 'I was certain he would pull through. I just had to believe it. In Los Angeles, when they talked about him being a vegetable, Ben and I knew there was intelligence in his eyes. It's just that he couldn't get the words out.'[7]

Within weeks of arriving at Doneraile Street Robert announced he was desperately in need of a holiday. After one further medical check-up, everyone went to Ann's farmhouse, L'Hermitan, in the South of France. Robert was always happy there and he later bought the surrounding land, including the ruins of another house, intending to create his own French retreat, as well as providing Ann with the security that her own property would never be hemmed in by holiday villas.

There was quite a gathering in France – Ann was accompanied by her daughters, Tor and Emma, plus Ben and Jo, Robert's daughter Sally and her daughter, Rosie. For a fortnight they laughed, ate, drank and swam in the sea, rejoicing in the obvious progress that Robert had made. But their optimism was cruelly dashed when one night, without warning, Robert suffered a heart attack.

For a while it was sheer chaos. Fortunately, one of France's leading heart surgeons, Dr Couve, was on holiday in the area and he was summoned to the hospital at St Tropez where Robert had been rushed by ambulance. Couve decided he could do little without first inspecting Robert's medical records and a frantic effort was made to acquire them. Since Ann's farmhouse lacked a telephone, Jo went down the road to call Gillian Harrison from a pay phone. 'It was a bank holiday in Britain,' said Gillian, 'and I couldn't get at the records. I also couldn't phone them back in France. It became a black farce. Eventually I found a houseman at the hospital who said he would break into the office and get Bob's medical records. We got the records and put them on a plane and I tracked down the doctor in the States who had done the bypass operation. It was pretty hairy and a miracle that he survived.'[8]

The black farce continued when Ben and Jo went to visit Robert the next morning. 'Ben came out of the room looking ashen,' said Jo. 'He said, "Dad's not there." I went in, looked at all the monitors and the tubes and then I noticed that one of the tubes seemed to fall to the floor, so I followed it and found Bob under the bed trying to fix his drip with a nail file. It squeaked when he moved, which annoyed him. That was so typical of him.'

Robert's truculence, which astonished and delighted the French doctors and nurses, found its expression in a postcard to Julie Laird: 'Well there – see I am at the Hospital for "Nervous Disorders" at St Tropez. Not at all painful – in fact nothing like painful – except for the hideous French voices screaming up and down the upstairs corridor. But he – the doctor – seemed to be so hideously disappointed at my general improvement that we did have to give him a go with the coloured pipes which he has hanging from the ceiling.'[9]

Getting him back to London was a nightmare [said Jo]. He went to the airport in an ambulance and we went in a car with his passport. Air France was on strike so everyone was trying to get on the British Airways plane. Nice Airport was like the fall of Saigon. We were told that Robert would be put on the plane separately from us but when we started to taxi he was nowhere to be seen. We looked out of the window and saw the ambulance on the tarmac but there was no sign of Bob.

Ben started to panic. He did a John Cleese and grabbed a stewardess and said in French, 'My father's having a heart attack' when he meant, 'My father's had a heart attack.' Ben's

French is always in the present tense. Anyway, we actually got the plane to stop. Then an amazing thing happened. We saw Robert in the first class section, draped over three seats, reading Wodehouse with half a bottle of champagne. We rushed up to him and he said, 'Benedict! What is the hold up?'

After that, we drank a lot and arrived at London Airport where Ann Queensberry had organised an ambulance. The drivers were identical twins and I remember we all looked from one to the other thinking we were seeing double.[10]

Robert Oxton Bolt was obviously as strong as an ox, except that he could barely walk or talk. Amazingly, the heart attack seemed to have had very little effect, beyond giving everyone a thorough scare. But now, back at 34 Doneraile Street, Ben and Ann needed sound advice and a strategy, a way of giving Robert constant speech therapy and mental exercise. They also had to have Robert's consent, since many stroke victims allow themselves to lapse into a vegetative state, waited on hand and foot, refusing the mental stimulation which leads to a partial recovery of their means of communicating. Robert had the choice of going forward or slipping back and staring at the wall. It was the actress Patricia Neal who put the choice to him in the starkest terms possible.

While Robert was in hospital in Los Angeles, Michael Caine had made contact with the author Roald Dahl whose wife, Patricia Neal, had suffered a series of strokes in 1965 which left her paralysed and unable to speak. 'I remember talking to Roald on the phone from the Caines' house,' said Ben. 'When Pat suffered brain damage, Roald was told she would never recover, just as we were told that my father would never walk or talk again. Roald refused to accept that and he coaxed Pat back to the point when she was able to act again in films. He did this by re-educating the portions of the brain that aren't used.'

Shortly after Robert's release from hospital he went to lunch with Dahl and Patricia Neal at their house in Great Missenden, Buckinghamshire. 'Dad couldn't talk and he was in a wheelchair,' said Ben. 'Pat told him what the therapy had been like for her, all the effort and the humiliation that she had suffered. She went on for about twenty minutes or half an hour, a monologue, and then she asked him if he wanted to do that. It was the moment of decision. He thought about it and seemed to make up his mind. He nodded solemnly and then we knew what we were going to be doing for the next year. This was a compact between him and his friends. If he hadn't agreed, he would have just vegetated. It was a tremendously brave thing for him to do.'[11]

Another key contributor to Robert's rehabilitation was Valerie Eaton Griffith, whose pioneering work with stroke victims began with a quirk of fate. She had been working for the cosmetics company, Elizabeth Arden, when surgery left her seriously disabled for three years. In 1965 she received a phone call from her neighbour, Roald Dahl, who asked if she might be willing to give up an afternoon to chat with his wife. Eaton Griffith's visit to Patricia Neal turned into a commitment, a vocation, and when Neal recovered enough to resume her acting career Eaton Griffith accompanied her everywhere, helping the actress learn her lines. Dahl then suggested that Eaton Griffith help a friend of his, the writer Alan Moorehead, whose condition was even worse than Patricia Neal's. As Eaton Griffith's work became more widely known, she obtained funding from a charity, the Chest, Heart and Stroke Association. A book followed – *A Stroke in the Family* – and missions to America and Australia, where Eaton Griffith established branches of her Volunteer Stroke Scheme. She was awarded the MBE in 1977.

When Robert went to see Eaton Griffith he was accompanied by Ben, Jo, Ann and his friend, the actor John Standing. They sat around Eaton Griffith's dining table and the questioning began.

'What do you like doing, Bob?' asked Eaton Griffith.

'Well . . . er . . . yes. I like . . . work. Yes,' said Robert.

'Writing plays is both work and pleasure, then?'

'Oh, yes. And . . . er . . .'

'You used to love painting,' said Standing.

Robert shrugged.

'How is your right hand?' asked Eaton Griffith.

'Not much . . . er . . .'

'We could try, though, couldn't we? And see if you enjoy it,' said Standing.

'Ben and I thought we'd take him to the theatre,' said Jo.

'Would you understand the words all right?' asked Eaton Griffith.

'If . . . um . . . if . . .'

'Perhaps we could avoid Bernard Shaw for a bit,' said Ben.

'How about trying rereading your own plays, Bob,' said Eaton Griffith. 'The very familiarity should be helpful.'

'I'll help you with that,' said Ann.

'Are there new plays inside your head?' asked Eaton Griffith.

Robert nodded instantly.

'Are pictures or words clothing the ideas?'

'I don't . . . I don't know,' said Robert.[12]

Eaton Griffith thought Robert was a fairly typical case, similar to Patricia Neal in his physical and speech difficulties. His constant swearing did not surprise her either:

'About thirty years ago, I met this lovely lavender-and-lace old lady who was in her eighties. She was so tiny that her wheelchair was meant for a child. When I was taken to meet her she picked up her good hand, banged it on the wheelchair and said, "Fuck fuck fuck!" You wouldn't have thought she even knew the word. Alan Moorehead was just the same. He was a bridge player and wanted to play again, so every time he picked up a card he said, "Bloody two of clubs." '[13]

After this initial consultation, which Eaton Griffith recorded on tape, she briefed everyone on how to proceed. The worst thing, she told them, was to leave Robert with nothing to do. 'That was absolute death,' she told them.

'Bob was very frightened,' said Ann. 'He'd pretend he could read but the book would be upside-down. He started to type but what he wrote never made sense. It was absolutely heart-breaking to turn the pages. But right from the start we did puzzles with him, with objects on a tray which we'd cover up and then get him to say and later on write down what they were. We had to make his brain function again. And it gradually started to work.'[14]

With no prospect of using his right hand again, Robert taught himself to write with his left – a slow, deliberate and jagged signature developed from 'Bob' to 'ROB' to 'Robert' to 'Robert Bolt' and sometimes 'Roberto.' Although the spelling and phraseology were often wobbly, the writing was always legible. And he started to talk. Single words became sentences, paragraphs, not always comprehensible, and invariably punctuated by 'Oh, fucking hell!' which momentarily purged the system of scrambled syllables. He was often vituperative and angry, with himself as well as with Ben and Ann, and he found some of the indignities hard to cope with – for instance, his food needed to be cut up for him, and he had to be helped to get dressed and undressed. 'He was, it has to be said, quite a tyrant in the house,' said Ben, 'and that was with my complicity. I elected to let him feel he was the head of the house and that he was running the house. We all did that in an effort to build up his self-esteem.'[15]

Each dawning day at Doneraile Street began with Robert shouting 'Oy!!' which meant that either Ben or Jo or Ann would have to get up and help him to the bathroom. 'Ben and I would be lying in bed thinking, well, who's it going to be this time,' said Jo. 'And if no one

went at once we'd hear the stomp, stomp of his stick on the floor.
Sometimes he'd throw the stick down the stairs which would make
us all rush out and we'd find him standing there with a huge grin on
his face.'[16]

'He was pretty difficult at times,' said Julie Laird. 'We went out for
dinner at a West End restaurant and he lost his temper with Ann. We
also went to Inigo Jones in Covent Garden, just the two of us. Robert
didn't mind what he looked like, which I thought was impressive,
and we were sitting down when Rex Harrison walked in. Robert saw
that Rex recognised him but didn't want to do anything about it. So
as we left Robert said, "Oh God, he's going to cut me." Because
Robert didn't want Rex to see how disabled he was, I put my arm
around him and as we walked past Rex's table I said, "Silly old
bugger, drunk again." Robert was very pleased about that.'[17]

One of the tactics advocated by Eaton Griffith was to have the
formal sessions of speech therapy conducted by friends or sometimes
strangers rather than by Ben or Ann. This not only served to
stimulate Robert's mind more actively, because of the concentration
involved, it also gave him a sense of obligation and encouragement,
since the friend or stranger was obviously there because he or she
wanted to be and was not doing it simply as a duty. For no matter
how caring, a wife or another family member often find themselves
turned into the target of insults and anger. So every single day Jo and
Ann organised a rota of visitors. 'He wasn't allowed to just sit,' said
Ann's daughter, Tor. 'Having been in command of everything, it was
horrible to see, because he couldn't do anything. My mother worked
so hard, to the exclusion of all else, really. It must have been terrible
for her as he had always been there if she had a problem. And now
there was just this blob, with this brain inside. She was so determined
that he would be all right.'[18]

There was a rota of people coming in every day to try and stretch
his brain, to give him mental therapy [said Gillian Harrison]. He
was immensely brave and had great physical courage, since this
wasn't a man who had just had a stroke. He'd also had major
heart surgery. He could barely walk and was rapidly becoming
very fat. But he'd go out on his own. He'd hire a taxi and fall
down getting into it and fall down getting out of it. I remember
he told me once that he had gone out for a haircut which gave
him immense pleasure. Given the state he was in, people must
have thought he was out of his mind. Then he said he was going
to drive again. I thought he was crazy but he bloody well did! He

was difficult to deal with because after a stroke all the inhibitions go. I didn't know that.[19]

John Standing was good as his word and started to teach Robert how to paint and draw. 'I would do a drawing myself and get him to copy it, which he had to do with his left hand,' said Standing. 'He was so charming and so sweet about it and so dastardly frustrated. "Oh, oh, oh fuck!" he used to go when he couldn't get through, when he couldn't happen, when the pencil went in a direction he didn't want it to go in. And then that great frame of his would shake with laughter, which was a great character trait of his, the ability to laugh at himself in appalling circumstances.'

Standing already had experience of this when his mother, the actress Kay Hammond, suffered a serious stroke when she was in her fifties:

When my mother had a stroke everyone was gentle and kind to her. They didn't try to push her along, make her do things. Everyone was just unrelentingly sympathetic, all of which is fine except you need that other force as well, to make the patient do things. We learned all this from Roald Dahl and Val Eaton Griffith who gave us a real talking to. And Ann Queensberry was fantastic, astonishing, and she'd been in love with Robert for ever.

I saw Robert about once or twice a week and quite often he'd come to see me or we'd go off to the National Gallery. He knew it was important for him to get out because if we always went to him he'd think it was just another lesson. He had to get out there, he was making the effort.[20]

Another friendly therapist was Kenneth Williams.

Kenny and Bob did orienteering [said Jo]. Kenny would arrive in a taxi, always with this big black driver, and they'd all go off with their maps, the idea being that Bob would have to find their way home. Of course, it didn't quite work out and the driver would usually ring up to say they'd all got lost. And when Bob learned to drive – he had this red Range Rover with a hydraulic lift – he once backed into Kenny's front wall and demolished it. Whenever he did anything like that, and it happened quite a lot, he'd just drive off and throw twenty pound notes out of the window. And if he got lost, which he often did, he couldn't ask the way home because people thought he was either mad or drunk.

Pat Neal, who was the living proof of what was possible, used to come by and sit with Bob doing jigsaw puzzles. Then once or twice R. D. Laing showed up. He wanted to give Bob LSD but Ben said to him, 'I think Dad has enough problems thank you.' But there were some people who just couldn't cope with it. I mean, if he wanted some sugar we would never say the word for him but wait until he said it himself. We let him struggle. That was one of the things Dahl told us to do. So some people thought we were really rough on him.[21]

One of Robert's oldest friends found the experience heart-breaking. 'I feel a certain amount of guilt that I didn't see much of him after his stroke,' said a clearly emotional Bernard McCabe. 'He was such a brilliant talker that I saw only a shadow of the man. It was very difficult . . . but no excuses. My fault.'[22]

Robert's grown-up daughter, Sally, was a regular visitor to Doneraile Street and his youngest girl, Joanna, moved in for weeks at a time. Robert's first wife, Jo, came with Gordon Riddett and so did Debbie Condon. But there was never any sign of David Lean, despite the fact that he had returned to London and was living about two miles away at the Berkeley Hotel, and for a whole year there was no sign of Sarah either.

Robert had always wanted Sarah to come home and she finally left LA in March 1980, putting her faith in their reconciliation on Venice beach. The letters that Robert and Sarah had exchanged were full of affection and concern for each other's predicament. On 1 February 1980 Robert wrote:

I am writing this (on the left-handed typing machine) first to let you no I am not mad and indeed far short of that. And second, far riskier, to adumbrate your smothered groans of sorrow.

The point is, you say, that you have not a single figure to whom you can point and say 'There – that is my friend.' Well the majority of sojourners on the earth have no one to whom they can truly point and say 'There – that is my friend.' You are so bedevilled by honesty (or whatever it is) that you do not hesitate the give her heavy little sentence pronouncement, once you seen it to be true. The majority of earthlings without ever having aceepted this truth. Also I think that so conceitied is your earlier years that you saw the wrong side of this, and made a boast of it. (I say so cofidentally because I saw the other side and the made the opposite judgment.) Now we both see the cutting edge of it.

So what do we decide to do about it? You spend lomg hours trying to debitate what I should do. I will tell you what I am going to do about it professionally. I am going to write about two or three plays about it. That is when my heroic helpers have done they're best. What am I to about it personally?

Here I must be very careful. I that I love you. I don't know what to make of this. Maybe it the best I can make, of the best we have been given. A thoroughly weak-kneed little plan. But I don't think so.

What do you think of it? Do you feelings sketch so far as that? We had the best know if its mere friendliness. Mere friendliness is be counted sort of actual love I believe. I don't mean the heart-tearing, castraphosic love of yesteryear; but more of the soulsearching spirit of the true feeling. Truth is the open searching daylight in this predicament.

Hooray for the told times; and the hooray for the new.

Sarah wrote back and asked if Robert thought about her during the night. He replied that he did. 'Whether you, or we don't do any thing further requires some further comment. Eh? Not that if requires some further comment; just one of the brushes in the pan so doubt.'

When Sarah arrived, Ann had already moved out, exhausted by the effort, and had returned to her house in Ashlone Road, Putney, which she was renovating. Robert was delighted to see Sarah and, because they seemed so happy and relaxed with each other, Ben and Jo took the opportunity and spent the weekend with Jo Riddett at Cuckoo Hill. Robert, Sarah and Tom had the house to themselves.

In her book, *Bolt from the Blue*, Sarah gives a compelling account of her first encounters with Robert – her writing is fluid, witty and undeniably poignant. But Ann Queensberry is a somewhat shadowy figure in these passages of Sarah's book, even though she had set up Doneraile Street and, with Ben and Jo, was the principal architect of Robert's recovery. For her part, Ann believes that she was somehow exorcised from the memory of Robert's first wife as well:

We sometimes went to stay with Jo and Gordon and these were enjoyable occasions. But later on, when Jo has talked to me she has blotted me out, as if I wasn't there, in the same way that Sarah has blotted me out. Jo would say, 'They all came down to stay,' as if I wasn't there. I think Sarah convinced herself that she was there all the time.

I remember that when Sarah was staying at Doneraile Street she read my hand. It was quite extraordinary. She said I would get married to a man I admired enormously. She went on and on, and she wrote it down as she said it. It was quite clear to me that this was Bob but I don't think it was clear to Sarah.[23]

On the morning of 16 March a letter arrived from Jo which Robert asked Sarah to read to him. 'The sound of my voice reading that letter still reverberates in my ears,' wrote Sarah. 'It was a lethal letter. It reminded me of how the whole world, me included, is rife with self-delusion. Everyone pointing the finger at others, unaware of the fingers pointing back at themselves.'[24]

It was a short letter and to the point. Jo Riddett simply said that she hoped Robert would come to stay at Cuckoo Hill, though he should not on any account bring Sarah who brought nothing but trouble with her. According to Sarah, when Robert heard this letter, he moaned and roared in anguish, like a mortally wounded bull elephant. Sarah called Ben for help who told her Robert wanted her to leave Doneraile Street. Devastated, Sarah left at once with Tom, going at first to her mother's in Brighton, then to a house she bought in Holland Park. For the next month Joanna looked after her father, then Ben and Jo moved back and life resumed as before. One letter had caused chaos and would change everyone's lives.

Within a few weeks of his return to London Robert had attempted to use his old typewriter, the manual on which he had written his plays and screenplays. But something strange happened in the millisecond between the thought forming in his mind and his left index finger striking the key on the typewriter. What he thought did not correspond with what he read on the paper in front of him. More often than not it was gobbledegook.

After a year of therapy, courage, frustration and downright rage, he was ready to make a serious stab at it. Robert desperately needed to work and it was vital to him to be regarded as a writer who *could* work. Without that, life would not be worth living and he would have no self-respect. Nor would he have enough money to pay for medical treatment, speech therapy, a house, everyday comforts and special needs such as the custom-made Range Rover and a collection of motorised wheelchairs.

He started on a screen adaptation of *The Thwarting of Baron Bolligrew* in the hope that Ben would direct it. But even though the words seemed to come easily, they were often the wrong words, the result of his dysphasia. He sent his various drafts to his brother Sydney, the first time that Sydney had ever been asked to read anything of his, and Sydney, in turn, sent Robert his writings. In the end, the *Bolligrew* screenplay was adapted into a novel, which Robert published in 1995. 'It was a huge labour for him,' said Gillian Harrison. 'I used to take his work home and try and make sense of it. I made a point of always going back to him with queries because I knew that was therapeutic. It was very, very difficult.'[25]

Robert explained his problems and his progress in a letter to Vaea, who was living in Paris trying to make a career as an artist: 'Please note I am writing this all at once; no fair copies to let me correct any mistakes in the first one. I conitue (or conictue) with the filmscript of the children's play; it is rotten but keeps me from falling into bottomless gloom. My mood, dear heart, alternates between unreal bottomless gloom (see above) and equally unreal high and mighty.'[26]

Roald Dahl and Patricia Neal recognised the effort he was making and urged him on: 'The Bolt Mechanism appears to be clean and well-oiled,' wrote Dahl. 'The firing-pin is extended, the cartridge in place, and now all you have to do is pull the trigger. Bang!'

When Robert suggested taking them out to lunch, together with Ann, Ben, Jo and Val Eaton Griffith Dahl refused the invitation, saying it would be a waste of money and that, anyway, the chef would probably spit in the food: 'Also, it's very good for Pat to cook for guests,' he said. 'It keeps her on her toes for a week. Say yes.'[27]

Now that Robert was fully intent on working again, which meant holding meetings with producers and directors, the drawbacks to Doneraile Street were becoming noticeable. Hearing of Robert's interest in moving, Margaret Ramsay suggested The Little Boltons in Kensington and Charlotte Taylor, the interior designer who had worked on the Old Manor, knew of a basement and ground floor flat for sale in that very street. After Charlotte had renovated it, Robert moved in with his daughter Joanna. Anxious to see his old friends and make it known that he was back in the social swirl of London, Robert announced his intention to hold a lunch party.

> I thought, oh no, this won't work, but he insisted [said Jo]. And it wasn't just a lunch party. I mean, Ralph Richardson, Michael Caine and others showed up. At one point, Robert said, 'I'm going to tell a joke.' The room went quiet and everyone listened. Robert said, 'About that actor . . . you know . . . an actor . . .'

Everyone drank their wine and waited. Then Robert said to John Standing, 'That actor, John, you know. . .' Poor John looked helpless. Then Ben came to the rescue and made signs – they had a system for males and females, crowns for a man and breasts for a woman. It was a man. Then suddenly Jeremy Kemp said, 'Is it Rex Harrison?' And Robert said, 'Fucking hell, Rex Harrison, yes!' We all breathed a sigh of relief. But Robert had forgotten the joke. It was nightmare charades.[28]

Robert was making considerable progress. He had evolved a pattern of speech which could be understood by those closest to him, even if it left strangers nodding or staring in blank incomprehension. It was the child's equivalent of writing: it was not joined up speaking, which was all but impossible. It was a way of talking which sep–ar–ated ev–ery word and ev–ery syll–able, laced with a still strong and sweet Mancunian accent.

His handwriting had also improved and an operation to sever a tendon in his right ankle had increased his mobility, reducing his reliance on wheelchairs. He delighted in going to restaurants – Meridiana, a swish Italian place in the Fulham Road, was his favourite, later supplanted by Bibendum – and he went regularly to the cinema and the theatre, often accompanied by Ben and Julie.

Now that Ben and Jo had resumed their careers and had returned to their own flat in Kensington, Robert decided that he should put his new house in order. In the Bolt scheme of things this meant getting married. His history proved that he was a constant husband and that he needed, or felt he needed, whatever security marriage offered. Things somehow seemed more permanent, more comforting, more moral, when a licence and solemn vows were involved. The problem had always been that his wives were rather less constant. But Ann Queensberry was as constant as he was, a friend for twenty-five years, and both of them had shared the pain of a separation and a divorce. One evening at The Little Boltons he said to Ann, 'I wonder why we've never married.'

'I imagine it's because you never wanted to,' said Ann.

'Well, I think we should do it,' said Robert.

After Ann had accepted his proposal, Robert wanted Ben's approval. 'I sat down with him and questioned him closely, as a father might question his son,' said Ben. 'I asked him whether he was sure he wanted to marry Ann, whether he was doing it out of expediency or any unsustainable motive. He convinced me that he simply loved Ann and wanted to marry her.'[29]

Once Robert and Ann had Ben's blessing, they went to her farm-house in France for a pre-honeymoon. 'He was in very good spirits,' said Ann, 'and there didn't seem to be any doubt in his mind that he could make love to me. And it was fine, he could. I think it made him realise that he was still a man. That gave him a lot of hope.'[30]

The wedding was held in late May, with only members of the immediate family present, as well as one or two of their closest friends, including Fernando Ghia. Robert's and Ann's daughters, Sally and Tor, were their witnesses. In order to maintain secrecy, invitations to a reception, to be held on 9 June, were not sent out until the eve of the wedding.

Robert's wedding present to Ann was vital to their honeymoon plans – a Volvo estate car which took them on a touring holiday in England to visit their far-flung friends and relatives. 'I didn't get the honeymoon right,' said Ann. 'We started in Dorset, at a guest house in Wool where Tess of the D'Urbervilles was supposed to have had her wedding night. Not a good idea, actually, considering what happened to Tess. I had booked a room with a four-poster bed but when we got there the woman said, "I knew you would understand but we have a younger couple and we've given them your room." So Bob and I had twin beds which I had to push together. Then Tor came over and we had a frightfully gloomy dinner where we all whispered to each other.'[31]

'Bob was still bad,' said Tor, 'but we had this meal and there was this young waitress who found Bob alarming. Every time she brought a plate laden with this stuff he'd go, "Oh fuck!!!" She'd shake and go bright red and run away. And there was this Labrador dog which was farting all the time.'[32]

Getting back to London was a relief and the wedding party was as lavish and as crowded with friends as they hoped it would be. And then, from Hollywood, came the best wedding present of all, a commission to write a screenplay.

Norman Lear was a Hollywood pro who had started out after World War Two as a writer for television. In 1959, in partnership with Bud Yorkin, he branched into feature films, including *Come Blow Your Horn*, *The Night They Raided Minsky's* and *Start the Revolution Without Me*. But Lear's real talent lay in television and he had a huge hit in the Seventies with *All in the Family*, the American version of the BBC comedy series *Till Death Us Do Part*. Lear's company also produced *Mary Hartman, Mary Hartman*, a send-up of TV soap operas.

Lear had bought the screen rights to a popular children's book by Madeleine L'Engle called *A Wrinkle in Time*. Published in 1962 and never out of print, it was the story of a ten-year-old girl and her younger brother whose father disappears during one of his secret scientific experiments for the American government. With the help of three witches, named Which, Whatsit and Why, the children 'tessaract' like their father before them and soar through time into another world. After a long and dramatic search, the family is happily reunited.

With its suburban family setting and science fictional elements, it was a forerunner of Steven Spielberg's *ET*, with more than a dash of *Peter Pan* and *The Wizard of Oz*. Lear thought it would make a fine movie, appealing to children and adults alike, and selected Robert to write the screenplay 'because he was the greatest screenwriter in the world'. While Lear had heard of Robert's illness, he made no attempt to discover how incapacitated he was. Lear just flew to London to meet him. 'His speech was a little slow,' he said, 'but the fact that he spoke hesitatingly in no way meant that he could only write that way. I recall we asked ourselves if he was the most suitable writer for the project and we thought that anybody who knows material the way he knows material, let him make the decision. He would be the first to say, "I don't think I can do this." But he joined the ranks of those who loved the book. He loved the father–daughter relationship and the brother–sister relationship. He came out to Los Angeles for some meetings and then went home to write the script.'[33]

If Robert felt drawn to L'Engle's story because of his own isolation as a father, he gives few clues in his completed screenplay. Only at the end, when the father is returned to the family home, does something strange happen: Robert denies the mother a meeting with her lost husband. The children, especially the bespectacled heroine, Meg, appear more English than American (they are from Connecticut) and are far from the baseball-hatted, Dunkin' Donut, computer-age nerds who populated Spielberg's films at the time. They are bright, recognise Shakespeare and behave rationally; their name should have been Darling, not Murray.

Robert's screenplay, despite some vivid passages, was all but unfilmable, a fact that Lear and his colleagues quickly realised. Half the action takes place within the 'wrinkle in time' and would have involved a sustained level of expensive special effects to make the story believable. Robert's screenplay called for mountains, deserts, flocks of giant birds, multicoloured lakes, flying children, star-bursts and a gigantic Orwellian city of sterile uniformity called Camatotz. 'Nobody could figure out how to make the movie,' said Lear, 'and it's likely there have been eight screenplays since. Nobody has beaten it, though I don't think anyone wrote a better screenplay than Bolt. When I told him it wasn't going to be made he was a big boy. I guess that had happened to him before. He was a gentleman.'[34]

Was it restlessness, an invalid's understandable sense of claustrophobia, or a genuine dislike of the The Little Boltons which compelled Robert to move again? It was as if moving house somehow proved to him that he was mobile.

Gordon Riddett called Ann to say he had seen a promising house advertised in the *Sunday Times*. The address was 29 Hartington Road in Chiswick. A large house, architecturally undistinguished, its principal virtue was the long garden which led right down to the Thames. 'I went to see it right away and we decided to buy it,' said Ann. 'It needed a lot doing to it and Bob wanted a big conservatory and a writing room right by the river. So we sold The Little Boltons and moved to my little house in Putney with Alice, Tom, three dogs and an au pair girl.'

While Ann threw herself into adapting Hartington Road, she also continued her acting career. She took roles in several major TV series, including *Love in a Cold Climate*, *Miss Morrison's Ghosts* and *Tenko*, in which she was happy to be killed off in the first episode.

Robert had pocketed a respectable fee for *A Wrinkle in Time*, about $150,000, and waited for further offers. The three changes of residence had cost a great deal of money – there was currently a boom in house prices – and Robert also felt responsible for some of his friends, notably Vaea who was having a tough time in Paris. He wrote to her:

> How am I? Well OK since I am throwing the effects of this serious, poisionous illness, and look like doing so for another year at least. Typing is improving, reading ditto, and my speech is improving hands over arm-pits. That is enough for me. Except that I still can't write at all, well hardly any way . . .
>
> Oh Hell, I wish I could help with your uphill struggle. Money. I wish I had enough to see my friends into and out of the liquiding putresence into they fall, just as often as me. I mean that Vaea, I am – well I well as bag as fix as you, but I don't know how I am going to get through the intervening period leading inevitably to death. Healthy or unhealthy. Strangely

enough of course one does. Oh I do wish I could help. Do keep writing my dear, even if my ever open pocket remains so firmly shut.[35]

By early 1981 Robert, Tom and Ann were firmly installed in Hartington Road. Ann had done a remarkable job on the house, adapting the interior down to the last detail – bannisters were deliberately roughened so that Robert could get a decent grip; the stairs themselves were bevelled to minimise the risk of him slipping; a conservatory had been, in Sarah's phrase, 'pooped out' at the back and the garden had been levelled off to make a firm foundation for Robert's writing room. What he needed was something to write.

It was David Puttnam and Hugh Hudson, whose film, *Chariots of Fire*, had just won the Academy Award as Best Picture of the Year, who really initiated the second phase of Robert's writing career. Puttnam already knew Robert quite well. When Robert was President of the ACTT, Puttnam was on the executive council and they had clashed over the South African issue. When a film called *Gold*, starring Roger Moore and Susannah York, was made on location in South Africa, the Union attempted to stop the film being completed at British laboratories. And when that failed, the Union tried to prevent the film from being shown in British cinemas. Robert quietly opposed this – he had, after all, broken union regulations himself by going to South Africa for *Ryan's Daughter* – believing that the film had provided employment for black South Africans and that cultural associations between Britain and the apartheid regime could only have beneficial results. After this storm died down – *Gold* enjoying a full release in Britain – Puttnam and Robert became good friends, mainly because they both recognised that their futures depended on finance from Hollywood, even though they supported the campaign for a partial nationalisation of the British film industry.

When Robert was obliged to relinquish the presidency of the Union on his return from Tahiti, it was Puttnam who went to the hospital to get Robert's signature. To Puttnam's horror, all Robert could do was to put a spidery 'X' on the piece of paper. 'I really liked Robert,' said Puttnam. 'I felt that what had happened to him was an amazing injustice.'[36]

In early 1981 Puttnam and Hugh Hudson asked Robert to write a screen adaptation of Robert Littell's 1976 novel *The October Circle*. A draft script had already been written and had not found favour in Hollywood, which led Puttnam and Hudson to make *Chariots of Fire* instead. But they both loved the material, feeling that it combined the narrative sweep of *Doctor Zhivago* with the moral argument of *A Man For All Seasons*.

The October Circle was a traditional Cold War drama about a Bulgarian champion cyclist who conceives a plan to pedal through the Iron Curtain to freedom in the West. Puttnam's wife, Patsy, apparently thought it was the best of her husband's current projects. It was also a ripping yarn with a political message about the tyranny of Soviet communism. In this respect Robert, Puttnam and Hudson found themselves on common ground.

Puttnam and Margaret Ramsay drew up a contract which was sensitive to Robert's condition. By 26 May he was obliged to deliver what was termed a 'First Segment' of a first draft screenplay. This segment, of unspecified length, was intended to give Puttnam and Hudson an idea of the quality of work Robert was capable of producing. If they approved it, Robert would be paid $25,000 and they would authorise the completion of the first draft screenplay, which would earn Robert another $25,000. If the film was made, Robert would receive an additional $50,000.

> I have almost started on a rewrite of the tale recently half-completed for David Puntam [Robert wrote to Charlotte Taylor]. Does that make sense? Well almost; about as much sense as my scripts make, I dare say. Never mind, I shall force on regardless. One day they will make sense I do not doubt.
>
> The script I am to do for Dave Puntam is on off a Bulgarian cycle race, which is all mixed up with the Czech portests about twelve years back. It signals hope. I cannot help noticing that 'hope' is not the flag which futters bravely from the turreted battlements of Eastern Europe; which seem to be very little changed. Still it's a good story.[37]

To everyone's delight, the 'First Segment' was approved. According to his contract, Robert now had until 1 July to complete the first draft and he decided to carry out his work at Ann's farmhouse in France. Ann was left behind in London and Robert's companion in France was her daughter, Tor, who was working on the ruined house which Robert had bought for himself. 'He came to stay for about two months, supposedly to write, but he didn't,' said Tor. 'He tried to write but at twelve o'clock on the dot we had to go out for a meal. For two months we went out every day for lunch and dinner. That was a lovely time because he was very relaxed.'[38]

On 3 August, a month after his deadline, Gillian Harrison flew to France to help Robert finish the last scenes and completely retype the whole 140-page script to make it presentable to Puttnam and Hudson. It has to be said that a little subterfuge went on, with the delay in the delivery of the script blamed on the poor woman – not Gillian Harrison – who was supposed to be typing the final copy. But if Puttnam and Hudson were impatient, they gave no sign of it and Hudson in particular worked closely with Robert, even though there were major problems of communication. There were long sessions at Hartington Road and at Hudson's impressive Georgian home on Upper Mall, Hammersmith, a house which Robert loved. 'Hugh Hudson was such a nice man,' said Ann. 'He used to come to the house and he gave Bob such encouragement. I think it helped him a lot.'

The October Circle was due to start shooting in September 1981, then the spring of 1982. But weaknesses in the screenplay, not entirely due to Robert's adaptation, and Hollywood's doubts about its commercial viability led to the project being shelved. Hudson turned his attention to another project, *Greystoke: The Legend of Tarzan, Lord of the Apes*, which was to have been produced by Puttnam who abruptly withdrew after the budget soared, along with Hudson's ambitions.

While the cancellation of *The October Circle* disappointed Robert, he was able to shrug it off, knowing that he could never allow himself to indulge in self-pity. He started work on a screenplay for Ben and took particular pleasure in the fact that he was writing for his son. They had become a family team. Robert told Charlotte Taylor about his latest idea:

> I don't know whether your last sojourn in this country took in the downfall of a very distinguished diplomat as the hands of a, very, backbench Tory (it needent be Tory, still it was) MP? He (the diplomat) was during the hey-day of his bustle about the world, covertly involved in some pornophary involving children. You understand he did nothing, but circulate some loving compiled mansupits (or however maniscipts is spelt) among other paedeophiles. Now the other one, the MP, turns out to have been ankle deep in some illicit affair, without having told his wife about it. I sense that a thrilling script among the dark places if high life will emerge from this. And to be sure some uplifting bits about his seaminer side of low-life.[39]

Work on what would have been a rare contemporary drama came to a sudden halt when, out of the blue, Bernie Williams called to say that *The Bounty* was now ready to sail. If Robert had given everyone the impression that his previous work with Lean had been done purely for the money, he now changed his tune. 'I am very attached to that script,' he wrote to Dino De Laurentiis's lawyer. 'Tell Dino he could not have a better person to work on it.'[40]

TWENTY-FIVE

RELATIVE VALUES

'It is a wise father that knows his own child.'

William Shakespeare

Robert needed help. The scripts for *A Wrinkle in Time* and *The October Circle* had been physically and mentally exhausting. In order to make his next screenplays better, easier to write and more polished, he took two important steps.

First of all, he retired his manual typewriter, which he had used for years and had taken to Tahiti. When Lean offered to buy Robert an electric IBM he said no, the manual was like a friend which never broke down. But now, Robert himself had broken down and the machine was almost impossible to operate one-handed. The keys and the carriage return were slow and heavy, and even putting a new sheet of paper into the machine required considerable dexterity. The old thing simply had to go. To replace it he bought an electric Olivetti called an Olityper, an early version of a word processor which could paste and correct sections of text, and printed automatically from a cassette of paper. By today's standards the machine was primitive, but for Robert in 1981 it was a godsend.

The second thing he did was to ask Julie Laird to help him write his scripts. Julie said:

Robert wanted to work again and that was crucial. As he didn't want the world to know how bad he was, we threw a protective blanket around him so that people wouldn't know. All his writing, all his spelling mistakes were put right by me. I knew he trusted me and I knew I could do it. As a writer, he always remained in control. Sometimes I might say, 'This seems a bit underwritten' or, 'I don't like that character' and he'd say,

'You're not seeing it in a picture.' He always wrote in a visual way.

We'd meet regularly. He loved coming up to London for lunch, first at Meridiana and then at Bibendum. He'd hire a car and driver, have a sherry before lunch, a bottle of house wine and then the best brandy available. He hated people who only drank water, so I had to share the brandy with him and then go back to work at the V&A. He'd go back to the car and fall asleep.

You could never buy him lunch. He thought he had a lot of money. At least, he needed to think he had a lot of money. So he always insisted on paying and not only that, he wanted to pay me for the time I spent having lunch with him. Of course, I never let him do that.[1]

It would be wrong to say that Robert's scripts were 'ghosted' by Julie Laird. She was his friend, confidante, researcher, script polisher and his Thesaurus. And working on the story of William Bligh and Fletcher Christian was just like old times.

After Robert suffered his stroke David Lean had returned to London and engaged Melvyn Bragg to complete the second screenplay, *The Long Arm*. But that partnership soon failed and Lean's attempts to finance the film – at United Artists, at Warner Bros again and with Sam Spiegel – failed also. With great reluctance and with even greater sadness, Lean finally admitted defeat. Lean and Sandy packed up their suite at the Beachcomber in Tahiti, collected their two Rolls-Royces in Los Angeles, drove across America, put the cars aboard the *QE2* and settled into the Berkeley Hotel in London. Almost immediately, Lean committed himself to making a film of E. M. Forster's *A Passage to India*.

Dino De Laurentiis, meanwhile, owned Robert's screenplays and also the ship which was dry-docked in New Zealand. The project would have died were it not for Bernie Williams.

I felt a commitment to get the *Bounty* made and when Lean went I felt everything had been wasted. Robert Bolt had had a stroke and been left paralysed, the ship had been built . . . and we were just going to let all this slip by the wayside? It just seemed wrong. Dino wanted the ship to be burned.

I was producing films for him but I fell out with Dino over *Ragtime* and went my own way. But then Dino called me and said he wanted me to move to New York and become his Vice President in charge of all his films. I didn't want to move to New York and he said, 'Bernie, you move to New York and you'll be a big fish in a small pool and in Los Angeles you're just a small fish in a big piece of shit.' So I said there was just one movie I wanted to make and that was *The Bounty*. He said I only wanted to make it because I was British but I said, no, it's a universal drama and this is a beautifully written script. He said okay as long as I helped him with his other movies.

I had lunch with Robert in London and he gave me his pledge that he would help me get these movies made. It was the first time I saw him after his stroke and it was very hard for me to carry on as if nothing had happened, which is what he wanted. I told him that I would always say when I didn't understand him. And he said, 'I prefer that because most people just let me talk and they don't understand a fucking thing I'm saying. They treat me like I'm a cabbage. The brain is still here, Bernie, it's as good as it's ever been. My outward appearance lets me down. People think I'm some kind of vegetable and should be put in a home.' I thought that was sad but human nature is that way. People would listen to him and say yeah, yeah, yeah, you want four pints of milk when he really wanted a beer.[2]

Robert and Ann flew to New York and stayed at the Carlyle. De Laurentiis had always liked Robert and as a producer he knew that the writer was often more important than the director. Having out-manoeuvred Lean, and having replaced Robert Altman and Nicolas Roeg on *Ragtime* and *Flash Gordon*, De Laurentiis was accustomed to seeing the freshly severed head of a director on his gleaming desk every morning. He satisfied himself that Robert was capable of working and a new contract was drawn up.

Since the original plan to make two films was still out of the question, Robert wrote a new treatment which sketched in the crucial events leading up to the mutiny and emphasised the search for the mutineers and the carnage on Pitcairn Island, the aspects of the story which had never been filmed before and which had attracted him to it in the first place. The original opening, in which Captain Edwards attends the play, *Pirates*, was retained, as was much of the intricate flashback structure. Robert's treatment, which he called *Pitcairn Island*, produced an extraordinary telex from De Laurentiis:

I am very pleased to work with you again. Regarding revisions here are my feelings:
  1   We must reduce the script to 100 pages . . .
  2   The first 26 pages should be cut and a new opening

written.
3   Bligh's trip should be shortened.
4   Reduce and shorten any scenes you see fit.
5   Invent a new ending.[3]

Keeping his dismay to himself, Robert was about to make his Olityper administer the electronic axe when De Laurentiis's backers, Paramount Pictures, had a brainwave: why not film the whole story, the original two films, as a mini-series for television? The Paramount executives had seen how productions such as *Roots* and *The Thorn Birds* had opened up a whole new market, generating massive audiences and advertising revenue by stretching a single story over six or eight hours and as many weeks. 'So we worked with the mini-series idea, which I hated,' said Williams who saw the film as Lean and Robert had always envisaged it, as a big-screen spectacle. 'Robert reworked his screenplays into eight episodes. Then after a year Paramount dropped it because they thought it wouldn't get any ratings with women. That pissed me off because Robert had worked so hard on it. And Dino was really pissed off.'

But the project had developed a momentum of its own, there were too many people committed to it and De Laurentiis had already spent too much money to stop it. Robert was now prevailed upon to convert what had become an eight-hour mini-series into a two-hour movie called *The Saga of HMS Bounty*.

Robert's script was far too long so we had to keep rewriting it [said Williams]. Then I got involved with a director called Alan Bridges and went all round the Pacific with him. We went to Fiji and the Cook Islands, then down to Australia and New Zealand, and back to Tahiti. One night he got drunk and starts saying, 'the movie I'm going to make . . .' I thought, the movie *you're* going to make? No, the movie *we're* going to make. Then he goes on, 'Bligh and Christian were obviously gay and had a falling out.' I said, 'Beg pardon? Is that you how see it?' He said, 'Well, yes.' So I said, 'Right, you're fired and when you're sober in the morning I'll tell you again.' I hadn't spent four years of my life trying to make a film about two gay guys on the high seas. Alan was outraged and said I couldn't fire him. So I called Dino and he went, 'What? He wants to make a picture about two fag men? I don't understand this stupid director! I fire him!' I said I already fired him. Dino says, 'I want to fire him again!' So Alan Bridges was fired again.[4]

De Laurentiis started to look for another director. He offered it to

Hugh Hudson, who was already committed to *Greystoke*, then to Michael Cimino, whose lavish Western, *Heaven's Gate*, had flopped spectacularly, bringing down with it United Artists, whose management team had turned down Lean's *Bounty* in favour of Cimino's project. Cimino agreed to direct *The Bounty* on the condition that he could sail the replica around Cape Horn.

> Then Dino offered it to Richard Attenborough who wanted two and a half million dollars [said Williams]. Eventually it gets to Lindsay Anderson who just made a movie called *Britannia Hospital* which I thought was sick but Dino figured that Anderson was British and could make *The Bounty*. Then Dino offers it to Roger Donaldson, a New Zealander who was under contract to make the second *Conan* movie. Donaldson was not a particularly well-educated man, he didn't really like the Brits and he brings in this actor called Ian Mune. Roger said Ian was going to rewrite Robert's script. I thought, *Ian Mune* is going to rewrite *Robert Bolt*?
>
> Robert is still doing rewrites but at one point he came to me and said, 'You know what Bernie? I've fallen out of love with something I loved very much. I cannot write any more. I am so sorry. I have to back off now, thank you so much, you'll always have my support.' I felt really sad.[5]

It says a great deal about Robert's stamina and his newly acquired patience that he could work so hard on a project which held so many painful memories for him. Robert's herculean effort is all the more remarkable when set beside the tragedy which befell him and his extended family in March 1982, right in the middle of his work on the picture.

Of all Robert's children, Sally appears to have been the brightest and the wittiest. By all accounts her paintings and embroideries were outstanding, and her surviving letters to Robert are marvellous to read – touching, richly descriptive and with the sort of sardonic perspective on everyday life that one relishes in the work of, say, Alan Bennett. She could have written the most wonderful comedies for television. Here she is on the charms of Tahiti: 'Do you know, Papeete (for my money) is as enticing as Bournemouth. Except Bournemouth has the edge in that you can get a fast train out of there.'

And on the qualities of January and Doris Lessing:

The weather is disgusting. I see no point in it at all. Dunno that God is Dead, necessarily. Probably gone to Khartoum with John Gielgud and the British Isles have slipped his mind. That's how you feel in January. Forgotten.

You ask what one's impressions are of the situation here. Practically none at all. I'd guess you're possibly not a huge fan of Doris Lessing – I'm getting to be. Anyway, have you read *Memoirs of a Survivor*? Come to think of it, here's a copy. I reckon she hits the nail on the head about political and social disintegration (and I reckon she does it compassionately even if she is a commy bastard!).

In another letter she writes of her ideal man: 'The mental and spiritual qualities of Francis of Assisi, Samuel Beckett, L Van Der Post, Benn Levy, Sir Walter Raleigh. The physical attributes of the young Marlon Brando and/or Apollo, and whoever wrote the Kama Sutra.'[6]

But beneath the banter and the bulletins on motherhood was a woman in obvious torment and there were at least two intimations of the tragedy which lay ahead. In December 1978 she wrote to Robert in Tahiti about her fear of being sexually frigid with a new boy-friend, knowing that Robert himself would understand 'what a nightmare it's been and that I believed it would never ever go away.' But having successfully overcome that fear, she still wrote about her sense of failure and entrapment: 'I'm getting a real taste for going out. Doesn't happen much what with baby-sitting problems, but I make the best of it. Once or twice I've seized up completely and sat speechless and paralysed in a corner. Not so terrible in itself except there's no way I can do it and not leave a severe dent on the atmosphere. It's dreadful when it happens and I wish myself dead.'[7]

A few years later she ended another letter with a poem:

> Back to the delights of soiled nappies
> And early to bed
> early to rise
> makes for a mother's
> untimely demise.
> Har. Har.

Robert always worried about Sally and even though he was initially thrilled to see her when she visited him in Tahiti, her departure left him with mixed emotions. Sally had gone to Tahiti not only because she wanted to show off her daughter, Rosie, she also wanted Robert's love and understanding since she had recently separated from her husband, Neil Simmons. But Robert found Sally's emotional appeals strangely repellent. 'As babies go,' he wrote from Tahiti, 'Rosie well above average. But Sally is impermissably absorbed in her, to Sally's detriment. And as a topic of conversation the alimentary and excretory rhythms of young mamalia are, though undoubtedly important, insufficient. . . . I know that Sal is dangerously and poignantly dissatisfied but she gives no hint as to what appetites are being denied. There's something simultaneously poignant and unreal about her just now which is unsurprising but terribly wearing. A bit parasitic to be blunt.'[8]

Two weeks later, Robert was still perplexed by Sally's visit: 'Sal was here, as you know,' he wrote. 'I found it odd and a bit depressing. . . she is as critical of other people and as little critical of herself as ever. I think she is pitifully frightened and lacking in confidence, but she won't let herself look at that. I tried to avoid deep discussion – having nothing at all deep to say – and concentrated upon severe practicalities. Thus I pointed out that if she were going to be a painter it would be necessary to obtain paint and paper and apply the one to the other with some regularity. And so on.'[9]

On Monday, 9 March 1982 Robert learned that Sally was dead. She was thirty-one years old.

Sally had married Neil Simmons in 1972 and Rosie was born five years later. In April 1978 Sally and Neil separated, though they started living together again eighteen months later. It seems that one of the reasons for the separation was Sally's suspicion that Neil was continuing to have an affair with a former girl-friend, who happened to be Ann Queensberry's daughter, Emma. Convincing herself that this rumour was true, Sally wrote to Robert to tell him and with characteristic humour said that Emma had been struck off her Christmas card list.

As a teenager, Sally had seemed listless. Robert had got her a place at Cambridge Technical College, where his brother Sydney ran the English Department and she had jumped for joy, then refused to go there, preferring an art school, from which she dropped out six months later. When she decided she wanted to go to India for six months and just bum around, Jo Riddett insisted she went as a volunteer worker.

Sally seemed to exist in a sort of isolation ward: her father had married someone virtually her own age; her mother had the love and security of Gordon Riddett; Ben was the son, which always carries privileges, and Joanna was the youngest, which involves different perks. But perhaps the crucial element in Sally's insecurity was her belief that she was the reason for her parents' marriage and, by extension, their divorce. Nothing Jo Riddett or Robert did was enough to convince Sally that she was ever anything less than a fly in the ointment.

At the time of her death Sally was having trouble completing the illustrations for a children's book she had written, a tale about a witch and a cat. On that fateful Sunday, 8 March, Sally and Neil had entertained a friend to lunch. After the friend had gone, Sally and Neil had had an argument and at 5.30 p.m. Sally left the house and went up the road to an off-licence called the Bottle and Basket which was managed by a friend of hers, Simon O'Connell, who lived above the shop with his wife. Also at the off-licence was another friend, a freelance writer named Dave Smith, who was a former manager of the Bottle and Basket.

Sally stayed at the off-licence until 1.40 a.m., drinking beer and whisky, chatting and playing backgammon. When she left she was very drunk. Dave Smith asked her where she was going. 'I'm going to kill myself,' she said. She returned home, went straight to the bathroom, passed Neil who was in the kitchen, and moments later left the house and drove away. Then Dave Smith arrived to tell Neil that he was worried about Sally. Both men went out immediately and started to look for her.

Sally had a blood alcohol level four times the legal limit for driving. She took Neil's car, a white Citroën CX2400, and drove the few hundred yards to Putney Embankment, a quiet road which begins at Putney Bridge, heads west and ends at a pedestrian footbridge marked by two squat ornamental columns on the pavement. At approximately 2 a.m. Sally's car crashed head-on into one of these columns. Ten minutes later a minicab driver spotted the wreck and called the emergency services from a phone box. Sally was pronounced dead on arrival at Queen Mary's Hospital in Roehampton.

It was a cold night and the Citroën's windscreen was frosted over. The police found evidence that Sally had tried to remove the frost with the windscreen wipers, though her visibility would still have been severely impaired. By using established mathematical and geometric formulae, the police estimated that Sally's car would have been travelling at a minimum speed of thirty-two miles per hour. She was not wearing a seat-belt and her internal injuries were in accordance with someone who had been propelled by the impact into the steering wheel.[10]

The site of the crash was not only within 100 yards of Ann Queensberry's house in Ashlone Road, it was also diametrically across the river from the entrance to Doneraile Street.

Although the accident was reported on the front page of the *Putney Chronicle*, no journalist ever made the connection between Sally Simmons and her famous father. That was perhaps the only blessing in the catastrophe.

The inquest was held on 11 May 1982 when the Coroner, Dr Paul Knapman, recorded an open verdict because the cause of the accident was unclear. However bizarre the circumstances – Sally's drunkenness, the iced windscreen, the slow speed of the car – Robert was convinced that Sally had ended her own life. 'I think the notion of her having *chosen* to be killed gave Dad a tiny degree of comfort,' said Ben. 'What he couldn't bear was the notion of her death being so completely arbitrary and pointless.'[11]

'I don't think she killed herself,' said Tor. 'I think she just drove down the towpath and crashed into the iron bridge. We had walked there together a hundred times.'[12]

Sally's ashes were scattered on Glastonbury Tor, that ancient funeral mound which overlooks the Somerset levels, so close to Butleigh and a vanished age of Robert's youthful ambition and idealism. Every year Jo and Joanna make a pilgrimage there, though Robert, after accompanying them on a few occasions, did not do so in future: 'I don't go to Glastonbury Tor on Sally's death,' he wrote, some time later. 'It is too far perhaps. It is good, but I don't like this making of it a day to be remembered with gloom.'[13]

Years before, in a television interview recorded in 1965 just after his divorce from Jo, Robert was asked by Malcolm Muggeridge if he loved children. 'Love them, yes,' he said. 'But I don't like them and I don't think I'm very good with them.'[14] He knew that as a father he had been a failure, absent for most of the time and perhaps too reliant on the cushion he had provided for them by way of the royalties from *A Man For All Seasons*. The trust would make sure that they were all right, even if Robert himself failed to see that this was far from being the case.

Tom in particular made him despair. He had been kicked around from pillar to post all his life, and worse was yet to come, but the boy's unceasing love for his father sometimes went unreciprocated. If Robert had grown closer to Tom when they lived together in Devon, Tom's brief stay in Bora Bora made Robert seem cynical and uncaring: 'He attended the village school at Bora Bora but instruction was rendered in French and Tahitian, of both which languages he has little command. So, what with his blue eyes and white hair and all, he became an object of awe, pity and admiration – three modes well calculated to bring out the worst in him. Now he is attending Port Regis school in Shaftesbury with a view to Bryanston. But I understand that Bryanston only accepts children able to read and write and count their fingers so perhaps the poor little sod will end up at Millfield. . . He really has had a very rough ride.'[15]

While Robert could be rather brisk, even brutal, with his own children, he doted on the children of his friends and liked to spend hours with students, predominantly American, who wrote to him for advice or were writing theses about the British theatre in general, or Robert's plays in particular. These students were bright, they were not his responsibility and, most important, they flattered him.

All Robert's children wanted to live up to him, not because he was a famous writer but because he was their father. 'It would have been the same if he'd been a button manufacturer,' said Ben. But their wish to please him even extended to their writing letters with sections composed as plays, complete with characters, dialogue and stage directions. In this way they abstracted their own problems and confessions into imaginary dramas.

Ben was determined to become a film director and, indeed, he quickly became one, following studies at the National Film School. But it has been a difficult process for him. After directing many distinguished dramas and documentaries for British television he moved to Hollywood and worked on the hit TV show *Hill Street Blues*. He looked like being on the verge of a major breakthrough in 1986 when David Puttnam, recently appointed Chairman and Chief Executive Officer at Columbia Pictures, hired him to direct a film called *The Big Town*, starring Matt Dillon and set in Fifties Chicago. The original director, Harold Becker, had left the project after three days' shooting and Ben was not only required to pick up the pieces, but also expected to make an authentic slice of Americana without having had much experience of America.

He had, too, to endure a sceptical producer, the veteran Martin Ransohoff, as well as Ray Stark, and the hostility of American reporters, who were determined to ridicule Puttnam and bring his controversial regime to an end. Puttnam had arrived at Columbia noisily condemning the profligacy and cronyism of Hollywood, and quickly set about slashing budgets and hiring all his old buddies from Britain. Despite some good reviews, *The Big Town* was a disaster at the box-office, though Puttnam subsequently gave Ben a 'first look' deal at Columbia which lasted until Puttnam's reign came to an abrupt end. Badly bruised by his experience, Ben returned to England and has made many fine television dramas but not, as yet, a second feature film.

By the age of twenty, Joanna had become a bit of a recluse, seemingly consumed by anomie and, in recent years, suffering from ME. She worked briefly for the theatre bookshop, Samuel French, then quit out of boredom. A plan to move to a kibbutz in Israel was foiled by a Middle East war after which, with the help of Bernard McCabe, she enlisted at Drew University in New Jersey, studying philosophy and history. The courses bored her and she felt homesick, which prompted her return to England and unpaid work for Amnesty International. In 1988 Robert wrote to her:

I have been thinking of you and wondering what the future holds for you. I can't control the future but I do bear a certain responsibility for the past. Tom said, quite passionately, words to the effect that 'Don't withdraw your love from me.' I was brought to a halt because I had no idea that I was in danger of giving that impression. Matters were soon made up with Tom but then I began to realise how much pain I must have given you all those years back. Unbearable pain, I think. I slipped out of the door when you weren't looking. I don't know what else I could have done, but I think I know what else a more courageous and quick witted person would have done. Forgive me. I must have given you the impression that pain comes from man, and even from such other circumstances as involve women, so that the only person you can hold on to must be yourself. You are a person that takes everything to their OWN heart, and you keep it there. If I am right, you carry round inside yourself a burden of consciousness of the world's pain. And in your heart you carry round a principal of unworthiness, which takes I think the form of actual physical pain. If I am wrong throw this letter in the waste basket. If I am one third right, think for a minute about it. Nobody has the right to shoulder so much pain. Anyway, forgive me.[16]

'Two good things about *The Bounty*,' said Bernie Williams. 'One was that we were able to invite Robert to Tahiti when we made the film, which he was thrilled about. And when we finished the movie I showed it to him and he said, 'You should never have left Britain because we need producers like you,' which was very nice of him. Robert was pleased with the film and liked it enough to say that he would support me in every way to make Part Two.'[17]

The Bounty is by far the best picture yet made on the subject, despite one grotesque historical distortion, devised by Roger Donaldson and Ian Mune, which suggests the mutiny occurred because of Bligh's determination to make a second attempt to round Cape Horn. But Williams and Donaldson created an exceptional portrait of British mercantile expansion in the South Pacific and they assembled a particularly impressive cast in Anthony Hopkins, Mel Gibson, Liam Neeson, Daniel Day-Lewis and Laurence Olivier. But the critics were kind rather than enthusiastic and the picture was a box-office failure, vindicating the original concerns of Warner Bros and De Laurentiis so many years before.

When he saw the finished picture, Robert was so impressed by Anthony Hopkins's performance as Bligh that he hoped to persuade him to play Sir Thomas More in a projected stage revival of *A Man For All Seasons*. But watching the picture, Robert would also have been thrilled by one shot above all others: against the grey-blue dawn of the South Pacific were the words 'Screenplay by Robert Bolt.' It was the first time that his name had appeared on the screen since *Lady Caroline Lamb* more than ten years earlier. He also knew that his name would appear again in two years' time, as the writer of *The Mission*, another project from the past which had begun to breathe again.

TWENTY-SIX

LEAVING HOME

'All unhappy families resemble one another, but each unhappy family is unhappy in its own way.'

Leo Tolstoy

Val Eaton Griffith's experience with Roald Dahl and others had proved to her that a stroke in the family often destroys that family, or at least the principal partnership between man and wife. 'Ann was so nice and so caring,' she said, 'but to me she was quite exceptionally jumpy and nervy. The thought did flit through my mind that a man in Bob's condition did not need a jumpy wife and when I heard they had parted I wasn't too surprised.'[1]

All was not well between Robert and Ann. While she had to tread the difficult path of being both a wife and a nurse, Robert resented being treated like an invalid. Ann's solution to the problem was to try to be patient, bury her own hurt and not complain. Robert's was to bury himself in work for four or five hours every morning and go out as often as possible, leaving Ann behind at home, wondering whom he was seeing. And when he got back he would go to bed or pass out in front of the television.

Sometimes he would take himself off to Dartmoor. If it was warm he would stay with the Salmons, who lived right on top of the moor, if cold he would stay with Mary Wesley, whose home in Totnes was centrally heated. She said:

He'd ring up and ask to stay for two nights and he'd stay for about twelve. He'd always bring his work with him and work all morning. Then he'd expect to be entertained and taken out and about.

To my mind, he had become a much nicer person. Before he

had his stroke he loved to talk, always held the floor, but now he had to listen. He became extremely benign, patient and compassionate. He wanted to know the whole story of my life so I told him things I wouldn't want anyone to know. I thought, meanly enough, that he would not be able to repeat them to anyone else. He was also interested in anyone who had a spiritual life because he was a non-believer. I think he rather envied me my faith.[2]

When Robert was in London he would lunch out almost every day of the week, invariably with women. Some, like Julie Laird, combined business with pleasure. Others were simply friends, like Charlotte Taylor, who was now Lady St Johnston, having married Sir Kerry St Johnston, the head of P&O. 'Robert had this monstrous army of women who loved him,' said Charlotte. 'Not for romance . . . he was just this dear man. He had a magnetism and he had to have people around him. So he'd come down for weekends with us and we'd have lunch in London once a week. Ann Queensberry could not have been anything but jealous.'[3]

At this time an old friend came back into Robert's life. Naomi Keanie, then Naomi Kellaway, was now Mrs Naomi May and she lived in Kew. A friend of hers had a house in Hartington Road and when she went to visit, Naomi was told of her friend's new and famous neighbour. Deciding to risk a rebuff, she wrote and asked him how he was, how his work was going and whether he was happy with Ann.

'Good God, what a surprise,' replied Robert. 'Regarding my rebirth to work that progresses satisfactorilly (apart from the spelling which is a bad as so see). The marriage is all marriages seem to me, part good part bad. Do lets meet in a little while – yes?'[4] They met about three weeks later for lunch at a local restaurant, Jasper's Oven on Kew Green.

> From then on [said Naomi], it was like the beginning, except there were no complications and we were both antique by then. There was the same warmth and attachment and the same freedom of being able to talk about everything under the sun. When I asked him about Ann he said, 'She's a very decent woman' and I thought, oh God. But when she came to our house later on I was astounded. I expected someone rather four-square but she was rather delicate.
>
> Bob and I had lunch at Jasper's once a fortnight. That was rather amusing because the waiters quickly knew who they'd got

and they fawned all over him. And Bob of course would shit all over them in return. He used to turn up looking like a tramp. He was in a miserable condition. He was paralysed all down his right side and his speech was atrocious but he had great willpower and every afternoon he went for speech therapy which he found gruellingly boring but he never missed it.

Talking with him and being with him in public was very difficult. A waiter would come over and ask us if we wanted drinks. Bob would say something which the waiter couldn't understand and then he'd say, 'Fuck it, stupid, fuck it, stupid, fuck it.' I never knew at which point I should translate and say, 'A gin and tonic.' Then he'd take his napkin and blow his nose on it.

He was obviously unhappy and very lonely. He said the stroke was a worldly lesson to him, that when you weep you weep alone, that the world had crawled to him and suddenly you were left alone. He said that the people he thought would stand by him didn't, and David Lean was one. They just didn't see him for dust. He also said that he was happy that he'd had the stroke. Naturally, I was shocked by this and when I asked him why he said, 'Because I had gone to ashes inside.'

He also had a kind of religious quest which was never satisfied except when he had his stroke. He told me he thought he was going to die, that he wanted to die, until he saw Ben by his bedside. He said that when he saw Ben he thought, 'I must fight this, I must live.' He told me that during that month he had a total belief in God and this was wonderful, lovely, though it didn't last. He also said to me, 'I have forgiven myself for Sally's death.' He couldn't let that haunt him. If he did, it would have destroyed him.[5]

One day, another old friend, Frith Banbury, dropped by. Banbury had just turned seventy and didn't look a day over fifty.

Ann Queensberry was working with Wendy Hiller [said Banbury] and knowing that Wendy was in the American production of *Flowering Cherry* she invited her to lunch in Chiswick. Wendy called me and asked me to accompany her.

I was warned how handicapped he was and was prepared to be shocked. And I was shocked. He had to have his food cut up for him and he couldn't finish a sentence. I longed to discuss the things we used to discuss and I wanted to ask him what he now felt about Sam Spiegel's yacht. But it was impossible to have a real conversation with him. He was like a ghost.

A little while later, Banbury received an invitation from Robert to dinner at Hartington Road: 'I remember the letter was addressed to "Banbury Frith" and for some reason, perhaps I was in America, I didn't see it for some time. When I rang, the person who answered the phone said he was a decorator and that the house was empty. I thought this was extraordinary, very peculiar, so I called Peggy Ramsay. She said, "He's left her my dear! He's living in Battersea." I said he couldn't have left Ann. She said, "Well, that's how it is, dear. He can't stand domesticity." '6

Another guest at Hartington Road was Kenneth Jupp, who was immediately struck by the tense atmosphere: 'I'd known Ann Queensberry since I was a student,' he said. 'Ann truly adored him. I was delighted when they got married because they were two of my favourite people. Then I had dinner at Hartington Road and the vibes were terrible, terrible. I really couldn't understand why. When I learned the marriage was over, Debbie called and said, "Only Robert could leave a woman in his condition." Here was this guy who could hardly speak, hardly walk, and he was leaving this woman! Most men would have been delighted to have someone like Ann to look after them.'7

No one has any doubt that Robert and Ann had a deep love for each other which stretched back many years, though people wondered if Robert had married her out of a sense of gratitude. In some ways their families were too large, and their histories too intertwined – so many wives, so many daughters and step-daughters, so many problems. Perhaps David Lean had a point: cutting people out of your life, as he did, simplified things. But Robert never did this. Even if he revelled in his position as a somewhat Tolstoyan figure, the centre of the universe for children, step-children and grandchildren, all in some ways dependent on him while he was dependent on them, he also found it stifling and emotionally draining.

Without telling Ann, Robert made his plans for leaving her. He went to see a flat in Battersea and he arranged for an estate agent to value the house in Hartington Road. And he also went to see Mary Wesley in Devon:

> I asked him, 'What's the marriage like, Robert? How are you getting on with Ann?' He said, 'She's a termagant.' I didn't know Ann but I'd heard she was a sweet and charming person. He said, 'No, no, no. Do you know a good solicitor?' I said,

'Yes, Robert, I do, but I'm not giving you his name.' He said, 'Ring him up, ring him up!' He obviously wanted a divorce. So I said, 'Well, if I ring him up, promise me you won't complain to me that he cost you an arm and a leg.' I picked up the phone, made an appointment and within three months he had his divorce. And he did write to me and complain about the cost.[8]

Ann said:

I think he resented me. I remember a real warning bell. Bob's doctor rang me and said that Bob had told him how nice it was to have someone who worried about him. I was amazed that the doctor would have thought for a moment that I didn't care.

From having this close, close friendship for so long, it changed. It was shattering. I remember Roald Dahl telling me that it was important that I didn't do therapy with Bob because he would resent it much more. I also felt that he and Tom were ganging up on me. When Tom was on his own with me he was very lonely and obviously I was very close to him. I really loved him. But it was different when his father was there and I felt that Bob would pander to this.

I found a therapist for Tom, who was really disturbed. The therapist said she wanted Bob and Sarah to attend the next session, which they did, while I sat outside. The therapist then said that Tom would be leaving to live with Sarah and Bob went with them to have tea. It was absolutely shattering. That night he was very miserable. He said, 'I've lost my daughter and now I've lost my son.' I began to think then that Sarah wanted him back. It wasn't a concrete thought, it just went through my mind. There was nothing I could do about it.

In the late summer of 1983, three years after they were married, Ann went to France to attend to her house, but was called back unexpectedly when her foster-son got into some trouble with the police. 'Bob was very sweet that night,' she said. 'He held my hand and said, "This marriage isn't working. I want a divorce." I said, "Well, do what you want." There were no great discussions about it.'[9]

'Mum called me to say they were splitting up,' said Tor Douglas. 'She was so tired, so tired. She had worked so hard looking after Bob and making Hartington Road beautiful for him. It was hard work because he was so irascible. It was an endless round of speech therapy and hospitals. He didn't mind so much not being able to move, it was being unable to speak and be understood. He used words like, "Pass the dinosaur" when he meant "Pass the milk." And he'd get crosser and crosser if you didn't get it. Mum had to cope with all that for years.'[10]

'Looking back,' said Ann, 'I wonder why I didn't fight. I really wanted him to do whatever made him happy. Whether it did or not, I don't know. The whole point of my life was getting Bob better again and writing again.'

When Robert walked out on Ann Queensberry he allowed himself to come under the influence of a man, an uncharacteristic step for someone who habitually surrounded himself by women.

Anthony Tancred was unusually tall and handsome, a man with film star looks and charm. Robert had known him, off and on, for years. Tancred had been at school with David Queensberry, he was Tor's godfather and he had drifted through life, always dabbling in new schemes, none of which ever made him rich. It was Tancred and his girl-friend Penny who became Robert's resident domestic staff and business advisers.

Within weeks of moving in with the Tancreds, Robert had changed his doctor, accountant and lawyer. Another casualty was Gillian Harrison, who was suddenly given the sack after more than ten years of devoted service. It was Gillian who had had to deal with much of the aftermath of the David Whiting affair; she had been Robert's principal contact between Tahiti and London and she had handled his legal and financial affairs, as well as his family problems, with remarkable skill and discretion. Robert's dismissal of her was as abrupt as it was untypical. People were shocked by Gillian's sad experience and they began to feel deeply concerned for Robert's well being. Ann said:

> I'd known Anthony Tancred since I was seventeen. He was six feet four and immensely good-looking. When Dave left me he was wonderful, a tremendous friend. Later, he was into faith healers and religious cults, and he once tried to get my daughter Alice involved. But I refused to let her go. He and his girl-friend, Penny, who was much younger, were very good cooks and they started a hotel near Bracknell. Occasionally, when we had the builders in, Bob used to go and stay with them. Then I heard that Sarah wanted to stay with them, which I thought was a terrible idea.
>
> Anthony had done the catering for our wedding. One day he

said to me, 'How much would you leave Bob for?' And I said, 'I would never leave him.' So he said, 'What about him leaving you?' Anthony had got Bob to buy a flat in Battersea before we split up and Bob put Hartington Road on the market without telling me. I only found out when an estate agent rang to ask if he could come to value it. So Bob went straight from our house to share the flat with this man. His relationship with Bob always reminded me of that film, *The Servant*. I've not heard from Anthony again. It was very weird.[11]

Anthony Tancred's present whereabouts are unknown – some believe he may have died, others that he may be living in Sardinia. While some people refused point blank to talk about him, others spoke of his sinister charm and how he easily exploited Robert's vulnerability. 'Absolute bollocks,' said Ben. 'The Tancreds were as sweet as anything to my father. They took a salary for looking after him as they were not independently wealthy. They all lived in this ghastly tower block in Battersea, so it was pretty isolated. It was a sterile existence for him for a while.'[12]

The flat in Battersea – in Valiant House, Vicarage Crescent – was luxurious and dismal, a high security complex which afforded views of the river as well as the rubbish tips on Chelsea Reach. Modern in every respect, it was not the sort of place to find Robert Bolt – a connoisseur of Georgian manses or medieval thatch. And there was no garden or conservatory. For Robert, life in Valiant House with the Tancreds was nothing more than a half-way house, an arid zone between one life and another.

The only way out, it seemed, was to find another woman. Not for the first time, he asked Julie Laird to marry him. 'It was beautifully done,' said Julie. 'He took me to that terrible thing with trains, *Starlight Express*, which he didn't like. We left at the interval and went to dinner at La Poule au Pot. He'd worked it all out and he said that marrying him would save me from the V&A. It was very humbly put and difficult to resist. But I did resist it and said no.'[13]

Another candidate was Kate Ganz, an art historian who was introduced to Robert by Mary Wesley at a dinner party at Valiant House. 'He was desperately lonely and wanted another woman,' said Wesley. 'When he met Kate he was like a pointer who'd spotted a partridge. He didn't talk to me all night. They became great friends and he wanted to marry her but she told me she couldn't dedicate her life to looking after him. It would take a very special person to do that. I think what he really wanted was to get Sarah back.'[14]

TWENTY-SEVEN

AN OLD FLAME

'If this were played upon a stage now, I could condemn it as an improbable fiction.'

William Shakespeare, *Twelfth Night*

After her return to London from California, and following her traumatic incursion into Doneraile Street, Sarah had started to work again. Her reputation in the film industry was low and she was at an age – just past forty – when good roles were hard to come by. She knew that in order to make a living she would have to make some rubbish. Thus she appeared in Michael Winner's remake of *The Big Sleep*, which reunited her with Robert Mitchum and John Mills, and an ophidian thriller called *Venom*. Of a slightly higher order was *Priest of Love*, an account of D. H. Lawrence in New Mexico, directed by her brother Christopher and in some ways a compensation for never making *The Plumed Serpent*. She also did some stage work, appearing as Lady Viola in *Twelfth Night* and as Lady Macbeth for a small theatre company in North London.

Sarah was a changed woman, even though many of Robert's friends still held her in contempt and viewed her return to London with the deepest suspicion. For her part, she had come through the stigma of being accused of David Whiting's murder and had reached what she called 'a new state of self-awareness'. This, she later claimed, began in 1975 when she was on location in Dartmouth, Devon, for *The Sailor Who Fell From Grace With the Sea*. Walking along the quayside one night, a mysterious voice started to whisper to her and when she got back to her rented cottage the voice told her to light a candle, which she did. Then it commanded her to control the flame by willpower, which she did, compelling the flame to flare and gutter. For Sarah, it was a shattering moment. For the rest of us, it may be easy to dismiss as twaddle – perhaps there was a draught coming through the window and she says she hoped there was one, that she searched for one – but Sarah believes it and she lives by the revelation. She hasn't tried the candle trick again, for what is faith other than belief without proof?

The world of meditation beckoned her. 'I just had silence,' she said. 'I saw silence as a friend, not as an enemy.'

She also drank her own urine, a fact first revealed by Robert Mitchum in a press interview which trapped Sarah into admitting it. This was not done in accordance with Gandhi's belief that drinking urine purges the stomach and the soul, but on the advice of her song coach, who said it would improve her voice and cure her allergies. 'He was an extraordinary man, a warlock, who had been coaching Alice Cooper, Bob Dylan and Barbra Streisand as well as me,' she said. 'He took me to this doctor who injected my urine into my bum. I took Tom along as well for the treatment and his asthma attacks vanished. The doctor was eighty but he looked no older than fifty, but because his sessions cost two thousand dollars for an eight-week course I thought, why should I pay him to inject me with my own urine? So I learned how to drink a tiny amount from the mid-flow, twice a day, and I still do it.'

According to Sarah, it was the same music teacher who advised her when she discovered that Tom had started to smoke pot. 'Because I never allowed smoking in the house, Tom started to stay out all night. So my music teacher told me I had to wean Tom off marijuana and the way to do it was to let him smoke it at home, a low power dope, and gradually reduce the amount. So that's what I did.'

As soon as Sarah started to give interviews and publish her memoirs, in which the urine drinking and the event with the candle were revealed, she was typecast as a fruitcake, a description which she resents very much.

Sarah had set up home in Holland Park, a leafy and affluent enclave above Kensington Palace. While Tom was a temporary resident there – he commuted between his father and mother – a young man from Newcastle, Charly Foskett, took up permanent residence. Foskett was an unemployed musician, influencing Tom in music-making. He built a conservatory, then a recording studio in the basement and helped Sarah with her song writing.

When he was married to Ann, Robert often sent Sarah little affectionate notes or called her on the phone. He also visited her regularly, driving across London in his specially adapted Range

Rover. And as his marriage to Ann started to go wrong, he saw more
of her. 'He was obviously unhappy,' said Sarah, 'especially when he
was living in Battersea with Anthony Tancred. He'd come round and
see me so often it seemed like every day. I knew that I could take care
of his needs better than anyone else.'

Robert finally resolved that he wanted Sarah back, had in fact
always wanted her back. People wondered why, after all Sarah had
done to him. But there is only one answer to that: he loved her, and
there was also Tom's topsy-turvy life and dubious future to consider.
As for Sarah, she knew only too well the sacrifices she would have to
make. Robert was an invalid, hardly able to walk, expanding into the
size of Orson Welles, bloody-minded at times and barely able to
speak coherently. Yet there was also a sweetness, a patience, which
was new to her.

Inevitably, there were people who were shocked and appalled by
the news and some of those who had been loyal to Robert and had
given him therapy sessions now slipped away discreetly. Julie Laird,
who had turned down Robert's two proposals of marriage, was one
of the first to know. 'Robert said to me, "I can live with her now
because it's like water off a duck's back. There were dramas and I
used to worry about them but I no longer worry." That must have
been difficult for Sarah because if you have a drama you want
someone to notice.'[1]

Roger and Liza Gard were invited to dinner shortly after Robert
and Sarah got back together again. 'When Sarah came back to him,'
said Liza, 'we had dinner with them on several occasions. Sarah had
always been a fantasy figure for him and after their divorce he'd
convinced himself that the fantasy wasn't good for him. But when
she came back, he was so pleased. He became rejuvenated. I said to
him, "Why did she come back to you?" He said, "I can't understand
it." So I said, "Well, she must really love you." "No, I don't think
so," he said. "I can't imagine why she should. I think it's a new role
for her to play." '

'That's the cynical explanation,' said Roger Gard. 'But Sarah
played that role for so long and with such consistency that she must
have loved him. Whatever one can say about Miss Miles, and
whatever is preposterous about her, she looked after him so well. I
remember at dinner she wouldn't fuss about him but would keep a
sharp eye out to see if he needed anything and then she'd discreetly
get it for him. She never made him feel as if he was being nursed.'[2]

'The man was madly in love with her, in every possible way,' said
Fernando Ghia. 'Even after they separated he would always come to

me and say she was doing this, or writing something and it was terrific. He was always a fan. And when she came back to him, perhaps with a lot of guilt, that was irresistible to him. And I think she was very good for him.'[3]

For Robert's friend in Devon, the novelist Mary Wesley, Sarah had always been:

> a monster in the background. I'd never met her and only knew her by reputation. I'd always got the impression, though, that Robert missed her terribly. Soon after they got back together again, I had lunch with them and thought what an enchanting person she was. Sarah is an original. She's as mad as a hatter who doesn't give a fuck about causing offence.
>
> Robert gobbled you up. He always needed constant attention yet I never saw Sarah lose her patience. She gave him her full attention yet she managed to lead her own life. I couldn't have done it. She'd jolly him along and you could see how happy he was to be with her again.[4]

Robert and Sarah found themselves a fine place to live. Robert had always coveted a house on Chiswick Mall which had belonged to William Morris. It had been owned by Faye Dunaway – who made her stage début in an American production of *A Man For All Seasons* – then by another client of Margaret Ramsay, Christopher Hampton. But Sussex House, just up-river, was almost as good, a four-square Georgian edifice on Upper Mall, Hammersmith. Originally built in the 1720s for the Duke of Sussex, it was later the home of C. S. Forrester. When Robert and Sarah bought it the house belonged to Hugh Hudson who had installed a jacuzzi in the basement. 'It was hilarious when we moved in,' said Sarah. 'Hudson had taken everything away with him. There was literally nothing left in the house, not even a light bulb.'

Sussex House had considerable drawbacks, though. Its view of the river was partially obscured by an olde worlde pub, the Dove, which attracted crowds of boozers throughout the year, some of whom used the high front and side wall of Sussex House as a public urinal. And the rear wall of the house bordered the A4, one of the busiest commuter routes in London. The noise of the four lanes of traffic made sitting in the well-shaded garden an ordeal. A further distraction was that it lay directly beneath the main flight path into Heathrow Airport. But if one shut the doors and closed the windows, Sussex House was a peerless residence on three floors, with vast, high-ceilinged rooms.

One of Sarah's original problems with Robert had been his ceaseless capacity for work, that he would lock himself away in his study for hours on end and not emerge if the very house was burning down around him. Even if he had been writing for her, she had still felt ignored. If Sarah thought that Robert's physical condition had lessened his work load from what she remembered of her time with him at Byfleet, she was in for something of a surprise. He was working as hard as ever, and between 1984 and 1986 he wrote elaborate screenplays about the Florence of Leonardo da Vinci, the Washington of Thomas Jefferson and the birth of the Irish Republican Army. There was also *The Mission*. But first of all there was a screen adaptation of *Twelfth Night* which was to be produced by David Puttnam and directed by the renowned opera director, Elijah Moshinsky. The project spanned the move from Battersea to Sussex House.

By the time he moved to Battersea Robert had got rid of his first word processor, the Olityper, and had bought himself an Apple Macintosh which, in those early days, looked like a prop from *1984*, yet contained every facility a micro-chip could provide. Sitting in his large chair, which was placed on a wooden turntable enabling him to swivel around his U-shaped desk, Robert developed a way of pecking one-fingered at the keyboard, using the computer's word-processing programme to produce many versions of the same scene. When he saw it, Moshinsky was amazed by the technology:

I spent a few days with Robert in Battersea and it was there that I first saw a computer. Everyone has a PC now of course but in those days I thought it was something that had been developed for people with his sort of disability. He would have the most violent arguments with his son, Tom, who would become apoplectic with rage. I was seriously worried but felt it was just part of the intensity in which Robert lived.

I found it difficult to talk with Robert at first, then suddenly it wasn't. He was a brilliant imaginer of scripts and what he wrote was not just an edited version of the play but a real screenplay. He had some terrific ideas and invented some scenes with were suggested in the background of the play.

But sadly no one wanted to make *Twelfth Night*. Even though David Puttnam discovered that no Shakespeare film had ever lost money, no one would finance it because it centres on a female performance which has to be passed off as a man. Now, of course, Kenneth Branagh and everyone else is making Shakespeare films.[5]

Undismayed by the lack of interest in *Twelfth Night*, Robert began work on *The Florentines* for Franco Zeffirelli, who was a Florentine himself: 'I would show just how it was that in one brief moment, at the very start of the Sixteenth Century, a single town could have housed such towering geniuses as Leonardo da Vinci, Michelangelo and Machiavelli. I imagine a film full of the beauty and pageantry of the period, yet also vibrant with the profound cultural ideas which surfaced during that all too fleeting explosion of talent.'[6] Zeffirelli presented Robert with a theme, not a story. After doing his customary research, he came to realise that the Renaissance was just that, a theme, an artistic movement without a story.

Robert's job was to find a story, the arms and the legs, and graft them on like a sculptor and not allow any cracks to show. 'The whole point was the personalities of Michelangelo and Leonrado,' he told Zeffirelli. 'In fact they had nothing much to share between themselves. And nothing to recommend them to the general public, apart from the fact that they were both superlative artists. So the plain tale of Biagio has to carry the main burden of plot. However it has the strength of supporting the principle class divisions of the present day. I have made it and the Medicis very much more important. The tale of Michelangelo and Leonrado I have made hang on the fact that one was on the side of the people; and the other on the side of the Megates, the people who get things done. I hope very much you like what I have done.'[7]

By the time Zeffirelli had studied the preliminary draft of *The Florentines* and failed to raise the finance, Robert was at work on something else: a six-hour television adaptation of Gore Vidal's 1973 novel, *Burr*, which was to be made for Ray Stark's company, Rastar, in Hollywood.

Vidal's novel told a great story. In 1804, when Aaron Burr was Vice-President of the United States, he shot and killed General Alexander Hamilton in a duel and was subsequently indicted for murder. Leaving his Washington career behind him, he raised a small army and tried to force the lands of the Louisiana Purchase to cede from the Union. He was put on trial for treason and narrowly escaped execution because of a legal technicality. After some mysterious activities with the French and the British, he ended his days as a New York lawyer.

Like so many of Robert's major characters – Thomas More, T. E. Lawrence, Lady Caroline Lamb, the *Bounty* mutineers or the missionaries of South America – Burr, with his extraordinary life, allowed for the broadest of brush strokes to evoke the political and philosophical climate of the time. And in the characters of Burr and his President, Thomas Jefferson, Robert also had a story about the foundations of American democracy.

Rastar's original financial offer seemed reasonable until Robert learned how much Frederic Raphael was getting paid by Warner Bros for a mini-series about Napoleon and Josephine. Consequently, Robert upped his asking price, which was quickly accepted. His contract required him to produce a 'bible' – a preliminary break-down of the story divided into episodes – for which he would receive $75,000. After everyone had agreed on the storyline, Robert would be paid $75,000 for each scripted episode. The plan was for three two-hour episodes, netting him a total of $300,000.

Robert managed to deliver his 'bible' to Rastar within the stipulated six weeks, even though during that time he underwent an operation for gallstones. The word back from Rastar was not encouraging. 'There is trouble along the way with *Burr*,' Robert told Margaret Ramsay. 'It appears that the network people, whoever they may be, want me to think of another theme. Needless to say, I shall not do that. And they want me to start with the climax – the killing, in a duel, of General Hamilton! Oh, they are stupid; the whole point of the thing is the special attraction of the extraordinary Burr for the newly formed United States of America.'[8]

Despite his misgivings, Robert went ahead and completed first and second drafts of his three scripts within a year. Although he had had a taste of writing for American television when he converted *The Bounty* into a mini-series, *Burr* brought Robert into contact with the teams of readers, researchers, producers and market research people who analysed every scene for its dramatic impact and, most important, for its impact on ratings. Only the need to work kept Robert going; that and the money. As always, the scripts were thoroughly sub-edited and corrected by Julie Laird.

When it was finally done, Robert wrote Ramsay a letter which is tragically revealing of his condition: 'Dear Peggy, Can you next me how you felt about my *Burr*. I think (apart from the numerous spelling erreros) it stood up well to was a have been doing, prior to the stroke, I mean, but perhaps I am wrong. You tell me. It's not that I shall give up trying but I need to now. Love, Bob.'[9]

To Ben he wrote: 'I have finished Version II of the *Burr* script. The thing is that I can't imagine how I let Version I past my fingers; it seems to me awful. Yet I was proud of it, when I had just finished it. Supposing the same is true of Version II? I seem to have lost my touch entirely, well almost entirely. Never mind, it is either coming back or it isn't.'[10]

As *Burr* fell into limbo, Robert received a call from Barry Spikings who ran EMI in London and had won an Oscar in 1978 for producing Michael Cimino's *The Deer Hunter*. Spikings had a potentially explosive idea, a film biography of Michael Collins, the founder of the Irish Republican Army who was assassinated by fellow Irishmen in 1922. A script, by Owen Harris, had already been written but Spikings, who had brought Cimino in as the director, wanted it rewritten. The picture was to be made on an epic scale, showing the Easter Rising of 1916, when Dublin's city centre became a battleground, as well as the complex series of diplomatic negotiations between Dublin and London. Because the modern IRA's campaign was causing death and destruction in Ulster and on the mainland, any film about Collins would have to tread extremely carefully in its political allegiances. 'I commissioned a script from Robert,' said Spikings. 'He was in recovery, needed every good cheer and was desperate to work. At the same time, I knew that Neil Jordan was working on a rival Collins project so it was a race between us.'

Michael Cimino had just been through the cauterising experience of *Heaven's Gate*, his monumentally ambitious Western which had brought United Artists to its knees. An enigmatic and delicately framed man who habitually wears gleaming cowboy boots, Cimino was a perfectionist who made David Lean seem almost careless by comparison.

The three of them – Spikings, Cimino and Robert – opted for a general approach to Collins's life. They also decided to emphasise one episode in particular, his love affair with Lady Hazel Lavery, a society hostess in London. As Robert, Spikings and Cimino saw it, Winston Churchill persuaded Lady Hazel to host a lavish reception for the Irish-American community, when she would seduce Collins and extract from him all the secrets of the IRA.

> But Collins showed up two hours late [said Spikings]. He arrived and looked across the room at Lavery and immediately fell in love with her. They went to bed that night and she told him she was working for Churchill. Collins's intelligence agents knew all along about Churchill's plan.
>
> Michael Collins dominated a room. He had a very commanding presence, a charisma just like a movie star. So we had a big budget and we wanted a big star. We held talks with

Kevin Costner and Robert Redford, but Liam Neeson always wanted to play it. 'If I don't,' he told me, 'I'll blow you up.'

The film was to have been a co-production between EMI and Columbia in Hollywood which was owned at the time by Coca-Cola. 'Columbia warned Coke that the film might be controversial,' said Spikings, 'and they started to get very nervous. They finally cancelled the production just weeks before we were due to start shooting. We had done recces and had designs done for the sets.'[11]

A few years later David Puttnam, when he was Columbia's CEO, tried to put the rival Neil Jordan script into production but ran into what he called 'a miasma of corporate paranoia. Coca-Cola worried what the effect would be if someone was blown up at their bottling plant in Northern Ireland and they worried even more when a British Army official hinted that if the film was made the army would switch from Coke to Pepsi.'[12]

If Coca Cola's nervousness put paid to both films, Robert's screenplay was never completed to Spikings's and Cimino's satisfaction. 'We never quite got there with Robert's script,' said Spikings.

When the film was cancelled, in late 1985, the rumour mill started in earnest. It was thought that Britain's Prime Minister, Margaret Thatcher, had intervened personally or that Loyalist terror groups had targeted the production. Somehow another rumour started: that the reason for the cancellation was due to Robert being late in his delivery of the screenplay. When this was published in the trade magazine, *Screen International*, Robert sued for libel and eventually won undisclosed damages. A man in his condition could not possibly allow that particular rumour to gain currency in Hollywood. 'Sarah was furious when the film was cancelled because her one concern was Robert's health and his career,' said Spikings. 'But Robert was a very proud and a very professional man. Yes, he was saddened and disappointed when a year's work led to nothing. But he was too proud to have made a big to-do about it.'[13]

To set beside Robert's disappointment over *Twelfth Night, Burr, The Florentines* and *Michael Collins*, came the exciting news that David Puttnam intended to make *The Mission*, which Robert had written for Fernando Ghia some seven years earlier. Much as Robert liked the subject, it was really Ghia's personal project and Robert loyally extended Ghia's option on it annually for a nominal amount. Ghia had hawked it around Hollywood for years without success, even though several directors showed an interest in it, including

George Roy Hill, Sydney Pollack, Franco Zeffirelli, Jack Clayton and Richard Attenborough. 'Finally,' said Ghia, 'that "gentleman" Puttnam approached Robert.'[14]

When David Puttnam decided to make *The Mission* he was still riding high on his Oscar success for *Chariots of Fire* and had just completed *The Killing Fields*, a drama about Pol Pot's genocidal rule of Cambodia. These two films had been partially funded by the British company, Goldcrest, with whom Ghia had been discussing *The Mission*. Puttnam, who was on the board of Goldcrest, knew of these discussions and began to see *The Mission* as the successor to *The Killing Fields*. Instead of approaching Ghia, who owned the project, Puttnam went straight to Robert and secured his agreement that the movie would be made by Goldcrest for Warner Bros. Only then was Ghia brought into the picture. 'Fernando is a very nice man and a complete idiot,' said Puttnam. 'Robert was very loyal to him and confused his friendship with Fernando's extraordinary lack of professional grip. The script had a certain cred to it but I think there was a point where I decided that Fernando was quite ambivalent to it being made. In a strange way, it was his calling card. He owned this Robert Bolt script which could be the greatest film ever made. And once it was made, part of Fernando's *raison d'être* was undercut. He's a very complicated man.'[15]

Ghia said: 'I was speaking to Sandy Lieberson who had just started at Goldcrest. I was planning to make the film with Hugh Hudson as the director. Then Sandy told me about a director I had never heard of, Roland Joffé, who had just finished *The Killing Fields*. The film was three hours and twenty minutes long when I saw it. It was a mess but the shooting was brilliant, I mean, brilliant. I said, yes, I'll go with this guy. So we made a deal.'[16]

Because Puttnam was exhausted by his work on *The Killing Fields*, which had been shot in Thailand, he decided to serve only as executive producer on *The Mission*, acting as the liaison between the production, Goldcrest and Warner Bros. Ghia, who was firmly established as the producer, immediately took Joffé and Iain Smith, the associate producer and another veteran of *The Killing Fields*, on the same tour of South America which Robert had done. Like Robert, Joffé was stunned by the Iguassu Falls and saw its visual potential. However, because the surrounding terrain was unsuitable, the decision was made to film the bulk of the story in Colombia. But the location recce proved to be a disaster. Joffé called Puttnam from Colombia saying he was unable to work with Ghia and that Puttnam should produce it himself. 'So I had to produce it,' said Puttnam, 'which was inconvenient because my daughter was getting married and I had to go to the Tokyo Film Festival. So Sandy Lieberson went to Colombia to cover for me because you couldn't leave Fernando on his own for two weeks. He is honestly the most genuinely incompetent person I have ever worked with, bar none. In fairness to him, he had a bad back and was in a lot of pain. But it was hopeless.'[17]

Ghia totally refutes Puttnam's view of events. 'I wanted to make the film so much,' he said, 'and because I knew that David was instrumental in the making of it, I agreed to withdraw. I was in Colombia for the start of shooting, just observing for about two weeks, and then I took over all the Argentina section, when we shot at Iguassu, because Britain had no relations with Argentina because of the Falklands War.'[18]

There is a theory, endorsed by Ghia, that Puttnam was not so much a cavalryman riding heroically to the rescue, as a man ruthlessly pursuing his own private agenda: by hijacking the film from Ghia, Puttnam could produce another potential Oscar winner and further his career. And produce it he did, sidelining Ghia and running the risk of alienating Robert. As for Ghia, he was trying to retain what he legitimately regarded as his moral rights over the project. He was also attempting to restrain Joffé from altering the script. 'Since Robert could not take meetings,' said Ghia, 'I was facing Roland who started to come up with some funny ideas. Now, Roland is great visually but his writing is terrible. The original screenplay provided two characters, the Jesuit priest, Gabriel, and the slave trader, Mendoza, who had killed his brother in a duel. The priest was a seventy year-old man, physically weak but with fantastic strength inside. Roland changed this to a younger man, so that Gabriel and Mendoza became like brothers. But Robert's script was about a father and son.'

In Robert's original screenplay there was a major scene between Gabriel and Mendoza, when the priest persuades the slave trader to lay down his sword and perform a penance for murdering his brother. It was a scene which crystallised the relationship between the man of the spirit and the man of the sword, recalling the debates about conscience in *A Man For All Seasons*. There are also echoes of *Lawrence of Arabia* in which the diplomat, Dryden, and General Allenby lay siege to Lawrence's soul, and further echoes of the scene in which Lawrence tells Allenby that he executed a man and enjoyed it. The scene from *The Mission* is published here for the first time:

Inside the spartan little cell MENDOZA lies on a spartan little cot. He is pale, unshaven, dirty and dull-eyed, a man (as we would say) in deep depression. His soiled shirt, still stained with his brother's blood, hangs out of his breeches.

GABRIEL goes into the cell. He is carrying MENDOZA's sword and scabbard. He sits in the only chair. MENDOZA is looking at the sword.

> GABRIEL
>
> Remorse?

MENDOZA looks at him resentfully, then looks away wearily.

> GABRIEL
>
> No, no remorse. Remorse makes people
> modest. And modest people are polite.

He gets up and goes to examine a dark little religious picture with an affectation of great interest, changing his spectacles from a soft leather pouch to do so. He rattles on, knowing that he has begun to catch MENDOZA's interest.

> And then of course, if you were remorseful,
> God would have forgiven you by now. And
> he hasn't, has he?

MENDOZA mutters something behind his back, inaudible. He turns from the picture.

> GABRIEL
>
> What?

> MENDOZA
> repeats, loudly
>
> I don't know!

> GABRIEL
> (cheerfully)
> Well you would if he had.

He returns to his seat.

MENDOZA looks at him, sits up and: Father, not to have done it, I would cut off both my hands.

He says it steadily, carefully, looking at his powerful wrists and meaning it. But:

GABRIEL
That's not remorse; that's just regret.

MENDOZA frowns; he can make nothing of it; shakes his head irritably.

GABRIEL
A lecherous husband regrets that he married. A banker regrets that he made a bad bargain. Regret is regret for the consequence; remorse is regret for the thing itself.

MENDOZA is listening intently, his eyes uneasy.

GABRIEL
(gently but firmly, breaking bad news):
And to be as good at anything as you appear to be at killing, my son, I'm afraid you have to enjoy it.

MENDOZA
(incredulous and horrified)
What?

GABRIEL
Do you know anyone who's really good at a thing he doesn't enjoy doing?

MENDOZA
thinks about this and then looks up and
Father, are you telling me that I'm a monster?

GABRIEL
No. No that's what you're telling yourself I think. But are you telling me that in the actual moment – not afterwards, mind, but in the moment – you can run a man through from front to back, with regret?

BIG CLOSE Mendoza. He opens his mouth to expostulate but, sharply:

GABRIEL
Think!

BIG CLOSE MENDOZA.

GABRIEL

SOUND OVER   The actual moment . . . the thing itself.

Fear dawns in MENDOZA's eyes. And:

FLASH SHOT. The tremendous thrust which killed Philippo. His own face absorbed and concentrated.

BIG CLOSE MENDOZA, in the cell again. He whispers:
    Oh Christ. . .

BIG CLOSE GABRIEL, watching him, carefully.

MENDOZA
No no, Father, I . . .

FLASH SHOT, the same blow; his own face now seeming to him gleeful. In the cell he stops as though winded and again:

MENDOZA
Oh Christ . . .

BIG CLOSE GABRIEL, as before.

MENDOZA
Father, am I damned?

GABRIEL
What do you think?

MENDOZA
I think I am.

GABRIEL
You're probably alright then, despair is not damnation, despair is not far off from grace. All that's missing is a bit of love. (He cocks his head and looks at him shrewdly.) You don't know much about love, do you?

MENDOZA
No.

GABRIEL
Well it's as hard as they make out. But . . .
(He frowns and contemplates the sword again, its beautiful blade and chasing,

respectfully, puzzled by a mystery.) . . . there's love gone into this, you see. I don't know why but it has. (He looks up at MENDOZA, keenly and dubiously) And if you're going to be a priest you'll have to give this up. And if you give up this, and all that goes with this, what will you be left with? What more have you got?

MENDOZA looks at the sword and thinks, 'that yard of metal is all I've got.' Nothing.

GABRIEL
It's a very strong man who can manage on nothing, even for a day. Are you sure you want to try?

MENDOZA
Yes.

'What I find so sad is that scene was one of the most beautiful ever written,' said Ghia. 'It was an extraordinary piece of writing which was totally fucked up. Puttnam and Roland never understood that changing Gabriel into a young man was not a matter of just rewriting the scene, it was a matter of rewriting the whole relationship.'[19]

Rather than ask Robert to condense and rewrite the scene himself, Joffé got John Mortimer to do it instead. 'We never cracked the problem of that scene,' said Puttnam. 'Roland can't get the wrap for that. It was an accident followed by expediency. We were nervous about the physicality of the part and Warners kicked hard about the passivity of the part.'

This and other changes to the original script were done partly for commercial reasons and partly because of a last-minute change of casting. When Robert de Niro was cast as the slave trader, Mendoza, the budget of the picture went up and that, in turn, necessitated a more populist approach. For De Niro, the role was a significant departure from the paranoid or otherwise disturbed modern Americans he was accustomed to playing. De Niro spent a great deal of time researching the period and he invited Robert and Sarah out to dinner, absorbing every single thought Robert had about the story and the character of Mendoza. De Niro was like a sponge and when there was nothing left within Robert to soak up, he sat silently and allowed Robert the privilege of paying the bill, even though Robert and Sarah were supposedly his guests. De Niro's self-absorption – if not downright meanness – made Sarah angry for a week.

But it was casting the role of the Jesuit, Gabriel, which caused all the problems. When he first wrote the script, Robert envisaged Cyril Cusack as Father Gabriel, though by the time the film was made Cusack was too frail to undertake an arduous production in the tropical jungle.

As part of his research, Robert went to Blackfriars, the Dominican priory in Oxford, to see his old friend Herbert McCabe. 'I can't remember being cross-examined,' said Brother Herbert. 'We just talked and strolled in the garden.' But nearly ten years later Brother Herbert was summoned to London to have lunch with Roland Joffé. 'I think I was being considered to play the part,' he said. 'Of course, I couldn't possibly have played it and, anyway, I had work to do in England.'[20]

Puttnam and Joffé next offered Gabriel to Dirk Bogarde, a startling idea which might also have been an inspired one. Sadly, his friend, Tony Forwood, became seriously ill, obliging Bogarde to withdraw from the project. It was then that Puttnam and Joffé decided to cast a younger man. That was a more commercial idea and, in view of the physical demands of the role, probably a safe one too. As a result of this Jeremy Irons – who just happened to be Cyril Cusack's son-in-law – was cast as Gabriel. In fact, Joffé had cast a clone of himself and asked Irons to wear a similar beard.

Shooting started on *The Mission* in April 1985. Although Robert was keen to visit the set in Colombia, Puttnam advised against it. The conditions were terrible and people were falling like flies, victims of dehydration, malaria and other tropical bugs. Joffé, who was himself in the sick bay for three days, did not want Robert on the set for fear that he would see how he was changing things. It fell to Puttnam to put Joffé's anxiety to Robert 'Your arrival,' he wrote, 'could create an additional tension among the artists and would also inhibit him in taking some liberties with both the text and the structure that are necessary to maintain our schedule. He believes, as I do, that every decision we make is in the best interests of the film but rather more realistically than I, he realises that these might not always appear to be strictly in the best interests of the text! If you feel, on reviewing selected takes once a week, that we are damaging your conception we will rely on you to holler. In this respect, no news will be good news!'[21]

Robert, anxious to avoid an argument, kept quiet about Joffé's changes to the script. Instead, he sent encouraging notes to him and by the time the film was being edited he told Joffé he felt, 'blissfully content to be in your hands. I am in seventh heaven about it.'[22] In particular, Robert loved Chris Menges's lustrous photography and Ennio Morricone's music, which immediately became an international hit. This famous score, though, was the source of another row between Puttnam and Ghia, who said:

> David is resentful because everything I said turned out to be right. He tried to make the music with George Martin who worked with the Beatles. But all Martin did was to suggest that we use the Adagio of Albinoni. Then Puttnam wanted to go with Leonard Bernstein, who was the godfather of my best friend in Rome. But I knew that Leonard wouldn't be able to do it.
>
> I had been pushing for Ennio Morricone well before we started shooting because music is so important to the story. Well, when the film finished shooting, I won the battle over Ennio and I was supported by Roland. And when the music proved to be the most successful part of the film, David had to accept and swallow that.[23]

Robert was in a dilemma, for the acrimony which existed between Ghia and Puttnam hurt him deeply. They argued about everything – the script, the budget, the music and over their screen credits which were eventually shared between them, with Ghia's name coming first.

Ghia had approved the budget of $17 million which, taking inflation into account, was similar to his budget of $10 million when he was trying to get the film made in the Seventies. But de Niro's fee pushed up the costs and so did Puttnam's and Joffe's insistence on importing a huge technical crew to Colombia, rather than take Ghia's advice and use the people there. The film eventually cost $23 million, for which Puttnam and Joffé must take responsibility. Along with Hugh Hudson's *Revolution* and Julien Temple's *Absolute Beginners*, the film's high cost and its disappointing reviews and box-office performance led directly to the collapse of Goldcrest.

'Privately,' said Sarah, 'Robert thought *The Mission* betrayed his script. But he always kept those thoughts to himself. In his position, he didn't want to upset anybody because he wanted another job.'

'I think Robert was proud of the film eventually,' said Puttnam. 'There were things he missed but he loved the music and the sweep of the film. I had enormous reservations about it but you do tend to park them when you win the Palme d'Or at Cannes.'[24]

Ghia argued strenuously against entering *The Mission* at Cannes because the film was not finished and because he knew that winning a prize there invariably led to a box-office flop in America. Again, Ghia was eventually proved right but he lost that argument – he has the Palme d'Or to prove it – and in May 1986 he flew to Cannes in a private jet with Robert, Sarah, Puttnam, Joffé and the film's editor, Jim Clark. In the cargo hold were twenty-four cans of 35mm film, twice the expected number since the film was being shown double-head, with picture and sound track on separate reels.

Ghia remembers arriving at Nice Airport as though it were yesterday. When the plane landed, every able-bodied man carried the heavy cans of film under his arms and walked 200 yards to the customs building. Since Ghia had a bad back, he found himself slipping behind the others. But as he reached the customs barrier, Puttnam came over to him and said, 'Fernando, you can't go on like this. Let me carry those.' Puttnam took Ghia's cans of film, turned a corner and was photographed by the press struggling out of the airport followed by an embarrassingly empty-handed Ghia.

> The next day [said Ghia], there were pictures of David carrying his film. I'm a total idiot about this kind of thing but David is a master at promoting himself.

Puttnam and Ghia's dispute is typical of two ambitious producers thrown together by circumstance; Robert, who loved them both dearly, was caught in the middle. Ghia's feelings about Puttnam run contrary to the commonly held view and are certainly coloured by his experiences on *The Mission* and the incident at Nice airport.

'The problem with David is this,' said Ghia. 'The man likes to appear for what he is not. A lot of people in this business do that but his case is extraordinary. He has an image of great morality, great principles, someone who doesn't care much about money. Well, he's a total fucking lie! He loves to appear very humble. Well, he's a total egomaniac. He has always loved to see it as 'David Puttnam's *Chariots of Fire*' and 'David Puttnam's *The Killing Fields*'. On *The Mission* he couldn't do that. He just used the film to see how much he could get out of it in terms of awards and prestige.'[25]

The acrimony between Ghia and Puttnam was never resolved and sadly reared its head again in 1991 when Puttnam contacted Morricone with the idea of turning *The Mission* into an opera, a project which might have involved Robert in writing the libretto. While Puttnam was anxious to sideline Ghia again, Morricone called Ghia to ask him what he knew about Puttnam's idea. 'I said I knew nothing,' said Ghia, 'and the project has never gone forward because Ennio wouldn't do it unless I was involved.'

Robert, meanwhile, saw a bitter dispute in the making and tried once again to remain loyal to both Ghia and Puttnam: 'The opera of *The Mission*,' he wrote to them both. 'If I am mentioned in the programme, I request that I am mentioned not as "Robert Bolt but as Robert Bolt and Fernando Ghia." I don't see what else I can do. Please, please, leave me out of it.'[26]

Throughout much of the writing of *Twelfth Night, Burr, The Florentines* and *The Mission* a terrible stench hung over Sussex House. To Robert and Sarah's shock and dismay, Tom was discovered to be in the final stages of heroin addiction. He was eighteen years old and seemed unlikely to reach nineteen.

When they moved into Sussex House, Tom took over the basement and soon converted it into a hovel. 'Let him live like a pig,' Robert told Sarah as she tried to pluck up the courage to go down there. When she did, she found an appalling mess. 'One morning,' she wrote, 'I could bear the stench no longer and took seven dirty coffee cups, swilling with half-smoked fags, dirty plates caked with dry food, underwear, knives, forks, spoons back up to the kitchen. I tried to comfort myself that all this was perfectly normal for a teenager's den, but the comfort dwindled sharply when I came across more coffee stains, cigarette burns plus a couple of burned spoons . . .'[27] At first, Sarah just thought he was smoking marijuana, as they had done in California. She herself continued to smoke dope occasionally when she returned to London, though she gave it up in 1984 during a trip to Nepal, a satisfyingly perverse place to do it, she thought. But Tom was thoroughly hooked and he had the money and the contacts to buy as much as he needed.

Tom had always been left alone to do as he liked. Shunted from parent to parent, from Ann Queensberry to other friends, from California to temporary homes spread across England, he had become self-sufficient. And utterly helpless. It was nearly a year before anyone noticed.

TWENTY-EIGHT

TOM'S STORY

'Who needs reasons when you've got heroin?'

John Hodge, *Trainspotting*

In late May 1997, Sarah was sitting in the garden of a cottage she was renting in Trefriw, a village on the River Conwy, just south of Llandudno. It was a rare day for North Wales. The sun shone from a cloudless sky, the rhododendrons blazed scarlet and the only sound was a tractor coughing in a field. She had been reading the preliminary draft of this book. Robert's life, and much of her own, were scattered across the lawn – loose pages everywhere, weighed down with pebbles and sometimes by one of Sarah's Yorkshire Terriers whose name is Oxton.

'Do you think Tom is a victim?' she asked.

'Do you think I've made him seem like one?' I said.

'Well, yes, I do, a bit,' she said. 'He's not a victim, you know. He's a one-off, with an amazing will. I was ineffective as a mother. That's a ghastly thing to say, but it's true. I could never cope with the power of the boy. Whatever I said, he'd do the opposite. He got expelled from his first school, the kindergarten, when he was two and a half and that was when Robert and I were living together in a state of bliss. He's not a victim. Tom was born a rebel.'[1]

'I hear you're making me out to be a victim,' said Tom on the phone that very evening.

'I think maybe I am,' I said. 'Would you like to tell me why you're not? Your side of the story?'

We met the following week at his home in West London. 'If I had to live my childhood again, I wouldn't change a thing,' said Tom.

'I'd do it all again in order to get where I am today. I don't want to blame anything on my parents. There are thousands, millions, of children who have a much rougher childhood than I had but they don't shove heroin into their arms.'

Tom was born into wealth, privilege and glamour. Not many English boys can have gone to Arizona to play cowboys, or to Bora Bora for three months, or had the chance to kick a ball about in the back garden with George Best, or attend the Monaco Grand Prix, where Sarah conned her way in by pretending Tom was Jackie Stewart's son and she his nanny. I wondered when he first realised that his parents were different from normal people, that they were famous and didn't have nine to five jobs.

'I don't think I ever realised that,' he said. 'It was just the way it was. I very much went along with things and I'm only finding out now what I felt when I was twelve years old.'

Although he can only dimly remember the year he spent in Ireland during the filming of *Ryan's Daughter* and the time his parents made *Lady Caroline Lamb*, he has a clear picture of *The Man Who Loved Cat Dancing*:

> I thought Burt Reynolds was the most happening thing since sliced bread. I was obsessed with guns, cowboy things, and was absolutely in my element. I was on the set once and they were doing a scene when Jack Warden and Burt Reynolds have this huge fight. Just before one of them flies through a window I shouted out 'Cut!'. Everything stopped and the director looked at me as if to say, 'What the fuck is he doing?' Mum said, 'Why did you say cut?' And I said, 'Because Jack Warden's gun is bent.' He had this gun made from rubber and the barrel had bent over. So the director came over and said, 'Thank you very much.'

Like his father and mother, Tom was useless at school. It did not matter if it was public or private, boarding school or day school, he always got into trouble and was often expelled. When he was about to leave his final school, he was officially diagnosed as dyslexic which he says, 'was a huge relief, a huge weight off my shoulder.' But he claims that no one realised it before then, not even Robert who had encountered many such pupils at Millfield – and Sarah herself suffered from dyslexia.

> Everybody thought I was stupid [said Tom]. I knew I was quite intelligent, as it were, and if I was just doing English, I could

invent things and write and write. But I would take exams and come out with zero. I looked at a page of questions with sheer terror. Just a single sentence, even a simple sentence, made no sense. I kept coming bottom of the class and people thought I was stupid. So I got very frustrated and became the joker in the class and was always quite a disruptive influence. I was always the bad boy. My school reports would always say things like, 'He would do well if he wasn't so disruptive.' I was disruptive because I wasn't doing well.

Although Robert and Sarah were always there for him, Robert's office was strictly off limits as it had been for Ben and his sisters.

I think if you are truly talented it's impossible to draw a line between work and responsibility. I think you can do that if you have a nine-to-five job at an office but you can't when your work encompasses your whole life, as it did with Mum and Dad. But like my father, I am obsessive. I was a heroin addict. Whatever I do, I do obsessively. Because of this, I don't hold any resentment towards my father. Although I don't have the talent he had, I have the drive, the obsession.

When Dad did take the time though, like when he took me fishing or played football with me, we had the most wonderful times. When he opened his arms for me the love that came out of him was overwhelming.

After Robert and Sarah separated, Tom was sent to a succession of boarding schools, which he hated. He just looked forward to the school holidays because he knew he would be flying to California to spend time with Sarah. It was while he was living with Sarah in Los Angeles that he took drugs for the first time.

'How old was I at the time?' he asked.

'About eleven,' I said.

'Well, although there are upsides to living a crazy childhood there were plenty of downsides. I moved around quite a lot, I needed friends and I think I matured much quicker than the normal child. So because other kids of my age didn't do that much for me, I hung out with kids who were twelve or thirteen. And, yeah, I started nicking weed off people at an early age.

'You've also got to remember, it was the Seventies, it was what people did. Weed was everywhere. My mother never sat me down and said, "Don't do that," because I would have just done the opposite. I just kept on smoking.'

When Tom went to live in Devon with Robert, it was a good time for both of them. 'I had a motor bike and my hobby was motor cross. I also had this huge thing about wanting to be liked. I was at a boarding school and saw people who were popular and I longed to be like them. So I targeted people I wanted to be friends with and offered them things like rabbits and skateboards. I can remember Dad coming to pick me up at school and these kids going up to him to demand their rabbit or their skateboard.'

Then he was whisked out of school to Bora Bora. While Robert and Julie Laird spent much of their time worrying about Tom's health and his education, Tom himself was exhilarated. He had found paradise.

> I hated any form of authority or restriction and then, suddenly, I was on this island. There wasn't a boarding-school, there wasn't any sort of regime, it was just a place I could be free. And I was with my dad.
>
> I didn't like the heat and Dad took me to hospital once because of it. And I remember I cut myself very badly on my knee when I jumped off a jetty into the water. You sometimes went right down to the bottom and I hit my knee on some coral. When I came out, my knee to my foot was bright red, pissing with blood. So they held me down, cut a lime in half and went wallop, right into the cut. The worst thing was that a pip got stuck inside the cut which they prised out with a stick. God, that was agony, and I spent the next two months wearing a huge bandage.

School in Bora Bora was swiftly subverted to his advantage. Knowing that learning French was totally beyond him, he changed places with the teacher, stood at the front of the class and gave them all English lessons. There was also the saga of the mangoes and Indian ink.

> In Bora Bora, I felt my first crush for a female who happened to be Raffaella De Laurentiis, Dino's daughter. I was just besotted with her, totally gaga. We'd have these dinners and I'd always stare at her and she'd always make me kiss her good-night. So I thought to impress I would tattoo her initials on my arm. But I thought her name was Raffaella Telaurentiis, so I tattooed RT not RDL.
>
> Anyway, I got a needle and scratched my arm and got some Indian ink and put it in. Some of the guys at school thought this

was pretty cool. Now, I was hooked on mangoes and I still am a complete mango freak. But the nice mangoes were at the top of the trees and I couldn't climb them. So I traded tattoos for mangoes. At lunch-break I would have a queue of kids waiting to be tattooed and they all came with their bags of mangoes. I felt like a king. I was kinda like the cool one, the one who did tattoos. Two or three days later, kid after kid came to school with their parents because their arms had gone septic. I think that's one of the things that contributed to my being sent home. But I'd do it all again, because it was fun.

Being sent home meant coming under the care of Ann Queensberry who was acting *in loco parentis*.

To me, it was just another move and I had begun to get sick of taking it on the chin. Although I'd met Ann when I was a kid, I didn't really know her at all. So it was an odd thing to show up at her door and say, I'm living here now. I resented her a lot though, looking back, she was probably absolutely wonderful with me. She was strict in a way, which was probably what I needed, but I was at boarding-school, I went home to Ann for the weekends, and I was absolutely miserable. I just wanted to be with my mum or my dad.

I also lived in immense fear of what I was going to do when I was older, which was amplified by my father and my mother being very successful. I hadn't a clue what I was going to do.

There was no one with whom Tom could share these worries, even if he'd wanted to. He always regarded Robert's other children as a separate, rather distant family and, anyway, they were much older than he was. He never gave any thought to confiding in Ann's three daughters because he could see no reason to do so. He just accepted everything that was happening to him: failing at school, causing havoc, pretending he was having a great time.

He was holidaying in Los Angeles when Sarah came home to tell him some bad news.

Mum took me into a small room at the bottom of the garden in Venice and explained that Dad had had a stroke. Now, this might give the impression that I was an uncaring wanker, but I can remember Mum explaining it to me and all I wanted to do was ride my bike which she'd bought me the day before. At that time, I was really out of contact with my emotions. I distanced myself from everything. So when she told me, it didn't really register.

I wanted Mum and Dad to get back together again and in LA she had told me there was a possibility of that happening and I thought, wow, that's what I want most of all. But it didn't happen and I found myself living with Dad and Ann Queensberry in Doneraile Street.

One of my problems there was that if I was told not to do something, I wanted my dad to tell me, not Ann. Even if there was negative feedback, I wanted it from my dad. But because of his stroke he wasn't really there.

I remember I was staying with Anthony Tancred when Dad arrived in the Range Rover with Ann, who brought loads of presents for me. The punchline was that they were getting married. I loathed the prospect, it was horrendous. I didn't think it was the right move for Dad and I just wanted him and my mum to get back together again.

Tom also inherited Ann's three daughters, who were living with them, and he was seeing a great deal more of his half-brother and sisters. Like Sarah, he felt as if he was a stranger, the black sheep of the family.

By the time we were living at Hartington Road I hadn't taken heroin but I was doing a lot of speed and coke every now and then. I got sent to a school in Victoria which, believe it or not, was for backward American children. For me, it was a complete licence to run riot. I started to do more drugs and then Dad said he wanted me to see a psychiatrist.

On my fourteenth birthday I snuck out with Ann's daughter, Alice, and we went to a club called the Whisky a-GoGo in Wardour Street. I was like a Fifties rockabilly at the time with this huge quiff and I wore my grandfather's baggy suits. I was dancing away and the drummer came up to me and said I danced really well. Being precocious I told him, yes, I did, and you should hear me sing. So I went for an audition and started to sing with this band, the Subway Sect, which became the Joe Boxers. Suddenly, I was a success. I had write-ups in *Smash Hits* and I had a lot of fans. My stage name was Tomcat.

My sister Sally came to see me perform at a huge gig. I adored Sally, I mean I really adored her. Sally had no pretences. Sally and I were both fucked-up, in different ways, so we had a rapport. When she heard me sing she didn't say, 'You were great' or 'You were brilliant'. She just said, 'You've made it, you've done it.' That made me feel so good.

Then a weird thing happened. My manager, who was also manager of the Clash, asked me to do a concert for Island Records. There were some big bands there, thousands of people, lashings of champagne. Malcolm McLaren, who was the most important producer around, heard me sing and said he was interested in me. If McLaren wanted to be your manager, you had it made.

I was with Ann's daughter, Alice, and she felt so strongly about what had happened to the Sex Pistols and Sid Vicious, who McLaren had managed, that she turned to him and said, 'Fuck off. We don't need you.' I remember that so well. I thought, there it goes ... I had become somebody and I thought, 'My father is a writer, my mother is an actor and I'm a singer' and how good that sounded. But Alice told McLaren to fuck off.

It had got to the stage when she was sort of chaperoning me and after a gig she'd ask me to go up to the microphone and say things like, 'Thank you, Alice, for doing my costume and my quiff.' Stuff like that. I was quite scared of Alice. She could be very domineering. Then I heard that the band didn't want me any more, so that was the end of Tomcat.

Two years later, my group was on *Top of the Pops* and had some top ten hits. Some years after that I met the drummer and he said, 'What happened to you?' I had been given loads of reasons why the band didn't want me any more and then I found out that they did want me. You know, I still haven't a clue what really happened.

Although Tom says he adored Sally, her death barely registered with him. 'I remember being told she was dead and went home in the evening and saw my father, Ben and Neil sitting at a table in this dark room. I thought, sorry guys, I'm leaving, so I spent the night with a friend. I was speeding off my head then, so I couldn't deal with it. I don't think I've ever truly mourned for Sally.'

Tom was fifteen when he first took heroin. He'd been expelled from his last school and marijuana was not giving him a buzz any more. He would even eat it as a means of getting as much inside his system without the incriminating smell of the smoke. Then, at a party, he was offered heroin. 'The first time I took heroin I was absolutely out of it. I threw up at our front door and the next morning I felt just awful. I thought, that was disgusting, I'm never doing that again. Three or four months went by. Then I woke up in the morning and, damn, I had to have some heroin. Very strange drug.'

It was around this time that Robert and Sarah got back together again and moved to Sussex House. A few years before, their reconciliation was what Tom wanted most of all. But now he saw things rather differently:

When Mum and Dad got together again, I think I was probably quite resentful about it. I was too far gone at that stage. I was a junkie. I thought they weren't there for my childhood and now that I'm an adult and a junkie they decide to get back together again.

At Sussex House I was very clever about concealing my heroin use though I never concealed my marijuana. Sometimes my mum would give me an ear-bashing about it and sometimes she wouldn't. And anyway, I was doing it in the basement and Dad couldn't manage the stairs. He didn't understand the seriousness of where I was at.

Sarah took Tom to Spain, where she was filming, in the hope that he might clean up. But he took a supply of methadone with him and the trip was a disaster for both of them. Back at Sussex House, things only got worse until Sarah called the police. 'I shopped my son,' she said.

'The next thing I knew, said Tom, 'I was in a Black Maria heading for a remand centre in Ashford. That was a total nightmare. The place was closed down shortly afterwards as it wasn't fit for human habitation. My cell had a broken window, so I just froze there for a month.'

For his court hearing, Robert and Sarah appointed a fine solicitor, who was to argue against a probable prison sentence of two years. 'I remember sitting outside the court,' said Tom, 'and got talking to this really nice guy who was wearing a smart suit and carrying a briefcase. He seemed to want to help me and we chatted for about twenty minutes. Then he said, I'm from the *Sun* and I've been sent to get your story. The paparazzi were outside and everything.'

Tom was sent not to prison but to a succession of drug rehabilitation centres. After one or two bad experiences, he finally thought he had conquered his addiction:

I went to Clouds in Wiltshire and then I was court-ordered to a half-way house. I remember booking myself out and going back to London. There was a drunk Scottish guy on the train who offered me a beer and I said no, thanks. I felt really great. I thought I didn't need this and all I wanted to do was to go to a Narcotics Anonymous meeting in Paddington.

I got off the train, forgot the meeting and half an hour later I was sitting in my room with a needle hanging out of my arm. I just could not understand how it had happened. I had no control over this thing.

My parents found out about my heroin addiction when a former girl-friend of mine wrote and told them about it. They asked me to leave home, which was the right thing to do. It's what I would do to my son or daughter.

I reached a level of bottom which most people don't reach until they are thirty or forty. I was seventeen, I hadn't even stopped physically growing. I ended up sleeping in cars because I was banned from my friends' houses. It was costing me around £350 a week and sometimes I spent a grand a week. I scammed, stole off my parents, forged my dad's cheques.

I remember being in Soho which was then a very dingy place, full of hookers, junkies and dealers. I'd just learned about AIDS and knew that I could catch it from needles. I had some smack but I didn't have a syringe so I went through a bin to find one. I remember saying to myself, this is a really stupid thing to do, but I didn't care. My attitude was, if I catch AIDS then that will just be the excuse. I didn't care if I died or not. Suicide was always an option for me.

When he was at his lowest ebb and physically very ill he contacted a former girl-friend and told her that he wanted somewhere to stay and go cold turkey. 'I stayed with her for two days, feeling like shit, running hot baths all the time. I was raging, absolutely just raging. The reason I loved heroin so much was because I'm a hyperactive person and heroin is about the only drug which brings you down, it lowers your blood pressure. That's why I loved it so much.'

Tom has a word for his hyperactivity. He calls it the 'bureau' and it's inside his head, always open, always busy. When he took heroin, the bureau shut down for the night. But going cold turkey in the girl's flat meant that the bureau was wide open and working.

The bureau would drive me crazy, make me berserk. So I thought, fuck it, I'm going to score. My friend had gone to work and I found her jewellery in a drawer. I thought, I need heroin more than I need breath right now. But, you know, a weird thing happened, I couldn't be bothered to take all this stuff to the pawn shop, to go to the West End, to score, to come back, to have a hit.

So I went to my dad and I said, 'I really want to give up.' He said, 'No, no, we've spent all this money and you'll never give it up.' I pleaded with him and he took me to a doctor.

Tom was given a stark choice. He either went to a treatment centre in America or he continued to take heroin and die within two months. Tom told the doctor, 'No, I don't want to go. I've been to treatment centres, I can talk a counsellor out of his trousers. It doesn't work.'

But he went to America, to a place in Minnesota called Hazleden. He was expecting some sort of palatial clinic, a tranquil retreat, with trees and a lake. It turned out to be a wooden shack in one of the drabbest parts of America. Tom mistook the place for a hamburger joint. The people there were slouching around, having affairs and doing drugs. 'But somehow, through all the withdrawals, I said "No". I had people offering me pills, stuff to help me come off, and I said "No". And I was able to say "No" because on the plane to America I really felt as if this was it. And I came through.'

Until Tom went to Minnesota, Robert and Sarah had been virtual spectators, coping as best they could with the emotional crises that came their way, dreading the thought that their son might die a junkie. Nothing could really be done unless Tom himself made the decision to 'face the Devil,' as they called it. In Minnesota he did just that and part of the treatment obliged him to face his parents in a communal therapy session. Bracing themselves, Robert and Sarah flew over to the States. 'It was horrific for them because I think Dad felt he hadn't spent the time with me he thought he should have done,' said Tom. 'I think he felt guilt over that.' 'Family Week', as it was called, was traumatic. In public, with total strangers, Robert and Sarah had to discuss themselves and the history of their parentage of Tom. Perhaps for the first time, both of them were behaving as parents were expected to behave, as a couple with a single purpose. While the tragedy that had befallen Sally had no beneficial side effects for anyone, at least Tom's heroin addiction and his rehabilitation brought Robert and Sarah closer to each other than they had ever been before.

When Tom was released from the rehab centre he decided to remain in America for a year. 'Suddenly I was the person I always wanted to be when I was at school. I had friends, I was quite popular with the girls, probably because I was English. And when I came back to England, things were great. Mum was living with Dad and everything looked like a normal way of living.'

Having satisfied themselves that Tom was totally 'clean,' Robert and Sarah set him up in a house in Chiswick. The only problem at first was that a few newspaper stories had made him briefly famous, so the neighbours feared the worst and the police kept a sharp eye on the house, which was defended by an alarm system and a fierce-sounding Staffordshire bull terrier named Bear.

Tom needed a job, though he already had an obsession. When he was nine years old, Robert picked him up from school and gave him a watch. It was a Timex with plastic bezels, not quite a toy, not quite a real watch. After he put the Timex on, Tom looked at Robert's watch which was a gleaming, stainless-steel Rolex. 'From that day on,' said Tom, 'I thought if you make it in life you have a Rolex on your wrist.'

After he came off drugs he was working in a warehouse in Brentford and thought he was ready for a Rolex. He paid £320 for a second-hand one and soon began to think he couldn't afford to have all this money on his arm. He only had £150 in his bank account. So he sold the Rolex and made a small profit. 'Slowly I learned about watches, so that's what I do. I enjoy it and it makes me a living. I know a fair amount about watches.'

Everyone says he's an expert.

Sometimes, when he and his wife go out and meet new people, Tom will accidentally drop a small piece of autobiography into the conversation. The effect is often one of total disbelief and Tom himself sometimes thinks his past history is not his at all, but someone else's, which is perhaps why he talks about it so objectively. 'It's true I didn't receive the care and attention that most children get,' he said. 'My dad had the bureau inside him as well and that's one of the things I share with him. But the flipside of not getting that attention – and it's a very important flipside – is that I had some invaluable life experience. I'm twenty-nine but I think I have lived the life of someone who is two hundred and fifty years old.'[2]

TWENTY-NINE

SKIPPING ON THE SURFACE OF LANGUAGE

'No one would remember the Good Samaritan if he'd only had good intentions. He had money as well.'

Margaret Thatcher

While Robert and Sarah were coping with Tom's drug addiction, they somehow managed to maintain their own careers. After years in the professional wilderness, Sarah was in demand again. John Boorman offered her a tremendous role, as the steadfast mother in his evocative film of the Blitz, *Hope and Glory*, which opened at the Cannes Festival to considerable acclaim. She made *Steaming*, which was Joseph Losey's final film, and she went to Kenya to make *White Mischief*, a story of colonial torpor and perversion, in which she rode astride the corpse of her murdered husband and sipped her own vaginal juices. A four-hour American TV movie, *Harem*, was rubbish but she got to work with Ava Gardner and Omar Sharif.

Robert, meanwhile, sat at his word processor in Sussex House and embarked on what would prove to be the final phase of his career.

Marlon Brando was in London making *A Dry White Season*, his first film for eight years. Unusually for Brando, he wasn't making it for the money but for union scale of around $4000 because he supported the film's opposition to the apartheid regime in South Africa. Brando had been cast as an anti-apartheid lawyer, Donald Sutherland was playing a naïve schoolteacher who slowly realises the evil at the heart of his country and Susan Sarandon a liberal journalist.

Based on a novel by André Brink, the film was being directed by

Euzhan Palcy, a young black woman from Martinique, whose screenplay had been reworked by many hands, including Colin Welland's, who ultimately received screen credit. As soon as Brando arrived at Pinewood Studios, sick with influenza, he said he wanted his scenes rewritten. Paula Weinstein, the film's producer, said:

> I had admired Robert from afar and was really stuck. I knew about his stroke so I called Puttnam to see what his experience had been and he said it was just wonderful. Because Brando felt that the earlier draft hadn't given him enough to work with, I called Robert and asked if he would do it. We were all thrilled when he said yes.
>
> For two weeks I went from the set to his house and he'd do the pages right in the room with me. He rewrote the character and made him an absolutely brilliant lawyer who worked just the way Marlon did, with all those little characteristics. Then Marlon changed a lot of it, rather in the humour vein, making his character more testy, sarcastic and flamboyant. I showed Robert what Marlon had rewritten and he was fine about it. Screen credit was never an issue with him.[1]

Another major Hollywood actor was also in town. For years, Charlton Heston had been a tireless champion of *A Man For All Seasons*, first performing it in Chicago in the mid Sixties and subsequently taking it on tour all over the world. Because a portion of the royalties from all stage performances went to the trust set up by Robert for his children, Heston was firmly established as Ben's favourite actor.

Heston had seen the play during its original run at the Globe and was stunned by it. 'I don't think there's been a better play written in English since that time,' he said. 'If you do a run of a play for two weeks or two months, you often feel you've exhausted all there is in it. That's not true with the old gentleman from Stratford and it's certainly not true with *A Man For All Seasons*. Having done it three times before, I was invited by Duncan Weldon to do it at the Savoy, with a tour of the provinces afterwards.'

Heston, who is well known for his love of history and for playing notable historical personages, brought his own interpretation of More, which differed substantially from that of Paul Scofield. Whereas Scofield's More was frail and stooped, Heston brought an unavoidable physicality to the part.

If you're six foot three with a broken nose and a bass voice, I did the only interpretation I could do [he said]. But, having done my research and having done the role probably more often than Scofield, I dare to offer a dissident opinion of him. I don't think his towering reputation will be tarnished by my opinion that, fine though his performance was, his More was some distance from the historic More.

Scofield's acerbic, dry style – I guess that's fair, that's basically his colour – has served him well. But More was a much more sanguine personality. He liked people, he liked hunting and going out to parties, he liked the Duke of Norfolk, he liked King Henry for heaven's sake. He was vigorously involved because it was fun, not because it was his job. He liked doing good, like Benjamin Franklin and Thomas Jefferson.

I saw Scofield's performance again in the film and of course he was very good but there was a kind of chilliness about it. But I think his reputation can survive my dissent.

Although Heston had once considered making a film version of *State of Revolution* – a plan which was abandoned after Robert wrote to Heston saying that the play had significant flaws and that it had not played well at the National – he had never met Robert personally and was anxious to do so. Heston decided to invite Robert to the final dress rehearsal. 'By the time I was at the Savoy he'd had his stroke and he found it very difficult to speak, let alone move. He came to the final dress rehearsal and sat up in the mezzanine. I went up to see him there and I'm still touched by the struggle it was for him. He said to me, "You . . . have . . taken . . me . . . over . . . the Moon." '[2]

Heston's new stage production ran at the Savoy, then toured Britain during the autumn of 1987. It was such a success that the media tycoon Ted Turner proposed that Heston direct and star in a film version. Made in 1988, and shown on the opening night of Turner's TNT cable network, Heston's film also starred John Gielgud, Vanessa Redgrave and Richard Johnson. As an adaptation of Robert's original play it is far more faithful than Fred Zinnemann's film because Heston decided to preserve the Comman Man.

For Robert, *A Dry White Season* was a breeze: two weeks' work, none of the normal pressures, no mountain of research, and a cheque for $100,000 at the end of it. And Charlton Heston's film of *A Man For All Seasons* brought an unexpected financial bonus in the sale of the film rights.

By the close of 1987, though, Robert found himself briefly out of work. He worried that he might have been rumbled, that the quality of his writing had deteriorated since his stroke and that producers like Franco Zeffirelli and Ray Stark had hired him solely on his former reputation. While the lawsuit over *Michael Collins* was a sort of victory, he still had to convince people that he was much fitter than he really was. In fact, he had reached his plateau of improvement; his speech was as good as it was ever going to get and his body still hurt like hell, especially his right leg. Much of his daily routine was taken up by speech therapy, physiotherapy and bottles of pills. Although he had been able to resist taking up smoking again, he drank considerable quantities of hard liquor and fine wine. And he still loved to lunch, either at Meridiana or at Bibendum in the art-deco Michelin building.

In addition to his regular lunch companions, such as Naomi, Julie Laird and Charlotte Taylor, Robert also renewed some old friendships, for example, Roy Battersby, his adversary from the ACTT and the Workers Revolutionary Party, who said:

> I had broken with the WRP because I discovered there were all sorts of horrors going on in the party and I had gone through some personal problems. . . I had deserted my family and people I loved the most. I was also feeling very much the loss of work because I came out of the WRP into fuck all and a blacklist. My career was very seriously harmed.
>
> I heard that Bob had had a stroke and never felt that I knew him well enough to make contact. But one day the phone went and it was him, inviting me to his house in Hammersmith. He was unwell and in bed. He'd been asked to write a screenplay from a book called *The Sealed Train*, about Lenin's journey back from Switzerland to Russia in 1917. I'd already read it and he asked me if I would direct it. It never came to anything but we started having long lunches together.
>
> I was overwhelmed by his dignity and courage. For the first time we talked without all that union division between us and we could just say, 'Great to see you' and discuss the cinema and the state of the nation. At first, he thought I was still the old Trot and what did I make of it all. Once, in a posh Italian restaurant in the Fulham Road where the staff knew him and looked after him, he said, 'Oh . . . you know . . . there's a minister . . . um . . . um . . . oh . . . fuck it!' The whole restaurant fell silent. Then he said, 'Oh . . .fuck it . . . Lamont!'

When you consider what he must have been going through, the pain and the frustration, but he always gave off the feeling that said, I continue, I'm going on, I won't be beaten. I always felt part of the pleasure for him was we could be a bit buoyant about things and not seriously explore each other's difficulties. We could just be together and be supportive. We were both well-blooded, albeit in different ways, and had enough to regret. We'd both been through the mill. I felt utterly comfortable with him. It was one of the most moving friendships I've ever had.[3]

Robert had little sympathy for the Workers Revolutionary Party, which Battersby had left and which was still supported by Vanessa Redgrave. Redgrave, though, was one of the few actors who maintained contact with Robert, even if he found her revolutionary socialism a little hard to swallow: 'Vanessa popped in and joined us on Boxing Day,' he told Charlotte Taylor, 'and apart from boring us rigid with forthcoming accounts of the coming revolution, was exceedingly nice. I go on liking her, revolution notwithstanding.'[4]

Robert's politics had not changed. He was still a traditional Labour supporter, even if under Michael Foot the party had adopted some extreme stances which caused its election manifesto of 1983 to be described as 'the longest suicide note in history.' Unsurprisingly, the Conservatives, under Margaret Thatcher, who was riding a wave of patriotism after the victory in the Falklands War, won a landslide victory. Mrs Thatcher appalled Robert, especially when she bought an ostentatiously huge modern residence in Dulwich, South London, which was initially explained away as her eventual place of retirement but seems to have been bought principally as an investment. Robert thought that Ben, who was living in Los Angeles, should be kept up to date about this:

Mrs Thatcher has bought a house; and the whole country is shocked by it, or up in arms against it; no one laughs at it. Price, say about £400,000. But the area could not have been chosen by anyone less *au fait* with her than she is herself. There is a drive up to it – just a little drive – then the full horror of grey stuccoe; a smug land round to the back, which faces on to a golf course. It is neither flamboyant nor is it ruggedly bourgeois; it is just what she, having reduced the country to rubble, would choose.

I have solved the mystery of her persona; she is exactly what one would think her to be; a upwardly striving, middle class mum; with no aspirations to our imperial past like say Churchill;

and no romantic dreamed of, superb townscape built on the proletarian hills of Lancashire. No wonder the Queen can't stand her. You see? She has made the Queen seem an outpost of some dignity.[5]

Much as Robert detested Mrs Thatcher, he worried about her losing the next General Election for fear that an incoming Labour government headed – likely as not – by Neil Kinnock would immediately rob the rich to pay the poor. 'It will be back to 95% of our earnings,' Robert told Ben. 'This doesn't seem right to me. Of course one has to make the allowance, a very large allowance, for the fact that one will probably fall within the brackets of the "wealthy". I worry about this quite a lot. Is it just that one is greedy, or is there something punitive about it?'[6]

In addition to his ruminations on politics, Robert was compelled to analyse himself. Val Eaton Griffith was writing a book and asked if she might record a conversation with him. It had been seven years since his stroke and Griffith wanted to know how he was getting on. When she arrived at Sussex House for her interview, she found his speech slow and careful, reluctant to trip over consonants, and when he couldn't find a word he'd worry it 'like a terrier'.

'Did you do all the things we planned?' asked Griffith.

'Of course,' said Robert.

'And you continued with your speech therapy?'

'Yes. And still today.'

'Excellent. What else did you do?'

'I watched television,' said Robert, laughing. 'Five or six hours.'

'Did you feel being surrounded by words would help?'

'I had not thought of that.'

'Have you found speech comes easier when you have something to say?'

'About this I have no doubt. When I was a young man I found that I could communicate ideas with a fresh slant to them, off the cuff. I had only to receive a proposition and lo and behold I was straight away on my feet to the evident admiration of the people whose idea it originally was, do you see? I found that I could do this with a typewriter. Hence I became a writer. Hence I became preoccupied with what ideas were mine and what were not, just borrowed. I take it that's the ancient puzzle of writers. But if it had crossed my mind that I would never be able to communicate with words, I think I would have folded up, or else become a vegetable. Lately I have sorrowfully concluded that I shall not again reach that skipping on the surface of the language that I once had.'

Griffith was also interested to learn how Robert's friends and family had helped him. 'When you came out of hospital,' she said, 'were Ben, Joanna, Ann and John able to help you?'

'Oh yes,' said Robert.

'How did your children manage?'

'First two years fantastic. Lovely. But they have parted from me now.'

'Because they are young with busy lives to lead?'

'Of course,' said Robert. 'Another thing. Most sad. The people who I know. Only one-fifth of them come near me.'

'Fair-weather friends?' said Griffith.

'No. It's not that. At least it is, but it is not the thing that keeps them away.

'What does?'

'Fear,' said Robert.

Griffith was surprised by the word and wondered if Robert had really meant it.

'Who knows?' said Robert. 'But it is fear. *Fear.* They greet me when they see me. "Oh hallo." They are all over me and they say they will ring. But they don't. Fear.'

'The question of shame crops up often following a stroke,' said Griffith. 'How did you feel? Did you feel ashamed?'

'Shame . . . I really don't know,' said Robert. 'I'll tell you what I did feel. Triumphant. Well, not triumphant exactly, but as though I had paid for all the many things that I had hitherto failed to do right back to my childhood, through greed, cowardice, pride and just not having bothered enough. I felt a terrific relief at having paid, at one fell swoop, for all that. I didn't feel shame exactly, but guilt, socially, at having to make a fuss about standing up or going on a journey. I felt something more, still feel it now, a discontent about not being able to put my thoughts in order before the conversation I am taking part in has switched to another point, leaving me with the final coping-stone upon the talk, unuttered. This is taken, as far as I can see, for wisdom. It is not, except for possessing my soul in patience.'[7]

On Saturday, 27 February 1988 Robert and Sarah remarried at a church in Hammersmith. The local vicar had urged them to take their vows. 'The way you look at each other,' he said. 'What a love story!' When Sarah told him she had previously married Robert in Woking Registrar's Office he said, 'All the more reason to do it properly this time.' It was a small family affair, followed by a reception at Sussex House. 'I wore pale pink,' wrote Sarah, 'subtly flattering Robert's sage green, and not a single child cried, candle dripped, daffodil died or dog crapped. We both had to admit that the vicar had been right, for we both felt very right being wed that second time. Why? Because the whole ritual of "getting married" and the ceremony itself weren't based on a youthful rush of hope or lust, but on the knowledge of a benevolent continuity.'[8]

There could be no honeymoon, since Sarah was embarking on what promised to be the most prestigious moment of her career, playing Imogen in *Cymbeline* at the National Theatre under the direction of Peter Hall. For his swan song as Director of the NT, Hall planned simultaneously to direct three lavish productions of Shakespeare: *Cymbeline*, *The Tempest* and *The Winter's Tale*. All three were intended to open in May 1988.

Since he had suffered his stroke, Robert had seen little of Peter Hall, though when the NT's company first learned of Robert's illness letters of goodwill and support arrived in force. When Hall bumped into Robert and Sarah at a Christmas party, he suddenly asked Sarah if she would be his Imogen. Sarah had misgivings but, urged on by Robert, she agreed on the condition that she did an audition, which she passed with flying colours.

Sarah was not Hall's first choice. He had originally cast an actress named Wendy Morgan, who had suddenly dropped out, claiming she wanted to spend time with her new baby. Hall's own daughter, Jennifer, had been cast as Miranda, raising eyebrows and accusations of nepotism. By the time Sarah arrived at the rehearsal room things were already sour. When Hall fired Robert Eddison, who was playing the King, Sarah was shocked and alone tried unsuccessfully to make Hall change his mind. But Hall was adamant: Eddison, who was seventy-nine and was to appear in all three plays, was having trouble with his lines and with the style of delivery which Hall wanted.

Sarah was having the same problem. Although she had considerable stage experience and had done her share of Shakespeare, the world of the National Theatre and Peter Hall was quite new to her. And, because Hall had *The Tempest* and *The Winter's Tale* to deal with, Sarah, who was word-perfect, felt she was being left to get on with it. She felt intimidated by her surroundings and deeply insecure, even though Robert, who attended a rehearsal, was clearly impressed by her performance. But Hall, in mid-April, just a month before the first night, telephoned Sarah on a Sunday afternoon and told her she was fired. Hall replaced her with Geraldine James. 'If you've got a dead play on your hands,' he said, 'you've got to do something about it. It's tragic in human terms, and I'm not proud of it because I wanted to be fair. I endangered the production and the company by leaving it to the last moment.'[9]

Sarah was distraught and saw her career collapse around her, as it had done in the aftermath of David Whiting's death. As for Robert, he was angry and frustrated. 'I can do nothing because I can't speak!' he cried when Sarah told him the news. Robert's thirty-year friendship with Hall was over.

At first, Sarah said she was unhappy with the role, an explanation for her departure which led the theatre critic, Sheridan Morley, to wonder if that might have been news to Shakespeare. But the truth of what had happened was soon discovered and the press had a field day, pitching the volatile and eccentric actress against an equally volatile and egocentric director. Neither of them came out of it well and any hopes Sarah might have had for reviving her stage career were dashed. She subsequently appeared in *Asylum* at her local theatre, the Hammersmith Lyric, then walked out of *Henry IV* – Pirandello's – before it reached the West End, having clashed with its star and producer, Richard Harris. 'If Peter Hall hadn't fired me,' she said, explaining her unexpected period of unemployment, 'we would never have found Chithurst. I have this to thank him for.'

Robert had become tired of London even though, contrary to Samuel Johnson, he was not yet tired of life. He found the city expensive, crowded and, towards the end of Mrs Thatcher's reign, dirty and distasteful. The restaurants were full of new young things with mobile phones and snazzy ties, and the pavements of beggars with scrawny-looking dogs. Negotiating London's traffic was a nightmare and if he got lost and asked someone the way he would be treated like a vagrant or a drunk.

One day, Robert was driving home when his Mercedes started billowing black smoke. He was in the middle of a busy London street. He got out of the car, lifted the bonnet and was pleased that he was able to fix the problem. Two smartly dressed men approached him and offered to start the car to see if it worked. Robert thanked them for their kindness, then watched as they got into it, switched on the engine and roared off. Shocked and completely stranded, he asked for help. 'Can – you – please – help – me?' he said, slowly and deliberately to passers by. No one wanted to know. Finally, he asked a policeman. 'Can – you – please – help – me?' The policeman said, 'I think you've had too much to drink.

Why don't you just go home?' Robert threw himself into the middle of the road, forcing a taxi to stop.

'Robert cried that night,' said Sarah. 'He said, "I am not weeping for myself. I am weeping for humanity."'

The drawbacks to Sussex House were also increasingly obvious. His doctor insisted that he take regular exercise but hemmed in by the traffic on one side and the pub on the other, Robert had nowhere to walk except to pace the noisy and noxious garden like a caged grizzly bear. He felt trapped and yearned once again for the unpolluted air of the countryside and a garden in which the birdsong was not drowned out by buses hurtling along to Heathrow Airport.

Robert and Sarah scanned the property pages and got themselves on the mailing lists of likely estate agents. Not Devon this time, which was too far from the doctors and hospitals, not to mention the producers and directors who came to discuss film projects. Something old and pretty was what they wanted, with woodland, water, and a chapel. When they saw the picture of Chithurst Manor they knew they had found exactly what they were looking for. It matched precisely a 'picture' Sarah once saw on the palm of her hand.

To get there, you leave the main road, then negotiate a series of narrowing lanes, a route which seems to shed a century or two with every mile. And there, among the trees, is a picture of England as Thomas More would have known it. Chithurst is an elongated copse with the River Rother flowing through it. Records date back to 1086, when Chithurst Manor – reputedly the smallest manor house in the land – was owned by Earl Roger, Lord of Arundel, and valued at four hides. A tiny church of the same period stands ruined on an artificial mound, while its cemetery wraps itself half-way round the manor's grounds. There are said to be ghosts, of course, and a natural spring down by the river, which bubbles up through pale sand, is mentioned in the 'Domesday Book'. The ground plan is eccentric, with two rooms off the entrance hall, as well as a passage way, intended for servants, which leads around the back towards another retiring room and the kitchen. Upstairs, there are three bedrooms and an attic. The house leans and groans with age, and because the windows are small and heavily mullioned, the sun rarely invades. It is an inner world of perpetual twilight, cosy yet far from claustrophobic.

Inevitably, a conservatory was swiftly appended, enabling Robert to admire from within a flowering walnut, if not a flowering cherry. Designed and built by Sarah's brother, Chuzzer, it was a major engineering enterprise, involving the construction of a retaining wall some six feet high. With the conservatory came a croquet lawn, several cats, one of whom was called Nice and then renamed Horrible when she perpetually hissed and clawed. It could be said that Sarah was endowing the cat with her own identity in reverse: at first she was horrible and then she was nice.

There was also a pack of Yorkshire terriers, one of which was christened Oxton. But Robert said he wanted a big dog, as big as himself, a woofer rather than a yapper. Sarah decided to give Robert a surprise. She located a breeder of English mastiffs, took delivery of a bitch puppy and laid it one day on Robert's bed. 'I only saw Robert cry three times,' said Sarah. 'Once was after his car was stolen, the next time was when he saw Chithurst and the third time was when he went up to his room and saw the mastiff on his bed.' Rather than call the mastiff Fucking Hell, which was the first option, she was christened Lovely, one of Robert's favourite words.

In Chithurst Manor, Robert had found the perfect place in which to live and to die.

THIRTY

MOONLIGHTING

'Some harbours of the earth are made difficult of access by the treachery of sunken rocks and the tempests of their shores.'

Joseph Conrad, *Nostromo*

Sitting under the shade of the walnut tree at Chithurst, with a glass of cool and honeyed Montrachet, a lesser man than Robert might have thought, 'fuck it, this is glorious, I'm sixty-four, seriously disabled, that's enough for me, I've retired, I've got a beautiful and devoted wife, let's enjoy what time is left.' Robert didn't think that for a moment; his compulsion to work was as strong as his constitution. And the work he was about to do would have destroyed a fit man half his age.

Robert had commandeered the largest and the brightest of the living-rooms as his study, filling it with his awards and the books he needed for immediate reference. While the rapidly growing Lovely draped herself across the hearth, slobbering and dreaming, Robert's Apple Macintosh burned bright. He now had a separate screen on which he could see a complete page of A4 typescript and a Microsoft programme designed for screenwriters, doing away with all those tricky tabulations. The computer was placed on a refectory table in front of the window, and on a parallel table Robert placed his research papers and notes. Between the two tables, Robert sat on his wooden turntable, swivelling himself around, pushing buttons on his computer and his fax machine, looking like Galileo in the age of *Star Trek*.

Everyone seemed to phone or fax at once. David Puttnam had an interesting idea; a man in Hong Kong named Ronnie Colsen had another; and what on earth did David Lean want? At one point, Robert had four screenplays and a novel on the go and was trying desperately hard to make each paymaster feel that he had his undivided attention. One morning the phone rang and Sarah answered it.

'Hello, Sarah,' said a silky and familiar voice. 'It's David Lean.'

Lean proceeded to tell Sarah that he was working on an adaptation of Joseph Conrad's *Nostromo* and that his collaborator on the project, Christopher Hampton, had suddenly quit after a year's work. Lean barely concealed his anger at Hampton and hoped that Robert might agree to take over. He didn't want Robert simply to take up where Hampton had left off. He wanted to started again from scratch, just like *Lawrence of Arabia* when Michael Wilson had deserted him.

'Is he capable of working with me again?' Lean asked Sarah.

'Ask Puttnam, not me,' she said.

'But I'm asking you, Sarah,' said Lean, anxious to enlist her support in the great enterprise which lay ahead.

'Robert felt very strongly,' said Sarah, 'that if David had grown up at all in the intervening years then let him signal that growth by being the first to bridge the differences. I remember very vividly the look of joy that radiated from Robert. It was a truly wonderful day, the day of that first phone call.'[1]

Lean's life had changed considerably since he had last met Robert in Tahiti. He had married Sandy Hotz in 1981, just before they left for India to prepare *A Passage to India*. By all accounts the shooting of the film in 1983 was a miserable experience: Lean was bad-tempered throughout, impeded by a modest budget and at odds with three of his leading cast members, Judy Davis, Peggy Ashcroft and Alec Guinness, as well as his cameraman, Ernie Day, who had been Freddie Young's assistant. Only the unfailingly loyal and stoical Eddie Fowlie managed to jolly Lean along.

When Lean returned to London to edit the film, Sandy was cut off from the production and denied permission to visit Lean in his cutting room. But every night there would be a wordless dinner, just the two of them, in the gloomily formal restaurant at the Berkeley.

Although Lean himself considered *A Passage to India* to be well below the standard of his best work, its release was greeted with enthusiasm. Having suffered for years at the hands of the critics, he was now welcomed back as the sole survivor and master exponent of the narrative movie; even Pauline Kael had some good words to say about him. After fifteen years in the wilderness, Lean was fêted with accolades and honours, including a knighthood.

Lean and Sandy decided to live permanently in London, buying a group of three disused warehouses on the river at Narrow Street, Limehouse, which they converted into one of London's most spectacular homes, complete with an indoor lift, a large waterfront garden and a turntable in the garage for the Rolls-Royce. Lean sank £7 million into the property. Sandy, though, would never live in Narrow Street. While they stayed at the Berkeley, waiting for the builders and designers to finish their work, Lean began an affair with another Sandra, Sandra Cook, an exotic-looking fifty-something art dealer whom he had met at Harrods. When Sandy found out about the affair she left Lean and subsequently set up house in Connecticut with John Calley, the Warner Bros executive who was the first to finance the *Bounty* project. By the time Narrow Street was completed Lean and Sandra Cook were living together.

It is a strange thing, this bouncing silver ball called *Nostromo* by Joseph Conrad. In the Fifties Robert had proposed it as a radio serial for the BBC but had given up, defeated by the novel's scope and complexity. Then, in the Sixties, as *Lawrence of Arabia* was opening in Britain and America, Robert proposed it to Lean, who dismissed the idea out of hand. In the late Seventies Christopher Hampton had written an adaptation for BBC television which was rejected because it was too expensive. In 1986 Hampton began work with Lean and completed a first draft, which was sent to Steven Spielberg who was going to produce it.

'Who's the hero?' Spielberg asked Hampton.

'The hero is Nostromo,' said Hampton.

'Who's the villain?' asked Spielberg.

'The villain is the money,' said Hampton thoughtfully.

Spielberg bowed out after that exchange and shortly afterwards Hampton did the same, worn down by Lean's fastidiousness. Feeling betrayed by Spielberg and Hampton, Lean might have been forced to abandon *Nostromo* were it not for a chance meeting with the French producer, Serge Silberman, who had resurrected the careers of two other ageing statesmen of the cinema, Luis Buñuel and Akira Kurosawa. Having secured Silberman's commitment to raise the finance, Lean took Hampton's last words of advice and called Robert. After a couple of exploratory lunches with Robert and Sarah at Narrow Street, Lean sent him away with Hampton's script. 'It is remarkable how close you have stuck to the original storyline,' Robert told Lean. 'Nevertheless, I would take a much freer line with it, make it more about Nostromo and less about the blessing (and curse) of the Gould silver. Excuse me if this is based upon pride but then the whole world is based upon pride. . . . Forgive all this, if this is a confounded cheek.'[2]

A contract was swiftly drawn up which gave Robert $300,000 for the screenplay, whether the film was made or not. He started work at once, driving up to Lean's home early in the morning and returning shortly after lunch, when he would pass out in front of the television.

The routine with Lean was the same as always – long silences, grunts, grimaces, Lean staring out of the window at the river, Robert folding his arms across his considerable girth, chuckling to himself. Together they created a bizarre, surreal image for a film industry run by thirty-year-olds for an audience of eighteen-year-olds: the positively Falstaffian Robert, barely able to speak, and the seventy-eight-year old Lean, barely able to decide on a single line of dialogue in a script based on a novel that no Hollywood executive had heard of, much less read.

The fact that Robert and Lean had not met or spoken to each other for ten years says much about their collective egos and guilt. Lean had been devastated that Robert refused to see him in hospital in Los Angeles and was convinced that Robert held him personally responsible for his illness. What followed was even uglier, when an act of generosity was interpreted as heartless expediency. Since no provision had been made to insure Robert while he was in Tahiti, and because Robert himself was in no position to sign a cheque, David Lean paid his medical bill of $25,600, while Michael Caine covered his air fare to London.[3]

Lean, though, began to have second thoughts, reasoning that if word got round that he had paid Robert's medical fees, this might be interpreted as proof of his culpability in Robert's illness. He felt that not only Ben blamed him, but so did Margaret Ramsay, even talking to the press about Lean's way of drawing every last drop of blood from his collaborators. Enough emotional damage had been done to ensure that Lean stayed well away from Robert and his friends and family. Robert, though, was unaware of all this and in September 1979, shortly after his heart attack in France, he asked Julie Laird to arrange a dinner party with Lean and Sandy. The response was disappointing: 'You will not be surprised to learn', wrote Julie, 'that I have received *total silence* in reply to my letter to the Leans at the Berkeley inviting them to dine with us.'[4]

Five years passed before Robert contacted Lean again, when he wrote to ask if a newspaper report of Lean's and Sandy's marriage was true or not. 'Yes,' replied Lean on a postcard. 'Sandy and I were married outside Zurich two to three years ago but kept it quiet until it was stale news for the press. I'm on a cutting marathon – except on Sundays – so forgive this short note.'

On the day of the British première of *A Passage to India*, Robert had been saddened by an article in the *Sunday Mirror* in which an anonymous source said that Robert blamed Lean for his stroke. He felt compelled to write to Lean again:

> I do not know the friend who pronounced me very bitter about the failure of our friendship. Suffice to say that it wasn't me, for the obvious reason that I don't feel very bitter about it; and don't in any case talk to the Press. Look:
>
> I had lunch with Jill Harrison the other week. She told me about your extraordinary generosity in coming forward to meet my hospital bill. She told me that I had met this. I literally do not know; all that passed me by in those two years, passed like a dream. It was open handed of you and now, five and a half years later, thank you from the bottom of my heart.[5]

There was still no response from Lean himself, not until he needed Robert to work with him on *Nostromo*. As Sarah wrote with pin-point accuracy: 'David's friendships were based on *use* and Robert hadn't been any *use* to David of late.'[6]

The writing of *Nostromo* took two years and what emerged was a skeleton of the novel, shorn of several of its characters and most of its political and philosophical meaning. The script – with its bands of marauding guerrilla armies, machismo posturing and wilting expatriates – recalled nothing less than a flaky spaghetti Western by Sergio Leone called *Duck You Sucker*. While Robert endeavoured to invest the story with contemporary relevance – it was *The Mission* with silver rather than religion at its core – Lean searched out those moments where he could create visual poetry, notably the scene in which Nostromo and Decaud take the silver ingots across the starlit bay and bury them on the island.

The project ebbed and flowed with Lean's health. One month it looked as if it was about to start shooting; the next, Lean would succumb to shingles and the whole thing seemed doomed. It was to be shot in Cuba, then Mexico. When Lean and Sandra went to live in France, where they had lavishly converted an old mill in the hills above Cannes, it was announced the film would be shot in Spain and at the Victorine Studios in Nice, where John Box was building the sets. The budget was $20 million, then $40 million. Brando was in, then out, and so it went on. While Robert naturally hoped the film would be made, he knew that *Nostromo* and Lean himself were slipping away. But while *Nostromo* was not Robert's entire life – he was moonlighting on at least three other projects – it was literally a matter of life or death for Lean. At his age, if this project failed he would never find another.

When the news broke that Lean and Robert had got back together again, Melvyn Bragg proposed making a documentary about their partnership for his arts programme, *The South Bank Show*. Bragg had taken over briefly from Robert on Lean's *Bounty* project and he had also made a splendid profile of Lean to coincide with the opening of *A Passage to India*. Bragg's idea was to film Lean and Robert working in Narrow Street and intercut this with separate interviews about their previous collaborations.

Robert was terrified that he would not be understood, that he would look drunk, a hopeless wreck when pictured alongside Lean, who could switch on a performance of imperial elegance as easily as turning on a light. But Bragg and his team were so skilful and sensitive that only a few of Robert's remarks needed to be subtitled. For the most part, Bragg developed a technique of asking a question and repeating Robert's answer as if he wanted to chew it over himself, though clearly this was meant for the audience. 'We all went down to Chithurst to see Melvyn's film,' said Ben's wife, Jo. 'Bob couldn't bear to look at it but we finally persuaded him. He'd never heard his own voice before and when he came on he said, "Darling, I can't understand a fucking thing I'm saying." '

If the *South Bank Show* was one triumph, the restoration of *Lawrence of Arabia* was another. This new version, which restored Freddie Young's 70mm photography to its original brilliance and put back scenes which had been cut in 1963, opened in America and Europe in 1989 to thunderous acclaim. Lean went round the world promoting it, shovelling all the blame for the cuts on the shoulders of the late Sam Spiegel. Promoted as the rebirth of a butchered masterpiece, only later, following Lean's death, was it revealed that the butcher in question was Lean himself.

The second David in Robert's life was David Puttnam, who had bought the rights to a book by Mollie Dickenson called *Thumbs Up* which told the story of President Ronald Reagan's press secretary, James Brady. On 30 March 1981 a young man named John Hinckley Jr broke out from a crowd in Washington and fired a pistol at the president. Reagan was wounded, as was Brady who had dived across the President in an attempt to save his life. Brady emerged from surgery seriously brain damaged, barely able to speak and confined to a wheelchair. It later transpired that Hinckley had been charged before with firearm offences and that his assassination attempt was

ROBERT BOLT

done to impress the actress Jodie Foster, on whom he doted. When Brady's wife, Sarah, initiated a campaign for gun control, a policy opposed by Reagan, Brady himself was put in a difficult position, being the victim of America's liberal gun laws, yet wishing to remain loyal to his boss. Only when Reagan had stepped down as President did Brady support his wife publicly. The resulting Brady Bill was later adopted as policy by President Clinton.

Puttnam had no hesitation in offering the project to Robert:

It seemed tailor made for him because it fused Robert's disability with the opportunity to say something about disability. And I had some amazing experiences with Bob and Jim Brady together, including lunch at the White House.

We shipped off in Brady's disability wagon to the White House. We got to Brady's office where everyone said, 'Hi, Jim.' One of the sweet things was that Brady never lost his title and that the other guy was always known as the Acting Press Secretary. It still said James Brady on the door. Suddenly, the door opened and this girl said, 'Jim, the President is free for lunch, why don't you all join him?' Now, I've got these two shipwrecks on either side of me, Bob and Jim, one on each arm. So off we go. We see Reagan at the door of the Oval Office, about twenty yards away, a distance one would normally cover in five seconds. It takes us a full fifty seconds, with Reagan saying 'Hi!' and Brady garbling 'Hi!' back to him. Eventually we get there and Reagan stretches out his hand to Brady. But it's the wrong hand. Then he stretches out his hand to Bob and it's the wrong hand again. There's a chaos of hands. Then we're ushered inside for a lunch with plastic forks.

I said to Reagan, 'Mr President, were you intimidated when you first sat down in this room?' And he said, 'Well, not really. I'd been Governor of California and this job is much the same, you know. But there's one difference. I get to meet a lot of foreigners.'

Then Robert said, 'Oh. You were a governor? Do you think that is a good training ground for presidents? Does that mean you will be voting for Governor Dukakis?' Robert's joke cracked Reagan up.[7]

As Robert prepared to write the *Brady* screenplay, he wrote a letter to his friend, Roger Gard, telling him about the lunch at the White House and his general feelings about the quality of his current work. Robert was in an ironic and mischievous mood, which always went down well with Gard:

The directors and producers think I have a sure footed way through they're contradicotory stepping stones, across their scripts. It may be so. The scripts are not what they once were – I am always willing to be amended on that point – Sarah tells me they are better, bless her heart – but they really are not; well I don't think so.

I am now doing one for David Puttnam, about President Reagan's Press Secretary who was gunned down by the assassin, who thought that this would put him higher on the visiting list of a film starlet; needless to say it didn't. I saw him (Jim Brady) and Reagan. Good, nice, heart warming people, but goodness me how prenaturally thick as three planks. The wife of the Press Secretary was really spiritual, a saint I shouldn't wonder.[8]

At first, the Brady project was to be a two-hour feature film for Warner Bros for which Robert would be paid $200,000 plus a bonus of $100,000 if the film went into production with his sole name as author of the screenplay.

Working with Robert was an associate of Puttnam, Colin Vaines, who spent many hours at Chithurst and came to regard Robert as a sort of father figure or mentor, someone he could ask for advice on the other projects he had running at the time.

As soon as Robert delivered his first-draft screenplay, Warner Bros had cold feet about the idea and put it into turnaround. Fortunately, the project was taken up by Home Box Office (HBO) as a made-for-television movie, its natural home. Barbara Bloom, who worked for HBO, was brought in as script editor. 'We loved the script,' said Bloom, 'even though it was long and needed to be condensed. I had one meeting with Robert at Puttnam's office and I thought, how am I going to give notes to Robert Bolt? He did another couple of drafts before we produced it.'[9]

As Robert was writing his various drafts, the title kept changing. It started as *Thumbs Up*, then became *Bear*, then *The Political Animal* and finally, *Without Warning: The James Brady Story*. What remained consistent was Robert's approach to the subject which was less political than humane, focusing on the relationship between the disabled Brady and his wife, Sarah, an uncanny coincidence.

Robert's problem was combining the human story with the political ramifications of the Brady Bill which HBO wanted to emphasise, lending the film the topicality which all made-for-TV movies strive for. After viewing a video of Brady's testimony to the Senate, Robert wrote to Puttnam:

I have been thinking about what you have said about the Brady Gun Control. The Brady testimony was heart rending. Look, I will try and get it into the script as it now stands. But the *main* point of the film is Jim's hauling himself back from death, isn't it? That's what I took it to be anyway. This can only be tampered with by the politication of Sarah and the liberalisation of Brady very, very sparsely. Otherwise we are trying to make two films out of one. What was it that made his testimony so moving? It was his soldiering on through the pages, her hand guiding his eyes, down the pages, turning them leaf by leaf. This is the thing that I thought you meant by your saying, 'You and you only, you could could do a film from the inside about this, Robert.' Well, I will try, honestly.[10]

Robert was never able successfully to combine the two elements of the story. Barbara Bloom found him strangely resistant to these requirements and finally, just before shooting started, another writer was brought in to politicise the script. Although the other writer never received screen credit, his existence meant that Robert was obliged to forfeit half his $100,000 bonus.

Without Warning: The James Brady Story was shown by HBO on 16 June 1991 and commanded rave reviews and a large audience. Directed by Michael Uno and starring Beau Bridges and Joan Allen, it was not shown in Britain until early 1997, when the massacre of the schoolchildren at Dunblane had made gun control a live issue. 'I am very proud of my part in the Brady story, I mean very proud,' Robert told Puttnam. 'I am particularly pleased about receiving a world's record fee for it – I'd no idea, but once again, thank you. However I can't agree about HBO really knowing more about the appetites of the viewers than either you or I. Why was it so hard to get it done? You forced it on them. And now they congratulate themselves on the critics.'[11]

Melvyn Bragg's *South Bank Show* had resulted in a torrent of fan letters, all of which were answered by Robert, Sarah or Julie Laird. The success of the *Brady* film now brought Robert some welcome personal publicity in America, enhancing his reputation in Hollywood and producing a further flood of letters from stroke victims and their carers or relatives. In particular, a profile by David Gritten for the *Los Angeles Times* conveyed Robert's life at Chithurst, his indefatigable optimism and his relationship with Sarah. 'I think of life as hard, yes,' Robert told Gritten, 'but I never wake up and think, Oh God, another day. I wake up and think, Oh good, another day.'[12]

Shortly after the *Los Angeles Times* piece was published, Robert received a letter from the wife of Burt Lancaster. 'As you may have heard,' she wrote, 'my husband suffered a stroke in November. Burt has been left paralyzed on the right side and he has difficulty with his speech. He is making steady progress and although his attitude remains positive most of the time, I am wondering if there are not things I might be doing that would enhance his comfort. Conversely, I'm concerned that I may be doing things that are annoying or counter-productive – little things – that he has not expressed to me. My hope is that you or your wife would be willing to share pieces of your own struggle – things you liked, things you didn't – so that I might better help Burt.'[13]

Robert replied immediately with a long and brutally honest letter:

I havn't the foggiest notion what to say, it is all up to Burt and to a lesser extent you what to do about it. If he, faced with a long row ahead doesn't want to be bothered, well good luck to him. It is a terribly uphill struggle. . . I took about a couple of years doing customary speech exercises. . . I could just drive my car, adapted, that was simply tremendous. I rember thinking how lucky my friends were to be invited out to lunch by me. I now realise that it must have been agony for them, but, this is the point. I would be the same if I had to do it again. They thought I was drunk or mad. He mustn't mind if people treaet him like that, it's part of the price one has to pay. Funny anyway.

Burt's paralysis sounds like mine. I have lost all my right side, arm and leg, well very nearly. I can walk abot a eighth of a mile before I must find a bench. The right hand side of my brain, so they tell me, too. But I don't believe them. It is amazing, how one works out the alenative routs to one's old patterns of thinking. All my dearest friends have got used to my croaking, slurred voice.

Tell Burt to get a WORD PROCESSOR. Mine is a Macintosh. It saved my life. Now, than God, I can do the Screenplay. You must all this under your hat.

It is up to him to let you know whether you are doing things he doesn't need doing or vice versa. It is not your fault. I was once, in the early staged of my attack, Burt came up to me in an LA office and shook me warmly by the hand. I have never fogortten it (Apogies for the spelling). Show this to Burt.[14]

One of the beneficial side effects of Robert's illness was that it brought him closer to his family than he had ever been before. His first wife, Jo Riddett, had become a novelist and Robert was generous with his praise and encouragement. Sarah, too, had become a writer, having abandoned her acting career in order to remain at Chithurst and attend to Robert's well-being. Robert had looked up to his brother Sydney from an early age and was always intimidated by his conspicuous intelligence. Robert also admired Sydney for never allowing his academic brilliance to overrun his socialist principles; as a result, Sydney taught at state run institutions and was never tempted by a Cambridge college stipend, even though he lived there. Until Robert suffered his stroke, Sydney was never shown any of Robert's scripts or screenplays and was rarely asked for advice. But all that changed after the stroke. Robert sent him his various works in progress and Sydney worked assiduously on them. If Robert wanted to mention the names of Picasso and Gertrude Stein in a script about Scott of the Antarctic, he would ask Sydney if this was appropriate or not. Sydney replied that it was not and suggested that a better name to drop would be Beerbohm. It was Sydney who served as the uncredited editor of Robert's novelisation of *The Mission*, as well as *The Thwarting of Baron Bolligrew*, which was his favourite of his brother's plays.

Robert's relationship with Ben also underwent a profound change. They began to exchange ideas, scripts and many letters, especially when Ben and his wife, Jo, were living in Los Angeles. If Ben was sent a script he invariably asked his father's opinion of it. In most cases this involved little more than a mutual dislike of the offer in hand, though one script in particular led to a long exchange of notes.

Colin Vaines had been asked by David Puttnam to produce a film about T.E. Lawrence's life after Arabia. It was such an obvious idea that the only surprise was that no one had already made it, for Lawrence's participation in the peace conference in Paris and his ambivalent approach to the fame which attended him provided a fascinating postscript to the epic adventure in the desert. A script, called *A Dangerous Man*, had been written by Tim Rose Price. Because Vaines had developed a close working relationship with Robert on the *Brady* film, he naturally sought the advice of the man who had written the screenplay for Lean's *Lawrence of Arabia*. Ben wanted Robert's advice as well because he not only saw several flaws in Price's script, he was reluctant to take on a project which had such close connections with his father. When Robert heard about the Lawrence project, he faxed Ben some advice about the subject and some prescient thoughts about David Puttnam: 'Make sure it is full of the facts, or the probable facts,' Robert told Ben. 'T. E. Lawrence wasn't a probable figure in that scramble for oil, not that that makes him a figure worth writing about, but watch your Producer. He is full of the finesse which would make him a knight or even a lord, you know. I mean no matter how many Directors faces he has to grind squashily to pulp. It may be very good, but it equally well may be oh so boring.'[15]

Ben sent Robert the script and asked: 'Is it good enough to do for the "keep working" philosophy? Or is it too boring, too redundant after your and Lean's legendary movie? Because if it is dull and redundant, it seems to me doubly dangerous for me to risk appearing to be trying to invoke or emulate *Lawrence of Arabia*.'[16]

Robert read Price's script and sent Ben a series of notes which almost amounted to a rewrite. 'I can't, as you know, spell,' wrote Robert to Ben. 'I have read *A Dangerous Man* at one sitting (quite remarkable for me) and I think that it's very nearly dangerously good and very nearly a run of the mill doctumentary. If you are given a free hand with the treatment of it I would say, do it. If you are not, I would say don't. I shall deny outright having read it.'[17]

Ben finally passed on *A Dangerous Man*, which was subsequently directed by Christopher Mensaul and won an Emmy Award as the best foreign television drama of the year. It was an impressive film which had an opening uncannily like that of Michael Wilson's original script for Lean, showing Lawrence attending a performance of Lowell Thomas's 'lecture' in London. The film, modest in scale, skilfully revealed Lawrence's complex and contradictory personality and in Ralph Fiennes it also revealed a major new screen actor.

While Robert was hard at work on the *Brady* film and *Nostromo*, he took on another gargantuan project, the story of the Buddha. Although Robert's lifelong interest in religions was one motive for starting work, and Sarah's interest in Buddhism and all things mystical was another, anyone with any sense or understanding of the film industry would have foreseen disaster and indeed, the project lumbered on for five frustrating years.

It began with Ronnie Colsen, the son of an industrialist, Walter Colsen, who had stolen a march on other Americans by setting up in Japan shortly after the war. Walter Colsen called his company Waco – a contraction of his name – and turned to electronics. By the Seventies he was producing car entertainment systems, video recorders and computers. Not one of Japan's industrial giants, Colsen nevertheless made a handsome living.

His son, Ronnie, who was based in Tokyo and Hong Kong, developed a keen interest in Eastern religions and thought of diverting some of his wealth into a lavish film about the Buddha. Having had no previous experience of the film industry, Colsen set up Waco Productions and decided personally to finance the preliminary research and the screenplay. Only when he had a completed screenplay and a commitment from a leading director would he look for production finance from Japanese, Taiwanese and Indian investors. And once he had the funding – estimated at $36 million – he felt confident he could sell the film to an American distributor. It sounded so easy since Colsen, who was in his mid-forties, was convinced that his own belief in the project, his own religious obsession, would be infectious. The picture would be the Nineties equivalent of *Gandhi*, not so much an epic movie, but a 'world event'. 'This movie seems a natural to me,' Colsen told the *Hollywood Reporter*, 'Buddha is the last great historical figure of whom a world-class movie hasn't been made. It's going to have lots of action and adventure but we're keeping historically very true to all the accounts available.'[18]

In need of a screenwriter, Colsen asked various people for advice. 'All put Robert as the number one choice, due to his record in writing historical and epic films,' said Colsen. 'I set up a meeting in London with him and my first impression was that, despite his age and state of health, he was energetic and jovial. I soon felt an affinity with him. From the outset, Robert was concerned about his lack of knowledge on the subject, but felt easier after I explained we needed a writer who was *not* an expert on the Buddha in order to better convey its themes to a Western audience.'[19] Robert would be paid $275,000 in instalments, a further $175,000 within six weeks of the start of photography, plus three and a half per cent of the profits when the picture recovered its production and marketing costs.

'I didn't want Robert to do the Buddha film,' said Sarah. 'He didn't believe in Enlightenment. He only believed in more money. I was shocked when he accepted it but when he did I helped him as much as I could.'

Robert's first job was to produce a fifteen-page outline which was to form the basis for two 'workshop-seminars' chaired by Colsen. The first was held at a Tibetan colony in the Dordogne and the second in Oxford. These seminars, which were also attended by an adviser to the Dalai Lama and Professor Richard Gombrich of Oxford, were intended to provide what Colsen called 'a forum for lively discussion of the best of the many possible approaches. Robert was accompanied by Sarah who was an added bonus due to her insight and feeling for the material. Robert assiduously absorbed those points which he felt could best be used for the script.

'Robert's stature had not made him lose his sense of humility which I believe made it easier for him to accept the need to work with experts, despite the difficulty that this entailed,' said Colsen.

The problem for Robert was similar to the one he encountered when dramatising the lives of Sir Thomas More and Gandhi: here was another saint who needed to be brought down to the level of a man. As he listened to the advice from the experts, Sarah went to do some research in Nepal, where she fell under the spell of Kense Rinpoche, the Dalai Lama's teacher.

'What did he teach you?' Robert asked her when she got back.

'He enabled me to touch upon the limitless capacity for inner contentment found in reverence and devotion,' she said.

'He was worth all that, was he?' said Robert.

'That and much more,' said Sarah. 'He was the jolly gentle giant, an eighty-year-old Sumo wrestler with hands and feet as young, unworn and untouched as a new born baby's.'

'Obviously never had to do the washing up,' said Robert.[20]

Colsen, meanwhile, had found his ideal director in Bernardo Bertolucci, a former Italian poet and devout Marxist who had made one great masterpiece, *The Conformist*, one worldwide *succès de scandale*, *Last Tango in Paris*, and a string of turgid flops notable only for the luscious photography of Vittorio Storaro. But in 1988 Bertolucci had won an Academy Award for his decorative if bloated epic of Chinese history, *The Last Emperor*. Bertolucci became Colsen's prime target.

Although Bertolucci had already committed himself to his next film – an adaptation of Paul Bowles's *The Sheltering Sky* – he asked to study Robert's work before making any promises. By October 1989, Bertolucci had agreed to direct *Buddha* and demanded a fee of $5 million, a fifty per cent share of the profits and total artistic control. The purity and the simplicity of Buddha's life, like that of Gandhi, would have a hefty price tag.

Colsen should have backed out then and there, if only because a director like Bertolucci, fresh from a triumph at the Oscars, brings with him dozens of lawyers, co-production partners and an army of sycophants; a novice like Colsen would have been sidelined in weeks. Instead, Colsen took out prestige advertisements in the trade press, guided Robert through the maze of Eastern mysticism and awaited Bertolucci's return from the Sahara, where he was filming *The Sheltering Sky*.

By the time Bertolucci had released his new film – a resounding flop everywhere – he had read Robert's second draft screenplay and had done a considerable amount of independent research into the life of the Buddha. The story he had in mind was radically different: Bertolucci wanted to use the Buddha's philosophy as a catalyst in the story of a young American who is believed to be the Buddha's reincarnated soul on earth. It was a Sixties concept, a retro hippie epic, with chiming bells, gorgeous scenery and a vague message about world peace. Teaming up with his regular producer, Jeremy Thomas, and two screenwriters – Rudy Wurlitzer and Mark Peploe – Bertolucci abandoned Colsen and Robert, taking from them the benefits of their work and research, and vanished to Nepal and Bhutan to make *Little Buddha*.

Colsen issued a lawsuit against Bertolucci and managed to capture the ear of a Warner Bros executive who sent Robert's screenplay to several directors, including Adrian Lyne who specialised in high-kink, such as *Fatal Attraction* and *Indecent Proposal*. But while Warner Bros were rounding up the makers of last year's hit movies, Colsen offered the project to Mira Nair, a thirty-year-old Indian woman whose 1987 film, *Salaam Bombay*, about a street urchin's misadventures, had won praise everywhere and had earned its director an Academy Award nomination. Nair compensated for her lack of experience in big-budget productions by what seemed to Robert and Sarah a genuine interest in the project: she spent several days at Chithurst and brought her own ideas about how the screenplay might be improved. Sitting on his turntable, surrounded by a mass of notes from Nair, Colsen and various academics, Robert tapped away for an additional $25,000.

After devoting a year to the project, Mira Nair threw in the towel. Writing from Kampala, Uganda, she told Robert she had spent a dismal two months in Hollywood 'talking Buddha, Buddha, Buddha. I would leave feeling so empty and disillusioned; it felt like work but I also felt like I was doing nothing at all. Anyway, Robert, there are no real takers right now. Not many understood or in any way "felt" the script; it was too alien for them, they said, emotionally distant and, to quote an oft-repeated term, "not transcendent" in any way. . . . I'm sorry to give you this news, Robert – but it is beyond my control. I have swiftly moved from being hired to direct an epic film on a very comfortable budget to raising money myself for what I'm used to making: an epic on a peanut.'[21]

Although Robert was earning substantial sums of money, he had become wearied by the project and felt that the revisions were leading nowhere. It was also a drain on his time as he was still working with Lean on *Nostromo* and with Puttnam and Vaines on *James Brady*. 'Buddha I regret I have taken on,' he wrote to Ben. 'There's no hint of humour anywhere in it, besides I don't know what he thought, well no more than a little – but I gladly take on lots of the rest, having the thing to do my level best at them, well nearly anyway. It keeps my hand in.'[22]

Keeping his hand in is what Robert did at all costs. It seems extraordinary that a man of his age and in his condition should not only be writing a film about the Buddha, but that he should also be working simultaneously on *Nostromo* and – his latest project – the life story of Richard Nixon for David Frost.

While the young Robert would readily abandon a play like *Gentle Jack* to devote himself to *Lawrence of Arabia* and shelve it again for *Doctor Zhivago*, the old and disabled Robert had turned into a circus conjuror, juggling Eastern religion, Washington politics and South American revolution with his left hand. Inevitably, the strain began to show – faxes to his script editor, Barbara Bloom, were addressed to Barbara Beale and David Puttnam's wife, Patsy, was addressed as Sarah. At least when he wrote to his producers he needed only to write 'Dear David', knowing that Lean, Puttnam and Frost would each believe the letter was for them.

The offers of work never ceased. Most of them hardly surprised Robert since they tended to be historical dramas. But Trevor Nunn came up with a real surprise by proposing a stage musical version of *Ryan's Daughter*.

'I hadn't seen much of Robert since *Bolligrew*,' said Nunn. 'I'd heard about his stroke of course and I spotted him once in a restaurant near the Roundhouse in Camden Town. He waved through the window and looked just like the old Robert. So I went in and was immediately shocked by his difficulty in speaking.'[23]

It was a few years after that chance meeting that Nunn turned his thoughts to *Ryan's Daughter*. Looking for another musical subject to follow his production of Andrew Lloyd Webber's *Sunset Boulevard*, Nunn was holding discussions with an Irish composer named Shaun Davey. They were searching for an existing story which contained all the right ingredients for a dramatic stage musical.

> We tossed aside a number of half-baked ideas [Nunn told Robert], which led us to discuss James Joyce and as we were going through story by story of *Dubliners* the Eureka thunder-flash happened and I shouted *Ryan's Daughter* for which you

conceived and wrote your superb film script.

That story has what is vital to a musical – a location which demands a particular musical idiom; a Romeo and Juliet-like forbidden love story, an epic environment of a political and racial struggle providing a constantly thrilling contrast between the public and the private, and a perfect range of characters who suggest the complete gamut of vocal demands. It has local ritual around which to build major musical set pieces, and in the central moral dilemma of the father's duplicity and the loss of his daughter, balanced by the unexpected courage and loyalty of the humiliated husband, it has hugely emotional crises and the optimism of human endurance.[24]

Nunn's letter was not only highly persuasive, it also contained what is perhaps the most perceptive appraisal of the film's themes that has ever been written. The fact that the movie's reputation was a fairly dismal one was of no consequence to Nunn and although the project fell into limbo, he hopes he might eventually stage it at the Royal National Theatre. 'I feel strongly that the National should not only be reviving musicals, such as *Guy and Dolls*, but presenting brand new ones,' he said.

Nunn's project merely required Robert's approval, which was given gladly. There was, too, at this time a sudden flirtation with Galileo, about whom Robert wrote a script – called *Messenger of the Stars* – for an American producer, Joe Feury, who had signed a deal with Carolco, the company which had made the *Rambo* films and which was destined to go bankrupt.

There was also an outbreak of skirmishes with British explorers. David Puttnam had a long-standing ambition to make a film about Ernest Shackleton which Hugh Hudson was slated to direct. Robert wrote a treatment for them and the project went into limbo, unable to find a sponsor in Hollywood.

John Heyman, a British producer, invited Robert to the Bahamas to discuss a film about Scott's and Amundsen's race to the South Pole in 1912. Robert signed a contract with Heyman, which would have paid him $500,000 if the film went into production, and two years later completed a screenplay called *The Tortoise and the Hare*, a clever title once one knew what it was about but an apparent children's film if one didn't.

The problem with Scott was his character, as Robert explained to Heyman: 'Can Scott have been such a heaven sent, toffee nosed ass and such a transformed hero as he was meant to be? He reminds me of those preunlimate, but never quite ulitamate, perfects of the schools I went to. He is hilarious and preternaturally touching, but never quite touching enough. Of course Amundsen is the true history of the globe trotting. But Scott is the other side of the tortoise and the hare and anyway which is the tortoise and which the hare? They were both hares if you ask me and Amundesen made it. That frightful Mrs Scott. Anyway a great subject for a film.'[25]

Robert sent Ben his script of *The Tortoise and the Hare* and received a penetrating analysis by return: 'I find the topic to be a dangerously hollow one. There's nothing at the Pole when you manage to get there – no mountain peak, no treasure, no bare-breasted girls. Is it possible to make more of a dramatic virtue of this? The hollowness of the achievement is a perfect metaphor for Scott's ambitions; but I'd like a clearer sense of why Amundsen made the journey.'[26]

If Robert found Scott a mysteriously compelling figure, he had little time for Dr Livingstone: 'I am waiting for two men to come from Los Angeles and interest me in a story about David Livingstone his life and times,' Robert wrote to Ben and Jo. 'As far as I know he was a humourless Scottish prick with all the virtues that go with that, lion-like courage, persistence and for all that, he was on the right side in reference to the slave trade re the Portese and the Arabs, ourselves he fogotten, but the awful religion, like my religion when I grew up, fortunately though I wasn't Scottish. A bad subject or a film. Downbeat and heavy.'[27]

On 16 April 1991 David Lean died of pneumonia. He had married Sandra Cook in France the previous Christmas, which was when he began to complain of a sore throat. He underwent surgery and radio therapy for throat cancer and seemed to be making a recovery until the pneumonia finally claimed him. When Robert heard the news, he was deeply shocked, even though he and Sarah had recently visited Lean and saw how close he was to death. More often than not, Lean was delirious, his mind wandering between memories of India and images from the unmade *Nostromo*.

Robert did not attend Lean's funeral, though he did go to the memorial service which was held at St Paul's Cathedral in October. Steadied by Sarah, Robert struggled to his feet and said, 'Oh dear. I'm here David. All of the style of film-making you taught me. . . I remember a unique friend.'

Lean's widow and Serge Silberman tried in vain to finance *Nostromo* with another director and Robert did all he could to assist them, even writing to Francis Coppola: 'I don't phone you because

I have had a stroke, and all that emerges is a series of gutteral grunts which would cause you to think you had a madman on the phone.'[28] Coppola declined the offer, as did everyone else. *Nostromo* seemed to die with Lean because no one was keen on making a film which had now become a celluloid monument to Lean's memory. Hugh Hudson, though, hoped to make his own film, using Christopher Hampton's screenplay, not Robert's, though he was beaten to it by none other than Fernando Ghia who filmed a lavish if flawed mini-series for the BBC, using yet another script. 'When Robert was working with Lean on the script,' said Ghia, 'I kept telling him that it was impossible to make *Nostromo* as a two- or three-hour film. It could only be done as a mini-series lasting six or seven hours and I made my version as a way of proving my theory to him. Sadly, he never saw it.'[29]

Several of Robert's friends wrote to express their commiseration at the loss of his old colleague. 'Yes, I find that a big hole has taken place in my life with David's passing,' he wrote to Bernard McCabe's sister, Eileen. 'I suppose that somebody may take up *Nostromo* where he left off but I simply don't know; I tell you, films – it is the Mafiah; a game of Monopoly with drawn pistols and poisons under the board. It was a goodish film. Never mind, I have been paid. Ah me.'[30]

If the passing of David Lean touched Robert deeply, Margaret Ramsay's death on 4 September 1991 affected him even more. She had been in ill-health for some years, though that did not stop her from putting in a full day at her offices in Goodwin's Court. But on 8 April there had been a major fire, destroying many files and manuscripts and that unexplained event, together with the death a few days later of her partner, Bill Roderick, quelled her fiery spirit. David Lean and Margaret Ramsay were Robert's yin and yang. They were almost exactly the same age – Ramsay was two months Lean's junior – and they both fed on Robert's talent and conscience like parental vultures. Lean and Ramsay barely knew each other – they may not even have met – though they knew only too well each other's strengths and weaknesses.

Robert regarded Lean as a constant irritation and a continuing inspiration. His view of Lean's personal fads – his gleaming white, tie-less shirts, his demand for a manicured world, his xenophobia and his general lack of learning – turned from amusement into contempt. He often drove Robert up the wall – how often had Lean said to him, 'All right, but let's go back and have a look at Scene One.' And yet he had given Robert the keys to international success and wealth. His influence on the younger man was profound.

Ramsay would doubtless have described that influence as baleful and destructive. As she acquired a new clutch of clients – Joe Orton, David Hare, Christopher Hampton – she offered them Robert's career as a terrible warning. Hampton had a dose of this when he left Lean and *Nostromo* in order to work on the film version of his successful play, *Dangerous Liaisons*. 'Peggy simply didn't enjoy films,' he said, 'and a lot of her attitudes were bound up with her early experiences with Bolt, who was held up as an example of what not to become.'[31]

When Ramsay became jealous of Lean's dominance, or Sarah's, she hissed and clawed like an alley cat in heat. 'The trouble is', she once wrote to Robert, 'no author is rich, because the more he earns the higher his station in life becomes. Motor cars are bought, *garçonières* are booked and wives are given the mink treatment.'[32] But if Ramsay was appalled by what Robert had become, she always had her ten per cent of it. Robert not only made her rich, he enabled her in 1963 to set up completely on her own. If Robert was not entirely her own creation, then she was a creation of his success. Her slice of Robert's cake gave substance to Ramsay's stubbornness and eccentricities and passion. Happily, Ramsay and Sarah had become friends, even to the extent of Sarah visiting her in Brighton. And Ramsay had liked a play Sarah had written called *Charlemagne*.

For thirty years, Robert had been caught like an iron filing between these two magnets. Lean had left him a legacy – of narrative structure, of getting the damn thing right, of what Ramsay called 'the corruption of the grand hotels' and what Frith Banbury summarised as 'Sam Spiegel's yacht'. Ramsay had left him with a different legacy – of drive, energy, principle and an agency still anxious to do his deals for him. And when Lean and Ramsay died, a significant part of the British cinema and the British theatre died with them. Amazingly, Robert had survived them both.

THIRTY-ONE

HOME FROM THE HILL

'Humour is emotional chaos remembered in tranquillity.'

James Thurber

In the spring of 1992, when Robert was still grappling with *Buddha*, David Frost suggested that he might be interested in writing a film about the early years of Richard Nixon. Frost had recorded a series of television interviews with the disgraced President in 1980 and felt that one of the fascinations about Nixon was that no one really knew him; that he was, in fact, a stranger even to himself. Nixon's rise and fall was in some ways the story of America itself, a fable about success and failure and the nature of power. It was a modern tragedy on a Shakespearian scale.

Having already written one White House drama, *Without Warning: The James Brady Story*, Robert was happy to tackle another. Unlike Frost, he had never met Nixon; the closest he had come was on 14 December 1972, shortly after *Lady Caroline Lamb* had opened, when he and Sarah were invited by the Prime Minister, Edward Heath, to a dinner at 10 Downing Street in honour of Nixon's daughter, Tricia, and her husband, Edward Cox.

The Nixon project was to be a co-production between HBO and Frost's company, David Paradine Television Inc., for which Robert had written *Augustus* in 1977. Since HBO's executives were pleased with *The James Brady Story*, they decided to engage Robert's script editor, Barbara Bloom, who had since left the company, as a producer and consultant. John Florescu, who was Frost's executive director in Los Angeles, would co-ordinate and produce the project with Bloom.

Although Robert knew relatively little about Nixon's life, he was drawn to the idea and saw in the disgraced former president a remarkably dramatic character. It was a story about a shy boy from a deeply religious, working-class background who was haunted by the deaths of his two brothers and also by the conviction that he was a perpetual outsider and that 'they' – the political and social establishment – were out to get him. When the project started Nixon was alive and had made a few appearances on the world stage in an effort to rehabilitate himself as a statesman. But while Robert was writing the script Nixon died, giving a new urgency to the project.

Robert's fee was the subject of protracted negotiation. Writers' fees for cinema and television films differ considerably, and since Robert's fee for *Brady* was scaled for a screenplay, even though it was eventually made for television, HBO insisted on paying him the reduced rate for a teleplay. Robert would receive $175,000 for the story outline and two drafts of the teleplay, plus a further $40,000 for any additional polish, plus a bonus of $60,000 if he ultimately received sole screen credit. The envisaged two-hour film, budgeted at $4 million, was to confine itself to Nixon's early life – his childhood, his wartime experience in the Pacific, his marriage to Pat and his first political campaigns, including his controversial persecution of Alger Hiss, culminating in his becoming Eisenhower's Vice-President.

Having only met Robert once before on the *Brady* film, Barbara Bloom flew with John Florescu to London for meetings at Chithurst. She said:

> We had worked at a distance on *Brady* but on the Nixon project we worked much closer and built up a lot of trust. We'd sit in his office, a very cold room, with his dog, Lovely. Robert would be in his night-shirt, sitting at his desk, and Sarah would serve us mugs of tea. Sometimes David Frost would sit in and tell us about his interviews with Nixon. He said that Nixon was socially very awkward, not a cool guy, and that he suddenly asked the crew, 'Have any of you done any fornicating lately?' Robert loved that and it went straight into the script. Robert became fascinated by Nixon. He'd hold up two fingers and squeeze them together so there was no space between them and then he'd say, 'He was this big! An awful man but I love him!'[1]

Although everyone was calling the project *Young Nixon*, HBO wanted something catchier, more commercial, and they came up with *Tricky Dickie*, a crass idea which suggested a lampoon. By the end of March 1993 Robert had completed his first draft and sent it to Florescu, Bloom and Hutch Parker at HBO. 'Here is the first draft of *Tricky Dickie*,' said Robert in his covering note to Parker. 'Tons of material missing naturally, but I think or guess it makes gripping reading as you go along. What a strange, overfull, prim creature he must be.'[2]

Inevitably, HBO had many queries and reservations about Robert's work. Although the script was often diffuse, one thing was clear: Nixon's early life was simply too interesting and too complex to compress into a two-hour film. Since Oliver Stone's 1991 film, *JFK*, had been a huge success and had run for more than three hours, HBO proposed making two films. Nixon's death brought about inflation: HBO wanted a mini-series of four hour-long episodes, later increased to six. Robert's fee was put up accordingly, if not entirely pro rata. The expansion of the project would enable him to write about Nixon's narrow defeat in 1960 by John Kennedy, the ensuing wilderness years, as well as Lyndon Johnson's presidency and the major political issues of the Sixties: the Cuban missile crisis, civil rights and the escalation of the Vietnam War. The mini-series would end with Nixon's election to the presidency in 1968, following the assassination of Robert Kennedy. No one felt it necessary to develop the story further: Nixon's White House years and the Watergate scandal had already been filmed many times, most notably in *All the President's Men* and several TV mini-series, such as *Washington Behind Closed Doors* and *Blind Ambition*. The last thing HBO wanted was another saga about CIA spooks, Cuban plumbers and chivalrous journalists lurking in underground parking lots. What they wanted was an epic which might explain an enigma.

Robert had been using Roger Morris's biography of Nixon as his principal source of research. Now he ordered up several more, as well as video transfers of the former President's most important speeches. HBO also sent him videos of their most recent mini-series so that he might acquaint himself with their 'house style'. John Florescu initiated research at the Richard Nixon Library and found them reluctant to co-operate. 'We only wanted to know the colour of his school football shirt and what his number was,' he said.[3]

Everyone at HBO and Paradine thought they had given Robert a full-time job. But he was a sly old fox who played one set of producers against another. With Julie Laird conducting some independent research for him and typing up his scripts, HBO and Paradine were kept in the dark about the true state of his writing and his health. Although Barbara Bloom and John Florescu were always welcome at Chithurst, Robert preferred that all discussions be conducted by fax. Consequently, Bloom and Florescu found themselves writing masses of notes when a phone call could quite easily have sufficed. For Robert, this procedure avoided talking and the risk of misunderstandings; but, more crucially, it slowed down the process, enabling him to prevaricate and continue work on *Buddha*, as well as new projects which came his way. He was moonlighting on a grand scale.

Shortly after he started work on the Nixon project Robert wrote his first script for British television. In 1992 Granada had a hit called *Prime Suspect*, about a woman detective played by Helen Mirren. When the screen rights looked like being sold to Universal in Hollywood, Granada decided to initiate a programme of large-scale films for cinema release. One of their ideas was a film about the Spanish Civil War. A production executive at Granada, Pippa Cross, had been impressed by *Doctor Zhivago* and how Robert had 'conveyed the macrocosm and also a personal story'. Before she contacted Robert, though, she checked him out with Colin Vaines. Having Vaines's complete endorsement, Cross approached the director, Jim Sheridan, who had made *My Left Foot* for Granada. 'Jim and I went down to see Robert,' said Cross, 'and we sat surrounded by dogs, drinking huge mugs of tea. Robert was already well informed about the Spanish Civil War, the war between the Right and the Left and the war between the Left and the Left. He also talked a great deal about his own days as a communist in ways people just don't talk any more. He and Jim got on really well together. They both flexed their intellectual muscles.'

Robert signed a contract with Granada and watched several hours of footage from a Granada documentary series which included interviews with Civil War veterans who spoke without fear of recriminations from Franco. His resulting script, which was called *The International Brigade*, told a human story about star-crossed lovers caught up in the conflict. 'Working with Bob was an extraordinary process, a flawed process,' said Pippa Cross. 'While his mental grasp was one hundred per cent, I think it's fair to say that he was grappling with the notion of giving speeches to characters he wasn't capable of writing.'[4]

Shortly after a second draft was commissioned, Granada's deal with Universal collapsed, putting paid to their co-production plans. The Spanish Civil War project was abandoned for good when Ken Loach and writer Jim Allen – two former Granada employees – announced their own film, *Land and Freedom*, which was released in 1995.

Taking up rather less of Robert's time was *The Proud and the Free*, a story of the American War of Independence which had been proposed to him by the actor Richard Dreyfuss. Based on a novel by the communist writer Howard Fast – best known for the novel, *Spartacus* – the story dealt with a localised event known as the January Mutiny, when immigrant soldiers rebelled against the harshness of their American officers. For relatively little money Robert hammered out a treatment for Dreyfuss, who was never able to secure the finance for a screenplay.

Ever since he had moved to Chithurst, Robert's health had been failing. At first, Sarah noticed an almost imperceptible slowing down. But the deaths of David Lean and Margaret Ramsay, as well as those of most his projects, hastened the decline.

Robert's weight, now fully twenty stone, was making it difficult for him to move about and his right leg was frequently swathed in bandages. He took to wearing a smock and a battered straw hat, and he carried a staff which was a present from Michael Bentine. He looked like a rustic who had just tramped across Edgon Heath. He also always carried an emergency bleeper which was connected to the local hospital. When the hospital called Sarah in the middle of the night to say that Robert had pressed his bleeper, she ran downstairs and found him unconscious, sweating profusely and his skin a purplish green. Since a heart transplant was out of the question – his body was too frail to undergo the shock of major surgery – he was put on more pills and advised to cut down on his work and on wine.

He was also persuaded to move his bedroom downstairs, having been told that his weight was damaging the ancient staircase, rather than the truth which was that the stairs were cracking his own timbers. The new arrangement meant that Sarah slept and worked alone upstairs. Her own writing room – she had now embarked on her series of memoirs and was always working on plays – was immediately above Robert's. She said that she felt his spirit wafting up through the floorboards, suffusing her own room and her work with his own creativity.

As a result of his declining health, Robert went up to London for lunch less often and his circle of friends accordingly narrowed. Hardly any of his colleagues, not even Fernando Ghia or David Puttnam, ever came to see him at Chithurst. Visits were largely confined to his three children and the grandchildren (Rosie, and Ben and Jo's daughter, Molly) as well as Jo and Gordon Riddett, whom

Robert would sometimes invite without informing Sarah of their imminent arrival.

Robert ignored his doctor's advice, cutting down on neither work nor wine. He still said yes to virtually everything that came his way and had become accustomed to saying goodbye after he had performed his task and had banked the cheque. To his amazement, Ronnie Colsen sent word that *Buddha* was now going ahead. 'We are finally getting Buddha together,' he said. 'The right director is finally on board, in tune with the spirit, harmony and great gift of the camera that this film always required.'[5]

Robert faxed back his 'flummoxed, staggered congratulations' and learned that the new director was Ron Fricke, an American who had just made a non-narrative feature called *Baraka* which juxtaposed images of religious serenity – the temples of Angkor, Luxor and Nepal – with the burning oilfields of Kuwait. Beautifully photographed and awesomely simplistic, *Baraka* was an audition for *Buddha* if ever there was one. Robert also learnt that Colsen had cast one of the leading roles: the Buddha's father would be played by Steven Seagal, a martial arts aficionado who had become a monosyllabic action movie hero for Warner Bros. Fricke's arrival meant further meetings, more revisions and additional money for Robert – an immediate $25,000 which brought his earnings to over $300,000 without a foot of film being shot. But even as Colsen and Fricke tried to breathe new life into the project, Bertolucci's *Little Buddha* had its world première in Paris, a sure sign of a stinker which is what it was when it later crept into British and American cinemas, shorn of some twenty minutes. The total failure of Bertolucci's film hardly helped Colsen's cause.

Just before the release of *Little Buddha*, Colsen had tried to prevent Bertolucci from using the word 'Buddha' in the title of his film. Despite Colsen's energetic campaign, reinforced by a signed statement issued by Robert, who also laid claim to the title 'Buddha', little or otherwise, the Motion Picture Association of America sided with Bertolucci. Another bulging file about another doomed project was consigned to Robert's archive. Ronnie Colsen, though, fights on: 'I felt a close personal friendship develop with both Robert and Sarah over the seven years which gives me all the more determination to assure that his script does indeed come to the screen.'[6]

The final collapse of *Buddha* and the abandonment of *The International Brigade* and *The Proud and the Free* should have left Robert's slate clean, apart from the never ending *Tricky Dickie*. But

there was one last epic in store for him, an adaptation of Jung
Chang's *Wild Swans* for Michael Wearing at the BBC. After a writing
career lasting forty years, it is peculiarly apt that Robert's first and
last commissions should have come from the BBC. It seemed to
complete a circle.

Chang's book – which bears an endorsement on its front cover
from Robert's friend, Mary Wesley – is a vast family saga spread over
three generations and covering China's rule by successive warlords
and communists. Banned in China, it rapidly became an
international best seller. The BBC bought the screen rights and
planned a lavish series, lasting six hours and costing £10 million.
One of the directors they had in mind was Jane Campion, who made
The Piano.

> We needed a top writer [said Wearing], and because Robert had
> written so many historical plays and films, he was the obvious
> choice, even though I thought his script for *Nostromo* was so
> undramatic it might have been made for the art houses. It
> condensed the novel so much that it seemed as if he just
> assumed the story was in the public ken.
>
> But I went with him because of his record and because *A Man
> For All Seasons* had made such an impact on me. At the
> beginning, Jung Chang and her agent were very keen to have a
> big name attached to it and Robert was very keen to do it as a
> last fling. He saw it as a human story set against the shifting
> politics of the times, something on the lines of *State of
> Revolution*. We paid him rather more than the going rate and I'd
> have lunch with him every now and then, always in London
> because he liked to get out and about.

Because Robert kept to his deadlines, Wearing had no idea that he
was also working simultaneously on *Tricky Dickie* – 'that's no
surprise,' he said, 'as Dennis Potter did that all the time.' Of the six
hour-long episodes, Robert completed all but the last one.

> It was a good first draft script [said Wearing] and I would have
> asked him to produce a second draft. But Jung Chang didn't
> particularly like the way Robert did it. She thought it was a
> Western intellectual's view of China and she started to insist
> that the film had to be made in the Chinese language by a
> Chinese director. This gave us all sorts of problems and the
> Chinese government refused to allow us to film there, mainly
> because the BBC had become a dirty word after Tianenman

Square. We hoped to finance it with Turner in America and then a German company suggested that we filmed it all in a studio using state-of-the-art effects. I don't know what will happen to it and our option on the book has expired. Frankly, it was a difficult working relationship with Jung Chang because she's a control freak.[7]

'We didn't hear about *Wild Swans* until very late in the game,' said Barbara Bloom. She had somehow assumed that Robert was working solely on *Tricky Dickie*.

'He was slow,' said John Florescu, 'and when we found out about *Wild Swans* we realised why he had missed a few deadlines. But because we liked him so much we held back on our criticisms. Normally we would have been much tougher editorially.'[8]

Tricky Dickie had taken the best part of three years and had become somewhat confused. Robert would receive faxes from people he had never heard of – 'Who is Glenn Whitehead?' he asked HBO when a fax arrived saying that the project should contain four chapters, rather than six hourly episodes. Refusing phone calls, Robert received regular faxes from Bloom and Florescu which suggested changes to existing scenes, additional ones and others to delete, all of which made Robert seem at times to be belligerent and unco-operative; he just wrote about Nixon the way he wanted to write about him. His third and final draft of the six-part, 397-page script was delivered over Christmas 1994.

HBO were now beginning to approach actors and directors. They had a meeting with Tom Hanks, who HBO and Florescu thought would make an ideal Nixon. HBO also sent Robert's script to Oliver Stone, who had made *JFK*, in the hope that he might want to direct the mini-series. 'Oliver or his people got back to us', said Florescu, 'and said they weren't interested in Nixon. Then, lo and behold, we heard that they were making their own picture. It became a case of who would blink first.'

Oliver Stone was not a blinking man; he had the 500 yard stare of the Vietnam veteran, as well as three Academy Awards. HBO had two options, both of them panic measures. To begin with, they considered combining the first two parts of Robert's script into a two-hour drama which could be broadcast well before Stone's picture opened in cinemas. This meant that Frost and HBO could claim they were first with the idea, possibly deter Stone from making his film and then produce the sequel. The second option was to wait until Robert's scripts had been polished by another writer and then go into production. But as these options were being considered Stone announced that he had signed Anthony Hopkins to play Nixon. Shooting would begin in March.

HBO put *Tricky Dickie* into turnaround, which gave David Frost a limited amount of time in which to secure funding from another studio. Frost worked tirelessly, sending Robert's scripts to Ted Turner's TNT, ABC, Showtime and Fox. But no one wanted it, mainly for fear of looking as if they were following in the wake of Oliver Stone. Someone had to tell Robert the bad news. 'I thought the best thing I could do', said Florescu, 'was to call Sarah and let her speak to Robert. I remember the conversation very well. I told her that the Oliver Stone film was on and that HBO were getting cold feet and would probably step aside or shelve it. She said, "I can't tell him, it will kill him." I didn't speak to Robert then and I never spoke to him again.'9

'How could I protect Robert from this brutal news?' wrote Sarah. 'The answer was, I couldn't. I knew it would be his death warrant. Robert went a ghastly ashen white, which remained with him to the end.'10

In one sense it is ironic that Oliver Stone should have been a protégé of Robert's and that people blamed him for the cancellation of Robert's project. But Stone, whose own *Nixon* bears no relation to the scripts which Robert wrote, is distressed by the suggestion and insists that Robert's project was cancelled because it was not good enough. 'My perception is that it was never serious as a teleplay,' he said. 'The scripts I read had nothing to do with what we did. It was the early Nixon, tricky Dick, and it took a very English attitude in that he was very much an asshole. I thought it was Robert's least successful movie and I think that was the reason it never got made. And HBO had it way before us and they could have made it if they liked it. On the contrary, they made *Nixon and Kissinger* for Showtime because we were making *Nixon*.'11

John Florescu and Barbara Bloom admit that Robert's scripts still needed fine tuning and that it was always planned to have another writer perform a final polish. 'Robert's script still needed work,' said Bloom. 'It was not an easy script. There were a lot of problems with it and cuts that needed to be made. There were things that were perfect and things that weren't and to get it right was a slow process. He was hospitalised in the middle of it and I think no one wanted to tell us he was too ill to work. But right to the end he was responsive and passionate about it.'12

On Monday, 13 February 1995 Robert sent a final fax to John

Florescu: 'Surely if Anthony Hopkins is to play the part it can only be with the last part of Nixon's life. A section we have left open for Stone? I hope that the version of our script that you have sent over to Ted Turner's has the altrations I have made . . .'

Seven days after he sent this fax, Robert was dead.

For the past year or so he had been in and out of hospital. A holiday with Sarah, Mary Wesley and their friend, Kate Ganz, had been disastrous, with the three women belatedly realising that Venice was quite possibly the worst place to take a twenty-stone man confined to a wheelchair. Shortly after returning from Venice, in October 1994, Robert made a great effort to attend Tom's wedding. That Tom had come finally through was a source of pride and joy to him and to Sarah. After that, though, Robert never left Chithurst, apart from visits to hospitals, always with his computer so that he could continue work on *Tricky Dickie* and *Wild Swans*. Sarah wondered why he did it: 'Money? Pride? Greed? I believe it was all about hiding from reality. Perhaps, for him, deadlines were lifelines, for living life is so much harder than working hard, and juggling secret deadlines is empowering.'[13]

Robert himself had often wondered why he carried on and he wondered what would happen to him if he didn't. In a letter to Charlotte Taylor, who had just returned from a long trip abroad, he couched these thoughts in a poetic little rumination on the life cycle of birds:

> It must look a great cheerful homecoming at this time of year; the great rooted blossomers standing ready to salute the winter surrounded by all the crunched under foot of the myriad of fallen nuts; and the hordes of swallows or whatever they are, darting low on the ground, some crying 'let us away, now, while there is yet time' and other more sedentary birds murmuring, 'No, no, no; there is lots of time yet, tomorrow, tomorrow' until one dawn they are there no more. And then one is faced with the Winter. Oh dear, I do not face it with so much energy as last time. I suppose it goes on like that, until one cloud wracked day one thinks, 'No, I have had enough' and closes one eyes for the last time. I hope it is like that anyway. Oh dear, I do wish I believed more firmly in some sort of after life. What do you credit the after times with? Something, something horrible, something beatific, or just nothingess?[14]

There perhaps came the point when he simply felt he'd had enough, thank you very much. 'I never had control over his pills and medicines,' said Sarah. 'He never let me near them.'

On the day he died, Monday, 20 February 1995 Robert had talked quite openly to Sarah about his imminent death. He seemed to have made up his mind about it and wanted his wishes known. Sitting at the kitchen table, eating a plateful of eels, he suddenly asked Sarah not to send him to a mortuary for embalming. The prospect of those indignities was quite repulsive. He said he wanted to be buried in the croquet lawn, in a cardboard box. Failing that, he said, he would like to be burnt on a funeral pyre, again on the croquet lawn. He was adamant there should be no religious paraphernalia. 'I am not a Christian!' he shouted.

Sarah asked if he wanted a big funeral.

'No! Tiny. Everyone to get pissed on champagne.'

She asked about his grave, the headstone.

'Just Robert Bolt. Make it a BIG Robert Bolt.'

Sarah had things to do that afternoon. Leaving Robert snoozing on his bed, with the enormous Lovely for company, she busied herself on a speech on alternative medicine that she was committed to give the following day at the House of Lords. She went out to see some neighbours and worked on her first novel. But all her instincts told her that this Monday would be Robert's last.

In the evening Sarah made mugs of tea and they watched the television news together. Then she went upstairs to wash her hair. By the time she returned Robert had died. A cat was fast asleep on the mountain of his breathless chest and Lovely lay alongside. Full of remorse for having missed his dying moment, Sarah remained in the silent room and was shortly joined by two friends, a Buddhist monk and a nun, who sat with her and Robert for the entire night. Then Sarah made the necessary phone calls.

Robert's wishes were carried out, for he never left Chithurst. Sarah declined to allow an autopsy and refused, too, to have the body removed from the house for any reason at all. Instead, she opened the windows to the February chill and arranged for Robert to lie peacefully in his room. Candles were lit and the animals slowly got used to the idea that Robert could not pet them any more. Ben, Joanna and Tom came to visit him and they all agreed on the plans for the funeral. Sarah vetoed the croquet lawn as the grave site – it would spoil her game – so Robert suggested he was buried beneath the upper lawn which afforded his favourite view of the house, a long shot framed by trees. Since this end of the garden adjoined the church graveyard, the border being marked by a flimsy wrought iron fence, the relevant officials – local council, water authority – had little difficulty in approving Robert's final resting place. Robert was buried at Chithurst Manor on 23 February. Sarah, Ben and his wife, Jo, daughter Joanna, son Tom and, at Sarah's invitation, Jo Riddett were there. Some of Robert's neighbours attended as well, including the Buddhists from the nearby monastery.

> I'd been preparing myself for his death but I was still devastated [said Tom]. I was very proud of my father and we had become very close in the last few years of his life. The week before he died he called me and asked me down to Chithurst. I said I couldn't because I had someone flying over from Italy to see me. Dad was quite insistent. He seemed to want to talk about something. But I didn't go.
> The funeral was perfecto. I read in the papers a few days later – Bolt buried in box in garden – that kind of shit. It was nothing like that. At formal funerals, people are never open to each other, but we could say what we wanted to say, we could be emotional with each other. It was a wonderful way for him to go.

Robert's grave was dug out of the hard, frozen earth of Chithurst by members of the family and by a couple of strong neighbours whom Robert adored and who loved him.

'It was such a beautiful painful and truthful affair,' said Ben, 'with occasional weeping forays to visit Dad for one last time.'

Robert was placed in a coffin made from chipboard. His twenty stones were carried up the garden, placed in the grave and covered over. There were songs, a violinist, candles, tributes, memories, champagne, laughing and crying. For a man who had written about all the world's major religions – Christianity, Islam, Buddhism – it was an aptly secular, even pagan ritual, the sort of funeral that might have been enacted on Glastonbury Tor 3000 years before.

The funeral mound at Chithurst later received its headstone, which reads: ROBERT BOLT and, above that, in smaller capitals, A MAN FOR ALL SEASONS.

In March 1978, when he was in Tahiti, Robert send his son Tom a letter. In it, on a separate piece of paper, was a poem:

Over the hill there may not be
Quite everything; but let me see –
Oh goodness yes, right off the cuff
I'm certain there's enough.
Come to think of it there's ample
Over the hill. For example:
Bread and butter, cats and dogs,
The telly and a fire of logs.
Steeples and peoples (as you point out)
And trees with leaves and, round about
This season I remember flights
Of Birds building nests and having fights,
New born lambs with trembling legs,
Hedges, cow-pats, bacon and eggs,
Brothers, sisters, fields and friends -
The list is long, it never ends.
In fact the only real care
I have just now is to be there,
Down in the valley, over the hill,
And it won't be long before I will.

ROBERT BOLT – A CAREER

1: BBC Radio Plays
The Thwarting of Baron Bolligrew (8 Oct. 52)
The Master (15 Feb. 53)
Fifty Pigs (1 Jun. 53)
A Man For All Seasons (26 Jul. 54)
Ladies and Gentlemen (26 Sep. 54)
Fair Music (21 Feb. 55)
The Banana Tree (25 Mar. 55)
The Last of the Wine (3 Apr. 55)
Mr Sampson's Sundays (16 Jul. 55)
Sir Oblong Fitz-Oblong and Baron Bolligrew (22 Jan. 56)
The Window (20 Dec. 56)
Sir Oblong Fitz-Oblong and the Bolligrew Island Dragon
(26 Feb. 57)
Sir Oblong Fitz-Oblong and the Magic Apple (26 Mar. 57)
Sir Oblong Fitz-Oblong and the Lost Treasure of the Bolligrews
(4 May 57)
Sir Oblong Fitz-Oblong and the Very Difficult Law (20 Jun. 57
Sir Oblong Fitz-Oblong Meets the Dragon Again (18 Jul. 57)
Sir Oblong Fitz-Oblong and the Siege of Bolligrew Castle
(15 Aug. 57)
The Drunken Sailor (10 Mar. 58)

2: Theatre productions
1957   The Critic And The Heart (Oxford Playhouse)
1958   Flowering Cherry (Haymarket)
1960   A Man For All Seasons (Globe)
1960   The Tiger And The Horse (Queen's)
1963   Gentle Jack (Queen's)
1965   The Thwarting Of Baron Bolligrew (RSC Aldwych)
1967   Brother and Sister (Brighton Festival)
1970   Vivat Vivat Regina! (Chichester Festival; Piccadilly)

1977   State Of Revolution (National)

3: Realised screenplays
1962   Lawrence of Arabia (dir. David Lean)
1965   Doctor Zhivago (dir. David Lean)
1966   A Man For All Seasons (dir. Fred Zinnemann)
1970   Ryan's Daughter (dir. David Lean)
1972   Lady Caroline Lamb (dir. Robert Bolt)
1984   The Bounty (dir. Roger Donaldson)
1986   The Mission (dir. Roland Joffé)

4: Television films:
1988   A Man For All Seasons (dir. Charlton Heston)
1991   Without Warning: The James Brady Story (dir. Michael
       Uno)

5: Uncredited Screenplays
1969   The Red Tent (dir. Mikhail K Kalatozov)
1989   A Dry White Season (dir. Euzhan Palcy)

6: Unrealised screenplays and teleplays
1977   Augustus (for Stella Richman; TV)
1978   The Lawbreakers (The Bounty Part I, for David Lean)
1979   The Long Arm (The Bounty Part II, unfinished, for David
       Lean)
1980   A Wrinkle in Time (for Norman Lear)
1981   The October Circle (for David Puttnam and Hugh
       Hudson)
1983   The Florentines (for Franco Zeffirelli)
1984   Burr (for Ray Stark; TV)
1984   The Michael Collins Story (for Barry Spikings and Michael
       Cimino)
1989   Nostromo (for David Lean)
1989   The Tortoise and the Hare (for John Heyman)
1989   Buddha (for Ronnie Colsen)
1992   The International Brigade (for Granada TV)
1993   Messenger of the Stars (for Joey Feury)
1995   The Proud and the Free (unfinished; for Richard Dreyfuss)
1995   Tricky Dickie (for David Frost; TV)
1995   Wild Swans (unfinished; for BBC-TV)˘

LAWRENCE OF ARABIA: AN APOLOGIA

What follows is Robert Bolt's intended introduction to the screenplay of
Lawrence of Arabia. *As described in Chapter 13, the screenplay was
never published due to the intervention of T. E. Lawrence's brother and
literary executor, Professor A. W. Lawrence. The Apologia is published
here for the first time.*

T. E. Lawrence was quite recently alive and several people still alive
remember him. Some of these loved him, some disliked him, all
agree that he was very remarkable. Any serious student of the period
whose studies bring him to the historical Lawrence should consult
these people or their written accounts. The accounts even of what he
did differ widely, and the accounts of what he was are flatly contradictory, but historians love conflicting evidence and a suspended
conclusion. And obviously he should consult Lawrence's own
account of himself in *Seven Pillars of Wisdom*. He will be told by some
authorities that parts of the book are untrue or so highly coloured as
to be virtually untrue, and he will find for himself in places an excess
of colour over fact, but even the undeniable minimum of it
constitutes a profound adventure of the body and the mind.

Many of the events in it are heroic, many morally shocking or
psychologically weird. They are not evaluated. The heroism is set
down without satisfaction, the horrors without apology. 'I do not say
that this was good or bad,' he seems to tell us, 'I say that this is how
it was. If you want to judge, judge without my help. I am indifferent.'
It gives the book consistent dignity even where the descriptive style
is, to my taste, unsuitably rhapsodic.

Seven Pillars of Wisdom was my prime, almost my only source for
the screenplay. It is a long book, diffuse and detailed. Ten different
dramas could be got from it. To chose which tenth you are going to
take for your one drama is an impudent enterprise but must be done.
You will choose of course what seems to you the most important
tenth. Which tenth seems to you the most important, and why, will

depend on yourself, not Lawrence, who at this point is made helpless.

A man's account of his deeds is already at one remove from the deeds themselves. A second man's evaluation of that account is at another remove again. His dramatisation of that evaluation is a further remove still. Historical plays (and screenplays) afford historical evidence not of the lives and times they purport to display but rather of the lives and times which produced them. *Richard III* tells us little that is reliable about Gloucester and the 15th century but a lot about Shakespeare and Elizabethan England.

By the time Shakespeare wrote his play, Richard had no surviving friends or relatives. Even if he had they might have been disarmed by the splendour of Shakespeare's verse. No such inhibition operates in my case and some of T. E. Lawrence's surviving friends have expressed indignation at my account. I am not indifferent to their reaction and feel now that it was perhaps a mistake to attempt to dramatise such very recent history even though the hero has almost forfeited his historical actuality and become a figure in contemporary mythology. So I am going to break the golden axiom which warns the writer never, never, when he's finished writing, to say 'What I meant was . . .'

Indignation has focused on the sequence in which the advancing Arab Army overtook and massacred a column of retreating Turks. Some authorities say that Lawrence was not actively involved in this at all. Captain Liddell-Hart suggests that when he says 'we' did this he really means 'they' (his Bedouin followers) did it, not himself. Professor Lawrence, Lawrence's brother, accepts that it was done but in a fit of righteous indignation such as anyone might have felt on discovering the Turkish atrocities in the village of Tafas.

Now if people who knew T. E. Lawrence, and knew him well, say that from their knowledge of him they know he could not have perpetrated the deed as he describes it, then their word is evidence which the historian should consider. But if they are right (I don't know how to put this delicately enough), they are calling Lawrence's veracity into question at a crucial – I would say the crucial passage of his book. For whatever he did on this occasion I don't think there is any real doubt as to what he says he did, as I hope to indicate below. And if we are to doubt his veracity here, why not elsewhere? I could not decently accept as truth whatever was suitable to a screen hero and reject as falsehood whatever wasn't. That, to my mind, really would have been a belittlement.

Lawrence's account is in Chapter CXVII of *Seven Pillars*. The advancing Arab Army came upon the village of Tafas. The retreating Turks had left the place a shambles. The Arabs cut them down (there were two thousand of them) to the last man.

First let us see what Lawrence says was the general nature of the action. 'In a madness born of the horror of Tafas we killed and killed, even blowing in the heads of the fallen and the animals.' It started in daylight and became, 'One of the nights when men went "crazy" and others' lives became toys to break and throw away.'

Now let us see what he says was his own measure of responsibility for this. First this: '*By my order* [my italics] we took no prisoners.' Now this: Lawrence had a personal Bodyguard (the famous 'cut-throats' who 'cut throats only to my order'). 'I said, "The best of you brings me the most Turkish dead," and we turned after the fading enemy, on our way shooting down those who had fallen out by the roadside, and came imploring our pity.'

Next let us see if he describes himself as a bystander or participant. I refer the reader to the last quotation above. I do not see how 'we' here can honestly be read as anything but 'we', the First Person (Plural). In a later passage he is even more specific. It is too long to quote in full but the reader may easily check it for himself. The last two hundred immediately available Turks had been taken prisoner: 'I had gone up to learn why it was,' being 'not unwilling' that they should be allowed to live. But at that moment the Arabs and Lawrence found another atrocity. It proved to be the work of this very two hundred: 'They said nothing in the moments before we opened fire. At last their heap ceased moving . . . we mounted again and rode home slowly in the gloom.' However, Lawrence could not rest and 'I had my other camel brought and with one of my bodyguard rode out into the night to join our men hunting the greater Deraa column'.

Finally, the question of motive, the nature of the emotion at work in all this. The atrocities which the Arabs found in Tafas were to the last degree horrible, and Lawrence's account heartrending. Righteous indignation was the natural response. Let us ignore what is a fact of common observation, that righteous indignation resulting in immediate cruelty is a highly suspect emotion, and merely ask how long righteous indignation can be thought to last? That a man, confronted by such a scene, should snatch up a weapon and kill in pure moral fury, this I can accept. That he should continue for some minutes from the same motive, this too I can accept with difficulty. But if he goes on for a day and a night, seeking out his victims and killing everything in his path, then something other than righteous indignation has risen up in him. Outraged morality cannot reasonably be offered as the mood in which prisoners, animals and wounded men are slaughtered for hours on end. Lawrence's words are 'madness' and 'crazy'.

In short he tells us that, triggered by the terrible Turkish crimes in Tafas, a further terrible crime was committed at his instigation, with his participation and in a mood of dreadful excitement. I do not see any other dispassionate reading of the text.

If the film was to be half-way honest then, the massacre had to be shown. Consider that. 'Others' lives became toys to break and throw away' is a statement, but a poeticised statement; it is all metaphor. To put it on the screen you have to uncover what it means in terms of concrete action (men kill other men, wantonly, foolishly, as children break toys), take a picture of that, and show it; the comforting blanket of metaphor has gone. It looks quite different and arouses a different response.

Moreover, it seemed to me that the massacre at Tafas could not be presented merely as one incident among others. A man must have supped full indeed of horrors if he could match it elsewhere in his life. It must be crucial. The seeds of it must have been in him from his past – unless we are to drag in some sudden aberration to explain it. It could not fail to mark his future – unless we are to think him merely brutish. Other incidents he tells of show him sensitive, compassionate, shrewd, immensely self-controlled. And deeply introspective. Whatever was in him blossomed at Tafas, he must have known of it. He was no mindless killer, though he killed.

And is it really very puzzling? Is a man containing gentleness and cruelty side by side abnormal? I think he is like all men. The abnormality lay in the heroic scale of his nature, not its disposition. And also, I think, in the abnormal sharpness of his self-awareness which was only just one pace behind him all the time.

For his heroic nature many reasonable explanations in terms of Freudian psychology and common sense have been put forward. These we only touched upon. To 'explain' in these terms means 'explain away'. We wanted not to do that nor to judge, but just to look.

For the unique circumstances, complex military and political forces were responsible. These simplified and contracted to the range of half a dozen characters I made the background to his story in the sense of plot. Thus Ali has to represent emergent Arab nationalism, Dryden represents European political skills, Feisal the opposing skill of the native people. Allenby is the one appointed to power, through whom Dryden must work. The present Lady Allenby has been shocked by my portrayal of this very considerable man. I want to say that as I wrote the part I admired him exceedingly and tried to show him as performing his duty – the duty given him by us, his people – perfectly and without relish. A weakness of historical drama is that individuals who could fairly claim to have been the instruments of impersonal forces must be made unreally conscious of their role in order that they may express it. (Consider that magnificent, necessary and implausible soliloquy of Gloucester's at the opening of *Richard*.) And thus, *vis-à-vis* the Arabs, the duplicity of British policy appears here like Allenby's own. *Vis-à-vis* Lawrence, the ruthlessness enjoined upon a field commander – our ruthlessness – looks like his.

For the rest, Brighton has to stand for the half admiring, half appalled disturbance raised by Lawrence in minds quite wedded to the admirable and inadequate code of English decency. Auda is meant to be Brighton's Bedouin equivalent. The Medical Officer who first strikes Lawrence in the face and then congratulates him, without real recognition either time, stands for the real, uncritical and, to my mind, unfeeling adulation which Lawrence underwent at the hands of the jingos. That adulation was fuelled by the popular Press, here rather cavalierly embodied in the person of Bentley, who also stands in for the facile Lawrence denigrators.

But in a deeper sense than that of plot, the background to the story is the Desert. Words cannot trap that landscape; the camera almost can, and did. It is the essence of the saga. The aesthete in Lawrence revelled in its fantasy and almost luscious colourings. The stoic in him bit hard on its inhumanities. And it was alien; he alone was in it. We tried to show, in short, a man awkward among his own, accepted by an alien people, but accepted by them as something he was not – 'posturing', as he says, 'in borrowed robes' – and not as a man among others but as a heaven sent leader. Thus he had the power, and no *mores* to guide him in the use of it.

That is the theme which I thought I found in *Seven Pillars* and tried to deploy in this filmscript. I sincerely regret whatever distress it has caused. I do not claim for it any authority to set against the opinion of people who knew him or have made a really deep study of him. I do claim that it is a reasonably faithful dramatisation drawn from his own account. As faithful, that is, as drama can be to a document.

SELECT BIBLIOGRAPHY

Attenborough, Richard, *In Search of Gandhi*, Bodley Head, 1982

Barber, Lynn, *Mostly Men*, Penguin, 1992

Bolt, Robert, *Flowering Cherry*, Samuel French, 1958

Bolt, Robert, *A Man For All Seasons*, Heinemann, 1970

Bolt, Robert, *The Tiger and the Horse*, Samuel French, 1961

Bolt, Robert, *Gentle Jack*, Samuel French, 1963

Bolt, Robert, *The Thwarting of Baron Bolligrew*, Heinemann, 1966

Bolt, Robert, *Vivat! Vivat Regina!*, Samuel French, 1971

Bolt, Robert, *State of Revolution*, Samuel French, 1977

Booker, Christopher, *The Neophiliacs*, Pimlico, 1992

Brownlow, Kevin, *David Lean*, Richard Cohen Books, 1996

Caine, Michael, *What's It All About?*, Turtle Bay, New York, 1992

Carpenter, Humphrey, *The Envy of the World: Fifty Years of the BBC Third Programme and Radio 3*, Weidenfeld & Nicolson, 1996

Chambers, Colin, *Peggy: The Life of Margaret Ramsay, Play Agent*, Nick Hern Books, 1997

Duff, Charles, *The Lost Summer*, Nick Hern Books, 1995

Eaton Griffith, Valerie, *'So they tell me' An Encounter with a Stroke*, Chest, Heart and Stroke Association, 1989

Fay, Stephen, *Power Play: The Life and Times of Peter Hall*, Hodder and Stoughton, 1996.

Goater, Michael, *Jack Meyer of Millfield*, Alan Sutton Books, 1993

Hall, Peter, *Diaries*, Hamish Hamilton, 1983

Hayman, Ronald, *Robert Bolt*, Heinemann Contemporary Playwrights, 1969.

Heston, Charlton, *In the Arena*, Simon and Schuster, New York, 1995.

McKern, Leo, *Just Resting*, Methuen, 1983.

Miles, Sarah (I), *A Right Royal Bastard*, Macmillan, 1993

Miles, Sarah (II), *Serves Me Right*, Macmillan, 1994

Miles, Sarah (III), *Bolt from the Blue*, Orion, 1996

Osborne, John, *Almost a Gentleman*, Faber, 1991

Redgrave, Vanessa, *An Autobiography*, Arrow, 1992

Rossiter, Anthony, *The Pendulum*, Gollanz, 1966

Swain, N. V., *A History of Sale*, Sigma Press, Wilmslow, 1987

Turner, Adrian, *The Making of Lawrence of Arabia*, Dragon's World, 1994

Walker, Alexander, *Hollywood, England*, Michael Joseph, 1974

Wesker, Arnold, *As Much As I Dare*, Century, 1994

Williams, Kenneth, *Diaries* (ed. Russell Davies), Harper Collins, 1994

Williams, Kenneth, *Letters* (ed. Russell Davies), Harper Collins, 1995

Zeffirelli, Franco, *Autobiography*, Weidenfeld and Nicolson, 1986

Zinnemann, Fred, *An Autobiography*, Bloomsbury, 1992.

NOTES AND SOURCES

All letters quoted from Robert Bolt come from the collections of Ben Bolt or Sarah Miles unless otherwise stated. Archival sources are abbreviated as follows:

AMPAS: The Academy of Motion Picture Arts and Sciences, Los Angeles.

BBCWA: The BBC's Written Archives Centre at Caversham, England.

CPA: The legal archive of Columbia Pictures Corporation, Los Angeles.

HRC: The Frith Banbury Collection held at the Harry Ransom Center for Humanities at the University of Austin, Texas.

MSA: The archive of the Millfield School Society.

MWP: The Michael Wilson Papers held at the Cinema and Theatre Arts Department at the University of California, Los Angeles.

TBC: The Ted Turner Broadcasting Corporation, Atlanta, where the legal documents of MGM are housed.

UoR: The University of Reading where Barbara Cole has deposited her collection of letters from David Lean, RB and others.

Other abbreviated forms appear in the Bibliography.

1: To the South Seas
1 RB letter to Mike Kellaway, 25 May 1967. Courtesy Michael Kellaway.
2 Stella Richman phone interview, 19 June 1996.
3 RB letter to David Lean, 14 May 1977.
4 RB letter to Phil Kellogg, 22 June 1977.
5 Stella Richman, op. cit.
6 Sarah Miles to AT, 31 July 1996.
7 Gillian Harrison to AT, 23 February 1996.
8 RB letter to Debbie Condon, 29 August 1977. Courtesy Debbie Condon.

2: The Littered Lagoon
1 RB letter to Sally, Ben and Joanna Bolt, 14 September 1977.
2 RB letter to Gillian Harrison, 13 November 1977.
3 Julie Nightingale to AT, 19 October 1996.
4 RB letter to Sally, Ben and Joanna Bolt, 16 December 1977.
5 Julie Nightingale to AT, 19 October 1996.
6 RB letter to Gillian Harrison, 23 November 1977.
7 Gillian Harrison letter to RB, 28 November 1977. Courtesy Gillian Harrison.
8 RB letters to Gillian Harrison, 13 & 20 November 1977. Courtesy Gillian Harrison.
9 RB letters to Sally, Ben and Joanna Bolt, 13 November 1977 & 16 December 1977.

10   Julie Nightingale to AT, 19 October 1996.
11   RB letter to Sally, Ben and Joanna Bolt, 16 December 1977.
12   Julie Nightingale to AT, 19 October 1996.
13   RB letters to Ann Queensberry, 18 December 1977 & 31 January 1978. Courtesy Ann Queensberry.
14   RB letter to Julie Laird, 10 January 1978. Courtesy Julie Nightingale.
15   Undated RB letter to Margaret Ramsay.
16   Ibid.
17   RB letter to Sally, Ben and Joanna Bolt, 11 March 1978.
18   RB letter to Gillian Harrison, 19 March 1978. Courtesy Gillian Harrison.
19   Ibid.
20   RB letter to Roger and Liza Gard, 2 April 1978. Courtesy Roger Gard.
21   Vaea Sylvain to AT, 3 May 1996.
22   RB letter to Charlotte Taylor, 26 June 1978. Courtesy Lady St Johnston.
23   Tor Douglas to AT, 15 April 1996.
24   RB letter to Margaret Ramsay, 5 May 1978.
25   RB letter to Charlotte Taylor, 26 June 1978. Courtesy Lady St Johnston.
26   Ibid.
27   RB letter to Margaret Ramsay, 5 May 1978.
28   Vaea Sylvain to AT, 3 May 1996.
29   Ben Bolt to AT, 29 October 1996.
30   RB letter to Vaea Sylvain, 14 December 1978. Courtesy Vaea Sylvain.
31   RB letter to Ann Queensberry, 16 September 1978. Courtesy Ann Queensberry.

3:   Falling Down
1   RB letter to Julie Laird, 2 December 1978. Courtesy Julie Nightingale.
2   Ibid.
3   RB letter to 'All', 22 November 1978.
4   RB letter to Julie Laird, June 1978. Courtesy Julie Nightingale.
5   RB letter to Julie Laird, 2 December 1978. Courtesy Julie Nightingale.
6   RB letter to Charlotte Taylor, 25 January 1979. Courtesy Lady St Johnston.
7   RB letter to Margaret Ramsay, 21 March 1979.
8   RB letter to Sarah Miles, 7 May 1978.
9   Margaret Ramsay letter to RB, 23 May 1978.
10   RB letter to Margaret Ramsay, 19 October 1978.
11   Margaret Ramsay letter to RB, 18 July 1978.
12   RB letter to Margaret Ramsay, 26 July 1978.
13   Bernie Williams to AT, 17 May 1996.
14   Ibid.
15   RB letter to Julie Laird, 28 January 1979. Courtesy Julie Nightingale.
16   RB letter to Julie Laird, 8 March 1979. Courtesy Julie Nightingale.
17   RB letters to Ann Queensberry, 8 & 12 March 1979. Courtesy Ann Queensberry.
18   RB letter to Charlotte Taylor, 25 January 1979. Courtesy Lady St Johnston.
19   Caine, p.429.
20   Fernando Ghia to AT, 11 April 1996.
21   Miles III, p.122-23.
22   Ibid

23 Fernando Ghia to AT, 11 April 1996.
24 Ben Bolt to AT, 24 October 1996.
25 Miles III, p.125.
26 Sarah Miles to AT, 22 May 1997.

4: Sale
1 Swain, p.85.
2 Swain, p.91.
3 Sydney Bolt to AT, 14 March 1996. All subsequent quotations from Sydney Bolt come from the same source.
4 Hayman, p.1.
5 Hayman, p.15.
6 Hayman, pp.1-2.
7 Ibid.
8 Hayman, p.8.
9 Hayman, pp.2-3.
10 Hayman, p.4.
11 Margaret Durden phone interview, 29 June 1997.
12 Hayman, p.5.
13 Bernard McCabe to AT, 8 August 1996.
14 Herbert McCabe to AT, 17 March 1997.
15 Hayman, p.9.
16 Lord Quinton to AT, 25 January 1996.
17 Ibid.
18 Len Smith to AT, 23 November 1995.
19 Hayman, p.10.
20 Len Smith to AT, 23 November 1995.
21 Hayman, p.10.
22 Hayman, p.11.
23 Hayman, pp.10-11.
24 RB letter to his parents, 24 August 1946.
25 Ibid.

5: Shotgun Wedding
1 Jaya Bolt to AT, 14 March 1996.
2 Sydney Bolt to AT, 14 March 1996.
3 Eric John phone interview, 23 June 1997.
4 *The Times*, 25 May 1977; Hayman, p.6.
5 Hayman, pp.3,7.
6 *Sunday Times*, 17 May 1970.
7 Naomi May to AT, 6 August 1996.
8 Jaya Bolt to AT, 14 March 1996.
9 Eric John phone interview, 23 June 1997.
10 Dora Wigg to AT, 7 February 1997.
11 Barbara Lover phone interview, 5 February 1997.
12 Herbert McCabe to AT, 17 March 1997.
13 Dora Wigg to AT, 7 February 1997.
14 Eric John phone interview, 23 June 1997.

6:   A Limited Amount of Good
1   From a speech made in 1947, q. Fred Blackburn, *George Tomlinson*, Heinemann, 1954, p.173.
2   Walter Stein, 18 February 1950, MSA.
3   Professor C. R. Cheney, 20 June 1949, MSA.
4   RB letter to his parents, 10 October 1949.
5   RB letter to his parents, 15 November 1949.
6   RB letter to his parents, 23 November 1949.
7   *Desert Island Discs* transcript, BBCWA.
8   RB letter to his parents, 6 October 1949.
9   RB letter to his parents, 7 November 1949.
10   RB letter to his parents, 23 November 1949.
11   RB letter to his parents, 23 November 1949.
12   Dora Wigg to AT, 7 February 1997.
13   RB letter to his parents, 2 February 1950.
14   RB letter to his parents, 16 March 1950.
15   RB letter to his parents, undated, but April 1950.
16   Den Back to AT, 15 October 1996.
17   Sheila Robbins to AT, 15 October 1996.
18   RB letter to his parents, 24 August 1950.
19   A combination of two RB letters to his parents, probably September-October 1950.
20   Den Back to AT, 15 October 1996.
21   Peter Wallis to AT, 14 October 1996.
22   Sheila Robbins to AT, 15 October 1996.
23   Peter Wallis to AT, 15 October 1996.
24   RB letter to his parents, undated but November 1950.
25   *Spectator*, 4 November 1960.
26   Terry Thompson phone interview, 3 October 1996.
27   RB letter to his parents, early December 1950.

7:   Drama in Dawlish
1   *Encore*, March–April 1961.
2   Peter Wallis to AT, 14 October 1996.
3   Bernard McCabe to AT, 8 August 1996.
4   RB letter to his parents, undated, but February 1951.
5   RB letter to his parents, 4 February 1951.
6   RB letter to his parents, 23 March 1951.
7   RB letter to his parents, 15 April 1951.
8   Some veterans of this production recall the title as *The Prince Who Tore His Trousers*.
9   Peter Wallis to AT, 14 October 1996.
10   Den Back to AT, 15 October 1996.
11   Terry Thompson phone interview, 3 October 1996.
12   *Dawlish Gazette*, 18 May 1951.
13   *Dawlish Gazette*, 25 May 1951.
14   Den Back to AT, 15 October 1996.

8: Avalon
1 *Times Educational Supplement,* 5 October 1951.
2 Jo Bolt letter to R. J. O. Meyer, 11 October 1951, MSA.
3 *Independent,* 10 March 1991.
4 Ibid.
5 Goater, p.132.
6 *Independent,* 10 March 1991.
7 Goater, pp.132–3.
8 Len Smith to AT, 23 November 1995.
9 Undated Meyer notes, MSA.
10 R. J. O Meyer letter to RB, 10 November 1951, MSA.
11 RB letter to RJO Meyer, 12 November 1951, MSA.
12 Undated RB letter to his parents, probably autumn 1952.
13 Len Smith to AT, 23 November 1995.
14 Wyndham Bailey to AT, 16 April 1996.
15 Len Smith to AT, 23 November 1995.
16 Wyndham Bailey to AT, 16 April 1996.
17 *The Times,* 16 March 1991.
18 Naomi May to AT, 6 August 1996.
19 Ibid.
20 Ibid.
21 RB letter to his parents, 8 September 1953.
22 Undated RB letter to his parents, probably October 1953.
23 Naomi May to AT, 13 August 1996.
24 Ibid.
25 Naomi May, letter to author, 9 September 1996.
26 Bernard McCabe, letter to author, 12 September 1996.
27 Naomi May, letter to author, 9 September 1996.
28 Jo Bolt letter to R. J. O Meyer, 18 February 1953, MSA.
29 Naomi May letter to author, 14 August 1996.
30 Naomi May, letter to author, 9 September 1966.
31 Mike Kellaway to AT, 6 February 1997.
32 Naomi May to AT, 13 August 1996.

9: On the Air
1 Len Smith to AT, 23 November 1995.
2 Carpenter, p.150.
3 RB letter, 12 February 1952, BBCWA.
4 RB letter to E. J. King Bull, 8 June 1952, BBCWA.
5 E. J. King Bull memo to Val Gielgud, 24 June 1952, BBCWA.
6 Donald McWhinnie letter to RB, 8 July 1952, BBCWA.
7 RB letter to Donald McWhinnie, 12 July 1952, BBCWA.
8 Helena Wood, Script Reader's Report, 24 October 1952, BBCWA.
9 Donald McWhinnie memo to Vivian Daniels, 30 October 1952, BBCWA.
10 *Radio Times,* Northern edition, 13 February 1953.
11 RB letter to his parents, 27 February 1953.
12 Donald McWhinnie memo to Leeds Drama Department, 27 March 1953, BBCWA.
13 RB letter to Charles Lefeaux, 15 April 1953, BBCWA.

14   Script Reader's Report, 27 May 1953, BBCWA.
15   RB letter to Charles Lefeaux, 13 June 1953, BBCWA.
16   RB letter to Charles Lefeaux, 25 July 1953, BBCWA.
17   RB letter to his parents, 21 November 1953.
18   RB letter to his parents, 11 August 1954.
19   Script Reader's Report, 10 January 1954, BBCWA.
20   RB letter to BBC, 26 January 1954, BBCWA.
21   Barbara Bray, Script Reader's Report, 27 August 1954, BBCWA.
22   RB letter to Mary Ellen, 24 January 1955, BBCWA.
23   *The Listener*, 8 July 1955.
24   RB letter to Barbara Bray, 7 March 1955, BBCWA.
25   Jo Bolt letter to Bursar, 21 October 1956.
26   *Radio Times*, 16 September 1955.
27   Script Reader's Report, 23 June 1954, BBCWA.
28   RB letter to Barbara Bray, 2 July 1954, BBCWA.
29   Barbara Bray to RB, 13 July 1954, BBCWA.
30   RB letter to Barbara Bray, 16 July 1954, BBCWA.
31   Barbara Bray letter to RB, 21 July 1954, BBCWA.
32   Script Reader's Report, 8 September 1954, BBCWA.
33   Donald McWhinnie, 2 December 1954, BBCWA.
34   RB letter to his parents, 22 November 1954.
35   Margaret Ramsay letter to Barbara Bray, 12 March 1955, BBCWA.
36   Margaret Ramsay letter to Murray Macdonald, 24 March 1955.
37   *Independent*, 6 September 1991.
38   RB tribute to Margaret Ramsay on her acceptance of a British Film Institute
     Fellowship, 26 June 1984.
39   Ibid.
40   RB letter to his parents, 6 November 1955.
41   Osborne, p.17.
42   John Perry letter to Margaret Ramsay, 1 December 1955.
43   Margaret Ramsay letter to Jack Minster, 26 July 1956.
44   Script Reader's Report, 16 April 1956, BBCWA.
45   RB letter to his parents, 1 April 1956.
46   RB letter to his parents, 18 February 1957.
47   Ibid.
48   *Daily Telegraph*, 2 April 1957.
49   *The Times*, 2 April 1957.
50   *New Statesman*, 5 April 1957.

10: His Name in Lights

1   *Intimations*, BBC-TV, Ex 28 December 1965.
2   Rossiter, pp.145–6.
3   Margaret Ramsay letter to Jack Minster, 27 March 1957.
4   Frith Banbury to AT, 27 November 1996.
5   Celia Johnson letter to Frith Banbury, 21 March 1957, HRC.
6   RB tribute to Margaret Ramsay on her acceptance of a British Film Institute
     Fellowship, 26 June 1984.
7   Frith Banbury to AT, 27 November 1996.
8   Margaret Ramsay letter to Barbara Bray, 9 October 1957. *Johnson Over*

Jordan, by J. B. Priestley, opened in London in 1939 and closed within a fortnight. A meditation on death and dying, it starred Ralph Richardson and, like *Flowering Cherry*, featured a cyclorama 'vision' at the end.

9   Frith Banbury to AT, 27 November 1996.
10 Margaret Ramsay letter to Frith Banbury, 22 August 1957.
11 Margaret Ramsay letter to Frith Banbury, 23 August 1957.
12 Margaret Ramsay letter to Hugh Beaumont, 18 October 1957.
13 Margaret Ramsay letter to Hugh Beaumont, 23 October 1957.
14 *The Times*, 28 June 1960.
15 RB letter to Mike Kellaway, 20 October 1957. Courtesy Michael Kellaway.
16 Margaret Ramsay letter to Frith Banbury, 24 October 1957.
17 Frith Banbury to AT, 27 November 1996.
18 This story is recounted at great length in Kate Fleming's memoir of her mother, Celia Johnson (Weidenfeld & Nicolson, 1991); in John Miller's *Ralph Richardson* (Sidgwick & Jackson, 1995); and in Charles Duff's *The Lost Summer* (Nick Hern Books, 1995).
19 RB letter to R. J. O. Meyer, 15 November 1957, MSA.
20 *Observer*, 24 November 1957.
21 *The Times*, 22 November 1957.
22 RB letter to Frith Banbury, 10 October 1957, HRC.
23 RB letter to Frith Banbury, 16 January 1958, HRC.
24 RB letter to Val Gielgud, 5 February 1958, BBCWA.
25 RB letter to Len Smith, 11 February 1958.
26 *Sunday Times*, 16 March 1958; *The Listener*, 13 March 1958.
27 *Evening Standard*, 13 January 1958.
28 RB letter to Bernard McCabe, 6 March 1959. Courtesy Bernard McCabe.
29 Frith Banbury to AT, 27 November 1996.
30 RB letters to his parents, 29 September & 1 October 1959.
31 RB letter to his parents, 19 October 1959.
32 *New York Times*, 22 October 1959.
33 Frith Banbury to AT, 27 November 1996.
34 *News Chronicle*, 5 December 1957.
35 *Evening Standard*, 18 January 1958.
36 Elaine Steinbeck phone interview, 17 April 1996.
37 John Steinbeck to RB, 8 April 1959. Robert bequeathed the dictionaries to his son, Ben.
38 RB letter to his parents, 17 January 1959.
39 *Intimations*, BBC-TV, tx 28 December 1965.
40 John Dunn to AT, 19 September 1996.
41 John Sergeant to AT, 20 September 1996.
42 RB letter to his parents, 17 January 1959.
43 Anthony Rossiter to AT, 16 April 1996.
44 Naomi May to AT, 13 August 1996.
45 RB letter to Mike and Naomi Kellaway, 4 January 1958. Courtesy Michael Kellaway.
46 Frith Banbury to AT, 27 November 1996.
47 Naomi May letter to author, 14 August 1996.
48 Michael Kellaway to AT, 6 February 1997.
49 RB letter to Bernard McCabe, 6 March 1959. Courtesy Bernard McCabe.

11: Burning Bright

1 RB letter to his mother, 24 April 1959.
2 Ibid.
3 Ben Bolt to AT, 24 October 1996.
4 RB letter to Mike Kellaway, 15 February 1959. Courtesy Michael Kellaway.
5 *Plays and Players*, November 1960.
6 *Daily Mail*, 19 August, 1960.
7 Frith Banbury letter to RB, 18 February 1959, HRC.
8 RB letter to Frith Banbury, 19 February 1959, HRC.
9 Michael Redgrave letter to Frith Banbury, 25 February 1959, HRC. Courtesy Lady Redgrave.
10 RB letter to Michael Redgrave, 27 February 1959, HRC.
11 RB letter to Frith Banbury, 2 March 1959, HRC.
12 Michael Redgrave letter to Hugh Beaumont, 21 July 1959, HRC. Courtesy Lady Redgrave.
13 RB letter to Frith Banbury, 12 June 1959, HRC.
14 RB letter to his father, 3 February 1960.
15 *The Times*, 28 June 1960.
16 RB letter to his parents, 3 February 1960.
17 RB letter to his father, 12 February 1960.
18 Frith Banbury letter to Hugh Beaumont, 29 February 1960, HRC.
19 Duff, p.215.
20 Paul Scofield letter to author, 13 March 1997.
21 Ibid.
22 *Observer*, 3 July 1960.
23 *Observer*, 17 July 1960.
24 Ibid.
25 *Financial Times*, 4 July 1960; *New Statesman*, 9 July 1960; *Daily Express*, 2 July 1960.
26 *Sunday Times*, 3 July 1960/1 January 1961.
27 Paul Scofield letter to author, 13 March 1997.
28 Ibid.
29 McKern, p.169–72.
30 Ibid.
31 Frith Banbury to AT, 27 November 1996.
32 Duff, p.213.
33 Frith Banbury to AT, 27 November 1996.
34 Redgrave, p.91.
35 Frith Banbury to AT, 27 November 1996.
36 *Daily Express*, 25 August 1960.
37 *Sunday Times*, 1 January 1961.
38 RB letter to his parents, 8 September 1960.
39 undated RB letter to Frith Banbury, HRC.
40 *News Chronicle*, 26 August 1960.
41 *Spectator*, 4 November 1960.
42 RB letter to his parents, 8 September 1960.
43 Margaret Ramsay letter to Frith Banbury, 14 August 1962, HRC.

12: Mad Dogs and Englishmen
1 Transcript of John Player Lecture, National Film Theatre, 18 June 1972.
2 RB letter to his parents, 8 September 1960. Walter Wanger was in London to prepare *Cleopatra*.
3 Transcript of John Player Lecture, National Film Theatre, 18 June 1972.
4 Frith Banbury to AT, 27 November 1996.
5 Sir Peter Hall to AT, 20 February 1997.
6 Ibid.
7 Ibid.
8 Undated Michael Wilson memo to Sam Spiegel, MWP.
9 RB contract, dated 17 February 1961, CPA.
10 Brownlow, pp.424-5.
11 *The South Bank Show*. LWT, tx 21 January 1990.
12 *Evening Standard*, 11 May 1989.
13 Brownlow, p.438.
14 Sir Anthony Nutting to AT, 8 May 1991.
15 Transcript of John Player Lecture, National Film Theatre, 18 June 1972.
16 David Lean letter to RB, 15 June 1964, UoR.
17 RB in brochure for the American Film Institute's Life Achievement Award to David Lean, 1990.
18 *Sunday Times*, 25 June 1961.
19 *Sunday Times*, 2 July 1961.
20 RB letter to Frith Banbury, 2 June 1962, HRC.

13: The Drake Hall One
1 Booker, pp.143–4.
2 Hayman, p.13.
3 *Sunday Times*, 29 January 1961.
4 *New Theatre Magazine*, July 1961, pp.8-9.
5 RB letter to his father, 24 February 1961.
6 Sydney Bolt to AT, 27 February 1997. The verse by C Day-Lewis comes from 'Where Are The War Poets?' (1943).
7 Williams, *Diaries*, p.176.
8 Ben Bolt to AT, 19 March 1996.
9 Hayman, p.14.
10 Wesker, p.508.
11 Redgrave, p.98.
12 Hayman, p.14.
13 Barber, p.81.
14 Hayman, p.14. Centre 42 was founded by Arnold Wesker as a means of taking theatre to real people by performing in factories and working men's clubs.
15 RB letter to his father, 16 October 1961.
16 Wesker, p.507.
17 Sir Peter Hall to AT, 20 February 1997.
18 Sian Phillips phone interview, 11 March 1997.
19 RB letter to David Lean, 25 May 1963, UoR.
20 *Variety*, 30 January 1963.
21 Brownlow, p.475.

22 *Observer*, 16 December 1962.
23 RB letter to David Lean, 22 January 1963, UoR.
24 RB letter to Edward Thompson, 25 January 1963. Heinemann papers, UoR.
25 Laurence Harbottle letter to Edward Thompson, 14 June 1963. Heinemann papers, UoR.
26 A. W. Lawrence letter to G. Wren Howard, 28 June 1963. Heinemann papers, UoR.
27 RB letter to Edward Thompson, 6 September 1963, Heinemann papers, UoR.
28 A. D. Evans letter to G. Wren Howard, 12 November 1963, Heinemann papers, UoR.
29 Michael Wilson letter to Adrian Scott, 25 June 1962, MWP.
30 Michael Wilson letter to Sam Spiegel, 7 November 1962, MWP.
31 Michael Wilson letter to Jim Johnson, 28 November 1962, MWP.
32 Michael Wilson letter to RB, 29 November 1962, MWP.
33 RB letter to Michael Wilson, 3 December 1962, MWP.
34 RB letter to Mike Frankovich, 3 July 1963, CPA.
35 John Lemont letter to Walter Jeffrey, General Secretary, Writers' Guild of Great Britain, 27 November 1989, MWP.

14: Not a Friendly Play

1 David Lean letter to RB, 23 December 1962, UoR.
2 Ibid.
3 Ibid.
4 RB letter to David Lean, 29 December 1962, UoR.
5 Sydney Bolt to AT, 6 March 1997.
6 Liz Kellaway to AT, 6 February 1997.
7 Ben Bolt fax to author, 29 January 1997.
8 RB letter to David Lean, 22 January 1963, UoR.
9 Sir Peter Hall to AT, 20 February 1997.
10 *Players and Players*, June 1977.
11 Michael Bryant phone interview, 11 March 1997.
12 RB letter to Kenneth Williams, 19 February 1963, KWA.
13 Williams, *Diaries*, p.208.
14 Williams, *Diaries*, p.213.
15 Michael Bryant phone interview, 11 March 1997.
16 Sian Phillips phone interview, 11 March 1997.
17 Michael Kellaway to AT, 6 February 1997.
18 *Sunday Times*, 1 December 1963.
19 RB letter to Len Smith, 8 February 1964. Courtesy the late Len Smith.
20 RB letter to Kenneth Williams, 7 February 1964, KWA.
21 John Dunn to AT, 19 September 1966.

15: Lara's Theme

1 RB letter to David Lean, 25 February 1963, UoR.
2 Brownlow, p.497.
3 RB letter to David Lean, 25 May 1963, UoR.
4 RB letter to David Lean, 7 July 1963, UoR.
5 RB letter to Margaret Ramsay, 19 September 1964.

6 David Lean letter to RB, 2 July 1963, UoR.
7 RB letter to David Lean, 7 July 1963, UoR.
8 RB letter to David Lean, 20 June 1964, UoR.
9 David Lean letter to Barbara Cole, 10 April 1964, UoR.
10 David Lean letter to RB, 15 June 1964, UoR.
11 RB letter to David Lean, 20 June 1964, UoR.
12 Bertrand Russell, *Autobiography*, Unwin, London 1978, p.661.
13 Malcolm Brown phone interview, 20 November 1996.
14 *Observer*, 24 May 1964.
15 *The Times*, 23 May 1964.
16 *Daily Herald*, 20 May 1964.
17 *Financial Times*, 27 May 1964.
18 David Lean letter to Robert O'Brien, 4 June 1964, UoR.
19 Ibid.
20 David Lean casting notes, 19 March 1964, UoR.
21 David Lean letter to Lee Steiner, 1 November 1964, UoR.
22 Margaret Ramsay letter to RB, undated but probably October 1964.

16: A Weird Vomiting of the Heart
1 Ann Queensberry to AT, 12 March 1996.
2 Ibid.
3 Ibid.
4 RB letter to David Lean, 4 November 1964, UoR.
5 RB letter to David Lean and Barbara Cole, 12 November 1964, UoR.
6 RB letter to Barbara Cole, 17 November 1964.
7 Lord Quinton to AT, 25 January 1996.
8 Kenneth Williams Diary, 26 November 1964, KWA.
9 RB letter to Mike Kellaway, 7 January 1965. Courtesy Michael Kellaway.
10 John Dunn to AT, 19 September 1996.
11 Carolyn Pfeiffer Bradshaw phone interview, 15 August 1996.
12 Kenneth Williams Diary, 7 January 1965, KWA.
13 RB letter to Kenneth Williams, 8 January 1965, KWA.
14 Ben Bolt fax to author, 29 January 1997.
15 RB letter to David Lean, 24 February 1965, UoR.
16 RB letter to David Lean, 14 June 1965.
17 Kenneth Williams Diary, 7 & 29 August 1965, KWA.
18 Kenneth Williams Diary, 10 September 1965, KWA.
19 Fred Zinnemann to AT, 8 February 1996.
20 Ibid.
21 McKern, p.47.
22 RB letter to Barbara Cole, 14 September 1965, UoR.
23 RB letter to David Lean, 13 September 1965, UoR.
24 RB letter to Barbara Cole, 14 September 1965, UoR.
25 Fred Zinnemann to AT, 8 February 1996.
26 Lord Dacre to AT, 24 January 1996.
27 Derek Bryan phone interview, 2 February 1996.
28 Lord Dacre to AT, 24 January 1996.
29 *SACU News*, November 1965.
30 Lord Dacre to AT, 24 January 1996.

31   Ibid

32   *SACU News*, December 1965

33   RB letter to David Lean, 24 October 1965, UoR.

34   Ibid.

35   RB letter to David Lean, 20 November 1965, UoR.

36   Fred Zinnemann to AT, 8 February 1996.

37   Paul Scofield letter to author, 13 March 1997.

38   Paul Scofield letter to Fred Zinnemann, 28 March 1967, AMPAS.

39   Paul Scofield letter to author, 13 March 1997.

40   Actors' fees from Fred Zinnemann Papers, AMPAS.

41   RB letter to David Lean, 20 November 1965, UoR.

42   Sir Peter Hall to AT, 20 February 1997.

43   Trevor Nunn to AT, 17 April 1997.

44   *Daily Mail*, 4 December 1965.

45   Paul Scofield letter to author, 19 April 1997.

46   Trevor Nunn to AT, 17 April 1997.

47   *Evening Standard*, 13 December 1965.

48   *Financial Times*, 13 December 1965.

49   *The Times*, 13 December 1965.

50   Sydney Bolt letter to author, 21 April 1997.

51   *Observer*, 5 December 1965; Hayman, p.88.

17: Sarah

1   Miles II, p.210.

2   Leslie Caron letter to author, 22 August 1996.

3   Sarah Miles to AT, 31 July 1996.

4   In her memoirs, Sarah claims that Robert first came into her consciousness when audiences for *Dazzling Prospect* booed because they were unhappy that *A Man For All Seasons* had been taken off at the same theatre. But since *A Man For All Seasons* had been replaced by a production of Anouilh's *The Rehearsal*, which ran for two months, Sarah's story is a little hard to credit.

5   David Thomson, *A Biographical Dictionary of Film*, Andre Deutsch, London 1994, p.509.

6   Sarah Miles to AT, 31 July 1996.

7   Michael Kellaway to AT, 6 February 1997.

8   Sarah Miles to AT, 31 July 1996.

9   Sarah Miles to AT, 5 December 1996.

10   Kenneth Jupp to AT, 30 January 1997.

11   RB letter to David Lean, 31 August 1966.

12   David Lean letter to Barbara Cole, 15 September 1966, UoR.

13   Ben Bolt fax to AT, 29 January 1997.

18: Great Soul

1   RB letter to David Lean, 10 January 1966, UoR.

2   RB letter to David Lean, 26 March 1966, UoR.

3   Sarah Miles to AT, 24 July 1996.

4   Ibid.

5   John Huston, *An Open Book*, Macmillan 1980, p.325. Huston makes no mention of the *Nefertiti* project in his memoirs.

6   RB letter to John Huston, 5 January 1967, AMPAS.
7   RB letter to John Huston, 24 April 1967, AMPAS.
8   Lord Attenborough to AT, 11 March 1996.
9   Ibid.
10   David Lean letters to Barbara Cole, 15 April 1963 & 15 September 1966, UoR.
11   RB letter to David Lean, 21 January 1966, UoR.
12   RB letter to David Lean, 10 February 1966, UoR.
13   Attenborough, p.142.
14   Fred Zinnemann to AT, 8 February 1996.
15   David Lean letter to Barbara Cole, 22 August 1966, UoR.
16   Laurence Harbottle letter to MGM, 16 December 1966, TBS.
17   Sarah Miles to AT, 24 July 1996.
18   Ibid.
19   David Lean letter to Barbara Cole, 18 November 1966, UoR.
20   Ibid.
21   Ibid.
22   Sarah Miles to AT, 24 July 1996.
23   Lawrence Harbottle to Frank E. Rosenfelt, 9 June 1967, TBS.
24   David Karr and Arthur Lewis to Robert O'Brien, 14 September 1967, TBS.
25   Sarah Miles to AT, 24 July 1996.
26   RB letter to Fred Zinnemann, 12 December 1967, AMPAS.
27   RB letter to Fred Zinnemann, 29 December 1967, AMPAS.
28   RB letter to Robert O'Brien, 1 February 1968, TBS.
29   RB memo, undated, but March 1968, TBS.
30   RB letter to Mike Kellaway, 5 May 1967. Courtesy Michael Kellaway.
31   *Hastings Evening Argus*, 25 April 1967.
32   *Oxford Mail*, 17 May 1967.
33   *Guardian*, 17 May 1967.
34   Margaret Ramsay letter to Frith Banbury, 21 May 1967.
35   Margaret Ramsay letter to RB, 1 September 1967.
36   Margaret Ramsay letter to RB, 15 September 1967.
37   Margaret Ramsay letter to Val May, 1 April 1968.
38   Miles II, p.270.
39   Ann Queensberry to AT, 21 March 1996.
40   Ben Bolt fax to AT, 29 January 1996.
41   Miles, pp.278–9.

19: Remarkable Women
1   Sarah Miles to AT, 24 July 1996.
2   Sydney Bolt to AT, 14 March 1996.
3   John Dunn to AT, 19 September 1996.
4   Bernard McCabe to AT, 8 August 1996.
5   Sarah Miles to AT, 8 July 1997.
6   Margaret Ramsay letter to RB, 15 September 1967.
7   Sarah Miles to AT, 8 July 1997.
8   Ibid.
9   RB letter to Len Smith, 18 March 1970. Courtesy Len Smith.
10   RB letter to David Lean, 31 August 1966, UoR.
11   David Lean letter to Barbara Cole, 15 September 1966, UoR.

12 Brownlow, p.553.
13 RB letter to David Lean, 21 January 1966, UoR.
14 RB letter to David Lean, 10 February 1966, UoR.
15 RB contract, *Michael's Day*, 23 January 1968. TBS.
16 Sarah Miles to AT, 31 July 1996.
17 RB letters to David Lean, 22 October & 2 November 1968.
18 Sarah Miles to AT, 31 July 1996.
19 Brownlow, p.554.
20 RB interview by Joseph Gelmis, *Sound on Film*, broadcast on Columbia University Radio, November 1970.
21 RB letter to Russell Thacher, 24 October 1968.
22 Fernando Ghia to AT, 27 March 1996. *The Red Tent* was released in America in the summer of 1971. Taking far longer to shoot than *Ryan's Daughter*, it was directed by Mikhail Kalatozov and the screenplay was credited to Ennio De Concini and Richard Adams who was a real person, not a pseudonym for Robert Bolt.
23 RB letter to David Lean, 24 October 1968.
24 Brownlow, p.558.
25 Sarah Miles to AT, 31 July 1996.
26 RB letter to David Lean, 28 October 1969.
27 Sarah Miles to AT, 31 July 1996.
28 Brownlow, p.579.
29 Sarah Miles to AT, 8 July 1997.
30 *The Times*, 16 May 1968.
31 *Johannesburg Star*, 23 May 1970.
32 Margaret Ramsay letter to Edward Thompson, 19 January 1970, Heinemann Archive, UoR.
33 Margaret Ramsay letter to Edward Thompson, 2 March 1970, Heinemann Archive, UoR.
34 *The Times*, 21 May 1970.
35 Sarah Miles to AT, 31 July 1996.
36 Trevor Nunn to AT, 17 April 1997.
37 Sarah Miles to AT, 8 July 1997.
38 *New Yorker*, 21 November 1970.

20: Lamb
1 Ben Bolt to AT, 17 October 1997.
2 *Daily Mail*, 13 March 1973.
3 *Esquire*, August 1973.
4 Ibid.
5 RB letter to John Dunn, 25 July 1972. Courtesy John Dunn.
6 Fernando Ghia to AT, 27 March 1996.
7 Bernie Williams to AT, 17 May 1996.
8 Jon Finch to AT, 26 January 1996.
9 Ibid.
10 RB letter to Mike Kellaway, 2 December 1972. Courtesy Michael Kellaway.
11 Oswald Morris to AT, 18 February 1997.
12 Bernie Williams to AT, 17 May 1996.
13 Oswald Morris to AT, 18 February 1997.

14 Jon Finch to AT, 26 January 1996.

15 Bernie Williams to AT, 17 May 1996.

16 Sarah Miles to AT, 8 July 1997.

17 Fernando Ghia to AT, 27 March 1996.

18 Jack Hazan to AT, 17 June 1997.

19 Bernie Williams to AT, 17 May 1996.

20 Oswald Morris to AT, 18 February 1997.

21 Fernando Ghia to AT, 27 March 1996.

22 Jack Hazan to AT, 17 June 1997.

23 *Private Eye*, 23 March 1973.

24 Bernie Williams to AT, 17 May 1996.

25 Oswald Morris to AT, 18 February 1997.

26 RB letter to John Dunn, 25 July 1972. Courtesy John Dunn.

27 Gillian Harrison to AT, 23 February 1996.

28 RB letter to John Dunn, 25 July 1972. Courtesy John Dunn.

29 RB letter to John Dunn, 26 February 1973. Courtesy John Dunn.

30 *Daily Cinema*, 20 January 1973.

31 RB letter to David Lean, 28 August 1973.

32 *Sunday Times*, 12 November 1972.

33 *Daily Cinema*, 25 November 1972.

34 *Observer*, 26 November 1972.

35 *Evening Standard*, 23 November 1972.

21: The Riddle of the Star-Shaped Wound

1 RB letter to David Lean, 3 February 1973.

2 *Esquire*, 'The Corpse as Big as the Ritz,' August 1973. All subsequent quotes from the inquest into David Whiting's death come from this source. The Gila Bend and Phoenix police stated to the author that all the files of the case have been destroyed.

3 Richard A Sarafian phone interview, 26 June 1996.

4 Reynolds, p.178.

5 Miles II, p.464.

6 Miles II, p.65.

7 *Esquire*, August 1973.

8 Sarah Miles to AT, 8 July 1997.

9 *Esquire*, August 1973.

10 Ibid.

11 Ibid.

12 Reynolds, p.178.

13 Richard Sarafian phone interview, 26 June 1996.

14 Ibid.

15 Sarah Miles to AT, 29 May 1997.

16 RB letter to David Lean, 26 February 1973.

17 *Esquire*, August 1973.

18 *Daily Mail*, 3 March 1973.

19 *Daily Mail*, 13 March 1973.

20 Sarah Miles to AT, 29 May 1997.

21 RB letter to David Lean, 29 December 1973.

22 RB letter to David Lean, 12 February 1974.

22: State of the Union

1 RB letter to Debbie Condon, 29 August 1977. Courtesy Debbie Condon.
2 Debbie Condon to AT, 13 May 1996 and fax to author, 25 February 1997.
3 Debbie Condon to AT, 21 January 1997.
4 Ibid.
5 Roger Gard to AT, 15 April 1996.
6 *Gandhi* contract, 29 March 1973, Part III (d), p.2. TBS.
7 Attenborough, p.149.
8 Richard Attenborough letter to Margaret Ramsay, 27 June 1973. Courtesy Lord Attenborough.
9 Lord Attenborough to AT, 11 March 1996.
10 *Gandhi* screenplay, pp.144–5.
11 RB letter to Margaret Ramsay, 10 July 1978.
12 Alan Sapper phone interview, 28 January 1997.
13 Roy Lockett to AT, 19 February 1996.
14 Roy Battersby to AT, 30 January 1996.
15 Roy Lockett to AT, 19 February 1996.
16 Ibid.
17 Roy Battersby to AT, 30 January 1996.
18 RB interviewed on *Arena Cinema*, BBC-TV, tx 17 November 1976.
19 RB letters to Debbie Condon, 9 & 19 January 1975. Courtesy Debbie Condon.
20 RB letter to Debbie Condon, 22 January 1975. Courtesy Debbie Condon.
21 Fernando Ghia to AT, 11 April 1996.
22 Oliver Stone to AT, 22 May 1996.
23 Fernando Ghia to AT, 11 April 1996.
24 Ibid. Ghia's extensive research into the period revealed that the experiment conducted by the Jesuits had been compared at the time to More's vision of Utopia as well as the proposals for a utopian commonwealth suggested by the Italian philosopher, Tommaso Campanella. The Jesuits also drew inspiration from Plato's *The Republic*.
25 Ibid.
26 RB letter to David Lean, 2 April 1975.
27 George Englund phone interview, 3 February 1997.
28 RB letter to Fernando Ghia, 19 October 1976. Courtesy Fernando Ghia.
29 Richard Sylbert was, and remains, a leading production designer whose credits include *The Manchurian Candidate, Who's Afraid of Virginia Woolf?, The Graduate, Chinatown, Reds* and *Dick Tracy*.
30 Undated RB letter to Ben Bolt.
31 Fernando Ghia to AT, 11 April 1996.
32 Kenneth Jupp to AT, 30 January 1997.
33 ibid.
34 Debbie Condon fax to author, 19 February 1997.
35 Liza Gard to AT, 15 April 1996.
36 Debbie Condon to AT, 21 January 1997.
37 Kenneth Jupp to AT, 30 January 1997.
38 Debbie Condon to AT, 21 January 1997.
39 Kenneth Jupp to AT, 30 January 1997.

23: State of Apathy
1   RB letter to Ann Queensberry, 14 May 1976. Courtesy Ann Queensberry.
2   Ibid.
3   Lady St Johnston to AT, 13 February 1997.
4   RB letter to Debbie Condon, 4 August 1976. Courtesy Debbie Condon.
5   Lady St Johnston to AT, 13 February 1997.
6   Undated RB letter to Debbie Condon. Courtesy Debbie Condon.
7   RB letter to Mia Farrow, 30 April 1977. Courtesy Mia Farrow.
8   Ibid.
9   David Salmon to AT, 16 October 1996.
10 Mary Wesley to AT, 15 October 1996.
11 John Fowles letters to author, 22 & 27 November 1996.
12 RB letter to Julie Laird, April 1978.
13 John Fowles letters to author, 22 & 27 November 1996.
14 *The Times*, 25 May 1977.
15 Michael Byrant phone interview, 11 March 1997.
16 Hall, p.295.
17 Christopher Morahan phone interview, 21 May 1997.
18 Hall, p.296.
19 Hall, p.297.
20 *The Times*, 28 May 1977.
21 *Morning Star*, 28 May 1977.
22 *Sunday Times*, 29 May 1977.
23 RB letter to Ben and Jo Bolt, 27 November 1977.

24: Deadlines and Lifelines
1   Gillian Harrison to AT, 23 February 1996.
2   Julie Nightingale to AT, 19 October 1996.
3   Undated RB postcard to Julie Laird. Courtesy Julie Nightingale.
4   Julie Nightingale to AT, 19 October 1996.
5   Ben Bolt to AT, 24 October 1996.
6   Ibid.
7   Ann Queensberry to AT, 21 March 1996.
8   Gillian Harrison to AT, 23 February 1996.
9   Undated RB postcard to Julie Laird. Courtesy Julie Nightingale.
10 Jo Bolt to AT, 23 January 1997.
11 Ben Bolt to AT, 24 October 1996.
12 Eaton Griffith, pp.161–62.
13 Valerie Eaton Griffith to AT, 31 January 1997.
14 Ann Queensberry to AT, 21 March 1996.
15 Ben Bolt to AT, 24 October 1996.
16 Jo Bolt to AT, 23 January 1997.
17 Julie Nightingale to AT, 19 October 1996.
18 Tor Douglas to AT, 15 April 1996.
19 Gillian Harrison to AT, 23 February 1996.
20 John Standing to AT, 10 January 1997.
21 Jo Bolt to AT, 23 January 1997.
22 Bernard McCabe to AT, 8 August 1996.
23 Ann Queensberry to AT, 21 March 1996.

24 Miles III, p.132.
25 Gillian Harrison to AT, 11 September 1996.
26 RB letter to Vaea Sylvain, 11 April 1980. Courtesy Vaea Sylvain.
27 Roald Dahl letter to RB, 12 March 1980. Courtesy Mrs Felicity Dahl.
28 Jo Bolt to AT, 5 March 1996.
29 Ben Bolt fax to author, 28 October 1996.
30 Ann Queensberry to AT, 21 March 1996.
31 Ibid.
32 Tor Douglas to AT, 16 April 1996.
33 Norman Lear phone interview, 2 July 1996.
34 Ibid.
35 RB letter to Vaea Sylvain, 1 October 1980. Courtesy Vaea Sylvain.
36 Lord Puttnam to AT, 24 January 1997.
37 RB letter to Charlotte Taylor, 22 March 1981. Courtesy Lady St Johnston.
38 Tor Douglas to AT, 15 April 1996.
39 RB letter to Charlotte Taylor, 22 March 1981. Courtesy Lady St Johnston.
40 RB letter to Fred Sidewater, 12 October 1991.

25: Relative Values

1   Julie Nightingale to AT, 19 October 1996.
2   Bernie Williams to AT, 17 May 1996.
3   Undated Dino de Laurentiis telex to RB.
4   Bernie Williams to AT, 17 May 1996.
5   Ibid.
6   Undated Sally Simmons letters to RB.
7   Sally Simmons letter to RB, 20 December 1978.
8   RB letter to private source, 27 June 1978.
9   RB letter to private source, 11 July 1978.
10 All facts and reported speech regarding the death of Sally Simmons are taken from the official records of the Inquest held at the Coroner's Court, Horseferry Road, London.
11 Ben Bolt fax to author, 27 June 1997.
12 Tor Douglas to AT, 5 April 1996.
13 RB letter to Ben Bolt, 5 March 1991.
14 *Intimations*, BBC-TV, tx 28 December 1965.
15 RB letter to Debbie Condon, 25 April 1978. Courtesy Debbie Condon.
16 RB letter to Joanna Bolt, 7 February 1988.
17 Bernie Williams to AT, 17 May 1996. Williams is still trying to make Part II.

26: Leaving Home

1   Val Eaton Griffith to AT, 31 January 1997.
2   Mary Wesley to AT, 15 October 1996.
3   Lady St Johnston to AT, 13 February 1997.
4   RB letter to Naomi May, 17 February 1982. Courtesy Naomi May.
5   Naomi May to AT, 13 August 1996.
6   Frith Banbury to AT, 27 November 1996.
7   Kenneth Jupp to AT, 30 January 1997.
8   Mary Wesley to AT, 15 October 1996.
9   Ann Queensberry to AT, 21 March 1996.

10 Tor Douglas to AT, 15 April 1996.
11 Ann Queensberry to AT, 21 March 1996.
12 Ben Bolt to AT, 24 October 1996.
13 Julie Nightingale to AT, 19 October 1996.
14 Mary Wesley to AT, 15 October 1996.

27: An Old Flame
1 Julie Nightingale to AT, 19 October 1996.
2 Liza and Roger Gard to AT, 15 April 1996.
3 Fernando Ghia to AT, 11 April 1996.
4 Mary Wesley to AT, 15 October 1996.
5 Elijah Moshinsky phone interview, 7 March 1997.
6 Zeffirelli, p.345.
7 RB letter to Franco Zeffirelli, 21 March 1984.
8 RB letter to Margaret Ramsay, 30 August 1984.
9 RB letter to Margaret Ramsay, 3 June 1985.
10 RB letter to Ben Bolt, 16 May 1985.
11 Barry Spikings phone interview, 14 March 1997.
12 Lord Puttnam to AT, 24 January 1997.
13 Barry Spikings phone interview, 14 March 1997.
14 Fernando Ghia to AT, 11 April 1996.
15 Lord Puttnam to AT, 24 January 1997.
16 Fernando Ghia to AT, 11 April 1996.
17 Lord Puttnam to AT, 24 January 1997.
18 Fernando Ghia phone interview, 21 April 1997.
19 Fernando Ghia to AT, 11 April 1996.
20 Herbert McCabe to AT, 17 March 1997.
21 David Puttnam letter to RB, 19 April 1985.
22 RB letter to Roland Joffé, 22 May 1986.
23 Fernando Ghia phone interview, 21 April 1997.
24 Lord Puttnam to AT, 24 January 1997.
25 Fernando Ghia phone interview, 21 April 1997.
26 RB letter to Fernando Ghia and David Puttnam, 16 December 1991.
27 Miles III, p.165.

28: Tom's Story
1 Sarah Miles to AT, 29 May 1997.
2 Tom Bolt to AT, 5 June 1997.

29: Skipping on the Surface of Language
1 Paula Weinstein phone interview, 24 May 1996.
2 Charlton Heston to AT, 23 May 1996.
3 Roy Battersby to AT, 30 January 1996.
4 RB letter to Charlotte Taylor, 8 January 1981. Courtesy Lady St Johnston.
5 RB letter to Ben Bolt, 19 August 1985.
6 RB letter to Ben Bolt, 16 May 1985.
7 Griffith, pp.163–65.
8 Miles III, p.206.
9 Fay, p.441-2.

30: Moonlighting

1   Sarah Miles letter to Kevin Brownlow, 13 July 1996.
2   RB letter to David Lean, 4 June 1988.
3   Although Robert had told his secretary that he had undergone tests in Tahiti for his medical insurance, it seems it was never part of his contract. Everyone just assumed that Robert was privately insured.
4   Julie Laird letter to RB, 9 September 1979. Courtesy Julie Nightingale.
5   RB letter to David Lean, 18 March 1985.
6   Miles III, p.230.
7   Lord Puttnam to AT, 24 January 1997.
8   RB letter to Roger Gard, 8 October 1988. Courtesy Roger Gard.
9   Barbara Bloom phone interview, 30 April 1997.
10   RB letter to David Puttnam, 23 July 1990.
11   RB letter to David Puttnam, 3 July 1991.
12   *Los Angeles Times*, 9 June 1991.
13   Susie Lancaster letter to RB, 10 August 1991. Courtesy Mrs Susie Lancaster.
14   RB letter to Mrs Susie Lancaster, 30 August 1991.
15   RB fax to Ben Bolt, 29 August 1990.
16   Ben Bolt fax to RB, 2 September 1990. Courtesy Ben Bolt.
17   RB fax to Ben Bolt, 6 September 1990.
18   *Hollywood Reporter*, 28 September 1989.
19   Ronnie Colsen fax to author, 7 February 1997.
20   Miles III, p.224.
21   Mira Nair letter to RB, 14 August 1992.
22   RB letter to Ben Bolt, 15 August 1990.
23   Trevor Nunn to AT, 17 April 1997.
24   Trevor Nunn letter to RB, 10 January 1992. Courtesy Trevor Nunn.
25   Undated RB fax to John Heyman.
26   Ben Bolt fax to RB, 13 October 1991. Courtesy Ben Bolt.
27   RB letter to Ben and Jo Bolt, 5 March 1991.
28   RB letter to Francis Coppola, 19 March 1992.
29   Fernando Ghia to AT, 27 March 1996.
30   RB letter to Eileen Chandler, 31 August 1991.
31   Chambers, p.252.
32   Chambers, p.92.

31: Home from the Hill

1   Barbara Bloom phone interview, 29 April 1997.
2   RB letter to Hutch Parker, 23 March 1993.
3   John Florescu phone interview, 21 May 1997.
4   Pippa Cross phone interview, 10 December 1996.
5   Ronnie Colsen fax to RB, 15 April 1993.
6   Ronnie Colsen fax to author, 7 February 1997.
7   Michael Wearing to AT, 15 May 1997.
8   John Florescu phone interview, 21 May 1997.
9   Ibid.
10   Miles III, p.252.
11   Oliver Stone to AT, 22 May 1996.
12   Barbara Bloom phone interview, 30 April 1997.
13   Miles III, p.252.
14   RB letter to Charlotte Taylor, 20 September 1984. Courtesy Lady St Johnston.

INDEX

Compiled by Gordon Robinson